HUMAN
RIGHTS
WATCH

# WORLD REPORT

W9-AUN-924

# 2018

EVENTS OF 2017

ISBN-13: 978-1-60980-814-3

Cover photo: *Abdul Kareem, a Rohingya Muslim,
carries his mother, Alima Khatoon, to a refugee
camp after crossing from Burma into Bangladesh
on Sept. 16, 2017.*
© 2017 Dar Yasin/AP

Cover and book design by Rafael Jiménez

**www.hrw.org**

**Human Rights Watch** defends the rights of people worldwide.

We scrupulously investigate abuses, expose facts widely, and pressure those with power to respect rights and secure justice.

Human Rights Watch is an independent, international organization that works as part of a vibrant movement to uphold human dignity and advance the cause of human rights for all.

Human Rights Watch began in 1978 with the founding of its Europe and Central Asia division (then known as Helsinki Watch). Today it also includes divisions covering Africa, the Americas, Asia, Europe and Central Asia, the Middle East and North Africa, and the United States. There are thematic divisions or programs on arms; business and human rights; children's rights; disability rights; the environment and human rights; health and human rights; international justice; lesbian, gay, bisexual, and transgender rights; refugees; terrorism and counter-terrorism; women's rights; and emergencies.

The organization maintains offices in Amman, Amsterdam, Beirut, Berlin, Bishkek, Brussels, Chicago, Geneva, Goma, Hong Kong, Johannesburg, Kiev, Kigali, Kinshasa, London, Los Angeles, Miami, Moscow, Nairobi, New York, Paris, San Francisco, São Paulo, Seoul, Silicon Valley, Stockholm, Sydney, Tokyo, Toronto, Tunis, Washington DC, and Zurich, and field presences in more than 40 other locations globally.

Human Rights Watch is an independent, nongovernmental organization, supported by contributions from private individuals and foundations worldwide. It accepts no government funds, directly or indirectly.

The leadership includes Kenneth Roth, Executive Director; Michele Alexander, Deputy Executive Director, Development and Global Initiatives; Iain Levine, Deputy Executive Director, Program; Nic Dawes, Deputy Executive Director, Media; Bruno Stagno Ugarte, Deputy Executive Director, Advocacy; and Chuck Lustig, Deputy Executive Director, Operations.

# Table of Contents

# Foreword

*World Report 2018* is Human Rights Watch's 28th annual review of human rights practices around the globe. It summarizes key human rights issues in more than 90 countries and territories worldwide, drawing on events from late 2016 through November 2017.

In his keynote essay, "The Pushback Against the Populist Challenge," Human Rights Watch Executive Director Kenneth Roth says that the surge of authoritarian populists appears less inevitable than it did a year ago. Then, there seemed no stopping a series of politicians around the globe who claimed to speak for "the people" but built followings by demonizing unpopular minorities, attacking human rights principles, and fueling distrust of democratic institutions. Today, a popular reaction in a broad range of countries, bolstered by some political leaders with the courage to stand up for human rights, has left the fate of many of these populist agendas more uncertain. "Where the pushback is strong, populist advances have been limited," Roth explains, "but where capitulation meets their message of hate and exclusion, the populists flourish."

Preoccupied with the internal domestic struggle over the populist agenda, many of the world's democracies, including the United States and the United Kingdom, have been less willing than before to promote human rights abroad. China and Russia have sought to fill that leadership void by advancing an anti-rights agenda. But several small and medium-sized governments, often backed by galvanized publics, have also stepped into the breach. They include France, the Netherlands, Canada, Belgium, Ireland, and even tiny Liechtenstein. Though lacking the clout of the major powers, they have succeeded in building coalitions that exert serious pressure on the anti-rights agenda and in trumpeting the advantages of governments that are accountable to their people rather than to their officials' empowerment and enrichment.

However, where other priorities stand in the way of a strong defense of human rights, the populists and autocrats have flourished. Roth cites Egypt, Turkey, Saudi Arabia, and Burma as examples of countries where a lack of international pressure has enabled governments to crush domestic dissent and, at times, to commit large-scale atrocities. "A fair assessment of global prospects for human rights," Roth concludes, "should induce concern rather than surrender—a call to action rather than a cry of despair." The populist surge is hardly inevitable and can be reversed if governments and the public are willing to make the effort.

The rest of the volume consists of individual country entries, each of which identifies significant human rights abuses, examines the freedom of local human rights defenders to conduct their work, and surveys the response of key international actors, such as the United Nations, European Union, African Union, United States, China, and various regional and international organizations and institutions.

The book reflects extensive investigative work that Human Rights Watch staff undertook in 2017, usually in close partnership with human rights activists and groups in the country in question. It also reflects the work of our advocacy team, which monitors policy developments and strives to persuade governments and international institutions to curb abuses and promote human rights. Human Rights Watch publications, issued throughout the year, contain more detailed accounts of many of the issues addressed in the brief summaries in this volume. They can be found on the Human Rights Watch website, www.hrw.org.

As in past years, this report does not include a chapter on every country where Human Rights Watch works, nor does it discuss every issue of importance. The absence of a particular country or issue often simply reflects staffing or resource limitations and should not be taken as commentary on the significance of the problem. There are many serious human rights violations that Human Rights Watch simply lacks the capacity to address.

The factors we considered in determining the focus of our work in 2017 (and hence the content of this volume) include the number of people affected and the severity of abuse, access to the country and the availability of information about it, the susceptibility of abusive forces to influence, and the importance of addressing certain thematic concerns and of reinforcing the work of local rights organizations.

The *World Report* does not have separate chapters addressing our thematic work but instead incorporates such material directly into the country entries. Please consult the Human Rights Watch website for more detailed treatment of our work on children's rights; women's rights; arms and military issues; business and human rights; health and human rights; disability rights; the environment and human rights; international justice; terrorism and counterterrorism; refugees and displaced people; and lesbian, gay, bisexual, and transgender people's rights; and for information about our international film festivals.

# The Pushback Against the Populist Challenge

### By Kenneth Roth, *Executive Director*

The surge of authoritarian populists appears less inevitable than it did a year ago. Then, there seemed no stopping a series of politicians around the globe who claimed to speak for "the people" but built followings by demonizing unpopular minorities, attacking human rights principles, and fueling distrust of democratic institutions. Today, a popular reaction in a broad range of countries, bolstered in some cases by political leaders with the courage to stand up for human rights, has left the fate of many of these populist agendas more uncertain. Where the pushback is strong, populist advances have been limited. But where capitulation meets their message of hate and exclusion, the populists flourish.

The playing out of this struggle has made many Western powers in particular more inwardly oriented, leaving an increasingly fragmented world. With the United States led by a president who displays a disturbing fondness for rights-trampling strongmen, and the United Kingdom preoccupied by Brexit, two traditional if flawed defenders of human rights globally are often missing in action.

Buffeted by racist and anti-refugee political forces at home, Germany, France, and their European Union partners have not always been willing to pick up the slack. Democracies such as Australia, Brazil, Indonesia, Japan, and South Africa have been heard actively defending human rights rarely, at best.

China and Russia have sought to take advantage of this vacuum. While focused on quelling any possibility of domestic mass protest against slowing economies and widespread official corruption, Presidents Xi Jinping and Vladimir Putin have aggressively asserted an anti-rights agenda in multinational forums and forged stronger alliances with repressive governments. Their avoidance of public oversight has attracted the admiration of Western populists and autocrats around the world.

The retreat of many governments that might have championed human rights has left an open field for murderous leaders and their enablers. Mass atrocities have proliferated with near impunity in countries such as Yemen, Syria, Burma, and South Sudan. International standards designed to prevent the most horrendous abuses, and emerging institutions of judicial response such as the International Criminal Court (ICC), are being challenged.

1

In this hostile environment, a number of small and medium-sized countries have begun to assume greater leadership roles. By building broad coalitions, they have shown themselves capable of exerting serious pressure in defense of human rights. In some cases, they have been backed by an increasingly mobilized public. They cannot wholly substitute for the powers that have withdrawn, but their emergence shows that the drive to defend human rights is alive and well.

## Responding to Populism

Real issues lie behind the surge of populism in many parts of the world: economic dislocation and inequality caused by globalization, automation, and technological change; feared cultural shifts as the ease of transportation and communication fuels migration from war, repression, poverty, and climate change; societal divisions between cosmopolitan elites who welcome and benefit from many of these changes and those who feel their lives have become more precarious; and the traumatic drumbeat of terrorist attacks that demagogues use to fuel xenophobia and Islamophobia.

Addressing these issues is not simple, but populists tend to respond less by proposing genuine solutions than by scapegoating vulnerable minorities and disfavored segments of society. The result has been a frontal assault on the values of inclusivity, tolerance, and respect that lie at the heart of human rights. Indeed, certain populists seem to relish breaking the taboos that embody these values. Invoking their self-serving interpretation of the majority's desires, these populists seek to replace democratic rule—elected government limited by rights and the rule of law—with unfettered majoritarianism.

Responding to this populist challenge requires not only addressing the legitimate grievances that underlie it but also reaffirming the human rights principles that populists reject. It requires trumpeting the advantages of governments that are accountable to their people rather than to their officials' empowerment and enrichment. It requires demonstrating that all of our rights are at risk if we allow governments to select which people deserve respect for their rights. It requires reminding ordinary people that they need human rights as much as dissidents and vulnerable groups.

The willingness of democratic leaders to take on this challenge and champion human rights has fluctuated. A year ago, as the populists seemed to have the wind at their backs, few dared. But in the past year, that has begun to change, to visible effect.

## Defending Rights

### France

France provided the most prominent turning point. In other European countries—Austria and the Netherlands, foremost—centrist and center-right politicians competed with populists by adopting many of their nativist positions. They hoped to pre-empt the populists' appeal but ended up reinforcing the populists' message.

Emmanuel Macron took a different approach during his presidential campaign. He openly embraced democratic principles, firmly rejecting the National Front's efforts to foment hatred against Muslims and immigrants. His resulting victory and his party's success in parliamentary elections showed that French voters overwhelmingly reject the National Front's divisive policies.

It remains to be seen how Macron governs. His move to make permanent many troubling aspects of France's emergency law was a disturbing early step. In foreign policy, he has shown leadership standing up to autocratic rule in Russia, Turkey, and Venezuela, and a willingness to support stronger collective European Union action against Poland's and Hungary's assault on rights. But he has been reluctant to confront widespread abuses in China, Egypt, and Saudi Arabia. Despite this mixed record, he showed during his campaign that a vigorous defense of democratic principles can attract broad public support.

### United States

In reaction to the election of Donald Trump, the United States saw a broad reaffirmation of human rights from many quarters. Trump won the presidency with a campaign of hatred against Mexican immigrants, Muslim refugees, and other racial and ethnic minorities, and an evident disdain for women. A powerful response came from civic groups, journalists, lawyers, judges, many members of the public, and sometimes even elected members of Trump's own party.

Trump was still able to take regressive steps by executive action—deporting many people without regard to their deep ties to the United States, reviving a

3

cruel and discredited policy of mass incarceration of criminal offenders, easing oversight against police abuse, and restricting global funding for women's reproductive health.

But the resistance limited the harm that might have been done, most notably his efforts to discriminate against Muslims seeking to visit or obtain asylum in the United States, to undermine the right to health care in the US, to expel transgender people from the military, and even, in some cases, to deport long-term resident immigrants.

Secretary of State Rex Tillerson largely rejected the promotion of human rights as an element of US foreign policy while more broadly reducing the role of the US abroad by presiding over an unprecedented dismantling of the State Department. He refused to fill many senior posts, dismissed several veteran diplomats, slashed the budget, and let the department drift. Many career diplomats and mid-level officials resigned in despair.

But as Trump embraced one autocrat after another, some of the remaining State Department officials, at times with Congressional support, did what they could to prevent a complete abandonment of the human rights principles that have played at least some role in guiding US foreign policy for four decades. They made it possible for Washington to still occasionally play a useful role, such as threatening targeted sanctions against the Burmese military officials behind the ethnic cleansing of the Rohingya minority.

**Germany**

Germany over the past year made headlines when the Alternative for Germany (AfD) became the first far-right party to enter its parliament in decades. That ascent cut into support for the ruling coalition including Chancellor Angela Merkel's Christian Democratic Union (CDU) party and complicated her task of forming a new governing coalition. Merkel's preoccupation with domestic politics, and her ongoing defense of her courageous 2015 decision to admit large numbers of asylum seekers to Germany, have ironically deprived Europe of a strong voice for the rights of refugees and immigrants—the most contentious issue on the continent today. That also left Macron without his most obvious European partner for resisting authoritarian populism.

Yet the German election also presented a lesson in how to address the far right. Beyond the economically depressed eastern parts of the country where widespread racism and xenophobia has not been tackled since the fall of the Berlin Wall, the AfD gained the most votes in wealthy Bavaria, where Merkel's governing partner, the Christian Social Union, adopted far more of the AfD's nativist positions than did Merkel's CDU. Principled confrontation rather than calculated emulation turned out to be the more effective response.

## Poland and Hungary

Central Europe has become especially fertile ground for populists, as certain leaders use fear of migration elsewhere in Europe to undermine checks and balances on their power at home. But there, too, the populists encountered resistance.

In Poland, amid large public protests and strong international criticism including from EU institutions, President Andrzej Duda vetoed the Polish government's initial attempt to undermine judicial independence and the rule of law, although the alternative he then advanced still fell short.

In Hungary, the threat of EU legal action—as well as international condemnation, including from the United States—impeded the government's plans to close Central European University, a bastion of independent thought that stood in opposition to the "illiberal democracy" championed by Prime Minister Viktor Orban. In the case of Poland at least, there is growing recognition in EU institutions and some member states that its assaults on democratic rule pose a threat to the EU itself. And given Poland's and Hungary's position as major beneficiaries of EU funding, a debate is beginning on whether that aid should be linked to upholding the EU's basic values.

## Venezuela

In Latin America, President Nicolás Maduro continued to eviscerate Venezuela's democracy and economy under the guise of standing up for the little people and against those whom he calls the imperialists. But as his rule became more brutal and autocratic, his corrupt and incompetent management of the economy became painfully apparent. This potentially wealthy nation was left destitute despite its vast oil reserves, with many people desperately searching for food and medicine amid raging hyperinflation.

People took to the streets in large numbers to protest. Some officials defected from his government. An unprecedented number of Latin American countries shed their traditional reluctance to criticize a neighbor's repression. Others followed, including the EU.

Maduro managed to stay in office, due largely to the violent repression he was willing to deploy. Taking advantage of a subservient Supreme Court and the Constituent Assembly that he created to take over legislative powers from the opposition-controlled National Assembly, he carried out a brutal crackdown on dissent. But as the Venezuelan people continue their descent into poverty and misery, it is unclear how long they will let Maduro cling to power.

## *A Struggle Deserving Support*

None of these examples of resistance to populist leaders is guaranteed success. Once in office, populists have the considerable advantage of being able to harness the power of the state. But the resistance shows that there is a struggle underway, that many people will not sit quietly as autocrats attack their basic rights and freedoms.

### Populists and Autocrats Fill a Vacuum

By contrast, where domestic resistance was suppressed and international concern lacking, the populists and other anti-rights forces prospered. President Recep Tayyip Erdoğan, for example, decimated Turkey's democratic system with impunity, as the EU shifted its focus to enlisting his help to halt the flight of refugees to Europe. President Abdel Fattah al-Sisi crushed public dissent in Egypt with little interference from the US or the EU. They bought into his narrative of combatting terrorism and ensuring stability, even though his ruthless suppression of any Islamic option in the country's political process was exactly what militant Islamists wanted.

With a seeming green light from Western allies, Saudi Arabia's new crown prince, Mohamed bin Salman, led a coalition of Arab states in a war against Houthi rebels and their allies in Yemen that involved bombing and blockading civilians, greatly aggravating the world's largest humanitarian crisis. Concern with stopping boat migration via Libya led the EU—particularly Italy—to train, fund, and guide Libyan coast guards to do what no European ships could legally do: forcibly return desperate migrants and refugees to hellish conditions of forced labor, rape, and brutal mistreatment.

Putin's efforts to repress opposition to his lengthening rule met little resistance from foreign governments more focused on his conduct in Ukraine and Syria than within Russia. Xi Jinping got away with little resistance to his imposition of the most intense crackdown since the brutal smothering of the 1989 Tiananmen Square democracy movement because other nations were afraid to jeopardize lucrative Chinese contracts by standing up for the rights of the Chinese people.

Indeed, when there was little international pushback to their behavior at home, repressive governments felt emboldened to manipulate and obstruct the international institutions that can defend rights.

China detained its citizens who hoped to engage with United Nations bodies on its rights abuse. Russia cast no less than 11 vetoes to block any attempt by the UN Security Council to address Syrian government war crimes. Russia also threatened to withdraw from a key European oversight body on human rights if it maintained sanctions for the occupation of Crimea, while Azerbaijan bribed some members of that body, and Turkey threatened to withhold its budgetary contribution. Burundi threatened UN rights investigators themselves with retaliation.

## Burma and the Rohingya

The cost of not standing up to populist attacks on human rights was perhaps starkest in Burma. Vitriolic nationalist rhetoric increasingly propagated by Buddhist extremists, senior members of the Burmese military, and some members of the civilian-led government helped to precipitate an ethnic cleansing campaign against Rohingya Muslims, following a militant group's attacks on security outposts. An army-led campaign of massacres, widespread rape, and mass arson in at least 340 villages sent more than 640,000 Rohingya refugees fleeing for their lives to neighboring Bangladesh. These are the very crimes that the international community had pledged never again to tolerate.

Yet the Western nations that had long taken an active interest in Burma were re-luctant to act, even by imposing targeted financial and travel sanctions on the army generals behind these crimes against humanity. In part, that reticence was because of geopolitical competition with China for the Burmese government's favor.

Also playing a part was the undue deference given to Aung San Suu Kyi, Burma's de facto civilian leader, even though she has no real control over the military and showed no willingness to pay the political price of defending an unpopular mi-nority. The result was the fastest forced mass flight of people since the Rwandan genocide, with little immediate hope of the Rohingyas' safe and voluntary return, or of bringing to justice the people behind the atrocities that sent them fleeing.

Ultimately, nations of the Organization of Islamic Cooperation (OIC) called for a special session of the UN Human Rights Council where they supported a resolu-tion condemning Burma's crimes against humanity. The effort was notable be-cause it represented a rare instance in which OIC members backed a resolution criticizing a particular country.

## *Pushing Back Can Work*

### Africa and the ICC

One of the most encouraging responses to anti-rights autocrats could be found in Africa. The year was already notable for the toppling of two long-time tyrants. Gambia's President Yahya Jammeh lost a free and fair election to Adama Barrow, and when he refused to accept the results, was eased out of office by the threat of West African troops.

Zimbabwe's President Robert Mugabe was ousted in a coup, though replaced by his former deputy, Emmerson Mnangagwa, a military leader with his own long record of abuse. Both countries saw large public protests against the long-serv-ing tyrants.

Yet the African defense of rights was most impressive in response to populist at-tacks on international justice. As recently as a year ago, many African leaders, some with blood on their hands and fearing prosecution, were plotting a mass exodus of their countries from membership in the International Criminal Court.

Using populist rhetoric against what they claimed was neo-colonialism, they sought to portray the ICC as anti-African because, having taken seriously crimes against African people, it had concentrated its attention on the responsible African leaders. (Its reach was also limited by the refusal of some governments to ratify the ICC's treaty and by the UN Security Council's reluctance to refer other situations for investigation).

But the mass exodus became a mass fizzle when only Burundi withdrew, in an ultimately unsuccessful effort to halt ICC investigation of alleged crimes against humanity committed under Pierre Nkurunziza as he violently extended his term as president. Gambia reversed its announced withdrawal after President Barrow took office. And the South African courts at least temporarily blocked President Jacob Zuma's attempt to withdraw after he was embarrassed for flouting a court order to prevent Sudanese President Omar al-Bashir, facing ICC warrants, from fleeing South Africa during a visit to avoid arrest.

An outpouring of popular support for the ICC by civic groups across Africa helped to persuade most African governments to continue to stand behind the court. The ICC prosecutor also sought to extend the court's reach by asking its judges for permission to investigate crimes by all sides in Afghanistan, including torture committed there by US soldiers and intelligence agents with impunity.

## *The Big Role of Small States*

The past year saw an impressive willingness by small and medium-sized states to step into leadership roles when the major powers fell silent in the face of mass atrocities or even obstructed efforts to address them.

This is hardly the first time that smaller states have taken the lead on rights issues. The ICC, the Mine Ban Treaty, the Convention on Cluster Munitions, the Optional Protocol on Child Soldiers, and the International Convention against Enforced Disappearance were all secured largely by global coalitions of small and medium-sized states operating without or despite the major powers. Yet the willingness of these alternative voices to take center stage was particularly important in the past year as major powers largely walked off the stage or even tried to upend it.

## Yemen

The effort at the UN Human Rights Council to open an independent international investigation of abuses in Yemen was illustrative. A coalition of Arab states led by Saudi Arabia pummeled Yemeni civilians; conducted airstrikes on homes, markets and hospitals; and blockaded urgently needed humanitarian aid and other goods. As a result, 7 million people faced starvation, and the country had nearly 1 million suspected cases of cholera.

Opposing Houthi forces and their allies also used landmines, recruited child soldiers, and blocked aid. Despite this grave situation, the idea of an investigation received at best lukewarm support from the United States, the United Kingdom, and France, all major sellers of arms to Saudi Arabia. None was eager to take a public stand. In that void, the Netherlands stepped in and took the lead, ultimately joined by Canada, Belgium, Ireland, and Luxembourg.

The task was not easy. Saudi Arabia threatened to cut diplomatic and economic ties with any nation that supported the investigation. Yet in part because of that threat, and its implicit message that the wealthy should stand above scrutiny for their atrocities, Saudi Arabia was forced to capitulate to a UN investigation once it became clear it would most likely lose a contested vote. The hope now is that a group of investigators looking over the shoulders of the combatants in Yemen will compel better behavior.

## Syria

In the case of Syria, Russia's repeated vetoes and veto threats at the UN Security Council, sometimes joined by China, barred the only immediately available route to the International Criminal Court. Despite a growing international effort to discourage use of the veto in situations of mass atrocities, Russia and China, as well as the United States, have not signed on to these initiatives.

To break that stalemate, the idea was floated to circumvent the Security Council's veto system by seeking action in the UN General Assembly, where no state has veto power. Leadership in this effort came from the tiny nation of Liechtenstein, which built a broad coalition of governments. With their support, the General Assembly ended up voting 105 to 15 to establish a mechanism to collect evidence and build cases for prosecution when venues ultimately become available—an important commitment to see justice done. It also opens the door to the General Assembly possibly creating a special tribunal for Syria should Russia continue to block a path to justice at the ICC.

The importance of this accountability was illustrated by the Syrian government's ongoing use of banned nerve agents such as sarin despite having supposedly relinquished all chemical weapons after its notorious August 2013 use of sarin in Eastern Ghouta. Russia offered a cover story for an April 2017 episode in the northwestern Syrian town of Khan Sheikhoun—that a Syrian conventional bomb supposedly hit a rebel cache of sarin—but that theory was conclusively disproved, so Russia responded by vetoing continuation of a UN investigation. When a permanent member of the Security Council is willing to use its power to cover the atrocities of an ally—in this case, while also providing military support—it is particularly important to explore alternative avenues for upholding the most basic rights.

## The Philippines

The Philippines presented an especially brazen and deadly example of a populist challenge to human rights. As he had done previously as mayor of Davao City, President Rodrigo Duterte took office encouraging the police to kill drug suspects. The resulting epidemic of police shootings—often portrayed as "shootouts" but repeatedly shown to be summary executions—had left more than 12,000 people killed in the roughly year and a half since Duterte took office. The vast majority of victims were young men from the slums of major cities—people who elicited little sympathy among many Filipinos.

The ongoing territorial dispute among China, the United States, and the Philippines over the South China Sea left little room for concern about executions. Donald Trump, as he has elsewhere, seemed mainly to admire Duterte's "strongman" qualities.

Instead, a major source of pressure to stop the slaughter came from a collection of states led by Iceland that issued statements at the UN Human Rights Council. Duterte tried to disparage these "bleeding hearts" but ended up, under pressure, transferring authority to combat drugs, at least for a while, from the murderous police to a far more law-respecting drug agency. When the police were withdrawn from anti-drug operations, executions dropped precipitously.

## Women's Rights

Several of today's populists display a misogynist slant. In the past year, Russia decriminalized certain acts of domestic violence. Poland, already possessing one of the most restrictive abortion laws in Europe, is now limiting access to emergency contraception.

Under Trump, the US government reintroduced an expanded "Global Gag Rule" that vastly reduces funding for essential health care for women and girls abroad.

Yet there were rising voices in response. The Women's March, convened initially as an American response to the election of Trump, morphed into a global phenomenon, with millions gathering in support of women's human rights.

Canadian Prime Minister Justin Trudeau and French President Macron both identified themselves as feminists, with Canada making the pursuit of gender equality a central part of its aid programs and France announcing new measures to combat gender-based violence and sexual harassment. The Dutch, Belgian, and Scandinavian governments led efforts to establish an international reproductive rights fund to replace US funding lost through the Global Gag Rule, and Sweden pursued a "feminist foreign policy" that prioritizes the rights of women and girls in places such as Saudi Arabia.

Responding in large part to the campaigning of women's rights activists, three Middle Eastern and North African states—Tunisia, Jordan, and Lebanon—repealed provisions in their penal codes that allowed rapists to escape punishment by marrying their victims.

## LGBT Rights

Sexual and gender minorities were a common target of governments seeking to rally conservative backers, often as a diversion from governance failures. Whether Putin in Russia, al-Sisi in Egypt, or Mugabe in Zimbabwe, leaders tried to stoke moral panic for their own political gain against lesbian, gay, bisexual, and transgender (LGBT) people. Police in Indonesia, Tanzania, and Azerbaijan targeted LGBT people in public and raided private spaces with impunity.

Regardless of its form, heightened persecution of LGBT people is a good indication that the government is failing to deliver on public expectations. Yet the assumption that persecution of LGBT people would inevitably meet with approval is becoming less certain.

Most Latin American countries have moved squarely into the pro-LGBT rights camp in international forums, joining Japan along with many North American and European countries. Mozambique, Belize, Nauru and the Seychelles have in recent years all decriminalized same-sex conduct.

This pushback manifested itself even in Russia. The detention, torture, enforced disappearance and murder of gay men by forces under Chechen President Ramzan Kadyrov met such widespread outrage that Putin was compelled to rein in his brutal ally, ending the purge in this southern Russian republic. Yet elsewhere other priorities still sometimes got in the way, as in the response to anti-LGBT crackdowns in Egypt, where donors seemed reluctant to raise the issue for fear of offending a counterterrorism ally.

## *Time to Act, Not Despair*

The central lesson of the past year is that despite the considerable headwinds, the defense of human rights can succeed if the proper efforts are made. Populists offer superficial answers to complex problems, but broad swathes of the public, when reminded of the human rights principles at stake, can be convinced to reject the populists' scapegoating of unpopular minorities and their efforts to undermine checks and balances against government abuse.

The inward orientation of Western powers wrought by the struggle over populism has led to an increasingly fragmented world where mass atrocities are too often left unchecked. Still, principled small and medium-sized countries can make a difference when they join forces and act strategically.

A fair assessment of global prospects for human rights should induce concern rather than surrender—a call to action rather than a cry of despair. As we enter the 70th anniversary year of the Universal Declaration of Human Rights, the challenge is to seize the considerable opportunities that remain to push back against those who would reverse hard-fought progress.

Human rights standards provide guidance but become operational only with champions among governments and ordinary people. Each of us has a part to play. The past year shows that rights can be protected from populist assaults. The challenge now is to strengthen that defense and reverse the populist surge.

# FORGOTTEN PEOPLE WITHIN
# A FORGOTTEN CRISIS

People with Disabilities at Risk in the Central African Republic

WORLD REPORT
2018

# COUNTRIES

HUMAN
RIGHTS
WATCH

"I Won't Be A Doctor,
and One Day You'll Be Sick"
Girls' Access to Education in Afghanistan

# Afghanistan

Fighting between Afghan government and Taliban forces intensified through 2017, causing high numbers of civilian casualties. Principally in Nangarhar province, government forces also battled the Islamic State of Khorason Province (ISKP), the Afghan branch of the extremist group Islamic State (also known as ISIS). A number of particularly deadly suicide attacks in urban areas, some claimed by ISKP, killed and wounded more than 2,000 people across the country. A growing number of these attacks targeted Afghanistan's Shia Hazara minority. Civilian casualties caused by government forces during ground fighting declined; however, US forces expanded their use of airstrikes, including drones, in military operations, causing increased civilian casualties.

Afghan National Security Forces (ANSF) continued to rely on irregular militia forces, some of which killed and assaulted civilians. War crimes suspect Gulbuddin Hekmatyar, one of several political figures accused of shelling Kabul during the 1990s, returned to Kabul as part of a 2016 peace deal with the government; clashes between his militia forces and rivals killed at least 20 civilians. Both the Taliban and ANSF used schools for military purposes, which, together with countrywide insecurity, deprived many children, especially girls, of access to education.

The government made some progress in adopting legislation to curb torture, but failed to prosecute serious offenders. Promised reforms to end the use of unscientific and abusive "virginity examinations" for women taken into custody, and the imprisonment of women for so-called morality crimes, did not materialize. Only a fraction of the reported cases of violence against women resulted in prosecutions. The government announced that district council and parliamentary elections would be held in July 2018, three years behind schedule. However, political infighting and security concerns threatened to delay the vote.

## Armed Conflict

The United Nations Assistance Mission to Afghanistan (UNAMA) documented 2,640 war-related civilian deaths and 5,379 injuries in the first nine months of 2017, a slight decrease over the same period in 2016. The Taliban and groups claiming allegiance to ISKP were responsible for two-thirds of these. Civilian deaths and injuries by pro-government forces and their allies during ground engagements declined; however, those from aerial operations by government and international forces increased by 52 percent to 205 deaths and 261 injured.

Insurgent attacks in major cities caused hundreds of civilian deaths and injuries. ISKP claimed responsibility for the March 8 attack on Kabul's Daud Khan hospital, the main treatment center for wounded Afghan soldiers, that killed at least 30 and wounded dozens. In that attack, insurgents reportedly dressed as doctors shot dead patients in their beds. The May 31 truck bomb that killed at least 92 and wounded more than 500 was the deadliest such attack ever in Kabul. Suicide attackers targeted Shia mosques in Kabul and Herat, killing more than 100.

On August 3-5, local Taliban forces in Sar-i Pul province launched an assault on the village of Mirza Olang, following weeks of fighting between insurgents and Afghan Local Police (ALP) forces. According to UNAMA, the Taliban separated women and children from men, and shot dead at least nine ALP and other pro-government militia members, along with 27 male civilians; among them were four boys ages 13 to 17, and 13 men over 60. They also killed one woman as she was trying to flee. The commander responsible, a relative of the Taliban "shadow governor," had self-identified as being affiliated with ISKP.

The number of internally displaced persons (IDPs) who fled from their homes due to the conflict surged as fighting intensified. More than 250,000 were displaced in the first 10 months of 2017, bringing the nationwide total to at least 1.7 million people. Among the displaced were hundreds of thousands of refugees coerced out of Pakistan with the support of the United Nations High Commissioner for Refugees (UNHCR) in 2016. Attacks on civilians contributed to depression and other mental disabilities; Afghanistan has few community-based mental health services to provide treatment.

## *Women's and Girls' Rights*

On March 12, the Attorney General's Office issued a report on prosecutions under the Elimination of Violence against Women (EVAW) law revealing that mediation remains the preferred route for most prosecutors, which women are often compelled to accept due to pressure from family and justice officials. Registered cases represent only a fraction of the actual crimes of violence against women. In late 2016, the Afghanistan Independent Human Rights Commission

(AIHRC) investigated 5,575 cases, noting that most cases of violence against women go unreported. A long-standing effort to reform family law, including divorce provisions, remained stalled.

On March 4, the revised penal code was adopted by presidential decree. It incorporated all the provisions of the EVAW law, while strengthening the definition of rape. However, because a number of conservative members of parliament have opposed the EVAW law, some activists campaigned to preserve the law in its stand-alone form decreed in 2009. In response to their efforts, in August President Ghani ordered the Ministry of Justice to remove the EVAW chapter from the new penal code. The controversial reversal has left the status of the law in limbo.

A long-promised plan by the Afghan government to implement UN Security Council Resolution 1325, which calls for women's equal participation in issues surrounding peace and security, was further delayed during the year. The Kabul Process peace talks in June included only two women among 47 government and international representatives.

Deaths and injuries among women in the conflict increased sharply in 2017, with 298 deaths and 709 injured in the first nine months of the year. Most occurred as a result of suicide bombings and aerial attacks.

## Arbitrary Detention, Torture, and Discriminatory Practices

An April report by UNAMA documented the highest levels of torture of conflict-related detainees in police custody since 2010. The report singled out the Kandahar police for torturing 91 percent of detainees by forcibly pumping water into their stomachs, crushing their testicles with clamps, suffocating them to the point of losing consciousness, and applying electric current to their genitals.

In a significant sign of progress in curbing torture, the government in March enacted anti-torture legislation, as part of the new penal code. The law left out a compensation system for victims of torture by state security forces, but in August the cabinet approved an annex to provide for victim redress.

Although the Afghan Constitution prohibits torture, the new provisions expand the definition in conformity with the UN Convention Against Torture, and create a new monitoring body, the Commission Against Torture; however, as of December it was not clear whether this would include staff from the AIHRC. The government did not prosecute any senior officials accused of torture.

In May, a report by the UN Committee Against Torture described "numerous and credible allegations" of severe human rights abuses, including torture and extra-judicial killings, and urged that all alleged perpetrators "be duly prosecuted and, if found guilty, convicted with penalties that are commensurate with the grave nature of their crimes."

In January 2017, the Afghan attorney general ordered nine of First Vice President Abdul Rashid Dostum's guards to answer questions in connection with the abduction, illegal imprisonment, and sexual assault of rival Uzbek politician Ahmad Ischi. Dostum refused to allow his guards to report to the attorney general, who then settled for interviewing seven of them on the premises of Dostum's compound. On November 1, seven of the bodyguards were convicted in absentia of sexual assault and illegal imprisonment, and sentenced to five years' imprisonment. As of December 2017, none was in custody.

In Afghanistan, same-sex relations are punishable by 5 to 15 years in prison under a law that bans all sex between individuals not married to each other.

## Freedom of Expression

The year looked likely to surpass 2016 as the bloodiest since 2001 for Afghan journalists, with 10 killed in the first six months of the year, most of them victims of insurgent bombing attacks. Since January, the Afghan Journalists Safety Committee (AJSC) recorded 73 cases of violence and threats against journalists, including deaths, detentions, beatings, and intimidation. Government officials and security personnel were responsible for slightly more than half of the cases; insurgent groups were responsible for the deaths of 10 journalists in suicide attacks in Kabul and Khost.

## Protests, Excessive Use of Force, and Freedom of Assembly

On June 2, civil society groups, political activists, and relatives of victims of the May 31 truck bomb attack converged in central Kabul to protest deteriorating security conditions. Some participants threw stones at police, and the group included some armed men among the crowd.

Security forces, principally the presidential palace guard, used water cannons to disperse the crowd, but then used live ammunition despite no real threat to public safety—first firing guns over the heads of demonstrators, injuring some protesters, then shooting into the crowd, killing seven. The government promised to conduct an investigation. As of December, the results of this investigation had not been made public.

The government subsequently accelerated its consideration of new legislation to restrict demonstrations. The Law on Gatherings, Demonstrations and Strikes narrows the definition of allowed venues for protests; prohibits "influential people" from "politically intervening" in any kind of protest, without clearly defining those terms; and limits protests only to those that have "reform objectives" rather than criticism of government policies alone. Civil society groups condemned the law, which as of December, was pending before parliament.

## Children's Rights

Despite the fact that the government in 2016 criminalized military recruitment of Afghans under 18 years old, the practice continued, most notably among the ALP and pro-government militias. The AIHRC reported on increased recruitment by groups affiliated with ISKP in Nangarhar. Both the ANSF and the Taliban continued to occupy or use schools for military purposes in contested areas, affecting the access to education of thousands of children, especially girls.

Afghanistan's new penal code criminalizes the sexual abuse of boys, known in Afghanistan as *bacha bazi*.

Conflict-related deaths and injuries of children continued at high rates, with 689 deaths and 1,791 injuries in the first nine months of 2017. Almost half of the children detained in relation to the conflict reported being tortured or mistreated.

## Key International Actors

On August 22, US President Donald Trump outlined a new US strategy for the war in Afghanistan, vowing to expand military operations to target criminal and terrorist networks, pressure Pakistan to end support for Afghan insurgents, and set no timetable for withdrawal.

In September, the Trump administration reportedly was considering a CIA request to carry out covert drone strikes in Afghanistan; the US military has had exclusive authority to carry out such strikes.

Trump authorized the deployment of an additional 3,900 troops, but the Pentagon acknowledged that actual troop levels were already close to 11,000, significantly higher than the 8,000 previously reported. US airstrikes increased through 2017, and the US provided Black Hawk helicopters and other equipment to support expanded Afghan government air operations.

In September, diplomatic sources indicated that the US was supporting an Afghan government initiative to create an additional village defense force, the Afghan National Army Territorial Force. The force would reportedly absorb some existing militias under army command, though it remained unclear how it would avoid replicating the record of the abusive Afghan Local Police. The US military command in Afghanistan also began classifying key data related to the development of Afghan security forces, most of which has been public since 2008.

In February, the European Union (EU) signed a new agreement with Afghanistan requiring it to accept rejected asylum seekers from Europe and undertake other measures to reduce migration. The agreement also included EU support for development, women's rights, ending corruption, and electoral reform. In July, the European Commission proposed a new EU strategy for Afghanistan, based on these objectives. In May, NATO members agreed to provide Afghan security forces with US$1 billion annually through 2020, and in November agreed to increase their troop commitments by an additional 3,000.

On November 20, the prosecutor of the International Criminal Court (ICC) asked the court's judges for permission to open an investigation into possible war crimes and crimes against humanity in Afghanistan committed by the Taliban and affiliated forces, Afghan National Security Forces, and US armed forces and the Central Intelligence Agency since May 1, 2003, when Afghanistan became a member of the court. The ICC's preliminary examination of allegations of serious international crimes in Afghanistan began in 2007.

# Algeria

Despite constitutional amendments passed in 2016, Algerian authorities continued to resort in 2017 to criminal prosecutions for peaceful speech, using articles in the penal code criminalizing "offending the president," "insulting state officials," and "denigrating Islam" as well as other articles on sharing "intelligence with foreign powers." They have also continued to ban demonstrations in Algiers.

President Abdelaziz Bouteflika was re-elected to a fourth five-year term in 2014, despite being in visibly frail health. In legislative elections held on May 4, 2017, the governing coalition, led by the National Liberation Front and the National Rally for Democracy, maintained its majority.

## *Freedom of Assembly*

Algerian authorities routinely violate the right to freedom of assembly, despite constitutional guarantees of that right. The penal code punishes organizing or participating in an unauthorized demonstration in a public place with up to one year in prison (article 98). Authorities in Algiers, the capital, banned public demonstrations indefinitely in 2001, when the country was under a state of emergency. Authorities did not rescind the ban when they lifted the state of emergency in 2011.

The ban on demonstrations in Algiers is strictly enforced by authorities, who mobilize large numbers of police to thwart demonstrations and detain participants, usually holding them for a few hours before releasing them.

For example, on September 6, 2017, dozens of protesters took to a square in central Algiers wearing t-shirts with the words "Article 102," referring to the constitutional article that stipulates a president can be removed from office if he cannot carry out his duties. At least six of them were detained for six hours before being released without charge, according to local media.

## *Freedom of Association*

In 2012, the government enacted Law 12-06, which requires all associations—including those that had already successfully registered—to re-file registration applications and obtain a registration receipt from the Interior Ministry before they can operate legally, in a cumbersome procedure akin to a new registration.

To date, major human rights organization such as the Algerian League for Human Rights (Ligue Algérienne des Droits de l'Homme, LADDH) and Youth Action Rally (Rassemblement Action Jeunesse, RAJ), and the Algerian division of Amnesty International, which all submitted compliance applications in January 2014 as provided for by Law 12-06, have still not obtained a receipt certifying their legal existence. Lack of a receipt means they are unable to open a bank account or rent an office in their own name or hire a public hall for a meeting. Moreover, members of an association that is "non-accredited, suspended, or dissolved" risk prison sentences of up to six months for conducting activities in its name.

Authorities used the association law to deny registration to a charitable organization formed by members of Algeria's tiny Ahmadiyya religious minority, basing its refusal on language in the law that gives authorities broad leeway to deny authorization if they deem that the content and objectives of a group's activities violate Algeria's "fundamental principles (*constantes nationales*) and values, public order, public morals, and the applicable laws and regulations."

## *Freedom of Speech*

Since the 1990s, Algeria has seen a proliferation of privately owned newspapers that enjoy a certain margin of freedom to criticize public figures and state policies. The 2014 Law on Audio-Visual Activities ended the formal state monopoly on audiovisual media. However, repressive press laws, dependence on revenues from public-sector advertising, and other factors limit press freedom. The Information Code, adopted in 2012, states that news journalism is to be "a freely practiced activity" as long as it respects "national identity, the cultural values of society, national sovereignty and national unity, as well as the requirements of national security, national defense, public order, and the country's economic interests, among others."

In 2017, authorities prosecuted a number of Algerians for critical speech.

On August 9, 2016, an Algiers appeals court upheld a two-year prison sentence for Mohamed Tamalt, a freelance journalist with dual Algerian and British nationality, for a video he posted on Facebook featuring a poem deemed offensive to

Algeria's president. Tamalt died in prison on December 11, 2016, after staging a hunger strike to protest his conviction. Authorities denied mistreatment but his family insisted that negligence or mistreatment contributed to his death.

Algerian authorities also prosecuted Marzoug Touati, a blogger and editor of the website *Al-Hogra*. Algerian security forces arrested Touati at his home in the coastal city of Béjaïa on January 18. According to his lawyer, security forces interrogated Touati about a video that he published online on January 9 containing a teleconferenced interview with an Israeli Foreign Ministry spokesman, who stated that Israel has maintained a liaison office in Algiers since before 2000.

A court in Béjaïa on January 22, 2017, ordered his pretrial detention on the charge of "talking to the agents of a foreign power with the intention of causing harm to Algeria's army, diplomatic relations, and financial interests," and "inciting citizens to carry weapons and gather illegally." He was still detained as of December 2017 in Oued Ghir prison, awaiting trial.

## Women's Rights

Algeria's constitution enshrines the principle of nondiscrimination based on gender and requires the state to take positive action to ensure equality of rights and duties of all citizens, men and women. In February 2016, parliament introduced an article proclaiming that the "state works to attain parity between women and men in the job market," and "encourages the promotion of women to positions of responsibility in public institutions and in businesses."

In 2015, parliament adopted amendments to the penal code specifically criminalizing some forms of domestic violence. Assault against one's spouse or former spouse can be punished by up to 20 years in prison, and the perpetrator can face a life sentence for attacks resulting in death. The amendments also criminalize sexual harassment in public places.

Despite adoption of the law, Algeria has yet to adopt the more comprehensive legal measures, such as protection orders to protect women from violence and specific obligations on law enforcement to respond to domestic violence. The law, moreover, makes women vulnerable to threats from the offender or relatives, by including a provision that a pardon by the victim puts an end to prosecution.

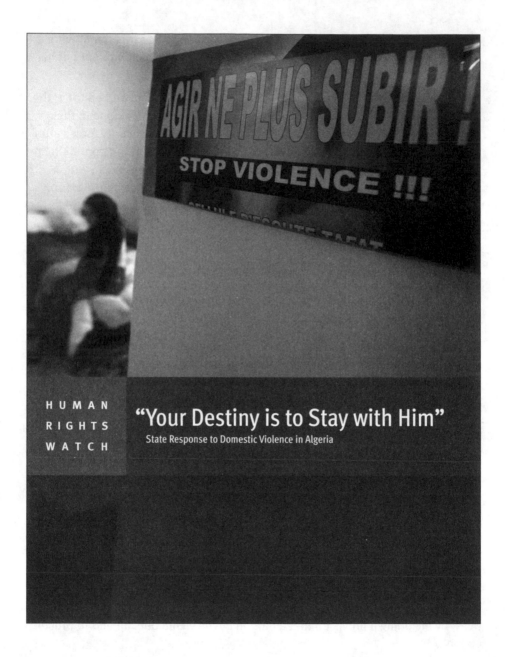

AGIR NE PLUS SUBIR !

STOP VIOLENCE !!!

HUMAN
RIGHTS
WATCH

"Your Destiny is to Stay with Him"
State Response to Domestic Violence in Algeria

Algeria's Family Code continues to discriminate against women despite some amendments in 2005 that improved women's access to divorce and child custody. Algeria also continues to retain article 326 in its penal code, which allows anyone who abducts a minor to escape prosecution if they married their victim.

## Freedom of Religion

More than 266 members of Algeria's tiny Ahmadi minority have been prosecuted since June 2016, and some imprisoned for up to six months. Senior government officials have at times claimed that Ahmadis represent a threat to the majority Sunni Muslim faith, and accused them of collusion with foreign powers.

Authorities charged them under one or more of the following charges: denigrating the dogma or precepts of Islam; participating in an unauthorized association; collecting donations without a license; and possessing and distributing documents from foreign sources that endanger national security. At least 20 have faced a charge of practicing religion in an unauthorized place of worship under Algeria's 2006 law governing non-Muslim religions, even though Ahmadis consider themselves to be Muslim.

On September 13, 2017, the court of First Instance in Ain Tedles, Mostaganem, sentenced Mohamed Fali, the president of the community, to a term of six months in prison, suspended, and a fine.

## Refugees and Migrants

From August to October 2017, authorities rounded up more than 3,000 sub-Saharan migrants of different nationalities living in and around Algiers and bused them 1,900 kilometers south to a camp in Tamanrasset, from which some were bused into Niger.

Those forcibly transported to Tamanrasset included migrants who have lived and worked for years in Algeria. Authorities then expelled several hundred to Niger.

## Sexual Orientation and Gender Identity

Algeria's penal code criminalizes same sex relations with a prison sentence of two months to two years. In 2015, several people were arrested for same-sex relations but none were prosecuted.

Activists state that during and after the 2014 presidential election, anti-LGBT rhetoric from politicians and media led to increased harassment and violence, leading many lesbian, gay, bisexual, and transgender community leaders to flee the country. Activists have documented recent cases of violence on the grounds of sexual orientation and gender identity within families, at universities, in the streets, and in prisons.

## Key International Actors

Algeria underwent its third Universal Periodic Review (UPR) at the United Nations Human Rights Council (UNHRC), on May 8, 2017. Algeria received 229 recommendations from states. Algeria failed to accept many of the most important recommendations, related to the abolition of the death penalty, ratifying the Rome Statute, decriminalizing same sex relations, and ending discrimination against women, among others.

Algeria continued during 2017 its noncompliance with longstanding requests for country visits by special procedures of the UNHRC including the special rapporteurs on torture, on human rights while countering terrorism, and on extrajudicial, summary and arbitrary executions, and the Working Group on Enforced and Involuntary Disappearances.

On April 2017, the special rapporteur on the right of everyone to the enjoyment of the highest attainable standard of physical and mental health, released his report on his 2016 visit to Algeria. While commending the government for improving basic health-related indicators, he also noted the prevalence of inequalities and discrimination against certain population groups, such as people living with HIV/AIDS, drugs users, men who have sex with men, migrants, and refugees and called for the decriminalization of homosexuality and sex work.

The European Union and Algeria adopted their shared Partnership Priorities for the period 2017-2020 at the Association Council of 13 March 2017. Strong emphasis was placed on the implementation of Algeria's new constitution. Notably, the EU pledged to assist Algeria in the areas of governance, democracy, promotion and protection of fundamental rights—including labor rights—strengthening the role of women in society, decentralization, judiciary, and civil society.

# Angola

Angola elected a new president, João Lourenço, in September, ending almost four decades of José Eduardo Dos Santos' repressive rule. Voting was peaceful, but marred by severe restrictions on freedom of expression and assembly, and limited access to information due to government repression and censorship in state media and in private media outlets controlled by ruling party officials.

The new president pledged to govern for all Angolans, and combat two of the country's major problems: corruption and mismanagement of public funds. Security forces continued to use excessive force, intimidation and arbitrary detention against peaceful protesters. Freedom of the press was threatened after a new media law was enacted, despite opposition from the journalist's union and other groups.

## *Freedom of Media*

Angolan media remained largely controlled by the government and people linked to the ruling party, the People's Movement for the Liberation of Angola (MPLA). The government continued to restrict freedom of expression by censoring state-run media and some private media controlled by ruling party officials, which remained the only outlets with nationwide coverage. During the election campaign, election observers from the African Union (AU), the Southern African Development Community (SADC) and Angola's journalists' union criticized the pro-ruling party coverage by state media.

With minimal debate, parliament on November 18, 2016, passed five laws that limit freedom of expression, despite opposition from the journalist's union and other groups. The government referred to the laws as the Social Communication Legislative Package (*Pacote legislativo da comunicação social)*. These laws, signed by then-President Jose Eduardo Dos Santos on January 23, are the press law, television law, broadcast law, code of conduct law for journalists, and statutes of the Angolan Regulatory Body for Social Communication (ERCA, *Entidade Reguladora da Comunicação Social Angolana)*.

The press law gives the Ministry of Social Communication the authority to oversee how media organizations carry out editorial decisions, and to fine or suspend the activities of violators. It also criminalizes publication of a text or image that is "offensive to individuals." Under the Angolan penal code, defamation and slander are punishable with fines and imprisonment for up to six months. The journalists union challenged the law before the Constitutional Court. At time of writing, the court had not ruled on the case.

## Freedom of Assembly

Authorities continued to violate international human rights law by denying citizens the right to peaceful protest. Security forces blocked peaceful anti-government protests with intimidation, excessive force and arbitrary detention.

For example, on February 24, police blocked a protest in Luanda of about 15 people who were calling for the resignation of the territorial administration minister, Bornito de Sousa. On the same day, police broke up a peaceful protest and detained two activists in Benguela Province who were also calling for the resignation of the minister. On April 19, a court in Luanda sentenced seven activists to 45 days in jail for resisting arrest during a protest against the voters registration process ahead of the August elections. On June 24, authorities detained at least 18 members of the Lunda Tchokwe Protectorate Movement, who were protesting for regional autonomy and an end to police brutality against movement activists. Ahead of the August 23 election, the Ministry of the Interior banned all protests by groups not contesting in the election, claiming that street protests planned by activists posed a security risk.

In a rare show of tolerance, authorities on March 18 allowed a group of women to protest against the criminalization of abortion. Authorities also allowed an opposition party, National Union for the Total Independence of Angola (UNITA), protest march against what the party called irregularities in the election process.

## Freedom of Association

On July 5, the Constitutional Court ruled that a presidential decree that imposed severe restrictions on civil society groups violated the Angolan constitution. The case was brought to the court by the Angolan Bar Association. The court ruled that parliament, not the president, has constitutional authority to regulate non-governmental organizations (NGOs).

The decree 74/15 required NGOs to go through onerous registration processes, including registering with multiple authorities, such as the Foreign Ministry, and obtaining a "declaration of suitability." It also allowed authorities to determine the programs and projects that the organizations implemented. Enforcement of the law in March 2015 led to several human rights groups facing difficulties accessing their bank accounts, as some banks demanded to see the required approvals, even though the government was not issuing such documents.

## Abortion Law

Women's reproductive rights were threatened after parliament approved an amendment to the abortion law on February 24, making all abortions illegal. As part of the process of replacing Angola's 1886 penal code, the government had proposed a bill that would criminalize abortion, except in cases of rape, or when the mother's health is in danger.

However, parliament rejected that proposal and made abortion, without exceptions, illegal and punishable by 4-10 years' imprisonment. Parliament passed the first reading of the bill without any public consultations, and activists accused parliamentarians of ignoring their views. The final vote on the draft penal code, which had been scheduled for March 23, was cancelled and the bill was withdrawn pending further debate after women marched on the streets supporting the right to abortion. At time of writing, a new version of the abortion bill had not been submitted to parliament.

## Abuses by Security Forces

Security forces continued to use excessive force with impunity. Authorities repeatedly failed to investigate and prosecute officers who committed abuses. In March, police beat activists with batons and set dogs on a peaceful protest, injuring at least four protesters. Responding to calls for the incident to be investigated, a police spokesman said the use of police dogs was necessary because the group was causing chaos.

In another incident in April, video footage showed a uniformed police officer in Luanda beating a protester with a disability until he fell off his wheelchair. The police then walked away from the scene, as a passersby struggled to lift the

man. The video also showed officers pulling banners and leaflets from other protesters with physical disabilities who gathered to protest inaccessible infrastructure and inequality. The police promised to investigate the incident, but at time
of writing had not published the results of the investigations. In June, at least
one person was reported killed, while 10 others were seriously injured when police fired into crowds of people protesting for the autonomy of the Lunda Chokwe
region, in Lunda Norte province.

## Election Violence

Reports emerged of violent incidents ahead of the August 23 general election involving members of the ruling MPLA and the main opposition party, UNITA. In
May, the governor of Benguela set up a commission of inquiry to investigate the
reports of political violence in the province.

On July 31, a senior UNITA official died and six people were injured when unidentified men attacked them in Benguela. UNITA blamed MPLA supporters for the incident. On September 15, during an election celebration, MPLA and UNITA
supporters clashed in the Bocoio region of Benguela Province. According to the
human rights group OMUNGA, several people were injured, houses and shops
were destroyed, and local residents hid in the bush for fear of fighting.

## Key International Actors

Angola has formally presented its candidature to the United Nations Human
Rights Council for the 2018-2020 term. As part of the process, on April 19 it
pledged to maintain interaction with civil society to better advocate for the rights
of migrants; adopt a national human rights action plan; and reinforce efforts to
achieve its goals of advancing the democratic process and diversifying the economy.

Following the August elections, the European Union pledged to support future
electoral processes, including efforts to ensure equal access and equitable coverage of all political parties in the media, and the reform of the electoral legislation in line with international principles of inclusiveness and transparency.

Both SADC and the AU expressed approval with the generally peaceful elections.
The two bodies advised the authorities to improve equitable coverage and ac-

cess to public media by all political parties. SADC also urged the government to improve the electoral framework in line with the Revised SADC Principles and Guidelines Governing Democratic Elections, for example by assigning voter registration to the National Electoral Commission. Currently, the voter registration process is organized by the Ministry of Territorial Administration.

# Argentina

Long-standing human rights problems in Argentina include police abuse, poor prison conditions, endemic violence against women, restrictions on abortion, difficulty accessing reproductive services, and obstacles keeping indigenous people from enjoying the rights that Argentine and international law afford them.

Impunity for the 1994 bombing of the AMIA Jewish center in Buenos Aires, vaguely defined criminal provisions that undermine free speech, and delays in appointing permanent judges are serious concerns.

In 2017, Argentina created a federal agency to ensure access to official information. Argentina continues to make significant progress protecting lesbian, gay, bisexual, and transgender (LGBT) rights and prosecuting officials for abuses committed during the country's last military dictatorship (1976-1983), although trials have been delayed.

## Confronting Past Abuses

As of November 2017, the Attorney General's Office reported 2,971 people charged, 818 convicted, and 99 acquitted of crimes allegedly committed by Argentina's last military junta. Of 613 cases alleging crimes against humanity, judges had issued rulings in 193.

Prosecutions were made possible by a series of actions taken in the early 2000s by Congress, the Supreme Court, and federal judges annulling amnesty laws and striking down pardons of former officials implicated in the crimes. As of September 2017, 125 people who were illegally taken from their parents as children during the 1976-1983 dictatorship had been located. Many were reunited with their families.

In May, the Supreme Court issued a controversial ruling on sentencing for crimes against humanity committed during the last dictatorship. It ruled that Luis Muiña, convicted of torture and kidnappings committed in 1977, could benefit from a 1994 law—known as the "2x1" Law, which aims to reduce the overuse of pretrial detention and incentivize speedy trials for people in detention. The court used provisions of the law to reduce his sentence from 13 to 9 years.

In July, a criminal court in Mendoza province sentenced four people who served as judges during the dictatorship to life in prison without possibility of parole for committing crimes against humanity, including arbitrary arrests, torture, killings, and enforced disappearances. Twenty-four military, police, and penitentiary agents were also convicted.

The large number of victims, suspects, and cases make it difficult for prosecutors and judges to bring those responsible to justice while respecting their due process rights. The Attorney General's Office reported in October that 533 pretrial detainees and convicted prisoners were under house arrest, a right that Argentine law provides to people older than 70. In 2016, the government said it would not appeal judicial rulings granting house arrest to these detainees and convicted prisoners.

The fate of Jorge Julio López, a torture victim who disappeared in 2006—a day before he was due to attend the trial of one of his torturers—remained unknown.

## *Freedom of Expression*

In January 2016, police detained Milagro Sala, a prominent social leader in Jujuy province, in connection with her participation in street protests. Sala and others had gathered in the provincial capital to protest a decree the governor had issued purporting to regulate organizations like Sala's, which implement government-funded housing and other welfare programs.

Sala was charged with instigating protesters to commit crimes and with sedition. Sala was also under investigation for alleged corruption. In July, she was transferred to house arrest, as mandated by precautionary measures that the Inter-American Commission of Human Rights (IACHR) had issued in her favor, but was returned to prison in October for allegedly failing to comply with the conditions of her home arrest.

In April 2017, the Argentine government committed to reforming the criminal code to modify and narrow the definition of sedition. However, it had yet to present a formal proposal to Congress at time of writing.

Upon taking office, President Mauricio Macri adopted a temporary set of decrees to regulate media, and created a new agency that reports to the Communications Ministry to implement the new rules. In July 2016, the government said it was drafting a communications law that it claimed would respect free speech. At time of writing, the law had not been presented to Congress. However, the new, supposedly temporary agency that lacks structural independence from the executive had already issued rulings regulating media.

In 2016, the Macri administration issued a resolution establishing transparent criteria to prevent favoritism in government purchases of media advertising. In August 2017, the president appointed the head of a national agency to ensure public access to information held by government bodies, implementing a 2016 law approved by Congress. However, some provinces and municipalities still lack such laws, undermining transparency.

## Prison Conditions and Abuse

Overcrowding, ill-treatment by guards, inadequate facilities, and inmate violence continue in Argentina's prisons. The National Penitentiary Office, which Congress created in 2003 to supervise federal prisons and protect detainees' rights, reported the violent deaths of eight federal prisoners between January and June 2017, although the statistics did not make clear the perpetrators. The office also documented 300 alleged cases of torture or ill-treatment in federal prisons between January and May 2017, after 608 cases in 2016.

Police abuse remains a serious problem. Security forces occasionally employ excessive force against protesters, despite a 2011 commitment by authorities in at least 19 of Argentina's 23 provinces to ensure that force is used proportionately.

The Provincial Commission for Memory, an autonomous public body created by the provincial legislature, reported that in 2016, one person a day either died in detention—mostly due to preventable causes, in facilities that are often plagued by poor medical treatment—or after being shot during clashes with police forces in Buenos Aires province.

On August 1, Santiago Maldonado, a 28-year-old artisan, went missing while visiting a Mapuche indigenous community in Cushamen, in the southern province of Chubut. On August 14, according to media reports, two members of the Mapuche community declared before the judge investigating the case that they saw the Gendarmerie—a federal security force—take Maldonado away from a demonstration. In October, his body was found near a river in the area. The judge investigating the case said that initial results of Maldonado's autopsy revealed he apparently did not have injuries caused by third parties, and some forensic experts reportedly claimed that his body had spent up to 60 days under the water. At time of writing, the judge was still investigating the circumstances of his death.

## Judicial and Prosecutorial Independence

The delayed appointment of permanent judges by the Council of the Judiciary has led to temporary appointments of judges who lack security of tenure, which the Supreme Court ruled in 2015 undermines judicial independence. As of November 2016, 254 of 979 lower-court judgeships remained vacant.

In 2017, President Macri asked Congress to initiate the process to remove Attorney General Alejandra Gils Carbó, arguing she did not have the "moral authority" required for the job. Other government officials, however, suggested it would be possible to oust Gils Carbó through an executive decree, so circumventing the legal requirement of a political trial.

## Impunity for the AMIA Bombing

Twenty-two years after the 1994 bombing of the Argentine Israelite Mutual Association (AMIA) in Buenos Aires that killed 85 people and injured more than 300, no one has been convicted of the crime.

The investigation stalled when Iran, which Argentina's judiciary suspects of ordering the attack, refused to allow Argentine investigators to interview Iranian suspects in Argentina. In 2013, Argentina and Iran signed a memorandum of understanding (MOU) that allowed an international commission of jurists to review evidence and question Iranian suspects—but only in Tehran—likely rendering the interviews inadmissible in an Argentine court. A federal court declared the MOU unconstitutional: the Macri administration said it would not appeal.

In August 2017, the government said it had asked Interpol to re-issue red notices—a form of international arrest warrant—to detain several Iranians implicated in the attack. In September, Vice-President Gabriela Michetti called on Iran to collaborate with the investigations during her speech at the United Nations General Assembly.

In January 2015, Alberto Nisman, the prosecutor in charge of investigating the bombing, was found dead in his home with a single gunshot wound to the head and a pistol beside him matching the wound. His death came just days after he had filed a criminal complaint accusing then-President Cristina Fernández de Kirchner and her foreign affairs minister of conspiring with Iran to undermine the investigation.

Later in 2015, a federal court dismissed Nisman's complaint. However, following an appeal by a federal prosecutor, in December 2016, the judiciary ordered the case reopened. In October 2017, a judge requested that Fernández de Kirchner provide a statement on the case. As of September 2017, courts had not determined whether Nisman's death was suicide or murder. A new Gendarmerie report published that month stated Nisman had been murdered.

In 2015, a court began the trial of several officials—including former President Carlos Menem, his head of intelligence, and a judge—for their alleged interference with the initial investigation into the bombing. The trial continued at time of writing.

## Indigenous Rights

Indigenous people in Argentina face obstacles in accessing justice, land, education, health care, and basic services. Argentina has failed to implement existing laws to protect indigenous peoples' right to free, prior, and informed consent when the government adopts decisions that may affect their rights—a right provided for in international law.

A survey of indigenous lands, required by law, is being conducted, but slowly. In November 2017, Congress approved a law extending the deadline for completing the survey to 2021.

## Women's and Girls' Rights

Abortion is illegal in Argentina, except in cases of rape or when the life of the woman is at risk. But even in such cases, women and girls are sometimes subject to criminal prosecution for seeking abortions, and have trouble accessing reproductive services, such as contraception and voluntary sterilization.

In 2017, "Belen," a 27-year-old woman from Tucumán province who had been sentenced to eight years in prison in 2016 for aggravated homicide after suffering a miscarriage, was acquitted and released.

Despite a 2009 law setting forth comprehensive measures to prevent and punish violence against women, the unpunished killing of women remains a serious concern. The National Registry of Femicides, administered by the Supreme Court, reported 254 femicides—the violent killing of women based on their gender—but only 22 convictions, in 2016.

In September 2017, Manuel Mansilla was found guilty of murdering his pregnant girlfriend, 14-year-old Chiara Páez, and sentenced to 21 years in prison. Páez's killing sparked a massive movement to protest violence against women in the country.

## Sexual Orientation and Gender Identity

In 2010, Argentina became the first Latin American country to legalize same-sex marriage. The Civil Marriage Law allows same-sex couples to enter civil marriages and affords them the same legal marital protections as opposite-sex couples, including adoption rights and pension benefits. Since 2010, local groups report, more than 16,200 same-sex couples have married nationwide.

## Key International Actors and Foreign Policy

In May, the UN Working Group on Arbitrary Detention (UNWAD), which had called for Milagro Sala's release arguing she had been arbitrarily detained, visited her in jail. The IACHR did so in June, and later issued precautionary measures requesting that Argentine government ensure her safety. In November, the IACHR sent the case to the Inter-American Court of Human Rights, arguing Argentina had not complied with the precautionary measures it had issued in her favor.

In August, the UN Committee on Enforced Disappearances requested that Argentina adopt "an integral and exhaustive strategy" to find Santiago Maldonado. Days later, the IACHR ordered Argentina to adopt all necessary measures to determine his whereabouts.

In February 2017, the Argentine Supreme Court ruled that an Inter-American Court's decision on a specific case, while binding on Argentina, could not reverse or overrule decisions by Argentine courts. The decision was related to a 2011 ruling by the Inter-American Court that established the state had violated the right to free speech of two journalists who were fined after publishing information of public interest.

President Macri has repeatedly and publicly criticized Venezuela's poor human rights record and called for the release of its political prisoners. His administration has allowed Venezuelans to apply for the same permits to stay in Argentina that are granted to residents of Mercosur member countries, despite Venezuela's expulsion from the regional trade bloc. The number of Venezuelans moving legally to Argentina has more than doubled every year since 2014, reaching 35,600 in May 2017.

In March, Argentina hosted delegations from 80 countries for the second international Safe Schools conference, taking stock of the implementation of commitments contained in the Safe Schools Declaration to better protect schools from attacks and military use during armed conflict.

# Armenia

Parliamentary elections, the first since the 2015 constitutional amendments moving the country from a presidential to a parliamentary system, failed to improve public confidence in the electoral system. The ruling Republican Party dominated the polls amid reports of irregularities. Authorities failed to bring to justice officials responsible for excessive use of force against protesters and journalists, including during largely peaceful protests in Yerevan in July 2016. The trials of 32 men accused of crimes committed during the violent takeover of a police station in Yerevan, which prompted the protests, were ongoing at time of writing. Four defendants have reported ill-treatment in detention.

Human rights defenders faced threats and harassment. Domestic violence persists as a serious problem. The government introduced in parliament a draft law on violence in the family, but women's rights groups opposed it, fearing it emphasized keeping families together rather than protecting victims. Many children with disabilities lack quality education and live in institutions separated from their families.

The government overhauled the onerous system for prescribing and accessing opioid pain medications. Discrimination against women and people with disabilities, and based on sexual orientation and gender identity, persisted.

## Parliamentary and Municipal Elections

International observers, led by the Organization for Security and Co-operation in Europe (OSCE), concluded that the April parliamentary elections "were well administered," but the polls were "tainted by credible information about vote-buying, and pressure on civil servants and employees of private companies." The ruling party won the May Yerevan municipal elections amid low voter turnout and reports of vote-buying and voter intimidation.

## Harassment of Human Rights Defenders

In April, 30 public school and preschool principals filed lawsuits against the nongovernmental organization (NGO) Union of Informed Citizens and its director Daniel Ioannisyan, for allegedly damaging their honor and dignity. The NGO had published audio recordings they claimed showed several principals recruiting supporters for the ruling party ahead of the parliamentary elections. The principals dropped the suit in July.

In June, Artur Sakunts, director of Helsinki Citizens' Assembly Vanadzor Office, reported death threats from a Facebook user, apparently in response to Sakunts' Facebook post the same day criticizing the government. The General Prosecutor's Office opened an investigation 10 days later, but no charges had been brought at time of writing.

Local rights groups continue to raise concerns about the harassment of, and spurious criminal embezzlement charges against, Marina Poghosyan, whose organization, Veles, provides legal support to victims of predatory lenders, including some with alleged links to local authorities.

## *Lack of Accountability for Abuses by Law Enforcement Officials*

The government has failed to ensure full accountability for police violence against largely peaceful protesters and journalists during protests in Yerevan in July 2016. While some police officers faced disciplinary actions, no officials have faced criminal charges.

At the same time, authorities aggressively prosecuted protest participants and leaders. Courts convicted 22 people, sentencing 11 to prison terms of one to three-and-a-half years. Seven others received conditional sentences, three were fined, and one received both a conditional sentence and a fine. Most pleaded guilty, for which they received a speedy trial or a lesser sentence. Charges included using violence during mass disorder and interfering with the work of a journalist. Trials of other protesters and protest organizers were ongoing.

Four men on trial for alleged crimes committed during the July 2016 armed takeover of a Yerevan police station alleged that police beat them in the court building in June. Officers removed the men from the courtroom after an argument broke out between them and police. The men said police beat them in basement holding cells. Authorities opened an investigation but no criminal charges have been brought. Some officers alleged to have participated in the beatings remained on duty in the courtroom.

## Attacks on and Harassment of Journalists

The Committee to Protect Freedom of Expression, a media freedom NGO, documented physical attacks and interference against journalists including during the parliamentary and municipal elections.

On May 11, four officers entered the home of Arpi Makhsydyan, a journalist with Civilnet.am, without a warrant, claiming they were searching for a criminal suspect. Makhsudyan refused the search. Police later claimed they wanted only to question her. Makhsudyan believes police sought to intimidate her for her critical journalism. She filed a complaint about police conduct, but authorities failed to effectively investigate.

## Palliative Care

In February, the government approved a National Strategy on Palliative Care and an Action Plan, specifying much needed reforms for delivery of adequate palliative care to patients with life-threatening illnesses. Authorities registered oral morphine in March, and in November overhauled onerous and time-consuming prescription and procurement procedures for accessing it.

## Children's Rights

Thousands of children are placed in residential institutions due to disability or poverty. Children can face neglect due to overcrowding. The government is transforming some institutions to community centers and supporting family-based care, but has not included children with disabilities equally. Children with disabilities frequently remain in institutions as adults indefinitely, stripped of their legal capacity.

Under law, education should be inclusive by 2025, with children with and without disabilities studying together in community schools. Physical barriers and lack of reasonable accommodations means children with disabilities may not always receive a quality education in many community schools. Many children with disabilities remain segregated in special schools or isolated at home with little or no education.

**HUMAN RIGHTS WATCH**

## "When Will I Get to Go Home?"

Abuses and Discrimination against Children in Institutions
and Lack of Access to Quality Inclusive Education in Armenia

## Women's Rights

The Coalition to Stop Violence against Women reported at least four women killed by their partners or family members in the first half of 2017, and at least 50 killed between 2010 and 2017. The coalition received 5,299 calls about domestic violence incidents through September 2017. In the same period, police received 602 complaints of various types of violence within the family and investigated 142 instances. Authorities brought criminal charges in 31 cases.

Several coalition activists and lawyers reported pressure and threats for their work. Despite years of pressure from local women's rights organizations, Armenia has no law criminalizing domestic violence and has not joined the Council of Europe's Istanbul Convention on Prevention and Combating Violence against Women and Domestic Violence.

In November, the government presented to parliament a draft law on prevention of violence in the family and protections for victims. Women's rights organizations opposed the law after the government introduced last minute changes, without public discussion, on "restoring harmony in the family," which they believe is designed to promote reconciliation and could undermine full protections for victims.

## Sexual Orientation and Gender Identity

Lesbian, gay, bisexual, and transgender (LGBT) people face harassment, discrimination, and violence. The LGBT rights organization PINK Armenia documented nine physical attacks based on sexual orientation or gender identity through August. Officials opened investigations in several cases, but the law does not include anti-LGBT bias as an aggravating circumstance. Fear of discrimination and public disclosure of their sexual orientation prevents many LGBT people from reporting crimes.

PINK Armenia Director Mamikon Hovsepyan reported a campaign of homophobic Facebook posts in May, including calls to attack the office and staff, following the Yerevan municipality's controversial removal of LGBT-themed social advertisements.

Days before the annual Golden Apricot International Film Festival in July, the Union of Cinematographers of Armenia (UCA) denied the festival's use of the main venue. The festival was unable to screen 40 films including two LGBT-themed films. Although officially the UCA justified the refusal citing the death of the UCA president more than a month earlier, local activists believe that inclusion of films on LGBT prompted the denial.

## *Key International Actors*

In November, Armenia and the European Union (EU) signed a Comprehensive and Enhanced Partnership Agreement, aiming to strengthen political dialogue, increase economic cooperation, and promote reforms, including on human rights and the rule of law. Following the EU-Armenia Human Rights Dialogue in May, the EU called for adoption of laws against domestic violence and discrimination, and for effective investigation and prosecution of crimes committed by law enforcement.

Also in March, Armenia endorsed the Safe Schools Declaration, committing to do more to protect students, teachers, and schools during times of armed conflict, including through implementation and use of the Guidelines for Protecting Schools and Universities from Military Use during Armed Conflict.

In a statement following his September visit, the United Nations special rapporteur on the right to health, Dainius Pūras, said that Armenia's approach to drug control "remains punitive and restrictive undermining the right to health of people who use drugs and of those in need of palliative care."

Following its March review, the UN Committee on the Rights of Persons with Disabilities commended the government's commitment to inclusive education by 2025 and other steps, but raised concerns about lack of accessibility; discrimination; institutionalization of children with disabilities; neglect, inhuman treatment, and deprivation of liberty of persons with disabilities in institutions; deprivation of legal capacity; inadequate support for living independently in communities; and barriers to accessing inclusive education.

The UN Committee against Torture's January concluding observations noted some improvements, but criticized excessive use of pretrial detention; lack of effective investigations into ill-treatment allegations; excessive use of force by police; violations of detainees' rights; attacks on journalists; domestic violence; and abuse of children in institutions.

In its November 2016 concluding observations, the UN Committee on the Elimination of All Forms of Discrimination against Women acknowledged some legislative and policy improvements, but noted the lack of comprehensive legislation on anti-discrimination and on preventing and prohibiting gender-based violence; persistence of gender-based violence and underreporting of crimes; and inadequate access to contraception and healthcare, among other concerns.

# Australia

Despite a strong tradition of protecting civil and political rights, Australia has serious unresolved human rights problems. Undeterred by repeated calls by the United Nations to end offshore processing, Australia continued in 2017 to hold asylum seekers who arrived by boat on Manus Island in Papua New Guinea and on the island nation of Nauru, where conditions are abysmal.

Indigenous Australians are overrepresented in the criminal justice system. Half the prison population has a disability, and inmates face violence, neglect, and extended periods of isolation. Abuses in juvenile detention centers and overbroad counterterrorism laws persist.

In October, United Nations member countries elected Australia to the UN Human Rights Council (UNHRC) for a three-year period for the first time.

## *Asylum Seekers and Refugees*

At time of writing, there were around 840 refugee and asylum seeker men in Papua New Guinea and 1,100 men, women, and children on Nauru, transferred by Australia. They are from countries including Afghanistan, Burma, Iran, Pakistan, Somalia, and Sudan, and most have been there for more than four years. Many suffer from mental health conditions, exacerbated by years of detention and uncertainty about their futures. At least nine refugees and asylum seekers have died on Manus and Nauru—three due to suspected suicide—since Australia introduced the offshore processing policy in 2013.

In September, the US accepted 54 refugees from Manus and Nauru, through a resettlement arrangement with Australia. Nauru and Papua New Guinea do not offer refugees meaningful opportunities for local integration or adequate and safe long-term settlement options.

These refugees and asylum seekers regularly endure violence, threats, and harassment from residents, with little protection from local authorities. Since June, refugees and asylum seekers on Manus have faced increased violent attacks and robberies by local men, with no police action. They endure unnecessary delays in, and at times denial of, medical care, even for life threatening conditions. Australian and Nauru authorities have ignored doctors' recommendations by blocking transfers to Australia for nearly 50 refugees and asylum seekers on Nauru.

Self-harm and suicide attempts are frequent. Two refugees with histories of mental health conditions reportedly committed suicide on Manus in separate incidents in 2017.

On October 31, the Australian and PNG governments closed the Manus Island regional processing center, ostensibly to implement a 2016 PNG Supreme Court ruling that detaining men at the main center was unconstitutional. Food, water, and power were stopped and refugees and asylum seekers urged to move to other less secure facilities in the main town.

For three weeks, hundreds of refugees and asylum seekers refused for to leave the closed facility, terrified by escalating violence against them in the main town and frustrated by the lack of a long-term solution to their predicament. Australia will pay PNG A$250 million (US$192 million) for the next 12 months of operations to provide services to about 840 refugees and asylum seekers.

In September, the Australian government settled a class action lawsuit agreeing to pay A$70 million (US$56 million) to men detained on Manus Island.

Reacting to a High Court challenge, in August the government introduced amendments to the Border Force Act to reduce the threat of criminal charges against service providers who speak out about abuse or neglect in offshore processing centers.

## Indigenous Rights

In May, over 250 Aboriginal and Torres Strait Islanders from 13 regions met and issued the "Uluru Statement from the Heart," which urged constitutional reforms, including the establishment of a First Nations voice in the constitution and a truth and justice commission. In October, Australia's government formally rejected the key recommendation of the Referendum Council to establish an Indigenous advisory body to parliament.

Indigenous Australians are significantly overrepresented in the criminal justice system, often for minor offenses like unpaid fines. Aboriginal and Torres Strait Islanders are 13 times more likely to be imprisoned than the rest of the Australian population. Aboriginal women are the fastest growing prisoner demographic in Australia.

In December 2016, the Western Australian state coroner found that the 2014 death in custody of a 22-year-old Aboriginal woman, Ms. Dhu, was preventable, and made a number of recommendations, including that Western Australia end imprisonment for unpaid fines. At time of writing, Western Australia had yet to implement the recommendation.

## Children's Rights

State inquiries have documented significant abuses against children in the criminal justice system. Incarceration disproportionately affects indigenous children, with a juvenile detention rate about 25 times the rate of non-indigenous youth.

In May, the Victorian Supreme Court ruled for the third time that detaining children at Barwon adult prison was unlawful. The government moved children to the maximum security prison following riot damage to a youth justice center in 2016, and decided to reclassify a section of the prison as a "youth justice facility" just days after the Supreme Court ruled against this move. Some of the detained children were as young as 15, and authorities isolated and handcuffed them for extensive periods.

In July, the Western Australia inspector of custodial services found a substantial increase in "critical incidents and self-harm" in a juvenile detention center. In November, the Royal Commission into the Protection and Detention of Children in the Northern Territory concluded that the territory's youth detention centers are "not fit for accommodating, let alone rehabilitating" the children they lock up, and called for their closure. The report recommended that the Northern Territory raise the minimum age of criminal responsibility from 10 to 12 years, and that children below the age of 14 should only be detained for the most serious offenses.

## Terrorism and Counterterrorism

Since 2014, the Australian government has introduced several draconian counterterrorism laws in response to the threat of "home-grown terrorism." Support for tough measures increased following a June siege in Brighton, in which a gunman who pledged allegiance to the extremist group Islamic State (ISIS) and Al-Qaeda killed a man and injured three police officers.

In July, Prime Minister Malcolm Turnbull proposed new legislation that would force tech companies to provide "appropriate assistance" to intelligence and law enforcement agencies to access encrypted communications, which risks undermining cybersecurity for all users. In December 2016, the government passed legislation that allows a judge to authorize detention for offenders who have served terrorism-related sentences but who pose an "unacceptable risk" of committing a serious offense if released.

In October, Australian authorities unveiled a proposal that would allow terrorism suspects as young as 10 to be held for up to two weeks without charge.

## Disability Rights

Over half the prison population has a physical, sensory, psychosocial (mental health), or intellectual disability.

Human Rights Watch research in 14 prisons across Western Australia and Queensland found that prisoners with disabilities experience bullying, harassment, physical, and sexual violence from fellow prisoners and staff. Due to a lack of staff sensitivity and training, prisoners with disabilities are frequently punished for behavior resulting from their disability and end up disproportionately represented in punishment units.

In 2016, the UN Committee on the Rights of People with Disabilities reviewed a communication against Australia concerning Marlon Noble who was incarcerated for more than 10 years in a Western Australian Prison and declared unfit to stand trial. The committee found that Noble could not exercise his right to due process and was deprived of liberty without trial. It recommended an effective remedy and to revoke the conditions attached to his release. The Western Australian government acknowledged significant failures in the way Noble's case was handled, and released its review of the Mentally Impaired Defendants Act in April 2016. At time of writing, no reforms had been enacted.

## Sexual Orientation and Gender Identity

In 2017, the Turnbull government held a non-binding postal survey on same-sex marriage. In November, Australians voted overwhelmingly in favor of marriage equality, and parliament passed a marriage equality law in December.

## Violence against Women

In February, UN Special Rapporteur on Violence Against Women Dubravka Ši-monović visited Australia. She expressed concern over inadequate policies to protect Aboriginal and Torres Strait Islander women, and the plight of asylum seekers and refugee women transferred from Nauru to Australia for medical treatment, including women who were raped.

The Australian Human Rights Commission released a report on sexual assault at Australian universities in August, finding 21 percent of students were sexually harassed in a university setting in 2016.

## Forced Labor

In August, Australia's justice minister proposed legal reforms to require the biggest companies in the country to report on practices to prevent forced labor in their supply chains. At time of writing, the government was consulting stake-holders on the proposal, which lacks meaningful due diligence requirements or penalties for noncompliance.

## Foreign Policy

Australia acted inconsistently and rarely showed leadership at the UN on human rights issues relating to particular countries. During the year Australia rarely raised human rights issues publicly in countries it works closely with on border security or trade, such as China, Cambodia, and Vietnam, preferring to engage in "quiet diplomacy."

In October, Australia deepened diplomatic ties with Cambodia while ignoring its sharp crackdown on civil and political rights. In November, it upgraded diplo-matic relations with Vietnam despite its escalating crackdown on freedom of ex-pression.

In October, Australia was elected to the UNHRC. The government said it would prioritize gender equality, freedom of expression, indigenous rights, good governance, and national human rights institutions, and that it would advocate for global abolition of the death penalty.

Australia has shown little transparency as a member of the US-led coalition conducting airstrikes against ISIS. In May, the Defense Department began releasing reports on strikes by the Australian air force, but more detailed reporting on civilian casualties in Iraq and Syria is needed. Australia has approved military exports to Saudi Arabia, despite concerns about alleged war crimes by the Saudi-led coalition in Yemen. Australia has not released information on the types or quantities of equipment sold.

## Key International Actors

In 2017, the UN special rapporteur on the human rights of migrants; the Committee on Economic, Cultural and Social Rights; and the High Commissioner for Refugees urged the Australian government to end offshore processing of asylum seekers.

Following his visit to Australia in December 2016, UN Special Rapporteur on Racism Mutuma Ruteere raised concerns that "xenophobic hate speech, including by elected politicians" was on the rise in Australia. The UN Special Rapporteur on the Rights of Indigenous Peoples Victoria Tauli-Corpuz said the "routine detention of young Indigenous children" was the "most distressing aspect" of her visit to Australia.

In February, the government announced it will ratify the Optional Protocol to the Convention against Torture and Other Cruel, Inhuman or Degrading Treatment or Punishment (OPCAT) by the end of 2017. Under OPCAT, independent inspecting bodies would monitor Australia's prisons, and juvenile and immigration detention facilities.

In November, the UN Human Rights Committee expressed strong concern for Australia's human rights record in key areas, including refugees, indigenous rights, lesbian, gay, bisexual, and transgender (LGBT) rights, and certain counterterrorism measures. The committee urged Australia to end its offshore detention arrangements, and condemned the same-sex marriage postal survey as "not an acceptable decision-making method."

# Azerbaijan

The government intensified its crackdown against critics in 2017. Courts sentenced at least 25 journalists and political and youth activists to long prison terms in politically motivated, unfair trials. Dozens more were detained or are under criminal investigation, face harassment and travel bans, or have fled. Draconian laws and regulations impede independent groups' work and ability to secure funding. Torture and ill-treatment in custody persist. In a violent campaign, police arrested and ill-treated dozens of gay men and transgender women.

Following years of scrutiny and several warnings, the Extractive Industries Transparency Initiative (EITI), an international coalition promoting better governance in resource-rich countries, suspended Azerbaijan for failing to ease restrictions on civil society groups.

## *Prosecuting Government Critics*

Authorities continued to use various criminal and administrative charges to stifle critics.

In January, courts sentenced 18 people, including prominent religious scholar Taleh Bagirzade, to long prison sentences following a trial marred by allegations of torture and ill-treatment. Authorities arrested the men in November 2015, during a raid in Nardaran, a Baku suburb known for its Shia religious conservatism and criticism of government policies. Charges included murder, terrorism, inciting religious hatred, organizing mass unrest, and illegal possession of weapons.

Also in January, a Baku court convicted youth activist Elgiz Gahraman, 31, to five-and-a-half years in prison on bogus drug-related charges. After his August 2016 arrest, police did not inform Gahraman's relatives of his whereabouts and denied him access to his lawyer for days. During the trial, Gahraman alleged police beat and threatened him with sexual assault to force him to confess to drug possession. Authorities failed to effectively investigate the allegations.

Three members of the opposition Azerbaijan Popular Front Party (APFP) were convicted during the year and at least nine were in prison on politically motivated charges. In July, a court convicted Faig Amirli, an APFP member and financial director of the now-closed pro-opposition *Azadlig* newspaper, on bogus charges of inciting religious hatred and tax-evasion. He received a suspended sentence. Fuad Ahmadli, a senior APFP member and social media activist, was sentenced in June to four years in prison on spurious charges of misusing personal data. In January 2017, a Baku court convicted senior APFP member Fuad Gahramanli to 10 years' imprisonment for inciting religious and ethnic hatred; he posted criticisms of the government on Facebook.

In May, authorities arrested APFP Deputy Chair Gozel Bayramli at the border with Georgia and charged her with smuggling. She remained in pretrial custody at time of writing.

Dozens of journalists and activists convicted in politically motivated trials remained in prison. Among them was Ilgar Mammadov, leader of the pro-democracy opposition movement Republican Alternative (REAL), imprisoned since February 2013. He remained in prison despite a 2014 European Court of Human Rights (ECtHR) judgment finding his imprisonment to be illegal, and repeated demands by the Council of Europe to release him. In November, in a separate case, the ECtHR found that Mammadov's right to a fair trial had been violated. Others behind bars include journalists Seymur Hazi and Nijat Aliyev; youth activists Ilkin Rustemzadeh, Bayram Mammadov, and Murad Adilov; and opposition politicians Mammad Ibrahim and Asif Yusifli.

None of the convictions of activists and journalists released in the last two years were quashed and some face travel restrictions, including award-winning investigative journalist Khadija Ismayilova and human rights lawyer Intigam Aliyev.

Authorities harassed relatives of activists living in exile. In February, police detained 12 relatives, including the two-year-old niece of Ordukhan Teymurkhan, a video blogger and social media activist living in the Netherlands. Teymurkhan recorded and published a call from a Baku police officer who blamed him for his relatives' detention. The next day the authorities released all of them except for Teymurkhan's older brother and adult nephew, who were sentenced to 30 days' detention for allegedly disobeying police orders.

In June, Vidadi Isganderli, a government critic living in Georgia, reported that five of his relatives were pressured to quit their jobs, apparently in retaliation for his activism.

In October, parliament adopted amendments banning lawyers without Bar membership from representing clients, likely to further limit the number of lawyers willing to take on politically sensitive cases. Observers have criticized the Azerbaijani Bar for lack of independence and its arbitrary powers to deny admissions of new members.

## Freedom of Media

Authorities continued to use bogus tax-related and other criminal charges to jail critical journalists and bloggers. At least 10 remained in prison. In March, a court sentenced Mehman Huseynov, a prominent journalist and blogger, to two years in prison for allegedly defaming the staff of a police station. Huseynov had publicized how several police officers arbitrarily detained and beat him in January.

A court sentenced Afgan Sadigov, the founder and editor-in-chief of AzelTV news website operating in a southern Azerbaijani region, to two-and-a-half years in prison in January on spurious hooliganism charges. Sadigov often reported on allegations of embezzlement of social benefits by local authorities.

In May, unidentified people abducted journalist and political activist Afgan Mukhtarli, in Georgia's capital, Tbilisi, and illegally brought him to Azerbaijan. Azerbaijani authorities then charged Mukhtarli with unlawful border crossing, smuggling, and resisting a representative of authority. Mukhtarli had lived in exile since 2015 out of fears for his security. He remained in custody in Baku at time of writing.

Also in May, police arrested Aziz Orujov, director of the Kanal13 online television channel, and sentenced him to 30 days' detention for allegedly resisting police. During his detention, authorities brought criminal tax-related charges against him. At time of writing Orujov remained in pretrial custody.

Authorities arrested Mehman Aliyev, director of Turan News Agency, the country's one independent news agency, in August on spurious criminal charges, but dropped the case in November.

In May, the government permanently blocked prominent independent and opposition media outlets' websites, including Radio Free Europe/Radio Liberty's Azerbaijani Service, the opposition newspaper *Azadlig*, and Berlin-based Meydan TV, claiming national security threats. Parliament passed laws tightening control over online media in March, and in June increased the maximum punishment for "insulting the honor and dignity of the president" to five years' imprisonment.

## Freedom of Association

Azerbaijan maintains highly restrictive and punitive regulations on nongovernmental organizations (NGOs), making it almost impossible for independent groups to fund and carry out their work. In January, under pressure from EITI, the Cabinet of Ministers adopted changes to certain regulations on international donor funding and grant agreement registration. The revisions did not eliminate the authorities' discretion to arbitrarily deny grant registration or the entrenched legal barriers to NGOs' operations.

Authorities continued to freeze the bank accounts of at least a dozen NGOs working on human rights and government accountability; the groups suspended their work or operated in exile. Some local groups involved in EITI gained access to their previously blocked accounts. Several NGO leaders continued to face travel bans, harassment, and interrogations.

## Ill-Treatment in Detention

Torture and other ill-treatment continued with impunity. At the January trial of those arrested in November 2015 in Nardaran, 17 men made credible allegations of ill-treatment in detention to coerce confessions and testimony against others. The men alleged that officers at the Interior Ministry Organized Crime Unit headquarters placed sacks on their heads, handcuffed them, and beat them with truncheons, including on their genitals and the soles of their feet. Some also said that officials used electric shocks on them and threatened to rape their wives or sisters. The men also alleged that police beat and kicked them in a police van upon detention. Authorities failed to effectively investigate the allegations.

In early January, several plainclothes officers attacked journalist Mehman Huseynov in downtown Baku. They bound his eyes and mouth, forced a bag over his head, used an electroshock weapon on his groin, and punched him before detaining him. The next day, a court found Huseynov guilty of disobeying police orders and fined him. After Huseynov publicized the abuse, a court convicted him to two years' imprisonment for defamation.

In an open letter posted on social media by his lawyer, activist Giyas Ibrahimov, serving a 10-year prison sentence since May 2016 for political graffiti, alleged guards chained his hands behind his back, beat and swore at him, and arbitrarily placed him in solitary confinement for 15 days in June. Authorities failed to conduct an effective investigation.

## *Sexual Orientation and Gender Identity*

In September, authorities detained dozens of people presumed to be gay or bisexual, as well as transgender women, on dubious disobedience charges. Police ill-treated many to coerce bribes and information about other gay men. Following unfair trials, they were either sentenced for up to 30 days' detention or released after they paid a fine. Authorities failed to investigate the allegations of torture and ill-treatment made by many of them during the appeal hearings.

## *Key International Actors*

The United States, European Union, and Azerbaijan's other bilateral and international partners continued to criticize the government's targeting of critics, but failed to effectively leverage their relationships with the government to secure meaningful rights improvements.

President Ilham Aliyev visited Brussels in February to inaugurate talks on a new EU-Azerbaijan partnership agreement to enhance political and economic ties. The EU failed to condition negotiations on the release of unjustly imprisoned journalists and activists, and an end to restrictions on NGOs.

A June European Parliament resolution condemned the abduction of Afgan Mukhtarli and urged Azerbaijan's authorities to release him and others detained on politically motivated charges.

In March, the EITI suspended Azerbaijan's membership for failing to comply with the group's civil society requirements. The government responded by withdrawing. While international financial institutions, like the World Bank, pledged support for EITI, they continued to fund extractives projects despite the government's failure to implement reforms required by EITI.

In June, the US expressed concern about the abduction and arrest of Afgan Mukhtarli as well as the arrest of APFP Deputy Chair Gozal Bayramli, and called on the government to release "all those incarcerated for exercising their fundamental freedoms."

In October, the Council of Europe's Committee of Ministers took the unprecedented decision to trigger infringement proceedings against Azerbaijan for failure to implement the European Court judgement on Ilgar Mammadov.

Also in October, the Parliamentary Assembly of the Council of Europe adopted two strongly worded resolutions, urging Azerbaijan to cease its unrelenting crackdown against critics.

In June, the Open Government Partnership, a voluntary initiative promoting government transparency and accountability, extended Azerbaijan's inactive status due to "unresolved constraints on the operating environment for NGOs."

# Bahrain

Bahrain's human rights situation continued to worsen in 2017. Authorities shut down the country's only independent newspaper and the leading secular-left opposition political society. The country's preeminent human rights defender remained in prison on speech charges. The government, ending a de facto moratorium on use of the death penalty, executed three people in January following unfair trials, despite their alleging that they had been tortured and their confessions coerced.

The government reversed two of the few substantive recommendations of the Bahrain Independent Commission of Inquiry (BICI) that it had previously implemented. In January, authorities restored arrest and investigation powers to the National Security Agency, despite its record of torture and abuse, and in April, King Hamad bin Isa Al Khalifa signed legislation authorizing trial of civilians before military courts.

Bahrain continued to deny access to special procedures of the Office of the UN High Commissioner for Human Rights, including the special rapporteur for torture. Authorities prevented dozens of rights advocates from traveling to Geneva ahead of Bahrain's third Universal Periodic Review (UPR) in May and the regular UN Human Rights Council (UNHRC) session in September.

## *Freedom of Expression, Association, and Peaceful Assembly*

On July 10, a court sentenced Nabeel Rajab, head of the Bahrain Center for Human Rights, to two years for "disseminating false news, statements and rumors ... that would undermine [Bahrain's] prestige and status," in relation to media interviews he gave in 2015. He faced 15 years in prison in a separate case for "insulting public authorities [the Interior Ministry]," "insulting a foreign country [Saudi Arabia]," and "spreading false rumors in time of war," in connection with tweets criticizing alleged torture and Bahrain's participation in the Saudi Arabi-led military operations in Yemen.

On June 4, the Information Affairs Ministry ordered the suspension of *Al Wasat*, Bahrain's only independent newspaper, ostensibly for a column about unrest in the Hoceima region of Morocco. On June 24, the newspaper's board told employees that the suspension forced the termination of their contracts.

On May 31, the High Civil Court, acting on the request of the government, dissolved the secular-left National Democratic Action Society (Wa'ad). The government charged Wa'ad with "incitement of acts of terrorism and promoting violent and forceful overthrow of the political regime," because the group condemned the January execution of three men on terrorism charges, calling them "martyrs," and for expressing solidarity with "a banned organization," referring to Al-Wefaq, the country's largest opposition society, which authorities had similarly dissolved in July 2016.

On June 6, Bahraini authorities declared that it would be a crime punishable by up to five years in prison to express "sympathy" with Qatar or criticize Bahrain's decision to break relations with that country and, together with Saudi Arabia, the United Arab Emirates, and Egypt, impose economic and movement restrictions.

In late April and again in late September, authorities summoned more than 20 rights activists, lawyers, and political opposition figures for questioning on charges of taking part in illegal gatherings. This restriction effectively placed these individuals under a travel ban, ensured that they could not go to Geneva for meetings in connection with Bahrain's third UPR at the UNHRC, which started on May 1, and the regular session of the Human Rights Council in September.

According to the London-based Bahrain Institute for Rights and Democracy (BIRD), as of late October authorities had stripped 105 persons of Bahraini citizenship, bringing the total since 2012 to 455.

## Security Forces

The government on January 5 restored arrest and detention authority to the National Security Agency (NSA), an intelligence agency. The decision reversed one of the few significant security sector reforms authorities had taken in line with a recommendation of the BICI, which had concluded that the NSA "followed a systematic practice of physical and psychological mistreatment, which in many cases amounted to torture."

King Hamad in April ratified a constitutional amendment giving military courts jurisdiction over civilians. The last time Bahraini military courts prosecuted civilians was in the aftermath of large anti-government protests in 2011, when they convicted some 300 people of political crimes. The explanatory note accompanying the February vote in the Council of Representatives approving the amendment said that it was needed to "make the military justice system flexible and speedy in investigating and sentencing."

On May 23, security forces appeared to have used excessive deadly force in a raid on a sit-in protest in the village of Diraz that left five demonstrators killed and dozens wounded. The sit-in had been in place since June 2016 outside the home of Sheikh Isa Qassim, widely regarded as the spiritual leader of the Al-Wefaq opposition group, after authorities had revoked his citizenship. The government said the objective was to "apprehend terrorists operating in the area and clear illegal roadblocks and obstructions."

Sayed Alawi, an employee of the state telecommunications company Batelco, was subjected to enforced disappearance when authorities arrested him on October 24, 2016. For several weeks, family members went from one security office to another, following instructions from officials, but was never able to make contact with him except for three brief phone calls about six weeks apart between late November 2016 and late February 2017, and a fourth call of about one minute on July 27.

The family submitted numerous complaints to the Interior Ministry's Ombudsman Office and Special Investigations Unit, and the Office of the Pubic Prosecutor. On September 11, the Ombudsman Office responded to an inquiry about the state of its investigation, saying that Allawi "had been transferred to be under the responsibility of another authority which is out of the Ombudsman's remit." On October 22, the official news agency announced that Allawi along with three others was in military custody and would face trial before a military court on terrorism-related charges.

## Death Penalty

On January 15, Bahrain ended a de facto moratorium since 2010 on executions when authorities carried out death sentences against Sami Mushaima, 42, Ali al-Singace, 21, and Abbas al-Sameea, 27. The men alleged they had been tortured and that their lawyers did not have access to all their hearings and could not cross-examine prosecution witnesses.

Mohamed Ramadan and Husain Ali Moosa remained on death row following a decision of the First Supreme Criminal High Appellate court in May 2015 upholding their death sentences for killing a policeman, despite their claims that their confessions had been coerced. On June 6, the Fourth Higher Criminal Court sentenced to death Sayed Ahmed al-Abbar, 21, and Husain Ali Mohamed, 20, in connection with an attack on a military patrol vehicle and the reported death of a security officer.

## Human Rights Defenders

Conditions of Nabeel Rajab's ongoing detention appeared at times to amount to arbitrary punishment. Authorities repeatedly denied him bail or release following his re-arrest in June 2016 on speech charges, although he posed no risk to himself or others, or risk of flight. He was kept in solitary confinement for significant periods of time. This denial of liberty also came despite medical conditions that required his prolonged hospitalization and repeated postponements of hearings. Rajab's family said that on one occasion authorities returned him to his jail cell two days after an operation, contrary to medical advice. On November 22, the High Criminal Court in Manama upheld a two-year prison sentence against Rajab, in relation to TV interviews from 2015 and 2016, accusing him of "disseminating false news, statements and rumors about the internal situation in the kingdom that would undermine its prestige and status."

Authorities at Bahrain International Airport interrogated human rights activist Ebtisam al-Sayegh in March, after she returned from meetings in conjunction with the UNHRC in Geneva. In May, following another interrogation, she alleged that NSA officers had subjected her to physical, verbal, and sexual abuse. Shortly before midnight on July 3 armed and masked men in civilian cars raided her home and arrested her again. Authorities charged al-Sayegh on July 18 with supporting terrorist activities, under the country's anti-terrorism law. According to Dublin-based Front Line Defenders, inmates at the Isa Town Women's Prison reported seeing her there with evident injuries, including a neck brace. Al-Sayegh was provisionally released from detention on October 22 but authorities made no announcement about the status of the charges against her.

On October 30, a criminal court in Manama sentenced three relatives of human rights defender Sayed al-Wadaei to three years in prison on dubious terrorism-related charges, despite due process violations and allegations of ill-treatment and coerced confessions. Targeting family members to silence activists amounts to collective punishment.

## Women's Rights, Gender Identity, and Sexual Orientation

Law 19/2009 regulates personal status matters only in Sunni religious courts, so that Shia women are not covered by a codified personal status law. Both Sunni and Shia women face discrimination in the right to divorce and other matters.

Adultery and sexual relations outside marriage are criminalized. No law prohibits discrimination on the grounds of gender, gender identity, or sexual orientation.

## Key International Actors

Bahrain continued to participate in the Saudi Arabia-led coalition military operations in Yemen.

US President Donald Trump, in a May meeting, told King Hamad that "there won't be any strain [in relations] with this administration." On September 8, the State Department announced it had approved a $2.78 billion sale of F-16V aircraft and other military equipment, a sale previously held up for unspecified human rights concerns. On August 15, in remarks on the release of the 2016 International Religious Freedom Report, Secretary of State Tillerson said, "Bahrain must stop discriminating against the Shia communities."

On July 10, the State Department criticized the sentencing of Nabeel Rajab and called for his release. The European Union, Germany, and Norway also criticized Rajab's sentencing; the United Kingdom failed to do so.

UN High Commissioner for Human Rights Zeid Ra'ad Al Hussein, in his September 11 address to the 36th session of the Human Rights Council, decried the "arrests, intimidation, travel bans and closure order, with increasing reports of torture" in Bahrain, saying that "democratic space in the country has essentially been shut down" and "no public relations campaign can paper over the violations being inflicted on the people of Bahrain." The UN Committee against Torture, in its observations on Bahrain's second and third periodic reports, expressed concern over "numerous and consistent allegations of widespread torture" and "the climate of impunity which seems to prevail."

# Bangladesh

Beginning in late August, Bangladesh received a massive influx of over 630,000 Rohingya refugees escaping a campaign of ethnic cleansing by the Burmese military after a militant attack in Rakhine State, Burma. Bangladesh sought urgent international humanitarian assistance to provide for the refugees.

Authorities failed to hold security forces responsible for serious human rights violations including secret detentions, enforced disappearances, torture, and extrajudicial killings.

Bangladesh took a massive step backward on women's and girls' rights in 2017, passing legislation in February permitting girls under 18 years old to marry under "special circumstances," eliminating the minimum age for marriages in this exception.

In response to protests in December 2016 by garment workers seeking higher wages, factory owners dismissed over 1,500 workers and authorities arrested 38 union leaders and workers on unsubstantiated criminal charges.

## Refugees

After an August 25 attack by the Arakan Rohingya Salvation Army on police posts in northern Rakhine State, the Burmese military began a catastrophic and systematic campaign of ethnic cleansing, carrying out armed attacks on Rohingya Muslim villagers, raping and sexually assaulting women and girls, and torching entire villages.

The over 630,000 Rohingya refugees created an unprecedented strain on Bangladesh's already meager resources. Humanitarian workers have struggled to meet needs in sprawling informal and formal refugee camps.

Bangladesh called for international pressure to ensure the swift return of refugees to their homes in Burma. In November, Burma and Bangladesh announced an agreement to repatriate the Rohingya refugees. However, at time of writing, serious concerns remained about the proposed repatriation process, including when and where the refugees would be resettled, if returns would be voluntary, the documentation required, freedom of movement, and the state of "temporary camps" called for as part of the resettlement process.

**HUMAN
RIGHTS
WATCH**

## "We Don't Have Him"
Secret Detentions and Enforced Disappearances in Bangladesh

## Security Force Abuse and Impunity

Bangladesh security forces—particularly the Detective Branch of the police, Bangladesh Border Guards (BGB), the Directorate General Forces Inspectorate (DGFI), and the Rapid Action Battalion (RAB)—have a long history of enjoying impunity for serious violations including arbitrary arrests, torture, enforced disappearances, and extrajudicial killings, a pattern that did not abate in 2017.

Law enforcement authorities continued to arrest opposition activists and militant suspects, holding them in secret detention for long periods before producing some in court. Several others, according to security forces, were killed in "gunfights," leading to concerns over extrajudicial killings. At time of writing, scores remained victims of enforced disappearances.

## Freedom of Expression and Attacks on Civil Society

Civil society groups faced pressure from both state and non-state actors, including death threats and attacks from extremist groups, and escalating harassment and surveillance by security forces. In June 2017, Islamist leaders threatened to "break every bone" of Sultana Kamal, a prominent Bangladeshi lawyer and rights activist, after she publicly opposed their campaign to dismantle a statue of Lady Justice outside the Supreme Court on the grounds that it constituted "idolatry," violating Islamic tenets.

Freedom of expression was severely limited as authorities used overly broad laws to stifle dissent or perceived criticism. The government continued to use Section 57 of the Information and Communications Technology Act (ICT Act) to punish critics. The draft Digital Securities Act, designed to replace section 57, proposed even harsher penalties for vaguely defined crimes under national security, defamation, and "hurting religious feelings."

In 2017, there were at least 30 assaults on journalists, including the February murder of Abdul Hakim Shimul, a reporter for the daily *Samakal* newspaper, while he covered political unrest in Shahjadpur. In August, the journalist Abdul Latif Morol was arrested for satirical reporting of the death of a goat on Facebook. In early September, police detained two Burmese journalists reporting on the Rohingya crisis and held them for a week before releasing them on bail. After significant international pressure, authorities dropped the charges on October 17 and allowed the two to return home.

The Foreign Donation (Voluntary Activities) Regulation Act to control nongovernmental organizations (NGOs) further hindered freedoms of expression and association. The Distortion of the History of Bangladesh Liberation War Crimes Act provides for imprisonment and fines if details of the 1971 war of independence are debated or disputed.

## Minorities

Sporadic attacks and threats against religious minorities continued in 2017. In mid-November, a mob of nearly 20,000 looted and burned down over 30 homes in the majority-Hindu Thakurpara village in Rangpur Sadar, in response to rumors that a villager had published a Facebook post defaming the Prophet Muhammad.

Indigenous groups in the Chittagong Hill Tracts (CHT) have for decades faced discrimination, forced displacement, assaults, evictions, and destruction of property by both Bangladeshi security forces and Bengali settlers from the mainland. In June, Bengali rioters burned 100 indigenous homes in Longadu, reportedly while army and police looked on.

## Environment

Bangladesh again failed to address its decades-long problem of arsenic in drinking water, with the World Health Organization estimating that 40 million people in the country are affected by arsenic poisoning. In February, three United Nations special rapporteurs published a joint letter raising their concerns which they had sent to the government the previous year, and to which the government had not responded.

In 2017, the government finally began to relocate about a third of the approximately 300 tanneries out of Hazaribagh, a residential area of Dhaka, to a dedicated industrial zone in Savar just outside the capital. The tanneries produce environmentally hazardous waste containing chemicals such as sulfur, ammonium, and chromium. However, many continue to operate in Hazaribagh, in contravention of multiple High Court orders, most recently in March. In November, the government announced that the move to Savar had been delayed again and would not be completed until 2019.

The Hill Tracts region suffered massive landslides in mid-June after several days of heavy rainfall, killing more than 160 people and displacing thousands. Environmental activists blamed decades of unregulated settlement and deforestation due to poor enforcement of existing laws.

The government pushed forward with plans for the controversial India-backed Rampal coal power plant in 2017, despite significant concerns about air and water pollution, and risk to the Sundarbans mangrove forest, a UNESCO world heritage site.

## *Labor Rights*

Bangladeshi authorities failed to implement their commitments under the Sustainability Compact in 2017, including amendments to the labor laws governing Export Processing Zones to bring them in line with international standards. In general, factory officials were not held accountable for attacks, threats, and retaliation against workers, particularly those involved with unions.

From December 2016 to February 2017, the government and garment manufacturers cracked down on workers for demanding higher wages, dismissing workers and arresting union leaders based on vague or repealed offenses from the draconian Special Powers Act of 1974.

Although the global garment union IndustriALL, the government, and the garment manufacturers' association reached an agreement in February after significant international and corporate pressure to release the 34 workers and union leaders, they continued to face criminal cases.

The Alliance for Bangladesh Worker Safety, a platform of North American retailers that sets timeframes and accountability for safety inspections and training programs, announced in 2017 that it would not extend its tenure after mid-2018. The Accord on Fire and Building Safety in Bangladesh, a European counterpart, decided to extend its tenure until 2021. Both were set up in the aftermath of the Rana Plaza building collapse in 2013 that killed more than 1,000 workers.

## Women's and Girls' Rights

With among the highest rates of early marriage in the world, the government had pledged to end marriage of children younger than 15 by 2021, and marriage younger than 18 by 2041. However, in February 2017, the government greatly undermined progress toward these goals by approving a law that permits girls under age 18 to marry under "special circumstances," such as "accidental" or "illegal pregnancy," with permission from their parents and a court. There is no age limit to how early girls can marry under this exception.

Stalking, sexual harassment, and violence against women and girls continued in 2017. In Bogra, a city in north Bangladesh, a university student accused Tufan Sarkar, a trade union leader linked to the ruling Awami League, of abducting and raping her in July. In an attempt to silence the victim, Sarkar picked up her and her mother, tortured them for hours, and then tonsured their heads, sparking widespread public outrage and protests in the city. Police arrested Sarkar, his wife, and several associates two weeks later, and filed charges in October.

Also in July, a student leader, and apparent repeat offender at Sirajganj Government College publicly harassed and assaulted a student because she protested against his repeated threats to sexually assault her. He was later arrested on assault charges.

Indigenous women and girls faced multiple forms of discrimination due to their gender, indigenous identity, and socio-economic status and were especially vulnerable to sexual and gender-based violence.

## Overseas Workers

Millions of Bangladeshis work abroad, sending home remittances worth billions of dollars. In 2017, 100,000 women migrated overseas, mostly to Gulf countries, for domestic work. Many Bangladeshi migrant workers have reported being deprived of food and forced to endure psychological, physical, and sexual abuse. In some cases, such abuses amounted to forced labor or trafficking.

Bangladesh has set a minimum salary for domestic workers in the Gulf equivalent to roughly US$200 per month, the lowest minimum salary of all sending countries. Its regional embassies do not provide adequate protection and assistance to many Bangladeshi nationals there.

## *Sexual Orientation and Gender Identity*

Although the government took some steps in recent years, such as declaring legal recognition of a third gender category for hijras, policy implementation remains weak and sexual and gender minorities remained under constant pressure and threat.

The government twice rejected recommendations during its Universal Periodic Review at the UN Human Rights Council (UNHRC) to repeal the colonial-era law forbidding same-sex conduct. In May, the Rapid Action Battalion raided a gathering in Dhaka, arresting 28 men and publicly accusing them of homosexuality and drug possession, flouting privacy rights.

## *Key International Actors*

The UN secretary-general and the UN High Commissioner for Refugees denounced the "ethnic cleansing" campaign in Burma against the Rohingya. Several governments pledged aid to assist the refugees, but humanitarian agencies asked for more. In December, Bangladesh sponsored a special session of the UNHRC to bring attention to the plight of Rohingya in Burma.

India and the United States remained largely silent on the country's human rights record in their public statements in 2017, save in relation to the Burmese Rohingya refugee crisis, when they expressed support for Bangladesh's efforts in dealing with the massive influx of refugees. However, the US did allocate $32 million in humanitarian aid for Rohingya in Bangladesh.

The UK government raised some concerns about the rights situation in Bangladesh, but without sufficient vigour or consistency, and preferred private statements to strong statements of public concern. In November, UK Prime Minister Theresa May publicly condemned the ethnic cleansing of the Rohingya and pledged to work with Bangladesh and other regional partners to deal with the crisis.

In February and March respectively, the UN Working Group on Enforced or Involuntary Disappearances and the Human Rights Committee raised concerns about the increasing number of enforced disappearances and the lack of investigations and accountability. The Bangladeshi government ignored the statements, as well as repeated requests for visits by UN special rapporteurs and the Office of the High Commissioner for Human Rights.

# Belarus

The government continued its crackdown on civil society in 2017. Authorities carried out the broadest wave of arrests of peaceful protesters since 2010. For the first time in 10 years, authorities registered a political opposition movement, but restrictive legislation continues to prevent rights groups from registering and operating freely. No new political party has been able to register since 2000.

Belarus remains the only European country to use the death penalty and in 2017 authorities made no efforts towards its abolition.

European governments and institutions continued to strengthen relations with Belarus despite a lack of tangible rights improvements.

In July, a vaguely worded law on "protecting children from information harmful for their health and development" entered into force. These provisions may be used to restrict dissemination of neutral or positive information about lesbian, gay, bisexual, and transgender (LGBT) people as "discrediting the institution of the family."

## Death Penalty

In November 2016 and April 2017 respectively, authorities executed Henadz Yakavitski and Siarhei Vostrykau, both sentenced to death in 2016. Kiryl Kazachok and Aliaksei Mikhalenya were sentenced to death on murder charges in December 2016 and in March 2017, respectively. Kazachok did not appeal. Mikhalenya's sentence was upheld on appeal in June. Ihar Hershankou and Siamion Berazhnou were sentenced to death in July 2017 on fraud and murder charges. Both were appealing at time of writing.

## Freedom Day Crackdown, Freedom of Assembly

February and March were marked by mass demonstrations in 13 Belarusian cities, protesting a new tax on the unemployed. Peaceful protests also took place on March 25, Freedom Day, the anniversary of the creation of the Belarusian People's Republic in 1918, and continued the following day.

Police arbitrarily detained at least 700 people in connection with the protests, including about 100 journalists and 60 human rights activists. Police punched, kicked, and clubbed many of the detainees. At least 177 people were charged with fabricated offenses, such as hooliganism or participating in unsanctioned protests, and sentenced to fines or up to 25 days' detention, following pro forma administrative court hearings. Many did not have access to lawyers and could not call defense witnesses.

Also in March, authorities arrested 35 people on criminal charges of "organizing mass riots" for the Freedom Day protests. Authorities obstructed their access to legal counsel. In April, authorities also charged 20 of those detained with "organizing an unlawful armed group." In June, authorities closed the rioting case due to lack of evidence, and released those who had been charged only with rioting. Also in June, authorities released all suspects in the case of "organizing an illegal armed group" on their own recognizance, but they continued to face charges. Some of the suspects are former members of White Legion, a disbanded nationalist organization.

In April, a Minsk court canceled the suspension of an earlier prison sentence against activist Dzmitry Paliyenka and ordered him to serve 18 months. The court said he had violated the terms of his suspended sentence by committing several administrative violations. In 2016, police detained Paliyenka for taking part in the apolitical Critical Mass cycling protest. After a flawed trial, a court handed him a suspended two-year prison sentence on trumped-up charges of spreading pornography and violence against a police officer.

## Human Rights Defenders

Hours before the March 25 protest, police in Minsk raided the Human Rights Center "Viasna," detaining 58 people. A Viasna lawyer had to be hospitalized for a concussion he sustained due to police mistreatment. Authorities refused to open an investigation.

Also in March, authorities arrested five activists from Viasna and the Belarusian Helsinki Committee while they monitored peaceful protests, and charged them with participating in an unauthorized gathering. All were sentenced to up to 15 days of detention.

In April, a Minsk court fined Viasna member Tatslana Reviaka for disorderly conduct and disobeying police during the March 26 rally.

73

Also in April, a court in Vitebsk sentenced Pavel Levinau to 15 days' detention for participation in an unauthorized rally that he was monitoring. Levinau had notified local authorities in advance of his intention to monitor the gathering as a member of the Belarusian Helsinki Committee.

## *Freedom of Association*

Laws and regulations governing public association remain restrictive, preventing human rights groups or political opposition movements from registering and operating freely. Involvement in a non-registered organization is a criminal offense. Most registration rejections are based on arbitrary bureaucratic pretenses.

In January, the founders of the Solidarity Committee for the Support of Entrepreneurship, which seeks to protect entrepreneurship and promote dialogue between authorities and entrepreneurs, appealed to the Supreme Court against the Justice Ministry's refusal to register the group. In February, the court upheld the ministry's refusal. Authorities had refused to register the group twice in 2016.

In August, authorities for the second time denied registration to Gender Partnership, a group that promotes gender equality, citing minor errors in registration documents.

In a positive development, in May, authorities registered Tell the Truth, an opposition movement that had repeatedly tried to register since 2010, making it the first political opposition group able to register in 10 years.

In August, the authorities charged staff of two independent trade unions, the Radio and Electronic Industry Workers' Union (REPAM) and the Belarusian Independent Trade Union of Miners (BITU), on suspicion of large-scale tax evasion. Henadz Fiadynich, leader of REPAM, was released on his own recognizance. Ihar Komlik, the union's accountant, remained in custody at time of writing. Local and international human rights groups said the charges were part of authorities' harassment against the unions and their leaders in retaliation for their criticism of the presidential decree imposing a tax on the unemployed, and taking part in the March demonstrations.

## *Freedom of Expression and Attacks on Journalists*

Between March and August, authorities detained at least 100 journalists, mostly while they were reporting on street protests, and sentenced at least 10 to up to 15 days' detention on trumped-up charges. Police beat six of them.

Authorities also prosecuted 20 journalists, for a total of 35 cases, for cooperating with unregistered foreign media, an increase since last year. All resulted in significant, sometimes repeated, fines.

On March 31, police searched the Minsk offices of Poland-based Belsat television, and seized the channel's equipment. The channel was able to continue operating, but the equipment was not returned. By October 2017, the total amount of fines imposed on Belsat journalists had exceeded US$11,000, according to the Belarusian Association of Journalists.

In December 2016, authorities arrested three bloggers with the Russian-language websites Regnum, Lenta.ru and EADaily, on charges of inciting extremism and sowing social discord between Russia and Belarus. All are in custody, pending investigation.

In July, authorities charged Ihar Pastnou, a psychiatrist in Vitebsk known for criticizing local officials, with making a knowingly false accusation of a crime, after he wrote on his social media page about beatings in one of the Vitebsk pretrial detention centers. Pastnou was at liberty pending investigation at time of writing.

## *Asylum Policy*

Belarus failed to provide meaningful protection to hundreds of asylum seekers, mostly from the Russian republic of Chechnya, who arrived in Belarus with the aim of crossing the border into Poland and requesting asylum. Belarus lacks a functioning asylum system. During 2017 it returned at least two asylum seekers from Chechnya back to Russia, which authorities view as a safe country of origin, putting them at grave risk of ill-treatment.

## Key International Actors

In July, the Organization for Security and Co-operation in Europe (OSCE) Parliamentary Assembly held its 26th Annual Session in Minsk.

The government continued to refuse to cooperate with United Nations Special Rapporteur on Belarus Miklos Haraszti, appointed in 2012. Haraszti visited Minsk in July at the invitation of the OSCE. In June, Haraszti issued a report on the human rights situation in Belarus, pointing out the "cyclical" nature of the repression of human rights and underscoring the vital importance of international scrutiny on Belarus. In June, the UN Human Rights Council extended Haraszti's mandate for another year.

In October 2016, the European Olympic Committees selected Minsk to host the second European Games, to be held in June 2019. The decision sparked concern about Belarus' long record of rights abuses, especially on media freedoms, in connection with major sporting events.

A rapporteur of the Parliamentary Assembly of the Council of Europe (PACE) visited Belarus in March. In its April resolution, the PACE condemned the March escalation of violence, and urged Belarus to respect freedoms of assembly, association, and expression.

In June, Belarus submitted a report to the UN Human Rights Committee for the first time since 1996.

In November 2016, in its concluding observations to Belarus' eighth periodic report to the UN Committee on Elimination of Discrimination against Women, the committee noted the need to adopt anti-discrimination legislation, and to review registration requirements for nongovernmental organizations working on human rights issues.

In November 2016, Belarus ratified the UN Convention on the Rights of Persons with Disabilities.

# Bolivia

Impunity for violent crime and human rights violations remains a serious problem in Bolivia. The administration of President Evo Morales has created a hostile environment for human rights defenders that undermines their ability to work independently.

Despite recent legal reforms, extensive use of pretrial detention—combined with trial delays—undermine defendants' rights and contribute to prison overcrowding. Threats to judicial independence, violence against women, and child labor are other major concerns.

In September 2017, supporters of President Morales in the Plurinational Assembly —the national legislature—brought a lawsuit to the Constitutional Court seeking to abrogate the constitution's one-time re-election limit, which would allow him to run for a fourth term. Partly due to a 2013 Constitutional Court ruling, President Morales has been able to run in three consecutive presidential elections, all of which he won. In February 2016, voters had rejected a national referendum that would have changed the constitution to allow him to run a fourth time.

## *Impunity for Abuses and Violent Crime*

Bolivia has prosecuted only a few of the officials responsible for human rights violations committed under authoritarian governments from 1964-1982, partly because the armed forces have at times refused to give information to judicial authorities about the fate of people killed or forcibly disappeared.

In August, the government established a truth commission to carry out non-judicial investigations of grave human rights abuses committed between 1964-1982, and the commander-in-chief of Bolivian armed forces, Gen. Luis Orlando Ariñez, said that the military would fully cooperate. The commission can provide information for judges to convict those responsible.

Impunity has led to mob attacks, or lynchings, of alleged criminals. In May, a mob in the eastern city of San Julián entered a courtroom where a judge was questioning an alleged killer of a local woman, dragged the suspect outside, killed him, and hanged him in a tree. Many such lynchings go unpunished.

## *Judicial Independence*

The government has sought to reform the Bolivian justice system, which has been plagued by corruption, delays, and political interference for years. While reforms are certainly called for, current efforts pose a serious risk to judicial independence in the country.

In June 2016, members of the three branches of government, as well as civil society groups and other stakeholders, discussed proposals during a "National Justice Summit." The summit's recommendations included reforming the selection process for high court judges, creating a new body to supervise judges, and assessing the work of current judges and prosecutors.

In January 2017, Congress created a commission to oversee implementing the recommendations. The commission has broad powers, including "controlling" the appointment of new judges and carrying out "all other actions necessary" to implement the recommendations. Five of the commission's nine members are either supporters of Morales in the Plurinational Assembly or government officials directly appointed by him.

In December 2016, government supporters in the Plurinational Assembly suspended four of the five members of the Magistrate's Council—the body in charge of appointing and removing judges—arguing that they had illegally named a judge to replace another judge who had been appointed but not sworn in. Faced with possible removal from office, three of them resigned in April.

In May, the Magistrate's Council new members ruled that all the judges who were appointed before the 2009 constitution was enacted were to be considered transitory and could be summarily removed by the council. That same month, the council summarily removed 88 judges.

At time of writing, voters were scheduled to elect high court judges in December 2017. Voters will choose judges from lists created by the Plurinational Assembly, where the Morales administration has a two-thirds majority.

In September, President Morales said in an interview that judicial independence was a "US doctrine" in the "service of the empire."

## *Due Process and Prison Conditions*

Around 68 percent of inmates in Bolivian prisons have not been convicted of a crime. Extended pretrial detention and trial delays overcrowd prisons and lead to poor conditions. As of December 2016, more than 15,000 inmates were packed into prisons built to hold a maximum of around 5,000.

Presidential decrees adopted between 2012 and 2017 allow the president to reduce the sentences of those convicted of minor crimes and pardon those held in pretrial detention for minor crimes. As of December 2016, more than 5,800 people had benefited from such pardons, according to official figures.

At time of writing, the Plurinational Assembly was discussing a government-sponsored criminal reform which would shorten the maximum periods of pretrial detention and limit the cases in which judges can apply it.

The Attorney General's Office has repeatedly used a 2010 anti-corruption law to prosecute alleged crimes committed before the law was enacted. International human rights law, however, prohibits such retroactive application of changes to criminal law, unless doing so is beneficial to the defendant.

In October 2016, the Attorney General's Office used the law to charge businessman and opposition leader Samuel Doria Medina with "anti-economic conduct" for allegedly transferring US$21 million from the government to a private foundation, when he was minister of planning in 1992. In January 2017, the Supreme Court rejected a request by the Attorney General's Office that Doria be held in pretrial detention, but ordered that he appear before prosecutors every month and forbade him from leaving the country.

At time of writing, Jorge "Tuto" Quiroga, former president of Bolivia and current opposition leader, was also being prosecuted for "anti-economic conduct." Prosecutors argued that officials in his administration negatively impacted the "interests of the state" by signing four oil agreements with foreign companies.

## *Human Rights Defenders*

Human rights defenders continue to face harassment, including from government officials, which undermines their ability to work independently.

A law and decree that President Morales signed in 2013 grant the government broad powers to dissolve civil society organizations. Under the decree, any government office may request that the Ministry of Autonomy revoke the permit of a nongovernmental organization (NGO) if it performs activities other than those listed in its bylaws, or if the organization's legal representative is criminally punished for carrying out activities that "undermine security or public order."

The decree also allows the Plurinational Assembly to request the revocation of an NGO's permit in cases of "necessity or public interest." These measures give the government inappropriately wide latitude to interfere with the operation of independent civil society groups.

Bolivian officials have repeatedly accused rights groups of engaging in an international conspiracy against the government, but have failed to present evidence to support such claims. In August 2017, for example, President Morales accused "some NGOs and foundations" of being "instruments of the empire to loot and intervene [in] countries"—a reference to the United States.

## *Freedom of Expression*

While public debate is robust, the Morales administration periodically lashes out against journalists, accusing them, without presenting evidence, of publishing what it calls lies and politically motivated distortions. The government has repeatedly accused media of participating in an international conspiracy against Bolivia and the president.

Bolivia lacks transparent criteria for using government funds to purchase media advertisements—an important source of media revenue—and some media outlets have accused the government of discriminating against those who criticize government officials by withholding advertising from them. In May 2017, President Morales said that media outlets that did not receive government advertisements were those that "lie, insult, slander, and discredit authorities."

## *Indigenous Rights*

The 2009 constitution includes comprehensive guarantees for indigenous groups' rights to collective land titling, intercultural education, prior consultation on development projects, and protection of indigenous justice systems.

Indigenous peoples' right to free, prior, and informed consent (FPIC) regarding legislative or administrative measures that may affect them is not fully embodied in Bolivian legislation. A current mining law limits FPIC to the exploitation phase of land concessions, but international standards call for FPIC through all stages of projects that impact on indigenous peoples' rights over land and natural resources.

In May 2017, President Morales signed a bill that authorizes the building of a highway in the Isiboro Secure National Park and Indigenous Territory (known as "TIPNIS"). The law is based on a 2012 consultation with local indigenous groups, which some rights groups say was not fully free nor fair.

## Gender-Based Violence and Reproductive Rights

Women and girls in Bolivia remain at high risk of gender-based violence, despite a 2013 law that sets forth comprehensive measures to prevent and prosecute violence against women. The law created the crime of "femicide" (the killing of a woman in certain circumstances, including of domestic violence) and called for the establishment of shelters for women, as well as special prosecutors and courts for gender-based crimes.

The Attorney General's Office reported 74 "femicides" in Bolivia from January-September 2016.

Women and girls face numerous obstacles to accessing reproductive health products, contraceptives, and services.

Under Bolivian law, abortion is not a crime when the pregnancy is due to rape or if the procedure is necessary to protect the life or health of a pregnant women. At time of writing, the Plurinational Assembly was discussing a government-sponsored criminal reform that would significantly ease abortion restrictions. Under the bill, abortion would be fully decriminalized for girls. Women would be allowed to end pregnancies in a range of circumstances, including if their lives or health are at risk, if the pregnancy is due to rape, and if the fetus suffers severe conditions not compatible with life outside the womb.

## Child Labor

In 2014, the Plurinational Assembly adopted legislation allowing children as young as 10 to work in activities that are not deemed "dangerous" or "unhealthy." The law contravenes international standards and makes Bolivia the first country in the world to legalize employment at such a young age. Under the law, the government had to carry out a census by July 2016 to identify the number of Bolivian children under 14 who are working. At time of writing, the census had yet to take place. The latest national census on child labor, from 2008, indicated that some 850,000 children under 17 were working in Bolivia.

## Sexual Orientation and Gender Identity

In May 2016, the Plurinational Assembly passed a bill that allows people to revise the gender noted on their identification documents without prior judicial approval.

In December 2016 a transgender woman, Luna, obtained her new birth certificate reflecting her identity as a woman. She married her husband on December 30, 2016, becoming the first transgender woman in Bolivia to legally marry a person of the same biological sex. However, in November, the Constitutional Court ruled that revision of gender did not grant the right to marry a person of the same biological sex.

Same-sex couples are not allowed to marry or engage in civil unions. Bolivia's 2009 constitution defines marriage as the union of a man and a woman.

## Key International Actors

In May, the Office of the US Trade Representative announced that it would initiate a review of whether Bolivia's child labor legislation disqualifies the country from a trade preference program that eliminates duties on certain products imported to the US.

The Office of the UN High Commissioner for Human Rights (OHCHR) in Bolivia was expected to close at the end of 2017, following the government's decision not to renew the 2007 agreement with it to establish an office in the country.

As a member of the UN Human Rights Council, Bolivia has regularly voted to prevent scrutiny of human rights violations, opposing resolutions spotlighting abuses in Syria, Burundi, and Iran.

# Bosnia and Herzegovina

There was little visible progress on human rights during 2017. Authorities failed yet again to end structural and political discrimination against Jews, Roma, and other minorities. There was limited progress towards accountability for war crimes in domestic courts. Journalists remain vulnerable to intimidation and threats. Lesbian, gay, bisexual, and transgender (LGBT) people face hate speech and threats. More than 98,000 people remain displaced from their original homes, despite the fact that conflict ended more than 20 years ago.

## Ethnic and Religious Discrimination

2017 marked another year in which the government and assembly failed to make progress amending the constitution to eliminate ethnic and religious discrimination in candidacy for the national tripartite presidency and the House of Peoples, despite a further pledge to do so by January 2017.

Currently, the constitution permits candidates for these institutions only from one of the three main ethnic groups—Bosniaks, Serbs, and Croats, thereby excluding Jews, Roma, and other minorities from political office. The European Court of Human Rights (ECtHR) ruled in 2009 and 2016 that the arrangements violate the European Convention on Human Rights.

## Asylum Seekers and Internally Displaced Persons

According to the Ministry for Human Rights and Refugees, the official number of internally displaced persons (IDPs) at the end of October was 98,574. By mid-November, 39 internally displaced families (107 individuals) and 16 refugee families (56 individuals) had returned to their pre-war homes since January, according to the United Nations High Commissioner for Refugees (UNHCR).

By mid-November, Bosnia and Herzegovina had registered 211 asylum applications and granted four people subsidiary protection. No one had been granted refugee status at time of writing. Most asylum seekers came from Syria, Pakistan, and Afghanistan.

## *Accountability for War Crimes*

There was slow progress in prosecuting war crimes in domestic courts.

The goal to finish the most complex cases in the War Crimes Chamber of the State Court by the end of 2015 has not been reached.

Between January and November 2017, the State Court War Crimes Chamber delivered 37 verdicts, 20 of them appeals. Out of 37 verdicts, the court reached seven acquittals, 22 convictions, and eight partial acquittals. The total number of final judgments since the court became fully operational in 2005 stands at 188.

A report in June by the Organization for Security and Co-operation in Europe (OSCE) Mission to Bosnia and Herzegovina identified progress made by national courts in addressing conflict-related sexual violence stemming from the 1992-1995 armed conflict in Bosnia and Herzegovina.

Between 2004 and 2016, 116 such cases were completed across all jurisdictions in the country. As of the end of 2016, 58 cases involving conflict-related sexual violence were ongoing in courts, and 128 cases remained under investigation. Many survivors have not accessed needed medical or psychosocial care, or financial compensation and support, in part due to lack of a comprehensive reparations scheme for wartime sexual violence.

Between September 2016 and September 2017, the cantonal courts issued 28 verdicts (11 acquittals, 17 convictions) in relation to 67 defendants. The district courts reached four verdicts (one acquittal and one conviction) in relation to nine people in the same period.

In January 2017, the State Court of Bosnia and Herzegovina confirmed the indictment against Boro Milojica and Zelislav Rivic. They are accused of participating in crimes against humanity in 1992 as members of Bosnian Serb forces, including widespread and systematic attacks on civilians in Prijedor and the murder and persecution of Bosniak, Croat, and Romani civilians.

In September 2017, the Prosecutor's Office of Bosnia and Herzegovina issued an indictment against Serbian national Nenad Bubalo for crimes against humanity over the killing and persecution of civilians in the Bihac municipality area in 1992, while serving as an officer in Bosnian Serb forces. The indictment was forwarded to the Court of Bosnia and Herzegovina, which had yet to confirm it at time of writing.

Cross appeals against the conviction and sentence filed in April 2016 by lawyers for Bosnian Serb wartime President Radovan Karadzic and prosecutors at the International Criminal Tribunal for the former Yugoslavia (ICTY), in relation to his March 2016 conviction for genocide, crimes against humanity and war crimes, were pending at time of writing.

On November 22, 2017, the ICTY convicted former Commander of the Republika Srpska Army, Ratko Mladic, of genocide in Srebrenica, war crimes and crimes against humanity in Bosnia, and sentenced him to life in prison.

## Human Rights Defenders and Civil Society

Between January and September 2017, Civil Rights Defenders, an international nongovernmental organization (NGO), documented an increased amount of freedom of assembly violations in Bosnia and Herzegovina. The most serious breach was the violent dispersal of a demonstration in Kruscica, where locals were protesting the building of a river dam.

## Freedom of Media

Journalists continue to work in an environment where threats and intimidation are common. The national journalists' association BH Novinari registered, in the first nine months of 2017, 45 cases involving assault on media freedom and expression, including nine physical attacks, seven death threats and six other threats, and two cases of defamation. The state response remains inadequate. Police investigations into attacks take too long and only rarely lead to criminal proceedings. Although the total number of cases of assaults declined, the number of physical attacks and death threats rose slightly compared to 2016. The difficult climate for journalists was also underlined in an August 2017 report by the Institution of Human Rights Ombudsman of Bosnia and Herzegovina, which recommended stronger criminal sanctions and training for police, prosecutors, and judges to tackle attacks on journalists.

## Sexual Orientation and Gender Identity

Between January and September 2017, Sarajevo Open Centre, an LGBT rights organization, documented 39 cases of hate speech, mostly on social networks and online portals, seven cases of discrimination, and 23 cases of hate crimes towards LGBT people. These cases included eight cases of illegal imprisonment and forced conversion therapies by family members, five cases of homophobic and transphobic violence in schools (of which three were committed against children), and 10 threats of violence, physical, verbal and psychological violence, or blackmail. The reaction of police and public authorities to these incidents was generally inadequate.

## Key International Actors

In its annual Human Rights Report published in March, the US Department of State highlighted the issue of child marriage in certain Romani communities in Bosnia and Herzegovina, affecting girls between the ages of 12 and 14, and the lack of government programs to tackle these issues. It noted that violence against women remains widespread and police response is inadequate. The report identified conditions in the country's prisons as harsh and sometimes life-threatening.

In July, the European Union (EU) delegation to Bosnia and Herzegovina expressed concerns over threats against journalists in Banja Luka and Sarajevo, and called for full investigations in such cases.

In its concluding observations adopted in May, the United Nations Committee on the Rights of Persons with Disabilities expressed concerns over the lack of a human rights-based concept of disability in Bosnia and Herzegovina's entities and cantons. The committee expressed concern at the lack of efforts to bring existing legislation in line with the Disability Rights Convention, and the exclusion of persons with disabilities from public life, especially women with disabilities.

In its concluding observations in April, the Human Rights Committee renewed its concern over the slow pace of accountability for war crimes in domestic courts, noting the failure to meet the goals in the National War Crimes Strategy to conclude most complex cases by the end of 2015.

In a November report, Council of Europe Commissioner for Human Rights Nils Muižniek expressed dismay that generations of children have been educated in segregated schools with little or no interaction with children from other ethnic groups. He also expressed concern over the low number of domestically prosecuted war-related crimes of sexual violence, and called on authorities to step up efforts in prosecuting war crimes.

# Brazil

Chronic problems plague Brazil's criminal justice system, including unlawful police killings and mistreatment of detainees. In Rio de Janeiro, killings by police are approaching record levels. In January 2017, more than 120 inmates were killed in gang-related violence.

Domestic violence remained widespread; thousands of cases each year are not properly investigated.

Thousands of Venezuelans poured into Brazil, fleeing repression and seeking food and medication. In response, Brazil facilitated residency permits for them, while it called for the re-establishment of democracy in Venezuela.

## *Public Security and Police Conduct*

Widespread violence, often perpetrated by criminal gangs, plagues many Brazilian cities. Abuses by police, including extrajudicial executions, contribute to a cycle of violence, undermining public security and endangering the lives of police officers. In 2016, 437 police officers were killed in Brazil, the vast majority of them while off-duty, according to official data compiled by the nonprofit Brazilian Forum on Public Security.

Police officers, including off-duty officers, killed 4,224 people in 2016, about 26 percent more than in 2015, according to the Brazilian Forum on Public Security.

After a two-year decline in killings by on-duty police officers in the state of São Paulo, the 494 killings from January to September represented a 19 percent rise from the same period in 2016. On-duty police officers in Rio de Janeiro killed 712 people from January to August, a 30 percent rise from the same period in 2016.

While some police killings result from legitimate use of force, others do not. Human Rights Watch has documented scores of cases in the past decade where there was credible evidence of an extrajudicial execution or a cover-up that were not properly investigated or prosecuted.

In Pará, police killed 10 farmers in May. Officers said they were responding to an attack, but witnesses and forensic data provide credible evidence that they executed the victims.

In July, the government deployed thousands of armed forces personnel in Rio de Janeiro to assist with policing. In October, Congress approved a bill, promoted by the army, that will shield soldiers accused of unlawful killings of civilians from prosecution in civilian courts, moving such trials to military courts. Under international norms, extrajudicial executions and other grave human rights violations should be tried in civilian courts.

## Prison Conditions, Torture, and Ill-Treatment of Detainees

In January, more than 650,000 adults were behind bars in Brazil, according to the National Council of Justice. The latest official data about overcrowding, from 2014, showed facilities housing 67 percent more inmates than they were designed to hold.

Overcrowding and understaffing make it impossible for prison authorities to maintain control within many prisons, leaving detainees vulnerable to violence. In January, more than 120 inmates died in three states, allegedly as a result of gang violence. Another 22 inmates had already been killed in October 2016.

Health and legal services are deficient in many prisons, and only a small percentage of inmates have access to educational and work opportunities. Pretrial detainees are routinely held with convicted prisoners, in violation of international standards and Brazilian law

Judges in only about 40 percent of jurisdictions see detainees promptly after arrest, as required by international law, according to the nonprofit Institute for the Defense of the Right to Defense. Such "custody hearings" help judges determine who should be in preventive detention and who should be set free pending trial. In the absence of custody hearings, detainees often wait many months to see a judge for the first time; 34 percent of people in Brazilian prisons were awaiting trial in January. At time of writing, Congress was examining a bill to make custody hearings mandatory countrywide.

Such hearings have the potential to be a powerful weapon against police abuse of detainees because they allow judges to detect mistreatment soon after arrest. In São Paulo, however, a 2017 report by the nonprofit Conectas found that Judges, prosecutors, and public defenders failed to ensure the proper investigation of allegations of mistreatment in hundreds of custody hearings.

HUMAN
RIGHTS
WATCH

"One Day I'll Kill You"
Impunity in Domestic Violence Cases in the Brazilian State of Roraima

## *Children's Rights*

Brazil's juvenile detention facilities were built to house about 19,400 children and young adults but held at least 24,000 in October 2016. These figures do not include the capacity of facilities and the number of detainees in six states, about which the federal government had no data.

In June, nine children were killed by other children in severely overcrowded detention facilities in Paraíba and Pernambuco. The National Council of Human Rights reported 40 children killed in confinement in Pernambuco from 2012 to 2016. The report did not make clear the assailants.

Investigations by the National Mechanism for the Prevention and Combatting of Torture and Human Rights Watch found scores of cases of mistreatment of children by staff and police in various states. Abuses are often not properly investigated or punished. An exception was the conviction in August of 12 staff members for torturing 85 children in São Paulo. Despite substantial forensic and video evidence, the case did not come to trial until 12 years after the abuse.

Instead of promoting rehabilitation and education, the physical infrastructure of juvenile detention facilities fosters isolation and punishment. Some children and young adults in the state of Ceará have no access to educational activities and are locked in their rooms most, if not all, day, as documented by Human Rights Watch.

At time of writing, Brazil's Congress was examining a bill to raise the maximum time of internment for children from 3 to 10 years—which would aggravate overcrowding—and a constitutional amendment to allow 16 and 17 year olds accused of serious crimes to be tried and punished as adults, in violation of international norms.

## *Freedom of Expression*

In December 2016, a panel of the Superior Justice Court ruled that a legal provision that punishes the "disrespecting" of public officials *(desacato)* with up to two years in prison violated freedom of expression and should be voided. But in May, the full criminal section of the court reversed that decision.

In Rio de Janeiro, where the armed forces have been deployed repeatedly to patrol the streets, scores of civilians have been tried in military courts for allegedly disrespecting soldiers under a *desacato* provision in the Military Criminal Code. Military Police forces have abused the provision to quell criticism, including in cases in which they detained artists during performances or people who had posted critical comments online.

Military police officers face broad restrictions on their own freedom of speech. State disciplinary codes and the military criminal code subject officers to expulsion from the force and prison sentences for offenses such as criticizing a superior officer or a government decision. Some commanders use those norms to impose disproportionate punishments on officers who advocate for police reform or voice complaints.

## *Women's and Girls' Rights*

Abortion is legal in Brazil only in cases of rape, when necessary to save a woman's life, or when the fetus suffers from anencephaly, a fatal congenital brain disorder.

Women and girls who abort pregnancies illegally not only risk injury and death but face sentences of up to three years in prison, while people convicted of performing unlawful abortions face up to four years. An estimated 416,000 Brazilian women had abortions in 2015, according to a survey. The Ministry of Health told Human Rights Watch that doctors administered only 1,667 legal abortions that year.

The Supreme Court is examining two petitions to decriminalize abortion. In April, Human Rights Watch submitted expert briefs in support of both cases. In November, a congressional committee approved a bill that would prohibit abortion under any circumstances.

An outbreak of the Zika virus in 2015 had particularly harmful impacts on women and girls. When a pregnant woman is infected, Zika can cause problems with fetal development, including microcephaly—underdevelopment of the brain. Inadequate investment in water and sanitation infrastructure, as well as limited reproductive health information and services, worsened the Zika outbreak, and

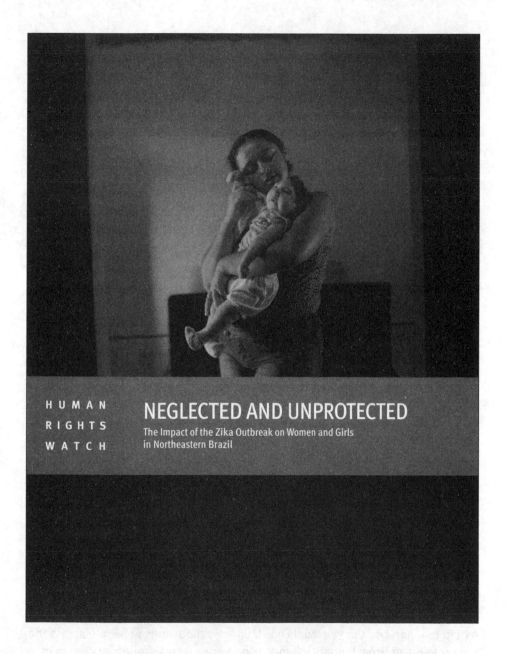

**HUMAN RIGHTS WATCH**

# NEGLECTED AND UNPROTECTED

The Impact of the Zika Outbreak on Women and Girls
in Northeastern Brazil

leave Brazilians vulnerable to future outbreaks. Children with Zika syndrome need additional state support.

Implementation of Brazil's anti-domestic violence legislation, the 2006 "Maria da Penha" law, is lagging. Specialized women's police stations have insufficient staff, are mostly closed during evenings and on weekends, and remain concentrated in major cities. Thousands of cases each year are never properly investigated, according to available data.

Unchecked domestic abuse typically escalates and may lead to death. In 2016, 4,657 women were killed in Brazil, according to official data compiled by the Brazilian Forum on Public Security. A 2013 study estimated that the attacker was a partner, former partner, or relative in half of all cases of killings of women.

## Disability Rights

In January 2016, a disability rights law came into effect, requiring public agencies to prioritize people with disabilities when providing services related to health, education, work, housing, culture, and sport.

In March 2016, a new civil procedure code revoked recently enacted provisions that guaranteed legal capacity for all persons with disabilities and mandated a move to systems of supported decision-making. Another bill under discussion would reinstate full legal guardianship in the country, a major setback for disability rights as it would impede certain people with disabilities from making their own decisions about their lives, such as where to live, with whom, whether to marry or have children, and whether to vote.

## Migrants, Refugees, and Asylum Seekers

In May, Brazil approved a new migration law that grants non-citizen immigrants equal access to public services, including education and health, and the right to join unions. The law allows the government to provide humanitarian visas to people from countries suffering "serious or imminent institutional instability, armed conflict, great calamity, an environmental disaster, or serious violation of human rights or international humanitarian law."

A humanitarian crisis in Venezuela has launched thousands of people across the border to Brazil. From January to June, 7,600 Venezuelans requested asylum In

Brazil, compared with 55 in all of 2013, according to government data. Brazil granted asylum to 14 Venezuelans in 2016, and denied it to 28, with the rest of cases still pending. From January to September 2017, Brazil did not make any decision on asylum applications from Venezuelans.

In March, Brazil approved a resolution allowing Venezuelans to apply for a two-year residency permit. In August, a federal judge exempted poor Venezuelans from paying the US$100 application fee, which had prevented many from requesting a permit.

## Sexual Orientation and Gender Identity

The national Human Rights Ombudsman's Office received 725 complaints of violence, discrimination, and other abuses against lesbian, gay, bisexual, and transgender (LGBT) people in the first half of 2017.

In February, men shouting homophobic insults beat, shot, and stoned to death Dandara dos Santos, a 42-year-old transgender person in the state of Ceará. A witness said he called the police twice during the attack. Police have not explained their delayed response. Police detained several suspects only after a video of the beating—apparently recorded by one of the aggressors—appeared on social media.

In September, a federal judge overruled a 1999 decision by the Federal Council of Psychology that banned conversion therapy—the attempt to change an individual's sexual orientation. The council appealed.

## Labor Rights

In 2016, the Ministry of Labor identified 885 cases of workers subjected to abusive conditions that under Brazilian law rise to the level of "slave-like," such as forced labor or degrading working conditions. While the number is lower than in previous years, the ministry conducted 25 percent fewer inspections. From December 2014 to December 2016, it imposed penalties on 250 companies for employing people in "slave-like" conditions.

In October 2017, the ministry issued a resolution that redefined "slave-like" conditions to apply only in circumstances when workers' freedom of movement is restricted. It also required that police participate in inspections and that the minister approve the publication of the names of companies penalized. A week later, a Supreme Court justice ruled the resolution was unconstitutional and suspended it until the full court decides on the issue.

## Environment and Land-Related Conflicts

Violence against rural activists and indigenous leaders involved in conflicts over land continued to climb. In 2016, 61 people involved in land conflicts died violently, the highest yearly number since 2003, and from January to October 2017, 64 were killed, according to the Pastoral Land Commission of the Catholic Church. Among those were nine rural workers killed in April in the state of Mato Grosso. Prosecutors assert a logger ordered the crimes to expel them from the land.

In 2016, 12 indigenous people were killed as a result of land conflicts, according to the Pastoral Land Commission. Prosecutors were investigating reports that illegal miners killed at least 10 members of a remote Amazon tribe in August.

The government almost halved the budget for Funai, the agency charged with protecting indigenous people, and maintained that indigenous people who were not occupying their lands in 1988, when the constitution was promulgated, should lose their right to those lands, a position opposed by the Federal Prosecutor's Office.

A federal law approved in July would grant titles to people occupying land illegally in the Amazon forest. Environmental and landless peasant organizations opposed it, arguing it would benefit large landowners and illegal loggers. The Federal Prosecutor's Office concurred, warning that the law could also increase the number of killings as a result of land conflicts, and petitioned the Supreme Court to declare it unconstitutional.

In May, a parliamentary inquiry commission dominated by the agribusiness caucus urged federal authorities to prosecute 67 indigenous leaders, anthropologists, public servants, and members of NGOs defending indigenous rights for alleged fraud, land invasion, and belonging to a criminal organization. At time of writing, federal authorities had not taken up that proposal.

In June, four rapporteurs from the United Nations and the Inter-American Commission on Human Rights (IACHR) stated that "indigenous and environmental rights are under attack" in Brazil. The government called the rapporteurs' allegations "groundless."

## Confronting Military-Era Abuses

The perpetrators of human rights abuses during military rule from 1964 to 1985 continue to be shielded from justice by a 1979 amnesty law that the Supreme Court upheld in 2010, a decision that the Inter-American Court of Human Rights quickly ruled violated Brazil's obligations under international law.

Since 2012, federal prosecutors have charged more than 40 former military officers and other agents of the dictatorship with killings, kidnappings, and other serious human rights abuses. Lower courts dismissed most of the cases, while the Supreme Court halted two, pending its re-examination of the validity of the amnesty law.

In May, the Inter-American Court of Human Rights held a hearing in the case of journalist Vladimir Herzog, who was tortured and killed by state agents in 1975. The court will have to address the amnesty law again when it decides the Herzog case.

## Key International Actors

In May, as part of the Universal Periodic Review (UPR), UN member states made 246 recommendations to improve Brazil's human rights record. They highlighted prison and police abuses, and the violation of rights of indigenous people and women, among other issues.

## Foreign Policy

The Brazilian government condemned violations of human rights in Venezuela and called for the reestablishment of democracy. In August, Brazil and the other founding members of the South American trading bloc Mercosur suspended Venezuela from the group for "breaking democratic order."

A Saudi-led coalition used Brazilian-made cluster munitions in Yemen on at least four occasions, the latest in February 2017, killing two civilians and wounding at least 12. Cluster munitions are prohibited by a 2008 treaty joined by 102 countries, but not by Brazil.

# Burma

Burma's stalled democratic transition gave way to a massive human rights and humanitarian crisis starting in August 2017, when the military launched a large-scale ethnic cleansing campaign against the Rohingya Muslim population in Rakhine State. By November, over 625,000 Rohingya had fled to neighboring Bangladesh to escape mass killings, sexual violence, arson, and other abuses amounting to crimes against humanity by the security forces.

2017 marked the country's first full year under the democratically elected civilian government led by the National League for Democracy (NLD) and de facto civilian leader Aung San Suu Kyi. The NLD-led government took some positive steps, including ratifying the International Covenant on Economic, Social and Cultural Rights, engaging in some efforts to resolve past land confiscation cases, and enacting minor reforms to laws regulating speech and assembly. However, the government increasingly used repressive laws to prosecute journalists, activists, and critics for peaceful expression deemed critical of the government or military.

Despite the appearance of civilian rule, the military remained the primary power-holder in the country. It continued to block efforts to amend the 2008 constitution, which allows the armed forces to retain authority over national security and public administration through control of the defense, home affairs, and border affairs ministries. The constitutional provision allowing the military to appoint 25 percent of parliamentary seats affords it an effective veto over constitutional amendments.

The peace process with ethnic armed groups made no meaningful progress. Fighting intensified in Kachin and northern Shan States, resulting in an increase in forced displacement and other abuses against civilians, primarily by government forces.

## *Crimes Against Humanity and Ethnic Cleansing of Rohingya*

On August 25, in response to coordinated attacks on security force outposts northern Rakhine State by militants from the Arakan Rohingya Salvation Army (ARSA), security forces launched a large-scale military operation against the Rohingya Muslim population.

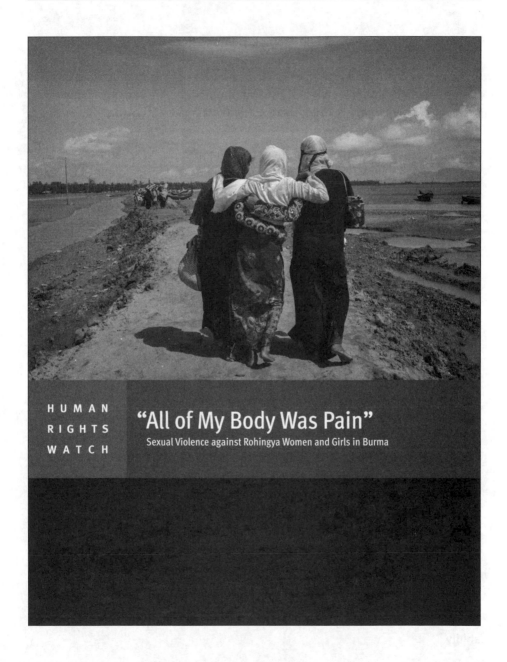

HUMAN RIGHTS WATCH

# "All of My Body Was Pain"

Sexual Violence against Rohingya Women and Girls in Burma

Military units, assisted by ethnic Rakhine militias, attacked Rohingya villages and committed massacres, widespread rape, arbitrary detention, and mass arson. Some Rohingya who fled were killed or maimed by landmines laid by soldiers on paths near the Bangladesh-Burma border. Satellite imagery showed that more than 340 primarily Rohingya villages were either substantially or completely destroyed.

Prior to August 25, the total Rohingya population in Burma was estimated to be more than 1 million, though precise figures do not exist as the Rohingya were excluded from the 2014 census. An estimated 120,000 Rohingya remain internally displaced in central Rakhine State from waves of violence in 2012. The military and government have denied that the Rohingya are a distinct ethnic group, effectively denying them citizenship, and calling them "Bengali" instead of "Rohingya" to label them as foreigners.

The military and government appointed multiple investigative commissions on the 2016-2017 violence, but each engaged in whitewashing, denying any unlawful killings. The Burmese government repeatedly stated it would not grant access to members of a United Nations Fact-Finding Mission, created by the UN Human Rights Council (UNHRC) in March 2017 following attacks on the Rohingya in late 2016.

In December 2017, the UN General Assembly passed a resolution urging Burma to give the mission full, unrestricted, and unmonitored access. The government denied access to affected areas in Rakhine State to independent journalists and human rights monitors. It also continued to heavily restrict access to humanitarian agencies, compounding the already-dire humanitarian conditions that internally displaced persons (IDPs) and other residents face.

## Ethnic Conflicts and Forced Displacement

As the peace process stalled, fighting between the military and ethnic armed groups continued over the year in Kachin and northern Shan States, with civilians endangered by indiscriminate attacks, forced displacement, and blockage of aid by the government. Approximately 100,000 civilians remain displaced in camps in the region, many near areas of active conflict, heightening their vulnerability.

In March, fighting broke out in the Kokang region of Shan State when the Myanmar National Democratic Alliance Army (MNDAA) attacked military posts and casinos in Laukkai. Over 20,000 temporarily fled across the border into China, and about 10,000 were displaced to central Burma. In June, fighting escalated in Tanai township in Kachin State, displacing thousands. Sporadic fighting in Chin State with the Arakan Army, comprised of ethnic Rakhine Buddhists, endangered civilians, forcing hundreds from their homes.

Reports rose of injuries and deaths caused by landmines, used by both government and ethnic armed forces. Landmine casualties in Burma over the past decade are the third highest in the world. Both government and ethnic armed groups unlawfully recruited children for their forces. The government did not adequately or effectively investigate alleged abuses by military personnel in conflict areas.

## Attacks on Free Expression and Media

The government increased its use of overly broad and vaguely worded laws to detain, arrest, and imprison individuals for peaceful expression. Activists and journalists reported an increase in surveillance, threats, and intimidation by security personnel or their agents. The rise in prosecutions of journalists has had a chilling effect on the country's media.

Prosecutions for critiques of government or military officials have surged since the NLD took office. Over 90 cases have been filed under section 66(d) of the 2013 Telecommunications Act, a vaguely worded law that criminalizes broad categories of online speech, with over 20 journalists among those charged.

In September, after parliament rejected a proposal to remove the law's criminal penalty, President Htin Kyaw signed into law amendments to the act that reduced the maximum prison sentence from three to two years and allowed for bail, but the majority of problematic provisions were retained.

In January 2017, the army filed defamation charges under section 500 of the penal code against nine students who performed a satirical play about armed conflict at a peace assembly in Irrawaddy Region. A local human rights defender was charged under section 66(d) in June for streaming a video of the play on Facebook. The chief editor of *Myanmar Now*, Swe Win, was arrested in July under section 66(d) for a Facebook post criticizing extremist Buddhist monk Wirathu. He was released on bail but has faced extensive pretrial delays.

Khaing Myo Htun, an environmental rights activist, was sentenced to 18 months in prison in October for violating sections 505(b) and (c) of the penal code, which criminalizes speech that is likely to cause fear or harm and incites classes or groups to commit offenses against each other. He had been detained since July 2016 for helping prepare a statement released by the Arakan Liberation Party, of which he was the deputy spokesperson, accusing the military of rights violations.

*The Voice* newspaper's chief editor Kyaw Min Swe and columnist Kyaw Zwa Naing were arrested in June under section 25(b) of the 2014 Media Law and section 66(d) of the Telecommunications Act for an article satirizing a military propaganda film, despite having printed an apology in May. Later that month, three journalists—Aye Nai and Pyae Phone Naing from the *Democratic Voice of Burma (DVB)*, and Lawi Weng from *The Irrawaddy*—were detained under section 17(1) of the 1908 Unlawful Associations Act while reporting on an event organized by the Ta'ang National Liberation Army (TNLA), an ethnic armed group, in northern Shan State. After a domestic and international outcry, the charges were dropped.

The government has long used the Unlawful Associations Act to restrict freedom of association and detain peaceful activists. In October, authorities sentenced two Kachin Baptist community leaders, Dumdaw Nawng Lat and Langjaw Gam Seng, to four years and two years in prison, respectively, under section 17(1). The two men were charged with allegedly supporting the Kachin Independence Army (KIA) after they assisted journalists documenting military damage to civilian areas in northern Shan State.

Despite changes to the Peaceful Assembly and Peaceful Procession Act, the right to protest is still limited. In October, the law was amended to remove the requirement of government consent to hold an assembly or processions, yet it retains several provisions that fail to meet international standards. The police announced in November a total ban on all public assemblies in 11 major townships in Rangoon.

A new privacy law enacted in March includes vague provisions on surveillance and data protection.

## *Freedom of Religion*

Religious minorities, including Hindus, Christians, and Muslims, continue to face threats and persecution in a country that is approximately 88 percent Buddhist. Religious activities are often tightly regulated and authorities threaten to fine or imprison those who conduct organized prayers in their homes.

In May, authorities sent a letter to a Christian man in Rangoon, warning him not to continue to pray in his home with others without first receiving approval from authorities. In Sagaing Region, a Buddhist mob attacked Christian worshippers, destroying homes and personal property.

The government took increasing action against Buddhist monks and organizations that used extremist and ultranationalist rhetoric. In May, the government banned the use of the name and logos of the Buddhist-monk-led Ma Ba Tha, or Association for the Protection of Race and Religion. Some but not all branches of the organization complied. A well-known extremist monk, Wirathu, was banned from public speaking for one year, but has on occasion violated the order without consequences.

In April, a mob of about 50 to 100 Buddhist ultranationalists put pressure on local officials and police in Rangoon's Thaketa township to close two Islamic schools. The authorities carried out the mob's demand and have not reopened the schools, denying several hundred students access to education. Following the closures, local officials charged seven Muslims who participated in a public prayer session on May 31. They faced up to six months in jail for holding public prayers under the Ward or Village Tract Administration Law.

## *Human Rights Defenders*

Accountability for attacks on human rights defenders remains impeded by the country's weak rule of law, corrupt judiciary, and unwillingness to prosecute members of the security forces.

On January 29, Ko Ni, a prominent Muslim lawyer and senior NLD advisor, was shot and killed outside the Rangoon airport. Ko Ni, a longtime advocate for interfaith dialogue and democratic reform, had been a proponent of controversial legislation including a hate speech bill and constitutional amendments. Authorities arrested four suspects, but have not apprehended the individual alleged to have engineered the attack. Aung San Suu Kyi was widely criticized for her silence after the killing.

Three recent murders of environmental defenders—rights activist Naw Chit Pandaing and investigative journalist Soe Moe Tun in late 2016, and community leader Lung Jarm Phe in February 2017—remain unsolved.

On November 1, a land rights defender in northern Shan State, Htay Aung, was killed by a mob while on his way to discuss a dispute over confiscated land.

## Land Rights and Government Land Seizures

The government took several steps toward reforming land laws that provide weak land tenure security for farmers and toward resolving decades-old claims of land confiscation that occurred under military rule.

However, progress was limited as attempts to reform laws and land governance structures failed to provide additional protections for landholders and did not incorporate provisions of the 2016 National Land Use Policy. Farmers faced threats and arrests for protesting about unresolved land confiscation claims. Poor redress mechanisms left many without a livelihood or compensation and facing increased barriers to health care and education.

## Human Trafficking

Human trafficking remained a serious problem in several areas, particularly in the north where armed conflict and widespread displacement exacerbated financial instability. Women and girls in Kachin and Shan States who went to China in search of work faced abuses. Many women and girls were sold to Chinese families as "brides" and often faced horrific abuses including being locked up, subjected to sexual slavery, forced to bear children of their "husbands" by rape, and forcibly separated from their children. The Burmese government put few measures in place to protect women and girls from these abuses or assist women and girls who escaped or sought to do so.

## *Key International Actors*

China continued to strengthen its ties with Burma, shielding the Burmese government from concerted international action and scrutiny over the Rohingya crisis. Large-scale infrastructure projects ramped up under China's "One Belt, One Road" initiative, including an eastern seaport development that offers strategic access to the Indian Ocean.

China attempted to play a larger role in Burma's peace process through ties to ethnic armed groups on the border. In November, China served as a mediator for talks between Burma and Bangladesh on the return of Rohingya refugees, but the resulting agreement failed to meet international standards for the protection and respect of rights of refugees.

Burma's civilian government continued to receive strong backing from Western donors, who remained hopeful about the reform process yet concerned about weak governance and the increased role and stature of the military.

In response to the Rohingya crisis, in September the UN Security Council held its first open discussion of the situation in Burma in eight years. A draft Security Council resolution was blocked by a veto threat from China. Instead, in November it adopted a Presidential Statement expressing grave concern over reports of human rights violations in Rakhine State by Burma's security forces and calling on Burma to cooperate with UN investigative bodies.

In December, the UN General Assembly adopted a resolution drafted by the Organisation of Islamic Cooperation (OIC) and co-sponsored by a broad cross-regional coalition that called for an end to military operations, unhindered access for humanitarian assistance and actors, the voluntary and sustainable return of refugees to their original places, accountability for violations and abuses, and full respect for the "human rights and fundamental freedoms" of the Rohingya population, including full citizenship. The resolution also requested the appointment of a special envoy to Burma.

In December, the UNHRC held a special session condemning the violations, urging the government to grant access to the council-created Fact-Finding Mission, and calling on the government to address root causes, such as statelessness and the denial of citizenship to Rohingya. The council said that returns should be safe, voluntary, dignified, and in accordance with international law, and requested additional reporting by the UN High Commissioner for Human Rights.

While Burma faced widespread international condemnation for the military's ethnic cleansing of the Rohingya, concrete action was less forthcoming. In September, the United Kingdom announced it was halting all engagement programs with the Burmese military. In October, the European Union suspended invitations to senior military officers and undertook a review of defense cooperation. The United States ceased consideration of travel waivers for current and former senior military officials and rescinded invitations for senior military officials to attend US-sponsored events. In October, citing the crisis in Rakhine State, the World Bank announced it would delay a loan for US$200 million, its first direct financial assistance to the government's budget since the institution suspended its lending to the country in the late 1980s.

The US government removed Burma from its annual list of governments using child soldiers, despite documentation of ongoing recruitment. Burma remains on the UN's annual "list of shame" for the military's use and recruitment of child soldiers. The US also upgraded Burma's designation in its global Trafficking in Persons (TIP) Report, despite continued violations and weak efforts by the government to end trafficking and punish those responsible.

# Burundi

The political and human rights crisis that began in Burundi in April 2015, when President Pierre Nkurunziza announced that he would run for a disputed third term, continued through 2017, as government forces targeted real and perceived opponents with near total impunity. Security forces and intelligence services—often collaborating with members of the ruling party's youth league, known as the Imbonerakure—were responsible for numerous killings, disappearances, abductions, acts of torture, rapes, and arbitrary arrests. Unknown assailants carried out grenade and other attacks, killing or injuring many people.

In September, a United Nations Commission of Inquiry, established by the Human Rights Council a year earlier, said it had "reasonable grounds to believe that crimes against humanity have been committed in Burundi since April 2015." During its session later that month, the council extended the commission's mandate for one year, but Burundi continues to refuse any form of cooperation with the commission. In October, judges of the International Criminal Court (ICC) authorized an investigation into crimes committed in Burundi since April 2015.

Also in October, Burundi's government adopted a plan to revise the constitution to allow President Nkurunziza to stand for two new seven-year terms. If passed by a vote in parliament or national referendum, Nkurunziza could possibly stay in power until 2034.

## Killings, Rapes, and Other Abuses by Security Forces and Ruling Party Youth

The violence in 2017 claimed scores of lives, according to Burundian and international human rights organizations. Dead bodies of people killed in unknown circumstances were regularly found across the country.

The Commission of Inquiry confirmed "the persistence of extrajudicial executions, arbitrary arrests and detentions, enforced disappearances, torture and cruel, inhuman or degrading treatment and sexual violence in Burundi since April 2015," blaming most violations on members of the intelligence services, the police, the army, and the youth league of the ruling party. The commission indicated that "some violations have been committed in a more clandestine, but equally brutal, manner since 2016."

The Commission of Inquiry collected several testimonies suggesting that "intelligence agents or members of the police" were involved in the disappearance of Oscar Ntasano, a former senator, in Bujumbura on April 21, 2017.

Human Rights Watch documented how in 2015 and 2016, members of the Imbonerakure and police—sometimes armed with guns, sticks, or knives—raped women whose male family members were perceived to be government opponents. In some cases, Imbonerakure threatened or attacked the male relative before raping the woman. Women often continued to receive threats after being raped. Human Rights Watch received credible reports that these abuses continued in 2017.

In early April, a video emerged showing about 200 members of the Imbonerakure gathered in northern Burundi, singing songs encouraging the rape of political opponents or their relatives. Incitement to hatred, violence, and rape, particularly by the Imbonerakure, has become common in Burundi, almost always without condemnation by authorities.

Security forces arrested, ill-treated, and illegally detained many opposition party members. Some detainees were held incommunicado in unknown locations. Several activists of the Movement for Solidarity and Democracy (Mouvement pour la solidarité et la démocratie, MSD) and National Liberation Forces (Forces nationales de libération, FNL) opposition parties were arrested in June. In early April, the government had suspended the MSD for six months and shut down its offices.

On January 24, unknown men attacked Camp Mukoni, a military base in Burundi's eastern Muyinga province. Seven soldiers, twelve civilians, and one policeman arrested after the attack were sentenced to heavy prison terms. Intelligence agents badly beat and tortured many defendants during interrogations, witnesses told Human Rights Watch.

## Abuses by Opposition Armed Groups and Unknown Actors

Several grenade attacks took place in bars and elsewhere across Burundi in 2017, killing and injuring many, including children. The identity of the perpetrators was often unknown.

The UN Commission of Inquiry found that "human rights abuses were also committed by armed opposition groups [since April 2015], but these proved difficult to document." Emmanuel Niyonkuru, minister of water, environment, land management, and urban planning, was killed on January 1. The commission was "unable to establish" who was responsible for this and several other "assassinations."

## Refugees

The number of Burundian refugees remained high in 2017, despite claims from the Burundian government that the country was "peaceful." More than 400,000 Burundians who fled the country since 2015 remained abroad at time of writing, most in Tanzania, Rwanda, Uganda, and the Democratic Republic of Congo.

In September 2017, the UN High Commissioner for Refugees (UNHCR) started repatriating hundreds of Burundian refugees back home from neighboring Tanzania. At least 12,000 Burundian refugees signed up for voluntary repatriation, sometimes because of the dire conditions in the refugee camps in Tanzania, while more than 234,000 refugees stayed in Tanzania.

On September 15, alleged members of the Congolese security forces used excessive force to quash a protest in Kamanyola, South Kivu province, in eastern Congo, killing around 40 Burundian refugees and wounding more than 100 others.

## Civil Society and Media

Most leading civil society activists and many independent journalists remained in exile, after repeated government threats in 2015 and arrest warrants against several of them, and after the Interior Minister banned or suspended 10 civil society organizations that had spoken out against government abuses in October 2016.

In January, two new laws allowed for increased control by authorities over the activities and resources of Burundian and foreign nongovernmental organizations. On January 3, authorities banned the Ligue Iteka, a prominent Burundian human rights organization.

On June 13, security forces arrested three members of Parole et Action pour le Réveil des Consciences et l'Évolution des Mentalités (PARCEM), one of the few remaining independent nongovernmental organizations in the country, while they were organizing a workshop on arbitrary arrests in Muramvya province.

The national intelligence agency detained Aimé Gatore, Emmanuel Nshimirimana, and Marius Nizigama from June 17 to 27, before they were transferred to Mpimba prison, in Bujumbura, and later to Muramvya prison, around 30 kilometers away from the capital. They remained in detention at time of writing, charged with "threatening state security."

Germain Rukuki, a human rights defender and former treasurer of Action by Christians for the Abolition of Torture (Action des Chrétiens pour l'Abolition de la Torture, ACAT) in Burundi, one of the banned organizations, has been detained since July 13 and faces several charges, including "rebellion." On August 25, UN experts called for Rukuki's release, adding that the charges against him formed "part of an overall context of threats and harassment against human rights defenders in Burundi."

Authorities continued to severely restrict media space in Burundi. Radio Publique Africaine, Radio Bonesha, and Radio-Television Renaissance—all private radio stations that the government had closed following an attempted coup d'état in May 2015—remained off the air at time of writing.

Other media were allowed to operate in 2017, but faced grave restrictions on their activities. On April 5, intelligence agents interrogated Joseph Nsabiyabandi, the editor-in-chief of Radio Isanganiro, another privately owned radio station, about his alleged collaboration with Burundian radios operating in exile in Rwanda. He was later criticized for having "incited the opinion and the population to revolt." Radio Isanganiro had been closed in May 2015, and then allowed by authorities to re-open in February 2016, after it signed an "ethical charter" with the Burundian National Communications Council, in which it committed to a "balanced and objective" editorial line, respectful of the "country's security."

## National and International Justice

Impunity for serious crimes committed in Burundi remains the norm. The justice system is manipulated by ruling party and intelligence officials and judicial procedures are routinely flouted.

Burundi became the first country to withdraw from the ICC on October 27, 2017. Two days earlier, ICC judges had authorized an investigation into crimes committed in the country since April 2015. The judges found that Burundi's withdrawal does not affect the court's jurisdiction over crimes committed while the country was a member.

## Discriminatory Laws

Since April 2009, Burundi has criminalized consensual same-sex conduct. Article 567 of the penal code, which penalizes consensual same-sex sexual relations by adults with up to two years in prison, violates the rights to privacy and freedom from discrimination. These rights are protected by Burundi's Constitution and enshrined in its international treaty commitments.

In May 2017, President Nkurunziza signed into law new regulations requiring unmarried couples to legalize their relationships through church or state registrations. In November, a new decree banned women from drumming and limited all "cultural shows" to official ceremonies authorized by the Ministry of Culture.

## Key International Actors

There was little progress in regional and international efforts to broker a dialogue between Burundian political actors, facilitated by former Tanzanian President Benjamin Mkapa. Most major donors have suspended direct budgetary support to the Burundian government, but some maintained humanitarian assistance. The US and the European Union maintained targeted sanctions on several senior Burundian officials and opposition leaders.

In addition to renewing the mandate of the Commission of Inquiry, the UN Human Rights Council also adopted another resolution on Burundi, on September 28, presented by the African Group, dispatching a mission of three experts to gather information on abuses to share with local judicial authorities.

In August, the UN Security Council said it remained "alarmed by the increasing numbers of refugees outside the country and disturbed by reports of torture, forced disappearances, and extra-judicial killings, as well as by the persisting political impasse in the country and the attendant serious humanitarian consequences."

A July 2016 Security Council resolution authorizing 228 UN police officers to deploy to the country was not implemented in 2017 due to continued rejection by Burundian authorities.

# Cambodia

The civil and political rights environment in Cambodia markedly deteriorated in 2017 as the government arrested the leader of Cambodia's political opposition on dubious charges of treason; dissolved the main opposition party and banned over 100 members from political activity; intensified the misuse of the justice system to prosecute political opposition and human rights activists; and forced several independent media outlets to close.

Authorities have detained at least 35 opposition and civil society leaders since July 2015, many of whom have been prosecuted and convicted in summary trials that failed to meet international standards. At least 19 remained in detention at time of writing.

The ruling Cambodia People's Party (CPP), which controls the country's security services and courts, has led the crackdown that began in 2016 and is likely motivated by Prime Minister Hun Sen's anxiety about national elections scheduled for July 29, 2018. The arbitrary arrests and other abuses appear aimed at preventing a victory by the opposition Cambodia National Rescue Party (CNRP), which made electoral gains during the 2013 national elections and the 2017 commune elections. Because of the dissolution of the CNRP in November, there will be no major opposition party to contest the CPP in the 2018 elections.

Throughout 2017 the government continued to deny Cambodians the right to free speech and peaceful assembly by suppressing protests and issuing a series of bans on gatherings and processions. Cambodia's anti-corruption authorities, rather than conducting investigations into suspicious government concessions and the questionable wealth of senior CPP leaders and their families, instead carried out politically motivated investigations of the CNRP and other organizations critical of the government.

## *Attacks on Political Opposition*

CNRP leader Sam Rainsy remained in exile in 2017 to avoid a two-year prison sentence stemming from a politically motivated criminal defamation charge from 2008.

On September 3, the government arrested CNRP's leader Kem Sokha on charges of treason. Kem Sokha, who had assumed leadership of the party after Sam Rainsy's exile and resignation, had already faced de facto house arrest in 2016 in a separate politically motivated case.

Several other elected opposition leaders, including parliamentarian Um Sam An, Senator Hong Sok Hour, Senator Thak Lany, and Commune Councilor Seang Chet, remained in detention after politically motivated prosecutions.

Commune elections on June 4 featured threats and harassment of the opposition and civil society groups. Prior to the election, Interior Ministry Gen. Khieu Sopheak acknowledged pre-election harassment of nongovernmental organizations (NGOs) and said the Interior Ministry had started an investigation "because we wanted to threaten those organizations to be scared."

Although voting day was peaceful, the overarching dynamic of the elections were unfair, with unequal media access for opposition parties, bias toward the CPP in electoral institutions, and lack of independent and impartial dispute resolution mechanisms.

The government used increasingly threatening political rhetoric throughout the year, including repeated threats of violence, to intimidate dissidents and civil society groups, especially in the lead-up to the commune elections. Prime Minister Hun Sen and other leaders repeated claims that any election victory by the opposition would lead to "civil war," and threatened to use violence against those who "protest" or seek a "color revolution," a term authorities use to portray peaceful dissent as an attempted overthrow of the state.

In May 2017, Hun Sen stated he would be "willing to eliminate 100 to 200 people" to protect "national security," and suggested opposition members "prepare their coffins." On August 2, Minister of Social Affairs Vong Sauth said that protesters who dispute the 2018 election results will be "hit with the bottom end of bamboo poles"—a reference to a torture technique used during the Khmer Rouge regime. After Kem Sokha's arrest, CPP officials insisted he had conspired with the United States to overthrow the government, citing US capacity-building support for political parties—support that was also given to the CPP.

The national assembly passed two rounds of repressive amendments to Cambodia's Law on Political Parties. The amendments empower authorities to dissolve political parties and ban party leaders from political activity without holding hearings and or an appeal process. The amendments also contain numerous restrictions that appear to have been tailored to use against the CNRP, most notably provisions that compel political parties to distance themselves from members who have been convicted of a criminal charge.

In October, Hun Sen used these provisions in a case brought in the Supreme Court to dissolve the CNRP. On November 16, the Supreme Court, chaired by a judge who is also a central committee member of the ruling CPP, dissolved the CNRP and banned 118 CNRP members of parliament and party officials from political activity for five years.

## Freedom of Media

Cambodia's General Department of Taxation, on the pretext of an unpaid tax bill, forced the independent *Cambodia Daily* newspaper to close on September 4, and brought tax-related criminal charges against its owners. At time of writing, two of its reporters were also being investigated for baseless charges of "incitement."

The government also cracked down heavily on independent radio in September, revoking the license of Mohanokor Radio and its affiliates, which broadcast Voice of America (VOA) and Radio Free Asia (RFA), and closing the independent radio station Voice of Democracy (VOD).

Authorities also forced the closure of RFA's bureau, and in November, a court charged two journalists with espionage for filing news reports for RFA. Other radio stations broadcasting VOA or RFA have come under pressure from the government and stopped broadcasting in August. Almost all domestic broadcast media is now under government control.

## Attacks on Civil Society

For most of 2017, the government detained four senior staff members of the Cambodian Human Rights and Development Association (ADHOC) and a former ADHOC staff member serving as deputy secretary-general of the National Election Committee (NEC). The group, commonly referred to as the "ADHOC Five," were arrested in 2016 on politically motived charges and held in pretrial detention for 427 days until their release in June. Each faces 5 to 10 years in prison if convicted.

Authorities continued to detain the land rights activist and women's rights defender Tep Vanny, who was arrested on August 15, 2016, during a "Black Monday" protest calling for the release of the ADHOC Five. After her arrest, authorities reactivated an old case against her stemming from a 2013 protest, and in February sentenced her to 30 months in prison. Authorities also continued to prosecute several other spurious legal cases against her.

In July, authorities announced an investigation into two groups that were monitoring the commune election. The government alleged that the groups violated the vague and undefined concept of "political neutrality" in Cambodia's Law on Associations and Non-Government Organizations (LANGO), which allows for the dissolution or denial of registration of NGOs, and had failed to register under LANGO.

On August 23, the Ministry of Foreign Affairs ordered the closure of the US-funded NGO National Democratic Institute (NDI), and expulsion of its non-Cambodian staff, citing LANGO and the 1997 Tax Law.

Throughout the year, authorities harassed Mother Nature, an environmental group, arrested members on spurious charges of incitement and making unauthorized recordings, and forced the group to deregister as an NGO in September. In October, the government suspended the registration for another NGO critical of the government, Equitable Cambodia, along with the Federation of Cambodian Intellectuals and Students.

## *Impunity*

A suspect was convicted in March in the July 10, 2016 murder of prominent political commentator Kem Ley, in proceedings that were highly flawed and did little to dispel concerns of government involvement in the killing. Kem Ley was killed five days after a Cambodian general publicly called on Cambodian armed forces to "eliminate and dispose of" anyone "fomenting social turmoil." Kem Ley had been a frequent critic of Hun Sen and, in the months before his killing, had given several media interviews in which he referenced the vast wealth of Hun Sen's family.

The convicted suspect, Oeuth Ang, was tried and sentenced to life imprisonment after proceedings that ignored improbabilities and inconsistencies in his confession and shortcomings in the investigation.

In June, Hun Sen brought a civil charge of defamation against another political commentator, Kim Sok, for suggesting that CPP authorities were behind the killing and authorities filed a criminal charge of incitement against him. In August, Kim Sok was sentenced to a year-and-a-half in prison and ordered to pay Hun Sen US$200,000. Opposition Senator Thak Lany was also convicted in absentia for similar offenses after commenting on the Kem Lay case.

## Labor Rights

Authorities carried out questionable legal investigations into trade unions under Cambodia's Trade Union Law, which has prevented some unions from legally registering and excluded them from collective bargaining and formally advocating for rights and improved working conditions.

## Key International Actors

China, Vietnam, and South Korea were key investors in 2017. China, Japan, and the European Union were Cambodia's leading providers of development-related assistance. The United States, once a key donor, is now regularly criticized by the Cambodian government as a hostile foreign power.

The United Nations Human Rights Council passed a resolution in September renewing the mandate of the UN special rapporteur on the situation of human rights in Cambodia for two years and requesting that the UN secretary-general report to the Human Rights Council in March 2018, ahead of Cambodia's national elections.

# Canada

Canada is a vibrant multiethnic democracy that enjoys a global reputation as a defender of human rights. Despite a strong record on core civil and political rights protections guaranteed by the Canadian Charter of Rights and Freedoms, the government of Prime Minister Justin Trudeau faces longstanding human rights challenges. Many of these relate to the rights of Indigenous peoples, including violations of their right to safe drinking water and police abuse of Indigenous women. Canada also grapples with serious human rights issues relating to detention, including the placement of children in immigration detention.

## *Indigenous Rights*

The government has yet to pay adequate attention to systemic poverty, housing, water, sanitation, healthcare, and education problems in Indigenous communities, particularly those in remote and rural areas. The United Nations Committee on the Elimination of Racial Discrimination in September urged the government to remedy what it found were persistent violations of the rights of Indigenous peoples.

Inadequate access to clean, safe, drinking water continues to pose a major public health concern in many Indigenous communities. The poor quality of water on First Nations reserves has a serious impact on health and hygiene, especially for high-risk individuals—children, elders, and people with disabilities.

In March, Canada provided an update on progress toward meeting Prime Minister Trudeau's commitment to end drinking water advisories in First Nations in five years, and committed to taking a new approach to fixing the drinking water crisis, including an online resource for tracking the number of advisories to increase transparency in its progress. At time of writing, the process to adopt safe drinking water regulations had stalled, with the largest First Nations organization in the country calling for the problematic law enabling regulations to be repealed.

Many residents of Grassy Narrows and Wabaseemoong (Whitedog), two First Nations communities along the English-Wabigoon River in northwestern Ontario, continue to live with mercury poisoning due to contamination from a now-closed chemical plant upstream in Dryden.

While the Ontario Environment Ministry said it was unaware of the contamination until 2016, a confidential report made public in October noted that provincial officials were told in the 1990s that the site was contaminated and that some groundwater samples taken at the site in recent years still show high levels of mercury.

The Prime Minister's Office announced in January 2017 that it would tackle the mercury contamination "once and for all," although the prime minister subsequently claimed it was a provincial issue. Federal and provincial-level responses to residents' health needs and the wider environmental contamination have been woefully inadequate, although the Ontario government pledged CAN$85 million in mid-2017 towards cleaning the river.

## Violence against Indigenous Women and Girls

Indigenous women and girls are more vulnerable to violence than their non-Indigenous counterparts in every province and territory of Canada. While Indigenous women only make up 4.3 percent of the female population, they account for 16 percent of the total female homicides and 11.3 percent of missing women in the country.

In its 2015 inquiry into the murders and disappearances of Indigenous women and girls, the Inter-American Commission on Human Rights affirmed that racial discrimination and socio-economic marginalization were root causes of the violence.

In September 2016, the Canadian government launched a two-year national inquiry into missing and murdered Indigenous women and girls. The inquiry is tasked with examining the root causes and institutional responses to high levels of violence.

Human Rights Watch and other groups have called on the national inquiry to closely examine how policing failures are contributing to Indigenous women's vulnerability to violence. To date, Canada has made only limited progress to ensure that police are accountable for these policing failures. Lack of accountability for policing abuses against Indigenous women exacerbates long-standing tensions between police and Indigenous communities in Canada.

## Children in Immigration Detention

Canada's federal government and the Canada Border Services Agency (CBSA) have shown willingness to reform the immigration detention system and have taken steps to address systemic issues within the immigration detention system. However, Canadian law and policy do not prohibit immigration detention of children and do not limit how long children can be held in immigration detention.

Human Rights Watch and other groups have called on Canadian authorities to ensure that children and families with children are not detained solely because of their immigration status; develop strong policies and guidelines about how the various alternatives to detention should be used; and review their practices to ensure that they are reflecting the best interests of the child in all decisions that affect them.

## Mining Industry Abuses

Canada's status as home to more than half of the world's mining companies and its dominant position in mining investment abroad create a key opportunity for the government to exercise global leadership on the human rights challenges that arise in the extractives context.

However, no Canadian law provides a mechanism to allow Canadian authorities to exercise meaningful scrutiny and oversight of the human rights impact of Canadian extractive companies operating overseas, or the extent to which those companies respect human rights in their operations. On these issues, Canadian companies operating overseas generally only must comply with the laws and regulations of the countries in which they work. This often means the bar is set far too low.

To date, victims of human rights abuses associated with Canadian mining companies operating abroad have had limited redress in Canada. However, in a potentially ground-breaking decision in November, the British Columbia Court of

Appeal ruled that a civil claim against the Canadian firm, Nevsun Resources, for alleged used of forced labor at an Eritrean mine could be heard in Canada.

Human Rights Watch and other groups have called on the government to establish an ombudsperson's office with a mandate to independently investigate and publicly report on complaints related to human rights issues involving Canadian mining companies. This would help strengthen the mining industry's human rights practices consistent with UN Human Rights Committee's recommendations to Canada to both establish an independent mechanism to investigate extractives companies operating abroad and a legal framework of remedy for abuses suffered by affected communities.

## Counterterrorism

In June, following a comprehensive national security review, the Trudeau government introduced Bill C-59 to address the human rights shortcomings in the country's Anti-Terrorism Act of 2015 (formerly Bill C-51).

The bill introduces some important reforms, such as increasing oversight over the security and intelligence agencies. But a coalition of Canadian civil society organizations voiced concerns in September that the proposed legislation does not provide the fundamental change needed to undo C-51's legacy, for example by substantially curtailing CSIS powers to disrupt a vast array of activities in the name of security, and ensure that human rights is at the core of Canada's national security framework.

In June, the Trudeau government overturned a previous government law that made it possible to strip dual citizens of their Canadian nationality if convicted of terrorism, treason, or espionage.

## Sexual Orientation and Gender Identity

Prime Minister Trudeau's government has taken significant steps domestically to advance the rights of lesbian, gay, bisexual, and transgender (LGBT) people, including passing legislation to protect transgender people from discrimination and creating a non-binary gender option on passports.

In June, Bill C-16 received royal assent amending the Canadian Human Rights Act to add gender identity and gender expression to the list of prohibited grounds of discrimination. The bill also amends the criminal code to extend protection against hate propaganda to any section of the public that is distinguished by gender identity or expression while deeming that any offence motivated by bias, prejudice, or hate based on gender identity and expression as an aggravating circumstance in sentencing.

In November, Prime Minister Trudeau apologized to members of the LGBT community for actions the government took through the late 1980s against thousands of workers in the military and the Canadian public service. The government also announced in May that it would pardon and expunge records for any Canadians who were charged, and who still have on their records, criminal offences that are no longer on the books.

## Foreign Policy

In her first major foreign policy address, Minister of Foreign Affairs Chrystia Freeland in June articulated the government's view that there is a need to renew and strengthen the postwar multilateral order and reaffirmed Canada's "unshakeable commitment to pluralism, human rights and the rule of law."

In September, Canada joined a successful Dutch-sponsored initiative at the UN Human Rights Council calling for an independent international investigation to address widespread human rights abuses in Yemen.

In August, Minister Freeland ordered an investigation into the alleged use of Canadian-made military vehicles by Saudi security forces in a violent crackdown in the Shia-populated city of Awamiyah in the Eastern Province. A government spokesperson told reporters that the minister would take action if it was found that Canadian exports had been used "to commit serious violations of human rights."

Canadian law limits the export of military technology to countries with a record of human rights violations. Human Rights Watch has documented a Saudi-led coalition of states committing repeated laws of war violations, some likely war crimes, in Yemen, and has repeatedly urged the Canadian government and others to stop selling weapons to Saudi Arabia until it credibly investigates and curtails its unlawful attacks.

## *Key International Actors*

In February, Canada endorsed the Safe Schools Declaration, thereby committing to do more to protect students, teachers, and schools during times of armed conflict, including through the implementation and use of the Guidelines for Protecting Schools and Universities from Military Use during Armed Conflict.

In May, the UN Committee on the Rights of Persons with Disabilities urged the Canadian government to collect much-needed disaggregated data and information about persons with disabilities and remedy persistent gaps in the equal enjoyment and exercise of rights.

In June, the UN Working Group on Business and Human Rights concluded its 10-day visit to Canada. The group urged Canada to "take a tougher line" on human rights abuses in the extractive sector, both domestically and overseas.

HUMAN
RIGHTS
WATCH

"They Said We Are Their Slaves"
Sexual Violence by Armed Groups in the Central African Republic

# Central African Republic

President Faustin-Archange Touadéra's government, with support from international partners, kept control of the capital, Bangui, and surrounding areas in the southwestern region of the Central African Republic. However, much of the country remained insecure, unstable, and beset by serious human rights violations. Armed groups still control key towns, despite the presence of United Nations peacekeepers.

Civilians continued to bear the brunt of fighting in central, northwestern, and eastern regions of the country, where predominantly Muslim Seleka rebel groups, largely Christian and animist anti-balaka militias, and other armed groups remained active. Armed groups killed hundreds of civilians, raped and sexually assaulted women and girls, and burned down villages. Survivors of sexual violence continued to face stigma, rejection, and other barriers to accessing essential services and justice.

Numerous armed groups signed ceasefire agreements in June and October, but the violence and abuses committed against civilians did not stop. While impunity for past abuses and war crimes continued, there was progress toward creating a Special Criminal Court, a hybrid court in the national justice system, and the International Criminal Court (ICC) continued investigations of crimes committed in the country.

The United Nations Human Rights Council renewed the mandate of the independent expert and scheduled a discussion with the independent expert, the UN, African Union (AU), government representatives, and civil society in March 2018 to focus on the impact of the peace and reconciliation process on the human rights situation.

## Attacks on Civilians

Human Rights Watch documented the killings of at least 249 civilians between May and September by various armed groups, as violence surged in many parts of the country, most notably in the Basse Kotto, Haut-Mboumou, Mboumou, Ouham and Ouham-Pendé provinces. The actual number of deaths is likely significantly higher.

The Union for Peace in the Central African Republic (*l'Union pour la Paix en Centrafrique*, UPC), a Seleka faction, carried out some of the worst attacks in and around Alindao, in Basse Kotte province, killing at least 188 people between May and August. The group established a military base in Alindao in February, after the UN peacekeeping mission asked the group to leave their former base in Bambari, Ouaka province. Human Rights Watch documented the rapes of at least 25 women, ages 18 to 50, by UPC fighters during attacks on local communities in Basse-Kotto in May.

On May 13, anti-balaka forces attacked the Muslim neighborhood of Tokoyo in Bangassou, Mboumou province. Nine survivors who fled to Bangui estimated that fighters killed at least 12 civilians, including the town's imam, as they tried to seek safety in the mosque. Peacekeepers transported Muslims from the mosque to the Catholic Church, where they continued at time of writing to provide protection to approximately 1,500 Muslim civilians.

In July, fighters from the Central African Patriotic Movement (*Mouvement Patriotique pour la Centrafrique*, MPC), a Seleka faction, attacked a displacement camp in Batangafo, in Ouham province, and surrounding neighborhoods, killing at least 15 people, including three with disabilities, and burning approximately 230 homes and makeshift huts in the camp.

In Zemio, Haut-Mboumou province, local armed Muslims without a clear link to the Seleka killed at least 28 civilians between late June and August, including during an attack on a displacement camp in the town on August 17.

Forces apparently from the UPC and Muslim civilians attacked and killed six volunteers working with the Red Cross in Gambo, Mboumou province, in August.

In October, the armed group "Return, Reclamation, Rehabilitation," or 3R, comprising of Muslim Peuhl under the command of General Sidiki Abass, took control of Bocaranga, a major town in Ouham-Pendé province, for several days. The UN mission forced them out of the town after several civilians were killed. Also in October, at least 20 Muslims were killed by auto-defense groups, local armed groups often linked to anti-balaka, in the town of Kembe in Basse-Kotto prefecture.

The Ugandan rebel group the Lord's Resistance Army (LRA) remained active in the southeast with allegations of killings and abductions of civilians.

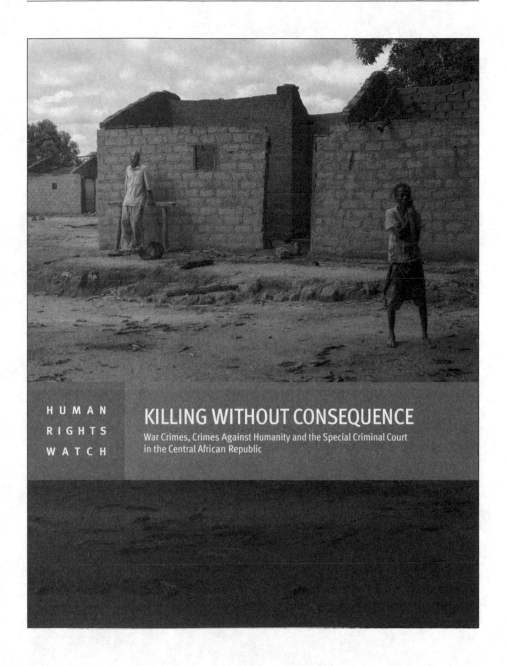

HUMAN
RIGHTS
WATCH

# NO CLASS
When Armed Groups Use Schools in the Central African Republic

## *Refugees and Internally Displaced Persons*

Fighting and attacks by armed groups forced tens of thousands of people to flee their homes since May, bringing the total number of internally displaced persons (IDPs) in the country, based on UN figures, to 601,600, and the total number of refugees to 538,400, the highest since mid-2014. Conditions for IDPs and refugees remained harsh. Many displaced people had little or no access to humanitarian assistance. Persons with disabilities at displacement sites faced barriers to access sanitation, food, and medical assistance.

About 2.4 million people, out of a population of 4.6 million, needed humanitarian assistance. The humanitarian response plan was only 34 percent funded, with a budget gap of US$328.3 million.

## *Regional and International Forces*

The United Nations peacekeeping mission, MINUSCA, deployed about 10,050 military peacekeepers and 2,000 police across many parts of the country, but struggled to establish security in key areas and to sufficiently protect civilians. The mission is authorized, by virtue of Chapter VII of the UN Charter, to take all necessary means to protect the civilian population from threat of physical violence and to "implement a mission-wide protection strategy." On November 15, the UN Security Council approved an additional 900 troops for MINUSCA and subsequently asked Brazil to send the additional peacekeepers.

The Regional Task Force (RTF)—the military component of the Regional Cooperation Initiative for the elimination of the LRA (RCI-LRA), an African Union effort to neutralize the LRA—withdrew from the country in early 2017. The presence of these forces, made up primarily of Ugandan soldiers and some American advisors, had a positive effect on general security in the southeast. Their withdrawal created a security vacuum that MINUSCA struggled to fill.

The Ugandan military, deployed in the country since 2009 as a part of the RTF, withdrew its troops as widespread allegations of sexual exploitation and abuse against women and girls resurfaced.

Despite its withdrawal from the RCI-LRA, the US will continue to train local forces in the Central African Republic. The EU military training mission, called EUTM RCA, trained the first of two planned army battalions in 2017.

## National and International Justice

Impunity remained one of the main challenges in addressing past and ongoing atrocities. Progress was made towards the operationalization of the Special Criminal Court, a hybrid court with national and international judges and prosecutors that will focus on grave international crimes committed since 2003. In February, President Touadéra appointed the court's chief prosecutor, Toussaint Muntazini Mukimapa, the former advisor to the military attorney general of the Democratic Republic of Congo, in a process perceived to be fair and transparent, with external partners observing all discussions.

In May, the UN released a mapping report documenting serious violations of human rights and humanitarian law committed over the past 13 years, founding that some may amount to war crimes or crimes against humanity. The report may aid the work of the Special Criminal Court and future justice mechanisms.

In April, Minister of Justice Flavien Mbata announced the appointment of two international judges, followed by the appointment of five national judges in May. In June, the president appointed a deputy international prosecutor.

The Netherlands, the US, and the UN were the principal donors to the Special Criminal Court, but the court's five-year budget remained only partially covered. The Special Criminal Court also continued to require technical assistance.

The Office of the Prosecutor at the ICC continued investigations into alleged war crimes and crimes against humanity committed in the country. The ICC issued no arrest warrants in 2017.

Jean-Pierre Bemba Gombo, a former vice president of the Democratic Republic of Congo and leader of the Movement for the Liberation of the Congo (*Mouvement pour la Libération du Congo*), was sentenced to 12-months in jail and fined €300,000 euros (approximately US$353,000) in March for bribing witnesses during an earlier war crimes trial at the ICC. ICC judges found Bemba and four associates guilty of witness tampering in October 2016. Bemba was found guilty of rape, murder and pillage in March 2016 for crimes committed in the Central African Republic in 2002 and 2003.

There was no progress in bringing to justice African Union peacekeepers from the Republic of Congo allegedly responsible for abuses in CAR in 2014. A mass grave exhumed at Boali in February 2016 appeared to contain the remains of 12 people allegedly killed by Congolese soldiers. In June 2016, the government of the Republic of Congo had announced that a judicial procedure was ongoing for this case. A forensic investigation and exhumation was concluded in November and a private report of this investigation was handed to the Central African investigating judge. The victim's remains were buried in Boali.

# Chile

Twenty-eight years after the Chilean dictatorship imposed a total abortion ban, and after a difficult process that included the intervention of the Constitutional Court, the government in September 2017 enacted a law decriminalizing abortion if the life of the pregnant woman is at risk, the fetus is unviable, or the pregnancy is due to rape.

The courts continue to prosecute those responsible for human rights violations committed during the military regime. In 2017, courts convicted or charged former military officers and state actors in three of the most egregious crimes of Augusto Pinochet's dictatorship from 1973 to 1990.

Cases of crimes committed by members of the armed forces and *Carabineros* (uniformed police) against civilians were transferred at the end of 2016 from military jurisdiction to civilian courts.

President Michelle Bachelet issued a decree that increased intrusive government access to personal data, violating Chileans' right to privacy. However, the *Contraloría General de la República* (Chile's Supreme Audit Institution) held that the decree was invalid and could not enter into force because the executive branch did not have legal authority to issue it.

After an investigation conducted by a Chamber of Deputies commission of inquiry revealed human rights violations against poor children under state care in the National Service for Minors (SENAME) network, the government proposed a set of bills to improve the centers and strengthen protection of children's rights. The government also presented a bill to legalize same-sex marriage.

## *Confronting Past Abuses*

In March, the Supreme Court convicted and sentenced 33 former state agents for the enforced disappearances of 5 members of the Manuel Rodriguez Patriot Front in 1987. The victims' bodies were fastened to railroad sleepers and thrown into the sea.

In April, an investigating judge charged the former army commander-in-chief, Juan Emilio Cheyre, with complicity in the extrajudicial execution of 15 people in the La Serena regiment, where he was a lieutenant during the military government.

In September, an investigating judge in Santiago filed murder and attempted murder charges against 13 retired members of the army in the death of Rodrigo Rojas and the injury of Carmen Gloria Quintana. Soldiers arrested the two young activists during a protest in 1986, doused them with gasoline, set them alight, and then abandoned them in a ditch.

In September, the Bachelet administration submitted a bill to Congress that would lift the 50-year veil of secrecy over testimony given before the National Commission on Political Prison and Torture, known as the Valech I Commission, from November 2003 to May 2004. The commission learned the places in which detention took place and the torture methods used by the dictatorship, and recognized 28,459 victims of political prison and torture (in a second revision, an additional 9,795 new torture victims were recognized).

The lifting of the secrecy order generated intense debate among those who believe that opening the testimony to judges investigating human rights crimes violates the victims' privacy and those who claim that the secret contributes to impunity enjoyed by the guilty.

## Prison Conditions

As of December 2016, 69 percent of the total prison population was convicted, and 31 percent was being held in pretrial detention.

As of August 2016, Chilean prisons were operating at 103.2 percent capacity, rising to 117.6 percent in the Metropolitan Region and exceeding 200 percent in some prisons. As of October 2016, the Santiago Sur Preventive Prison Center, which has a maximum capacity of 2,384 people, held 5,057 inmates.

In 2017, the National Human Rights Institute (INDH) filed dozens of lawsuits for mistreatment of prison inmates, including for the new crime of torture, which was incorporated into the criminal code in November 2016.

## Privacy

President Bachelet issued a decree that would have dangerously increased government access to the personal data of all citizens. The decree required telecommunications companies to retain, for at least two years, data that would have allowed the government to know individuals' location and with whom they communicate. The decree did not explicitly require a court order to access this stored data.

It also prohibited telecommunications companies from using technology that prevents interceptions, which could have been understood as a ban on protecting information through encryption. In November, the *Contraloría General de la República* held that the decree did not pass the *ex ante* control of legality (*toma de razón*), because the legal authority to issue such a regulation belongs with the legislative branch, not the executive.

## Children's Rights

The living conditions that children endure under state care in the National Service for Minors (SENAME) network are in dire need of improvement. Between January and June 2016, 34 children died under SENAME's care. At time of writing, the public prosecutor was conducting an investigation into the deaths of 259 children in the last decade. The victims were living in SENAME centers when they died.

In 2017, the INDH visited 171 SENAME centers, 83 percent of the total in the country. Of 405 children interviewed, 197 reported violations of their rights, including neglect, physical abuse, psychological abuse, and sexual abuse or exploitation.

The scandal generated when these figures were publicized produced a response from the government, which presented or accelerated the processing of a set of bills that seek to replace and strengthen the institutional structure of state's services for children in need.

The Court of Appeals in la Serena ordered the Prison Police Force to refrain from conducting invasive body checks and stripping children who visit detained relatives.

## Women's Rights and Reproductive Rights

In August 2017, the Chilean Congress approved a law that ended the absolute prohibition of abortion the military dictatorship imposed at the end of its mandate in 1989. The Constitutional Court upheld a law decriminalizing abortion under three circumstances: if the life of the pregnant woman is at risk, the fetus is unviable, or the pregnancy is due to rape. However, the Constitutional Court extended the right to conscientious objection beyond the medical doctor carrying out the abortion to all personnel present in the operating room, and even to institutions.

In January 2017, the government presented to Congress a bill regarding women's access to a life free of violence. As of September 15, 2017, 29 women had died at the hands of spouses or partners and 79 attempted killings of women by their spouses or partners were recorded. The bill addresses forms of violence that Chilean law does not currently recognize as distinct criminal offenses, such as violence in non-cohabiting couples and violence experienced by women in public spaces.

## Sexual Orientation and Gender Identity

In June, after four years of deliberation, a bill recognizing the right to gender identity was passed by the Senate and submitted to the House of Representatives for consideration. The bill allows for unmarried individuals over 18 years old to legally change their name and gender marker on their government-issued identity documents and requires medical certification.

In August 2017, President Bachelet introduced a bill to Congress that would legalize same-sex marriage and grant same-sex couples the right to access assisted reproduction techniques and adoption. The presentation of the bill corresponds to a commitment adopted by the Chilean State in the friendly settlement agreement signed on June 11, 2016, following a petition submitted to the Inter-American Commission on Human Rights (IACHR). The bill does not regulate, however, the situation of children of same-sex couples not united by marriage.

## *Indigenous Rights*

In June, President Bachelet publicly apologized to the Mapuche people for all social injustices that their communities have historically endured and that were committed or tolerated by the state.

In the context of the current Chilean constitutional-making process, indigenous people demand the recognition of Chile as a multinational State, collective rights, access to political rights such as self-determination, special political representation, and territorial rights to land, ancestral waters, and natural resources.

In 2017, conflict between the government and Mapuche communities was marked by acts of violence. In criminal cases against Mapuche activists accused of violent acts, the public prosecutor has insisted on applying the counterterrorism law, which does not guarantee due process and defines terrorism in excessively broad terms.

## *Migrant Rights*

In May 2017, the government launched the "Chile Reconoce" project, which will grant Chilean nationality to more than 2,000 children and adults born in Chile between 1995 and 2014 and denied Chilean nationality because of their parents' irregular migratory status.

In August 2017, the legislative process for a new immigration law began, aimed to replace legislation enacted in 1975.

## *Key International Actors*

In October, the UN special rapporteur on the rights of indigenous peoples, the UN Working Group on Arbitrary Detention, and the UN special rapporteur on counterterrorism, urged Chile not to prosecute Mapuche people accused of violent crimes under the country's counterterrorism legislation.

# China

The broad and sustained offensive on human rights that started after President Xi Jinping took power five years ago showed no sign of abating in 2017. The death of Nobel Peace Prize laureate Liu Xiaobo in a hospital under heavy guard in July highlighted the Chinese government's deepening contempt for rights. The near future for human rights appears grim, especially as Xi is expected to remain in power at least until 2022. Foreign governments did little in 2017 to push back against China's worsening rights record at home and abroad.

The Chinese government, which already oversees one of the strictest online censorship regimes in the world, limited the provision of censorship circumvention tools and strengthened ideological control over education and mass media in 2017. Schools and state media incessantly tout the supremacy of the Chinese Communist Party, and, increasingly, of President Xi Jinping as "core" leader.

Authorities subjected more human rights defenders—including foreigners—to show trials in 2017, airing excerpted forced confessions and court trials on state television and social media. Police ensured the detainees' compliance by torturing some of them, denying them access to lawyers of their choice, and holding them incommunicado for months.

In Xinjiang, a nominally autonomous region with 11 million Turkic Muslim Uyghurs, authorities stepped up mass surveillance and the security presence despite the lack of evidence demonstrating an organized threat. They also adopted new policies denying Uyghurs cultural and religious rights.

Hong Kong's human rights record took a dark turn. Hong Kong courts disqualified four pro-democracy lawmakers in July and jailed three prominent pro-democracy student leaders in August.

China's growing global influence means many of its rights violations now have international implications. In April, security officials at the United Nations headquarters in New York City ejected from the premises Dolkun Isa, an ethnic Uyghur rights activist, who was accredited as a nongovernmental organization (NGO) participant to a forum there; no explanation was provided.

In June, the European Union failed for the first time ever to deliver a statement under a standing agenda item at the UN Human Rights Council (UNHRC) regard-

HUMAN
RIGHTS
WATCH

THE COSTS OF
INTERNATIONAL ADVOCACY
China's Interference in United Nations Human Rights Mechanisms

ing country situations requiring the council's attention. This stemmed from Greece blocking the necessary EU consensus for such an intervention due to its unwillingness to criticize human rights violations in China, with which it has substantial trade ties. Chinese officials continued throughout the year to pressure governments around the world to forcibly return allegedly corrupt mainland officials despite a lack of legal protections in China or refugee status determination procedures outside China.

Despite the high costs, many in China continued to fight for rights and justice in 2017. Activists, including those working on women's, disability, and lesbian, gay, bisexual, and transgender (LGBT) rights, continued to take cases to court to seek limited redress and raise awareness. In a small but significant step, in July a court in Henan province ruled against a public hospital for forcing a gay man to undergo discriminatory "conversion therapy." In its narrow ruling, the court found that admitting the plaintiff to the hospital against his will violated his rights.

## Human Rights Defenders

The death of Nobel Peace Prize laureate Liu Xiaobo in 2017 laid bare authorities' ruthlessness towards peaceful proponents of human rights and democracy. In July, after serving nearly nine years of his 11-year prison sentence for "inciting subversion," Liu Xiaobo died from cancer in a Shenyang hospital, heavily guarded by state security. During his hospitalization, authorities isolated Liu and his wife, Liu Xia, from family and supporters, and denied Liu's request to seek treatment outside the country. Since Liu's death, authorities have forcibly disappeared Liu Xia. The government also harassed and detained a group of Liu's supporters for commemorating his death.

In 2017, authorities continued politically motivated prosecutions of human rights activists and lawyers who were rounded up in a nationwide crackdown that began in July 2015. Lawyer Wang Quanzhang and activist Wu Gan remained in police custody, awaiting trial or verdict on baseless charges. In November, lawyer Jiang Tianyong was sentenced to two years in prison on charges of "inciting subversion of state power."

A number of those caught in the "709 crackdown" were freed, but they continue to be closely monitored and isolated from friends and colleagues; some revealed that they were tortured and forced to confess while in detention. Authorities also continued to harass and intimidate the lawyers who represent the detainees, ordering them not to speak to media and disbarring several after giving them failing marks in China's annual lawyers' evaluation.

In March, a court in Guangdong province, in separate trials, convicted women's rights activist Su Changlan and online political commentator Chen Qitang on baseless charges of "inciting subversion" and sentenced them to prison terms of three years and four-and-a-half years, respectively. Su was released in October after serving her sentence. Her health deteriorated sharply while in detention due to inadequate medical care and poor conditions in detention. In March, a Sichuan court sentenced artist Chen Yunfei to four years in prison on charges of "picking quarrels and provoking trouble" in connection with his activities commemorating the 1989 Tiananmen Massacre.

The government also tried to eliminate the country's few independent human rights news websites by jailing their founders. In August, a Yunnan court sentenced citizen journalist and protest chronicler Lu Yuyu to four years in prison on charges of "picking quarrels and provoking trouble." Also in August, authorities charged Liu Feiyue, founder of the website Civil Rights and Livelihood Watch (□□□□) with "leaking state secrets" and "inciting subversion of state power." Liu could face life imprisonment if convicted. Veteran activist and founder of the human rights website 64 Tianwang, Huang Qi, suffers from kidney disease and has been denied adequate medical care since his detention in November 2016.

In August, prominent rights lawyer and activist Gao Zhisheng disappeared from his home in Shaanxi province. Authorities subsequently informed Gao's family that he had been taken into police custody.

China continues to detain non-citizens for promoting human rights in China. In March, Guangdong authorities arbitrarily detained Taiwan democracy activist Lee Ming-che. After holding him incommunicado for six months, denying him access to family, a court in Hunan province sentenced Lee to five years in prison for "subverting state power." Mainland activist Peng Yuhua, who was tried alongside Lee, was given a seven-year sentence on the same charge.

## *Freedom of Expression*

Authorities adopted new measures to limit access to circumvention tools that allow netizens to scale the Great Firewall to access the uncensored global internet. In January 2017, the Ministry of Industry and Information Technology issued regulations making it unlawful to provide circumvention tools without the ministry's pre-approval.

In March, Chongqing authorities made public a regulation that bans unauthorized use of internet circumvention tools in the city. Anyone—from individuals to companies—who does so would be ordered to disconnect and receive a warning. The regulation was unprecedented in banning all use of these tools. The same month a Guangdong court sentenced Deng Jiewei to nine months in jail for illegally selling virtual private networks, or VPNs, which protect user privacy by shielding browsing activities from service providers or state surveillance.

In July, Apple removed dozens of VPNs from its App store in China, citing compliance with government regulations. In August, the Cyberspace Administration of China (CAC) ordered five websites, including shopping giant Alibaba, to remove vendors that offered access to VPNs. In September, police detained Zhen Jianghua, activist and founder of a website that teaches people how to circumvent internet censorship, on suspicion of "inciting subversion." In November, in a letter to two US senators, Apple confirmed that it had removed 674 VPNs from its App store in China this year, citing compliance with government regulations.

Authorities further tightened screws on social media. In June, they shut down dozens of entertainment news and celebrity gossip social media accounts after calling on internet companies to "actively promote socialist core values" and stop the spread of "vulgar ... sentiments." In August, the CAC announced additional new regulations on the requirement of real-name registration. In September Weibo barred users who had not registered with their real names from posting messages on their own microblogs or comment on others.

In September, the CAC promulgated measures to make creators of online chat groups such as those on QQ and Wechat liable for information other users shared in the groups. The rules also require the service providers to establish credit rating systems for chat group users. Those who violate Chinese laws and regulations will have their credit scores lowered.

In September, Beijing police arrested Liu Pengfei, the creator of a WeChat group that had discussed political and social issues.

Authorities continued their assault on academic freedom. In January, Sun Yat-sen University in Guangzhou banned staff from criticizing the Communist Party. In June, the Central Commission for Discipline Inspection, the party's discipli-nary body, issued a report accusing 14 top universities of ideological infractions after a months-long investigation. Several professors were fired for speaking crit-ically of the Chinese government on social media. In August, Shi Jiepeng, a pro-fessor of classical Chinese at Beijing Normal University, was sacked for "improper comments"; Shi had called Mao Zedong a "devil."

In August, Cambridge University Press admitted it had blocked access in China to more than 300 articles published in its journal *China Quarterly*, following or-ders from the Chinese government. The international backlash against the deci-sion compelled the publishing house to restore the articles. In November, Springer Nature pulled access to over 1,000 articles in China. The publisher said the decision was to comply with Chinese regulations.

In March, authorities issued new measures to reduce the number of foreign chil-dren's titles published in Chinese. In August, the Ministry of Education issued new national editions of primary and middle school liberal arts textbooks, with added emphasis on traditional culture and "core socialist values."

Gui Minhai, a Swedish national and publisher of books critical of the Chinese leadership, was abducted in Thailand in October 2015. After holding Gui for two years in secret detention in China, the Chinese government in October told Swedish diplomats that Gui had been "released."

## Hong Kong

Civil liberties in Hong Kong are increasingly being undermined by the growing in-terference of the central government, 20 years after the city returned to Chinese sovereignty in 1997.

Opposition political parties and their supporters faced greater harassment from authorities. In April, the Companies Registry rejected the application of the Hong Kong National Party on grounds that the promotion of "Hong Kong independence is against the Basic Law." During President Xi's visit to Hong Kong, local and mainland police followed, harassed, and arrested some peaceful pro-democracy protesters.

In April, Hong Kong police arrested 11 pro-democracy advocates on charges including "unlawful assembly" and "obstructing police." The charges stem from the advocates' protest against a decision by China's top legislative body forcing Hong Kong courts to disqualify two pro-independence legislators. In July, a Hong Kong court disqualified four more pro-democracy lawmakers for modifying their oaths swearing allegiance to China in a 2016 ceremony.

In March, two mainland government advisers said the central government will rely more on "legal means"—suggesting manipulation of the territory's legal system—to strengthen central control. In April, the chief of legal affairs at the China Liaison Office in Hong Kong said the "one country, two systems" principle could be abolished altogether if the city "fails to actively defend the sovereignty" of China. In June mainland officials declared that the Sino-British Joint Declaration, which states that Hong Kong enjoys "a high degree of autonomy" except in foreign affairs and defense, "no longer has any realistic meaning."

In August, a Hong Kong appeals court sentenced pro-democracy student leaders Alex Chow, Nathan Law, and Joshua Wong to six to eight months in prison. The three had earlier been convicted of crimes related to "unlawful assembly" for peaceful protests at the time of the 2014 Umbrella Movement, and were given community sentences by a lower court. In a politically motivated move, the secretary of justice, a political appointee, sought a harsher prison sentence for the trio.

Also in August, the same court convicted 13 defendants of unlawful assembly for another anti-government protest in 2014. The 13, who had previously been sentenced to community service, were given prison terms of between 8 and 13 months after the Justice Department sought a review of their sentences. In October, the Court of Final Appeal released Chow, Law, and Wong on bail, pending appeal.

## Xinjiang

The Chinese government has long conflated peaceful activism with violence in Xinjiang, and has treated many expressions of Uyghur identity, including language and religion, as threatening. Uyghur opposition to government policies has been expressed in peaceful protests but also through violent attacks. However, details about protests and violence are scant, as authorities severely curtail independent reporting in the region.

In 2017, the Chinese government continued its 2014 "strike-hard" campaign in Xinjiang, which vowed to adopt "unconventional tactics" in countering terrorism. After Party Secretary Chen Quanguo was transferred from Tibet to Xinjiang in August 2016, the Xinjiang regional government expanded its already pervasive security measures by hiring thousands more security personnel. In July, authorities forced residents in a district of Urumqi, the capital city of Xinjiang, to install surveillance apps on their mobile phones. In 2017, the Xinjiang government also waged a campaign against "two faced" Uyghur cadres thought to oppose the party's stance on Uyghurs. In April, 97 officials in Hotan prefecture were reprimanded.

Authorities increasingly restricted and punished Uyghurs' foreign ties. Since October 2016, authorities have arbitrarily recalled passports from residents of Xinjiang. Since about April, 2017 authorities have arbitrarily detained thousands of Uyghurs and other Muslims in centers where they were forced to undergo "patriotic education."

Authorities also ordered Uyghur students studying abroad, including in Egypt, to return to Xinjiang; and in July, Egyptian authorities rounded up those who had failed to return, possibly at China's behest. By September, about 20 Uyghurs were forcibly repatriated to Xinjiang while 12 were released. Some of those who returned were detained; a Xinjiang court sentenced Islamic scholar Hebibulla Tohti to 10 years in prison after he returned with a doctorate degree from Egypt's Al-Azhar University.

In February, a video believed to be released by the extremist group Islamic State (also known as ISIS) showed Uyghur fighters who pledged to return to China and "shed blood like rivers"—the first reported direct threat by the group against Chinese targets. A 2016 study reported that at least 114 Uyghurs had joined ISIS, but estimates vary widely and the level of participation remains unconfirmed.

In April, the Xinjiang Counter-Extremism Regulations, which prohibit the wearing of "abnormal" beards or veils in public places, became effective. Also in April,

Xinjiang authorities issued a new rule banning parents from naming children with dozens of names with religious connotations, such as Saddam and Medina, on the basis that they could "exaggerate religious fervor."

## Tibet

Authorities in Tibetan areas continue to severely restrict religious freedom, speech, movement, and assembly, and fail to redress popular concerns about mining and land grabs by local officials, which often involve intimidation and arbitrary violence by security forces. In 2017, officials intensified surveillance of online and phone communications.

Six UN special rapporteurs sent a communication to the government of China expressing concern about the late 2016 mass expulsion of monastics (monks and nuns) and demolition of living quarters at the Larung Gar monastery in Kandze, Sichuan. Similar expulsions and demolitions were reported at the Yachen Gar monastery in Kandze in August 2017.

Several thousand Tibetans traveling on Chinese passports to India for a January 2017 teaching by the Dalai Lama were forced to return early when officials in Tibetan areas attempted to confiscate passports, threatening retaliation against those travelling abroad and their family members back home.

In June, residents of Palyul county, Sichuan, demonstrated against land grabs; in July and August, Qinghai residents peacefully protested against several official policies. One solo protest in central Lhasa on June 23 ended in the protester's suicide. Between October 2016 and March 2017, there were at least six protests in Ngaba, Sichuan, alone, but details are scant due to extreme surveillance and intimidation.

Tibetans continue to self-immolate to protest Chinese policies. At time of writing, four had done so in 2017.

## Freedom of Religion

The government restricts religious practice to five officially recognized religions in officially approved religious premises. Authorities retain control over religious bodies' personnel appointments, publications, finances, and seminary applications. The government classifies many religious groups outside its control as "evil cults," and subjects members to police harassment, torture, arbitrary detention, and imprisonment.

In February 2017, Beijing police detained Sun Qian, a businesswoman and Canadian citizen, on suspicion of "using cults to sabotage law enforcement." Sun is a follower of the Falun Gong, a meditation-focused spiritual group banned since 1999. Sun was reportedly pepper-sprayed, put in handcuffs attached to foot shackles, and deprived of sleep.

In May, authorities detained Shao Zhumin, a Catholic bishop of an underground church in Wenzhou, Zhejiang province. Shao's church had refused to join the state-affiliated Chinese Catholic Patriotic Association. Beijing and the Vatican have continued negotiations on the normalization of diplomatic ties, but the dialogue remains strained by disputes over who has authority to appoint bishops in the country.

In September, China passed revisions to the 2005 Regulations on Religious Affairs. The document, which comes into effect in February 2018, introduces new restrictions designed to "curb extremism" and "resist infiltration," including banning unauthorized teaching about religion and going abroad to take part in training or meetings. Donations from foreign groups or individuals that are over 100,000 RMB (US$15,000) are also prohibited. The new rules also expand the role of local authorities in controlling religious activities.

Authorities in Yunnan province charged more than a dozen Christians in 2017 with "using cults to sabotage law enforcement." In October, at least three of the charged were given prison sentences of four years. One of their lawyers said the arrests were due to the group not gathering at officially designated churches.

## Women's and Girls' Rights

According to a report by World Economic Forum, China ranked 100th out of 144 countries for gender parity in 2017, falling for the ninth consecutive year since 2008, when it ranked 57th. The Party Congress, concluded in October, was marked by a striking absence of women in top political posts. Women and girls in China continue to confront sexual abuse and harassment, employment discrimination, and domestic violence.

The Chinese government remains hostile to women's rights activism. In February, internet company Sina suspended the microblog of Women's Voices, run by outspoken feminists, for 30 days. Between May and June, Guangzhou police forced five activists from their homes in retaliation for their campaign to raise awareness about sexual harassment on public transportation. In September, authorities finally lifted a 10-year travel ban on activist Wu Rongrong, enabling her to travel to Hong Kong for studies.

## Disability Rights

China ratified the Convention on the Rights of Persons with Disabilities in 2008. However, persons with disabilities continue to face discrimination in areas including education and employment.

In February, authorities released long-awaited Regulations of Education of Persons with Disabilities to replace out-of-date 1994 regulations. While the new regulations have some positive aspects, they do not go far enough in removing discriminatory obstacles that prevent many children with disabilities from being placed in mainstream schools. They require that students with disabilities be evaluated by a quasi-governmental expert committee and placed according to their "physical conditions and ability to be educated and adapt to [mainstream] schools." Preventing children with disabilities from attending mainstream schools, or failing to provide them with support needed to attend such schools, is itself a violation of the CRPD.

In March, state press reported the death of a 15-year-old with autism in a Guangdong "care center" for the homeless, focusing attention on neglect in these facilities.

In a welcome move in April, the Ministry of Education issued a new rule to accommodate students with disabilities in college entrance exams, known as gaokao. While a 2014 decision already required schools to provide people with visual impairments access to braille or electronic paper in gaokao exams, the new rule provides more details on implementation and includes accommodation for people with other disabilities, including for deaf students.

HUMAN
RIGHTS
WATCH

"Have You Considered
Your Parents' Happiness?"
Conversion Therapy Against LGBT People in China

## Sexual Orientation and Gender Identity

While China de-criminalized homosexuality in 1997, it lacks laws protecting people from discrimination on the basis of sexual orientation or gender identity, and same-sex partnership is not legal.

In May, Chinese authorities shut down a popular dating app for lesbians. In June, the government banned "abnormal sexual lifestyles," including homosexuality, from online video programs. In July, authorities forced the LGBT group Speak Out to cancel a conference in Chengdu. An earlier Speak Out event scheduled for May in Xi'an was also cancelled after police briefly detained the organizers and told them that LGBT events were "not welcome" in the city.

## Refugees and Asylum Seekers

Beijing also appeared to step up its campaign to forcibly return North Korean refugees and asylum seekers in 2017: between July and August, 41 people were detained; 51 had been detained in all of 2016.

## Key International Actors

While the European Parliament, United States Congress, the UN High Commissioner for Human Rights, and individual members of governments and parliaments publicly expressed some concern about the deteriorating human rights situation in China in 2017, the response of "like-minded" governments to negative developments, such as jail sentences for peaceful protestors in Hong Kong, was even more muted than in previous years. Although the United States delivered a joint statement on behalf of a dozen countries at the March 2016 session of the UNHRC expressing concern at human rights violations in China, it did not present a follow-up joint statement at any of the council's 2017 sessions.

In January 2017, UN Secretary-General António Guterres introduced President Xi at an event closed to civil society at the Palais des Nations in Geneva. Guterres made no reference to China's deteriorating human rights environment or to human rights as a pillar of UN work.

At a summit in Brussels on June 1-2, the EU Council and Commission presidents publicly "expressed concern" about human rights abuses in China, but did not call for the release of political prisoners, including EU citizens, or the repeal of abusive laws. The EU did raise concerns about China at the UNHRC in September.

In June, German Chancellor Angela Merkel publicly challenged Chinese authorities to fulfill their commitments to register German NGOs under China's new Foreign NGO Management Law, which went into effect in 2017.

Also in June, Italian police briefly detained and later released Dolkun Isa, a prominent Uyghur activist and German citizen, as he tried to enter the Italian Senate, where he had been invited to speak. Italian authorities refused to clarify whether China had requested Isa's detention.

Australia failed to ratify an extradition treaty with China after protests from Australian politicians arguing Australia should not send people to China because the country's judicial system is plagued with human rights abuses.

Businessmen linked to China's government have made significant foreign donations to political parties in Australia, raising concerns about Chinese attempts to influence Australian policy. An Australian parliamentary inquiry in March called for a ban on political donations from foreign sources, and the government ordered a review of espionage laws.

In July, the United States issued several statements condemning China's failure to allow Liu Xiaobo the freedom to seek medical treatment wherever he chose. Yet within hours of Liu's death US President Donald Trump referred to President Xi as a "terrific guy" and "a great leader."

## *Foreign Policy*

In May, China hosted its largest-ever gathering for the "One Belt, One Road" (OBOR) initiative, a development program spanning 65 countries that China says will involve investments of more than $1 trillion. Many participating states have a history of countenancing serious human rights violations in major development and infrastructure projects.

Key international financial institutions, including the Asian Development Bank, the Asian Infrastructure Investment Bank, and the World Bank, have not taken adequate steps to ensure that they place strong human rights conditions on any participation in OBOR-related projects.

At the UN Security Council, China joined Russia in February in a double veto of a resolution that would have imposed sanctions related to use of chemical weapons in Syria. In September, the council held closed-door discussions on Burmese military atrocities against Burma's Rohingya Muslim minority; diplomats said China opposed language recognizing the right of return of the more than 630,000 Rohingya refugees who fled to Bangladesh. While senior UN officials described the military campaign as "ethnic cleansing," Chinese state media endorsed it as a firm response to "Islamic terrorists."

# Colombia

The government and the Revolutionary Armed Forces of Colombia (FARC) reached an agreement in 2016 to end their 52-year armed conflict. The agreement provides a historic opportunity to curb human rights abuses, but its justice component contains serious shortcomings that risk letting war criminals escape justice. At time of writing, the Special Jurisdiction for Peace, the judicial system the parties created to try wartime abuses, had yet to be put in place.

In June 2017, the United Nations mission in Colombia verified that the FARC had handed over its weapons and demobilized. However, civilians continue to suffer serious abuses by the National Liberation Army (ELN) guerrillas and paramilitary successor groups that emerged after a demobilization process a decade ago. Violence associated with the conflict has forcibly displaced more than 7.7 million Colombians since 1985, generating the world's largest population of internally displaced persons (IDPs). Human rights defenders, trade unionists, journalists, indigenous and Afro-Colombian leaders, and other community activists face death threats and violence, mostly from guerrillas and successor groups. Perpetrators of these abuses are rarely held accountable.

In February 2017, the government and the ELN started peace talks in Quito, Ecuador, after more than two years of exploratory negotiations. In September, days before Pope Francis' visit to Colombia, the parties agreed to hold a bilateral ceasefire between October 2017 and January 2018. The ELN also agreed to stop certain abuses, including recruiting children under 15 and using antipersonnel landmines.

Also in September, "Otoniel," leader of the Gaitanist Self-Defenses of Colombia (AGC), the country's largest paramilitary successor group, said he was willing to negotiate ending the groups' crimes. The reported negotiations remained confidential at time of writing.

## Guerrillas

On June 27, 2017, the UN political mission in Colombia verified that FARC guerrillas who accepted the agreement with the government had demobilized and handed their weapons to the mission. In September, the demobilized guerrilla group formally announced its political party, the Revolutionary Alternative Force of the Common People (FARC).

However, a minority of dissident guerrilla fighters rejected the terms of the peace agreement, have not disarmed, and continue to commit abuses. In May, guerrillas of the FARC's dissident First Front kidnapped a consultant of the UN Office on Drugs and Crime (UNODC) in Guaviare province. They released him in July.

The ELN continued in 2017 to commit serious abuses against civilians, including, for example, killings, forced displacement, and child recruitment in the province of Chocó. On October 25, ELN guerrillas reportedly killed an indigenous leader in Chocó, despite having agreed with the government to stop abuses.

The ELN continued in 2017 to use antipersonnel landmines. The government reported that landmines and unexploded ordnances killed four civilians and injured 22 between January and October 2017.

## *Paramilitaries and Successors*

Between 2003 and 2006, right-wing paramilitary organizations with close ties to security forces and politicians underwent a deeply flawed government demobilization process in which many members remained active and reorganized into new groups. These successor groups continue to commit such widespread abuses as killings, "disappearances," and rape. They have at times benefited from the tolerance and even collusion of state agents.

In its conflict with the ELN, the AGC continues to engage in serious abuses in Chocó province. In April, two boat drivers were found dead in an Afro-Colombian community in southern Chocó. Credible evidence indicates that AGC members abducted and killed them.

Implementation of the Justice and Peace Law of 2005, which offers dramatically reduced sentences to demobilized paramilitary members who confess their crimes, has been slow, despite significant progress since 2014. As of July 2016, 182 of the more than 30,000 paramilitary troops who officially demobilized had been sentenced under the law. The convictions cover a small portion of the more than 4,000 defendants seeking the law's benefits.

In June 2017, the Attorney General's Office sent Santiago Uribe, the brother of former President Alvaro Uribe, to trial on charges of murder and conspiracy for his alleged role in the paramilitary group "The 12 Apostles" in the 1990s.

"Parapolitics" investigations and prosecutions of members of Congress accused of conspiring with paramilitaries continued in 2017. From 2006 through August 2015, 63 legislators were convicted of crimes related to "parapolitics."

## Abuses by Public Security Forces

From 2002 through 2008, army brigades across Colombia routinely executed civilians. Under pressure from superiors to show "positive" results and boost body counts in their war against guerrillas, soldiers and officers abducted victims or lured them to remote locations under false pretenses—such as promises of work—and killed them, placed weapons on their bodies, and reported them as enemy combatants killed in action. There has been a dramatic reduction in cases of alleged unlawful killings attributed to security forces since 2009, though credible reports of some new cases continue to emerge.

As of September 2017, the Attorney General's Office was investigating more than 3,600 alleged unlawful killings from 2002 through 2008, and had achieved convictions in cases against more than 1,200 mid and low-level soldiers, including convictions against the same individual in different cases.

Authorities have largely failed, however, to prosecute senior army officers involved in the killings and instead have promoted many of them through the military ranks. In November, the Defense Ministry proposed to elevate in rank five officers against whom there is credible evidence of involvement in "false positives." The process before the Senate remained pending at time of writing.

Gen. Rodríguez Barragan continued, at time of writing, to command the armed forces, despite strong evidence implicating him in false-positive killings. Retired Gen. Jaime Alfonso Lasprilla Villamizar was Colombia's defense attaché in Washington between November 2015 and May 2017. According to the Attorney General's Office, he commanded a brigade likely responsible for the killing of 55 civilians between 2006 and 2007.

In January, the Attorney General's Office sent retired Gen. Henry William Torres Escalante to trial for his alleged role in the killing of two farmers in 2007. No meaningful progress had been achieved in other cases against generals allegedly responsible for false-positive killings. In March 2016, prosecutors summoned retired Gen. Mario Montoya Uribe, who commanded the army when killings peaked, for a hearing in which he was to be charged. The Attorney General's Office later backtracked; Montoya had yet to be charged at time of writing.

In April 2017, however, Gen. Alberto José Mejía Ferrero, the current head of the army, organized an event to honor the "principles and values" of Sgt. Carlos Eduardo Mora, who in 2007 disobeyed an order to commit a "false positive" and later became a star witness in the prosecution of such cases.

In May, policemen used excessive force against people in Buenaventura who were participating in street demonstrations the protesters called a "civic strike" to demand better living conditions, including access to basic public services, economic opportunities, and justice. The Ombudsman's Office received 161 reports of alleged police abuses during the protests, including of 20 individuals who said they were shot with rubber bullets.

In October, seven farmers were killed in the southern municipality of Tumaco during a peaceful protest against delays in the implementation of programs to replace illicit crops. The Defense Ministry initially said FARC dissidents had shot at protesters; survivors blamed the police. Days later, the National Police announced it had suspended four officers who had "allegedly triggered firearms" during the protest.

## Peace Negotiations and Accountability

The peace agreement provided that a Special Jurisdiction for Peace should be created to try those responsible for gross human rights violations committed during the conflict, including FARC guerrillas and members of the armed forces. Individuals responsible for crimes against humanity and serious war crimes who fully cooperate with the new jurisdiction and confess their crimes will be subjected to up to eight years of "effective restrictions on freedoms and rights," but no prison time.

In December 2016, Congress passed an amnesty law, with the stated purpose of excluding human rights violations from amnesty. The law, however, has language that could allow people responsible for atrocities to benefit from amnesties. As of September, the Constitutional Court was reviewing the law's constitutionality.

In April 2017, lawmakers passed a constitutional amendment creating the Special Jurisdiction for Peace. The amendment establishes a definition of "command responsibility"—the rule that determines when superior officers can be held responsible for crimes of their subordinates—for the armed forces that departs from established norms of international law in a way that could severely weaken accountability. In November, the Constitutional Court ruled that the "command responsibility" definition was constitutional.

## Human Rights Defenders, Journalists, and Trade Unionists

Rights advocates and journalists continue to be targeted with threats and attacks. Despite an Interior Ministry program that assigns protection to human rights defenders, trade unionists, and journalists, the Office of the UN High Commissioner for Human Rights (OHCHR) documented the killings of 53 prominent rights advocates and community activists from January through October 2017. In July, the Attorney General's Office said it had achieved convictions in 5 of more than 80 killings documented by the OHCHR since January 2016.

The Foundation for a Free Press, a Colombian nongovernmental organization (NGO) that monitors press freedoms, reported that 1 journalist was killed and 136 suffered threats between January and October 2017.

Former President Uribe, currently a senator, continued in 2017 to lash out against journalists and other critics, accusing them, without evidence, of being complicit with guerrilla groups.

## Internal Displacement and Land Restitution

More than 7.7 million Colombians have been internally displaced by conflict-related violence since 1985, government figures reveal. More than 48,000 were displaced between January and November 2017. Nationwide, forced displacement has significantly decreased since 2015, although it remains high in many areas. In Litoral de San Juan, in southern Chocó, the number of people displaced in 2016 represented 20 percent of the population.

The government's implementation of land restitution under the 2011 Victims' Law continues to move slowly. The law was enacted to restore millions of hectares of land that was abandoned or stolen during the many years of conflict to internally displaced Colombians. As of August 2017, the courts had issued rulings in just 5,400 of more than 106,000 claims received.

## Gender-Based Violence

Gender-based violence is widespread in Colombia. Lack of training and poor implementation of treatment protocols impede timely access to medical services and create obstacles for women and girls seeking post-violence care. Perpetrators of gender-based violence crimes are rarely brought to justice.

In July 2015, "femicide"—defined, in part, as the murder of a woman because of her gender—became a crime. The law established comprehensive measures to prevent and prosecute gender-based violence, including recognizing the rights of victims and their relatives to specialized legal assistance.

## Sexual Orientation and Gender Identity

In recent years, authorities in Colombia have taken several steps to recognize the rights of lesbian, gay, bisexual, and transgender (LGBT) people. In June 2015, the Justice Ministry issued a decree allowing people to revise the gender noted on their identification documents without prior judicial approval. In November 2015, the Constitutional Court ruled that no one can be barred from adopting a child because of their sexual orientation. In April 2016, the court upheld the right of same-sex couples to marry. In May 2017, lawmakers rejected a legislative proposal to hold a referendum that would have put progress in jeopardy by asking voters to decide whether same-sex couples and single people should be allowed to adopt children.

## Indigenous Rights

Indigenous people in Colombia suffer disproportionate limitations on their enjoyment of social and economic rights. From January through August 2017, at least 24 children indigenous—the majority of them belonging to Wayuu communities—died in the province of La Guajira of causes associated with malnutrition.

Many of these deaths are caused by limited access to drinking water. The Inter-American Commission of Human Rights (IACHR) had asked the government in December 2015 to take measures to curb these deaths. In January 2017, the IACHR expanded the request to cover pregnant and breastfeeding women.

## Key International Actors

The United States remains the most influential foreign actor in Colombia. At time of writing, the US Congress was moving forward with approval of more than US$390 million in aid; mostly for development and drug enforcement. A portion of US military aid is subject to human rights conditions, which the US Department of State has not rigorously enforced.

The Office of the Prosecutor of the International Criminal Court (ICC) continues to monitor Colombian investigations of crimes that may fall within the court's jurisdiction, and the prosecutor, Fatou Bensouda, conducted a mission to the country in September 2017. Upon request of the Constitutional Court, in October, Bensouda issued an amicus curiae before the court expressing concern about the definition of "command responsibility" and flaws in the amnesty law.

In September 2017, Pope Francis visited Colombia. He supported the peace process with the FARC and asked Colombians to "welcome every person who has committed offences, who admits their failures, is repentant and truly wants to make reparation."

In January 2016, the UN Security Council, at the government's request, established a political mission under a tripartite mechanism—the UN, the government, and FARC—to monitor and verify the peace agreement's definitive bilateral ceasefire and cessation of hostilities, and the laying down of arms. In July 2017, the Security Council created a second mission in charge of verifying the reintegration of FARC guerrillas.

In 2017, the Colombian government supported regional efforts to help solve the human rights crisis in Venezuela. In August, Colombia's foreign affairs minister signed, along with those of 11 other nations, the Lima Declaration, a comprehensive statement condemning the rupture of democratic order and the systematic violation of human rights in Venezuela.

Since 2014, when the crisis started to deepen, thousands of Venezuelans have migrated to Colombia. In July 2017, the Colombian government created a special permit that allows Venezuelan citizens who entered the country legally, but have overstayed their visas, to regularize their status.

# Côte d'Ivoire

Cote d'Ivoire continued the process of moving away from the successive and bloody political crises of 2000-11, with the United Nations ending a 13-year peacekeeping mission in June. However, ongoing indiscipline by members of the security services and violent army mutinies demonstrated the precariousness of the country's newfound stability.

President Alassane Ouattara promulgated a new constitution in January, which establishes a vice president position and a second legislative chamber, with one-third of its members appointed by the president. While the new constitution removed a divisive nationality clause, requiring a presidential candidate's father and mother to be Ivorian, many of the other root causes of past conflict remained unaddressed, particularly a politicized judiciary and simmering conflicts over land.

The prevalence of arbitrary arrests, mistreatment of detainees, and unlawful killings by the security forces lessened again in 2017, but investigations and prosecutions of those who commit abuses were rare. Although Côte d'Ivoire's press largely operated without restrictions, laws criminalizing publication of false information were on occasion used to unfairly detain journalists and several pro-opposition newspapers were temporarily suspended.

Progress in delivering justice for victims of the 2010-11 post-election violence remained slow, with the vast majority of perpetrators of human rights abuses—from across the military-political divide—not yet held accountable. The International Criminal Court (ICC) continued the trial of former President Gbagbo and Charles Blé Goudé, a former youth minister and leader of a pro-Gbagbo militia, and is also investigating crimes committed by pro-Ouattara forces during the 2010-11 crisis.

## Conduct of Security Forces

At least 15 people died in a wave of mutinies and demonstrations by demobilized soldiers. Thousands of soldiers mutinied in January and May, demanding unpaid bonuses and backpay. On both occasions, soldiers seized control of Bouake, Côte d'Ivoire's second largest city, for several days and blocked roads in

Abidjan and other towns, killing at least four people, several from stray bullets. The mutineers only returned to their barracks after the government paid them 12 million CFA (US$21,000).

The mutinies triggered sporadic demonstrations by other elements of the security forces and demobilized fighters, leaving 11 more dead, including four ex-soldiers killed in a clash with police on May 23. Serving and demobilized soldiers were also implicated in a series of attacks on police and gendarme installations.

Many members of the security forces, including senior army officers, continued to engage in racketeering and extortion. Several army commanders allegedly responsible for atrocities during the 2002-03 armed conflict and 2010-11 crisis were promoted in January.

Mutinying soldiers in May discovered an arms cache in Bouake, underscoring the failure of Côte d'Ivoire's disarmament process to secure weapons hidden in private arsenals. The owner of the property where the arms were discovered, a senior aide to National Assembly president Guillaume Soro, was arrested and detained on October 9.

## *Accountability for Past Crimes*

Ivorian judges continued to investigate crimes committed by both sides during the 2010-11 post-election crisis, but the deeply flawed trial of former First Lady Simone Gbagbo, acquitted on March 28, raised doubts about Ivorian courts' ability to effectively try serious human rights cases.

Côte d'Ivoire's Special Investigative and Examination Cell, established in 2011, continued its investigations into human rights crimes committed during the 2010-11 violence. The cell has charged high-level perpetrators from both sides, including several pro-Ouattara commanders now in senior positions in the army. However, the only national civilian trials so far are those of Simone Gbagbo and General Dogbo Blé, the ex-leader of President Gbagbo's Republican Guard, convicted April 14 with five others for the kidnapping and murder of four foreigners on April 4, 2011.

Human rights groups acting on behalf of victims refused to participate in Simone Gbagbo's trial, which was marred both by fair trial concerns and the prosecution's failure to present sufficient evidence to fully explore her role during the

2010-11 crisis. Simone Gbagbo is also wanted by the ICC on four counts of crimes against humanity, but so far the Ivorian government has refused to transfer her to The Hague. Neither the special cell nor the ICC are investigating crimes committed during election-related violence in 2000 or the 2002-2003 armed conflict.

The ICC trial of Laurent Gbagbo and the former youth minister and militia leader Charles Blé Goudé for crimes against humanity committed during the 2010-11 crisis continued in 2017. The ICC also intensified its investigations into crimes committed by pro-Ouattara forces during the crisis, but has yet to issue arrest warrants. President Ouattara has said that all further cases related to the 2010-11 crisis will be tried in national courts.

Côte d'Ivoire's reparations body was disbanded in April, having registered more than 316,000 victims. Having first awarded cash payments and medical care to 4,500 victims, the government began a second phase of largely non-monetary assistance in October.

## Freedom of Assembly and Expression

Six journalists were detained on February 12 for 48 hours on charges of publishing false information after reporting on alleged bonuses paid to mutineers from the army's special forces. Two other journalists were detained on July 31 for 24 hours on similar charges after alleging that bank accounts belonging to National Assembly leader Soro had been frozen. The trial of an online news editor, charged with divulging false news in May 2016 after publishing an interview with ex-President Gbagbo's son, Michel, was adjourned October 20 after several earlier delays.

The government in May indefinitely delayed a parliamentary vote on a new press law, which was criticized by media freedom groups for stipulating harsh penalties for vaguely defined media offenses.

In a violation of the right to freedom of expression, Sam Mohammed, a businessman and opposition supporter, was sentenced to six months' imprisonment on March 31 for slander and defamation, after he questioned President Ouattara's Ivorian nationality at a public rally.

Although the Ivorian constitution protects freedom of assembly, Ivorian law requires opposition parties to request permits for public rallies. Three opposition politicians were given disproportionate 30-month sentences May 26 for their role in a banned opposition rally in May 2015.

## Land Reform and Instability in the West

Recurring disputes over land ownership remain an important source of intercommunal tension, particularly in western Côte d'Ivoire. In October and November, at least 10 people were killed during clashes between rival groups for control of territory in protected forests in western Côte d'Ivoire. Ivorian judges have yet to complete an investigation into violent intercommunal clashes between pastoralists and farmers in Bouna in March 2016, which left at least 27 people dead and thousands more displaced.

Implementation of a 1998 land law, which aims to reduce conflicts by converting customary land ownership to legal title, remains extremely slow, with less than four percent of rural land registered. The government in 2016 created a new rural land agency to streamline the land registration process, with the agency to become operational in 2018.

Côte d'Ivoire, which has lost vast swathes of forest to cocoa farming, announced in September a policy to devolve responsibility for reforestation to private businesses. Past, government-led reclamation efforts, such as the 2016 eviction of farmers from Mont Péko national park, led to widespread forced evictions.

## Judicial System

Gradual efforts to strengthen the judicial system continued, demonstrated by the more frequent organization of *cour d'assises* sessions in Abidjan and two regional courts and the establishment of a legal aid fund. However, fundamental problems remain, including excessive use of pretrial detention and a lack of judicial independence, particularly in political trials. Dozens of former President Gbagbo supporters arrested for their alleged role in the post-election crisis or subsequent attacks against the state remain in extended pretrial detention.

Prisons are severely overcrowded and detainees lack adequate access to medical care and suffer extortion by prison guards and fellow inmates. Close to 130 detainees escaped in a series of prison breaks in August and September, although at least 42 were subsequently recaptured.

Côte d'Ivoire continues to struggle with violent crime by street gangs, including by children, which has led to public beatings and lynching of suspected criminals. Abidjan's juvenile detention center is housed inside an adult prison, and children in pretrial detention are often detained with adults.

## Sexual Orientation and Gender Identity

Côte d'Ivoire does not criminalize same-sex conduct, although the criminal code establishes higher minimum sentences for public indecency for same-sex couples. An antidiscrimination provision in Côte d'Ivoire's new constitution, promulgated in January 2017, does not include protection against discrimination on grounds of sexual orientation. Incidents of discrimination against lesbian, gay, bisexual, and transgender (LGBT) persons, including physical assaults, are common.

## Gender-Based Violence

Although the UN reported in January 2017 that the number of reported cases of sexual and gender-based violence has progressively decreased since 2014, social stigma and widespread impunity prevents many victims from reporting abuses. The holding of *cour d'assises* sessions has enabled some trials and convictions for rape, but many sexual assaults are reclassified as lesser offenses or settled out of court.

## Protection of Human Rights Defenders

Three years after the passage of a law strengthening protections for human rights defenders, the government finally adopted a decree necessary for the law's implementation in February 2017. The decree lacks detail on how the law's implementation will be monitored.

## Key International Actors

Côte d'Ivoire's international partners failed to apply public pressure on the government to address longstanding impunity. The UN Operation in Côte d'Ivoire (UNOCI) concluded its 13-year peacekeeping mission on June 30, 2017, leaving the European Union, France, and the United States as Côte d'Ivoire's principal partners on justice and security-sector reform.

The mandate of the UN independent expert on human rights in Côte d'Ivoire expired June 30 and was not renewed by the Human Rights Council. In June, Cote d'Ivoire was elected to the UN Security Council for the 2018-2019 term.

# Cuba

The Cuban government continues to repress and punish dissent and public criticism. The number of short-term arbitrary arrests of human rights defenders, independent journalists, and others was significantly less than in 2016, but still remained high, with more than 3,700 reports of arbitrary detentions between January and August 2017. The government continues to use other repressive tactics, including beatings, public shaming, travel restrictions, and termination of employment.

US President Donald Trump announced in June that he would reverse the previous administration's policy toward Cuba by reinstating travel and commercial restrictions that had been eased in 2015.

## *Arbitrary Detention and Short-Term Imprisonment*

The Cuban government continues to employ arbitrary detention to harass and intimidate critics, independent activists, political opponents, and others. The number of arbitrary short-term detentions increased dramatically between 2010 and 2016, from a monthly average of 172 incidents to 827, according to the Cuban Commission for Human Rights and National Reconciliation, an independent human rights group that lacks official authorization and the government considers to be illegal.

The number of detentions dropped significantly in 2017, with 4,537 reports of arbitrary detentions from January through October, a decrease of 50 percent compared to the same period in 2016.

Security officers rarely present arrest orders to justify detaining critics. In some cases, detainees are released after receiving official warnings, which prosecutors can use in subsequent criminal trials to show a pattern of "delinquent" behavior.

Detention is often used preemptively to prevent people from participating in peaceful marches or meetings to discuss politics. Detainees are often beaten, threatened, and held incommunicado for hours or days. The Ladies in White (Damas de Blanco)—a group founded by the wives, mothers, and daughters of political prisoners—like the Cuban Commission on Human Rights, lacks official authorization and is therefore considered illegal by the government. Police or state security agents continue to routinely harass, rough up, and detain its members before or after they attend Sunday mass.

In April, political activist Eliécer Ávila from the group Somos+ was arrested twice in three days for recording and broadcasting a protest message after authorities confiscated his computer in the Havana airport. The first arrest occurred on April 6, when he arrived from Colombia. He was released the following morning and returned to the airport to reclaim his computer. The following day, his documents and electronic devices were seized and police arrested him at home, according to media reports. He was released the same day on bail.

## *Freedom of Expression*

The government controls virtually all media outlets in Cuba and restricts access to outside information. A small number of journalists and bloggers who are independent of government media manage to write articles for websites or blogs, or publish tweets. The government routinely blocks access within Cuba to these websites and only a fraction of Cubans can read independent websites and blogs because of the high cost of, and limited access to, the internet. In September 2017, Cuba announced it would gradually extend the home internet service to all the provinces in the country.

Independent journalists who publish information considered critical of the government are subject to smear campaigns and arbitrary arrests, as are artists and academics who demand greater freedoms. Henry Constantín Ferreiro, editor of *La Hora de Cuba* magazine and a regional vice president of the Inter American Press Association, was detained on February 20 in Camagüey airport, along with journalist Sol García Basulto, a *La Hora de Cuba* colleague and correspondent for the independent news website 14ymedio.

García Basulto was released without charges. Constantín was held incommunicado for about 36 hours for allegedly fomenting "enemy propaganda," based on information from a computer that had been confiscated when he was previously briefly detained in November 2016. The charge was dropped in February, but in March, both journalists were accused of practicing journalism without proper certification, according to press reports, and prohibited from traveling abroad. Basulto was placed under house arrest on July 24.

Members of the Committee of Citizens Defenders of Human Rights (Comité de Ciudadanos Defensores de los Derechos Humanos), José Carlos Girón Reyes, the brothers Alberto Antonio and Leonardo Ramírez Odio, and their father Alberto de la Caridad Ramírez Baró, were detained on July 26 after staging a public protest calling for "justice, freedom and democracy." The activists said they had been beaten in custody. Girón was released without charge on August 2; the other three remained behind bars until October 18.

## Political Prisoners

The Cuban Commission for Human Rights and National Reconciliation reported scores of political prisoners—including 54 members of the group Cuban Patriotic Union (Unión Patriótica de Cuba)—as of May 2017. The government denies access to its prisons by independent human rights groups, which believe that additional political prisoners, whose cases they cannot document, remain locked up.

Cubans who criticize the government continue to face the threat of criminal prosecution. They do not benefit from due process guarantees, such as the right to fair and public hearings by a competent and impartial tribunal. In practice, courts are subordinated to the executive and legislative branches, denying meaningful judicial independence.

Dr. Eduardo Cardet Concepción, leader of the Christian Liberation Movement (Movimiento Cristiano Liberación), was sentenced three years in prison on March 20. He was detained on November 2016 after criticizing in interviews with international media former President Fidel Castro shortly after he died.

The activist Jorge Cervantes García, from the Cuban Patriotic Union, was detained allegedly for "contempt" and "resistance" in May, weeks after posting online videos addressing ill-treatment in a Cuban prison and corruption by Cuban authorities. After a 39-day hunger strike, he was transferred to a maximum-security facility. Cervantes was released in August after being held for 85 days.

## Travel Restrictions

Reforms to travel regulations that went into effect in January 2013 eliminated the need for an exit visa to leave the island. Exit visas had previously been used to deny people critical of the government, and their families, the right to travel. Since then, many people who had previously been denied permission to travel have been able to do so, including human rights defenders and independent bloggers.

Nonetheless, the reforms gave the government broad discretionary powers to restrict the right to travel on the grounds of "defense and national security" or "other reasons of public interest." Such measures have allowed authorities to deny exit to people who express dissent.

The government restricts the movement of citizens within Cuba through a 1997 law known as Decree 217, which is designed to limit migration to Havana. The decree has been used to harass dissidents and prevent those from elsewhere in Cuba from traveling to Havana to attend meetings.

According to the Cuban Commission for Human Rights and National Reconciliation, the government imposed restrictions mainly on people heading to Latin American countries to attend conferences. In June, the commission registered the highest number of restrictions on freedom of movement in many years: at least 29 people were prevented from traveling abroad to attend international conferences and other events.

## Prison Conditions

Prisons are overcrowded. Prisoners are forced to work 12-hour days and are punished if they do not meet production quotas, according to former political prisoners. Inmates have no effective complaint mechanism to seek redress for abuses. Those who criticize the government or engage in hunger strikes and other forms of protest often endure extended solitary confinement, beatings, restrictions on family visits, and are denied medical care.

While the government allowed select members of the foreign press to conduct controlled visits to a handful of prisons in 2013, it continues to deny international human rights groups and independent Cuban organizations access to its prisons.

## Labor Rights

Despite updating its Labor Code in 2014, Cuba continues to violate conventions of the International Labour Organization that it has ratified, specifically regarding freedom of association, collective bargaining, protection of wages, and prohibitions on forced labor. While the law technically allows the formation of independent unions, in practice Cuba only permits one confederation of state-controlled unions, the Workers' Central Union of Cuba.

## Human Rights Defenders

The Cuban government still refuses to recognize human rights monitoring as a legitimate activity and denies legal status to local human rights groups. Government authorities harass, assault, and imprison human rights defenders who attempt to document abuses.

On September 2016, police raided Cubalex, a six-year-old organization that investigates human rights violations and provides free legal services to free-expression activists, migrants, and human-rights defenders. Officers confiscated files, strip-searched four men and a woman, and arrested two attorneys, one of whom was still in detention at time of writing.

## Key International Actors

US and Cuba restored diplomatic relations in 2015, after the United States eased decades-old restrictions on travel and commerce. But in June 2017, President Trump declared that he would reverse the previous administration's deal.

The US government expelled 15 Cuban diplomats from the embassy in Washington in October, after American diplomats in Havana reported a series of mysterious illnesses. In November, the US administration reinstated restrictions on Americans' right to travel to Cuba and to do business tied to the Cuban military, security, or intelligence services. It also voted against the UN resolution condemning the US embargo on Cuba, reversing the previous abstention in 2016.

For the first time in years, Cuba agreed to allow a United Nations human rights investigator to visit the island. In April, the UN special rapporteur on trafficking in persons visited Cuba and called for new laws and stronger action targeting human trafficking.

The UN independent expert on human rights and international solidarity also visited Cuba in July 2017, and encouraged Cuba to ratify core international treaties—the International Covenant on Civil and Political Rights, and on Economic, Social and Cultural Rights, and their Optional Protocols.

OAS Secretary General Luis Almagro was denied entry to Cuba because Cuban officials considered the reason for his visit "an unacceptable provocation." Almagro was to receive a democracy award in honor of the late government opponent Oswaldo Payá, issued by the Latin America organization Youth for Democracy (Jóvenes por la Democracia). The government also denied visas to former Chilean Minister Mariana Aylwin, former Mexican President Felipe Calderón, and members of the Youth for Democracy.

In May, the European Union held its third high-level discussion on human rights with Cuba. In July, the European Parliament approved the first agreement with Cuba to strengthen economic and political ties and bring an end to the EU's 1996 "Common Position on Cuba," which conditions full EU economic cooperation with Cuba on the country's transition to a pluralist democracy and respect for human rights. The agreement entered into force provisionally in November 2017, but at time of writing was still pending ratification by member countries for its full application.

On October 2016, Cuba was re-elected to the Human Rights Council for the 2017-2019 term.

HUMAN
RIGHTS
WATCH

"Special Mission"
Recruitment of M23 Rebels to Suppress Protests
in the Democratic Republic of Congo

# Democratic Republic of Congo

Political violence and government repression continued in 2017, as President Joseph Kabila held on to power beyond his constitutionally mandated two-term limit, which ended on December 19, 2016. As authorities stalled plans to organize elections, government officials and security forces systematically sought to silence, repress, and intimidate the political opposition, human rights and pro-democracy activists, journalists, and peaceful protesters. Government security forces and numerous armed groups attacked civilians across the country with devastating consequences.

A power-sharing agreement mediated by the Catholic Church and signed in late 2016 called for elections by the end of 2017 and for a number of steps to de-escalate political tensions, including the release of political prisoners. Many of the main tenets of the agreement were largely ignored.

In March, the Catholic bishops withdrew from their mediation role. In June, the bishops blamed the country's dire security, human rights, economic, and political crises on the failure of those in power to hold elections in accordance with the constitution, and they called on the Congolese people to "stand up" and take their destiny into their own hands.

In November, days after the United States ambassador to the United Nations, Nikki Haley, visited Congo and called for Kabila to hold elections by the end of 2018, the national electoral commission published a calendar, setting December 23, 2018 as the date for presidential, legislative, and provincial elections, while noting numerous constraints that could impact the timeline.

Congolese civil society and political opposition leaders denounced the calendar as merely another delaying tactic to allow Kabila to stay in power. They called on him to step down by the end of 2017 and proposed a brief post-Kabila transition to organize credible elections, led by people who cannot run for office themselves.

## Freedom of Expression and Peaceful Assembly

Security forces killed at least 62 people and arrested hundreds of others during protests across the country between December 19 and 22, 2016, after Kabila refused to step down at the end of his second term. In total, security forces killed at least 171 people during protests in 2015 and 2016.

Human Rights Watch research found that senior Congolese security force officers had mobilized at least 200 and likely many more former M23 rebel fighters from neighboring Uganda and Rwanda in late 2016 to protect Kabila and quash anti-Kabila protests, after they had integrated into Congolese military and police units. M23 fighters were again brought into the country between May and July 2017 to prepare for "special operations" to protect the president.

Throughout 2017, government officials and security forces repeatedly and systematically banned opposition demonstrations, shut media outlets, and prevented opposition leaders from moving freely. They jailed more than 300 opposition leaders and supporters, journalists, and human rights and pro-democracy activists, most of whom were later released. Many were held in secret detention facilities, without charge or access to family or lawyers. Others have been tried on trumped-up charges. Many were arrested while planning or starting peaceful protests, which often prevented the protests from going forward. When larger protests were organized, security forces fired teargas and in some cases live bullets to disperse the demonstrators. Security forces killed five people, including an 11-year-old boy, and wounded 15 others during a protest in Goma on October 30.

Security forces killed at least 90 people as part of a crackdown against members of the Bundu dia Kongo (BDK) political religious sect in Kinshasa and Kongo Central province between January and March, and in August. Some of the BDK members also used violence, killing at least five police officers.

In July in Lubumbashi, unidentified armed men shot and nearly killed a judge who refused to rule against opposition leader and presidential aspirant Moïse Katumbi.

Authorities prevented international and Congolese journalists from doing their work, including by arresting them, denying access, or confiscating their equipment and deleting footage. At least around 40 journalists were detained in 2017. The government shut down Congolese media outlets and periodically curtailed access to social media. Authorities lifted a nine-month block on Radio France Internationale (RFI)'s signal in Kinshasa in August, but they refused to renew the accreditation for the RFI correspondent in Congo in June, and the visa for the Reuters correspondent in August.

## Attacks on Civilians by Armed Groups and Government Forces

Between August 2016 and September 2017, violence involving Congolese security forces, government-backed militias, and local armed groups left up to 5,000 people dead in the country's southern Kasai region. Six hundred schools were attacked or destroyed, and 1.4 million people were displaced from their homes, including 30,000 refugees who fled to Angola. Nearly 90 mass graves have been discovered in the region, the majority of which are believed to contain the bodies of civilians and militants killed by government security forces using excessive force against alleged militia members or sympathizers.

In March, two United Nations investigators—Michael Sharp, an American, and Zaida Catalán, a Swedish and Chilean citizen—were summarily executed by a group of armed men while investigating serious rights abuses in the Kasai region. Human Rights Watch investigations and an RFI report suggest government responsibility for the double murder. A seriously flawed trial in Congo began in June 2017.

In the southeastern province of Tanganyika, more than 200 people were killed, 250,000 others displaced, and numerous villages and displacement camps burned during intercommunal violence between July 2016 and September 2017.

More than 100 armed groups remained active in eastern Congo's North Kivu and South Kivu provinces and many continued to attack civilians, including the Democratic Forces for the Liberation of Rwanda (FDLR) and allied Nyatura groups, the Allied Democratic Forces (ADF), Nduma Defense of Congo-Renové (NDC-R), the Mazembe, Charles, and Yakutumba Mai Mai groups, and several Burundian armed groups. Many of their commanders have been implicated in war crimes, including ethnic massacres, rape, forced recruitment of children, and pillage.

A new coalition of armed groups in South Kivu known as the National People's Coalition for the Sovereignty of Congo (Coalition nationale du peuple pour la souveraineté du Congo, CNPSC) clashed repeatedly with the Congolese army and took control of numerous villages along Lake Tanganyika. The group's stated goal is to topple Kabila's government, which they say is illegitimate following Kabila's refusal to step down in December 2016. More than 100,000 people have been displaced since the fighting began in June, and the Congolese army reportedly arrested scores of local youth suspected of having links with the coalition.

Also in South Kivu province, alleged Congolese security force members used excessive force to quash a protest in Kamanyola in September, killing around 40 Burundian refugees and wounding more than 100 others.

The humanitarian situation in Congo has severely worsened, with the country facing Africa's largest displacement crisis in 2017, famine expected to affect 7.7 million Congolese, and a national cholera epidemic spread across the country. Meanwhile, the level of international humanitarian funding was at a 10-year low.

## *Justice and Accountability*

On July 26, militia leader Ntabo Ntaberi Sheka surrendered to the UN peacekeeping mission in Congo (MONUSCO), which then transferred him to Congolese judicial officials. Sheka has been implicated in numerous atrocities in eastern Congo, and he had been sought on a Congolese arrest warrant since 2011 for crimes against humanity for mass rape. His trial was yet to begin at time of writing.

Authorities continued to keep warlord Gédéon Kyungu Mutanga, who surrendered in October 2016, in house arrest instead of transferring him to prison to serve the remainder of his 2009 sentence for crimes against humanity.

Sylvestre Mudacumura, military commander of the FDLR armed group, remained at large. The International Criminal Court (ICC) issued an arrest warrant against him in 2012 for attacks on civilians, murder, mutilation, cruel treatment, rape, torture, destruction of property, pillage, and outrages against personal dignity, allegedly committed in 2009 and 2010 in eastern Congo.

The trial continues at the ICC for Bosco Ntaganda, who is accused of 13 counts of war crimes and five counts of crimes against humanity allegedly committed in northeastern Congo's Ituri province in 2002 and 2003.

## *Key International Actors*

On May 29, the European Union announced targeted sanctions against eight senior Congolese government and security officials and a militia leader who had long been implicated in serious abuses in Congo. On June 1, the United States imposed targeted sanctions against Gen. François Olenga, the personal military chief of staff of President Kabila and on a resort owned by General Olenga outside Kinshasa. The sanctions include travel bans, assets freezes, and a ban on making funds or economic resources available to, or engaging in transactions with, the listed individuals and entity.

In June, former UN Secretary-General Kofi Annan and nine former African presidents launched an "urgent appeal" to Kabila and other Congolese leaders for a peaceful, democratic transition. They warned that the future of the country is in "grave danger." Also in June, the UN Human Rights Council authorized an international investigation into the violence in the Kasai region. In September, the council also decided to boost and continue scrutiny over the broader situation in the country for another year, including in the context of the electoral process.

# Ecuador

In May, Lenin Moreno took office after winning a closely contested presidential election. Unlike his predecessor, Rafael Correa, President Moreno has publicly embraced respect for free speech and promised to deliver a more tolerant government.

Ecuador still faces serious human rights challenges, including laws that give the government broad powers to limit free speech; limited judicial independence; poor prison conditions; and far-reaching restrictions on women's and girls' access to reproductive health care.

In September, President Moreno initiated the process to carry out a plebiscite in early 2018 in which Ecuadoreans can vote on a series of proposals, including reversing indefinite re-election of public officials, and ending statutes of limitations for sexual crimes against children.

## *Freedom of Expression*

President Moreno has said he will respect press freedom, and ended his predecessor's practice of publicly threatening and harassing independent journalists, human rights defenders, and critics. He also appointed a new team to head public media outlets, which have begun to adopt an editorial line independent of the government.

However, a 2013 communications law that gives the government broad powers to limit free speech remains on the books. It requires that all information disseminated by media be "verified" and "precise," opening the door to retaliation against media critical of the same government that decides what meets these vague criteria. It also prohibits "media lynching," defined as "repeatedly disseminating information with the purpose of discrediting or harming the reputation of a person or entity." And it prohibits "censorship," defined as the failure of private media outlets to cover issues the government considers to be of "public interest." A government plan to reform the law had not yet materialized at time of writing.

Since its creation, the Superintendency of Information and Communication (SUPERCOM), a government regulatory body created by the 2013 communications law and separate from the Communications Ministry (SECOM), has in dozens of cases ordered media outlets and journalists to "correct" or retract reports, including opinion pieces and cartoons, or to publicly apologize for their content. SUPERCOM has also accused outlets of engaging in "censorship" by not publishing information that officials deem important.

In April, President Correa said on TV that media had engaged in censorship for failing to reproduce reporting by an Argentinian newspaper that claimed to implicate the opposition's presidential candidate in a corruption scandal. Days later, SUPERCOM fined seven media outlets for the same offence.

SUPERCOM has drastically diminished the amount of sanctions imposed since Moreno took office.

Criminal defamation remains a potent means of punishing government critics, despite a 2014 legal reform narrowing the crime's definition. In April, before leaving office, Correa brought a defamation case against Martin Pallares, a journalist who had published an article that was critical of Correa. In October, an appeals court confirmed Pallares' innocence. The ruling cited case law from the Inter-American Court of Human Rights that states that public officials are subject to greater scrutiny.

The former president, his political party and its members, state media outlets, and state agencies have repeatedly sought to make use of US copyright law in efforts to have critical images and documents removed from the internet. Users sometimes manage to restore content, after a legal process that can take weeks. In 2017, several Twitter accounts were reportedly blocked after publishing information critical of the government or its officials.

## Freedom of Association

In 2015, President Correa issued a decree confirming broad government powers to intervene in the operations of nongovernmental organizations (NGOs), including the power to dissolve them if authorities deem that they had "compromise[d] public peace" or had engaged in activities different from those they identified when registering with the government.

In December 2016, the Ministry of the Interior asked the Environment Ministry to shut down Acción Ecológica, an environmental organization. Two days earlier, the group had called for an investigation into attacks against indigenous and environmental rights in Morona Santiago province, where a state of exception was in force until February 2017.

The Ministry of the Interior requested the dissolution, alleging that Acción Ecológica incited and supported violent acts. The accusation was related to the organization's efforts to inform and mobilize the public against the San Carlos-Pananza mining concession. The Ministry of the Interior also accused the organization of deviating from its objectives and interfering with public policy. After a national and international outcry—which included condemnation by a group of UN human rights experts—the Environment Ministry rejected the request to dissolve the group.

In October, President Moreno replaced Correa's decree with a new one that limits some of its vaguely worded language, but maintains ambiguous grounds for dissolving civil society organizations. A proposal to adopt a law that could enact Correa's presidential decree permanently, but may be modified during its discussion in Congress, was pending before the National Assembly at time of writing.

In November, the Environment Ministry authorized the Pachamama Foundation, an environmental group that was arbitrarily closed using Correa's decree in 2013, to start operating again.

## *Judicial Independence*

Corruption, inefficiency, and political interference have plagued Ecuador's judiciary for years. President Correa received a popular mandate in a 2011 referendum to overhaul the justice system.

As part of its sweeping judicial reforms, however, the Council of the Judiciary, which in practice lacks independence from the executive, appointed and removed hundreds of judges, including all magistrates of the National Court of Justice, undermining judicial independence.

In August, a series of leaked emails suggested that President Correa, his private secretary, the Council of the Judiciary, and the Justice Ministry pressured judges, prosecutors, and public defenders to adopt specific decisions in several court cases. President Correa did not deny the authenticity of these emails, and claimed he was "doing his job." After the leak, dozens of judges who had been punished by the Council of the Judiciary made public allegations of political interference in their decision-making.

## Prosecutions of Indigenous Leaders

On December 14, 2016, a police officer died and several others were injured during a confrontation between the military and indigenous Shuar people in Morona Santiago province, when a small group of Shuar people attempted to take over a mining camp that they claim was built on ancestral lands without their consent.

The government mobilized nearly 1,000 military and police officers and declared a state of emergency, suspending certain rights in the province, which ended in February. Indigenous leader Agustin Wachapá, president of the Interprovincial Federation of Shuar Peoples, was charged with allegedly "inciting discord" with a Facebook post on December 18, 2016, in which he called on the Amazonia people to mobilize against the military presence, and said he did not recognize Correa as Ecuador's president. Wachapá spent four months in pretrial detention in a maximum security prison before being released in April 2017. His trial was ongoing at time of writing.

In June, President Moreno pardoned five citizens from Pastaza province who had been sentenced to 6 to 12 months in prison for the vaguely defined crime of "resistance" during nationwide protests in 2015. A sixth activist from Morona Santiago province was also pardoned. In July, a court acquitted 12 Saraguro indigenous people who had been accused of interrupting public services in 2015 by closing roads during indigenous rights demonstrations.

In May, CONAIE, an umbrella group of indigenous organizations, submitted a proposal to the National Assembly, requesting that legislators issue an amnesty in favor of nearly 200 of members of indigenous peoples whom they claim have been arbitrarily prosecuted. In November, Congress' Justice Commission recommended that all of the requests be archived, except for one individual's case that remains under consideration.

## Prison Conditions

Prison overcrowding and poor prison conditions are longstanding human rights problems in Ecuador. Since 2012, the government has spent millions of dollars building new detention centers.

In 2016, a series of videos were leaked to the public showing prison guards beating inmates, some of them naked, and subjecting them to electric shocks at the Turi detention center in Azuay province. Public defenders filed a habeas corpus request, demanding that measures be implemented to protect prisoners. A judge approved the petition. The Attorney General's Office opened an investigation, but later watered it down by changing its grounds from torture to the possibility that the guards were responsible for "overreaching in the execution of an act of service."

In February, the Attorney General's Office declined to accuse 34 out of the 49 officers implicated, and decided that it could not assign individual responsibility to any officer. In August, the judge dismissed charges against all of the officers who had been charged.

## Accountability for Past Abuses

A truth commission set up by the Correa administration to investigate government abuses from 1984 to 2008 (from the beginning of the repressive presidency of León Febres Cordero until Correa took office) documented 136 cases of gross human rights violations involving 456 victims, including 68 extrajudicial executions and 17 disappearances. A special prosecutorial unit created in 2010 to investigate the cases has initiated judicial procedures in fewer than 10 of them, and progress on those has been slow.

## Reproductive Rights

The right to seek an abortion is limited to instances in which a woman's health or life is at risk, or when a pregnancy results from the rape of a "woman with a mental disability." Fear of being criminally prosecuted for having an abortion drives some women and girls to have illegal and unsafe abortions and impedes health care and services for victims of sexual violence. The Prosecutor's Office reports that 184 women have been prosecuted since August 2014 for having a "voluntary abortion."

Government statistics released in 2010, the latest year for which data is available, indicate that one in four women and girls over 15 years old in Ecuador has been a victim of sexual violence.

## Sexual Violence against Children

In October, after a series of scandals regarding sexual violence against children were made public, the Education Ministry revealed that it had recorded 882 such cases that had occurred in schools between 2014 and 2017. Impunity in those cases remains the norm.

## Sexual Orientation and Gender Identity

Same-sex couples are not allowed to marry in Ecuador. Since 2008, civil unions are recognized but do not accord the full range of rights enjoyed by married couples, including the ability to adopt children.

## Key International Actors and Foreign Policy

The government continued in 2017 to refuse to participate in hearings before the Inter-American Commission on Human Rights (IACHR), and said it would not comply with the commission's recommendations.

In August, the UN Committee on the Elimination of Racial Discrimination asked Ecuador to investigate allegations by rights groups that the conflict with the mining company in Morona Santiago province and the deployment of security forces to the region had caused the forced displacement of dozens of Shuar families.

In February, the Inter-American Court of Human Rights ruled that Ecuador was responsible for an enforced disappearance in 1995 and for failing to conduct a diligent investigation into the case. Despite the fact that an official Truth Commission report had concluded the victim had been forcibly disappeared, Ecuador denied before the court that state agents were responsible.

Throughout 2017, the UN Committees on Migrant Workers, on the Elimination of Racial Discrimination, and on Enforced Disappearances evaluated Ecuador's compliance with UN treaties. They raised concerns, including lack of protection of indigenous peoples in voluntary isolation; lack of measures to prevent violence against rights defenders; insufficient efforts to confront human trafficking; lack of due process and proper judicial remedies for people facing deportation; and slow progress made in prosecuting cases documented by the Truth Commission, among other concerns.

In September 2017, the Human Rights Council completed its third Universal Periodic Review of Ecuador.

In August, Moreno expressed concern about the existence of "political prisoners" in Venezuela, a radical departure from Correa's strong support of the Nicolás Maduro government. More than 39,000 Venezuelans have entered Ecuador since Venezuela's crisis deepened in 2016, according to official data. Most request temporary residency permits. Many Venezuelans have applied for refugee status, but local groups were not aware at time of writing of any case in which they had been granted such status by Ecuador's government.

# Egypt

President Abdel Fattah al-Sisi's government maintained its zero-tolerance policy towards dissent, introducing repressive legislation, notably a nongovernmental organization (NGO) law that may end independent associations, reinstating a state of emergency and continuing near-absolute impunity for abuses by security forces under the pretext of fighting "terrorism."

Security forces rounded up hundreds of dissidents, mainly targeting the outlawed Muslim Brotherhood. The Ministry of Interior's National Security Agency arbitrarily detained, disappeared, and tortured people. There were numerous incidents of what appeared to be extrajudicial killings, including of previously detained persons in staged "shoot-outs."

Authorities placed hundreds of people on terrorism lists and seized their assets for alleged terrorism links without due process.

The government imposed a media blackout on its counterterrorism operations in Northern Sinai. Wilayat Sinai, an affiliate of the extremist group Islamic State (ISIS) operating there, targeted civilians as well as security forces.

Military prosecutors continued to send hundreds of civilians to military trials in cases related to political dissent, whether violent or peaceful. President al-Sisi has approved in August 2016 a five-year extension of a 2014 law that expanded, to an unprecedented extent, grounds for trying civilians before military courts. Between October 2014 and September 2017, authorities sent at least 15,500 civilians were sent to military courts including over 150 children.

## *Security Forces Abuses*

The Interior Ministry's National Security Agency (NSA), operating with near-absolute impunity, was responsible for the most flagrant abuses, including widespread and systematic use of torture to coerce confessions. Torture techniques included beatings, prolonged painful stress positions, and electrocutions. Prosecutors rarely investigated torture claims and almost never dropped torture-tainted confessions.

President al-Sisi declared a nation-wide state of emergency in April following church bombings claimed by the Islamic State that killed 47. At time of writing,

HUMAN
RIGHTS
WATCH

"We Do Unreasonable Things Here"
Torture and National Security in al-Sisi's Egypt

he had extended the state of emergency twice since then. The 1958 Emergency Law gives unchecked powers to security forces to arrest and detain and allows the government to impose media censorship and order forced evictions.

The Egyptian Commission for Rights and Freedoms, an independent rights group, said that as of mid-August, 378 persons had been disappeared over the previous 12 months and the whereabouts of at least 87 remained unknown. These numbers do not include those who were found killed after having gone missing.

In May, security forces arrested Hanna Bard al-Din, a co-founder of the Association of Families of the Disappeared. Prosecutors charged her with "joining a banned group" and kept her in pretrial detention. National Security agents secretly detained lawyer Ibrahim Mentally, a co-founder of the same association, in September as he was leaving for a meeting of the United Nations Working Group on Enforced or Involuntary Disappearances in Geneva. Prosecutors subsequently charged Mentally with "propagating false news" about enforced disappearance and espionage on behalf of foreign entities.

In April two judges, Husham Rauf and Assam Abdi al-Gabber, faced disciplinary proceedings for their earlier efforts to advocate for a law prohibiting torture. An investigation continued against prominent human rights lawyer Egad al-Bora, with whom they worked on the project. The judges risk dismissal for being "involved in politics" and al-Bora risks a lengthy prison sentence on charges that included implementing human rights activities without a license and receiving foreign funds.

Human Rights Watch documented three incidents in 2017 in which individuals were killed in alleged shootouts after having been detained. The Egyptian Coordination for Rights and Freedoms, another independent group, said that police "liquidated" at least 37 people in the first half of 2017. The government undertook no known investigations into these killings and provided little or no information to the families. In some cases, the NSA delayed the delivery of the bodies and forced families to bury the dead relatives without funerals.

## *Death Penalty*

Since July 2013, Egyptian criminal courts have sentenced over 800 people to death. The Cassation Court, Egypt's highest appellate court, has overturned many of those sentences and ordered retrials. In 2017, the Cassation Court upheld death sentences of 22 persons at least, who remain on death row, while 103 more death sentences were awaiting final court decisions at time of writing. Military courts have issued over 60 death sentences of civilians since July 2013 and 6 of those were executed. In 2017, the Supreme Military Court of Appeals confirmed 15 more death sentences.

## *Freedom of Association*

President al-Sisi ratified a new law on associations in May 2017 that, when implemented, could eliminate the little remaining space for civil society and end the work of decades-old human rights and other independent associations. The law criminalizes the work of NGOs, providing for up to five-year prison terms for failing to adhere to its provisions such as operating or receiving funds without government approval.

It also provides for day-to-day monitoring by officials, including security agencies, and prohibits activities that "harm national security, public order, public morality, or public health," vague terms that authorities can use to outlaw legitimate work. The new law gives organizations until May 23, 2018 to comply with its provisions or be dissolved. As of November, the government had not yet published implementing regulations.

The protracted criminal investigation into NGO workers involved in Case 173 of 2011, known as the "foreign funding" case, continued. As of October, the investigating judge had summoned 61 staff members for interrogation and charged 15 leading rights activists from four organizations. Authorities banned 27 from traveling outside the country. A criminal court also ordered asset freezes of 10 activists and 7 NGOs. Those summoned in 2017 included Mohamed Zarea, deputy director of the Cairo Institute for Human Rights Studies, released on 30,000 (US$1,700) bail, Mostafa al-Hassan, head of the Hisham Mubarak Law Center, and Abd al-Hafiz al-Tayel, director of the Egyptian Center on the Right to Education, released on 20,000 ($1,130) bail each.

## *Freedom of Expression and Assembly*

The government placed two independent newspapers, *Al-Borsa* and *Daily News Egypt*, and two independent news websites, Masry al-Arabiya and Cairo Portal, on the terrorist entities lists. The placement led to asset freezes and brought the four outlets under the administration of the government-owned *Akhbar al-Youm* newspaper, according to Reporters Without Borders (RSF).

In March, an appeals courts reduced a two-year prison sentence to one-year suspended sentence for the former head of the Journalists' Syndicate, Yehya Qallash, and two former board members, Khaled al-Balshy and Gamal Abdel Rahim. A final appeal was ongoing before Egypt's highest appellate court, the Cassation Court.

According to RSF, as of late October, 17 journalists remained in jail. On October 21, journalist Hisham Gaafar had spent more than two years in pretrial detention, the maximum allowed by Egyptian law, on charges of receiving foreign funds for his institution, Mada Media Foundation, and joining a banned group. Authorities denied him proper medical care for prostate disease. Ismail al-Iskandrani, a journalist who reported on Sinai, will have entered his third year of pretrial detention in December 2017. He faces charges of spreading false news and joining a banned group.

In May, the government blocked 21 websites of political groups and news outlets. As of October, the Association for Freedom of Thought and Expression, an independent Egyptian group, said that the number of websites blocked reached more than 425, including rights groups such as Human Rights Watch and RSF.

President al-Sisi signed parliamentary amendments to the 2013 protest law intended to meet a Supreme Constitutional Court ruling, but they did not affect the highly restrictive nature of the law, and peaceful gatherings remain effectively banned and penalized.

Security forces rounded up activists preemptively, ahead of anticipated protests. For example, at the beginning of April, security arrested 190 political activists, mostly in home raids, ahead of the mid-June parliamentary approval of the controversial government decision to cede two Red Sea islands to Saudi Arabia.

Al-Sisi pardoned a total of 705 prisoners in March and June, most of whom had been convicted in cases related to peaceful protests.

## Conflict in Sinai

The government continued to effectively isolate North Sinai from the outside world, imposing a near-absolute media blackout and shutting down communications for weeks at a time. Extensive military operations encompassed more areas, including al-Arish, the capital of the governorate.

Between January and August 2017, 209 government forces and 430 armed group members were killed in Sinai, according to the Tahrir Institute for Middle East Policy, based on military statements that are hard to verify.

The fighting in Sinai has been marred by widespread government abuses including secret detentions, extrajudicial executions, and military trials of civilians. In April, a video confirmed to be authentic showed army officers and pro-army militia members executing at close range blindfolded detainees, later claiming the detainees were "terrorists" killed in "clashes."

The Islamic State-affiliate Wilayat Sinai targeted civilians perceived as collaborators and Christians, as well as security forces. In many cases, attacks against government forces also killed civilians. Seven Christians were murdered in Sinai between January 30 and February 23 in attacks that bore the hallmarks of Islamic State killings, though no group claimed responsibility. As a result, hundreds of Christian families fled to cities and towns outside Sinai, leaving almost no Christian families there.

On at least two occasions, in February, armed men who identified themselves as ISIS fighters stopped buses carrying women teachers on the way to work close to Rafah to warn them they faced punishment if they did not adhere to the "Islamic" dress code they described.

## Freedom of Religion

On Palm Sunday, April 9, bombings later claimed by the ISIS targeted two churches in Tanta and Alexandria, killing at least 45. They were the deadliest ISIS attack since a suicide-bomber attacked Egypt's main Coptic Orthodox Cathedral in Cairo, killing 25, in December 2016. Since then, the government stepped up security around churches.

In Minya governorate in May 2017, ISIS claimed an attack on a bus carrying Coptic passengers travelling to a monastery that killed 29.

In September, representatives of Egypt's Orthodox Church submitted a list of more than 2,000 churches that lack any license needed legalize their status according the 2016 discriminative law. Sectarian violence around construction or repair of churches still exists and when violent incidents do occur, as in Kom al-Lofy in Minya governorate in April, the government sponsored "customary reconciliation" sessions in place of criminal investigations and prosecutions.

## Social and Labor Rights

Floatation of the Egyptian Pound in late 2016, apparently as part of a $12 billion loan agreement with the International Monetary Fund, nearly halved its exchange value from $0.112 to 0.057 and inflation reached almost 35 percent.

Egypt's economic crisis also featured constricting space for workers' mobilization. Workers' Strikes remain criminalized in the Egyptian law. Authorities arrested or charged at least 180 workers for peaceful workplace strikes and protests in 2016 and 2017, mostly over bonuses and delayed wages. In September, for example, security forces arrested at least eight Tax Authority workers and independent union leaders prior to anticipated protests. Independent trade unions remained effectively banned. The parliament largely approved in November a new trade unions law that will keep in place many restrictions and does recognize independent unions.

In 2018, the government-controlled Egyptian Trade Union Federation, the only officially-recognized union, begins its 12th year without board elections, and the government continued to appoint its leaders in violation of International Labour Organization conventions that grant the right to organize and freedom of association.

## Refugee Rights

Egypt remained a destination, transit, and source country for refugees and asylum seekers. As of September, the UN Refugee Agency (UNHCR) said that 211,104 persons from 63 nationalities were registered as refugees and asylum-seekers in Egypt, mostly from Syria, Sudan, Ethiopia, Eritrea, and South Sudan.

A law on combating irregular immigration came into force in late 2016. A misdemeanor court for minor offenses sentenced 56 defendants to terms ranging from 1 to 14 years in one mass trial. The defendants faced smuggling charges related to the 2016 capsizing of a boat off the coast of Rashid on the Mediterranean coast, killing over 200 migrants. The government has released little information, if any, about where apprehended migrants are routinely held and in what conditions.

In June, police arrested dozens of Uyghur students, a Chinese Muslim minority, some of whom were registered as refugees or asylum seekers with the UNHCR. The arrests seemed to have been at the request of the Chinese government, which ordered the Uyghur students abroad, including in Egypt, to return home. The government deported some of them of them to China, where they faced a high risk of torture. As of October, a lawyer confirmed that authorities released at least 60 of the students and allowed them to leave to a country of their choice while 16 remained in custody.

## Violence and Discrimination against Women and Girls

In May, according to *Al-Masry al-Youm* newspaper, the Justice Ministry's Forensic Medical Authority said that they investigated three cases of female genital mutilation (FGM) referred by prosecutors since the government amended the penal code to introduce harsher penalties in August 2016.

Also in May, the National Program for Combating FGM reported a decline in the percentage of girls aged 15 to 17 who underwent FGM from 74 percent in 2005 to 55 percent in 2015.

In September, the Supreme Constitutional Court took a step backwards when it ruled unconstitutional a 2008 law that prohibited the official registration of marriages for children under 18, although the prohibition against child marriages remained in place. President al-Sisi publicly spoke against child marriage after the 2017 national census in September revealed that there were 118,000 girls married under 18. "It hurts me and it should hurt anyone with true conscience," al-Sisi said.

Sexual harassment and violence against women remained endemic. Women police officers, part of a special unit started in 2013 to combat violence against women, became more visible in public places especially during crowded holidays. But prosecution of perpetrators was still rare. Two years passed since the declaration of the National Strategy to Combat Violence against Women but local groups were skeptical of the results because of the lack of monitoring mechanisms.

The government remained unresponsive to local groups' campaigns aiming at amending the highly restrictive abortion laws.

Women continued to face discrimination under Egypt's personal status law on equal access to divorce, child custody, and inheritance.

## Sexual Orientation and Gender Identity

In September and October, security forces arrested as many as 75 gay and transgender people and activists after a few activists raised a rainbow flag, a sign of LGBT activism, at a concert in Cairo. Supreme State Security Prosecution charged two with "joining an illegal group" aiming at overthrowing the constitution. Courts sentenced over 40 of the arrested to prison terms of up to 6 years under vague "debauchery" laws.

## Key International Actors

Egypt's international allies continue to support Egypt's government and rarely offer public criticism. United States President Donald Trump, in April during al-Sisi's visit to Washington, said "he has done a fantastic job in a very difficult situation."

In August the United States cut $100 million and held back another $195 million of its aid to Egypt, citing human rights violations, in particular the NGO law. An August 22 State Department memo to Congress, required by law for a national security waiver to allow US assistance, reportedly stated: "The overall human rights climate in Egypt continues to deteriorate," noting lack of access to conflict areas in Sinai.

In September, the US resumed the Bright Star joint training exercises with the Egyptian Army, after eight years of suspension. The US Senate Appropriations Committee approved withholding 26 percent of the $1 billion in military assistance for fiscal year 2018 until the secretary of state can certify Egyptian has taken "effective steps for advance democracy and human rights," specifying release of political prisoners and holding security officials accountable. While the bill approved by the committee was not law at time of writing, it would also withhold $75 million in economic aid until the convictions of NGO staff in the "foreign funding" case are quashed or set aside.

In July, the European Union-Egypt Association Council convened for the first time in seven years. The Council released the revised adopted partnership priorities, but downplayed human rights, only mentioning them under the heading of "enhancing stability," despite shortcomings highlighted in the European Commission's report on EU-Egypt relations, including the restrictions on independent groups.

The United Kingdom publicly supported the Egyptian government's counterterrorism efforts in Sinai, despite the massive rights violations associated with this initiative. The UK was largely silent about the wider human rights crisis in Egypt.

In September, Italy and Egypt exchanged the return of ambassadors despite the unresolved case of the torture and murder of Italian PhD student Giulio Regeni in 2016.

German Chancellor Angela Merkel visited Cairo in March, and in April the German parliament approved a security agreement with Egypt's Interior Ministry that had weak human rights provisions and risked making German authorities complicit in torture in Egypt. Later in October, the German government said it had canceled a training for Egyptian police on combating cybercrimes saying that the skills could be "used to pursue other groups."

France's then-defense minister, Sylvie Goulard, and foreign minister, Jean-Yves Le Drian, visited Cairo in early June to discuss "military and security cooperation." Neither minister commented publicly on human rights issues. Following a meeting in Paris with President al-Sisi on October 24, French President Emmanuel Macron refused to criticize Egypt's human rights record, citing respect for state sovereignty and the struggle to defeat terrorist groups.

In May, Egyptian warplanes launched airstrikes in eastern Libya against armed groups allegedly involved in attacks on churches and Egyptian Christians in Egypt. Egypt released almost no information about the size and nature of troops that joined the Gulf countries in the war in Yemen.

# Equatorial Guinea

Corruption, poverty, and repression of human rights continue to plague Equatorial Guinea under President Teodoro Obiang Nguema Mbasogo, the world's longest serving president, who has been in power since 1979. Vast oil revenues fund lavish lifestyles for the small elite surrounding the president, while little progress has been made on improving access to key rights, including health care and primary education, for the vast majority of Equatorial Guineans. Mismanagement of public funds, credible allegations of high-level corruption and repression of civil society groups and opposition politicians, and unfair trials, persist.

In April, police detained the two leaders of the Center for Development Studies and Initiatives (CEID), the country's leading civic group and a member of the national steering group of the Extractive Industries Transparency Initiative (EITI), creating yet another obstacle toward the government's stated goal of reapplying for EITI membership. EITI promotes a standard by which information on the oil, gas, and mining industry is published, requiring countries and companies to disclose key revenue information. In September, police arrested an artist whose drawings frequently lampoon government officials; he remained in detention and had not been charged at time of writing.

Equatorial Guinea won a seat on the Security Council beginning in January 2018. Its victory was assured after the United Nations' African group submitted a non-competitive slate for the annual election of non-permanent council members. Governments and rights groups in a number of countries have initiated money-laundering investigations against government officials.

In October, President Obiang's eldest son, Teodorin, was convicted by a French court of embezzling more than €100 million (US$119 million) in state funds to purchase a Parisian mansion, exotic sports cars, and luxury goods. In an apparent attempt to shield him from accountability, Obiang appointed Teodorin vice president in 2016, shortly after French prosecutors concluded their investigation. Another money-laundering prosecution implicating government officials is making its way through the Spanish courts, and Swiss authorities started investigating Teodorin for alleged money-laundering activities in 2016.

HUMAN
RIGHTS
WATCH

"Manna From Heaven"?
How Health and Education Pay the Price for Self-Dealing
in Equatorial Guinea

## *Economic and Social Rights*

Equatorial Guinea is among the top five oil producers in sub-Saharan Africa and has a population of approximately 1 million people. According to the United Nations 2016 Human Development Report, the country had a per capita gross national income of $21,517 in 2015, the highest in Africa and more than six times the regional average.

Despite this, Equatorial Guinea ranks 135 out of 188 countries in the Human Development Index that measures social and economic development. Available data, including from the World Bank, the International Monetary Fund (IMF) and a 2011 joint household survey by government and ICF International, a US firm specializing in health surveys, reveal that Equatorial Guinea has failed to provide crucial basic services to its citizens.

In 2016, 42 percent of primary school age children were not registered as students, the seventh highest proportion in the world, according to UNICEF. Only half of children who begin primary school complete it. And according to the 2011 survey, about half the population lacks access to clean water and 26 percent of children exhibited stunted growth, a sign of malnutrition. Equatorial Guinea has among the world's lowest vaccination rates; 25 percent of children received no vaccinations at all, according to the 2011 survey.

In August 2014, Equatorial Guinea reaffirmed its commitment to rejoin EITI, an initiative from which it was expelled in 2010, in part due to its failure to guarantee an "enabling environment" for civil society to fully participate in EITI's implementation. Since then, the tripartite EITI steering committee made up of government officials, oil company representatives, and civil society has met five times, including in April and September 2017.

## *Freedom of Expression and Association*

Only a few private media outlets exist in the country, and they are largely owned by persons close to President Obiang. Freedom of association and assembly are severely curtailed, and the government imposes restrictive conditions on the registration and operation of nongovernmental organizations. The few local activists who seek to address human rights-related issues often face intimidation, harassment, and reprisals.

On April 17, 2017, the police detained Enrique Asumu and Alfredo Okenve, who head the leading civil society group CEID. The two men visited the National Security Ministry after security officers prevented Asumu from boarding a domestic flight, apparently on the ministry's orders. The minister interrogated them for five hours and then prevented them from leaving. Authorities did not charge them or bring them before a judge, as is required under Equatoguinean law, but, after several days' detention, conditioned their release on a fine of 2 million CFA francs (US$3,325). Asumu, who has health problems, was released on April 25, and Okenve on May 3, after both paid the sum demanded.

The detentions are the latest in a series of government efforts to impede CEID's work. In March 2016, the minister of interior, who also headed the National Electoral Commission, suspended the organization one week before the government called for early presidential elections. CEID resumed activities in September 2016, and prior to the detentions high-level officials attended its events and it took part in EITI meetings.

On September 16, state security arrested a political cartoonist, Ramón Nsé Esono Ebalé, whose drawings are harshly critical of President Obiang and other senior government officials. At time of writing, he remains in prison without charge.

## Elections and Political Opposition

The ruling (PDGE) party's virtual monopoly over political life and government continued in 2017, as did harassment of the political opposition. President Obiang won a new seven-year term in April 2016 in an election the US embassy in Malabo said was marred by political harassment. PDGE and aligned parties won the entire 70-seat senate in November 12 elections, and only one opposition representative won a seat in the 100-member House of Deputies. Obiang elevated his son to the position of vice president in June 2016, four weeks after French prosecutors formally requested he be brought to trial in an apparent attempt to shield him from prosecution over corruption allegations.

On June 23, police briefly detained two journalists, Samuel Obiang and Justo Enzema, while they were attending a press conference held by political opposition groups covering the French money laundering trial of Teodorin Obiang, according to EG Justice, an independent rights group. Four days later, police arrested

Joaquin Elo Ayeto, a member of the opposition party Convergence for Social Democracy (CPDS) and held him for three days without charge.

Ayeto told Human Rights Watch that police accused him of inciting violence because he and others had attended the funeral of a taxi driver killed during a protest and distributed pamphlets denouncing government violence. He was also held for approximately one month without charge in December 2016, which he said was retaliation for writing an internet post about an officer he observed at a toll booth who refused to pay the toll.

## *International Corruption Investigations*

On June 19, Teodorin Obiang was tried in absentia by a French court on charges of corruption, money-laundering, and embezzlement. He was convicted on October 27 and sentenced to a three-year suspended sentence and €30 million (US$35 million) suspended fine. During the investigation, French authorities seized assets belonging to Teodorin, including a mansion, 11 luxury cars, and a €22 million (approximately $24 million) art collection. At the time the purchases were made, Teodorin was minister of agriculture, for which he earned less than $100,000 annually. The prosecution presented evidence they claimed showed that at least €110 million (US$119 million) was transferred from the public treasury into Teodorin's accounts.

Teodorin was not present at the trial, but his lawyers' argued that the charges were politically motivated and that there are no domestic conflict-of-interest laws barring Teodorin from amassing such wealth from public contracts. They also claimed that Teodorin should be immune from prosecution as vice president.

Teodorin had unsuccessfully claimed immunity as second vice-president in a separate money-laundering case brought against him by the US Department of Justice following his purchase of a $30 million Malibu mansion and a $38.5 million private jet. That case was settled, with Teodorin agreeing to forfeit $30 million to US authorities that would be repatriated for the benefit of Equatoguineans. The US is expected to determine which charities will receive the funds imminently.

A Spanish judge unsealed the files in a separate corruption case implicating several senior government officials, including the president. A trial is expected in early 2018. The complaint alleges that the named officials purchased homes in Spain through a private company that a US senate investigation revealed had received $26.5 million in government funds at around the same time of the purchases. In September 2015, police arrested a Russian couple and their son who are accused of facilitating the transactions.

# Eritrea

Eritrea remains a one-man dictatorship under President Isaias Afewerki, now in his 26th year in power. It has no legislature, no independent civil society organizations or media outlets, and no independent judiciary. The government restricts religious freedoms, banning all but four groups.

Every Eritrean must serve an indeterminate period of "national service" after turning 18, with many ending up serving for well over a decade. Some are assigned to civil service positions, while most are placed in military units, where they effectively work as forced laborers on private and public works projects.

Largely because of the oppressive nature of the Isaias rule and the prolonged national service, about 12 percent of Eritrea's population has fled the country. In 2016 alone, 52,000 escaped, according to the latest United Nations High Commissioner for Refugees (UNHCR) report.

In June, the United Nations special rapporteur on Eritrea reported to the Human Rights Council that there can be "no sustainable solution to the refugee outflows until the government complies with its human rights obligations." The council echoed her call for reform in a resolution calling on Eritrea to end indefinite conscription and forced labor. It also urged the African Union (AU) to investigate government abuses so that perpetrators can be brought to justice.

## Indefinite Military Service and Forced Labor

Abuse in national service is rampant and is the principal reason why thousands flee the country annually. Service lasts over a decade although the proclamation establishing national service limits conscription to 18 months. A UN Commission of Inquiry in 2016 characterized the system as "enslavement."

Conscripts are subjected to 72-hour work weeks, severe arbitrary punishment, rape by commanders if female, and grossly inadequate food rations. Pay increased after 2014, but deductions for food limited the increase, and net pay remained inadequate to support a family.

## *Freedom of Speech, Expression, and Association*

President Isaias, freed from all institutional restraints, uses well-documented tactics of repression, showing little signs of easing up in 2017. The populace is closely monitored. Offenses include seeming to question authority attempting to avoid national service or to flee the country, practicing an "unrecognized" religion, or simply offending someone in authority. After witnessing the ordeal family members and others face when trying to exercise their rights, ordinary citizens have come to realize they are not allowed any rights.

Eritreans are subject to arbitrary imprisonment. Arrest and harsh punishment-including torture, are at the whim of security force commanders without trial or appeal. Few are told the reason for their arrests. Imprisonment is indefinite and often incommunicado; some arrestees disappear altogether. For example, an individual was arrested and held since 2002 but never charged and not allowed visits or other communications with his family for 15 years. His body was released to his family in August.

The government issued a new criminal procedure code in 2015 but its significant procedural safeguards, requiring warrants for arrest, access to defense counsel, and the right to habeas corpus petitions, remain largely unimplemented.

In September 2001, the government closed all independent newspapers and arrested their editors and leading journalists. None were brought to trial. They remain in solitary detention. There are reliable reports that about half of them had died. In May 2017, Dawit Isaac, not seen since 2005, received United Nations Educational, Scientific and Cultural Organization's World Press Freedom Prize.

Eleven former high-level officials who criticized Isaias's rule have also been imprisoned and held incommunicado since 2001. Eritrea has ignored calls by the African Commission on Human and Peoples' Rights and the Human Rights Council to release them or at least bring them to trial.

After a former minister defected in 2012, Isaias had his then-15-year old daughter, a United States citizen, his 87-year-old grandfather, and 38-year-old son arrested. All three remain jailed without trial.

## *Freedom of Religion*

In 2002, Eritrea required all religious groups to register but refused to register any except Sunni Islam and the Eritrean Orthodox, Roman Catholic, and Evangelical (Lutheran) churches.

The government exercises strict control over these religious groups. It deposed the Eritrean Orthodox patriarch in 2006, placed him under house arrest, and imposed a successor on the church. In July 2017, the octogenarian former patriarch was brought to a church service for the first time in 11 years but not allowed to speak. A contemporaneous church announcement blamed the patriarch for association with heresy but claimed the "issue" had been resolved. He has not been seen since.

Reliable sources reported as many as 170 arrests of Evangelical Christians in May to June alone. Some reportedly were sent to an infamous Red Sea Dahlak Island prison. It has become usual in Eritrea for security personnel to raid private homes where devotees of unrecognized religions meet for communal prayer. Repudiation of their religion is typically the price of release.

In October, the government suppressed protests by students at a private Islamic school in Asmara, Al Diaa, against a planned government takeover. The protests were triggered by the arrest of the school's nonagenarian honorary president after he objected to the takeover. Arrests of other school officials followed. The government had previously announced it planned to convert all religious schools into government-administered institutions.

Jehovah's Witnesses remain especially persecuted. As of August, 53 were imprisoned for attending religious meetings or for conscientious objection, including three arrested over 23 years ago, in 1994.

## *Refugees*

Fleeing Eritreans faced increased hostility in several countries. Sudan forcibly returned over 100 asylum seekers, including about 30 minors, to Eritrea in 2017. UNHCR criticized the expulsions as "a serious violation of international refugee law." In 2016, Sudan had repatriated 400 Eritreans who were promptly arrested upon their return, according to a UN Commission of Inquiry report. Whether any have been released since is speculative because of government secrecy and the absence of independent monitors.

Until early 2013, Israel prevented tens of thousands of Eritreans from lodging asylum claims. As of end of 2015, Israel had recognized only five Eritrean asylum seekers as refugees. It has tried to coerce others to leave by imprisoning, or threatening to imprison indefinitely, those who refuse to leave "voluntarily." In August 2017, the Israeli High Court of Justice held that authorities could detain those who refuse to leave for no longer than 60 days. The justice minister immediately proposed amending Israeli law to circumvent the court decision.

A Swiss court held in 2017 that an Eritrean woman who had not proved she had deserted national service could be presumed not to face punishment on return. The UN special rapporteur on migration criticized a similar earlier Swiss court decision because the court had no real evidence that involuntary returnees would not be prosecuted. Eritreans make up the largest group of asylum seekers in Switzerland.

Eritreans traveling from the Horn of Africa to Europe face grave dangers during their journey, including rape, being held for ransom, torture by smugglers, and drowning in the Mediterranean when boats sink. Nonetheless, thousands remain undeterred.

## Key International Actors

In July, Qatar suddenly withdrew its 450 troops guarding the Eritrea-Djibouti border. The two countries had fought a two-day battle inside Djibouti in 2008, and the UN Security Council concluded that Eritrea was the aggressor. The two ultimately agreed to have Qatar mediate the dispute and patrol the border. The only result of the mediation was that Eritrea released four prisoners-of-war in 2016, after eight years of captivity; Djibouti claims Eritrea holds a dozen more. At Djibouti's request, the AU proposed sending a fact-finding mission to the border but Eritrea did not respond. By year's end the border remained quiet.

Relations with Ethiopia remain tense but no major incidents occurred in 2017. The two nations fought a bloody border war in 1998-2000, and Ethiopia occupies territory identified by an international boundary commission as Eritrean, including the town of Badme. President Isaias uses the "no-war, no-peace" situation with Ethiopia to continue his repressive domestic policies, including protracted national service.

The UN Security Council retained arms embargo against Eritrea until at least April 2018 after receiving a report from its Monitoring Group on Somalia and Eritrea. Eritrea again refused to cooperate with the group in 2017. The group reported it had no evidence Eritrea was sending arms to Al-Shabab in Somalia, but Eritrea continued to arm and train anti-Ethiopia and anti-Djibouti militias in violation of the UN embargo.

Eritrea receives substantial income from foreign companies mining gold, copper, zinc, and nickel in the country. Government has 40 percent ownership in these companies. Two mines, SFECO Group's Zara Mining Share Company and Sichuan Road & Bridge Mining Investment are Chinese majority-owned; another, at Bisha, is majority-owned by Canada's Nevsun Mining.

All are required by the government to use government-owned construction firms for infrastructure development, thereby indirectly profiting from national service conscript labor. In November, a Canadian appellate court allowed a suit against Nevsun by former national service conscripts complaining of forced labor at Bisha to proceed

Absent evidence that Eritrea had implemented democratic reforms and ended its human rights abuses, the European Parliament in July once again denounced as unwarranted further disbursements from the European Union's 2015 €200 (US$238) million aid package, awarded to try to stem migration from Eritrea.

**HUMAN RIGHTS WATCH**

# "Fuel on the Fire"

Security Force Response to the 2016 Irreecha Cultural Festival

# Ethiopia

Ethiopia made little progress in 2017 on much-needed human rights reforms. Instead, it used a prolonged state of emergency, security force abuses, and repressive laws to continue suppressing basic rights and freedoms.

The 10-month state of emergency, first declared in October 2016, brought mass arrests, mistreatment in detention, and unreasonable limitations on freedom of assembly, expression, and association. While abusive and overly broad, the state of emergency gave the government a period of relative calm that it could have used to address grievances raised repeatedly by protesters.

However, the government did not address the human rights concerns that protesters raised, including the closing of political space, brutality of security forces, and forced displacement. Instead, authorities in late 2016 and 2017 announced anti-corruption reforms, cabinet reshuffles, a dialogue with what was left of opposition political parties, youth job creation, and commitments to entrench "good governance."

Ethiopia continues to have a closed political space. The ruling coalition has 100 percent of federal and regional parliamentary seats. Broad restrictions on civil society and independent media, decimation of independent political parties, harassment and arbitrary detention of those who do not actively support the government, severely limited space for dissenting voices.

Despite repeated promises to investigate abuses, the government has not credibly done so, underscoring the need for international investigations. The government-affiliated Human Rights Commission is not sufficiently independent and its investigations consistently lack credibility.

## *State of Emergency*

Ethiopia spent much of 2017 under a state of emergency first imposed in October 2016 following a year of popular protests, renewed for four months in March, and lifted on August 4. Security forces responded to the protests with lethal force, killing over 1,000 protesters and detaining tens of thousands more.

The state of emergency's implementing directive prescribed draconian and overly broad restrictions on freedom of expression, association, and assembly across the country, and signaled an increasingly militarized response to the situation. The directive banned all protests without government permission and permitted arrest without court order in "a place assigned by the command post until the end of the state of emergency" and permitted "rehabilitation"—a euphemism for short-term detention that often involves forced physical exercise.

During the state of emergency military were deployed in much larger numbers across Oromia and Amhara regions, and security forces arbitrarily detained over 21,000 people in these "rehabilitation camps" according to government figures. Detainees reported harsh physical punishment and indoctrination in government policies. Places of detention included prisons, military camps, and other makeshift facilities. Some reported torture. Artists, politicians, and journalists were tried on politically motivated charges.

Dr. Merera Gudina, the chair of the Oromo Federalist Congress (OFC), a legally registered political opposition party, was charged with "outrages against the constitution" in March. He joins many other major OFC members on trial on politically motivated charges, including deputy chairman Bekele Gerba. At time of writing, at least 8,000 people arrested during the state of emergency remain in detention, according to government figures.

## *Freedom of Expression and Association*

The state tightly controls the media landscape, a reality exacerbated during the state of emergency, making it challenging for Ethiopians to access information that is independent of government perspectives. Many journalists are forced to choose between self-censorship, harassment and arrest, or exile. At least 85 journalists have fled into exile since 2010, including at least six in 2017.

Scores of journalists, including Eskinder Nega and Woubshet Taye, remain jailed under Ethiopia's anti- terrorism law.

In addition to threats against journalists, tactics used to restrict independent media include harassing advertisers, printing presses, and distributors.

Absent a vibrant independent domestic media, social media and diaspora television stations continue to play key roles in disseminating information. The government increased its efforts to restrict access to social media and diaspora media in 2017, banning the watching of diaspora television under the state of emergency, jamming radio and television broadcasts, targeting sources and family members of diaspora journalists. In April, two of the main diaspora television stations—Ethiopian Satellite Television (ESAT) and the Oromia Media Network (OMN)—were charged under the repressive anti-terrorism law. Executive director of OMN, Jawar Mohammed, was also charged under the criminal code in April.

The government regularly restricts access to social media apps and some websites with content that challenges the government's narrative on key issues. During particularly sensitive times, such as during June's national exams when the government feared an exam leak, the government blocked access to the internet completely.

The 2009 Charities and Societies Proclamation (CSO law) continues to severely curtail the ability of independent nongovernmental organizations. The law bars work on human rights, governance, conflict resolution and advocacy on the rights of women, children, and people with disabilities by organizations that receive more than 10 percent of their funds from foreign sources.

## Torture and Arbitrary Detention

Arbitrary detention and torture continue to be major problems in Ethiopia. Ethiopian security personnel, including plainclothes security and intelligence officials, federal police, special police, and military, frequently tortured and otherwise ill-treated political detainees held in official and secret detention centers, to coerce confessions or the provision of information.

Many of those arrested since the 2015/2016 protests or during the 2017 state of emergency said they were tortured in detention, including in military camps. Several women alleged that security forces raped or sexually assaulted them while they were in detention. There is little indication that security personnel are being investigated or punished for any serious abuses. Former security personnel, including military, have described using torture as a technique to extract information.

There are serious due process concerns and concerns about the independence of the judiciary on politically sensitive cases. Outside Addis Ababa, many detainees are not charged and are rarely taken to court.

Individuals peacefully expressing dissent are often charged under the repressive anti-terrorism law and accused of belonging to one of three domestic groups that the government has designated as terrorist organizations. The charges carry punishments up to life in prison. Acquittals are rare, and courts frequently ignore complaints of torture by detainees. Hundreds of individuals, including opposition politicians, protesters, journalists and artists, are presently on trial under the anti-terrorism law.

The government has not permitted the United Nation's Working Group on Arbitrary Detention to investigate allegations despite requests from the UN body in 2005, 2007, 2009, 2011, and 2015.

## Somali Region Security Force Abuses

Serious abuses continue to be committed by the Somali Region's notoriously abusive Liyu police. Throughout 2017, communities in the neighboring Oromia regional state reported frequent armed attacks on their homes by individuals believed to be from the Somali Region's Liyu police. Residents reported killings, assaults, looting of property, and displacement. Several Somali communities reported reprisal attacks carried out by unknown Oromo individuals. Human Rights Watch is not aware of any efforts by the federal government to stop these incursions. Several hundred thousand people have been internally displaced as a result of the ongoing conflict.

The Liyu police were formed in 2008 and have a murky legal mandate but in practice report to Abdi Mahmoud Omar (also known as "Abdi Illey") the president of the Somali Regional State, and have been implicated in numerous alleged extrajudicial killings as well as incidents of torture, rape, and attacks on civilians accused of proving support to the Ogaden National Liberation Front (ONLF). No meaningful investigations have been undertaken into any of these alleged abuses in the Somali Regional State.

Abdi Illey's intolerance for dissent extends beyond Ethiopia, and family members of Ethiopian Somalis living outside of the country are frequently targeted in the Somali Region. Family members of diaspora have been arbitrarily detained, harassed, and had their property confiscated after their relatives in the diaspora attended protests or were critical of Abdi Illey in social media posts.

## *Key International Actors*

Despite its deteriorating human rights record, Ethiopia continues to enjoy strong support from foreign donors and most of its regional neighbors, due to its role as host of the African Union and as a strategic regional player, its contributions to UN peacekeeping, regional counterterrorism efforts, its migration partnerships with Western countries, and its stated progress on development indicators. Ethiopia is also a country of origin, transit, and host for large numbers of migrants and refugees.

Both the European Parliament and US Senate and House of Representatives have denounced Ethiopia's human rights record. The European Parliament urged the establishment of a UN-led mechanism to investigate the killings of protesters since 2015 and to release all political prisoners. In April, European Union Special Representative (EUSR) for Human Rights Stavros Lambrinidis visited Ethiopia, underscoring EU concern over Ethiopia's human rights situation. Other donors, including the World Bank, have continued business as usual without publicly raising concerns.

Ethiopia is a member of both the UN Security Council and the UN Human Rights Council. Despite these roles, Ethiopia has a history of non-cooperation with UN special mechanisms. Other than the UN special rapporteur on Eritrea, no special rapporteur has been permitted to visit since 2006. The rapporteurs on torture, freedom of opinion and expression, and peaceful assembly, among others, all have outstanding requests to visit the country.

**HUMAN RIGHTS WATCH**

"Like Living in Hell"
Police Abuses Against Child and Adult Migrants in Calais

# European Union

Xenophobic populists hostile to human rights shaped politics even when they failed to win at the ballot box, and European governments seemed determined to keep migrants away at all costs. Yet there were hints in the response to the crisis in Poland that European Union leaders were beginning to recognize that the bloc's future depends on a willingness to stand up for human rights and the rule of law.

## *Migration and Asylum*

The EU and its member states intensified efforts to prevent arrivals and outsource responsibility for migration control to countries outside the EU's borders. In Libya, in particular, the EU pursued a strategy of containment in cooperation with Libyan authorities, despite overwhelming evidence of pervasive and routine brutality against asylum seekers and other migrants arbitrarily detained by those authorities, or otherwise deprived of their liberty. Libya has not signed the Refugee Convention, and does not have a functioning asylum system.

By mid-November 2017, just over 150,000 people reached Europe by sea, less than half the arrivals for the same period in 2016, with a significant decrease in arrivals on Greek islands and dip in boat departures from Libya. There was a large increase in boat migration in the western Mediterranean, from Morocco to Spain, though the overall numbers remained low. The Western Balkan route remained largely closed, aided by an abusive border regime in Hungary and migrant pushbacks by Croatia.

The Mediterranean remained deadly, with almost 3,000 dead or missing by mid-November 2017. Nongovernmental organizations (NGOs) performed roughly 40 percent of all rescues in the central Mediterranean in the first half of 2017, but by September several NGOs had suspended activities due to security concerns and increased interceptions, sometimes reckless and accompanied by abuse, by Libyan coast guard forces. Backed by EU institutions, Italy imposed on NGOs a code of conduct governing rescues following a campaign to delegitimize and even criminalize their efforts.

Despite calls for expanded safe and legal channels, including family reunification and humanitarian visas, EU institutions and member states moved forward only on resettlement of recognized refugees. The European Commission announced in September that member states had resettled 22,518 refugees over the past two years, and recommended a plan to resettle 50,000 refugees to Europe over the next two years. Member states were slow to respond to the earlier commission call for resettlement pledges.

Member states less affected by direct arrivals remained reluctant to share responsibility for asylum seekers. The two-year binding plan to relocate almost 100,000 asylum seekers out of Greece and Italy officially ended in September, with only 29,401 people actually transferred, less than one-third of the final target. Some countries continued to relocate, however, and over 2,000 more had been relocated by mid-November. In June, the European Commission initiated infringement proceedings against Hungary, Poland, and the Czech Republic for failure to comply with the plan. In September, the EU Court of Justice (CJEU) dismissed the case against the relocation plan brought by Hungary and Slovakia.

EU countries continued to return asylum seekers to Italy, and resumed returns to Greece, under the Dublin Regulation, which requires the first EU country of entry to take responsibility for asylum claims in most cases. In March, the European Court of Human Rights (ECtHR) ruled that Hungary was in violation of its human rights obligations for the way it detained asylum seekers and returned them to Serbia under the "safe third country" argument, and in April the United Nations High Commissioner for Refugees (UNHCR) called for a suspension of returns to Hungary under the Dublin rules. Germany officially suspended such returns in late August, and a number of other EU countries took a similar approach.

Little progress was made on reform of EU asylum laws. Problematic proposals would make it easier to summarily reject claims, send people to countries outside the EU based on the "safe third country" concept, and revoke refugee status. Meanwhile, asylum seekers continued to face widely varying recognition rates across the union.

## Discrimination and Intolerance

Populist extremist parties exercised an outside influence over European politics during the year. While they came second rather than first in presidential elections in France and Austria and the parliamentary vote in the Netherlands, radical right populists entered the German parliament, and at time of writing were in talks to become part of the coalition government in Austria, following elections in October. Worse still, elements of their anti-immigration, anti-refugee and anti-Muslim policy agenda continue to be embraced by mainstream political parties in many EU countries.

Racist, xenophobic, and anti-Muslim sentiment and violence persisted across the EU. Muslims experienced widespread hostility and intolerance. Anti-Semitism, including hate crimes, remained a serious concern.

In its June annual report, the Council of Europe's Commission against Racism and Intolerance (ECRI) noted that nationalistic populism and xenophobic hate speech had entered the political mainstream in the region. In an April report, the EU Fundamental Rights Agency (FRA) noted that many hate crimes in the EU remain unreported and invisible, leaving victims without redress, and urged member states to improve access to justice for victims.

In an August assessment on strategies aimed at helping Roma, the European Commission found that as many as 80 percent of Roma are at risk of poverty across the EU, calling for further efforts to improve access to schooling and employment.

In August, the Council of Europe's Commissioner for Human Rights Nils Muižnieks identified the right to live in the community and deinstitutionalization; the right to legal capacity; and the right to an inclusive education as key challenges affecting persons with psychosocial and intellectual disabilities in Europe. In September, Muižnieks called for an end to school segregation for children with disabilities, Roma children and refugee and migrant children.

A March decision by the CJEU backing private sector workplace bans on headscarves seriously undermined women's right to equality and non-discrimination. In July, the ECtHR upheld Belgium's ban on burqas and full-face Islamic veils.

In a June resolution, the Council of Europe Parliamentary Assembly called for an end to impunity of sexual violence and harassment of women in public by prosecuting perpetrators. In June, the EU signed the Istanbul Convention on preventing and combatting violence against women. Eleven EU member states—including the United Kingdom, Greece, and Hungary—have yet to ratify the convention.

In May, Council of Europe Secretary General Thorbjørn Jagland warned that attacks against lesbian, gay, bisexual, and transgender (LGBT) people are widespread in Europe, and highlighted the need for strong and effective anti-discrimination laws. In April, the ECtHR ruled that requiring transgender people to undergo sterilization in order to have their gender recognized violates human rights.

## Terrorism and Counterterrorism

Attacks in Belgium, Finland, France, Greece, Spain, Sweden and the UK, together killed over 60 people and left hundreds injured. All the mass casualty incidents among these were claimed by the Islamic State (also known as ISIS). Some incidents were attributed to or claimed by far-right, left-wing and regional separatist armed organizations. During the year, attacks specifically targeting police officers or soldiers took place in France, Poland, Spain, Sweden, and the UK.

France, Germany, and the Netherlands passed laws permitting or enhancing existing powers of the executive, to order administrative controls restricting the movement and association of people considered a threat to national security.

In March, a new EU directive to combat terrorism, strengthening the existing EU framework, was approved by governments. The directive requires states to criminalize "public provocation to commit a terrorist offence" and various preparatory acts that fall short of direct participation in attacks. Human rights groups expressed concern about insufficient safeguards and vague terminology in the directive, and its impact on freedom of expression.

During the year, people in France and Spain were convicted of terrorism offences for posting comments online that were treated as glorification of or apology for terrorism, in some cases without evidence of any direct link to incitement to violence.

In June, the European Commission accelerated existing plans to combat radicalization and remove online terrorist content. An Anglo-French action plan published the same month included proposals to remove extremist material online, and to access encrypted content, raising concerns about freedom of expression and privacy.

Criminal investigations into alleged complicity by Polish and Lithuanian authorities remained stalled, and a judicial review of a 2016 decision by prosecutors to close the investigation into alleged UK complicity in renditions by the Central Intelligence Agency (CIA) to Libya remained pending. A ECtHR case brought against Lithuania and Romania over their complicity in CIA torture and secret detention remained pending.

## Croatia

By August, 1,262 people claimed asylum in Croatia in 2017, including people returned to Croatia from other EU member states under EU asylum rules. Only 76 asylum seekers had been granted some form of protection in 2017 at time of writing. Croatia relocated 78 asylum seekers from Greece and Italy by late September.

During the year, Croatia forced back asylum seekers and migrants who entered the country from Serbia without examining their asylum claims. In July, the CJEU ruled that Croatia breached EU law by allowing asylum seekers and migrants to cross into Slovenia and Austria without first examining their asylum claims.

Asylum seekers and refugees continued to face social isolation and difficulties in accessing language classes, education, and employment. Unaccompanied migrant and asylum children continued to be placed in residential institutions for children without adequate arrangements for their protection and care. Out of 30 registered unaccompanied children, only one had been enrolled in school for the academic year of 2017/2018.

People with disabilities continued to be denied the right to legal capacity and to live in the community. Adult persons with disabilities continued to be placed in residential institutions without their consent.

Members of national minorities, in particular ethnic Serbs and Roma, continued to face discrimination, ethnic intolerance, and hate speech. Thousands of Roma remain stateless. Roma children are effectively segregated in schools.

The Croatian judiciary continued to make slow progress on war crimes accountability.

## Estonia

The number of stateless persons continued to decline in Estonia in 2017, although the naturalization rate is very slow. According to the Interior Ministry, in 2016, only 1,450 stateless people acquired citizenship by naturalization and as of January 2017, leaving 79,438 stateless persons residing in Estonia, compared to 82,561 in January 2016. Stateless persons, most of whom are ethnic Russians who lost their citizenship in 1991 after the collapse of the Soviet Union, continue to face significant barriers to social and economic integration. Not only do they lack full political and employment rights, they are also unable to pursue certain careers in national and local civil service, police, and customs.

While Estonia has made some strides in reducing child statelessness in recent years, the government has only partially addressed the problem. Children between 15 and 18 and those born outside Estonia to parents who are stateless residents of Estonia still cannot automatically obtain citizenship. In February 2017, the UN Committee on the Rights of the Child recommended that Estonia "fast track the naturalization of children with undetermined citizenship" between 15 and 18 years old.

In January 2017, Estonia became the first former Soviet republic to recognize same-sex marriages entered into abroad. In July 2017, Estonia held its first Pride Parade in 10 years. Despite these significant steps, the government has yet to implement the 2016 Cohabitation Act that would give people in same-sex civil partnerships the same rights as married couples, including in relation to property and adoption.

As of September 25, 2017, the government had relocated 141 asylum seekers under the EU relocation scheme.

## France

France continues to rely on abusive counterterrorism powers introduced following November 2015 attacks.

The state of emergency that permitted the use of security powers without adequate safeguards was extended in December 2016 and July 2017. The state of emergency ended on November 1, when the new Law to Strengthen Internal Security and the Fight against Terrorism entered into force, following its adoption by parliament in October.

Despite widespread concern from rights bodies, both domestically and abroad, the law incorporates some of the powers utilized under the state of emergency. These include powers that have led to significant abuse, such as the power to order people considered a threat to national security to live in an assigned place of residency, and to carry out house searches without judicial authorization.

The French Ombudsman, the French National Consultative Commission of Human Rights (CNCDH) and a large coalition of NGOs criticized the law for granting the executive the power to restrict freedom of worship, assembly, free movement and the right to privacy, without adequate judicial safeguards.

A report by the French ombudsman in January confirmed earlier CNCDH's findings that young men from visible minorities are overrepresented in police checks, and are 20 times more likely to be stopped by the police than members of the majority population. The new security law expands police check powers at and around borders, including international train stations, raising concerns that the use of discriminatory identity checks could be expanded.

An April report by the CNCDH records a 44.7 percent decrease in anti-Semitic and anti-Muslim incidents in 2016 compared to 2015.

There were reportedly between 500 and 1,000 migrants, including up to 200 unaccompanied children, in the Calais area, as of October, despite the dismantling of the squalid, informal camp at the end of 2016. The French ombudsman and local organizations reported dire living conditions for migrants there, as well as police harassment and abuse against migrants and aid workers, concluding that they contributed to "inhuman living conditions." The report of an investigation ordered by the interior minister, published in October, found that police had abused migrants in Calais.

Despite several court orders, local authorities in Calais continued to obstruct the work of aid groups and refused to provide water and sanitation. By the end of October, the central government had opened four new short-term shelters and provided running water, toilets, and showers.

By late September, France relocated 377 asylum seekers from Italy and 4,091 from Greece.

In an annual report in March 2017, the inspector of prisons found that women in prison face difficulties "accessing psychiatric care."

In February, France became the first permanent member of the UN Security Council to endorse the Safe Schools Declaration.

## *Germany*

Arrivals of asylum-seekers and migrants fell for the second year in a row. By the end of July, 105,000 new asylum-seekers had been registered. Authorities made decisions on over 408,000 asylum applications in the first half of the year, many pending from the previous year. By August, Germany had accepted 1,730 resettled refugees, of whom 1,700 were Syrian. By late September, Germany had relocated 3,641 asylum seekers from Italy and 4,838 from Greece.

In the first half of 2017, authorities recorded 143 attacks on asylum shelters and 642 attacks on refugees and asylum seekers outside their home.

Germany's federal parliament approved a series of surveillance measures during the year that raise concerns about the rights to privacy and freedom of expression. One measure, which would allow law enforcement agencies to install malware on mobile phones, tablets and computers to circumvent encryption, had not entered into force at time of writing. A second came partly into force in October, requiring social media companies to take down "illegal content," a poorly defined term including hate speech, or face large fines. A third, which entered into force in July, permits law enforcement authorities at the border to examine data on the mobile phones of refugees and migrants, without a prior court order, a reasonable suspicion of a criminal offense, or consent.

An amendment to the Federal Criminal Police Act, in force since July, allows the pre-emptive electronic tagging and imposition of restrictions on the movement of people considered to pose a risk to national security (*Gefährder*), but who had not yet committed any crime. An immigration power allowing similar restrictions on foreign nationals pending deportation came into effect the same month.

German authorities continued to investigate serious international crimes related to the conflict in Syria and Iraq. Trials for war crimes are underway or have been concluded against members of ISIS, former Jabhat al-Nusra members, and various armed groups opposed to the Syrian government.

In June, Federal Parliament approved the recognition of equal marriage rights for same-sex couples, and the law came into force on October 1.

## Greece

A December 2016 European Commission plan for Greece recommended tougher measures aimed at increasing the number of returns of asylum seekers to Turkey, including weakening protections for vulnerable groups, expanding detention, and curbing appeal rights. As a result, Greece increased detention capacity and forced people identified as "vulnerable" to remain on the Aegean islands until their asylum claim is heard.

Despite progress, access to asylum remained difficult and subject to delay while there were particular concerns with low refugee recognition rates on the islands.

The policy under the EU-Turkey deal of containing asylum seekers on the islands trapped thousands in overcrowded and abysmal conditions, while denying most access to adequate asylum procedures or refugee protection.

According to UNHCR data, there were more than 46,000 asylum seekers and migrants in mainland Greece, and 13,652 on the islands, as of October.

The Greek authorities' failure to properly identify vulnerable asylum seekers for transfer to the mainland impeded their access to proper care and services.

The policies, conditions, uncertainty and the slow pace of decision-making contributed to deteriorating mental health for some asylum seekers and other migrants on the islands, while creating tensions that sometimes erupted into violence.

Greek police were criticized for excessive use of force against asylum seekers during a July protest at the hotspot on Lesbos, and ill-treatment of some of those who were detained following ensuing clashes. At time of writing, an inquiry was ongoing.

In September, the Council of State ruled that two Syrian asylum seekers could safely be removed to Turkey without their claims being heard, paving the way for large scale returns of Syrians under the EU deal. The wider impact of the ruling had yet to be felt on the islands at time of writing, and no asylum seekers had been returned under the conditions permitted in the ruling.

More than 1,390 migrants had been removed to Turkey by the end of October, after their claims were rejected on the merits or because they did not file an asylum claim or agreed to return voluntarily. In June, the Greek ombudsman launched an inquiry into allegations of pushbacks, including of Turkish nationals, at the Greek-Turkish land border.

An estimated 3,150 unaccompanied migrant children entered Greece as of October 31. In July, the Greek ombudsman criticized the prolonged detention of unaccompanied children at police stations and refugee camps while they await placement in the overburdened shelter system. At time of writing, an estimated 2,016 were waiting to be placed in a dedicated facility, including 107 who were detained.

Greece opened afternoon preparatory classes to integrate asylum-seeking and migrant children into public schools on the Greek mainland, but failed to cover hundreds of children on the islands. At time of writing, the education ministry was planning to extend classes to children on the islands, but plans excluded children older than 15 and those living in camps.

Far-right groups regularly attacked asylum seekers on the island of Chios. In April, two men were convicted for racially-aggravated crimes over the incidents.

In a landmark ruling in March, the ECtHR ordered Greece to pay some €600,000 in damages for failing to protect from forced labor 42 migrant strawberry pickers who were shot at by farm foremen in 2013 when they protested about unpaid wages.

In September, parliament adopted a new law on legal gender recognition, removing medical requirements to change a person's legal gender.

## Hungary

Hungary saw a decrease in asylum applications in 2017, with 3,035 asylum seekers registered in the first ten months of the year, compared to more than 26,000 during the same period in 2016, according to UNHCR. Most asylum seekers in 2017 came from Afghanistan, Iraq and Syria.

A March law allows for automatic detention of all asylum seekers, including children over 14 years, in two transit zones at Hungary's border with Serbia for the entire duration of the asylum procedure. Coupled with recent restrictive amendments to the asylum law, which bar asylum seekers from meaningful access to the asylum procedure, authorities limited daily entry of asylum seekers to 20, leaving thousands stranded in Serbia in poor conditions.

In September, UN High Commissioner for Refugees Filippo Grande called on Hungary to Improve access for people seeking asylum, and to dismantle the transit zones at the borders.

The construction of a second line of fencing on Hungary's border with Serbia in April, and violent and other pushbacks of asylum seekers at the border also contributed to the significant drop in arrivals.

By mid-November, there were 455 asylum seekers detained in the two transit zones, including 243 children, among them 19 unaccompanied children, according to UNHCR.

The government engaged in a campaign to discredit civil society organizations, particularly those funded by philanthropist George Soros, describing them as foreign paid traitors, to smear Soros himself.

In February, the UN special rapporteur on the situation of human rights defenders raised concerns about the government's continued stigmatization of human rights defenders.

In April, the government passed a law forcing all civil society organizations receiving more than US$27,000 per annum in foreign funding to register with authorities as foreign funded, and to report that fact on all published materials. Failure to comply results in a fine and could ultimately mean deregistration. To date, over 200 organizations have declined to register, while 20 complied.

A group of 23 organizations, including prominent human rights organizations, filed a complaint to the constitutional court in August, challenging the law. The EU Commission started infringement proceedings against Hungary in April as a result of the law.

Also in April, parliament adopted a law targeting the Central European University in Budapest, introducing requirements that would make its operations in Hungary impossible, and undermine academic freedom. The law triggered protests in Budapest and drew significant international criticism, including from the US

Department of State and the European Commission, which also initiated infringement proceedings against Hungary.

In May, the European Parliament adopted a resolution characterizing the human rights situation as one that risked breaching EU values and calling for action under article 7 of the EU treaty.

Many media outlets are under state control or owned by people with close ties to the government. In September, pro-government online publication *888.hu* published a list with names of eight journalists, accusing them of pursuing a foreign agenda sponsored by Soros.

Roma continued to face discrimination in housing, education, and public health care. In May, the European Commission launched infringement proceedings against Hungary for on-going discrimination of Roma children in education.

The UN Working Group on the issue of discrimination against women in law and in practice highlighted domestic violence in Hungary in a report to the Human Rights Council in June, and urged authorities to ratify the Istanbul Convention and improve training for law enforcement officials.

In June, the appeals court in Budapest ordered the retrial of a Syrian man sentenced in November 2016 to 10 years in prison for terrorism, for throwing stones during 2015 clashes between Hungarian security forces and migrants and asylum seekers at the Serbian-Hungarian border.

## *Italy*

Over 114,000 migrants and asylum seekers had reached Italy by sea by mid-November, according to UNHCR, significantly straining the country's reception system. The government adopted harsher policies amid a toxic political debate over migration.

In the first seven months of the year, the number of new asylum applications almost doubled compared to 2016, while authorities granted some form of protection in 43 percent of cases. The majority received temporary humanitarian leave to remain in the country, including for abuses suffered as migrants in Libya.

In February, the government introduced measures to accelerate the asylum procedure, including by limiting appeals against negative decisions, and announced plans for new immigration detention centers around the country.

The central government faced problems finding accommodation for asylum seekers across Italy, with many communities refusing to host reception centers. Many reception centers lack care and support for sexual violence survivors, as well as survivors of other traumatic violence. Italy's failure to provide long-term support to individuals granted international protection was on stark display in August, when police violently evicted hundreds of homeless Eritrean refugees from an occupied building in Rome.

Children made up 15 percent of new arrivals, with many traveling on their own. In March, parliament adopted a law to improve protections for unaccompanied children, including prioritizing their placement with foster families rather than institutions and ensuring every child is appointed a legal guardian.

A government proposal to make it easier for those born in Italy to obtain citizenship faced significant opposition and remained blocked in parliament at time of writing.

In July, parliament adopted a law finally making torture a crime, but with a definition and statute of limitations that do not meet international standards.

The Council of Europe's Committee for Prevention of Torture published a report in September calling on authorities to address prison overcrowding and conditions, and improve investigations into alleged ill-treatment by law enforcement agents.

In July, the UN women's rights committee recommended stronger measures against gender-based violence, including improving identification and protection in asylum reception centers and adequate anti-trafficking mechanisms.

## Latvia

In 2017, Latvia made little progress in reducing its stateless population, which as of late 2016 was 242,736 persons, according to UNHCR. Stateless persons, most of whom are ethnic Russians, do not have full political rights and continue to experience social and economic discrimination. They are also unable to pursue certain careers in civil service, among other professions, and face restrictions on property rights.

In September, the parliament rejected amendments to Latvia's citizenship law submitted by the country's president earlier the same month, which would allow all children born in Latvia automatically to receive Latvian citizenship, unless their parents opt out or they already have another nationality. Under current legislation, non-citizens may register their children as Latvian citizens, but this process is not automatic.

The Latvian State Language Center continues to sanction individuals for failing to use Latvian in professional communications. During 2016, the center issued 160 warnings and fines, a sharp decrease from the previous year. For a second year, the mayor of Riga was among those fined.

In December 2016, Council of Europe Commissioner for Human Rights Nils Muižnieks published recommendations following his visit to Latvia in September 2016, calling on the Latvian authorities to ensure greater protection for women, children, and LGBT people. Latvia has yet to ratify the Istanbul Convention, which it signed in 2016.

By late September, Latvia had accepted a total of 321 asylum seekers from Italy and Greece under the EU relocation plan.

## *The Netherlands*

Anti-immigrant, anti-Muslim rhetoric pervaded the election platforms of mainstream parties in the run-up to the general election in March. The incumbent prime minister published an open letter to voters telling immigrants who did not accept Dutch values "to act normal or leave."

The time-limited and conditional support offered by the Dutch government to rejected asylum seekers continued to raise concern. In July, the UN Committee on Economic, Social and Cultural Rights criticized a law making health, education and welfare assistance contingent on rejected asylum-seekers' "demonstrated willingness to return to their country of origin."

In 2017, the Central Agency for the Reception of Asylum Seekers (COA) reduced its shelter capacity from 48,700 to 31,000 places and closed 45 locations, claiming it reflected a decrease in asylum seeker numbers.

In March, new counterterrorism powers entered into force, allowing authorities to impose restrictions on people suspected of involvement in terrorism, including reporting obligations, geographic limits on movement, contact bans, prohibitions on leaving the country, and extending the power to strip Dutch nationals as young as 16 of their citizenship while abroad if suspected of joining a terrorist group. In August, the acting justice minister confirmed the first use of the power to strip Dutch nationality from a person convicted of a terrorism offense.

In July, parliament took the final step to adopt sweeping new surveillance legislation, despite widespread criticism that it violated the right to privacy. Domestic rights groups criticized as inadequate the body established by law to oversee the exercise of the broad powers given to the intelligence services to intercept communication.

## Poland

The government continued to undermine the rule of law and human rights protection during the year.

Using its parliamentary majority, the government introduced a series of laws in July that threaten judicial independence and the rule of law. One law would give the minister of justice control over judicial appointments. A second law, approved in the same month, would remove all sitting supreme court judges, except those chosen by the government, and together with its power to appoint judges, would give it control of the court.

Following significant international criticism, Poland's president vetoed both laws and submitted his own proposals to parliament, which also fail to adequately guarantee the independence of the judiciary. The president signed a third law giving the justice minister power to appoint the presidents of lower courts, lower the retirement age for judges and dismiss the president of any court.

The efforts to undermine the independence of the judiciary met with significant international opposition, including from the Organisation for Security and Co-operation in Europe (OSCE), the Council of Europe, and the UN special rapporteur on the independence of the judiciary.

The EU Commission initiated infringement proceedings against Poland in July over the law on common courts. The commission also made further recommendations under the rule of law framework and expressed willingness to trigger article 7 of the EU Treaty if Polish authorities did not address concerns. EU member states twice debated rule of law in Poland in the General Affairs Council during the year, with many expressing support for the commission's efforts, but without the council reaching a firm conclusion. In November, the European Parliament adopted a resolution on Poland to take steps needed for the parliament to make a formal request to the council to trigger article 7 in relation to Poland.

In September, the Polish parliament passed a law with adverse effects on civil society organizations. It establishes a government controlled body in charge of overseeing the distribution of public funds to NGOs. Prior to its adoption, the OSCE's Office for Democratic Institutions and Human Rights raised concerns about the law, and urged lawmakers to provide safeguards limiting government interference in the body's work. State-funded NGOs working on asylum and migration, women's rights, and LGBT rights reported difficulties and delays during the year accessing the state funds granted to them.

Asylum seekers, the majority from the Russian republic of Chechnya and Central Asia, who arrived at the Polish-Belarus border crossing were routinely denied the right to access the Polish asylum procedure, and summarily returned to Belarus. Polish authorities on five occasions in 2017 ignored binding ECtHR interim orders to halt the removal of asylum seekers to Belarus.

In June, the Polish parliament adopted a law restricting access to emergency contraception, even in cases of rape.

## Spain

Catalonian authorities held an independence referendum on October 1, even though Spain's Constitutional Court had ordered it to be suspended and later declared it unconstitutional. The vote was marred by excessive use of force by Civil Guard and national police officers.

UN High Commissioner for Human Rights urged Spanish authorities to ensure thorough, independent, and impartial investigations into all acts of violence.

Central authorities used constitutional powers to dissolve the Catalan regional government and impose direct rule on October 27, and called for elections in De-

cember. In November, prosecutors began criminal proceedings against 14 representatives of the dissolved Catalan government for sedition and other offenses.

Attacks in Barcelona and Cambrils by an armed extremist cell in August left 16 dead and more than 100 wounded. ISIS claimed responsibility. The Barcelona attack was the deadliest in Spain since 2003.

Public officials warned against Islamophobia in the wake of the attacks. Reported anti-Muslim incidents included an assault on a 14-year-old Moroccan child. A Pakistani man began a case against Spain at the ECtHR in May, for police use of ethnic profiling, a perennial problem in the country.

The increased numbers of migrants reaching Spain by sea faced substandard conditions in police facilities and obstacles to applying for asylum. Over 16,000 people arrived by sea in the first ten months of 2017, a significant increase over the previous year. Over 5,000 crossed land borders into Ceuta and Melilla, many by scaling fences around Spain's enclaves.

In October the ECtHR found that the 2014 summary return from Melilla to Morocco of two sub-Saharan African men constituted collective expulsions. The ruling means Spain should reform a 2015 law formalizing this practice, which continued periodically throughout 2017. Asylum seekers in Spain's enclaves faced delays in transfers to the mainland, including LGBT asylum seekers, despite vulnerability to abuse.

In January, an appeals court reopened the investigation into the February 2014 deaths of 15 migrants in Ceuta waters after Guardia Civil officers fired rubber bullets and tear gas into the water.

As of September, Spain had relocated only 1,257 asylum seekers of the 9,323 it had committed to taking from Greece and Italy. While it pledged to resettle 1,449 refugees from outside the EU, at time of writing it had resettled only 631.

The CJEU issued two rulings against Spain, in December 2016 and January, for unfair mortgage practices, paving the way for consumer lawsuits against banks.

## United Kingdom

More than six months after the government formally triggered the start of Brexit, significant concerns remained about the status of rights and protection for all UK residents derived from EU law after the UK leaves the EU. A draft law to move EU law into domestic law after Brexit raised serious concerns about granting broad powers to the executive to amend laws undermining rights without parliamentary scrutiny, and excluding rights currently protected under the EU Charter of Fundamental Rights.

In June, a fire destroyed an apartment block in London, of which significant parts were social housing, raising troubling questions about the state's fulfilment of its duty to ensure safe and adequate housing. Seventy-one people died, and hundreds were left homeless. The government established a public inquiry into the immediate circumstances surrounding the fire.

Despite allegations of serious abuse in immigration detention centers, the UK persisted in not imposing a maximum time limit for immigration detention, and continued to detain asylum-seeking and migrant children.

By June, the UK had resettled 8,535 Syrians, part of a commitment to resettle 20,000 by 2020. Separately, in April the government reversed a much-criticized decision in February to curtail a program to bring unaccompanied asylum-seeking children in Europe without family ties to the UK.

No new anti-terrorism laws were proposed in response to attacks in London, Manchester, and Northern Ireland that resulted in 36 deaths and more than 250 injuries. Three attacks inspired by or claimed by ISIS caused most of these casualties. The government linked its efforts to press internet companies to remove content deemed extremist to the ISIS-related attacks.

A case at ECtHR on the privacy implications of the UK's mass interception of communications data remained pending at time of writing.

The Iraq Historic Allegations Team, a body set up to investigate alleged abuses of civilians in Iraq by UK armed forces between 2003 and July 2009, was shut down by the government in June 2017. A preliminary examination by the Office of the Prosecutor of the International Criminal Court into alleged war crimes committed by UK personnel in Iraq remained open.

Although access to abortion remained restricted in Northern Ireland, in June, the UK health minister announced that women and girls from the region who travel to access abortion services in England each year would no longer have to pay to do so.

## *Foreign Policy*

While the European Union and its member states continued to pledge their commitment to human rights, foreign policy initiatives were often undermined by other national interests, including security, trade and access to natural resources; a desire to prevent refugees, asylum seekers and other migrants from arriving in Europe; and a failure of the EU's External Action Service to provide principled leadership on behalf of human rights.

In April, EU foreign ministers adopted a strategy on Syria that included justice for war crimes, the release of thousands of prisoners, clarification about enforced disappearances, lifting of sieges, and the end of unlawful attacks and the use of illegal weapons, despite the lack of effective EU action to realize these priorities. Also in April, the EU co-hosted an international donors' conference to secure continued support for Syrian refugees and host countries in the region. The EU and its member states became the biggest donors to the International Impartial Independent Mechanism to investigate atrocity crimes committed in Syria.

EU member states supported the United Nations Security Council's establishment of a mechanism for crimes committed by ISIS in Iraq, without insisting that Iraq become a member of the International Criminal Court (ICC), which would have jurisdiction over crimes committed by all parties.

The EU and its member states continued to denounce Israeli settlement expansion, displacement of Palestinians, and demolitions of their homes and other structures in the Occupied West Bank as violations of international law and obstacles to lasting peace.

In the Arab Gulf states, the EU did not publicly insist on the release of numerous jailed human rights defenders, including EU nationals and a Sakharov prize winner.

The EU often stayed silent about severe human rights violations in countries along the Mediterranean migration route such as Egypt, Libya and Sudan, while engaging these countries in efforts to curb migration flows.

The EU and its member states strengthened diplomatic and business ties with Iran, and remained a staunch supporter of the Iran nuclear agreement. The EU and Iran also began discussions to establish an Iran-EU human rights dialogue. But, by and large the EU and Its member states did not use their political and economic leverage to press for the release of jailed journalists and human rights defenders and for effective human rights reforms in the country.

The EU repeatedly expressed concerns over the arrests of human rights defenders, journalists, and political opposition members in Turkey. While the European Parliament responded to negative developments in Turkey by voting to cut pre-accession funding, there was disagreement among member states on the way forward.

Despite disputes among member states, the EU issued numerous public statements deploring the human rights crackdown in Russia, and exhibiting support for the embattled human rights community.

The EU failed to leverage talks on a new partnership agreement with Azerbaijan to secure concrete rights improvements.

At the UN Human Rights Council, the EU took the lead on the establishment, and later the extension of the mandate, of a Fact-Finding Mission (FFM) to investigate and report on abuses in Burma's Rakhine State. EU foreign ministers condemned atrocity crimes in Rakhine state, urged the Burmese government to cooperate with the FFM, insisted on Rohingya refugees' right to return to their homes, and demanded that those responsible for serious human rights violations be held accountable. However, at time of writing, the EU had not adopted targeted sanctions against Burmese military officials responsible for crimes against humanity. The EU, and its member states, were the biggest humanitarian donors supporting Rohingya refugees in Bangladesh.

In June, the EU high representative issued an unheeded call to China to allow the terminally ill Nobel Prize laureate, Liu Xiaobo, to travel abroad with his wife to receive medical treatment. Several EU member states echoed that call, and Germany used the G20 Summit in Hamburg to press the Chinese president to let Liu Xiaobo go, but China refused. Meanwhile the EU did not seriously challenge the broader crackdown on dissent and freedom of expression in China.

The EU and the European Parliament condemned Cambodia's crackdown on political opposition and media freedom and the decision to dissolve the Cambodian National Rescue Party, and stated that respect for human rights is a "prerequisite for Cambodia to continue to benefit from the EU 's preferential 'Everything but Arms' scheme."

The EU's commissioner for trade raised concerns over the Philippines' anti-drug campaign involving extrajudicial killings of alleged drug users and dealers. The European Parliament adopted a resolution decrying abuses, and called for the release of Senator Leila de Lima, who received a visit from a delegation of MEPs.

The EU and its member states decried the crackdown on human rights in Venezuela, and imposed an embargo on arms and material that can be used for internal repression. EU foreign ministers also adopted a legal framework to impose targeted punitive sanctions against individuals responsible for abuses, but at time of writing had not named any people to its sanctions list. The European Parliament awarded the 2017 Sakharov Prize to the democratic opposition and political prisoners in Venezuela.

# Gambia

The human rights climate in Gambia improved dramatically as the new president, Adama Barrow, and his government took steps to reverse former President Yahya Jammeh's legacy of authoritarian and abusive rule.

After winning the December 2016 election and taking office in January, Barrow moved quickly to distinguish his government from Jammeh's, whose security forces used arbitrary arrests, torture, and extrajudicial killings to suppress dissent and independent media during his 22 years in power. The new government promised to make Gambia the "human rights capital of Africa," released scores of political prisoners, and began to strengthen the judiciary and reform the security services. It also reversed Jammeh's planned withdrawal from the International Criminal Court (ICC).

President Barrow committed to investigate those most responsible for human rights abuses during the Jammeh era. During 2017, the government took meaningful steps to uncover past abuses, including by announcing that it would establish a truth, reconciliation and reparations commission, beginning the trial of nine former intelligence officials for the April 2016 death of an opposition activist, and establishing a commission of inquiry into Jammeh's abuse of public funds.

The Economic Community of West African States (ECOWAS) played a critical role in convincing Jammeh to leave office after he lost the elections, and, at time of writing, maintains a 500-strong peacekeeping force in Gambia.

The international community provided significant financial backing to the Barrow government, including support for the investigation of past human rights abuses and reform of the security forces and judiciary.

## *Political Developments*

Following his defeat in the December 1, 2016 presidential election, Jammeh initially conceded defeat and promised to peacefully cede power to Barrow. Eight days later he rejected the results "in totality" and called for new elections, holding on to power despite widespread condemnation from ECOWAS, the African Union, and the UN. The security forces arrested soldiers perceived as loyal to

Barrow, closed independent radio stations and detained opposition supporters, causing many to flee the country. Barrow himself left Gambia on January 13 and was sworn in as president in Dakar, Senegal, on January 19.

On January 20, after a last attempt at mediation by regional leaders and with ECOWAS troops at the Gambian border, Jammeh agreed to step down and left for Equatorial Guinea the next day. Barrow returned to Gambia on January 26 and was officially inaugurated February 18.

Gambia held peaceful legislative elections on April 6, 2017, with most seats won by the United Democratic Party (UDP). Barrow was a UDP member when he was elected to head the opposition coalition during the 2016 presidential elections.

## Political Prisoners

Following Jammeh's election defeat, and particularly after his departure for exile, Gambian courts and prisons released dozens of people wrongfully imprisoned during Jammeh's time in office. This included opposition leader Ousainou Darboe, serving a three-year prison term after being detained during a 2016 peaceful protest, who was released in December 2016 along with 40 other opposition supporters.

## Judicial and Prison Reform

President Barrow's government took steps to reform the judiciary, which was heavily politicized during Jammeh's time in office, by appointing a slate of new judges, including a respected new supreme court head. Prison conditions, however, remained dire, with prisoners lacking appropriate housing, sanitation, food, and adequate medical care. The government significantly reduced prison overcrowding by pardoning more than 250 prisoners in February and March 2017. On September 21, Barrow signed a UN treaty committing Gambia to abolish the death penalty.

Proposed legislation on the creation of a human rights commission, which was drafted in 2016 with UN assistance, was presented to the National Assembly for adoption in November.

## *Accountability and Truth Telling*

In the first trial for human rights abuses committed during the Jammeh era, a Gambian court in March began the trial of nine officials of the National Intelligence Agency, including its former head, for the April 2016 murder of opposition activist Solo Sandeng.

The minister of justice, Aboubacarr Tambadou, has not provided a timeline for further prosecutions of human rights abusers, citing the need to strengthen the justice sector before further trials. Gambian human rights groups are concerned that the government has not taken steps to preserve documentary and physical evidence of security force abuses. In October 2017, Gambian victims, civil society organizations, and international human rights groups formed a coalition to campaign to bring Jammeh and his accomplices to justice.

The bodies of four people suspected of being forcibly disappeared during the Jammeh era were exhumed in March 2017, including that of Solo Sandeng. The Ministry of the Interior also in February 2017 created a specialized police unit, the Panel on Missing Persons, to investigate enforced disappearances during the Jammeh era.

The Gambian government formally informed the UN secretary-general on February 10 that it was reversing Jammeh's withdrawal from the ICC. Ousmane Sonko, minister of the interior from 2006 until he fled the country in September 2016, is being investigated in Switzerland for alleged crimes against humanity committed during the Jammeh era.

The Ministry of Justice in October drafted legislation establishing a Truth, Reconciliation and Reparations Commission to document violations committed from 1994 to January 2017 and oversee reparations to victims. The government in August conducted an extensive consultation process into the commission's mandate and structure, envisioned to be established by years end.

The government has frozen assets suspected of belonging to Jammeh and has established a commission of inquiry to investigate Jammeh's alleged abuses of public finances. The commission began hearing evidence in public sessions on August 10.

## Security Sector Reform

President Barrow in May 2017 underscored the need for comprehensive security sector reform, describing security institutions as "polluted" because of their ties to Jammeh-era abuses. In February 2017, the National Intelligence Agency, which during the Jammeh era oversaw arbitrary detention and torture, was renamed the State Intelligence Services and its powers of detention eroded. However, while Barrow's government has replaced the heads of the army, police, intelligence and prison services, at time of writing it had not yet begun a wider vetting of these agencies.

At least 12 soldiers arrested between July and November on suspicion of plotting against Barrow's government were held in military detention, without charge, until being brought to court on November 17. Gambia's constitution requires that anyone suspected of a crime be brought to court within 72 hours. The family of one soldier alleged that he was hospitalized after being beaten in detention. At least 10 soldiers implicated in human rights abuses during the Jammeh era are still being held in military detention and have not yet been brought before a judge.

## Freedom of Expression and Assembly

During 2017, Barrow's government largely respected media and opposition freedoms and promised to repeal laws that curtail freedom of expression, including those criminalizing sedition, defamation and the publication of "false news." Many journalists who fled Gambia during the Jammeh era, often after being arbitrarily detained and even tortured, have returned to Banjul. The government announced in November that it will comply with judgments of the ECOWAS Community Court against Gambia regarding the forced disappearance of two journalists and torture of another, including by negotiating compensation payments with victims' families.

The government publicly apologized after a journalist, Kebba Jefang, was beaten by supporters of the ruling coalition after a March 5 press conference.

The Gambian government has not yet amended laws that require a permit for public rallies, an infringement of freedom of assembly. A November 12 peaceful protest against electricity and water shortages, which the government had initially authorized but then prohibited on November 11, was dispersed by riot police.

One person died and at least six were injured when Senegalese peacekeepers fired live ammunition to disperse demonstrators near Jammeh's former residence in Kanilai on June 2. The government promised an investigation but at time of writing no report or findings had been published.

## Sexual Orientation and Gender Identity

President Barrow's government has promised not to prosecute same-sex couples for consensual sexual acts, which sharply contrasted with Jammeh's hate-filled rhetoric toward lesbian, gay, bisexual, and transgender (LGBT) persons. However, the government has not repealed laws that criminalize same-sex conduct, including an October 2014 law that imposes sentences of up to life in prison for "aggravated homosexuality" offenses.

## Key International Actors

West Africa regional body ECOWAS played a critical role in convincing Jammeh to accept the results of the December 2016 election. After high-level ECOWAS delegations on December 13, 2016, and January 13, 2017, failed to convince Jammeh to step down, ECOWAS authorized the deployment of a military force (ECOWAS Mission in The Gambia, ECOMIG).

With military intervention imminent, Guinean President Alpha Condé and Mauritanian President Mohamed Ould Abdel Aziz convinced Jammeh to leave office on January 21, 2017. The same day, hundreds of ECOMIG forces, largely made up of Senegalese troops, entered Gambia to maintain peace and security for a transitional period. ECOMIG's mission was extended for 12 months on June 4.

The European Union, United Kingdom, and United States, which were strong critics of Jammeh's human rights abuses and provided little or no foreign assistance to his government in 2016, committed significant funds to address the dire economic situation inherited by the Barrow government. China also provided significant bilateral assistance. The World Bank in July committed US$56 million in budget support, with the International Monetary Fund in June approving a $16 million loan.

The United Nations, both through the United Nations Development Programme (UNDP) and the Office of the UN High Commissioner for Human Rights (OHCHR), provided financial and technical support to the proposed creation of the Truth, Reconciliation and Reparations Commission. The OHCHR also facilitated visits to Gambia by the Working Group on Enforced or Involuntary Disappearances and the special rapporteur on the promotion of truth, justice, reparation and guarantees of non-recurrence.

# Georgia

The ruling Georgian Dream party rushed in 2017 to approve constitutional reforms to complete Georgia's evolution to a parliamentary system of governance, without securing broader political consensus. Lack of accountability persisted for abuses committed by law enforcement. Georgia maintained punitive criminal drug policies for drug users. Other areas of concern included privacy rights, labor rights, media freedom and the rights of lesbian, gay, bisexual, and transgender (LGBT) people.

## *Constitutional Reform*

Opposition parties, the president, and nongovernmental organizations (NGOs) criticized the new constitution for postponing critical electoral reforms until 2024. The Venice Commission, the Council of Europe's advisory body on legal affairs, positively assessed the reform, but saw postponement of the move to a fully proportional electoral system as "highly regrettable" and "a major obstacle to reaching consensus." It welcomed the ruling party's commitment to amend the new constitution to alleviate the negative effects of postponing implementation of a fully proportional electoral system, including allowing party blocs and a one-time reduction of the election threshold to 3 percent in the 2020 elections.

## *Lack of Accountability for Police, Security Service Abuse*

Georgia does not have an effective independent mechanism for investigating abuse by law enforcement officials. Investigations, if launched, often lead to charges that carry lesser, inappropriate sanctions, like abuse of office, and rarely result in convictions. Authorities often refuse to grant victim status to those who allege abuse, depriving them the opportunity to review investigation files.

Since November 2016, the Georgian Young Lawyers' Association (GYLA), a leading human rights group, received at least 20 allegations of torture and ill-treatment by police, and five by prison staff. According to GYLA, authorities did not effectively investigate the allegations.

At the ombudsman's request, the prosecutor's office launched investigations into 63 cases of alleged torture and ill-treatment since 2014. The investigations did not lead to a single criminal prosecution.

In May, Azerbaijani journalist and political activist Afgan Mukhtarli vanished from central Tbilisi. Less than 24 hours later, he resurfaced in Azerbaijani border police custody, facing fabricated illegal border crossing and other charges. Mukhtarli, who lived in political exile in Georgia, alleged that several people wearing Georgian police uniforms and speaking Georgian stopped him near his house, put a bag over his head, pushed him into a car, beat him, and drove him away. Authorities promptly launched an investigation and denied security service involvement. Later, facing increasing international and domestic criticism, they suspended a number of counterintelligence and border police officials, pending the investigation's outcome.

## *Drug Policy*

Although numbers have decreased in recent years, authorities continued to use harsh drug laws to criminally prosecute people who use drugs, while treatment options remain limited. In response to a 2015 Constitutional Court decision declaring imprisonment for marijuana possession unconstitutional, parliament amended legislation in July 2017 to remove imprisonment as a penalty for cannabis possession of up to 70 grams, but retained it as a felony for larger amounts. Drug-related felonies often result in disproportionately long sentences, prohibitive fines, and deprivation of other rights. Police compelled thousands of people to take drug tests, in some cases by detaining them for up to 12 hours.

In June, police arrested two rappers, Mikheil Mgaloblishvili and Giorgi Keburia, on charges of illegal purchase and possession of large quantities of illicit drugs. Mgaloblishvili and Keburaia claimed that police planted the drugs in retaliation for their video mocking police. After a public outcry, authorities released both on bail and investigated their allegations of police misconduct. Both investigations were pending at time of writing.

## *Right to Privacy*

In March, parliament adopted a new surveillance bill, establishing a new agency within the State Security Services to carry out surveillance operations. In 2016, the Constitutional Court ruled unconstitutional legislation that allowed state security services to have direct, unrestricted access to telecom operators' networks to monitor communications. The court found this system allowed mass collection of personal information in real time without effective oversight, and required independent oversight of mass surveillance. Several nongovernmental organizations, supported by the president and the ombudsman, filed a lawsuit against the new law, claiming that it does not guarantee the right to privacy, as the new agency is not sufficiently independent.

## *Sexual Orientation and Gender Identity*

The new constitution defined marriage "as a union of a woman and a man," entrenching the definition that had existed for years in the civil code. Rights groups feared that using the constitution to reinforce a barrier to same-sex marriage could feed widespread homophobia. The Venice Commission said the clause should not be interpreted "as prohibiting same-sex partnership" and urged Georgia to provide legal recognition of civil unions for same-sex couples.

In May, a small group of gay rights activists and supporters gathered in front of the main government building in Tbilisi to mark International Day Against Homophobia and Transphobia, amid heavy security presence. Police erected fences to block counter demonstrators, assembled activists at two locations beforehand, and escorted them to and from the area on municipal buses.

In August, unidentified persons in Batumi assaulted three transgender women and two activists with the LGBT rights group Equality Movement, inflicting bruises on activists Levan Berianidze and Tornike Kusiani. The assailants shouted homophobic slurs. Police standing nearby did nothing to stop the assailants.

Instead, they pushed Berianidze and Kusiani to the ground, kicked them, and took them to a police station, where police allegedly subjected them to verbal abuse. The next day, a court fined them for disorderly conduct and disobeying police. Rights groups and the ombudsman demanded timely investigation into alleged police ill-treatment and the homophobic nature of the assault. Authorities launched an internal probe, which was pending at time of writing.

In July, the Constitutional Court declared unconstitutional the ban on gay and bisexual men donating blood.

## Labor Rights

Every year dozens of workers die and hundreds suffer injuries as a result of occupational accidents. According to the ombudsman, 270 people died in the past five years because of unsafe working conditions, 18 of them in the first half of 2017. The ombudsman and NGOs criticized the Labour Inspection Department under the Ministry of Labour, Health, and Social Affairs, for having no executive authority to enforce standards, thus failing to introduce effective health and safety measures at the workplace. Investigations into workplace incidents rarely lead to accountability.

## Freedom of Media

The ownership dispute over Georgia's most-watched television broadcaster, Rustavi 2, now in its third year, continued in 2017 and raised concerns over ongoing government interference with media. In March, the Supreme Court ruled that the station's ownership should revert to Kibar Khalvashi, a businessman who owned it from 2004 to 2006, and who alleged he had been improperly forced to sell the station at below market value by then-president Mikheil Saakashvili. The court issued a unanimous decision the same day it examined the case, declining to allow the parties to make oral arguments. The European Court of Human Rights (ECtHR) ordered the Supreme Court decision suspended until further notice and instructed Georgian authorities to refrain from interfering in the station in the interim.

In February, the new leadership of the Public Broadcaster announced it would suspend several political talk shows, citing plans to upgrade the station's equipment and content. In June, it stopped airing two joint programs with Radio Free Europe/Radio Liberty. A regional TV station, Adjara TV, picked up both cancelled shows.

## *Key International Actors*

A June European Parliament resolution condemned the abduction of Afgan Mukhtarli and urged Georgian authorities to ensure an effective investigation into his disappearance in Georgia and "illegal transfer to Azerbaijan," and to bring the perpetrators to justice.

In its January resolution on media freedom in Europe, the Parliamentary Assembly of the Council of Europe highlighted concerns about the Rustavi 2 ownership dispute, and called on Georgia "to continue strengthening the independence and diversity of the public and private media."

In March, following the Supreme Court ruling on Rustavi 2, the Organization for Security and Co-operation in Europe (OSCE) representative on media freedom called on the authorities to ensure media independence and pluralism.

Concluding observations on Georgia by the United Nations Committee on the Rights of the Child, issued in March, noted some progress, including the adoption of the Juvenile Justice Code, but expressed concern regarding, among other things, corporal punishment, sexual exploitation and abuse, and the rights of children with disabilities and of internally displaced children.

During his visit in August, US Vice President Mike Pence highlighted the ties that bring the two countries together, including "freedom, democracy, and the rule of law."

In his September report to the Human Rights Council, the United Nations High Commissioner for Human Rights highlighted Georgia's lack of an independent "framework" to investigate torture and ill-treatment, violations of the right to privacy, and media freedom. Despite lack of access to Georgia's breakaway regions, the commissioner noted that some practices there "appear to amount to discriminatory patterns based on ethnic grounds."

The International Criminal Court (ICC) continued its investigation into war crimes and crimes against humanity allegedly committed in the lead-up to, during, and after the August 2008 war between Russia and Georgia over South Ossetia.

# Guatemala

Guatemala continued to make progress in prosecuting human rights and corruption cases, due in significant part to the collaboration of the Attorney General's Office with the United Nations-backed International Commission against Impunity in Guatemala (CICIG), established in 2007 to investigate organized crime and reinforce local efforts to strengthen the rule of law. At time of writing, CICIG and the Attorney General's Office were prosecuting more than a dozen current and former Congress members, as well as former President Otto Pérez Molina and former Vice-President Roxana Baldetti—who were arrested on corruption charges in 2015.

The work of CICIG produced a strong backlash from public officials in 2017. In August, President Jimmy Morales ordered the expulsion of CICIG Commissioner Iván Velásquez from the country—two days after CICIG and the Attorney General's Office sought to lift the president's immunity to investigate his alleged role in illicit campaign financing.

In September, the Guatemalan Congress voted to reduce the maximum penalty for campaign finance crimes to 10 years and to allow prison sentences of 10 years or less to be commuted to monetary fines—a change that would allow the president and many members of congress to avoid prison sentences if they are convicted of crimes for which they are being investigated. Both efforts provoked strong criticism within Guatemala and abroad and were blocked by Guatemala's Constitutional Court.

## Public Security, Corruption, and Criminal Justice

Violence and extortion by powerful criminal organizations remain serious problems in Guatemala. Gang-related violence is an important factor prompting people, including unaccompanied youth, to leave the country.

Guatemala suffers from high levels of impunity, partly because criminal proceedings against powerful actors often suffer unreasonably long delays due to excessive use of motions by criminal defendants. Those delays are compounded by courts often failing to respect legally mandated timeframes and suspended hear-

HUMAN
RIGHTS
WATCH

# RUNNING OUT THE CLOCK
How Guatemala's Courts Could Doom the Fight against Impunity

ings may take months to reschedule. Intimidation against judges and prosecutors and corruption within the justice system continue to be problems.

Despite these obstacles, investigations by CICIG and the Attorney General's Office have exposed multiple corruption schemes, implicating officials in all three branches of government, and prompting the resignation and arrest of the country's then-president and vice-president in 2015, for their alleged participation in a scheme to defraud the customs authority by collecting bribes instead of customs duties.

Prosecutors also pressed charges against scores of officials—including more than a dozen current and former members of Congress from six different political parties—for hiring people in Congress who never performed any work for the institution (or already received a salary from another employer) and pocketing the wages for those "phantom jobs."

At time of writing, these corruption cases were still in pretrial proceedings.

## *Accountability for Past Human Rights Violations*

In July 2017, an appellate court confirmed the conviction of two former military officers for crimes against humanity in the form of sexual violence and domestic and sexual slavery. The victims were 14 Maya Q'eqchi' women. One of the officers was also found guilty of the homicides of three females, and the other one of the enforced disappearance of the husbands of seven of the female victims. They were sentenced to 120 years and 240 years in prison respectively.

In March 2017, a judge ordered a trial for five former military officers for the enforced disappearance of Marco Antonio Molina Theissen and the rape of his sister in 1981. The suspects include Benedicto Lucas García, former top military officer and brother of former military dictator Romeo Lucas García. At time of writing, a trial date had not been set.

Former Guatemalan dictator Efraín Ríos Montt was ordered to stand trial in April 2017 for his role in the 1982 Dos Erres massacre, in which Guatemalan army special forces killed around 200 civilians. In 2011 and 2012, five former members of the military were convicted for their roles in the massacre. At time of writing, no trial date for Ríos Montt had been set.

In May 2013, Ríos Montt was found guilty of genocide and crimes against humanity for the assassination of over 1,771 Mayan Ixil civilians in 105 massacres, when he was head of state in 1982 and 1983. He was sentenced to 80 years in prison, but 10 days later the Constitutional Court overturned the verdict on procedural grounds. The retrial began in March 2016 but was suspended two months later. In May 2017, the Constitutional Court ruled that because Ríos Montt was mentally unfit for a public trial, proceedings against him would take place behind closed doors, but those against his co-defendant, José Mauricio Rodríguez Sánchez—the former intelligence director—would be public. The trial date for each defendant had yet to be scheduled at time of writing.

## Human Rights Defenders and Journalists

Journalists are targets of harassment and violence. In June 2017, TV journalist Carlos Rodríguez survived a gunshot to the head. In June 2016, radio journalist Álvaro Aceituno was killed, and in March 2015, journalists Danilo López and Federico Salazar were assassinated. In January 2017, investigations by CICIG and the Attorney General's Office implicated Congressman Julio Juárez from government party FCN-Nación in the latter crime. Juárez' political immunity was lifted in November 2017.

## Women's and Girls' Rights

In March 2017, 41 adolescent girls were killed in a fire in the Hogar Seguro government-run shelter. Fifty-six girls had been locked up for the night in a space that could hold only 11, without access to water or a restroom, following a protest against the poor living conditions and treatment received in the shelter—including reports of sexual violence stretching back years. The guards' failure to open the door when fire broke out meant that 41 girls burned to death and 15 were injured. In August 2017, a judge sent the former presidential secretary for social welfare and the former director of the Hogar Seguro to trial for involuntary manslaughter and breach of duty, among other charges. At time of writing, proceedings against five other public officials were ongoing.

Guatemalan law makes it a crime to obtain abortions, except in cases in which the life of the woman might be at risk. Women and girls who terminate pregnancies in any other circumstances face prison sentences of up to three years.

## Sexual Orientation and Gender Identity

In April 2017, lawmakers presented a legislative proposal, supported by over 30,000 signatures, to explicitly prohibit same-sex marriage. The bill also aimed to restrain public schools from teaching students about sexual diversity and "gender ideology".

## Key International Actors

The UN-backed CICIG plays a key role in assisting Guatemala's justice system in prosecuting violent crime. CICIG works with the Attorney General's Office, the police, and other government agencies to investigate, prosecute, and dismantle criminal organizations operating in the country. It is empowered to participate in criminal proceedings as a complementary prosecutor, to provide technical assistance, and to promote legislative reforms.

After President Jimmy Morales ordered the expulsion of CICIG Commissioner Iván Velásquez in August 2017, UN Secretary-General António Guterres reaffirmed the UN's commitment to supporting CICIG and maintaining Velasquez at its helm. The attempt to remove Velásquez was also condemned by the UN High Commissioner for Human Rights, the administration of US President Donald Trump, and members of the US Congress and the European Parliament. The Constitutional Court's annulment of Morales' order ensured that Velásquez would continue to lead CICIG, at least until its mandate expires in September 2019.

The US Congress approved US$655 million in assistance for 2017 for the Plan of the Alliance for Prosperity in the Northern Triangle, a five-year initiative announced in 2014 that intends to reduce incentives to migrate from Guatemala, El Salvador, and Honduras.

The aid aims to reduce violence, strengthen governance, and increase economic opportunity. Fifty percent of it is conditioned on the US Department of State annually certifying progress by the beneficiary countries in strengthening institutions, fighting corruption and impunity, and protecting human rights. In 2017, Guatemala received certification for continued full funding under the plan. The assistance for 2017 included $7 million for CICIG.

# Haiti

Political instability in 2017 hindered the Haitian government's ability to meet the basic needs of its people, resolve long-standing human rights problems, or address continuing humanitarian crises. The United Nations peacekeeping mission operating in Haiti for the past 13 years ended in October. A smaller mission replaced it.

More than 175,000 individuals remained displaced in the aftermath of October 2016's Hurricane Matthew, and many more faced food insecurity due to widespread damage to crops and livestock.

As of September 2017, authorities had failed to assist many of the nearly 38,000 individuals still living in displacement camps since the 2010 earthquake in resettling or returning to their places of origin. The country's most vulnerable communities continue to face environmental risks, such as widespread deforestation, pollution from industry, and limited access to safe water and sanitation. Almost one-third of people live with food insecurity due to the ongoing drought affecting much of the country.

Since its introduction by UN peacekeepers in 2010, cholera has claimed more than 9,500 lives and infected more than 800,000 people. Cholera cases surged in October 2016 in communities most impacted by Hurricane Matthew. There were more than 41,000 suspected cases and 440 deaths in 2016. The number of cases has since declined significantly due to intensified cholera control efforts, including an ambitious campaign in which more than 800,000 people were vaccinated. Only 11,916 suspected cases of cholera and 118 deaths had been reported from January to October 2017.

## *Electoral Crisis*

In October 2015, elections were deferred indefinitely due to allegations of fraud. To thwart a constitutional crisis when President Michel Martelly's term ended in February 2016 without an elected successor, the National Assembly selected Jocelerme Privert as a provisional president until a new one could be elected.

In June 2016, a special commission confirmed fraud and irregularities in the 2015 presidential and run-off parliamentary elections and scheduled a new first-round presidential election to be held in October. The elections were further postponed due to Hurricane Matthew and finally took place in November 2016. Jovenel Moïse won 56 percent of the vote. In response to fraud allegations made by opponents, an electoral tribunal conducted a verification process and confirmed Moïse's victory in January. Moïse was sworn in on February 7, 2017.

## Criminal Justice System

Haiti's prison system remained severely overcrowded, with many inmates living in inhumane conditions. In 2016, the United Nations estimated that nearly all inmates in Haiti's national prison system have access to less than one square meter of space and most are confined for 23 hours a day. According to the UN, overcrowding is largely attributable to high numbers of arbitrary arrests and the country's large number of pretrial detainees. In May 2017, Haitian prisons housed more than 10,000 detainees, 71 percent of whom were awaiting trial.

## Illiteracy and Barriers to Education

Illiteracy is a major problem in Haiti. According to the UN Development Fund, approximately one-half of all Haitians age 15 and older is illiterate. The quality of education is generally low, and 85 percent of schools are run by private entities that charge school fees that can be prohibitively expensive for low income families. More than 500,000 children and youth remain out of primary and secondary school. Hurricane Matthew significantly impacted access to education, damaging 1,633 out of 1,991 schools in the most hard-hit areas.

## Accountability for Past Abuses

The Human Rights Committee has called on Haiti to continue investigations into financial and human rights crimes allegedly committed during former President Jean-Claude Duvalier's tenure as president from 1971-1986. It has called on Haiti to bring to justice all those responsible for serious human rights violations committed during that time. Allegations of violations include arbitrary detentions, torture, disappearances, summary executions, and forced exile.

Duvalier died in 2014, six months after the Port-of-Prince Court of Appeal ruled that the statute of limitations could not be applied to crimes against humanity and ordered that investigations against him should continue. As of November 2017, a re-opened investigation into crimes committed by Duvalier's collaborators remained pending.

## Violence against Women

Gender-based violence is a widespread problem. Haiti does not have specific legislation against domestic violence, sexual harassment, or other forms of violence targeted at women. Rape is only criminalized according to a 2005 ministerial decree.

In March 2016, the UN Committee on the Elimination of Discrimination Against Women called on Haiti to expedite the adoption of a draft law on violence against women. The political crisis prevented progress towards consideration of the bill or a similarly pending criminal code reform that would address gaps in protection. Destruction from Hurricane Matthew has forced many people to migrate to Port-au-Prince, leaving women and children in temporary shelters and camps, where they are more vulnerable to abuse.

## Sexual Orientation and Gender Identity

Lesbian, gay, bisexual, and transgender (LGBT) persons continue to suffer high levels of discrimination. In June 2017, the Haitian Senate introduced a bill regulating conditions for the issuance of the Certificat de Bonne Vie et Mœurs, a document that many employers and universities require. The bill lists homosexuality, alongside child pornography, incest, and commercial sexual exploitation of children, as a reason to deny a citizen a certificate.

In August 2017, the Haitian Senate passed another bill calling for a ban on gay marriage, as well as any public support or advocacy for LGBT rights. The bill states that "the parties, co-parties and accomplices" of a homosexual marriage can be punished by three years in prison and a fine of about US$8,000.

The Senate approved both these bills, which were awaiting a vote in the Chamber of Deputies as of November 2017.

## Children's Domestic Labor

Widespread use of child domestic workers—known as restavèks—continues. Restavèks, most of whom are girls, are sent from low-income households to live with wealthier families in the hope that they will be schooled and cared for in exchange for performing light chores. Though difficult to calculate, some estimates suggest that between 225,000 and 300,000 children work as restavèks. These children are often unpaid, denied education, and physically or sexually abused. Haiti's labor code does not set a minimum age for work in domestic services, though the minimum age for work in industrial, agricultural, and commercial enterprises is 15. In February 2016, the UN Committee on the Rights of the Child called on Haiti to criminalize the practice of placing children in domestic service.

## Deportation and Statelessness for Dominicans of Haitian Descent

At least 200,000 Dominicans of Haitian descent and Haitian migrants working in the Dominican Republic re-entered Haiti between June 2015 and May 2017, after Dominican officials deported more than 27,000 people, along with another 24,254 who were deported without official documentation—in accordance with a controversial 2015 regularization plan for foreigners in the Dominican Republic. Many others left under pressure or threat. Many deportations did not meet international standards and many people have been swept up in arbitrary, summary deportations without any sort of hearing.

Some of the poorest arrivals live in unofficial camps in the Anse a Pitres area, in harsh conditions with little or no access to basic services. Humanitarians relocated 580 families from these camps into housing in April and May 2016.

## Key International Actors

In March, as insisted upon by Haiti, the UN Human Rights Council abruptly discontinued the mandate of the independent expert on the situation of human rights in Haiti, established in 1995.

The UN Stabilization Mission in Haiti (MINUSTAH) has been operating since 2004 and has a mandate to contribute to efforts to improve public security, protect vulnerable groups, and strengthen the country's democratic institutions. Following the end of MINUSTAH's mandate in October 2017, the UN adopted a new, smaller peacekeeping mission, the UN Mission for Justice Support in Haiti (MIN-UJUSTH). This successor mission began on October 16, 2017, and was slated to run for an initial six months.

In October 2016, the UN deputy secretary-general announced the UN's new approach to cholera in Haiti, which included intensifying efforts to treat and eliminate cholera, and establishing a trust fund to raise $400 million to provide "material assistance" to those most affected by the epidemic. In a special session of the UN General Assembly in December 2016, the secretary-general apologized on behalf of the UN's role in the cholera outbreak, calling the provision of material assistance a "concrete expression" of the organization's "regret" for the suffering of many Haitians. As of November 2017, only $13 million had been pledged to the New Approach from 33 member states.

As of November 2017, no consultations had taken place between the UN and victims of cholera on the development of the material assistance package. Meanwhile, the UN has stated a preference for moving forward with community-based assistance projects instead of individual assistance for those whose family members have died from cholera. Victim advocates have criticized this as a departure from the promise to place victims at the center of the development of the new package.

In August 2016, a United States federal court dismissed an appeal filed in 2013 by the Institute for Justice and Democracy in Haiti and the Bureau des Avocats Internationaux on behalf of 5,000 victims of the epidemic. In August 2017, a federal judge dismissed the only remaining class-action suit seeking compensation for Haitians from the UN, affirming the organization's assertion of immunity.

According to figures from the UN Office of Internal Oversight Services, at least 102 allegations of sexual abuse or exploitation have been made against MINUS-TAH personnel since 2007.

The Temporary Protected Status (TPS) for Haitians in the US is set to end in July 2019, and would affect an estimated 60,000 Haitians who were permitted to stay in the US following the 2010 earthquake. After that time, they will lose permission to work legally in the US and face deportation back to Haiti.

# Honduras

Violent crime is rampant in Honduras. Despite a downward trend in recent years, the murder rate remains among the highest in the world. Journalists, environmental activists, and lesbian, gay, bisexual, and transgender (LGBT) individuals are among those most vulnerable to violence. Efforts to reform the institutions responsible for providing public security have made little progress. Marred by corruption and abuse, the judiciary and police remain largely ineffective. Impunity for crime and human rights abuses is the norm.

The Mission to Support the Fight against Corruption and Impunity in Honduras (MACCIH), established in 2016 through an agreement between the government and the Organization of American States (OAS), has successfully promoted the passage of legislation aimed at curbing illegal funding for political campaigns.

## Police Abuse and Corruption

In January 2017, President Juan Orlando Hernández announced that the Special Commission for Police Reform Restructuring will extend its mandate until 2018. As of May, nearly 4,000 of the more than 9,000 police officers evaluated by the commission had been removed, including many for alleged involvement in corruption or criminal acts. However, none of the police officers expelled upon orders of the commission has been convicted to date for alleged involvement in criminal activities including human rights abuses.

## Judicial Independence

Judges face interference from the executive branch and others, including private actors with connections in government. On June 30, the former vice-president of the defunct Judiciary Council, Teodoro Bonilla, was found guilty of influence peddling. Using his authority as a senior official of the judicial oversight body, Bonilla pressured two judges into favoring relatives of his who were charged with illegal weapons possession and money laundering.

## Attacks on Journalists and Freedom of Expression, Association, and Assembly

Twenty-five journalists were murdered between 2014 and 2016 according to the human rights ombudsman, CONADEH, which also revealed in its 2016 report that 91 percent of killings of journalists since 2001 remain unpunished. Most recently, journalist Carlos William Flores was shot and killed by unidentified gunmen on a motorcycle in Cortes, near the Guatemalan border. Flores directed a television program, "Sin Pelos en la Lengua," which was critical of major agribusiness enterprises linked to deforestation in the area.

In February 2017, Congress approved a new penal code making it a criminal offense—punishable by a four to eight-year prison sentence—for individuals or media outlets to engage in the "apology, glorification, [or] justification" of terrorism. The new legislation also defines as terrorist offenses any form of "illegal association" and acts "causing fear, putting in grave risk, or systematically and indiscriminately affecting the fundamental rights of the population or a part of it, the internal security of the State or the economic stability of the country." These vague and unreasonably broad provisions could conceivably be used to bar peaceful protests and association meetings as terrorism.

The Inter-American Commission for Human Rights (IACHR) and the Office of the UN High Commissioner for Human Rights (OHCHR) both expressed concern about the ambiguous formulation of the law and its potential to arbitrarily restrict freedom of expression and of the press.

## Attacks on Lawyers, Human Rights Defenders, and Environmental Activists

Lawyers and human rights defenders suffer threats, attacks, and killings. In 2016, CONADEH registered 16 violent attacks against lawyers, including 13 killings. The IACHR described Honduras in August 2016 as one of the "most hostile and dangerous countries for human rights defenders" in the Americas.

To date, eight men have been charged with the murder in March 2016 of environmental and indigenous rights activist Berta Cáceres, including an army major and the former environment manager of Desarrollo Energético S.A. (DESA), the company behind the Agua Zarca dam project that Cáceres was campaigning against at the time of her death.

The Mechanism for the Protection of Journalists, Human Rights Defenders and Operators of Justice, created in 2015, suffered from a lack of adequate resources and staffing, according to local activists.

## Sexual Orientation and Gender Identity

Homophobic violence is a major problem in Honduras. Several UN agencies working in Honduras have noted that sexual violence against LGBT individuals forces them into "internal displacement" or to flee the country in search of international protection.

In July 2017, David Valle, project coordinator of the Center for LGBTI Cooperation and Development, was stabbed by a stranger in his home in Tegucigalpa. Valle had received repeated threats in the past. He survived the attack.

## Women's Sexual and Reproductive Rights

Under the criminal code, abortion is illegal without any exceptions in Honduras, and women and girls who terminate pregnancies can face prison sentences of up to six years. On May 5, 2017, the National Congress of Honduras voted against modifying the existing criminal code to allow abortion in cases of rape, grave fetal malformations and grave risks to the health of the woman. The law that remains in force also sanctions abortion providers and those who assist with procedures.

## Children's Rights

In July 2017, the Honduran Congress unanimously passed a bill making all child marriage illegal. The new bill replaces legislation that previously allowed for girls to marry at 16 with permission from family. According to UNICEF, a third of Honduran girls are married before 18.

In May 2017, President Juan Orlando Hernández launched an initiative to revise the criminal code to allow children as young 12 to be prosecuted as adults, rather than through the existing juvenile justice system, in violation of international standards.

## *Prison Conditions*

Inhumane conditions, including overcrowding, inadequate nutrition, and poor sanitation, are endemic to Honduran prisons. Designed to hold up to 8,000 inmates, the country's penal institutions held more than 17,500 in 2016, the last year for which reliable figures were available. Prison guards at many facilities have effectively relinquished control over the prison grounds to the inmates.

## *Key International Actors*

At the behest of the Mission to Support the Fight against Corruption and Impunity in Honduras (MACCIH), Congress passed the Law on Clean Politics, which came into force in March 2017. The law created a framework to prevent organized crime from contributing to political campaigns and to hold parties and candidates accountable for financing their campaigns illegally. In July 2017, the MACCIH announced that it would investigate the funding and government concession granted to DESA for the Agua Zarca Dam project for possible corruption and money laundering.

For fiscal year 2017, the US Congress allotted US$95.3 million in bilateral aid to Honduras. Members of Congress reintroduced the "Berta Caceres Human Rights in Honduras Act" (H.R. 1299) on March 2, 2017. The bill would suspend US funding for the country's police and military operations until the Honduras government prosecutes and convicts those who ordered and carried out the murder of Cáceres, in addition to other killings and attacks against other activists; investigate and prosecute members of military and police forces who have allegedly violated human rights; withdraw the military from domestic policing; establish effective protections for human rights defenders; and strengthen rule of law.

In May 2016, after prosecutors filed murder charges against an employee of DESA, the Dutch development bank, FMO, and the Finnish Fund for Industrial Cooperation, Finnfund, announced they would suspend payments of their loans to the Agua Zarca Dam. In June 2017, both funders told the *Guardian* that they would withdraw completely from the Agua Zarca project. The third and largest investor in the project, the Central American Bank of Economic Integration (CABEI), also announced that it would no longer fund the project.

# India

Vigilante violence aimed at religious minorities, marginalized communities, and critics of the government—often carried out by groups claiming to support the ruling Bharatiya Janata Party (BJP)—became an increasing threat in India in 2017. The government failed to promptly or credibly investigate the attacks, while many senior BJP leaders publicly promoted Hindu supremacy and ultra-nationalism, which encouraged further violence. Dissent was labeled anti-national, and activists, journalists, and academics were targeted for their views, chilling free expression. Foreign funding regulations were used to target nongovernmental organizations (NGOs) critical of government actions or policies.

Lack of accountability for past abuses committed by security forces persisted even as there were new allegations of torture and extrajudicial killings, including in the states of Uttar Pradesh, Haryana, Chhattisgarh, and Jammu and Kashmir.

Supreme Court rulings in 2017 strengthened fundamental rights, equal rights for women, and accountability for security forces violations. In August, the court declared the right to individual privacy "intrinsic" and fundamental under the country's constitution, and emphasized the constitution's protections, including free speech, rule of law, and "guarantees against authoritarian behaviour."

That month, the court also ended the practice of "triple *talaq*," allowing Muslim men the right to unilaterally and instantaneously divorce their wives.

In July, the court ordered an investigation into 87 alleged unlawful killings by government forces in Manipur state from 1979 to 2012.

## *Violent Protests, Impunity for Security Forces*

In the first 10 months of 2017, there were 42 reported militant attacks in the state of Jammu and Kashmir in which 184 people were killed, including 44 security force personnel. Several were killed or injured as government forces attempted to contain violent protests.

In May, the army gave a commendation to an officer who used a bystander unlawfully as a "human shield" to evacuate security personnel and election staff from a mob in Jammu and Kashmir's Budgam district.

In a setback for accountability for security force abuses, the Armed Forces Tribunal in July suspended the life sentences of five army personnel who were convicted in 2014 for a 2010 extrajudicial killing of three villagers in the Machil sector in Jammu and Kashmir.

The government failed to review and repeal the abusive Armed Forces Special Powers Act (AFSPA), in force in Jammu and Kashmir and in parts of India's northeastern region, which gives soldiers who commit violations effective immunity from prosecution. At time of writing, the government had yet to comply with a Supreme Court ruling civilian authorities should investigate all allegations of violations by troops.

Several parts of India witnessed violent protests in 2017. In August, at least 38 people were killed during protests in Haryana and Punjab led by supporters of a popular spiritual guru, after he was convicted of raping two female followers. In June, the West Bengal state government's decision to make Bengali language mandatory in all schools triggered protests in Darjeeling district over the long-standing demand for a separate Gorkhaland state, killing eight. Five farmers were fatally shot in June in Madhya Pradesh state, allegedly by police, during protests demanding debt relief and better prices.

In April, 26 paramilitary soldiers from the Central Reserve Paramilitary Force were killed in an ambush by Maoists in Chhattisgarh's Sukma district.

In June, Manjula Shetye died in a Mumbai prison after six prison staff allegedly beat and raped her. The case drew attention to mistreatment in custody, but police reforms remained stalled.

## *Treatment of Dalits, Tribal Groups, and Religious Minorities*

Mob attacks by extremist Hindu groups affiliated with the ruling BJP against minority communities, especially Muslims, continued throughout the year amid rumors that they sold, bought, or killed cows for beef. Instead of taking prompt legal action against the attackers, police frequently filed complaints against the victims under laws banning cow slaughter. As of November, there had been 38 such attacks, and 10 people killed during the year.

In July, even after Prime Minister Narendra Modi finally condemned such violence, an affiliate organization of the BJP, the Rashtriya Swayamsevak Sangh (RSS), announced plans to recruit 5,000 "religious soldiers" to "control cow smuggling and love jihad." So-called love jihad, according to Hindu groups, is a conspiracy among Muslim men to marry Hindu women and convert them to Islam.

Two people died in caste clashes between Dalits and members of an upper caste community in Uttar Pradesh in April and May. Between April and July, 39 people reportedly died from being trapped in toxic sewage lines, revealing how the inhuman practice of "manual scavenging"—disposal of human waste by communities considered low-caste— continues because of the failure to implement laws banning the practice.

In November, following a two-week official visit to India, the United Nations special rapporteur on the human rights to safe drinking water and sanitation, Léo Heller, called on the government to incorporate a human rights perspective into its national programs on water and sanitation, including the flagship Swachh Bharat Mission. As part of his preliminary findings, he said the government's emphasis on constructing toilets to end open defecation should not "involuntarily contribute to violating fundamental rights of others," including specific castes engaged in manual scavenging, or marginalized people, including ethnic minorities and those living in remote rural areas.

Tribal communities remained vulnerable to displacement because of mining, dams, and other large infrastructure projects.

## Freedom of Expression

Authorities in India continued to use sedition and criminal defamation laws against government critics. In June, police in Madhya Pradesh state arrested 15 Muslims on sedition charges for allegedly celebrating Pakistan's victory over India in a cricket match, despite Supreme Court directions that sedition allegations must involve actual violence or incitement to violence. After a public outcry, the police dropped the sedition case but charged them with disturbing communal harmony. Also, in June, the Karnataka state assembly punished two editors for articles that allegedly defamed two of its members.

In March, authorities in Maharashtra state charged a journalist for spying and criminal trespass for reporting that officers improperly used subordinates for personal work, filming on army premises without permission, and using a hidden camera.

Journalists faced increasing pressure to self-censor due to threat of legal action, smear campaigns and threats on social media, and even threats of physical attacks. In September, unidentified gunmen shot dead publisher and editor Gauri Lankesh, a vocal critic of militant Hindu nationalism, outside her home in Bengaluru city.

State governments resorted to blanket internet shutdowns either to prevent violence or social unrest, or to respond to an ongoing law and order problem. By November, they had imposed 60 internet shutdowns, 27 of these in Jammu and Kashmir. In August, the government issued rules to govern temporary shutdown of the internet and telecommunications services in the event of "a public emergency or public safety [issue]." However, the rules do not specify what the government considers to be a public emergency, or a threat.

## Civil Society and Freedom of Association

Activists and human rights defenders faced harassment including under the Foreign Contribution Regulation Act (FCRA), which governs access to foreign funding for NGOs.

In April, the government canceled the FCRA license of the Public Health Foundation of India (PHFI), one of country's largest public health advocacy groups, accusing it of diverting foreign funds to lobby parliamentarians, media, and the government.

Although FCRA may be revoked if the groups violate procedures laid down in the law, the government's political motivations became evident after the Centre for Promotion of Social Concerns (CPSC) challenged the government's decision in the Delhi High Court. A January 2017 government affidavit in response accused CPSC of using foreign funding to share information with United Nations special rapporteurs and foreign embassies, "portraying India's human rights record in negative light." In November 2016, India's National Human Rights Commission questioned the government's decision not to renew the FCRA for CPSC and concluded: "Prima-facie it appears FCRA license non-renewal is neither legal nor objective."

## Women's and Girls' Rights

Multiple high-profile cases of rape across the country during the year once again exposed the failures of the criminal justice system. Nearly five years after the government amended laws and put in place new guidelines and policies aimed at justice for survivors of rape and sexual violence, girls and women continue to face barriers to reporting such crimes, including humiliation at police stations and hospitals; lack of protection; and degrading "two-finger" tests by medical professionals to make characterizations about whether the victim was "habituated to sex."

Rape survivors also lack adequate support services including health care, quality legal assistance, and compensation. While women and girls should have access to safe abortions if they become pregnant after rape, several rape victims have had to petition courts in 2017, including in Delhi and Chandigarh, seeking safe abortion when denied by doctors.

In a setback for women's rights, in July the Supreme Court passed several directives on section 498A of the penal code—the anti-dowry law—to curb what it said was "abuse" of the law, directing police not to make arrests until complaints are verified by family welfare committees, bodies the court recommended be comprised of members of civil society, not police.

## Children's Rights

The murder of a 7-year-old boy in a private school in Haryana state in September highlighted that child sexual abuse is disturbingly common in homes, schools, and residential care facilities.

In a deadly outcome resulting from state corruption and neglect, over 60 children died in a public hospital in Uttar Pradesh state in August when a private supplier cut off the oxygen supply after government officials failed to pay long-pending dues.

Children's education was frequently disrupted in areas facing conflict and violent protests. Clashes between protesters and security forces in Jammu and

HUMAN
RIGHTS
WATCH

"Everyone Blames Me"
Barriers to Justice and Support Services for Sexual Assault Survivors in India

Kashmir state that began in July 2016, continued to simmer throughout 2017, leading to frequent closing of schools and colleges. In May 2017, a student was killed by paramilitary forces inside a government school in Anantnag district during a violent protest.

Schools and colleges also faced disruptions in Darjeeling district in West Bengal state after violent protests and strikes erupted in June over demands for a separate Gorkhaland state.

In October, the Supreme Court ruled that sex with a girl younger than 18 was unlawful, regardless of whether she is married or not, saying the exception for married girls was arbitrary and discriminatory.

## Sexual Orientation and Gender Identity

In August, the Supreme Court, in its ruling that privacy is a fundamental right, gave hope to lesbian, gay, bisexual, and transgender (LGBT) people in India by stating that section 377 of India's penal code, which effectively criminalizes same-sex relationships between consenting adults, had a chilling effect on "the unhindered fulfilment of one's sexual orientation, as an element of privacy and dignity."

In July, a parliamentary committee submitted a report examining the draft Transgender Persons (Protection of Rights) Bill, introduced in parliament in August 2016. The report recommended that the bill adopt a 2014 Supreme Court ruling, guaranteeing transgender people the right to self-determine their gender identity. The committee also recommended the bill recognize transgender people's right to marriage, partnership, divorce, and adoption.

No date has been set for the Supreme Court to hear a set of curative petitions, filed in 2014, challenging the 2013 ruling that reinstated section 377 after a High Court had struck it down in 2009.

## Rights of Persons with Disabilities

In April, India enacted a new mental health law that provides for mental health care and services for everyone and decriminalizes suicide. However, disability rights groups say much remains to be done to ensure that the law is properly enforced.

## Death Penalty

There were no executions in 2017 but nearly 400 prisoners remained on death row. The number of people sentenced to death nearly doubled from 2015 to 2016, from 70 to 136. Most crimes for which capital punishment was handed down included murder, and murder involving sexual violence.

## Foreign Policy

In May, India did not attend China's Belt and Road Initiative (BRI) summit in Beijing, citing sovereignty and procedural issues. The initiative is China's major development campaign to build infrastructure connecting it to countries across Asia and beyond.

Despite concerns over China's influence, India intervened in Nepal to persuade the government to adopt inclusive policies that accommodated minority communities in the southern part of the country.

India continued to abstain, and even played a negative role, in country-specific resolutions at the UN Human Rights Council (UNHRC) and General Assembly.

In September, Prime Minister Modi visited Burma amid a growing humanitarian crisis as more than 600,000 Rohingya Muslims in Rakhine State fled to Bangladesh in the face of ethnic cleansing by Burmese security forces following attacks by a Rohingya militant group. India committed to providing aid for large-scale infrastructure and socio-economic development projects in Rakhine State, but did not call on the government to check abuses by its security forces or to amend its discriminatory citizenship law that effectively keeps the Rohingya stateless. At home, BJP leaders threatened to deport Rohingya refugees, saying they were illegal immigrants.

## Key International Actors

In May, at India's Universal Periodic Review at the UNHRC, countries raised numerous human rights issues and reminded India to fulfil its past commitments to ratify human rights conventions, including the Convention against Torture. Several countries, including the US, Norway, South Korea, Czech Republic, Switzerland, Canada, Germany, and Sweden raised concerns over restrictions on civil society and called on India to ensure freedom of association.

During Modi's visit to the United States in June, a US-India joint statement reiterated cooperation on increasing trade and combating terrorism, including calling upon Pakistan to ensure that its territory is not used to launch terrorist attacks on other countries. There was not even a token mention of pressing human rights issues in India, including limits on free speech and attacks on religious minorities.

China's attempt to extend an unpaved road on the Doklam Plateau in June, part of the disputed territory between China and Bhutan, led to a three-month military standoff between India and China. India, competing with China for influence in the region, saw this as a move by China to extend its control. In August, both sides agreed to de-escalate tensions ahead of September's BRICS (Brazil, Russia, India, China, and South Africa) Summit in Xiamen, China.

# Indonesia

Indonesian President Joko "Jokowi" Widodo's government took small steps in 2017 to protect the rights of some of Indonesia's most vulnerable people. In September, the Attorney General's Office announced that it had rescinded a job notice that not only barred lesbian, gay, bisexual, and transgender (LGBT) applicants, but suggested homosexuality was a "mental illness." The government also quietly reduced its population of Papuan political prisoners from 37 in August 2016 to between one and five in August 2017.

But the Jokowi government has consistently failed to translate the president's rhetorical support for human rights into meaningful policy initiatives. Religious minorities continue to face harassment, intimidation from government authorities, and threats of violence from militant Islamists. Authorities continue to arrest, prosecute, and imprison people under Indonesia's abusive blasphemy law. Papuan and Moluccan political prisoners remain behind bars for nonviolent expression. And Indonesian security forces continue to pay little price for committing abuses, including unlawful killings of Papuans.

The government's acquiescence in 2017 to generals and powerful thugs who seek to stifle discussion of the army-led 1965-66 massacres made Jokowi's promised reconciliation mechanism for those atrocities appear increasingly unlikely. Jokowi and senior police generals also advocated adopting Philippine President Rodrigo Duterte's approach to suspected drug users and dealers: shoot-to-kill orders that have been accompanied in the Philippines by more than 12,000 summary executions of suspects.

Following a 2016 deluge of government-driven anti-LGBT rhetoric, authorities in 2017 continued to target private gatherings and LGBT individuals—a serious threat to privacy and public health initiatives in the country.

## Freedom of Religion

In March, a Jakarta court handed down five-year prison terms for blasphemy to two leaders of the Gerakan Fajar Nusantara (Gafatar) religious community, founder Ahmad Moshaddeq and president Mahful Muis Tumanurung; the group's vice-president, Andry Cahya, received a three-year sentence.

On May 9, a Jakarta court sentenced former Jakarta governor Basuki "Ahok" Pur-nama, a Christian, to a two-year prison sentence for blasphemy against Islam. That conviction followed the success of Islamist militant groups in making his blasphemy prosecution a centerpiece of efforts to defeat him in Jakarta's guber-natorial election in April 2017.

On August 21, Siti Aisyah, the owner of an Islamic school in Mataram, Lombok Is-land, was sentenced to 30 months in prison on blasphemy for "strange teach-ings." In August, municipal governments in Java took steps to effectively shut down two mosques that espoused the ultra-conservative Wahabhi strain of Islam—Al Arqom mosque in Pekalongan and the Ahmad bin Hanbal mosque in Bogor—due to concerns that they could fuel "social turmoil."

In a landmark ruling in November, the Constitutional Court struck down a law prohibiting adherents of native faiths from listing their religion on official identi-fication cards. The ruling will help protect adherents of more than 240 such reli-gions from prosecution under Indonesia's dangerously ambiguous blasphemy law.

In early 2017, the Ministry of Religious Affairs drafted a religious rights bill that would further entrench the blasphemy law as well as government decrees mak-ing it difficult for religious minorities to obtain permits to construct houses of worship. The draft law, still pending at time of writing, would also impose exces-sively narrow criteria for a religion to receive state recognition.

## Freedom of Expression and Association

On April 5, the Constitutional Court ruled that the central government could no longer repeal local Sharia (Islamic law) ordinances adopted by local govern-ments in Indonesia. It deprived the Home Ministry of the power to abolish ordi-nances that threaten universal rights to freedom of expression and association and violate the rights of women and LGBT people.

On July 12, President Jokowi issued a decree amending the law that regulates nongovernmental organizations, enabling the government to fast-track the ban-ning of groups it considers "against Pancasila or promoting communism or advo-cating separatism." Pancasila, or "five principles," is Indonesia's official state philosophy. Days later the government used the decree to ban Hizbut ut-Tahrir, a

SOMETHING TO HIDE?
Indonesia's Restrictions on Media Freedom
and Rights Monitoring in Papua

conservative Islamist group that supports the creation of a Sharia-based Islamic caliphate.

## Women's and Girls' Rights

Indonesia's official Commission on Violence against Women reports that there are hundreds of discriminatory national and local regulations targeting women. They include local laws compelling women and girls to don the jilbab, or head-scarf, in schools, government offices, and public spaces.

Indonesian female domestic workers in the Middle East continue to face abuse by employers, including long working hours, non-payment of salaries, and physical and sexual abuse. Indonesia's ban on women migrating for domestic work in the Middle East, imposed in 2015, has led to an increase in irregular migration of women seeking such work, increasing the risk of abuse and exploitation.

## Papua and West Papua

In March 2017, the Indonesian government loosened its tight controls on visits by foreign observers to Papua, allowing Dainius Pūras, the United Nations special rapporteur on the right to health, to make a rare two-day visit. But foreign journalists seeking to report from Papua continue to face harassment, intimidation, and deportation despite Jokowi's May 2015 commitment to lift the restrictions.

In March, Indonesian authorities deported French journalists Jean Frank Pierre and Basille Marie Longchamp from Timika. On May 11, six Japanese journalists were arrested and deported while filming in Wamena without reporting visas.

In September, a police ethics panel inquiry ruled that four police officers were guilty of "improper conduct" when they deliberately opened fire on Papuan protesters in the Deiyai region on August 1, killing a young man. The panel ruled that their punishment should be limited to demotions and public apologies rather than criminal prosecution.

## *Sexual Orientation and Gender Identity*

On April 30, police raided a private gathering of gay men in Surabaya, arrested and detained 14 men, and subjected them to HIV tests without their consent.

On May 21, police raided the Atlantis club in Jakarta, arrested 141 men, and charged 10 for holding an alleged gay sex party. Officers allegedly paraded the suspects naked in front of media and interrogated them still unclothed, a claim the police deny.

On May 23, Aceh, Indonesia's only province that implements Sharia, flogged two gay men each 83 times. The two, ages 20 and 23, were found in bed together by vigilantes who entered their private accommodation in March. This was the first caning of gay men in Indonesia.

On June 8, government officials in Medan apprehended five "suspected lesbians" and ordered their parents to supervise them—then shared a video of the raid and the names of the five women with reporters.

On September 2, police and local government officials unlawfully raided the homes of 12 women in Bogor, West Java, alleging they were "suspected lesbians." Police recorded the women's personal details and ordered them to relocate from the area within three days.

## *Military Reform and Impunity*

In August, Indonesian police and military personnel forced the cancellation of a public workshop on financial compensation for victims of the state-sanctioned massacres of 1965-66, in which the military and military-backed militias and vigilantes killed an estimated 500,000 to 1 million people. Victims included suspected members of the Communist Party of Indonesia (PKI), ethnic Chinese, trade unionists, teachers, activists, and artists. Security forces "interrogated and intimidated" organizers, claiming they lacked a permit.

On September 16, authorities prevented the Jakarta Legal Aid Institute from hosting a seminar about the massacres. Police and military officers surrounded the compound, preventing participants from entering the building on the pretext that the organizers lacked a permit for the gathering.

## Children's Rights

Thousands of children continue to perform hazardous work on tobacco farms. They are exposed to nicotine, toxic pesticides, and other dangers, which can have lasting impacts on health and development.

The government pledged to eradicate child labor by 2022. In meetings with Human Rights Watch in late 2016 and 2017, government officials said they had begun activities to raise awareness about the health risks to children of tobacco farming. However, authorities have not changed laws or regulations to protect children from hazardous work on tobacco farms.

## Disability Rights

Despite a 1977 government ban on the practice, families and traditional healers continue to shackle people with psychosocial disabilities, sometimes for years at a time. Enforcement of the ban has been long delayed, but in 2017 the government announced steps to improve access to mental health services, a key component of its campaign to eliminate shackling.

Health ministry officials claim that in 2017 the government accredited about 2,000 community health centers, certifying their capacity to respond to 155 conditions including psychosocial disabilities, and oversaw the training of some 25,000 trainers, people who are to in turn train primary health staff on improved responses to and community outreach around a range of health issues, including mental health.

In April, UN Special Rapporteur on Health Dainius Pūras urged the government to scale-up its campaign against shackling and ensure it is not replaced by other forms of restraint that violate human rights.

## Extrajudicial Killings

On July 20, National Police Chief Gen. Tito Karnavian called for combating drugs in Indonesia by shooting drug dealers. The next day, President Jokowi issued an order instructing police who encounter foreign drug dealers who resist arrest to "Gun them down. Give no mercy."

According to a University of Melbourne analysis, Indonesian police killed an estimated 49 suspected drug dealers in the first six months of 2017, a sharp rise from the 14 such killings in all of 2016 and 10 in all of 2015.

## Key International Actors

In September 2017, Indonesia rejected 58 human rights recommendations made by United Nations member states as part of Indonesia's Universal Periodic Review before the UN Human Rights Council. The recommendations targeted issues including threats to the rights of LGBT people, the abusive blasphemy law, and the death penalty. An Indonesian Ministry of Foreign Affairs official responded weakly, describing the recommendations as "hard to accept" given "Indonesian conditions."

On July 14, Indonesia announced that it was renaming a part of the South China Sea the "North Natuna Sea." The newly named body of water encompasses a region of the sea north of Indonesia's Natuna Island that partly falls within the infamous "nine dash line," marking the area of the South China Sea that China claims as its own. The Chinese government has condemned the renaming as "not conducive to the effort of the international standardization of the name of places."

In September, Indonesia took the initiative to provide humanitarian aid to ethnic Rohingya refugees along the Burma-Bangladesh border. Jokowi deplored the violence against the Rohingya and dispatched his foreign minister, Retno Marsudi, to meet with Burmese de facto leader Aung San Suu Kyi to express Indonesia's concern about the Rohingya's plight.

In October, the National Security Archive, a US nongovernmental public transparency organization, released 39 declassified documents from the US Embassy in Jakarta that show US diplomatic personnel were fully aware of army-orchestrated mass killings as they were unfolding in late 1965 and early 1966 in Indonesia. The documents underscore the need for the US and Indonesian governments to fully disclose all related classified materials to provide an accurate historical record of the killings and to provide justice for the crimes.

# Iran

President Hassan Rouhani secured a second four-year term in office in May 2017, in an election marked by debate over the state of civil and political rights in Iran. Executions, especially for drug-related offenses, continued at a high rate. Authorities in the security apparatus and Iran's judiciary continued to target journalists, online media activists, and human rights defenders in an ongoing crackdown that showed blatant disregard for international and domestic legal standards.

## *Death Penalty*

The judiciary continued to execute individuals at a high rate, particularly for drug offenses. Human rights groups reported that Iran executed at least 476 individuals as of November 27, 2017, including five individuals who were sentenced to death for crimes they allegedly committed as children.

On August 13, the Iranian parliament approved a long-awaited amendment to the country's drug law that significantly raises the bar for a mandatory death sentence for drug-related offenses. The Guardian Council, a body of 12 Islamic jurists, approved the amendment in October and the law went to force on November 14. On November 21, Abbas Jafari Dolatabadi, prosecutor of Tehran, stated that 3,300 individuals convicted of drug offenses have filed appeals under the new law.

Under Iran's penal code that went into force in 2013, judges can use their discretion not to sentence children to death. However, a number of individuals who were retried under this provision for crimes they allegedly committed as children have been sentenced to death anyway.

Iranian law considers acts such as "insulting the prophet," apostasy, same-sex relations, adultery, and certain non-violent drug-related offenses as crimes punishable by death. On August 28, Mahmoud Alizadeh Tababi, the lawyer of Mohammadi Ali Taheri, a spiritual teacher and the founder of the spiritual group of Erfan-e-Halghe (Circle of Mysticism), announced that his client was sentenced to death for the second time on a charge of "sowing corruption on earth." Previously, in 2011, a revolutionary court had sentenced Taheri to five years in prison, but in 2015 tried him again for corruption on earth and sentenced him to death. The Supreme Court rejected the ruling in 2016.

## Due Process Rights and Treatment of Prisoners

Iranian courts, and particularly revolutionary courts, regularly fell short of providing fair trials and used confessions obtained under torture as evidence in court. Authorities routinely restrict detainees' access to legal counsel, particularly during the investigation period.

Several individuals charged with national security crimes suffered from a lack of adequate access to medical care in detention. In August, authorities refused to allow the hospitalization of Arash Sadeghi, a 30-year-old human rights defender, who suffers from digestive complications following his long-term hunger strike in February. Zeinab Jalalian, a Kurdish prisoner who is serving a life in prison sentence in Khoy prison in West Azarbaijan province, is reportedly in urgent need of medical treatment for her eye. In 2017, several political prisoners in Rajai Shahr and Evin prisons, including Saeed Shirzad, a child rights activist, embarked on a hunger strike to protest their prison conditions.

## Freedom of Expression, Association, and Assembly

On December 19, 2016, President Rouhani announced the Charter on Citizens' Rights, which largely reiterated rights and protections that already exist in the constitution and domestic law. In the absence of a mechanism for enforcement, however, it is unclear whether the charter will add real protections.

Authorities continued to restrict freedoms of expression, association, and assembly and prosecuted dozens of journalists, online media activists, and trade unionists on charges of "acting against national security," "propaganda against the state," and "assembly and collusion to disrupt national security," merely for exercising their legitimate rights.

On August 29, Ali Mojtahedzadeh, the lawyer of six administrators of channels on the social media application Telegram who were close to reformists arrested before the May presidential elections, told Ilna news agency that Branch 15 of Tehran's revolutionary court had sentenced his clients to three to five years in prison.

In March, the Intelligence Ministry arrested journalists Hengameh Shahidi and Zeinab Karmianian and detained them for nearly five months. They were released on August 29.

Authorities from the Judiciary Intelligence Agency arrested Sasan Aghaei, 34, deputy editor of the reformist daily Etemad, and Yaghma Fashkhami, a journalist for the Didban Iran website, at their offices in Tehran on August 13 and 22, respectively. As of November, authorities have not charged either individual with a recognizable crime.

Authorities sent back to prison several prominent trade unionists whom they had sentenced to prison for peaceful activities but later released. Authorities arrested Ismael Abdi, secretary general of the Teachers' Union, and Mahmoud Beheshti Langeroudi, the union's spokesperson, on June 7 and September 13, respectively, while they were out on furlough. On August 9, Reza Shahabi, a prominent labor activist, returned to prison to serve the remainder of his six-year prison sentence in order to prevent the judiciary from seizing his bail. Shahabi had been released on medical grounds in May 2014.

## Human Rights Defenders and Political Prisoners

Scores of human rights defenders and political activists remain behind bars for their peaceful activism. Atena Daemi, a child rights activist, is still serving a seven-year prison sentence from November 2016 for peaceful activism. Abdolfatah Soltani, a prominent human rights lawyer who has been in prison since 2011, is serving a 13-year prison sentence for his human rights work, including co-founding the Defenders of Human Rights Center. Zia Nabavi, a student activist, is serving a 10-year prison sentence in Karoon prison in the city of Ahvaz.

On March 16, Narges Mohammadi, a prominent human rights defender who was arrested in June 2015 to serve the remainder of her six-year prison sentence, began serving a new sentence of 10 years in prison on charges including "membership in the banned campaign of Step by Step to Stop the Death Penalty."

Over the past three years, authorities have prosecuted, on charges of cooperating with foreign states, several Iranian dual nationals and foreign nationals who have traveled to Iran. These include Siamak Namazi, a businessman, and his 81-

HUMAN
RIGHTS
WATCH

"It's a Men's Club"
Discrimination Against Women in Iran's Job Market

year-old father Baquer, as well as Nazanin Zaghari Radcliffe, Nizar Zakka, and Xiyue Wang.

Former presidential election candidates Mehdi Karroubi and Mir Hossein Mousavi, as well as Mousavi's wife Zahra Rahnavard, who is a scholar, have remained under house arrest without charge or trial since February 2011. Their families have reported that the health of all three has deteriorated and that they have been denied access to adequate healthcare.

## Women's Rights

Iranian women face discrimination in personal status matters related to marriage, divorce, inheritance, and child custody. A virgin woman needs her male guardian's approval for marriage regardless of her age, and Iranian women cannot pass on their nationality to their foreign-born spouses or their children. A married woman may not obtain a passport or travel outside the country without the written permission of her husband. Under the civil code, a husband is accorded the right to choose the place of living and can prevent his wife from having certain occupations if he deems them against "family values."

In 2017, Human Rights Watch documented how in this discriminatory environment, and in the face of government policies that do not afford adequate protection against discrimination in the public and private sectors, women are marginalized in the economy, constituting only 16 percent of the workforce. The rate of unemployment for women is 20 percent, twice that of men.

During his reelection campaign, President Rouhani criticized women's marginalization in the economy and vowed to increase their presence in decision-making roles in his government. He did not, however, select a female minister despite expectations that he would do so by many, including members of parliament.

On June 9, Iran reportedly allowed 300 women to attend a volleyball game between Iran and Belgium national teams, but only 30 of those tickets were sold to the public. Authorities, prevent girls and women from attending certain sporting events, including men's soccer.

## Treatment of Minorities, Migrants, Rights of People with Disabilities

Iranian law denies freedom of religion to Baha'is and discriminates against them. At least 92 Baha'is were held in Iran's prisons as of November 2017. On September 18 and October 31, Mahvash Sabet, Fariba Kamal Abadi, and Behrouz Kamali, three of the seven members of the former leadership group of the Baha'is in Iran, were released from prison after serving their 10-year prison sentence. The government also discriminates against other religious minorities, including Sunni Muslims, and restricts cultural as well as political activities among the country's Azeri, Kurdish, Arab, and Baluch ethnic minorities.

On August 2, Molavi Abdolhamid, a prominent Sunni leader, wrote a letter to Supreme Leader Ayatollah Khamenei asking him to remove restrictions on the appointment and employment of Sunnis in Sunni-majority areas and to remove restrictions on Friday prayer assemblies in major cities in Iran. Ayatollah Khamenei reportedly responded that Iranian law and Sharia oblige officials not to discriminate between Iranians based on religion or ethnicity according to law and Sharia.

On October 8, the court of administrative justice suspended Sepanta Niknam, a Zoroastrian member of the Yazd City Council, because of his religion.

In 2015, Iran reportedly allowed all Afghan children, including undocumented ones, to enroll in schools after Ayatollah Khamenei issued a ruling emphasizing that "no Afghan child, even the undocumented ones, should be left out of school." On September 14, 2017, Seyed Mohammad Bathaie, Iran's Minister of Education, announced that 370,000 Afghans and other foreign students have enrolled in schools in Iran.

In 2017, Human Rights Watch documented that Iran's Islamic Revolutionary Guards Corps (IRGC) had recruited Afghan children residing in Iran to fight as combatants in Syria in its Fatemiyoun division.

Under Iranian law, same-sex conduct is punishable by flogging and, in the case of two men, can be punished by the death penalty. Although Iran permits and subsidizes sex reassignment surgery for transgender people, no law prohibits discrimination against them. On September 14, Nasser Atabati, prosecutor of

Ardebil province, told media that six people have been arrested in Ardebil for promoting homosexuality on the Telegram messaging platform.

In March 2017, before the Committee on the Rights of the Child, Iran denied allegations that coercive treatment and electric shocks were being used against lesbian, gay, bisexual, and transgender (LGBT) people.

On April 12, in its concluding observation, the Committee on the Rights of Persons with Disabilities expressed concerns over violation of disability rights by the Iranian government in many areas including preventing and punishing violence and abuse, access to justice, and denial of legal capacity. The committee also recommended that Iran brings its legislation in line with the Convention on the Rights of Persons with Disabilities, which Iran ratified in 2009. At time of writing, a new Bill on Protecting Rights of Persons with Disabilities was under consideration in a specially designated commission in the parliament.

## *Key International Actors*

Iran continues to provide the Syrian government with military assistance and plays an influential role alongside Russia and Turkey in the Syria negotiations currently taking place in Astana, Kazakhstan. Human Rights Watch has documented a pattern of deliberate and indiscriminate attacks on civilians, as well as torture by the Syrian government.

On October 13, US President Donald Trump announced he was not certifying Iran's compliance with the nuclear agreement signed in 2015 between Iran and the five permanent members of the UN Security Council, plus Germany and the European Union. Instead, Trump asked Congress to re-evaluate conditions for re-imposing sanctions on Iran. The International Atomic Energy Agency (IAEA) has maintained that Iran is complying with the terms of the agreement.

HUMAN
RIGHTS
WATCH

# FLAWED JUSTICE
Accountability for ISIS Crimes in Iraq

# Iraq

Multinational military operations in Iraq against the extremist group Islamic State (also known as ISIS) intensified over 2017, including major operations to retake Mosul and Telafar. Iraqi armed forces, including army, federal police, Popular Mobilization Forces, and Kurdistan Regional Government (KRG) forces, were supported by Iran and the 73-nation Global Coalition against ISIS, led by the United States.

Fighting displaced at least 3.2 million Iraqis, over 1 million of them to the Kurdistan Region of Iraq (KRI). ISIS used civilians as human shields, carried out chemical attacks and targeted fleeing civilians, before being defeated in most of Iraq. In their battle against ISIS, Iraqi forces summarily executed, tortured, and forcibly disappeared hundreds of ISIS suspects. Communities in former ISIS-controlled territory took actions of collective punishment against families of suspected ISIS members, displacing them and destroying their property with the complicity of government forces.

Since 2014, mostly Shia armed groups under the authority of a government body known as the Popular Mobilization Forces (the PMF or Hashd al-Sha'abi), have played a significant military and security role in the battle against ISIS. Over 2017, authorities integrated more armed groups made up predominately of other religious groups into the PMF, some with very little formal military training.

On September 25, despite the opposition of the federal Iraqi government and most of the international community, the KRG held a non-binding referendum on independence in the Kurdistan Region of Iraq as well as in disputed territories under KRG de facto control. After the referendum, which passed, the federal Iraqi government issued a set of demands including that Kurdish authorities nullify the results of the referendum and withdraw from Kirkuk, a major city in the disputed territories 85 kilometers south of Erbil, and surrounding military and oil installations. On October 16, a range of Iraqi forces retook parts of the disputed territories some of which had been under de facto KRG control since 2003. In the context of the operations, thousands of Kurdish families fled their homes as Iraqi forces arrived, and some Iraqi forces looted and burned homes in the town of Tuz Khurmatu.

## ISIS Abuses

Since 2014, ISIS forces have carried out the most serious human rights abuses, war crimes and crimes against humanity. The United Nations-mandated Independent International Commission of Inquiry (COI) on abuses in the conflict in neighboring Syria, where ISIS is also active, found that ISIS forces were responsible for acts of genocide. ISIS's struggle for power since 2011 has been marked by hundreds of suicide and car bombing attacks, killing thousands of civilians, including through the use of child soldiers. In territory under its control in 2017, fighters continued to resort to ill-treatment, including sexual violence, as well as public beheadings and other grotesque killings and acts of torture as a method of governing through fear.

ISIS's Diwan al-Hisba (Moral Policing Administration) subjected the mostly Sunni populated areas under its control to severe restrictions and punishments, including executions of allegedly gay men, stonings of individuals for alleged adultery, and prohibition on the use of cell phones and cigarettes. It imposed severe restrictions on women and girls' clothing and freedom of movement. Sunni women and girls have said that they were only allowed to leave their houses dressed in full face veil (*niqab*) and accompanied by a close male relative. These rules, enforced by beating or fines on male family members or both, isolated women from family, friends, and public life.

ISIS also taxed families living under its control, confiscated property of those that fled, raided banks and stole money, gold and other valuables. ISIS destroyed mosques, shrines, churches, statues, tombs, and other religious and archaeological sites throughout areas under its control, and looted and sold valuable cultural artifacts to help finance its operations. In June 2017, its fighters destroyed the Grand al-Nuri Mosque in Mosul, where its leader Abu Bakr al-Baghdadi declared the caliphate three years earlier. These acts represent war crimes.

In its battles against anti-ISIS forces, the group also has carried out chemical attacks and launched ground-fired munitions into civilian populated areas. Fighters have hidden themselves among civilians in protected objects like hospitals, using civilians as human shields during operations, and firing on civilians trying to flee. In the midst of its battles, ISIS has also carried out mass executions of civilians under its control, leaving many mass graves in its wake.

## *Treatment of ISIS Suspects*

Iraqi and KRG forces are screening people leaving ISIS-controlled areas in order to arrest ISIS suspects. The screening process relies on official wanted lists or identification by community members. As part of this process, KRG forces have stopped hundreds of families fleeing ISIS-controlled areas, for weeks or even months at a time, citing security concerns about ISIS fighters present among them or their affiliation with ISIS. In many cases they stopped families at checkpoints on the frontlines of fighting, preventing their access to more secure areas and to humanitarian assistance.

The judicial systems of both the federal Iraqi and the KRG authorities are prosecuting thousands of ISIS suspects under their respective counterterrorism legislation, primarily for membership in or providing support to ISIS, as well as for killings and other acts enshrined in counterterrorism legislation. Authorities have made no efforts to solicit victims' or witnesses' participation in the trials.

Authorities are detaining ISIS suspects in overcrowded and in some cases inhumane conditions. They are failing to segregate some detained children from adult detainees. Authorities are also systematically violating the due process rights of ISIS suspects, such as guarantees in Iraqi law for detainees to see a judge within 24 hours, to have access to a lawyer throughout interrogations, and to have families notified of their detention and to able to communicate with them. Numerous detainees have alleged that authorities forced them to confess by using torture.

ISIS convicts may be entitled to release in federal Iraq under the General Amnesty Law passed in August 2016 (no.27/2016). The law offers amnesty to those who can demonstrate they joined ISIS or another extremist group against their will and did not commit any serious offense before August 2016. According to the Justice Ministry, by February 2017 authorities had released 756 convicts under the Amnesty Law, but it is unclear whether judges are consistently applying this law and the percentage of those convicted for ISIS affiliation among the released. The KRG has not passed any amnesty law, and a KRG spokesperson said none was under consideration.

## Collective Punishment of Families of Suspected ISIS-Affiliates

Local officials have forcibly displaced hundreds of families of suspected ISIS-members in Anbar, Babil, Diyala, Salah al-Din, and Nineveh governorates. Iraqi forces have done little to stop these abuses, and in some instances participated in them, moving the families to open-air prison camps. In May, local communities in Nineveh carried out grenade and other attacks on ISIS families, and issued threatening letters and demands to deny the families humanitarian assistance. As a result, many of these families were forced to move to nearby camps housing families displaced by the fighting in Mosul. At time of writing, Iraqi authorities were detaining around 1,400 foreign women and children who had been in Iraqi custody since they surrendered with ISIS fighters in late August.

## Abuses by Anti-ISIS Forces

### Ill-Treatment and Executions

The battle against ISIS has afforded Iraqi government and KRG forces the latitude to carry out serious abuses under the guise of fighting terror. For example, during the operations to retake Mosul, Iraqi forces tortured and executed those captured in and around the battlefield with complete impunity, sometimes even after posting photos and videos of the abuses on social media sites.

### Indiscriminate Bombardment

Iraqi and US-led coalition forces bombarded civilian objects including homes and hospitals in ISIS-held areas. They have fired inherently imprecise ground-fired munitions, including mortars, grad rockets and Improvised Rocket-Assisted Munitions (IRAM), into densely populated civilian areas. In addition, aircraft have dropped explosive weapons with wide-area effects on these areas. By the coalition's own admission, its aircraft have unintentionally killed at least 624 civilians.

Prime Minister al-Abadi said that between 970 and 1,260 civilians were killed during the battle to capture Mosul but provided no details on how those numbers were reached. It is likely that Iraqi and coalition forces have killed many thousands of civilians in the course of their military operations against ISIS.

## *Death Penalty*

Iraq has long had one of the highest rates of executions in the world, ranked number four after China, Iran, and Saudi Arabia. Iraqi law permits the death penalty against adults for a range of crimes, including offenses under the counterterrorism law. In the Kurdistan Region of Iraq, the KRG implemented a de facto moratorium on the death penalty in 2008, banning it "except in very few cases which were considered essential," per a KRG spokesperson.

Currently, federal Iraqi authorities are conducting executions without publicizing any official numbers or sharing this information with international actors. Human Rights Watch is aware of at least 78 executions of individuals convicted of ISIS affiliation. In August, the Higher Judicial Council stated that the Nineveh counterterrorism court had sentenced four ISIS suspects to death, three of whom had been ISIS police and one responsible for recruiting fighters.

A judge at the court told Human Rights Watch that the court had issued many more death sentences but could not provide numbers. The expedited nature of the ISIS trials in Nineveh's court, with the completion in six months of 5,000 conviction hearings now in the sentencing phase, raises the concern that courts will issue many death sentences despite serious due process shortcomings.

The Iraqi criminal code prohibits the use of the death penalty against children. However, Prime Minister al-Abadi stated in September that judges are deciding whether to sentence to death a German girl for communicating with ISIS, a crime under the counterterrorism law.

## *Women's Rights*

Women have few legal protections to shield them from domestic violence. Iraq's criminal code includes provisions criminalizing physical assault, but lacks any explicit mention of domestic violence. While sexual assault is criminalized, article 398 provides that such charges be dropped if the assailant marries the victim. A 2012 Ministry of Planning study found that at least 36 percent of married women reported experiencing some form of psychological abuse from their husbands, 23 percent reported verbal abuse, 6 percent reported physical violence, and 9 percent reported sexual violence. While more recent national studies are not available, women's rights organizations continue to report a high rate of domestic violence.

In 2015, Iraqi officials published a deeply flawed draft domestic violence law, but parliament has yet to pass it or to consider a range of amendments for which women's rights advocates have been petitioning.

Iraq's criminal code does not prohibit same-sex intimacy, although article 394 makes it illegal to engage in extra-marital sexual relations.

## *Key International Actors*

The US-led Global Coalition against ISIS, including Australia, Belgium, Canada, Denmark, France, the Netherlands, and the United Kingdom, as well as Iranian and Turkish forces, have supported Iraqi and Kurdish troops in the war against ISIS since 2014.

The US-led coalition carried out over 24,160 airstrikes on ISIS targets since August 2014. The United States, with 5,000 troops in Iraq, was the largest provider of equipment to the Iraqi military, and Germany the largest provider to the KRG's Peshmerga forces. In light of the rampant impunity of Iraqi security forces, Human Rights Watch called on foreign governments to end military assistance to units involved in laws of war violations and explain publicly any suspension of military assistance, including the grounds for doing so.

# Israel and Palestine

The Israeli government continued to enforce severe and discriminatory restrictions on Palestinians' human rights; restrict the movement of people and goods into and out of the Gaza Strip; and facilitate the unlawful transfer of Israeli citizens to settlements in the occupied West Bank. Punitive measures taken by the Palestinian Authority (PA) exacerbated the humanitarian crisis in Gaza caused by the closure enforced by Israel. The PA in the West Bank and Hamas in Gaza escalated crackdowns on dissent, arbitrarily arresting critics, and abusing those in their custody.

In February, the Knesset, Israel's parliament, passed the Regularization Law, which allows Israel to retroactively expropriate private Palestinian land on which settlements have been built, though it agreed in March to suspend implementation pending a ruling by the High Court of Justice on its legality. Between July 2016 and June 2017, Israeli authorities authorized construction work on more than 2,000 new housing units for settlers in the West Bank, excluding East Jerusalem.

Israel operates a two-tiered system in the West Bank that provides preferential treatment to Israeli settlers while imposing harsh conditions on Palestinians. While settlements expanded in 2017, Israeli authorities destroyed 381 homes and other property, forcibly displacing 588 people as of November 6, in the West Bank, including East Jerusalem, as part of discriminatory practices that reject almost all building permit applications submitted by Palestinians.

Israel continued to maintain its decade-long effective closure of Gaza, exacerbated by Egypt's keeping its own border with Gaza largely sealed, and to impose restrictions that limit supply of electricity and water, restrict access to medical care and educational and economic opportunity, and perpetuate poverty. Approximately 70 percent of Gaza's 1.9 million people rely on humanitarian assistance.

Periodic shutdowns of Gaza's only power plant, a result of a dispute between Fatah and Hamas over who should pay for fuel needed to operate the plant, and the decision by the Israeli government in June to accede to a PA request to cut the electricity it sells to the PA for use in to Gaza, significantly reduced electricity supply in Gaza, leaving households for stretches with four hours or less of electricity a day. Power outages jeopardize water supply, interfere with sewage treatment, and cripple hospital operations.

Tensions around the Al-Aqsa/Temple Mount compound in July-August 2017 triggered an escalation in violence. Israeli security forces used lethal force against demonstrators and against suspected attackers in the West Bank and at the Gaza border. Palestinian assailants, most of them apparently acting without the formal sponsorship of any armed group, carried out stabbings and occasional shootings against Israelis.

Between January 1 and November 6, 2017, Israeli security forces killed 62 Palestinians, including 14 children, and injured at least 3,494 Palestinians in the West Bank, Gaza and Israel, including protesters, suspected assailants or members of armed groups, and bystanders. Palestinians killed at least 15 Israelis during this same time, including 10 security officers, and injured 129 in conflict-related incidents in the West Bank and Israel.

In April and May, hundreds of Palestinian prisoners spent 40 days on hunger strike seeking better conditions. As of November 1, Israeli authorities incarcerated 6,154 inmates on what they consider security grounds, the overwhelming majority Palestinian, including 3,454 convicted prisoners, 2,247 pretrial detainees and 453 administrative detainees held without charge or trial, according to the Israel Prison Service.

The PA and Hamas arrested activists who criticized their leaders, security forces, or policies, and mistreated and tortured some in their custody. The Independent Commission for Human Rights in Palestine (ICHR), a statutory commission charged with monitoring human rights compliance by the Palestinian authorities, received 205 complaints of torture and ill-treatment by PA security forces and 193 such complaints against Hamas security forces as of October 31. Hamas authorities executed six people during this same period following trials that lacked appropriate due process protections.

## *Gaza Strip*

### Closure

Israel's near-total closure of the Gaza Strip, particularly restrictions on movement of people and on outgoing goods, together with Egypt keeping its border with Gaza mostly closed, continued to have severe consequences for the civilian population.

Travel through the Ere Crossing, Gaza's passenger crossing to Israel, the West Bank, and the outside world, is limited to what the Israeli military calls "exceptional humanitarian cases," meaning mostly medical patients, their companions, and prominent businesspersons.

In the first 10 months of 2017, an average of about 230 Palestinians exited Erez each day, compared to the average of more than 24,000 Palestinians who crossed each day in September 2000, just before the second "Intifada" or Palestinian uprising, began. Outgoing goods in the same period averaged 207 truckloads per month, mostly produce to be sold in the West Bank and Israel, just 19 percent of the average 1,064 truckloads per month that exited prior to the June 2007 tightening of the closure.

Israeli restrictions on the delivery of construction materials to Gaza and a lack of funding have impeded reconstruction of the 17,800 housing units severely damaged or destroyed during Israel's 2014 military operation in Gaza. About 29,000 people who lost their homes remain displaced. The Israeli government sought to justify the restrictions by saying that construction materials can be used for military purposes, including fortifying tunnels; it allowed only limited quantities to enter, under the supervision of international organizations.

Measures taken by the PA to pressure Hamas further exacerbated the impact of the closure. Its decision in January to stop buying fuel from Israel that it had been supplying to Hamas authorities and its request in May for Israel to cut the electricity the Israeli government sells to the PA for use in Gaza significantly reduced already limited electricity supply, imperiling critical health, water, and sanitation services.

Patients in Gaza seeking treatment outside Gaza faced lengthening delays in obtaining approvals from the PA. While the PA approved 99 percent of applications

**HUMAN RIGHTS WATCH**

# UNWILLING OR UNABLE
Israeli Restrictions on Access to and from Gaza
for Human Rights Workers

within seven days of submission between January and May, that number dropped to 36 percent between June and August and 32 percent in September, according to the World Health Organization (WHO). In addition, in September, Israel authorities denied or delayed permits with no response by the time of the appointment to 45 percent of patients seeking treatment outside Gaza. As of August, 40 percent of medications on the "essential drug list" were are at zero stock in Gaza, according to the WHO.

Egypt also blocked all regular movement of goods at the crossing with Gaza that it controls, with narrow exceptions mostly for medical patients, those holding foreign passports, residencies or visas, including students, and pilgrims to Mecca. Between January and October, an average of about 2,766 persons monthly crossed through Rafah in both directions, compared with an average of 40,000 per month in the first half of 2013, prior to the overthrow of Egyptian President Mohamed Morsy.

## Israel

As of November 6, lethal force by Israeli forces resulted in the killing of 17 and injuring of at least 215 Palestinians in Gaza, the UN Office for the Coordination of Humanitarian Affairs (OCHA) reported.

The Israeli authorities have declared an area inside Gaza near the border with Israel to be a "no-go" zone, justifying it as a means to prevent cross-border attacks. Israeli soldiers fire at people who enter that zone and at fishermen who venture beyond six nautical miles from the shore—the area to which Israel restricts Gaza fishing boats. Israel temporarily expanded the fishing zone to nine miles between May and June and again between October and December. Israel says it restricts access to the sea to prevent the smuggling of weapons into Gaza.

## Hamas and Palestinian Armed Groups

In 2017, Palestinian armed groups launched 10 rockets into Israel from Gaza as of October 31, causing no casualties but generating fear and disruption in affected cities and towns. These rockets cannot be accurately aimed at military objectives and amount to indiscriminate or deliberate attacks on civilians when directed at Israeli population centers. Hamas, which has internal control over

Gaza, is responsible for policing the border and the territory it controls and acting to ensure that unlawful attacks do not take place.

Hamas authorities arrested scores of protesters following demonstrations in January related to the electricity crisis in Gaza as well as activists, journalists, and critics throughout the year.

In addition, Gaza's civilian authorities executed three men in April convicted of collaboration with Israel and three men in May convicted of killing a Hamas leader after trials rife with due process violations, including reliance on confessions in a system where coercion and torture are prevalent.

In Gaza, where laws differ somewhat from those in the West Bank, having "unnatural intercourse" of a sexual nature, understood to include same-sex relationships, is a crime punishable by up to 10 years in prison.

## West Bank

### Israel

In the West Bank, as of November 6, Israeli security forces fatally shot 42 Palestinians and wounded at least 3,279, including passersby, demonstrators, and those suspected of attacking Israelis. In many cases, video footage and witness accounts strongly suggest that forces used excessive force. In this same period, attacks by settlers killed three Palestinians, injured 49, and damaged property in 106 incidents, according to OCHA.

In February, an Israeli military court sentenced to 18 months in prison soldier Elor Azaria, who had been convicted of manslaughter for the 2016 killing at close range of a Palestinian who lay immobilized on the ground after stabbing another Israeli soldier. The IDF chief of staff reduced the sentence to 14 months in September.

The conviction marked a rare exception, as Israeli authorities continued in 2017 to fail to hold accountable security forces and settlers who attack Palestinians and destroy or damage Palestinian mosques, homes, schools, olive trees, cars, and other property. Between 2013 and 2016, police closed 91.8 percent of cases of reported settler violence against Palestinian persons and property tracked by the Israeli human rights group Yesh Din without indicting anyone.

## Settlements, Discriminatory Policies, Home Demolitions

Israel continued to provide security, administrative services, housing, education, and medical care for about 607,000 settlers residing in unlawful settlements in the West Bank, including East Jerusalem. Israel's building of 2,000 new settlement housing units in the period between July 2016 and June 2017 marked an 18 percent decrease over the same period in 2015-2016, but Israeli authorities approved plans for 85 percent more housing units in the first half of 2017 than all of 2016, according to the Israeli group Peace Now. International humanitarian law bars an occupying power's transfer of its civilians to occupied territory.

Building permits are difficult, if not impossible, for Palestinians to obtain in East Jerusalem or in the 60 percent of the West Bank under exclusive Israeli control (Area C). This has driven Palestinians to construct housing and business structures that are at constant risk of demolition or confiscation by Israel on the grounds of being unauthorized. Palestinians in these areas have access to water, electricity, schools, and other state services that are either far more limited or costlier than the same services that the state makes available to Jewish settlers there.

Of the 381 Palestinian homes and other property demolished in the West Bank (including East Jerusalem) in 2017 as of November 6, displacing 588 people, Israeli authorities sought to justify most for failure to have a building permit. Israel also destroyed the homes of families in retaliation for attacks on Israelis allegedly carried out by a family member, a violation of the international humanitarian law prohibition on collective punishment.

## Freedom of Movement

Israel maintained onerous restrictions on the movement of Palestinians in the West Bank, including checkpoints and the separation barrier, a combination of wall and fence in the West Bank that Israel said it built for security reasons. Israeli-imposed restrictions designed to keep Palestinians far from settlements forced them to take time-consuming detours and restricted their access to agricultural land.

Israel continued construction of the separation barrier, 85 percent of which falls within the West Bank rather than along the Green Line separating Israeli from

Palestinian territory, cutting off Palestinians from their agricultural lands and isolating 11,000 Palestinians on the western side of the barrier who are not allowed to travel to Israel and must cross the barrier to access their own property as well as services in the West Bank.

## Arbitrary Detention and Detention of Children

Israeli military authorities detained Palestinian protesters, including those who advocated nonviolent protest against Israeli settlements and the route of the separation barrier. Israeli authorities try the majority of Palestinian children incarcerated in the occupied territory in military courts, which have a near-100 percent conviction rate.

Israeli security forces arrested Palestinian children suspected of criminal offenses, usually stone-throwing, often using unnecessary force, questioned them without a family member present, and made them sign confessions in Hebrew, which most did not understand. The Israeli military detained Palestinian children separately from adults during remand hearings and military court trials, but often detained children with adults immediately after arrest. As of June 30, Israeli authorities held 315 Palestinian children in military detention.

As of October 2017, Israel held 453 Palestinian administrative detainees without charge or trial, based on secret evidence, many for prolonged periods. Israel jails many Palestinian detainees inside Israel, violating international humanitarian law requiring that they not be transferred outside the occupied territory and restricting the ability of family members to visit them.

## Palestinian Authority

PA security services arrested dozens of journalists, activists and opposition members. In September, the PA detained for seven days human rights defender Issa Amro over a Facebook post. Amro also faces charges in Israeli military court for his role in a protest. In June, the PA issued a new cybercrime law, granting the government vast authority to control online activity and blocked access in the West Bank to at least 29 news websites affiliated with Hamas and Fatah factions opposed to Palestinian President Mahmoud Abbas. Complaints persisted of torture and ill-treatment carried out in the West Bank by PA security services. Arbitrary arrests and torture violate legal obligations that the state of Palestine assumed after it ratified the International Covenant on Civil and Political Rights and the Convention against Torture in 2014.

## Israel

Israeli authorities have continued to narrow the space for criticism of its policies toward Palestinians. In March, the Knesset passed a law barring entry to foreigners who call for boycotting Israel or settlements. Authorities continue to impose onerous reporting requirements on nongovernment organizations receiving most of their funding from foreign government entities.

Palestinian Bedouin citizens of Israel who live in "unrecognized" villages in the Negev suffered discriminatory home demolitions on the basis that their homes were built illegally, even though most of those villages existed before the state of Israel was established or were created in the 1950s on land to which Israel transferred Bedouin citizens.

The Israeli government continued its openly stated policy of rendering "miserable" the lives of the roughly 40,000 Eritrean and Sudanese asylum seekers present in the country in order to induce them to depart. These measures include prolonged detention; restrictions on freedom of movement; ambiguous policies on permission to work; and restricting access to health care. On August 28, the Israeli High Court ruled that authorities could not detain rejected asylum seekers refusing transfer to Rwanda for longer than 60 days and that they could only use force to transfer them if Rwanda agreed to that approach.

## *Key International Actors*

Under commitments stemming from the 1978 Camp David accords, the United States allocated US$3.1 billion in military aid to Israel in 2017 fiscal year. It also allocated $362 million in assistance to Palestinian security forces and economic support to the PA. The International Criminal Court (ICC) Office of the Prosecutor is conducting a preliminary examination into the situation in Palestine to determine whether the criteria have been met to merit pursuing a formal investigation into crimes committed in and from Palestine.

In December 2016, the UN Security Council unanimously adopted a resolution, with the US abstaining, that said settlements have "no legal validity," are a "flagrant violation" of international law and a "major obstacle" to peace between Israel and the Palestinians.

The UN Human Rights Council requested the High Commissioner for Human Rights to create a database of businesses that have enabled or profited from the construction and growth of the settlements. Originally scheduled for March, the council accepted the High Commissioner's request to defer submission of the database report until the end of 2017 at the latest.

# Japan

Japan is an established democracy with rule of law and an active civil society. After Prime Minister Shinzo Abe dissolved the lower house of the Diet in September, Japanese voters went to the polls on October 22, 2017. Prime Minister Abe's ruling coalition kept the two-thirds majority that increased the chance that he will realize his long-time ambition of amending the post-World War II constitution.

## *Refugees and Asylum Seekers*

Japan's asylum and refugee determination system is tilted strongly against granting refugee status. In 2016, the Ministry of Justice reported that 10,901 people applied for asylum (the highest number ever), but the government rejected most of them and granted formal recognition as a refugee to only 28 applicants. Japan classified another 97 asylum seekers as having humanitarian status, which spares them from being forcibly returned to their home country.

## *Abuse of Foreign "Technical Intern Trainees"*

Japan provides only weak legal protections for the approximately 230,000 foreigners— most of them from Vietnam and China—working in the country as part of the Technical Intern Training Program. Created in response to labor shortages for low-level jobs, the program is a main framework through which foreign migrant workers are permitted to work in Japan.

Abuses that program participants faced include payment of sub-minimum wages, illegal overtime, dangerous or unhygienic working conditions, restrictions on changing employers, forced return to their home countries, as well as requirements to pay unreasonably high fees to labor-sending agencies, and penalty fees if the trainee does not successfully complete the training. Sexual abuses and rules that violate privacy (for example, prohibitions on owning a cell phone, or having romantic relationships) are also significant problems.

In November 2016, the Diet responded by passing the so-called Technical Training Act. These stronger regulations, which took effect in November 2017, established the Organization for Technical Intern Training as the program execution body and introduced more criminal penalties against rights violations. However, key issues the reforms failed to address included restrictions related to changing employers and reliance on often exploitative labor-sending agencies.

In March 2017, the Tokyo Organizing Committee of the Olympic and Paralympic Games announced the adoption of the Sustainable Sourcing Code ahead of the 2020 games, which includes a comprehensive protection clause for migrant workers throughout supply chains for provision of goods and services for the committee. However, the committee has not yet established an effective implementation system for the code, including a grievance mechanism for affected individuals including workers and contractors.

## Racial and Ethnic Discrimination

Reflecting the recent rise of anti-ethnic Korean groups, Tokyo Governor Yuriko Koike, for the first time in a decade, did not send a eulogy to the annual memorial service on September 1 for ethnic Korean victims of the 1923 Kanto Great Earthquake. Ethnic Koreans (Zainichi) were massacred in the aftermath when demagogues claimed Koreans were looting and committing arson. Historically, ethnic Koreans have faced widespread social and economic discrimination in Japan, attitudes that persist in ultra-nationalist political groups.

## Women's Rights

In July, revisions to the penal code strengthening criminal penalties against sexual violence entered into force. The new provisions add additional offenses including in cases of abuse within families, increase sentences, permit prosecutors to proceed in cases where victims refrain from lodging a criminal complaint, and make provisions regarding sex offenses gender neutral rather than applicable only to female victims.

## Sexual Orientation and Gender Identity

In December 2016, the National Personnel Authority, which handles rules and policies involving national government officials, revised its interpretation of rules on prohibiting sexual harassment to include harassment based on sexual orientation or gender identity.

In revising the government's policy on bullying prevention, the Ministry of Education, Culture, Sports, Science and Technology (MEXT) specified for the first time that sexual and gender minority students should be protected from bullying, and required schools to promote accepted understanding of the issues among teachers and take other necessary measures. Unfortunately, in March, the MEXT failed to include information about sexual and gender minority students in its once-in-a-decade review of the national educational curriculum. As a result, the national curriculum still only refers to heterosexuality, rather than also referring to homosexuality.

A multi-party group in the parliament failed to make progress in its goals to enact legislation to address discrimination based on sexual orientation and gender identity. Similarly, parliamentarians were unable to advance their efforts to revise an existing law to eliminate the requirement that transgender persons seeking legal recognition according to their gender identity undergo sterilization surgery.

## Disability Rights

In February, the Japan Federation of Bar Associations pressed the Ministry of Health, Labor and Welfare to provide a formal government apology and financial compensation to the approximately 84,000 persons mostly with genetic disorder (including 16,500 persons forced to have sterilization surgery) victimized under the Eugenic Protection Act between 1948 and 1996.

Use of restraints in psychiatric hospitals again came under scrutiny when Kelly Savage, 27, an English teacher from New Zealand, died in a psychiatric hospital in Kanagawa Prefecture in May. He allegedly died from cardiopulmonary arrest, after officials had held him continuously in restraints on his hands, legs, and waist for 11 days. A survey shows that psychiatric hospitals in Japan use physical restraints on patients with mental health conditions for very long periods—about 96 days on average.

## Children's Rights

In August, the Ministry of Health, Labor and Welfare endorsed that children younger than preschool age shall in principle not be institutionalized in alternative child care centers, in line with the "family-based care'" principle in the amendment of the Child Welfare Act in May 2016. The government also endorsed new goals, such as lifting national foster placement rate to 75 percent for pre-school children within seven years, and reforming temporary custody institutions.

## Death Penalty

Japan continued to use the death penalty in 2017, executing two people in July. One had filed an appeal for a retrial, the first time since December 1999 that an inmate seeking retrial was executed.

## Foreign Policy

Japan states that it pursues "diplomacy based on the fundamental values of freedom, democracy, basic human rights, and the rule of law." However, some important diplomatic actions were inconsistent with this commitment. In December 2016, Japan abstained from the United Nations Security Council resolution on South Sudan including arms embargo, along with seven other council members. Japan's abstention helped ensure the resolution was not adopted. In March, when the UN Human Rights Council established the international Fact-Finding Mission to Burma, Japan stated it did not support the mission. Japan subsequently abstained from Burma resolutions at the UN General Assembly in November and the Human Rights Council Special Session in December, which called for an end to violence against ethnic Rohingya and requested that access be given to the Fact-Finding Mission.

In September, Japan presented the resolution on Cambodia at the UN Human Rights Council. The resolution fell short of adequately responding to the rapidly deteriorating situation on the ground and ultimately failed to include robust reporting and discussion ahead of Cambodia's national elections in July 2018.

In 2017, Japan held human rights dialogues with Burma, Iran, and Cambodia. As in the past, there was either no prior announcement, or only last minute notice, about these dialogues.

The Japanese government did hold a formal dialogue with nongovernmental organizations based in Cambodia before the human rights dialogue with the Cambodian government, a modest but significant step forward.

# Jordan

In February 2017, a royal committee convened by King Abdullah II released sweeping proposals to reform Jordan's judiciary and justice system. In June, parliament passed a new disabilities law that includes the concept of "informed consent" and prohibits discrimination against persons with disabilities.

Despite these reforms, Jordan continued to violate human rights, including restrictions on free expression, free assembly, and women's rights.

Bassel Tarawneh, Jordan's governmental human rights coordinator, facilitated government interaction with local and international nongovernmental organizations (NGOs) and held open consultation sessions on human rights issues.

## *Freedom of Expression*

Jordanian law criminalizes speech deemed critical of the king, foreign countries, government officials and institutions, and Islam, as well as speech considered to defame others.

On January 12, Jordanian authorities arrested eight men, including a former member of parliament and a retired senior intelligence officer, apparently in response to critical comments online and peaceful anti-corruption advocacy. Authorities held the men on suspicion of "undermining the political regime," a vague provision under the "Terrorism" section of Jordan's penal code, but released them on February 8 without formal charges. On October 31, authorities briefly detained well-known cartoonist Emad Hajjaj for publishing a cartoon deemed offensive to Christians.

In 2017, authorities proposed amendments to the country's 2015 Electronic Crimes Law that criminalize hate speech, defining it vaguely as "any word or action that incites discord or religious, sectarian, ethnic, or regional strife or discrimination between individuals or groups." The amendments require parliamentary approval and the king's endorsement to become law.

In July 2017, high-level Jordanian officials used an inquiry into the legality of a Jordanian online magazine to issue statements against lesbian, gay, bisexual, and transgender (LGBT) people. The ministers of justice and interior wrote separate official letters to the minister of political and parliamentary affairs declaring

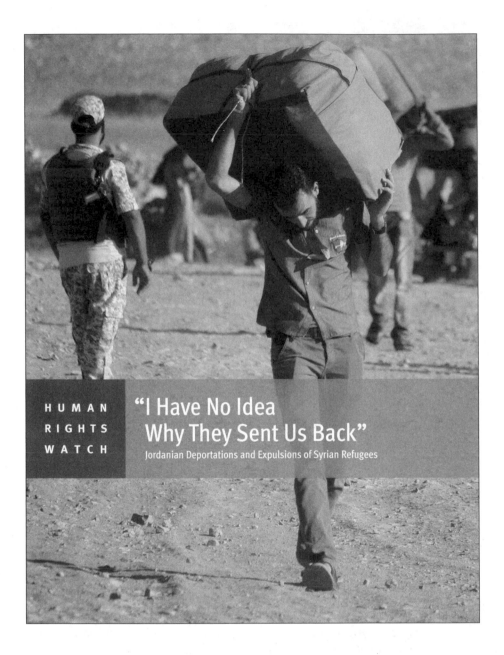

HUMAN RIGHTS WATCH

"I Have No Idea Why They Sent Us Back"

Jordanian Deportations and Expulsions of Syrian Refugees

their broad intolerance of LGBT people and making it clear that the government would not defend the rights of LGBT Jordanians.

## Freedom of Association and Assembly

In September, authorities threatened the Center for Defending Freedom of Journalists (CDFJ), a regional media freedom organization, over its receipt of foreign funding. The authorities said that CDFJ's registration category prohibits it from receiving foreign funding under government rules. But prior to 2017 the organization operated without incident or official complaint for 19 years. The group works on behalf of journalists detained across the region and hosts annual workshops and events on media freedom.

Since the amended Public Gatherings Law took effect in March 2011, Jordanians no longer require government permission to hold public meetings or demonstrations. However, organizations and venues continued to seek permission from Jordan's Interior Ministry to host public meetings and events. In some cases, the ministry cancelled public events without explanation.

In May, Jordan's Supreme Administrative Court upheld a Ministry of Political and Parliamentary Affairs decision denying registration to the Jordanian Civil Gathering Party because some of its founders have "dark skin." The court argued that Jordan's political parties law forbids formation of parties on an ethnic basis, even though the party's platform has no reference to ethnicity or race.

## Refugees and Migrants

Between 2011 and 2017, over 655,000 persons from Syria had sought refuge in Jordan, according to the United Nations High Commissioner for Refugees (UNHCR). Of these, approximately 79,000 were housed at the Zaatari Refugee Camp in northern Jordan; 53,000 were registered in Azraq Camp, 100 kilometers east of Amman; and 7,100 were at the Emirates Jordan Camp in Zarqa Governorate. The rest were living outside refugee camps. In 2017, Jordan did not permit Syrians to enter the country to seek asylum.

Jordanian officials stated that the country did not receive enough international financial assistance in 2017 to cope with the effects of the refugee crises on its public infrastructure, especially in the areas of public education and health. The

UNHCR Jordan office, which coordinates the refugee response, said that by November it had raised only 42 percent of its US$1.2 billion budget goal for 2017.

In 2017, Jordan deported hundreds of Syrian refugees—including the collective expulsion of large families—without giving them a meaningful chance to challenge their removal and failing to consider their need for international protection. During the first five months of 2017, Jordanian authorities deported about 400 registered Syrian refugees each month. In addition, approximately 300 registered refugees each month returned to Syria during that time under circumstances that appeared to be voluntary. Another estimated 500 refugees each month returned to Syria under circumstances that are unclear.

In 2017, authorities continued the implementation of the Jordan Compact, which aims to improve the livelihoods of Syrian refugees by granting new legal work opportunities and improving the education sector. By 2017, labor authorities had issued at least 60,000 work permits for Syrians.

Data compiled by the Jordanian government and published in April found that only 125,000 out of approximately 220,000 school-age Syrian refugee children were enrolled in formal education in Jordan, lower than previous estimates. Jordan implemented programs to reach out-of-school refugee children and waived documentation requirements for them to enroll in school.

Between January and June 2017, Jordanian authorities allowed limited deliveries of humanitarian aid to the tens of thousands of Syrians in unorganized camps along the border with Syria facing limited access to food, water, and medical assistance. In October, authorities announced that no more aid deliveries would be permitted from Jordanian territory.

## Women's and Girls' Rights

Jordan's personal status code remains discriminatory, despite a 2010 amendment that included widening women's access to divorce and child custody. Marriages between Muslim women and non-Muslim men, for instance, are not recognized.

Article 9 of Jordan's nationality law does not allow Jordanian women married to non-Jordanian spouses to pass on their nationality to their spouse and children. In 2014, Jordanian authorities issued a cabinet decision purporting to ease restrictions on non-citizen children of Jordanian women's access to key economic and social rights. By September 2017, the government distributed at least 66,000 special ID cards, but affected persons reported officials' lack of follow-through on promised reforms, especially regarding the acquisition of work permits and drivers' licenses.

In August, Jordanian lawmakers abolished article 308 of the country's 1960 penal code, an infamous provision that allowed perpetrators of sexual assault to avoid punishment if they married their victims. Lawmakers also amended article 98 to state that perpetrators of crimes "against women" cannot receive mitigated sentences. The provision leaves a loophole, however, under article 340 of the same law, which allows for mitigated sentences for those who murder their spouses discovered committing adultery.

## Criminal Justice System and Police Accountability

In 2017, Jordanian lawmakers overhauled the country's criminal procedure law, making positive changes that guarantee all suspects the right to access a lawyer from the time of arrest and during interrogations and create a legal aid fund to provide lawyers for suspects who cannot afford them.

Under the changes, the law states that pretrial detention is an "exceptional measure" rather than the norm and only allowed under limited circumstances. Pretrial detention for minor offenses cannot exceed a maximum of three months, and courts can only extend pretrial detention for serious offenses and to a year or 18 months. For the first time, anyone sent for pretrial detention has the right to appeal.

Jordanian executed 15 Jordanian men on March 4 by hanging. Those executed included 10 convicted in six terrorist attacks between 2003 and 2016, and five convicted in murder cases. They were the first executions since February 2015.

In May, authorities detained policemen allegedly involved in the death in custody of an 18-year-old man. The "torture" trial of five policemen in the Police Court relating to the September 2015 death in detention of 49-year-old Omar al-Nasr remained ongoing as of December 2017.

Local governors continued to use provisions of the Crime Prevention Law of 1954 to place individuals in administrative detention for up to one year, in circumvention of the Criminal Procedure Law. The National Center for Human Rights reported that 30,138 persons were administratively detained in 2016, some for longer than one year.

## Key International Actors

Jordan received approximately US$1.279 billion in economic and military assistance from the United States in 2017, according to the Congressional Research Service. The US did not publicly criticize human rights violations in Jordan in 2017, except in annual reports.

Jordan is a member of the Saudi-led coalition fighting the Houthis in Yemen. Human Rights Watch has documented 87 apparently unlawful coalition attacks in Yemen, some of which may be war crimes, which have killed nearly 1,000 civilians. Jordan did not respond to Human Rights Watch inquiries regarding what role, if any, it has played in unlawful attacks in Yemen and if it was undertaking investigations into the role its own forces played in any of these attacks.

On March 29, Jordan failed to arrest Sudanese President Omar al-Bashir after allowing him to enter the country to attend the 28th summit of the Arab League even though al-Bashir has been a fugitive from the International Criminal Court (ICC) since 2009 and Jordan is an ICC member.

In March, commenting on Jordan's execution of 15 people convicted for terrorism, the EU reiterated its strong opposition to death penalty. In June, the EU report on EU-Jordan relations highlighted some shortcomings in freedom of expression and women's rights. In July, the EU and Jordan held their 12th Association Council meeting.

# Kazakhstan

As the Kazakh government hosted high-profile international events, including EXPO 2017, an annual international exhibition, and several rounds of Syria peace talks, its human rights record further deteriorated. Authorities suppressed independent trade union activity and continued to target government critics, including journalists, with politically motivated criminal charges and other harassment. Several activists and union leaders remain wrongfully imprisoned. The government is considering legislative amendments that appear to propose even further restrictions on freedom of religion. Impunity for torture and ill-treatment in detention persist.

## *Civil Society*

In January 2017, tax officials ordered two human rights groups, International Legal Initiative and Liberty, to pay substantial fines on alleged undeclared profits despite laws that exempt nonprofit organizations from taxes on grants. The groups unsuccessfully challenged the fines in court.

Maks Bokaev and Talgat Ayan, activists imprisoned in November 2016 after protesting land reform proposals, continued to serve five-year sentences. Bokaev was transferred to prison medical units due to health complications in July and October. In April, the United Nations Working Group on Arbitrary Detention deemed Bokaev's and Ayan's deprivation of liberty arbitrary, and called on the government to release and compensate them.

On October 29, an unknown assailant attacked Marat Zhanuzakov, an activist in Kokshetau, northern Kazakhstan, wounding him in the head. Police investigated but later claimed Zhanuzakov fell on his own. Zhanuzakov linked the attack to his critical political commentary on social media.

Activist Vadim Kuramshin continued to serve a 12-year prison sentence, despite fair trial violations and concerns that his December 2012 conviction was retribution for government criticism. Government critic Natalya Ulasik, whom a court found mentally incompetent in October 2016, remained in forced psychiatric detention.

Authorities continued to misuse the vague and overbroad criminal charge of "inciting discord" to target outspoken activists and others. On August 1, an Almaty court convicted Olesya Khalabuzar of "inciting national discord" for preparing leaflets criticizing proposed constitutional changes to land ownership rights. Bogus charges of "inciting religious discord" brought against atheist writer Aleksandr Kharlamov in 2013 remain pending. On October 25, an Almaty region court acquitted four people charged with allegedly "inciting ethnic discord" for comments they posted on Facebook and the Russian social media network VKontake.

## Freedom of Media

Independent and opposition journalists continued to face harassment, physical attacks, and spurious criminal prosecutions. Unknown assailants stabbed journalist Ramazan Yesergepov in May as he traveled by train to Astana to meet with diplomats. Yesergepov linked the attack to his public calls for sanctions against Kazakh officials who commit human rights violations. Officials opened an investigation, but at time of writing no one has been held accountable. The European Union delegation in Astana called for a swift, thorough investigation to bring those responsible to justice.

In September, an Almaty court convicted Zhanbolat Mamay, editor of the independent *Sayasy Kalam: Tribuna* newspaper, on politically motivated money laundering charges. The court banned Mamay from journalism for three years among other restrictions. The Organization for Security and Co-operation in Europe (OSCE) Media Freedom Representative Harlem D'esir criticized the ban.

Kazakhstan's Supreme Court ruled in August to overturn and return to a lower court a 2016 defamation conviction against Tamara Eslyamova, editor of the independent newspaper *Uralskaya Nedelya* and the newspaper's founders. The lower court ruled against Eslyamova in October, but reduced total damages to 300,000 tenge (US$900) from 3.5 million tenge ($10,500).

In November, a court granted parole to Seitkazy Mataev, head of the National Press Club, whose six-year prison sentence was halved in April. Mataev, along with his son, Aset, also a journalist, were imprisoned in October 2016 on spurious embezzlement charges. Aset remained in prison.

Parliament is considering some media and information law amendments that could undermine media freedoms, including by introducing an overly vague definition of "propaganda." In an open letter, human and media rights groups in September urged parliament to create a working group to draft a new media law instead.

## Labor Rights

The independent labor movement faced a concerted crackdown in 2017. In January, a court closed the Confederation of Independent Trade Unions of Kazakhstan (KNPRK) for failing to register in accordance with the restrictive trade union law. A court convicted KNPRK President Larisa Kharkova on politically motivated embezzlement charges in July, and imposed travel and other restrictions for four years, and banned her from trade union leadership positions for five years.

A court found illegal a January hunger strike by approximately 400 oil workers in Aktau protesting the closure of KNPRK. Nearly 50 workers were fined or ordered to pay compensation to their employer. In April and May, courts sentenced two participants, Amin Eleusinov and Nurbek Kushakbaev, to two-and-a-half and two years' imprisonment, respectively, in apparent retaliation, and barred them from union activities for two and five years.

In June, the International Labour Organization's (ILO) Committee on the Application of Standards reviewed Kazakhstan for the third year in a row for freedom of association violations, and called on authorities to revise the Trade Union Law and ensure that KNPRK operates. At time of writing, the government has not addressed the ILO's conclusions.

## Freedom of Assembly

Kazakh authorities regularly deny permits for gatherings aiming to criticize government policies. Police break up unauthorized protests and arbitrarily detain and sanction organizers and participants. For example, in February, police detained three activists for attempting to organize a rally in Almaty supporting detained journalist Mamay. A court sentenced one of them to 15 days' detention.

## *Torture and Ill-Treatment*

Six years after violent clashes brought an end to an extended oil sector labor strike in Zhanaozen, the authorities still have not credibly investigated torture allegations made by those subsequently detained and prosecuted.

In March, the UN Human Rights Committee found that Zhaslan Suleimenov, sentenced to eight years in prison in 2011 on terrorism-related charges, was tortured in custody and denied an effective remedy. Despite a 2014 UN Human Rights Committee decision, authorities have not held accountable those who tortured Rasim Bayramov, detained in 2008 on suspicion of robbery.

## *Freedom of Religion*

Courts convicted at least 22 people on criminal charges of "inciting religious discord" or "membership in a banned organization," in violation of their right to freedom of religion or belief, according to international religious freedom watchdog Forum 18. Among them were 15 members of the Tabligh Jamaat movement, five men who worked or studied in Saudi Arabia, and two Jehovah's Witnesses. In October, the UN Working Group on Arbitrary Detention called for the immediate release of Jehovah's Witness Temir Akhmedov, imprisoned in May.

In July, an Almaty Region court fined a Protestant pastor and five foreign visitors for illegal missionary activity for an outdoor baptism. Authorities imposed three-month bans on Protestant and Jehovah's Witness churches in Almaty in March and June, respectively, and on a Protestant church in Ust-Kamenogorsk in August, for violating the restrictive religion law.

The government is proposing amendments to the religion law, which would increase restrictions and sanctions on religious teaching, proselytizing, and publications. At time of writing, the draft had not yet been submitted to parliament.

## *Women's and Girls' Rights*

In July, President Nursultan Nazarbaev signed amendments to the criminal code decriminalizing battery and light bodily harm, including in cases of domestic violence. The law does not envisage criminal sanctions for repeat offenses.

## Counterterrorism

Amendments to counterterrorism and extremism-related legislation, which increase restrictions on travel abroad for religious purposes and tighten censorship of religious literature, took effect in January 2017. An October 2016 report by the OSCE Office for Democratic Institutions and Human Rights found the amendments could unduly restrict freedom of movement, expression, and religion.

In July, President Nazarbaev signed into law amendments that allow deprivation of citizenship for certain terrorism-related crimes and that bar independent candidates from running for president.

## Sexual Orientation and Gender Identity

Many lesbian, gay, bisexual, and transgender (LGBT) people hide their sexual orientation or gender identity out of fear of reprisals or discrimination. On rare occasions when LGBT people report abuse, they can face indifference and hostility from authorities. Transgender people must undergo humiliating and invasive procedures—including a psychiatric diagnosis and coerced sterilization—to change gender on official documents. Feminita, an Almaty-based lesbian, bisexual and queer (LBQ) group, reported that "police not only use vulgar, evil, insulting jokes, but also blackmail, [and] sometimes violence," based on interviews with LBQ people across Kazakhstan in 2016 and 2017.

## Key International Actors

Many of Kazakhstan's international partners did not use key opportunities to insist that the government improve the human rights situation. Public criticism remained muted.

During his June tour of Central Asia, UN Secretary-General António Guterres named Kazakhstan a "pillar of stability," but failed to condemn politically motivated prosecutions and imprisonment of activists, journalists and union leaders. Guterres did not meet independent groups or activists in Kazakhstan.

In statements in advance of and during EXPO 2017, US officials continued to downplay human rights concerns. In June, US Secretary of State Rex Tillerson praised Kazakhstan for "its commitment to democracy, religious tolerance, and free speech."

German President Frank-Walter Steinmeier met President Nazarbaev on July 12, to mark 25 years of diplomatic relations, and to discuss political and economic cooperation. Steinmeier urged the Kazakh government to pursue rule of law reforms, and pledged technical assistance.

European Parliament hearings on ratification of the EU-Kazakhstan Enhanced Partnership and Cooperation Agreement, signed in December 2015, began in August but had not concluded at time of writing.

Following her September visit, the UN special rapporteur on the rights of persons with disabilities, Catalina Devandas, acknowledged the government's stated commitment to the rights of people with disabilities, but criticized continued institutionalization, denial of legal capacity, involuntary medical treatment, and lack of inclusive education.

# Kenya

On August 8, Kenya's electoral commission declared incumbent President Uhuru Kenyatta winner for a second term, amid opposition and civil society claims of fraud. The elections were marred by excessive use of force against residents, especially in opposition strongholds in Nairobi, the coast and western Kenya.

On September 1, the Supreme Court nullified the election after the leading opposition candidate Raila Odinga of the National Super Aliance (NASA) successfully challenged the results. The ruling Jubilee party responded to the court decision with threats and intimidation of the Supreme Court Judges and moved to change elections laws in a bid to weaken accountability measures for election offences. A fresh election was held on October 26, from which Odinga withdrew and Kenyatta was declared the winner, with the court dismissing all petitions challenging his win.

Impunity for abuses committed during the country's 2007-2008 post-election violence (PEV) persists, after the International Criminal Court (ICC) dropped cases against Kenyatta, his deputy William Ruto, and four others. The government has yet to develop a plan to implement a reparations fund it established in 2015 to support the PEV victims. Although it has taken steps to help some victims from the 2007 political violence such as internally displaced persons (IDPs), the government has not assisted rape survivors who still need medical treatment and financial help. Three men wanted by the ICC since 2013 and 2015 for witness interference in one of the cases have yet to be surrendered. Challenges to the arrest warrants or surrender are pending in Kenyan courts.

Dropping water levels in Kenya's Lake Turkana following the development of dams and plantations in Ethiopia's lower Omo Valley threaten the livelihoods of half-a-million indigenous people in Ethiopia and Kenya.

## Security Forces Abuses

Kenyan and international human rights organizations documented a range of rights abuses by the security forces in military and law enfrocement operations between 2016 and 2017 across the country. In Laikipia county of the Rift Valley, where herders looking for pasture for their livestock are in conflict with private ranch owners, Human Rights Watch found in June 2017 that police and the mili-

"Kill Those Criminals"

Security Forces Violations in Kenya's August 2017 Elections

tary were implicated in beating and killing herders and their livestock from the Pokot community.

Police killings in Mathare and other informal settlements in Nairobi such as Dandora, Kayole, Huruma, Eastleigh, Kibera, and Kariobangi have not been investigated. In May 2017, a report by Mathare Social Justice Center, a community based human rights organization, found that between 2016 and 2017 alone, police had extrajudicially killed at least 57 young men and women.

Kenyan security forces have also been implicated in serious human rights violations, including extrajudicial killings, enforced disappearances of those suspected of links to Al-Shabab, the Somalia based Islamist armed group, and abusive policing operations mostly targeting Kenyan and non Kenyan Somalis and Muslims. In a letter to President Uhuru Kenyatta in December 2016, Kenyan and international human rights organizations, incuding Human Rights Watch, called for a commission of inquiry into these killings and disappearances. The president had not responded at time of writing.

## Security Forces Abuses During Elections

Both the August and October 2017 elections were marred by serious human rights abuses. In early August, a technology manager with the electoral commission, Chris Musando, was abducted and his body found two days later on the outskirts of Nairobi. The opposition alliance, NASA, said the killing was a step toward manipulating polling technology and the tallying of results.

During and after the August 8 polling, Kenyan police and other security agencies used excessive force against protesters, primarily in opposition strongholds. The protests erupted following allegations by Raila Odinga that the August 2017 elections had been rigged.

Police also carried out violent house to house operations, beating or shooting primarily male residents, even though they also beat female residents for failing to produce the males suspected of participating in demonstrations. At least 67 people were shot or beaten to death by police nationwide, and hundreds more were injured during these operations. There were troubling reports of rape and sexual harassment during police operations in Kisumu and Nairobi. At time of

**"Not Worth the Risk"**
Threats to Free Expression Ahead of Kenya's 2017 Elections

HUMAN
RIGHTS
WATCH

ARTICLE 19

writing, the Independent Policing Oversight Authority (IPOA) was investigating just about six of the cases of killings.

## Freedom of Expression and Media

Over the past five years, Kenyan authorities have used legal, administrative, and informal measures to restrict media. In the lead up to the 2017 elections, journalists and bloggers reporting on sensitive issues such as land, corruption, and security faced threats, intimidation, arbitrary arrests, and physical assaults.

At least two Kenyan journalists were arrested before and after the August elections. On June 18, police officers arrested *Daily Nation* journalist Walter Menya and released him without charge after two days. Police alleged Menya had solicited for a bribe, but the Nation Media Group argued that he was being targeted for reporting how government officials flouted election campaign laws with impunity.

On August 12, police arrested two television journalists, Duncan Khaemba, and Otieno Willis, whom they wrongly suspected of wearing bullet-proof vests without relevant approval documents. The arrests appear to have been designed to obstruct their work in covering police abuses.

In May, Human Rights Watch documented at least 50 cases of journalists and bloggers who faced a range of abuses in the last three years across Kenya, including beatings and threats. At least two journalists were killed by unknown people in the past two years. In some cases, Kenyan authorities have withdrawn advertisements or withheld payment to media houses in a bid to pressure individual media outlets to stop criticism of the government.

Despite receiving formal complaints from journalists and bloggers, police have rarely investigated the attacks or threats and perpetrators have rarely been held to account.

## Threats to Civil Society

NGOs working on a range of issues, particularly accountability, security forces abuses, and elections, continue to face hostile rhetoric and restrictions, including threats of closure by authorities.

In December 2016, Kenyan authorities suspended a civic education program, "Kenya Electoral Assistance program, KEAP 2017," worth US$20 million that was funded by USAID and being implemented by International Foundation for Electoral Systems (IFES). The NGO regulatory body, the NGO Board accused IFES of not being duly registered. IFES denied the accusation, but halted the implementation of the program.

On August 14, the NGO Board announced the cancellation of the registration of the Kenya Human Rights Commission (KHRC)—one of the oldest human rights groups in Kenya— citing alleged tax evasion and other reasons, but the cabinet secretary for interior suspended the move. On August 16, police and Kenya Revenue Authority (KRA) officials visited the offices of another NGO, AfriCOG, which focuses on governance issues and had challenged the 2013 elections in which Kenyatta was declared winner, but were successfully resisted by AfriCOG's lawyers.

In November, the NGO Board summoned Inuka Kenya, Katiba Institute and Muslims for Human Rights (MUHURI) over, among other allegations, lacking proper registration documents. The officials of these organizations said they believed the threats to deregister them were aimed at stopping them from challenging the August election results in court.

## Refugees

In February, the High Court of Kenya stopped the government order to shut down Daadab refugee camp, home to 240,000 mainly Somali refugees. The number of refugees in the camp had fallen by half, from about 465,000 living there in 2011, as a result of government threats of closure and significant cuts in services and food rations by the UN Refugee Agency, UNHCR. About 32,000 returned to Somalia in 2017. Kenyan authorities said in May 2016 they would close the camp and forcefully return Somali refugees, accusing Somali refugees of harboring terrorists and disbanded the department of refugee affairs, which is responsible for registration of new refugees.

In January, human rights lawyer, Samuel Dong Luak, and his colleague, Aggrey Idris, were abducted by unknown people in Nairobi and are suspected to have been forcibly returned to South Sudan where they were at risk of being tortured or persecuted. Kenyan government failed to prevent or even investigate these and other abductions and forcible return of South Sudanese refugees and human rights defenders to South Sudan.

## Sexual Orientation and Gender Identity

Constitutional challenges regarding Kenya's anti-homosexuality laws and the use of forced anal examinations remained pending before the courts. The Kenya Medical Association condemned forced anal exams. The attorney general established a task force in May 2017 to study policy reforms regarding intersex persons.

## Key International Actors

Kenya remains a regional hub in the global counterterrorism efforts largely supported by the United States, United Kingdom, European Union, and the United Nations.

Kenya is a troop contributor to the African Mission to Somalia (AMISOM) and the UN peacekeeping mission in South Sudan (UNMISS). In November, the UN sacked the Kenyan peace keeping force commander for the mission, prompting Kenya to withdraw all its troops. In January 2017, Kenya agreed to redeploy troops following negotiations between President Kenyatta and UN Secretary-General António Guterres in Addis Ababa, Ethiopia.

The international community deployed significant resources to observe the August 2017 elections and to assess the potential for violence and human rights violations. The African Union, EU, Commonwealth, and two US organizations, National Democratic Institute (NDI), and The Carter Cente monitored the August elections, but significantly scaled down during the October 26 repeat election.

Observers and the international community in general were more guarded in their endorsement of the October 26 election than they were in the August election, and did not congratulate Kenyatta for winning the October poll. Despite concerns about the credibility of the August elections, the US and UK missions urged the opposition to accept the outcome and concede defeat. The Office of the UN High Commissioner for Human Rights (OHCHR) deployed human rights monitors in parts of Kenya during both elections and urged restraint by security forces.

# Kuwait

In January 2017, Kuwait carried out its first executions since 2013, hanging seven people.

Despite recent reforms, migrant workers do not have adequate legal protections, and remain vulnerable to abuse, forced labor, and deportation for minor infractions.

In October, Kuwait's Constitutional Court found that an overbroad 2015 law that required all Kuwaiti citizens and residents to provide DNA samples to authorities violated the right to privacy.

Provisions in Kuwait's constitution, the national security law, and other legislation continue to restrict free speech, and were again used in 2017 to prosecute dissidents and stifle political dissent.

Kuwait continues to exclude thousands of stateless people, known as Bidun, from full citizenship despite their longstanding roots in Kuwaiti territory. In 2017, Kuwait reportedly deported 76 men on suspicion of being gay.

Kuwait is a member of the Saudi-led coalition fighting Houthi-Saleh forces in Yemen, with media reporting that Kuwait had deployed 15 aircraft. Human Rights Watch has documented 87 apparently unlawful coalition attacks in Yemen, some of which may amount to war crimes, yet coalition members have provided insufficient information about the attacks to determine which countries are responsible.

Unlike many of its Gulf neighbors, Kuwait continued to allow Human Rights Watch access to the country and engaged in constructive dialogue with the organization on a range of human rights issues.

## *Migrant Workers*

Two-thirds of Kuwait's population is comprised of migrant workers, who remain vulnerable to abuse despite recent reforms.

In 2015, Kuwait issued a new standard contract for migrant workers, and a 2016 administrative decision allowed some migrant workers to transfer their sponsorship to a new employer after three years of work, without their employer's consent. However, these reforms do not include migrant domestic workers.

In 2015, the National Assembly passed a law granting domestic workers the right to a weekly day off, 30 days of annual paid leave, a 12-hour working day with rest, and an end-of-service benefit of one month a year at the end of the contract, among other rights. In 2016 and 2017, the Interior Ministry passed implementing regulations for the law, and mandated that employers must pay overtime compensation. The ministry also issued a decree establishing a minimum wage of KD60 (US$200) for domestic workers.

Protections for domestic workers are still weaker than those in Kuwait's labor law. The domestic worker law also falls short by failing to set out enforcement mechanisms, such as inspections of working conditions in households. The law also does not set out sanctions against employers who confiscate passports or fail to provide adequate housing, food, and medical expenses, work breaks, or weekly rest days.

Migrant workers remain vulnerable to abuse, forced labor, and deportation for minor infractions including traffic violations and "absconding" from an employer. In April, a video, apparently filmed by her employer, captured an Ethiopian domestic worker falling from the seventh floor of an apartment building. Authorities reportedly charged the employer for failing to assist the worker.

## *Freedom of Expression*

Kuwaiti authorities have invoked several provisions in the constitution, penal code, Printing and Publication Law, Misuse of Telephone Communications and Bugging Devices Law, Public Gatherings Law, and National Unity Law to prosecute journalists, politicians, and activists for criticizing the emir, the government, religion, and rulers of neighboring countries in blogs or on Twitter, Facebook, or other social media.

Prosecutions for protected speech are ongoing in Kuwaiti courts. Kuwaiti officials and activists reported that many, if not most, initial complaints in these cases are filed by individuals, underscoring the need to further amend broadly written or overly vague Kuwaiti laws to ensure adequate protections for speech and expression. Kuwaiti courts continued to issue deportation orders in some of these cases, including against members of the Bidun population, although Kuwaiti officials reported these orders would not be implemented.

In 2016, Kuwait amended the election law to bar all those convicted for "insulting" God, the prophets, or the emir from running for office or voting in elections. The law is likely to bar some opposition members of parliament from contesting or voting in future elections.

The Cybercrime Law, which went into effect in 2016, includes far-reaching restrictions on internet-based speech, such as prison sentences, and fines for insulting religion, religious figures, and the emir.

## Treatment of Minorities

Kuwait has a population of about 100,000 stateless persons, known as Bidun, whose predicament dates to the foundation of the Kuwaiti state.

After an initial registration period for citizenship ended in 1960, authorities shifted Bidun citizenship claims to administrative committees that for decades have avoided resolving the claims. Authorities claim that many Bidun are "illegal residents" who deliberately destroyed evidence of another nationality to receive benefits.

Members of the Bidun community have taken to the streets to protest the government's failure to address their citizenship claims, despite government warnings that Bidun should not gather in public. Article 12 of the 1979 Public Gatherings Law bars non-Kuwaitis from participating in public gatherings. In September, a Bidun man reportedly set himself on fire to protest the status and conditions of the Bidun in Kuwait.

## Terrorism

In October, Kuwait's Constitutional Court found that an overbroad 2015 law that had required all Kuwaiti citizens and residents to provide DNA samples to authorities violated the right to privacy. The law was introduced after the June 2015 suicide bombing of the Imam Sadiq Mosque. Authorities reported to local media at the time that anyone failing to comply with the law would be subject to sanctions, including cancelling their passports and a possible travel ban. In 2016, the United Nations Human Rights Committee found the law imposed "unnecessary and disproportionate restrictions on the right to privacy."

## Women's Rights, Sexual Orientation, and Gender Identity

Kuwaiti personal status law, which applies to Sunni Muslims who make up most Kuwaitis, discriminates against women. For example, some women require a male guardian to conclude their marriage contracts; women must apply to the courts for a divorce on limited grounds unlike men who can unilaterally divorce their wives; and women can lose custody of their children if they remarry someone outside the family. Men can marry up to four wives, without the permission or knowledge of the other wife or wives. A man can prohibit his wife from working if it is deemed to negatively affect the family interests. The rules that apply to Shia Muslims also discriminate against women.

Kuwait has no laws prohibiting domestic violence or marital rape. A 2015 law establishing family courts set up a center to deal with domestic violence cases, but requires the center to prioritize reconciliation over protection for domestic violence survivors. Article 153 of the Kuwaiti penal code stipulates that a man who finds his mother, wife, sister, or daughter in the act of adultery and kills them is punished by either a small fine or no more than three years in prison.

Kuwaiti women married to non-Kuwaitis, unlike Kuwaiti men, cannot pass citizenship to their children or spouses.

Adultery and extramarital intercourse are criminalized, and same-sex relations between men are punishable by up to seven years in prison. In 2017, Kuwait reportedly deported 76 men on suspicion of being gay. Transgender people can be arrested under a 2007 penal code provision that prohibits "imitating the opposite sex in any way."

## Death Penalty

Kuwait maintains the death penalty for nonviolent offenses, including drug-related charges. In January, it carried out seven executions by hanging, the first executions since 2013. Human Rights Watch has documented due process violations in Kuwait's criminal justice system that have made it difficult for defendants to get a fair trial, including in capital cases.

## *Key International Actors*

Kuwait joined the Saudi-led coalition that began attacking Houthi and allied forces in Yemen on March 26, 2015, with media reporting that Kuwait had deployed 15 aircraft. Human Rights Watch has documented 87 apparently unlawful coalition attacks in Yemen, some of which may amount to war crimes, that killed nearly 1000 civilians and repeatedly hit markets, schools, and hospitals. Kuwait did not respond to Human Rights Watch inquiries regarding what role, if any, it has played in unlawful attacks in Yemen and if it was undertaking investigations into the role its own forces played in any of these attacks.

# Kyrgyzstan

The 2017 presidential election was won by Sooronbai Jeenbekov and marked the second time since independence in 1991 that Kyrgyzstan experienced a peaceful transfer of presidential power. International observers found the election to be competitive and orderly, but noted concerns about abuse of public resources, pressure on voters, and vote buying. Prior to the election, authorities banned public assemblies in central Bishkek and introduced restrictions on domestic election monitors, such as limiting the number of civil society observers per polling station to one.

Human rights defender Azimjon Askarov continued to serve a sentence of life imprisonment, notwithstanding his wrongful conviction and ill-treatment. Impunity for ill-treatment and torture remain the norm. The situation for media freedoms deteriorated, with the Prosecutor General's Office bringing unjustified multimillion Som (tens of thousands of US dollars) lawsuits against critical media. Several foreign human rights workers are banned from Kyrgyzstan.

Parliament in April adopted in its first reading a draft ombudsman law, aimed at bringing the institution into compliance with the Paris Principles, the international standards that frame and guide national human rights institutions. The government has yet to ratify the United Nations Convention on the Rights of Persons with Disabilities.

## Access to Justice

Authorities continue to deny justice to victims of the June 2010 inter-ethnic violence in southern Kyrgyzstan, and took no steps to review torture-tainted convictions delivered in its aftermath. Ethnic Uzbeks were disproportionately affected by the violence, which left more than 400 dead and led to numerous cases of arbitrary detention, ill-treatment and torture, and house destruction.

Instances of courtroom violence occurred in 2017. In April, relatives and friends of a murdered police officer hit and threatened Osh-based lawyers Muhayo Abduraupova and Aisalkyn Karabaeva, and their client, a relative of two men accused of the officer's murder. At time of writing, no one had been held accountable.

In a March 2017 ruling, the UN Human Rights Committee determined that four ethnic Uzbeks from southern Kyrgyzstan were arbitrarily detained following interethnic violence in Osh in 2010, and ill-treated or tortured in custody. The committee concluded that Kyrgyzstan must investigate the authors' torture allegations and provide adequate compensation. At time of writing, authorities had taken no steps to fulfill the decision.

## Civil Society

The government continued to ignore its obligation to fulfill the 2016 UN Human Rights Committee decision to release rights defender Azimjon Askarov and quash his conviction, handed down after a trial marred by torture and violence. On January 24, a Bishkek court upheld Askarov's life sentence. In September, a Bazar-Kurgon court found unlawful the authorities' efforts to confiscate Askarov's family home.

In May, the Supreme Court ruled against human rights defender Tolekan Ismailova, who in 2016, along with fellow rights defender Aziza Abdurasulova, had sued President Almazbek Atambaev for defamation after he publicly smeared them. On October 30, a Bishkek court found that Kyrgyzstan's National Security Committee (GKNB) had in January disseminated false information about the human rights group Bir Duino, and ordered the GKNB to refute the information in media.

In July, following Russian human rights activist Vitaly Ponomarev's participation in a conference on countering violent extremism, authorities banned him from Kyrgyzstan. Human Rights Watch Central Asia researcher and Bishkek office director Mihra Rittmann remained banned from Kyrgyzstan.

## Freedom of Expression

In March and April, Kyrgyzstan's prosecutor general brought five defamation lawsuits against media outlet *Zanoza*, its founder Narynbek Idinov, and editor Dina Maslova; Radio Azattyk, the Kyrgyz branch of Radio Free Europe/Radio Liberty; and human rights defender Cholpon Djakupova. The prosecutor accused them of discrediting the president's honor and dignity and spreading false information.

Courts ordered Idinov's and Djakupova's bank accounts frozen and seized their property as collateral, and banned Idinov, Maslova, and Djakupova from leaving Kyrgyzstan. The prosecutor general in May withdrew the lawsuit against Radio Azattyk, but pursued lawsuits against *Zanoza*, Idinov, Maslova, and Djakupova. In rushed hearings in late June, Bishkek courts awarded crippling multi-million som damages, which were upheld on appeal in August. In another defamation lawsuit, a Bishkek court on October 5 awarded then-presidential candidate Jeenbekov 10 million som (US$143,000) against news portal 24.kg and Kabay Karabekov, a journalist and former member of parliament. In November, a Bishkek court banned the chief editor of Tribuna.kg, Yrysbek Omurzakov, from leaving Kyrgyzstan.

Authorities in June charged Ulugbek Babakulov, a freelance journalist and contributor to Moscow-based Ferghana News, an independent news website, with inciting ethnic hatred after a May article about the increase of nationalist and anti-Uzbek sentiments in social media. On June 10, a Bishkek court ordered Ferghana News' website to be blocked. Babakulov, fearing for his safety, fled Kyrgyzstan in June.

On August 22, a Bishkek court ordered the closure of Sentyabr television station for disseminating "extremist material." Authorities did not inform Sentyabr of the allegations or the court case until two hours before the hearing began. Sentyabr is tied to the opposition politician Omurbek Tekebaev, who in mid-August was imprisoned for eight years for corruption, charges which his supporters claim were politically motivated.

On September 29, a Bishkek appeals court reduced Zulpukar Sapanov's four-year prison sentence to a two-year suspended sentence and released him. Sapanov was convicted on September 12 for inciting religious discord after his book was determined to "diminish the role of Islam as a religion and create a negative attitude toward Muslims."

## *Freedom of Assembly*

Authorities took steps to limit freedom of peaceful assembly. In February, a Bishkek court imposed a three-week ban on public assemblies in the Leninskii district, citing the need to ensure public order. In mid-March, five protest participants were detained during a peaceful march to support freedom of speech.

A Bishkek court in July banned public assemblies at central locations in Bishkek, including Ala-Too Square, from July 27 to October 20, citing concerns about public security before the elections. On August 9, police detained Ondurush Toktonasyrov, an activist who held a single-person protest outside the Central Election Committee building, for violating the ban. Toktonasyrov was issued a warning and released.

On November 8, a Bishkek court, citing the then-upcoming presidential inauguration on November 24, banned public gatherings in several locations in central Bishkek until December 1.

## Torture and Ill-Treatment

Impunity for torture remains the norm, and investigations into ill-treatment and torture allegations remain rare, delayed, and ineffective. Kyrgyzstan's Coalition Against Torture, a group of 16 nongovernmental organizations working on torture prevention, reported in February that the prosecutor's office had registered 435 complaints of ill-treatment in 2016, but declined to open investigations into 400 cases. Sardar Bagishbekov, a representative of the coalition, noted that, on average, the prosecutor's office declines to investigate torture allegations in over 90 percent of cases.

## Violence against Women

In April, Kyrgyzstan adopted a new Law on the Prevention and Protection against Family Violence, which requires police to register any domestic abuse complaint, and recognizes physical and psychological abuse, and "economic violence," which includes restricting access to and use of financial resources or other assets. The law mandates police and judicial response to domestic violence, and ensures victims' access to shelter, psychosocial support, and legal aid. Some provisions of the law lack specificity and survivor protections.

Despite positive legislative changes, domestic violence remains widespread. Pressure to keep families together, stigma, economic dependence, and fear of reprisals by abusers, or limited services and police hostility and inaction hinder survivors from seeking assistance or accessing protection or justice.

## Sexual Orientation and Gender Identity

Lesbian, gay, bisexual, and transgender (LGBT) people continued to experience ill-treatment, extortion, and discrimination by both state and non-state actors. There is widespread impunity for these abuses. Consideration of an anti-LGBT bill, which would ban "propaganda of nontraditional sexual relations," remained stalled in parliament.

Several days before a peaceful public gathering planned for September 23, five law enforcement officers arrived unannounced at Labrys, a Bishkek-based LGBT rights group, threatening members not to hold the gathering. Labrys cancelled the event.

## Terrorism and Counterterrorism

The government stepped up counterterrorism measures following deadly attacks abroad that investigators linked to armed extremists of Central Asian origin, arresting scores of people for storage of vaguely defined "extremist" materials, an offense which carries a mandatory prison sentence of three to five years. As of August, 191 people had been imprisoned for terrorism or extremism-related offenses. Many were ethnic Uzbeks who alleged they had been arrested based on false testimony or evidence planted by the police, and that they were tortured and otherwise abused in police custody.

An overly broad constitutional amendment approved in December 2016 aims to revoke citizenship of Kyrgyz nationals who join international terrorist organizations. The measure awaited enabling legislation.

## Key International Actors

In January, the European Union timidly reacted to a Bishkek court's decision to uphold Askarov's life sentence. EU leaders failed to publicly call for Askarov's release during meetings with President Atambaev in February and in November, nor has the EU publicly made any other reference to Askarov's case at time of writing.

Brussels hosted the 8th annual EU-Kyrgyzstan human rights dialogue in June. The EU commended Kyrgyzstan for its new domestic violence legislation, and called on the government to ensure media freedoms, enable transparent presidential elections, and protect the rights of ethnic minorities. Concrete outcomes were not known at time of writing.

In a meeting with President Atambaev in June, UN Secretary-General António Guterres failed to express concern about worrying media freedom developments, and instead praised the government for upholding the rule of law, protecting human rights, and serving as a "pioneer of democracy in Central Asia." Guterres did not meet activists in Bishkek.

The Organization for Security and Co-operation in Europe (OSCE) announced in April that as of May 1, it would downgrade its presence in Kyrgyzstan to an "OSCE Programme Office."

# Lebanon

In June, Lebanon adopted a new electoral law and set parliamentary elections for May 2018, the first such elections since 2009. In November, Prime Minister Saad Hariri announced his surprise resignation while visiting Saudi Arabia, raising the likelihood of a renewed period of political instability in the country. At time of writing, the actual impact of the resignation was uncertain.

Lebanese authorities continue to prosecute individuals for peaceful use of free speech, and in June soldiers beat protesters demonstrating in downtown Beirut against a third extension of parliament.

Human Rights Watch continues to document reports of torture by Lebanese security forces, including Internal Security Forces and the Lebanese Armed Forces. A new torture law falls short of Lebanon's obligations under international law.

Lebanon has 15 separate religion-based personal status laws, which discriminate against women. Marital rape and child marriage both remain legal in Lebanon. In a positive development, parliament repealed article 522 of the criminal code, which had allowed rapists to escape prosecution by marrying the victim.

Lebanon's waste management crisis has led to widespread open burning of waste, risking a range of short term and long-term health effects among local residents.

As the Syrian refugee crisis continued, an estimated 80 percent of the approximately 1.5 million refugees lack legal status, leaving them vulnerable to arrest, abuse, and exploitation; contributing to poverty and child labor; and restricting their access to education and healthcare. Lebanon waived burdensome residency fees for some Syrians in February.

## *Lengthy Pretrial Detention, Ill-Treatment, and Torture*

Human Rights Watch continued to document reports of torture by Lebanese security forces, including Internal Security Forces, the Lebanese Armed Forces, and Military Intelligence. In October, parliament passed a new anti-torture law that, while a positive step, falls short of Lebanon's obligations under international law.

HUMAN
RIGHTS
WATCH

"It's Not the Right Place for Us"
The Trial of Civilians by Military Courts in Lebanon

On July 4, 2017, the Lebanese military issued a statement saying four Syrians died in its custody following mass raids in Arsal, a restricted access area in northeast Lebanon. A doctor with expertise in documenting torture reviewed photos of three of the men, provided by their families' lawyers to Human Rights Watch, and found the injuries "consistent with inflicted trauma in the setting of physical torture." The army said the men had died of natural causes but has not publicly released the results of its own investigation.

In 2016, parliament passed legislation creating a national preventative mechanism to monitor and investigate the use of torture. However, Lebanon has still not established the mechanism, allocated funding, or announced its members.

## *Freedom of Assembly and Expression*

While freedom of expression is generally respected in Lebanon, defaming or criticizing the Lebanese president or army is a criminal offense carrying penalties of up to three years in prison. The Lebanese penal code also criminalizes libel and defamation of other public officials, authorizing imprisonment of up to one year.

In 2017, Lebanese authorities continued to detain and charge individuals for social media posts critical of government officials.

In June, soldiers were captured on video kicking and beating protesters who had gathered to demonstrate against a third extension of parliament's term. The army said it had opened an investigation but has not publicly released the results.

## *Military Courts*

Lebanon continues to try civilians, including children, in military courts, in violation of their due process rights and international law. Those who have stood trial in the military courts describe incommunicado detention, the use of confessions extracted under torture, decisions issued without an explanation, seemingly arbitrary sentences, and a limited ability to appeal.

In one prominent case, 14 protesters, arrested in 2015 for demonstrating against corruption and the government's failure to resolve a trash crisis, were charged before the Military Tribunal though some of the charges were transferred to a civilian court in March.

## *Migrant Workers*

An estimated 250,000 migrant domestic workers, primarily from Sri Lanka, Ethiopia, the Philippines, Nepal, and Bangladesh, are excluded from labor law protections. The *kafala* (sponsorship) system subjects them to restrictive immigration rules and places them at risk of exploitation and abuse.

The most common complaints documented by the embassies of labor-sending countries and civil society groups include non-payment or delayed payment of wages, forced confinement, refusal to provide time off, and verbal and physical abuse. Migrant domestic workers suing their employers for abuse face legal obstacles and risk imprisonment and deportation due to the restrictive visa system. Several migrant domestic workers in Lebanon committed suicide or attempted to commit suicide in 2017.

In 2016 and 2017, Lebanon's General Security agency detained and deported migrant domestic workers, apparently for having children in Lebanon.

## *Women's and Girls' Rights*

On August 16, Lebanon's parliament repealed article 522, which had allowed rapists to escape prosecution by marrying the victim, but left a loophole with regard to offences relating to sex with children aged 15-17 and seducing a virgin girl into having sex with the promise of marriage.

A lack of coordination in the government's response to sex trafficking continues to put women and girls at risk. Syrian women appear to be at particular risk of being trafficked into forced prostitution and sexual exploitation.

Women continue to face discrimination under the 15 distinct religion-based personal status laws. Discrimination includes inequality in access to divorce, residence of children after divorce, and property rights. Unlike Lebanese men, Lebanese women cannot pass on their nationality to foreign husbands and children and are subject to discriminatory inheritance laws.

Lebanon has no minimum age for marriage for all its citizens. Instead, religious courts set the age based on the religion-based personal status laws, some of which allow girls younger than 15 to marry. Parliament has failed to take up draft bills that would set the age of marriage at 18.

A 2014 Law on the Protection of Women and Family from Domestic Violence established important protection measures and introduced policing and court reforms. But it failed to criminalize all forms of domestic violence, including marital rape. Some women continued to face obstacles in pursuing criminal complaints of domestic violence, mostly due to lengthy delays.

## Sexual Orientation and Gender Identity

Sexual relations outside of marriage—adultery and fornication—are criminalized under Lebanon's penal code. Furthermore, article 534 of the penal code punishes "any sexual intercourse contrary to the order of nature" with up to one year in prison. In recent years, authorities conducted raids to arrest persons allegedly involved in same-sex conduct, some of whom were subjected to torture including forced anal examinations.

In January, a judge challenged the legal basis of the arrest of men for same-sex conduct, declaring in a court ruling that "homosexuality is a personal choice, not a criminal offence."

## Refugees

More than 1 million Syrian refugees are registered with the United Nations High Commissioner for Refugees (UNHCR) in Lebanon. The government estimates the true number of Syrians in the country to be 1.5 million.

Lebanon's residency policy makes it difficult for Syrians to maintain legal status, heightening risks of exploitation and abuse and restricting refugees' access to work, education, and healthcare. According to humanitarian organizations, an estimated 80 percent of Syrians in Lebanon now lack legal residency and risk detention for unlawful presence in the country. In February, Lebanon waived residency fees for some Syrians in Lebanon.

More than 200,000 school-age Syrian children were out of school during the 2016-2017 school year, largely due to parents' inability to pay for transport, child labor, school directors imposing arbitrary enrollment requirements, and lack of language support. Secondary school-age children and children with disabilities faced particular barriers.

HUMAN
RIGHTS
WATCH

"As If You're Inhaling Your Death"
The Health Risks of Burning Waste in Lebanon

An estimated 10,000 Syrians returned from Arsal, a restricted access border area in northeast Lebanon, to Syria between June and August, under deals largely negotiated by Hezbollah. Refugees told Human Rights Watch that military raids and lack of residency permits were the primary reasons they felt pressured to return.

In 2017, Lebanon continued to impose entry regulations on Syrians that effectively barred many asylum seekers from entering Lebanon. Human Rights Watch has also documented isolated forcible deportations of Syrians and Palestinians back to Syria, putting them at risk of arbitrary detention, torture, or other persecution.

Approximately 45,000 Palestinians from Syria have also sought refuge in Lebanon, joining the estimated 260-280,000 Palestinian refugees already in the country, where they face restrictions, including on their right to work.

## Open Burning of Waste

Lebanon has never implemented a national waste management system and continues to face a waste management crisis. There are hundreds of open dumps across the country, many of which are being burned, posing a range of short and long term health risks to populations living nearby. Open burning disproportionately affects poorer areas of the country, and children and older persons among local residents are at particular risk.

## Legacy of Past Conflicts and Wars

Lebanon has failed to advance justice or accountability for the families of the estimated 17,000 kidnapped or "disappeared" during the 1975-1990 civil war. In October 2012, Justice Minister Shakib Qortbawi put forward a draft decree to the cabinet to establish a national commission to investigate the fate of those "disappeared" during the country's 1975-1990 civil war and its aftermath, but no further action was taken. In September 2014, the government finally provided the families of the disappeared with the files of the Official Commission of Inquiry appointed in 2000. These showed that the government had not conducted any serious investigation.

## *Key International Actors*

Syria, Iran, and Saudi Arabia maintain a strong influence on Lebanese politics through local allies and proxies, increasingly so as the conflict in neighboring Syria drags on.

Many countries, including the United States, United Kingdom, members of the European Union, Canada, and various Gulf countries, have given Lebanon extensive, albeit insufficient, support to help it cope with the Syrian refugee crisis and to bolster security amid spillover violence.

Lebanese armed forces and police also receive assistance from a range of international donors, including the US, EU, UK, France, and Saudi Arabia. Some of these actors have tried to ensure the forces adhere to international human rights law, but compliance remains weak.

# Libya

Political divisions and armed strife continued to plague Libya as two governments vied for legitimacy and control of the country, and United Nations' efforts to unify the feuding parties flagged. The UN backs the Government of National Accord (GNA), based in Tripoli, in the west, but not the rival Interim Government based in the eastern cities of al-Bayda and Benghazi.

Clashes between militias and forces loyal to these governments decimated the economy and public services, including the public health system, law enforcement, and the judiciary, and caused the internal displacement of over 200,000 people.

Armed groups throughout the country, some of them affiliated with one or the other of the competing governments, executed persons extrajudicially, attacked civilians and civilian properties, abducted and disappeared people, and imposed sieges on civilians in the eastern cities of Derna and Benghazi.

The extremist armed group Islamic State (also known as ISIS) lost control of its Libya "capital" Sirte in December 2016. In January 2017, remaining ISIS forces in Benghazi fled the city. ISIS-affiliated fighters remained present in areas south of Sirte and Bani Walid.

Most of the more than 200,000 migrants and asylum seekers who reached Europe by sea in 2017 departed in boats from Libya. Migrants and asylum seekers who ended up in detention in Libya faced beatings, extortion, sexual violence, and forced labor in unofficial and quasi state-run detention centers, at the hands of guards, militias, and smugglers. Coast guard forces also beat migrants they intercepted at sea and forced them back to detention centers with inhumane conditions. Between January and November, 2,772 migrants died during perilous boat journeys in the central Mediterranean Sea, most having departed from the Libyan shore.

## *Political Transition and Constitution*

The GNA struggled to gain authority and control over territory and institutions. Between February and May, militias aligned with it overran positions in Tripoli held by militias that supported a third authority, the Government of National Salvation (GNS).

In the east, Libyan National Army forces (LNA), under the command of General Khalifa Hiftar and allied with the Interim Government, continued to expand control over territory in the east and south. Libya's legislative body, the House of Representatives, remained allied with the LNA and Interim Government, and failed to approve a slate of ministers for the GNA.

## *Armed Conflict and War Crimes*

In March, the LNA ended its siege of nearly two years on the Benghazi neighborhood of Ganfouda, which fighters of the Benghazi Revolutionaries Shura Council (BRSC) had controlled. When LNA forces entered, they committed what appeared to be war crimes, killing civilians and summarily executing and desecrating the bodies of opposition fighters.

On May 18, forces aligned with the GNA, including the Third Force from Misrata, the Benghazi Defense Brigades, and other local units from the south, attacked an LNA airbase at Brak Al-Shati, in the south of the country, summarily executing as many as 51 individuals, most of them LNA fighters captured during the attack.

Clashes between pro- and anti-GNA militias for the control of Tripoli lasted between March and May. Hostilities left many injured and resulted in the deaths of scores of fighters, and some civilians before militias and security forces aligned with the GNA took control of the capital.

Several videos recorded between June 2016 and July 2017 emerged on social media seemingly implicating LNA fighters in summary executions and the desecration of bodies of captured enemy fighters in eastern Libya. On August 15, the prosecutor of the International Criminal Court (ICC) issued an arrest warrant against Mahmoud al-Werfalli, an LNA commander implicated in these recordings. On August 18, the LNA announced they had arrested al-Werfalli for questioning. As of September, the LNA had not provided any update on the status of the alleged investigation against him.

On August 23, unidentified gunmen beheaded nine LNA fighters and two civilians in an attack on a LNA-controlled checkpoint in al-Jufra region. According to the LNA, ISIS carried out the attack.

In August, the LNA intensified a 14-month siege against the eastern city of Derna, which remained controlled by the Derna Mujahedeen Shura Council (DMSC), an alliance of armed groups that opposed Khalifa Hiftar and the LNA. Local council members, activists, and journalists reported on an impending humanitarian crisis in the city, where the LNA intermittently imposed strict measures that included cutting delivery of cooking gas, food items, and fuel.

On October 4, unidentified armed men including a suicide bomber, attacked a courthouse in Misrata where regular criminal proceedings were taking place, killing at least four and injuring several people. ISIS claimed it carried out the attack.

In October, unidentified forces conducted air strikes in Derna killing 16 civilians, including 12 children. There was no claim for responsibility.

Also in October, armed groups loyal to the LNA appear to have summarily executed 36 men in the LNA-controlled eastern town of al-Abyar.

## *Judicial System and Detainees*

The criminal justice system has all but collapsed since 2014. Civilian and military courts in the east and south remained mostly shut, while elsewhere they operated at reduced capacity.

Prison authorities, often only nominally under the authority of the ministries of interior, defense, and justice of the two rival governments, continued to hold thousands of detainees in long-term arbitrary detention without charges. Militias that operated their own informal and often-secret detention facilities also held detainees in similar circumstances.

According to the Tripoli-based Judicial Police, the body responsible for managing prisons under the GNA Justice Ministry, 6,400 detainees were held in prisons managed by it in the east, west, and south of the country, of whom only 25 percent had been sentenced for a crime. The rest were held in pre-charge or pretrial detention. The Defense and Interior Ministries of both governments in Libya held an unknown number of detainees, in addition to militia-run secret detention facilities.

Hundreds of civilians, mostly women and children and including non-Libyan nationals, remain held without charge in two prisons in Tripoli and Misrata and in a camp run by the Libyan Red Crescent in Misrata for their apparent link to alleged ISIS fighters, without prospect for release due to their uncertain citizenship status and lack of coordination with countries of origin.

On May 26, The Tripoli Revolutionaries Brigade, a militia allied with the GNA Interior Ministry, overran the al-Hadba Correctional Facility in Tripoli and transferred from there to another location in Tripoli Gaddafi-era officials detained there, including former intelligence chief Abdullah Sanussi, former Prime Minister Abuzaid Dorda, and al-Saadi Gaddafi, a son of ousted Libyan leader Muammar Gaddafi.

## International Criminal Court

The ICC prosecutor has a mandate to investigate war crimes, crimes against humanity, and genocide committed in Libya since February 15, 2011, pursuant to UN Security Council Resolution 1970.

In April, the ICC unsealed an arrest warrant for Mohamed Khaled al-Tuhamy, a former chief of the Internal Security Agency under Gaddafi, for war crimes and crimes against humanity during the 2011 uprising. His whereabouts were unknown at time of writing.

Saif al-Islam Gaddafi, a son of Gaddafi, continued to be subject to an arrest warrant issued by the ICC to face charges of crimes against humanity. In 2015, the Tripoli Court of Assize sentenced Gaddafi to death in absentia for crimes committed during the 2011 uprising. The Abu Baker al-Siddiq militia in Zintan, which had held him since 2011, reported it released him on June 9, 2017, citing an amnesty law issued passed by Libya's parliament. His release could not be confirmed; independent international observers have not seen or heard from Gaddafi since June 2014.

## Death Penalty

The death penalty is stipulated in over 30 articles in Libya's penal code, including for acts of speech and association that are protected activities under international human rights law. Civil and military courts around the country have imposed the death penalty since the overthrow of Gaddafi in 2011, often after trials marred by due process violations. An unknown number of people were sentenced to death by Libyan civil and military courts since 2011, yet no death sentences have been carried out since 2010.

## Internally Displaced Persons

The International Organization for Migration (IOM) estimated that 217,000 people were internally displaced in Libya as of September. According to the IOM, most displaced people originated from Benghazi, Sirte, Misrata, and Ubari.

Militias and authorities in Misrata continued to prevent 35,000 residents of Tawergha from returning to their homes, despite the announcement on June 19 by the GNA that it had ratified a UN-brokered agreement between them and Tawerghans to end their disputes and allow Tawerghans to return to their homes. Misrata representatives, who accused Tawerghans of having committed serious crimes as supporters of Libyan leader Muammar Gaddafi during the 2011 uprising that ousted him, demanded, as stipulated in the agreement, that the GNA establish a fund to compensate persons who had been detained and the families of victims who went missing or were killed, between February and August 2011. At time of writing, the GNA had yet to establish such a fund, and Misrata forces continued to block displaced families from returning to their homes in Tawergha.

According to the Benghazi municipal council based in "exile" in Tripoli, approximately 3,700 Benghazi families have been forcibly displaced since 2014 and have sought shelter in the western cities of Tripoli, Misrata, Khoms, and Zliten, after militias affiliated with the LNA threatened them, attacked, burnt or appropriated their homes, and accused them of being terrorists. Authorities in Misrata and Tripoli have detained a number of people displaced from Benghazi, often on dubious terrorism allegations. An additional 9,200 families from Benghazi were internally displaced in western Libya due to the conflict in the east.

## Freedom of Speech and Expression

Armed groups intimidated, threatened, and physically attacked activists, journalists, bloggers, and media professsionals.

Security forces affiliated with the LNA in Benghazi arrested AFP photographer Abdullah Doma twice within one week—on March 28 and April 2—for a day each time. According to Doma's family, the arrests were for his coverage of Earth Hour, a global event that took place on March 25 to raise awareness of climate change. Security forces also briefly arrested four of the organizers of the event, slamming it as "offensive to Islam" for allowing men and women to mix.

In August, members of militias and armed groups in both east and west Libya threatened in phone calls and on social media the contributors and editors of *Sun on Closed Windows*, a book of essays and fiction, accusing them of "immoral content." Militias briefly arrested two participants in the book launch in the city of Zawiyah.

In November, a force affiliated with the GNA Interior Ministry, reportedly arrested participants of a comic book convention in Tripoli under the pretext that it breached the country's "morals and modesty."

## Freedom of Religion

Since 2011, militias and forces affiliated with several interim authorities, as well as ISIS fighters, have attacked religious minorities, including Sufis and Christians, and destroyed religious sites in Libya with impunity.

In July 2017, the Supreme Fatwa Committee under the General Authority for Endowments and Islamic Affairs, the religious authority of the Interim Government, issued a religious edict calling the minority Ibadi sect of Islam "a misguided and aberrant group," and "infidels without dignity." The Ibadi faith is practiced by many Amazighs, mostly in western Libya. Amazighs number between 300,000 and 400,000 of Libya's total population of 6.5 million. The GNA responded by condemning the religious edict.

In August, unidentified armed groups in Benghazi reportedly kidnapped or arrested 21 Sufi adherents, a minority Muslim group, at different times and different locations. As of September, none of the 21 had been released.

## Women's Rights, Sexual Orientation, and Gender Identity

Libyan law does not specifically criminalize domestic violence. Personal status laws continue to discriminate against women, particularly with respect to marriage, divorce, and inheritance. The penal code allows for a reduced sentence for a man who kills or injures his wife or another female relative because he suspects her of extramarital sexual relations. It also allows rapists to escape prosecution if they marry their victim under article 424.

On February 16, Abdelrazeq al-Nadhouri, chief of staff of the LNA, issued an order requiring women who wished to travel abroad by land, air, or sea to be accompanied by a male guardian. Al-Nadhouri rescinded the order on February 23 after public pressure, and replaced it with another order requiring all men and women ages 18 to 45 to acquire clearance by relevant security agencies ahead of any international travel from east Libya.

The penal code prohibits all sexual acts outside marriage, including same-sex relations, and punishes them with up to five years in prison.

## Abductions and Enforced Disappearances

Militias linked with various government authorities in east and west of the country and criminal gangs kidnapped or forcibly disappeared scores of people for political gain, ransom, and extortion. Tripoli-based activist, Jabir Zain, remained missing after an armed group linked to the GNA Interior Ministery abducted him in Tripoli on September 25, 2016. Civil society activist Abdelmoez Banoon and Benghazi prosecutor Abdel-Nasser Al-Jeroushi, both abducted by unidentified groups in 2014, remained missing.

In August, an armed group affiliated with the GNA kidnapped former Prime Minister Ali Zeidan during a visit to Tripoli and released him nine days later.

## Migrants, Refugees, and Asylum Seekers

Libya remained a major hub for refugees, asylum seekers, and migrants on their way to Europe. As of November, the IOM recorded over 161,010 arrivals to Europe by sea since January, most of whom departed from Libya. According to the UN Refugee Agency (UNHCR), at least 2,772 died or went missing while crossing the central Mediterranean route to Europe. As of November, the IOM reported that 348,372 migrants and asylum seekers were present in Libya.

Italy and the EU provided training and material support to Libyan coast guard forces to boost their capacity to intercept boats in territorial and international waters and return migrants and asylum seekers to Libyan territory, where many were exposed to physical abuse including beatings, sexual violence, extortion, abduction, harsh detention conditions, and forced labor.

In November, after revelations of alleged "slave auctions," Rwanda offered to resettle 30,000 African "slaves" from Libya.

The Department for Combating Illegal Migration (DCIM), which is part of the GNA-aligned Interior Ministry, managed the formal migrant detention centers, while smugglers and traffickers ran informal ones.

## Key International Actors

The United States announced in September 2016 that it had ended its military campaign against ISIS targets in Libya. In September 2017, the US conducted what it called "precision airstrikes" against purported ISIS targets south of Sirte. There were no reports of civilian casualties.

In June, the UN Security Council extended an arms embargo on Libya, effective since 2011, for another 12 months. On June 1, the UN Panel of Experts of the Libya Sanctions Committee, established pursuant to UN Security Council resolution 1973 (2011), issued its report on human rights abuses, violations of the arms embargo, and misappropriation of funds.

In February, the UN Support Mission to Libya published a report on the 2014 and 2015 trial proceedings against 37 former members of the Gaddafi government who were accused of crimes during the 2011 uprising, concluding that proceedings violated both international fair trial norms and Libyan law.

Members of the European Council met in Malta in February, and pledged to train, equip, and support Libyan coast guard forces, and, together with UNHCR and the IOM, improve reception capacities and conditions for migrants in Libya. The EU pledged a total of €200 million for migration-related projects in Libya to support migrant detention centers and coast guard forces, despite evidence of abuse.

In July, the EU Council extended the mandate of its anti-smuggling naval operation in the central Mediterranean, Operation Sophia, until December 2018. Operation Sophia's mandate is to disrupt migrant smugglers and human traffickers, including training Libyan Coastguard and Navy forces, and contributing to the implementation of the UN arms embargo in international waters off Libya's coast.

On July 25, France's President Emmanuel Macron hosted a meeting between Libyan leaders Prime Minister Fayez Serraj and General Hiftar in a bid to break the stalemate between them. The meeting resulted in a declaration of principles, mainly to a conditional ceasefire, and plans for future elections.

In September, the EU renewed sanctions for six months against three Libyans seen as threatening the peace, security, and stability of Libya, and obstructive to the implementation of the LPA: Agila Saleh, president of the House of Representatives; Khalifa Ghweil, prime minister of the National Salvation Government; and Nuri Abu Sahmain, president of the self-declared General National Congress.

# Malaysia

Malaysia's government continued its crackdown on critical voices and human rights defenders in 2017. With corruption allegations casting a shadow over Prime Minister Najib Razak, the government strengthened abusive laws and facilitated a societal shift toward a more conservative and less tolerant approach to Islam.

## *Freedom of Expression*

Although Prime Minister Najib claimed, at a speech in April 2017, that freedom of speech was "thriving" in Malaysia, the reality is far different. The Communications and Multimedia Act (CMA) has been used repeatedly to investigate and arrest those who criticize government officials on social media. Section 233(1) of the CMA provides criminal penalties of up to one year in prison for a communication that "is obscene, indecent, false, menacing or offensive in character with intent to annoy, abuse, threaten or harass another person." It has been used against, among others, a blogger who posted an image showing Najib behind bars and, in 2017, individuals who criticized former Chief Minister Adenan Satem after his death.

In May 2017, the government launched its CMA prosecution of the CEO and the editor-in-chief of online news portal *Malaysiakini* over a video the news portal carried criticizing Attorney General Mohamed Apandi Ali for clearing the prime minister of corruption allegations.

In April, the government threatened to withdraw the publishing license of Chinese language newspaper *Nanyang* because it published a satirical cartoon about the debate in parliament on Sharia, or Islamic law. The threat was withdrawn only after the newspaper withdrew the cartoon and apologized.

In August, authorities used Malaysia's restrictive Film Censorship Act to require the deletion of scenes from a film by a Malaysian investigative journalist implicating Malaysian immigration officials in the trafficking of Rohingya girls. Authorities also banned in its entirety *Kakuma Can Dance*, a film by a Swedish filmmaker about refugees and hip-hop dance in Kenya. Both films were scheduled to be shown during the annual Refugee Festival in Kuala Lumpur.

## Criminal Justice System

Malaysia continues to detain individuals without trial under restrictive laws. Both the 1959 Prevention of Crime Act and the 2015 Prevention of Terrorism Act give government-appointed boards the authority to impose detention without trial for up to two years, renewable indefinitely, to order electronic monitoring, and to impose other significant restrictions on freedom of movement and freedom of association, with no possibility of judicial review.

In August, the government passed amendments to the Prevention of Crime Act that effectively eliminated the right of a detainee to be heard. The amendments abolished the detainee's right to appear before or make representations to either the inquiry officer responsible for presenting the case for detention or to the government-appointed Prevention of Crime Board (POCB) that makes the detention decision.

The similarly restrictive Security Offences (Special Measures) Act, which allows for preventive detention of up to 28 days with no judicial review for a range of "security offenses," was renewed for an additional five years in April.

Malaysia retains the death penalty for various crimes, and makes the sentence mandatory for 12 offenses, including drug trafficking. Nearly 1,000 people are estimated to be on death row. The government is not transparent about when and how decisions are made to carry out executions, and executed two men for murder on short notice in March 2017 despite a pending clemency petition.

## Human Rights Defenders

Human rights defenders continue to face legal attacks and arbitrary restrictions on their rights. In March, authorities investigated three members of the Citizen Action Group on Enforced Disappearances (CAGED) under section 505(b) of the Penal Code for making statements with "intent to cause fear and alarm in to the public" after they used the phrase "enforced disappearances" to refer to the unsolved abduction of Pastor Raymond Koh and the disappearance of several other individuals connected to the Christian church.

In the same month, a court sentenced Lena Hendry to pay a fine of RM$10,000 (US$2,062) or face one year in prison for her role in arranging a showing of the documentary film *No Fire Zone*. In June, lawyer Siti Kassim was charged with "obstructing a public servant" for her actions in challenging the authority of officials conducting a raid on a transgender beauty pageant in April 2016.

The government also regularly takes action to block foreign human rights activists from attending events in Malaysia. In June, immigration authorities detained Singaporean activist Han Hui Hui when she attempted to enter the country to attend a human rights event and sent her back to Singapore. In July, government officials detained Adilur Rahman Khan, head of the prominent Bangladesh human rights nongovernmental organization (NGO) Odhikar, when he arrived to attend a conference on the death penalty. Authorities held him for more than 15 hours at the airport before putting him on a plane back to Dhaka.

## Police Abuse and Impunity

Police torture of suspects in custody, in some cases resulting in deaths, continues to be a serious problem, as does a lack of accountability for such offenses. In February, detainee Chandran Muniandy was hospitalized with multiple injuries to his head and body and most of his toenails missing; police claimed his injuries resulted from a fall in the toilet.

The Enforcement Agency Integrity Commission (EAIC) announced that it would investigate the death of S. Balamurugan, who died in custody in February, only after a post-mortem found evidence of blunt force injuries. In October, one police inspector was charged with "voluntarily causing hurt" to Balamurugan to extort a confession. At time of writing, no one has been arrested or disciplined in the Munianty case. During the year, at least two other individuals died in custody as a result of untreated medical conditions.

## Refugees, Asylum Seekers, and Trafficking Victims

Malaysia is not a party to the 1951 Refugee Convention, and refugees and asylum seekers have no legal rights or status in the country. Over 150,000 refugees and asylum seekers, most of whom come from Burma, are registered with the UN Refugee Agency, UNHCR, in Malaysia but are unable to work, travel, or enroll in government schools. Asylum seekers arrested by authorities are treated as "illegal migrants" and locked up in overcrowded and unhealthy immigration detention centers.

No Malaysians have been held responsible for their role in the deaths of over 100 ethnic Rohingya trafficking victims whose bodies were found in 2015 in remote jungle detention camps on the Thai-Malaysian border. The 12 policemen initially charged in the case were all exonerated and released in March 2017.

The Malaysian government has failed to effectively implement amendments passed in 2014 to Malaysia's 2007 anti-trafficking law, in particular by taking the necessary administrative steps to provide assistance and work authorization to all trafficking victims who desire it, while ensuring their freedom of movement. Despite these clear failures, the US State Department upgraded Malaysia to Tier 2 in its annual Trafficking in Persons (TIP) Report.

## Freedom of Assembly and Association

Malaysian authorities regularly prosecute individuals who hold peaceful assemblies without giving notice or participate in "street protests." The Societies Act restricts freedom of association by requiring that organizations with seven or more members register with the registrar of societies. The law gives the minister of home affairs "absolute discretion" to declare an organization illegal, and grants the Registrar of Societies authority over political parties.

In July, the Registrar of Societies compelled the opposition Democratic Action Party to hold new elections for its central executive committee, finding that a previous election was invalid. In November, it threatened to deregister opposition party Bersatu, claiming the name of its youth wing was illegal.

## Freedom of Religion

Malaysia has continued its shift towards a more conservative approach to Islam, the majority religion. A bill to increase the punishments that can be imposed by state Sharia courts remains pending in parliament, and in July 2017 the state of Kelantan passed legislation to permit public canings imposed by Sharia courts.

In August, a government minister called for "atheists" to be tracked down, and statues of winged women were removed from a local park after complaints that they were "offensive" to Muslims. In September, Turkish academic Mustafa Akyol, author of a book arguing for liberal Islam, was detained and interrogated by the Federal Territories Islamic Religious Department (JAWI) for giving a talk on

Islam without official credentials from religious authorities. Dr. Ahmad Farouk Musa, who organized the talk, was charged with abetting Akyol in the offense and faces up to three years in prison if convicted. The home minister subsequently banned Akyol's book, along with a collection of scholarly articles by the G25 organization calling for a more moderate approach to Islam.

The abduction of Christian Pastor Raymond Koh by 15 masked men in February, followed by the unexplained disappearance of three other people linked to Christian churches, raised serious fears among the Christian community. At time of writing, all four persons remained missing.

## Sexual Orientation and Gender Identity

Discrimination against lesbian, gay, bisexual, and transgender (LGBT) people is pervasive in Malaysia. Numerous laws and regulations attributed to Sharia prohibiting a "man posing as a woman," sexual relations between women, and sexual relations between men effectively criminalize LGBT people.

Violence against LGBT people remains a serious concern, highlighted by the murder of a transgender woman Sameera Krishnan in February, and the rape and murder of 18-year-old T. Nhaveen, a young man whose assailants taunted him with anti-LGBT slurs, in June. In a positive development, the Health Ministry, in response to strident criticism from activists and the general public, reframed the terms of a youth video competition, removing language and criteria that stigmatized LGBT identities in favor of language that appears to affirm them.

## Domestic and Sexual Violence

Malaysia took a step forward in the protection of women's rights in 2017 by amending its domestic violence law to provide better protection for victims of domestic violence. It also passed a law expanding criminal sanctions for sex offenses against children. Efforts to pass a law to end child marriage were defeated, however, and Malaysia is one of the few countries that does not collect data on the number of children marrying. Marital rape is not a crime in Malaysia.

## *Key International Actors*

Malaysia positions itself in the UN and the international community as a moderate Muslim state prepared to stand up to Islamist extremism, earning support from the US and its allies. Malaysia also has continued its engagement with China, its largest trading partner.

HUMAN
RIGHTS
WATCH

MALI CONFLICT AND AFTERMATH
Compendium of Human Rights Watch Reporting, 2012-2017

# Mali

Insecurity in Mali worsened as Islamist armed groups allied to Al-Qaeda dramatically increased their attacks on government forces and United Nations peacekeepers. The peace process envisioned to end the 2012-2013 political-military crisis stalled in 2017. Government forces conducted counterterrorism operations that resulted in arbitrary arrests, summary executions, torture, and ill-treatment.

In the north, armed groups made scant progress on disarmament and the government made inadequate progress on the restoration of state authority. This deepened a rule of law and security vacuum, facilitating rampant banditry and displacement. In central Mali, Islamist armed group presence and intimidation of the population steadily increased through the year, resulting in numerous serious abuses including summary executions of local officials and alleged government informants.

Intercommunal violence in central and northern Mali left scores dead, displaced thousands, and was exploited by ethnically aligned and abusive vigilante groups to garner recruits. Banditry and attacks undermined the delivery of basic health care, education and humanitarian assistance.

Some effort was made toward ensuring justice for victims of abuses committed during the 2012-2013 armed conflict, but the judiciary was reluctant to investigate ongoing abuse by the armed forces. Rule of law institutions remained weak, and corruption endemic, further impeding Malians' access to basic health care and education.

The spread of militant attacks from north to central Mali and across borders into Burkina Faso and Niger sparked increased diplomatic and military engagement by the international community, leading to a United Nations sanctions regime and the creation of a five-nation counterterrorism military force, the G5 Sahel Joint Force.

## *Abuses by Armed Groups in North and Central Mali*

A suicide bombing in Gao claimed by Al-Qaeda in the Islamic Maghreb (AQIM) killed over 50 former members of armed groups. Islamist armed groups summarily executed numerous local government officials and members of armed groups they accused of being government informants. At least two victims were beheaded.

In central Mali, Islamist armed groups increasingly imposed their version of Sharia (Islamic law), establishing courts that did not adhere to fair trial standards. They threatened villagers collaborating with authorities, recruited children, destroyed schools, and beat villagers who engaged in cultural practices they had forbidden.

Several civilians were killed during fighting between armed groups, as well as by explosives planted by the groups on major roads. In 2017, humanitarian agencies suffered scores of attacks, mostly by bandits, which undermined their ability to deliver aid.

At least 23 UN peacekeepers with the Multidimensional Integrated Stabilization Mission in Mali (MINUSMA) were killed and 103 wounded in attacks by Islamist armed groups in 2017, bringing the total to 92 killed since MINUSMA's creation in 2013.

At time of writing, Islamist armed groups still held six foreigners hostage, including a Colombian nun, a French aid worker, American and Swiss missionaries, a Romanian mine worker, and an Australian doctor, all kidnapped within the Sahel region from 2015 to 2017. A Swede and a British-South African held hostage since 2011 were released in 2017. In November, 11 Malian security force personnel kidnapped during operations in 2016 and 2017 were inadvertently killed during a French airstrike on armed Islamists.

## *Abuses by State Security Forces*

Government forces took steps to protect civilians by patrolling and intervening to stop communal tension, but military operations to counter the growing presence of Islamist armed groups resulted in serious violations of human rights and international humanitarian law including extrajudicial killings, enforced disappearances, torture, and arbitrary arrest.

During 2017, soldiers allegedly killed and buried at least 15 suspects in common graves, while more than 25 were subjected to enforced disappearance. Dozens of other suspects were subjected to severe ill-treatment during interrogations.

Numerous men and some children accused of crimes against the state and terrorist-related offenses were detained by the national intelligence agency without respect for due process. Some members of the security forces were also implicated in acts of extortion, bribe-taking, and theft, including from detainees.

The military made little effort to hold to account soldiers or militiamen implicated in abuses. However, they took steps to ensure the presence of military police—responsible for monitoring respect for international humanitarian law—during military operations, made progress in operationalizing the Military Justice Directorate in Bamako, and, in October, promised an internal investigation into alleged abuses by their forces in central Mali.

## *Recruitment of Child Soldiers and Children's Rights*

Armed groups in the north and center, including those allied with the government, continued to recruit and use child soldiers. Numerous children suspected of supporting armed groups were detained in state-run detention centers, in contravention of a 2013 protocol stipulating that children were to be placed in a care center managed by UNICEF.

During 2017, over 150,000 children were denied the right to education because of insecurity, threats against teachers and school closures in northern and central Mali. Numerous teachers were directly threatened and schools vandalized or destroyed by armed Islamist groups. At least 10 children died during crossfire, intercommunal violence, or explosions.

## *Accountability for Abuses*

The Justice Ministry took steps to improve its case management system, and, in late December 2016, set up a special investigations cell to address serious crimes, attached to the Specialized Judicial Unit on Terrorism and Transnational Organized Crime. At year's end, implementation of the decision had not moved forward.

The August conviction of Aliou Mahamane Touré, former head of the Islamic police force in Gao for crimes against the state, indicates progress towards accountability. The trial of former coup leader Gen. Amadou Haya Sanogo and 17 other members of the Malian security services for the 2012 killing of 21 elite "Red Beret" soldiers was suspended in December 2016.

Judicial authorities failed to open investigations into ongoing violations against civilians by security forces and made little progress in ensuring justice for the victims of violations committed during Mali's 2012-2013 armed conflict.

## Truth and Reconciliation Mechanism and Independent Human Rights Commission

The Truth, Justice and Reconciliation Commission, established by presidential executive order in 2014 with a three-year mandate to investigate crimes and the root causes of violence dating back to 1960, made meaningful progress in 2017. The 25-member commission operationalized five regional offices and took over 5,000 statements from victims and witnesses. However, the credibility of the commission was undermined by government's inclusion of nine armed group members, while excluding victims' group representatives.

The mandate of the National Commission for Human Rights was strengthened with improved funding and the appointment in May of nine full-time commissioners. However, the commission showed reluctance to investigate abuses by security force personnel.

## Judiciary and Legal Framework for Human Rights

The Malian judiciary was plagued by neglect and mismanagement, and insecurity led many judicial personnel to abandon their posts in northern and central Mali. Due to the courts' inability to adequately process cases, hundreds of detainees have been held in extended pretrial detention. However, some effort was made to rehabilitate and improve prison conditions.

In March, under pressure from international donors, the government established the Central Office for the Fight against Illegal Enrichment, mandated by a 2016 law to coordinate anti-corruption efforts.

In April, a new Ministry of Human Rights and State Reform was created by a presidential decree to oversee activities related to rule of law and transitional justice. However, the minister was reluctant to investigate or denounce violations by security force personnel.

In April and October, the National Assembly extended the state of emergency, first declared in 2015. The constitution review process stalled amid protests by opposition parties and civil society that the process had been hijacked by the executive and that proposed changes increased executive powers.

## Key International Actors

Mali remained a top political priority for France, which, together with the United States, took the lead on military matters. The European Union led on training and security sector reform, and the UN led on rule of law and political stability. These actors were largely reluctant to publicly call for investigations into past and ongoing government violations.

Regional actors acted to combat the spread of Islamist militancy in the Sahel. In January, Mali, Burkina Faso, and Niger established a joint task force to combat rising insecurity along their shared borders.

In July, Mali, Mauritania, Burkina Faso, Niger, and Chad launched the G5 Sahel multinational counterterrorism military force. The creation of G5 Sahel was endorsed by the African Union and welcomed by the UN Security Council. The EU pledged $56 million, the US $60 million and Saudi Arabia $100 million in support of G5-Sahel.

MINUSMA meaningfully contributed to training government forces and members of the judiciary. While the forces increased patrols, MINUSMA struggled to implement its more robust 2016 civilian protection mandate, largely due to persistent lack of equipment and assets.

Operation Barkhane, the 4,000-strong French regional counterterrorism operation, conducted numerous operations in Mali. The EU Training Mission in Mali (EUTM) and the EU Capacity Building Mission (EUCAP) continued to train the Malian army, national guard, gendarmerie, and police forces.

The situation in Mali remained under investigation by the International Criminal Court (ICC) since 2012. In August, the court ordered former Ansar Dine leader Ahmad Al Faqi Al Mahdi to pay US$3.2 million in reparations after his 2016 conviction for his role in the 2012 destruction of historical and religious monuments in Timbuktu. ICC prosecutor Fatou Bensouda visited Mali in October. Investigations are ongoing but limited due to the precarious security situation.

The UN, EU, Netherlands, Swiss, and Canada took the lead in programs to support the justice sector and address corruption. The United States supported reform of military justice.

In March, the UN Human Rights Council renewed the mandate of the independent expert on Mali and decided to hold a discussion with the independent expert and government representatives in March 2018 to focus on justice and reconciliation.

In September, UN Security Council Resolution 2374 imposed an asset freeze and travel ban against those who obstruct the 2015 peace accord, commit human rights abuses, recruit child soldiers, hinder aid delivery, or conduct attacks on peacekeepers and other UN personnel. The sanctions will be monitored by a panel of experts.

# Mexico

During the administration of President Enrique Peña Nieto, which began in 2012, security forces have been implicated in repeated, serious human rights violations during efforts to combat organized crime—including extrajudicial killings, enforced disappearances, and torture. The government has made little progress in prosecuting those responsible for recent abuses, let alone the large number of abuses committed by soldiers and police since former President Felipe Calderón initiated Mexico's "war on drugs" in 2006.

In April, the Mexican Congress passed legislation to curb torture and the use of coerced evidence during judicial proceedings. Implementation of the law remained pending at time of writing.

## *Enforced Disappearances*

Since 2006, Mexico's security forces have carried out widespread enforced disappearances.

In August 2017, the government reported that the whereabouts of more than 32,000 people who had gone missing since 2006 remain unknown. Prosecutors and police routinely fail to take basic investigative steps to identify those responsible for enforced disappearances, often telling the missing people's families to investigate on their own. Authorities have routinely failed to identify remains of bodies or body parts found in various locations, including in clandestine graves, throughout the country.

The federal government has pursued potentially promising initiatives to find people who have gone missing, but they have produced limited results. In 2013, it created a unit in the Attorney General's Office to investigate disappearances, which became a Special Prosecutor's Office in October 2015. However, the office has made only limited progress in investigating and prosecuting cases of forced disappearance.

In 2015, Congress approved a constitutional reform giving it authority to pass general laws on enforced disappearances and torture that would establish a single nationwide definition for each of the crimes and facilitate their prosecution in all 31 states and Mexico City. The law was passed in November 2017. At time of writing, its implementation remained pending.

Mexican authorities have failed to make progress in determining what happened to 43 missing students from the teachers college in Ayotzinapa who disappeared in 2014 and are believed killed. Only one of the students has been positively identified among remains that the government says are those of the students. The Attorney General's Office has failed to conduct in-depth investigations following recommendations made by the Interdisciplinary Group of Independent Experts (GIEI), established through an agreement between the government and the Inter-American Commission on Human Rights (IACHR).

At time of writing, more than 100 people had been charged with alleged involvement in the abductions, yet prosecutors had neither presented accusations against state or federal authorities nor against members of the armed forces, despite indications of their involvement.

An August 2016 internal report from the Attorney General's Office about the Ayotzinapa investigations established that investigators had broken the law and had engaged in arbitrary detentions and the coercion of alleged suspects. The inspector general who wrote the report claimed that the Attorney General's Office asked him to step down shortly after he presented the report to his superiors. The report was rewritten, and the version that the Attorney General's Office eventually published concluded that only a handful of minor violations had been committed.

## Extrajudicial Killings

Unlawful killings of civilians by Mexican security forces "take place at an alarmingly high rate" amid an atmosphere of "systematic and endemic impunity," according to the United Nations special rapporteur on extrajudicial, summary, or arbitrary executions in 2014.

In August 2016, the National Human Rights Commission (CNDH) concluded that federal police arbitrarily executed 22 of 42 civilians who died in a confrontation in 2015 in Tanhuato, Michoacán State. Police fatally shot at least 13 people in the back, tortured two detainees, and burned a man alive, the CNDH concluded, then altered the crime scene by moving bodies and planting guns to justify the illegal killings. At time of writing, nobody had been charged and a federal investigation into the Tanhuato killings remained open.

## Military Abuses and Impunity

Mexico has relied heavily on the military to fight drug-related violence and organized crime, leading to widespread human rights violations by military personnel. As of July 2016, the CNDH had received almost 10,000 complaints of abuse by the army since 2006—including more than 2,000 during the current administration. It found in more than 100 cases that military personnel committed serious human rights violations.

In November 2017, the Chamber of Deputies approved the Law on Internal Security, authorizing military involvement in domestic law enforcement activities—including intelligence gathering—without including meaningful measures to improve accountability. At time of writing, the proposal was under discussion in the Senate.

In 2014, Congress reformed the Code of Military Justice to require that abuses committed by members of the military against civilians be handled by the civilian criminal justice system rather than the military system, which had a history of routinely failing to hold members of the military accountable for abuses.

In May 2016, provisions included in a new Military Code of Criminal Procedure and in reforms to the Code of Military Justice granted military prosecutors and judges broad powers to order the search of homes and public buildings, and to listen to private telecommunications, without a judicial order issued by a civilian judge. In June 2016, the CNDH challenged the constitutionality of these provisions. At time of writing, a Supreme Court decision was still pending.

In the case of Tlatlaya, where soldiers killed 22 civilians in 2014—witnesses and the CNDH reported that they extrajudicially executed at least 12 of them—nobody has been convicted of the killings. In May 2016, a civilian, federal court absolved the last of eight soldiers charged with homicide. However, in July 2017, a judge ordered the Attorney General's Office to investigate the case in-depth, including the responsibility of military commanders and the alteration of the crime scene. The Attorney General's Office appealed the ruling. The appeal was pending resolution at time of writing.

## *Torture*

Torture is widely practiced in Mexico to obtain confessions and extract information. It is most frequently applied in the period between when victims are detained, often arbitrarily, and when they are handed over to civilian prosecutors, a period in which they are often held incommunicado at military bases or illegal detention sites.

According to a survey of more than 64,000 people incarcerated in 370 Mexican prisons located throughout the country in 2016, performed by Mexico's national statistics office (Instituto Nacional de Estadística y Geografía – INEGI), 57.8 percent of the prison population reported having suffered some type of physical violence at the time of their arrest. Of these people, 19 percent reported receiving electrical shocks; 36 percent being choked, held underwater, or smothered; and 59 percent being hit or kicked. In addition, 28 percent reported that they were threatened that their family would be harmed.

In April 2017, the Mexican legislature approved the Law to Investigate, Prevent, and Sanction Torture, aimed at curbing torture and excluding testimony obtained through torture from judicial proceedings. At time of writing, implementation of the law remained pending.

As of June 30, 2017, the Specialized Unit for the Investigation of the Crime of Torture—a unit within the Attorney General's Office—had 4,390 ongoing investigations into alleged cases of torture. Additionally, between September 2016 and June 2017, courts ordered more than 750 criminal investigations into allegations of torture.

The Interdisciplinary Group of Independent Experts, established through an agreement between the government and the IACHR concluded in April 2016 that 80 percent of the suspects detained in connection with the case showed bodily injuries possibly due to ill-treatment and torture. As of September 2017, the Attorney General's Office was conducting six investigations related to the alleged torture of 31 people. None of the investigations had been finalized at time of writing.

According to the CNDH, Mexico State prosecutors sought to cover up military wrongdoing in the Tlatlaya case by using torture to coerce false testimony from witnesses. Four police officers were sentenced to three years and eight months' imprisonment for the crime. As of September 2017—more than three years after the massacre—nobody has been convicted in connection with the cover-up.

## Criminal Justice System

The criminal justice system routinely fails to provide justice to victims of violent crimes and human rights violations. Causes of failure include corruption, inadequate training and resources, and complicity of prosecutors and public defenders with criminals and abusive officials. The failure of law enforcement has contributed to the emergence of armed citizen self-defense groups in several parts of the country.

In 2013, Mexico enacted a federal Victims Law intended to ensure justice, protection, and reparations for crime victims. Reforms to the law, intended to reduce bureaucracy and improve access to aid and reparations for victims, were approved in January 2017.

## Attacks on Journalists and Human Rights Defenders

Journalists, particularly those who report on crime or criticize officials, face harassment and attack by both government authorities and criminal groups. Journalists are often driven to self-censorship as a result.

From 2000 through October 2017, 104 journalists were killed and 25 disappeared, according to the Attorney General's Office. The nongovernmental organization (NGO) Article 19 documented eight cases of journalists killed and one disappeared between January and July 2017.

Authorities routinely fail to investigate crimes against journalists adequately, often preemptively ruling out their profession as a motive. The CNDH reported in 2016 that 90 percent of crimes against journalists in Mexico since 2000 have gone unpunished, including 82 percent of killings and 100 percent of disappearances. Since its creation in July 2010, the Special Prosecutor's Office for Crimes against Freedom of Expression has opened more than 1,000 investigations into crimes against journalists. As of October 2017, it has brought charges in 115 cases and obtained only 3 convictions.

In July 2017, an investigation by Citizen Lab, a research center at the University of Toronto, showed that at least 11 human rights activists and journalists (as well as the 16-year-old son of a journalist) and members of the GIEI had been targets of a spyware campaign conducted with sophisticated software bought by the Mexican government. A senator and two high-ranking members of the main opposition party were also targeted. The affected activists filed complaints with the Attorney General's Office, which opened an investigation.

By October 2016, 617 people had received protection under a 2012 law to protect journalists and human rights defenders. However, protection has been slow to arrive or, in some cases, insufficient.

## Women's and Girls' Rights

Mexican laws do not adequately protect women and girls against domestic and sexual violence. Some provisions, including those that make the severity of punishments for some sexual offenses contingent upon the "chastity" of the victim, contradict international standards.

Eighteen of Mexico's 31 states have passed laws establishing that there is a right to life from the moment of conception. Although the Supreme Court ruled in 2010 that all states must provide emergency contraception and access to abortion for rape victims, many women and girls face serious barriers accessing abortions after sexual violence, including official intimidation.

## Unaccompanied Migrant Children

Apprehensions of unaccompanied children from the Northern Triangle countries of El Salvador, Guatemala, and Honduras decreased sharply in the first seven months of 2017 compared with the same period in 2016, and asylum recognition rates for unaccompanied children from these countries have risen in recent years. Even so, less than 1 percent of those apprehended each year received international protection, far short of the likely need: the UN High Commissioner for Refugees (UNHCR) has estimated that as many as half of the unaccompanied children who arrive in Mexico from the Northern Triangle have plausible asylum claims that should be seriously considered.

## Sexual Orientation and Gender Identity

Same-sex marriage has been legal in Mexico City since 2010. It is also permitted in 10 additional states (eight of which have reformed their local legislation to allow it and two where the Supreme Court invalidated articles of the local Civil Code, therefore permitting it without a legislative change). In 2015, the Supreme Court opened the door to recognition in all states by ruling that defining marriage exclusively as a union between a man and a woman constitutes discrimination and thus violates Mexico's Constitution.

In May 2016, President Peña Nieto introduced bills to recognize same-sex marriage in the constitution and the Federal Civil Code. This would have also removed sexual orientation and gender identity as barriers to adoption. However, the federal bill was rejected when two committees in the Chamber of Deputies voted against the initiative in November 2016.

At the same time, President Peña Nieto instructed federal agencies to recognize gender identity through the reissuance of birth certificates and passports, without a doctor's involvement. He also instructed the Secretariat of Education to include sexual diversity among the new educational materials. It had yet to do so at time of writing.

## Disability Rights

In a 2014 report, the UN Committee on the Rights of Persons with Disabilities found that, despite new laws and programs protecting the rights of the disabled, serious gaps remained, including in access to justice, legal standing, and the right to vote; access to buildings, transportation, and public spaces; violence against women; and education.

In 2015, Disability Rights International reported that conditions were inhumane in Mexico City's government-funded facilities for people with disabilities, including one institution that locked children in cages. The report also documented that women with psychosocial disabilities at state-run clinics in Mexico City were sometimes pressured into being sterilized or, when pregnant, into having abortions.

Mexico made no progress in the implementation of the right to legal capacity for persons with disabilities. In addition, it amended the General Education Law in

June 2016, enabling the special education of children with disabilities in schools.

In February 2016, Mexico's Supreme Court determined the requirement that people on the autistic spectrum obtain a certificate of ability to work violates Mexico's Constitution, as well as international human rights standards.

## Key International Actors

In September, the UN Committee on Migrant Workers published a preliminary report in which it expressed its concern about the "grave irregularities" in the identification of the victims and those responsible for the mass murders of migrants committed between 2010 and 2012 in the states of Nuevo León and Tamaulipas. It also urged the state to guarantee the rights of migrants in transit and called upon Mexican authorities to "only use the detention of migrants as a measure of last resort," to improve conditions of detention, and to "immediately put an end to" the detention of migrant children.

In January, after his visit to the country, the UN special rapporteur on human rights defenders raised concerns about attacks against human rights defenders and criminalization of their activities. In May, the special rapporteurs on freedom of expression from the UN and the IACHR issued a joint statement urging the Mexican government "to end [the] epidemic of violence against journalists."

In April, the UN working group on human rights and business had also urged the government to better protect human rights defenders and journalists, as well as to implement mechanisms to create social dialogue about large-scale projects and improve efforts to combat gender-based discrimination in the workplace.

The IACHR published a report in March 2016 documenting a wide range of abuses in Mexico—including disappearances; extrajudicial executions; torture; and insecurity for women, children, migrants, human rights defenders, and journalists—which they concluded amounted to a "crisis of gross human rights violations." The government criticized the report, responding that there was no "human rights crisis" in Mexico. Later that month, Mexican authorities denied UN Special Rapporteur on Torture Juan Méndez permission to return before the end of his term, rejecting his conclusion that torture was widespread and accusing him of acting "unethically."

In October 2016, the Office of the UN High Commissioner for Human Rights (OHCHR) issued 14 recommendations to Mexico on the need to address impunity for human rights violations, adopt laws to regulate the use of force and eliminate torture and enforced disappearances, and establish an independent forensic institution with adequate resources. In May 2016, the UN special rapporteur on extrajudicial, summary, or arbitrary executions released a report on Mexico identifying continuing serious violations, including extrajudicial killings and excessive use of force by security forces, impunity, and lack of reparations for victims.

Since 2007, the United States has allocated more than US$1.6 billion in aid through the Mérida Initiative to help combat organized crime. In 2015, the US secretary of state withheld $5 million in security aid, saying the State Department could not confirm that Mexico had met the agreement's human rights criteria, but Mexico received its full Mérida aid the following year. In 2017, the Mérida aid was $139 million.

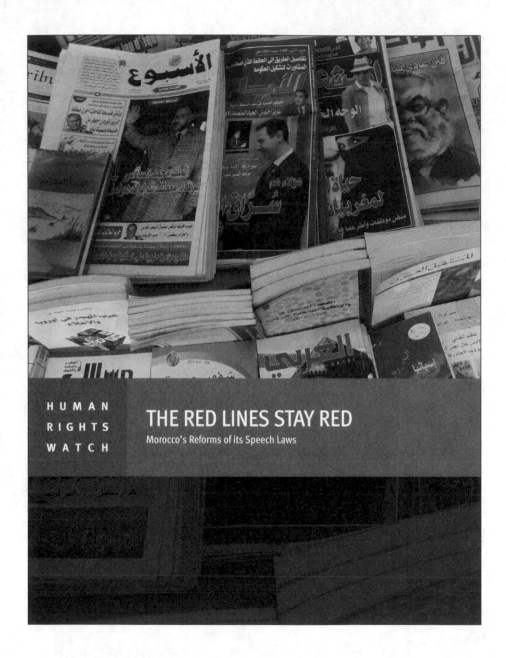

# Morocco/Western Sahara

Morocco responded to ongoing demonstrations in the restive Rif region throughout 2017 with its characteristic vacillation between tolerance and repression. Security forces allowed many street protests to proceed against the central government's alleged neglect of the region's needs, but, starting in May, moved to arrest activists of the so-called Hirak Rif movement, beating and abusing many of them. Some were subsequently imprisoned after unfair trials. A court imprisoned a well-known journalist-commentator on dubious charges relating to inciting the Hirak Rif demonstrations.

The political process for self-determination of Western Sahara, a territory under Moroccan control, remained stalled with little international mediation or attention. Morocco proposes autonomy under its continued rule but rejects a referendum on independence. The government systematically prevented gatherings in Western Sahara supporting Sahrawi self-determination.

A new trial before a civilian court of 24 Sahrawis accused of involvement in the deaths of policemen during 2010 clashes resulted in their conviction and lengthy prison sentences, an outcome similar to the one in their first trial before a military tribunal. The trial was tainted by apparent due process violations such as the reliance on testimony allegedly obtained under coercion without properly examining allegations of torture.

Authorities continued throughout 2017 to restrict the activities of Morocco's biggest independent human rights organization, the Moroccan Association for Human Rights, and of international human rights groups seeking to conduct research visits.

## *Freedom of Expression*

The Press and Publications Code, adopted by parliament in July 2016, eliminates prison sentences yet imposes fines and court-ordered suspensions of publications or websites as punishment for many nonviolent speech offenses.

Meanwhile, the penal code maintains prison as a punishment for a variety of nonviolent speech offenses, including for crossing Morocco's long-standing "red lines," that is "causing harm" to Islam, the monarchy, the person of the king, and the royal family, and "inciting against" Morocco's "territorial integrity," a reference to its claim to Western Sahara. Prison also remains a punishment for insulting state institutions and for speech and writings that are perceived as an "apology for terrorism."

On September 11, 2017, the al-Hoceima Appeals Court increased the three-month prison sentence handed down by a lower court against website editor and journalist Hamid Mahdaoui on July 25, 2017, for inciting participation in an unauthorized demonstration, to one year. The case was based on comments that Mahdaoui made in a public square in al-Hoceima on July 19, supporting the Hirak Rif movement and condemning the government's decision to ban a demonstration planned for July 20. Among the several citizen journalists and web activists prosecuted in connection with the Rif protests was Ilyass Akallouch, whom the al-Hoceima Court of First Instance sentenced on August 24 to eight months in prison and a MAD20,000 (US$2,000) fine for social media posts that "incite others to participate in unauthorized demonstrations."

Authorities require but often refuse to issue permits for foreign broadcast media to film in Morocco. On July 25, they deported two Spanish journalists who were covering the Rif protests, including one, Jose Luis Navazo, who had been living in Morocco for 17 years.

## *Freedom of Assembly and Association*

Authorities tolerated many marches and rallies throughout the year demanding political reform and protesting government actions, but often forcibly dispersed protests, even when they were peaceful.

In the Rif region, security forces had arrested over 450 Hirak Rif protesters, as of October. The protests began in October 2016, after a fishmonger in al-Hoceima was crushed to death in a garbage truck while trying to rescue his goods that authorities had confiscated.

Many of the detained protesters alleged beatings by police during arrest and said police forced them to sign written statements unread. Some of these allegations were corroborated by reports prepared by forensic doctors appointed by the National Human Rights Council, who had examined detained protesters. Courts convicted protesters on charges that included insulting and physically assaulting members of the security forces, armed rebellion, and destruction of public goods, sentencing them to terms in prison that were mostly 18 months or less.

Officials continue to arbitrarily prevent or impede associations from obtaining legal registration, although the 2011 constitution guarantees freedom of association.

Authorities have kept sealed since 2006 houses belonging to at least two members of the Islamist movement al-Adl wal-Ihsan (Justice and Spirituality), an Islamist movement that questions the king's claim of spiritual authority, without providing a formal legal basis.

Authorities frequently impeded events organized by local chapters of the Moroccan Association for Human Rights (AMDH), by denying access to planned venues. In a typical instance, on July 8, authorities in the village of Zaouiat Cheikh prevented access of participants to the community center, where AMDH had planned a public conference on human rights. They also sometimes prevented efforts by chapters to comply with document-filing requirements, placing some of these chapters in legal jeopardy.

The government has continued to impose a de facto ban on research missions by Amnesty International and Human Rights Watch since 2015, despite relative unimpeded access of the two organizations for nearly 25 years before then.

As in previous years, authorities expelled several foreign visitors who came to witness human rights conditions in Western Sahara or attend human rights events there. On July 4, Spanish citizens Laura Moreno and Andrea Sáez, who had come to meet with Sahrawi human rights activists were not allowed to deplane in El-Ayoun and were sent back.

## *Police Conduct, Torture, and the Criminal Justice System*

Courts failed to uphold due process guarantees in political and security-related cases.

The Code of Penal Procedure, amended in 2011, gives a defendant the right to contact a lawyer after 24 hours in police custody or a maximum of 36 hours if the prosecutor approves this extension. In cases involving terrorism offenses, the prosecutor can delay access to a lawyer for up to six days. The law does not give detainees the right to a have a lawyer present when police interrogate or present them with their statements for signature.

The 2003 counterterrorism law contains an overly broad definition of "terrorism" and allows for up to 12 days of *garde à vue* (precharge) detention in terrorism related cases.

The Rabat Appeals Court conducted a new trial of 24 Sahrawis convicted by a military court in 2013 for their alleged role in violence that erupted after security forces entered to dismantle a protest encampment set up in Gdeim Izik, Western Sahara. The violence resulted in the deaths of 11 security force members. The appeals court sentenced nearly all of the defendants to prison terms of between 20 years and life, similar to the sentences that the military court handed them in 2013. In its verdict, the court relied on the original police statements from 2010, which the defendants rejected as false. They said they were either coerced or physically forced into signing the statements, including through the use of torture. The court ordered medical examinations, which concluded that torture could neither be proven nor disproven, an unsurprising conclusion given that these examinations, the first of a forensic nature of these defendants, were taking place seven years after the alleged torture took place.

On March 9, a Rabat court of appeals upheld the conviction of French citizen Thomas Gallay on charges of materially aiding persons who harboured terrorist aims, but reduced his prison sentence from six to four years. Gallay's lawyer, who was not present when the police questioned him, said that police used pressure and deceit to persuade him to sign statements in Arabic, a language that he could not read. The court also convicted Gallay's eight Moroccan co-defendants, sentencing them to prison terms of up to 18 years. Hundreds of others were serving prison terms on terrorism charges, some of them following unfair mass trials, like those arrested in the "Bellarij" case in 2008.

Between January 1 and October 1, Morocco's highest court upheld the death penalty in three cases; 11 other death sentences that lower courts pronounced in 2017 were still under review at time of writing. Authorities have not carried out any executions since the early 1990s.

## Migrants and Refugees

A draft of Morocco's first law on the right to asylum had yet to be adopted. Since 2013, Morocco's ad hoc inter-ministerial commission charged with refugee issues has granted refugee cards and one-year renewable residency permits to almost every person that the United Nations High Commissioner for Refugees (UNHCR) recognized as a refugee, totalling 745 persons since 2013, most of them sub-Saharan Africans. As of September 30, UNHCR said it had 2,995 Syrian asylum seekers in its registry. While Morocco has not formally recognized these Syrians as refugees, it allows them to reside in Morocco and to access essential public services, such as health and education, according to UNHCR.

Morocco also granted one-year renewable residency permits to thousands of sub-Saharan migrants who were not asylum-seekers but who met criteria set forth in a 2013 plan.

On June 21, Moroccan authorities granted temporary residence status to 28 Syrian asylum seekers who remained blocked in no-man's land between Algeria and Morocco after a two-month-long stand-off between the two countries during which time neither agreed to admit them.

## Women's and Girls' Rights

The 2011 constitution guarantees equality for women, "while respecting the provisions of the constitution, and the laws and permanent characteristics of the Kingdom."

The 2004 Family Code, which improved women's rights in divorce and child custody, discriminates against women with regard to inheritance and procedures to obtain divorce. The code raised the age of marriage from 15 to 18, but judges routinely allowed girls to marry below this age.

Criminalization of adultery and sex outside marriage has a discriminatory gender impact, in that rape victims face prosecution if they file charges that are not later sustained. Women and girls also face prosecution if they are found to be pregnant or bear children outside marriage.

On March 17, 2016, the government adopted a revised bill on combatting violence against women (Bill 103-13), and the House of Representatives passed it on July 20, 2016. The draft law remained with the House of Councillors, the parliament's second chamber, at the end of 2016.

## Domestic Workers

A 2016 law on domestic worker rights is scheduled to go into effect in October 2018, following the adoption in 2017 of necessary implementing regulations. The law requires written contracts for domestic workers and sets 18 as the minimum age for such employment, after a five-year phase in during which 16- and 17-year-olds can work. It limits weekly working hours and guarantees 24 continuous hours of rest per week and sets a minimum wage and provides for financial penalties for employers who violate the law.

Despite a current prohibition on employing children under the age of 15, thousands of children under that age—predominantly girls—are believed to still work as domestic workers.

## Disability Rights

Parliament in 2016 adopted Framework Law 97.13 on the rights of persons with disabilities, a step toward harmonizing legislation with the Convention on the Rights of Persons with Disabilities, which Morocco ratified in 2009. However, the Framework Law fell short in some areas, such as in guaranteeing access to inclusive education for children with disabilities, and in affirming the right of legal capacity.

## Sexual Orientation and Gender Identity

Moroccan courts continued to jail persons for same-sex conduct under article 489 of the penal code, which stipulates prison terms of six months to three years for "lewd or unnatural acts with an individual of the same sex."

In December 2016, a court in Marrakech acquitted two teenage girls who had been detained for one week and charged with "sexual deviancy" for allegedly hugging and kissing in private. On February 24, two men were sentenced on charges that included violating article 489, to six months in prison and a fine of MAD1,000 (US$107) by a Tangiers court of first instance, after a video showing them engaging in consensual sex was shared on social media.

## *Key International Actors*

On December 21, 2016, the Court of Justice of the European Union concluded that 2012 bilateral EU-Morocco agreements liberalizing trade in agriculture and fish were not applicable to Western Sahara, due to the separate and distinct status guaranteed to that territory under the Charter of the United Nations and the principle of self-determination of peoples. The court however overturned a 2015 court decision invalidating the trade agreement.

Despite its own mixed record on eradicating torture, Morocco is a founding member of the Convention against Torture Initiative, a campaign by states to get the UN Convention against Torture universally ratified and better implemented by 2024.

# Mozambique

A ceasefire in December 2016 ended armed clashes between the government and the former rebel group, now political party, Resistência Nacional Moçambicana (Mozambican National Resistance, or RENAMO). But members of government security forces and RENAMO-linked armed groups continued to commit abuses with impunity during armed clashes that started in late 2014, including killings, enforced disappearances, kidnappings, arbitrary arrests, and destruction of property.

The country further endured an economic crisis, mainly due to the disclosure of state-owned companies' debt to foreign banks, which led donors to freeze their contributions to the state budget. Authorities failed to prosecute government officials implicated in the debt scandal, despite an international audit that detailed the transactions and named individuals involved in the process.

## *Impunity and Unresolved Killings*

Mozambican law enforcement continued its practice of not investigating a range of serious crimes. The cases of 10 high-profile figures, including senior opposition members, state prosecutors, and prominent academics, who were either killed or injured in apparently politically motivated attacks in 2016, remained unresolved. Likewise, the government provided no new information about 15 unidentified bodies found scattered under a bridge between the central provinces of Manica and Sofala, in May 2016. A parliamentary commission established in June 2016 to investigate the case did not publish an account of its findings or state when it would complete its work.

Authorities also failed to investigate human rights abuses allegedly committed by government security forces in 2015 and 2016 in relation to clashes with armed men from RENAMO, such as enforced disappearances, arbitrary arrests and property destruction. In 2016, the United Nations High Commissioner for Human Rights said at least 14 RENAMO officials were killed or abducted across the country in the first quarter of 2016.

Mozambique's leading human rights group, Liga dos Direitos Humanos (LDH), said that government security forces abducted and summarily executed at least

83 people in the provinces of Manica, Sofala, Tete and Zambezia between November 2015 and December 2016.

In cases investigated by Human Rights Watch, family members of "disappeared" people said that government officials had failed to provide them with information, despite strong evidence that security forces had detained their relative. Authorities also failed to investigate the destruction of homes and crops by security forces in Manica and Sofala provinces, or provide compensation to those affected.

There was also no significant progress in the investigation into a major financial scandal involving three state-owned companies that illegally borrowed over US$2 billion from Credit Suisse and VTB of Russia in 2013 and 2014 without parliamentary approval. The case led to the International Monetary Fund (IMF) suspending its Mozambique program and all 14 international donors freezing aid to the annual budget, pending an investigation and independent audit of the loans. In June, the attorney general published the audit report conducted by Kroll, a British audit firm, which detailed the transactions and individuals involved in the process, including former ministers and former heads of the state intelligence and security service. At time of writing, the government claimed to be investigating the case, but no individual mentioned in the report had been charged.

## *Abuses in the Mining Industry*

In July, videos shared on social media appeared to show Mozambican security forces assaulting artisanal miners at the ruby mines in Namanhumbir, Montepuez, northern Cabo Delgado province, which are co-owned by the British company Gemfields and former generals linked to the ruling party.

The footage showed uniformed officers beating the miners and ordering some of them to beat others who were tied to trees or had their heads buried in the sand. Reacting to the videos, a police spokesman said on July 26 that the officers involved were under investigation but provided no details.

In August, the Bar Association's human rights commission, after a mission to the Montepuez region, found that security forces in the region had committed abuses against miners, such as killings, beatings, and extortion. The commission urged authorities to investigate and hold perpetrators to account.

These events followed accounts from media and activists in February 2017 that Mozambican police had beaten and raped some Tanzanian miners while they were being deported for working illegally in the country. Mozambique denied the accusations and Tanzania said it was investigating how its nationals were treated.

## Attacks on Children and Adults with Albinism

The killings, kidnappings, and physical attacks against people with albinism continued, despite government efforts to stop the violence, including several arrests. In Mozambique and some neighboring countries, people with albinism are hunted for their body parts, which are used for witchcraft.

In March 2017, the United Nations independent expert on the enjoyment of human rights by persons with albinism, Ikponwosa Ero, told the UN Human Rights Council that the situation of people with albinism in Mozambique "requires urgent and immediate attention." She estimated that more than 100 attacks against people with albinism had occurred in Mozambique since 2014. Many of the victims are children. In September 2017, according to the police, a 17-year-old boy with albinism was killed and his brain removed, in Tete province. Four months earlier, police uncovered an attempt by two parents to sell their child with albinism in the same province. In June, the Malawian press reported that a 12-year-old Malawian boy with albinism had been killed in Mozambique, and police had arrested five people allegedly connected with the crime.

## Sexual Orientation and Gender Identity

Two years since the decriminalization of homosexuality in Mozambique, the government had still not registered the country's largest lesbian, gay, bisexual, and transgender (LGBT) group, Lambda. Since January 2016, the government has not made a public statement about Lambda or the rights of homosexuals in the country, despite constant appeals by the UN Human Rights Council for the government to register nongovernmental organizations that work on issues of sexual orientation and gender identity. Homosexuality is widely tolerated in

Mozambique, but LGBT people and local activists point to frequent discrimination at work and mistreatment by family members.

## Prison Conditions

Prison overcrowding continued to be a major problem, with prisons that have a total capacity of just over 8,000 holding more than 18,000 people. Authorities blame the overcrowding on slow judicial processes, the large number of illegal detentions, and a lack of alternative forms of punishment for petty crimes. The attorney general has also expressed concern about the overcrowding, which, according to her, was the highest it has been since 2014.

## Domestic Violence

Domestic violence was in the spotlight with two high-profile cases making headlines. In December 2016, the daughter of former President Armando Guebuza was shot dead by her husband during a domestic dispute in their home. As of late November, the case was awaiting trial. In February, the daughter of former President Samora Machel won a court case against her ex-boyfriend, who beat her so badly she lost an eye.

Reacting to the cases, the Association of Women in Legal Careers said the government often fails to investigate and prosecute cases of domestic violence. According to the group, family pressure and obstruction by the police caused many cases to be dropped. Domestic violence against men also made headlines in 2017, after at least three women, in separate cases, allegedly tried to kill their husbands. In reaction to the cases, police said that in the first three months of the year they had registered 210 cases of domestic violence against men and women.

## Impact of the Economic Crisis

Mozambique's economic crisis had a significant impact on the country's finances, making it harder for people to enjoy basic economic and social rights. The health authorities struggled to purchase medicine, and in March, media reported that there were temporary shortages of basic medicine, such as paracetamol, in at least three provinces: Inhambane, Manica, and Zambezia. In June, media reported that due to the financial crisis, hospitals in Inhambane province did not have food for patients.

## Key International Actors

In August, the European Union and the United States congratulated President Filipe Nyusi and RENAMO leader Afonso Dhlakama for having their first meeting since February 2015. Held on August 6, the meeting raised expectations for a potential peace agreement by the end of 2017, though no agreement was reached. The EU encouraged the two leaders to work toward a deal that would allow 2018 local elections and 2019 general elections to take place in a climate of peace.

In September, the US pledged US$400 million to fight HIV/AIDS in Mozambique, as part of the president's Emergency Plan for AIDS Relief (PEPFAR). In August, the IMF said it would not resume its assistance programs in Mozambique until authorities provide all information on money that state-owned companies had borrowed from foreign banks.

# Nepal

Shifts in Nepal's political landscape continued throughout 2017, with a new prime minister taking office in June. Local district elections, held for the first time in 20 years, were a significant step in the country's political transition following the 1996-2006 civil war. However, public differences between political parties and interest groups over power sharing underscored the country's deep, ongoing rifts, which had intensified with the 2015 constitution.

Successive administrations stalled on delivering justice for atrocities committed during the decade-long civil war between government forces and insurgent Maoist forces. The slow pace of reconstruction efforts around the devastating 2015 earthquakes, mired by corruption, reinforced social and economic marginalization.

Severe flooding during the monsoon season from June to August affected an estimated 1.7 million people, with 65,000 homes destroyed and 461,000 displaced.

## Transitional Justice and Accountability

Nepal's transitional justice process has been plagued by a lack of political will from all parties, as well as the military. At least 13,000 people were killed and over 1,300 were forcibly disappeared during the country's decade-long conflict, yet political leaders continue to neglect calls for accountability.

Although the mandate for the Truth and Reconciliation Commission (TRC) and the Commission of Investigation on Enforced Disappeared Persons (CIEDP) was extended for another year in February 2017, political and resource constraints obstructed their work. The government failed to amend the commissions' enacting law, despite pledges and two separate Supreme Court rulings that found the act contravenes international norms due to amnesty provisions.

In August, the commissions began preliminary investigations into the more than 65,000 complaints they received. However, reports of flawed implementation, including lack of transparency and weak engagement with victims, sustained concerns among stakeholders.

Authorities consistently ignored court orders for investigations, prosecutions, and convictions. They failed for years to enforce repeated court summons and an arrest warrant for three army officers charged with the 2004 murder of a 15-year-old girl tortured to death in military custody. In April, the officers were sentenced to life imprisonment in absentia, but the government has yet to take measures to locate the convicted and uphold the landmark verdict. A fourth officer tried in the case, Maj. Niranjan Basnet, was acquitted, which the district prosecutor declined to appeal in May.

In October, Maoist leader and former parliamentarian Bal Krishna Dhungel was arrested and sentenced to 12 years in prison on a conviction from 2004 for a 1998 murder, which he had long evaded through political protection. The Supreme Court had issued an order for his immediate arrest in April, yet he remained free for a further six months until a second contempt of court was filed against the police chief for failing to act. Dhungel's party staged protests calling for his release.

## Earthquake Reconstruction

Marginalized groups have been disproportionately affected by challenges in the rebuilding process from the 2015 earthquakes that left 3.5 million homeless. The widening gap in recovery efforts has significantly impacted lower caste and indigenous ethnic groups, people with low income and education levels, and persons living with disabilities.

Government corruption also obstructed dispersal of aid, with the estimated US$4 billion raised by the international community remaining largely undistributed.

## Elections

Nepal held local district elections in three phases in May, June, and September, and provincial and national parliamentary elections in November and December. In February, protests flared up over demands for constitutional amendments from Terai-based political parties seeking a greater role in governance. In March, four people were killed and dozens injured after security forces used live ammunition to disperse crowds protesting a campaign event in Saptari district. While investigating the deaths, National Human Rights Commission (NHRC) officials were attacked in their vehicle by supporters of parties boycotting the election.

Although there were some incidents of violence, and a section representing Madhesi communities in the south maintained their call to boycott the polls, the elections were largely considered free and fair.

## Migrant Workers

More than 2 million Nepalis work abroad—about 10 percent of the population—although the numbers are likely higher as many workers migrate through unofficial channels. The migrant workforce contributes 30 percent of the country's annual revenue in funds sent home.

Government reforms have failed to protect migrant workers from abusive recruitment agencies. In 2015, Nepal introduced a "free visa, free ticket" policy, through which employers in Gulf countries and Malaysia bear the costs of visas and flights tickets. After two years, however, the policy's implementation remains inadequate.

Authorities' failure to enforce protections has allowed agencies to continue charging exorbitant fees for jobs abroad. Other exploitative practices include confiscation of travel documents and false depictions of the work. In tangent with recruitment debts, these leave migrants highly vulnerable to forced labor and other abusive conditions.

In 2016, Nepal lifted the ban on domestic workers migrating to the Gulf and introduced new guidelines on employers and recruitment agencies in countries of employment. In April 2017, the parliament's labor committee recommended the ban be re-implemented.

## Sexual Orientation and Gender Identity

In line with a 2007 Supreme Court decision, the government has gradually introduced a legal third gender on various documents, including citizenship certificates and passports. In 2017, the court issued a new judgment to emphasize the government's responsibility to issue such documents. Activists remain frustrated with the lack of implementation of a Supreme Court-mandated committee recommendation that the government recognize same-sex relationships.

## *Women's and Girls' Rights*

Nepal has the third highest rate of child marriage in Asia—37 percent of girls are married before 18, and 10 percent by 15. Progress toward ending the practice has stalled. In 2016, the government launched a national strategy to end child marriage by 2030, but they have yet to announce any practical action plan.

Chaupadi, a practice that forces menstruating women and girls from their homes, was criminalized under a new law in August after a series of publicized deaths of women and girls in menstrual sheds. However, the Supreme Court had already outlawed the practice in 2005 with little practical outcome.

Women won 41 percent of seats in the local district elections as a result of compulsory quotas, yet higher level posts remained predominantly male. While the constitution reserves one-third of seats in parliament for women, only 7 percent of direct polling candidates for the parliamentary elections were women.

## *Key International Actors*

In the face of strained relations with India, Nepal's ties with China grew stronger over 2017, particularly as tensions between China and India flared during a standoff over the disputed Doklam plateau near Bhutan.

In April, Nepal and China held their first joint military exercise. In May, Nepal signed China's One Belt, One Road Initiative, which India strongly opposes, establishing wide-ranging plans for infrastructure projects including an airport and hydropower plants. The partnership posed an increased risk to Nepal's population of Tibetan refugees due to increased cooperation between Nepal and China's border security forces.

In October, Nepal was elected to the United Nations Human Rights Council for a three-year term, pledging to "remain committed to addressing the cases related to violations of human rights that occurred during the conflict period and providing justice to victims."

The Office of the United Nations High Commissioner for Human Rights and the international community were largely silent on the transitional justice process, despite the country's refusal to bring its laws into compliance with Supreme Court and international law directives.

# Nigeria

The ongoing Boko Haram conflict in the northeast, cycles of communal violence between pastoralists and farmers, and separatist protests in the south defined Nigeria's human rights landscape in 2017.

Notably absent for much of the year was President Muhammadu Buhari, who traveled overseas on two extended medical leaves for an undisclosed illness. Vice President Yemi Osinbajo acted as interim president on both occasions.

While the Nigerian army made considerable gains against Boko Haram, the toll of the conflict on civilians continued as the extremist group increasingly resorted to the use of women and children as suicide bombers. Over 180 civilians have been killed in suicide bomb attacks since late 2016, mostly in Maiduguri, the Borno state capital. In August, female suicide bombers killed 13 people and injured 20 others in an attack near a security checkpoint in Borno. Three suicide bombers also killed 27 people and wounded 83 in coordinated attacks at a market and an internally displaced persons (IDP) camp in Maiduguri in August. Bomb attacks in September killed at least 25 IDPs in two camps at Banki and Ngala.

Nigeria's eight-year conflict with Boko Haram has resulted in the deaths of over 20,000 civilians and a large-scale humanitarian crisis. Approximately 2.1 million people have been displaced by the conflict while 7 million need humanitarian assistance; in February the United Nations secretary-general, together with key UN agencies, warned Nigeria was facing famine-like conditions due to insecurity triggered by the war. In June, Nigeria helped Cameroonian authorities unlawfully force almost 1,000 asylum seekers back to Nigeria.

In May, after negotiations brokered by Switzerland and the International Committee for the Red Cross, 82 Chibok schoolgirls were released. Boko Haram fighters had abducted 276 schoolgirls from Chibok, Borno state, in April 2014. More than 100 of the girls and hundreds other captives, including over 500 children from Damasak, Borno, remained in Boko Haram captivity at time of writing.

## *Abuses by Boko Haram*

Boko Haram retained control over a small portion of Nigerian territory after numerous offensives to dislodge the group by security forces from Nigeria and Cameroon. The extremist group, however, continued its violent campaign in the northeast, particularly in Borno and some parts Yobe and Adamawa states. The group used suicide bombers in markets, universities and displacement camps; ambushed highway convoys; and raided and looted villages.

At least 300 civilians died in the group's attacks in 2017. In perhaps its deadliest 2017 attack, Boko Haram ambushed an oil exploration team from the Nigerian National Petroleum Corporation in July, killing at least 69 people in Magumeri, approximately 30 miles outside Maiduguri.

Boko Haram mostly used women and girls as suicide bombers, forcing them to detonate bombs in urban centers. According to the UN Children's Fund, UNICEF, 83 children were used as suicide bombers since January: 55 girls and 27 boys, one was a baby strapped to a girl. The group abducted 67 women and children in 2017.

On October 9, authorities began closed-door trials in a Kainji Niger state military base of more than 2,300 Boko Haram suspects, some detained since the insurgency's inception in 2009. Concerns about due process and fair hearing heightened when, within four days of trial, 45 of the first batch of 565 defendants were convicted and sentenced to between three to 31 jail terms for undisclosed charges. The court threw out charges against 34, discharged 468, and referred 25 defendants for trial in other courts.

Prior to October, only 13 Boko Haram suspects had faced trial, out of which nine were convicted for alleged involvement in crimes committed by the group.

## *Conduct of Security Forces*

On January 17, the Nigerian air force carried out an airstrike on a settlement for displaced people in Rann, Borno State, killing approximately 234 people according to a local official, including nine aid workers, and injuring 100 more. The military initially claimed the attack was meant to hit Boko Haram fighters they believed were in the area, blaming faulty intelligence. After six months of investigations, authorities said they had mistaken the settlement of displaced people for insurgent forces. At the time, the settlement was run by the military.

In June, a military board of inquiry made up of seven army officers and two lawyers from the National Human Rights Commission concluded that there was no basis to investigate allegations of war crimes committed by senior army officials in the northeast conflict and elsewhere. The allegations they investigated included extrajudicial killings, torture, and arbitrary arrests of thousands.

Authorities have failed to implement a December 2016 court order for the release of Ibrahim El Zakzaky, leader of the Shia Islamic Movement of Nigeria, IMN. Zakzaky and his wife Zeenat, as well as hundreds of IMN members, have been in detention without trial since December 2015, when soldiers killed 347 IMN members in Zaria, Kaduna state.

In August, acting President Osinbajo established a presidential judicial panel to investigate the military's compliance with human rights obligations and rules of engagement. The seven-person panel, which began hearing complaints in September, was set up in response to allegations of war crimes committed by the military across the country, including the December 2015 Shia IMN incident in Zaria, the killing of pro-Biafra protesters in the southeast, and the killing, torture, and enforced disappearance of Boko Haram suspects in the northeast.

## Inter-Communal Violence

Violence between nomadic and farming communities spread beyond the north-central region to southern parts of the country in 2017. Hundreds of people were killed, and thousands displaced. In July, two days of clashes between herdsmen and farmers killed over 30 people in Kajuru village, 31 miles outside the city of Kaduna, Kaduna state. A similar attack in Jos, Plateau State left 19 dead and five injured in September. The governor of Kaduna state called for the intervention of the regional bloc, the Economic Community of West African States (ECOWAS), to end the perennial violence between the two groups.

In April, Nnamdi Kanu, leader of the separatist Indigenous People of Biafra (IPOB) was released from detention on the orders of a court. He was arrested in October 2015 and detained on treason charges. In response to calls for Igbo independence by IPOB, in June a northern-interest pressure group, the Arewa

Youth Consultative Forum (AYCF), issued a notice demanding that Igbos leave northern Nigeria before October 1, or face "visible actions." Following condemnation by various interlocutors, including UN independent experts, the AYCF withdrew the quit notice in late August.

## Public Sector Corruption

Corruption continues to plague Nigeria despite the Buhari administration's increased efforts at reform and oversight. In October, President Buhari sacked Secretary to the Federal Government, Babachir Lawal, on corruption allegations, and National Intelligence Agency head, Ayodele Oke, after the Economic and Financial Crimes Commission (EFCC) found US$43 million in cash in his apartment. The EFCC accused Diezani Alison-Madeke, the former oil minister, of bribery, fraud, money laundering and misuse of public funds. In August, a court ordered forfeiture to the government of $44 million worth of property and $21 million from bank accounts linked to Alison-Madeke.

## Sexual Orientation and Gender Identity

The passage of the Same Sex Marriage (Prohibition) Act (SSMPA) in January 2014 effectively authorized abuses against the lesbian, gay, bisexual, and transgender (LGBT) community in 2017. The law has undermined freedom of expression for members of the LGBT community, human rights organizations, and others. In July, authorities arrested over 40 men attending an HIV awareness event at a hotel in Lagos and accused them of performing same-sex acts, a crime that carries up to 14 years in jail. In April, 53 men were arrested for celebrating a gay wedding, and charged with "belonging to a gang of unlawful society."

In addition to the SSMPA, under the Nigeria Criminal Code Act of 1990, "carnal knowledge of any person against the order of nature" carries a maximum sentence of 14 years in prison. The Sharia penal code adopted by several northern Nigerian states prohibits and punishes sexual relations between persons of the same sex, with the maximum penalty for men being death by stoning, and whipping and/or imprisonment for women.

## *Freedom of Expression, Media, and Association*

Nigerian press, bolstered by strong civil society, remains largely free. Journalists, however, face harassment, and the implementation of a 2015 Cyber Crime Act threatens to curtail freedom of expression.

In January, police arrested two journalists, the publisher and judiciary correspondent of an online publication, Premium Times, in Abuja for articles that allegedly showed "deep hatred for the Nigerian army." In June, Ibraheema Yakubu, a journalist with the Hausa radio service of the German Deutsche Welle, was arrested and detained while covering a procession by the Muslim Shiites group in Kaduna. He told media that policemen beat and slapped him. In August, police arrested and detained journalist Danjuma Katsina in Katsina state for posting "injurious comments" about a politician on Facebook. The two journalists were released after a day each in detention following the intervention of officials of the Nigerian Union of Journalists.

The director of defense information announced in August that the military would monitor social media for "hate speech, anti-government and anti-security information." The government also directed the National Broadcasting Commission to sanction any radio or television station that broadcasts hate speech. It threatened to charge people found to spread yet-to-be defined hate speech under the Terrorism Prevention Act.

A "Bill to provide for the Establishment of Non-Governmental Organizations (NGOs)," described by local groups as an attempt to crackdown and monitor NGOs has passed two readings in the House of Representatives.

## *Key International Actors*

International actors, notably the United States and the United Kingdom, have continued their support for the Nigerian government in the fight against Boko Haram, providing military equipment, funding, and humanitarian aid for the crisis in the northeast.

In August, the US finalized the sale of $593 million-worth of military equipment to Nigeria. The sale, which was initially delayed under the Obama administration because of human rights concerns, included 12 A-29 Super Tucano light attack aircrafts, laser guided rockets, unguided rockets and other equipment. While members of Congress expressed concern about this sale, there was no attempt to block it.

Following an August visit to Nigeria by the UK secretary of state for foreign and commonwealth affairs, the UK pledged $259 million over five years in an emergency assistance package to provide food, medical treatment, and education assistance in Nigeria's beleaguered northeast.

In February, the UN humanitarian agency OCHA co-hosted a donor conference that raised $700 million in Oslo, Norway to address the humanitarian crisis in the Lake Chad Basin in the northeast. Despite an August army raid on a UN compound in Maiduguri, allegedly to search for arms, UN relations with Nigeria remain intact.

The Office of the Prosecutor of the International Criminal Court (ICC) continued its preliminary examination into allegations of atrocities committed by all sides in the Boko Haram conflict. The office also has an ongoing analysis of the December 2015 event between soldiers and Shia IMN members.

In May, Nigeria was reviewed by the UN Committee on the Protection of the Rights of All Migrant Workers and Members of their Families, but failed to submit its report to the committee or send a delegation to the review. The committee expressed concerns, including about harassment and exploitation of domestic migrant workers and lack of information on measures taken by Nigeria to ensure non-discrimination for all migrant workers in law and in practice.

When reviewing Nigeria in July, the UN Committee on the Elimination of Discrimination against Women expressed concerns regarding access to justice; female genital mutilation; sexual exploitation in IDP camps; gender based violence, including domestic violence; trafficking for the purpose of sexual and labor exploitation; and continued abduction, rape, and sexual slavery under Boko Haram.

## Foreign Policy

Nigeria currently sits on the UN Human Rights Council, as well as the Economic and Social Council. In January, Nigeria's minister of environment Amina Mohammed assumed office as UN deputy secretary-general. In August, government officials joined the UN High Commissioner for Human Rights in the condemnation of ethnic cleansing of Rohingya Muslims in Burma, and called on the UN to invoke the principle of "responsibility to protect" to end the abuse.

Africa has been the focus of Nigeria's foreign policy for many years, but at the African Union 28th Summit in January, the country failed to secure any leadership position in the body. In January, President Buhari played an important role with other ECOWAS leaders in ending Gambia's political crisis.

Nigeria took a stand in support of justice for grave crimes by publicly opposing ICC withdrawal at the African Union's January 2017 summit in Addis Ababa.

# North Korea

North Korea is one of the most repressive authoritarian states in the world. In his sixth year in power, Kim Jong-un—the third leader of the dynastic Kim family and head of the ruling Workers' Party of Korea (WPK) who exercises almost total political control—intensified repressive measures; tightened domestic restrictions on travel and unauthorized cross-border travel with China; and punished North Korean for contacting the outside world. The government continued to generate fearful obedience from citizens by means of threatened and actual execution, detention, and forced labor under harsh, sometimes fatal, conditions.

During 2017, North Korea fired 23 missiles during 16 tests and conducted its sixth nuclear test, sending tensions between the US and its allies and North Korea to their highest level in decades. Personal insults and threats traded between US President Donald Trump and Kim Jong-un in September and October further worsened the situation.

On human rights, the international community continued to press for action on the findings of the United Nations Commission of Inquiry (COI) report on human rights in the Democratic People's Republic of Korea (DPRK or North Korea) that found the government committed crimes against humanity, including extermination, murder, enslavement, torture, imprisonment, rape and other forms of sexual violence, and forced abortion.

On December 9, 2016, for the third consecutive year, the UN Security Council put North Korea's egregious human rights violations record on its formal agenda as a threat to international peace and security. On March 24, the Human Rights Council adopted without a vote a resolution that authorizes the hiring of "experts in legal accountability" to assess cases and develop plans for the eventual prosecution of North Korean leaders and officials responsible for crimes against humanity.

The North Korean government restricts all basic civil and political liberties for its citizens, including freedom of expression, religion and conscience, assembly and association. It prohibits any organized political opposition, independent media and civil society, and free trade unions. Lack of an independent judiciary, arbitrary arrest and punishment of crimes, torture in custody, forced labor, and executions maintain fear and control.

North Korea discriminates against individuals and their families on political grounds in key areas such as employment, residence, and schooling by applying *songbun*, a socio-political classification system grouping people into "loyal," "wavering," or "hostile" classes. Pervasive corruption enables some room to maneuver around the strictures of the *songbun* system, and some people who bribe government officials can receive permission, pursue market activities, or travel domestically or abroad.

## Vulnerable Groups

North Korea refuses to cooperate with either the Office of the UN High Commissioner for Human Rights (OHCHR) Seoul office or the UN special rapporteur on the situation of human rights in North Korea, Tomás Ojea Quintana. However, in 2017, the DPRK engaged with two UN human rights treaty bodies and invited a UN thematic special rapporteur to visit for the first time ever.

On December 6, 2016, the North Korean government ratified the Convention on the Rights of Persons with Disabilities (CRPD). From May 3 to 8, Catalina Devandas-Aguilar, UN special rapporteur on the rights of persons with disabilities, met with government officials, visited schools and rehabilitation centers, and spoke with some people with disabilities. Although her schedule was tightly controlled and authorities did not grant her request to visit a mental health facility, Devandas-Aguilar acknowledged the DPRK's commitment to advance the realization of the rights of persons with disabilities.

Following a long delay in submitting overdue reports required under the Convention on the Rights of the Child (CRC) and the Convention on the Elimination of All Forms of Discrimination against Women (CEDAW), North Korea submitted reports on both conventions in 2016. North Korean officials had their record on children's rights examined by the CRC committee on September 20, 2017, and appeared before the CEDAW committee on November 8, 2017.

The CEDAW committee expressed concerns about a broad range of violations affecting women, including discrimination; stereotyping; non-criminalization of marital rape; sexual harassment and violence, including in the workplace; trafficking; lack of political participation; and lack of an independent human rights institution, civil society organizations, or other means to enable independent monitoring and promotion of the rights of women.

Despite such engagement, North Korea often refuses to acknowledge its own rights violations or accept committee recommendations. When the CRC committee raised concerns about the North Korean government requiring unpaid labor from children, subjecting children to physical punishment and violence, and discrimination against children on political grounds, DPRK officials denied these allegations. The government did acknowledge the possibility that schools or individual teachers may have forced children to work, but offered no further details.

## Women's and Girls' Rights

Women in North Korea face a range of sexual or gender-based abuses, as well as violations of other rights in common with the rest of the population. These include punishment for acts of their husband or other relatives, torture, rape and other sexual abuses in detention facilities, sexual exploitation, or forced marriages of North Korean women in China, and other forms of sexual and gender-based violence and discrimination.

Gender-based discrimination starts from childhood, with girls constantly exposed to and compelled to comply with stereotyped gender roles. It is harder for women than it is for men to be admitted to university and to join the military and the ruling Korean Workers' Party, which serves as the gateway to any position of power. State authorities are sometimes perpetrators of abuses against women, and fail to offer protection or justice to women and girls facing gender-based or sexual abuse.

## Border Tightening

Kim Jong-un's government bolstered efforts to prevent people from leaving North Korea without permission by increasing the number of border guards, CCTV cameras, and barbed wire fences on its border with China. Tactics included jamming Chinese cellphone services at the border and targeting those communicating with people outside the country. China also increased checkpoints on roads leading from the border.

During the summer of 2017, Chinese authorities also apparently intensified crackdowns on both North Koreans fleeing through China and the networks guiding them, resulting in fewer North Koreans being able to complete the arduous overland journey to Laos or Thailand, and from there, most often, to South Korea.

The Ministry of People's Security classifies defection as a crime of "treachery against the nation." Harsh punishments apply to North Koreans forcibly returned by China, including potentially a death sentence. Former North Korean security officials told Human Rights Watch that those forcibly returned face interrogation, torture, sexual violence, humiliating treatment, and forced labor.

The severity of punishment depends on North Korean authorities' assessments of what returnees did while in China. North Koreans caught working or living in China are sent to different types of forced labor camps, long-term (*kyohwaso*) or short-term prisons (*rodong danryeondae*). Those discovered trying to reach South Korea are treated as enemies of the country, and may disappear into North Korea's horrific political prison camp system (*kwanliso*), where prisoners face torture, sexual violence, forced labor, and other inhuman treatment.

North Koreans fleeing into China should be considered refugees *sur place* regardless of their reason for flight because of the certainty of punishment on return. China treats them as illegal "economic migrants" and fails to meet its obligation to protect refugees as a state party of the 1951 UN Refugee Convention and its 1967 protocol. Beijing regularly denies the staff of the UNHCR, the UN Refugee Agency, permission to travel to border areas where North Koreans are present.

## Key International Actors

On May 9, South Korea elected Moon Jae-In, a former student activist and human rights lawyer, as South Korea's new president, following a bitter race prompted by President Park Geun-Hye's impeachment and removal from office. President Moon proposed dialogue with the North Korean leadership, resumption of humanitarian reunions of families separated between the north and south since the Korean War (1950-1953), and offered to share with the DPRK the privilege of hosting the 2018 Winter Olympics. The DPRK rejected these offers.

In a policy shift from Park's administration, the Moon administration allowed humanitarian and development groups to engage in projects with North Korea.

To date, the Moon administration has not announced its policy on various North Korean human rights issues. These include the creation of a foundation based on the North Korean human rights law that went into effect in September 2016; assistance for North Korean escapees detained in China; and the seven South Korean nationals currently detained in the DPRK. On September 21, South Korea approved a US$8 million aid package for North Korean children and women at risk that will be distributed at an "appropriate time" and monitored by UNICEF and the UN World Food Program (WFP).

North Korea's relations with Malaysia and other Southeast Asian states suffered serious damage when Kim Jong-nam, the half-brother of Kim Jong-un, was assassinated on February 13 in a public area of Kuala Lumpur International Airport in a plot many believe North Korea planned.

Japan continues to demand the return of 12 Japanese citizens whom North Korea abducted in the 1970s and 1980s. Some Japanese civil society groups insist the number of abductees is much higher.

In January and October 2017, the US government imposed targeted sanctions for human rights abuses on five institutions, including the Military Security Command (the military's secret police), the Ministry of Labor, and 14 North Koreans, including Kim Yo-Jong, Kim Jong-un's younger sister and vice director of the Workers' Party's Propaganda and Agitation Department.

# Oman

Sultan Qaboos bin Said al Said, 77, has ruled Oman since 1970. He holds several positions of authority, including prime minister, supreme commander of the armed forces, minister of defence, minister of finance, and minister of foreign affairs. Omani authorities continued in 2017 to harass activists and restrict publications by local independent magazines and newspapers critical of the government, violating international standards of freedom of expression.

Oman's *kafala* (sponsorship) immigrant labor system and lack of labor law protections leaves the country's more than 160,000 female migrant domestic workers exposed to abuse and exploitation by employers, whose consent they need to change jobs. Those who flee abuse—including beatings, sexual abuse, unpaid wages, and excessive working hours—have few avenues for redress and can face legal penalties for "absconding."

## *Freedom of Expression*

Authorities, particularly from the Internal Security Service (ISS), continued to target pro-reform activists, often for views they expressed on social media platforms like Facebook and Twitter. Several bloggers and online activists were harassed, arrested, and sometimes detained up to several months for criticizing the authorities' policies. Courts across the country sentenced activists to prison terms on the basis of vaguely defined laws that limit free speech, including crimes such as "insulting the Sultan" and "undermining the prestige of the state."

Authorities often have relied on provisions in the 2002 Telecommunications Act and 2011 Cybercrime Law to restrict freedom of expression online.

In 2017, several activists remained behind bars for views they expressed either online or in their writings.

Former diplomat and online activist Hassan al-Basham remains in prison serving a three-year sentence on charges that include insulting God and Sultan Qaboos bin Said al Said. He has been detained since May 3, 2016.

On October 5, Oman's Supreme Court ordered *Azamn* newspaper to permanently close. In August 2016, authorities ordered the immediate closure of the paper, after arresting the editor-in-chief, Ibrahim al-Ma'mari; deputy editor, Zaher al-Abri; and another journalist Yousef al-Haj, following the publication of an article that alleged corruption within the judiciary.

Al-Ma'mari and al-Haj were charged with "disturbing public order," "misusing the internet," "publishing details of a civil case," and "undermining the prestige of the state," and al-Abri with using "an information network [the internet] for the dissemination of material that might be prejudicial to public order." A Muscat court convicted them and sentenced them to prison terms and fines. On appeal, al-Ma'mari and al-Haj had their sentences reduced and al-Abri was acquitted. On October 23, al-Haj was released from Muscat prison after serving one year in prison.

Omani authorities have also closed down other publications that have been critical of the government. The Gulf Centre for Human Rights (GCHR) reported that on May 3, the ISS ordered the website of the local independent magazine *Mowaten* to be blocked throughout the country. Human Rights Watch reported in February that Omani authorities had barred the family of *Mowaten's* editor-in-chief and founder, Mohammad al-Fazari, who currently lives in the United Kingdom, from traveling outside Oman.

In February, the Omani Center for Human Rights reported that the management of Muscat's annual International Book Fair withdrew two books that were critical of the government. One was a compilation of *Mowaten* articles and the other an anthology by the poet Ahmed al-Raimi titled, "To You No Loyalty."

On May 23, the Court of First Instance in Muscat sentenced a writer and researcher, Mansour Bin Nasser al-Mahrazi, to three years in prison for his 2016 book, *Oman in the Square of Corruption*. The court issued the sentence despite the fact that the writer himself removed the book from the Omani book market, according to the Omani Center for Human Rights. On the same day, the court ordered the release of al-Mahrazi on bail, the human rights group reported.

## Freedom of Assembly and Association

All public gatherings require official approval in advance; authorities arrest and prosecute participants in unapproved gatherings. Some private gatherings are also prohibited under article 137 of the penal code, which prescribes a punishment of up to three years in prison and a fine for anyone who "participates in a private gathering, including at least 10 individuals with a view to commit a riot or a breach of public order." Authorities sharply increased the penalties under article 137 after the pro-reform demonstrations of 2011.

On May 4, 2016, Dr. Talib al-Maamari, a former Shura Council member from Liwa, in Al Batinah Region, northern Oman, was released from prison three months prior to the end of his prison sentence, reportedly by a royal decree from Sultan Qaboos. In August 2014, a court of appeals in Muscat had sentenced him to four years in prison on charges of "illegal gathering" and calling for anti-government demonstrations.

The United Nations Working Group on Arbitrary Detention in December 2014 had characterized Dr. Talib al-Maamari's detention as arbitrary and stated that the government should release him immediately and compensate him.

## *Women's Rights, Sexual Orientation, and Gender Identity*

Article 17 of the Basic Law states that all citizens are equal and bans gender-based discrimination. In practice, however, women continue to face discrimination. The Personal Status Law discriminates against women on matters such as divorce, inheritance, child custody, and legal guardianship. For instance, women can lose child custody if they re-marry, and men continue to hold guardianship of the child regardless of whether they have custody.

Oman has no laws prohibiting domestic violence and marital rape. Cases can only be brought under general provisions that criminalize assault. Oman's penal code explicitly excludes marital rape, and does not criminalize sexual harassment.

Oman's penal code criminalizes sexual relations outside marriage and provides three months to one-year imprisonment when the person is unmarried, and one to three years' imprisonment when the person is married. Criminalization of such offenses apply disproportionately to women whose pregnancy can serve as evidence of the offense. Oman's penal code provides for six months to three years in prison for consensual sex between two people of the same sex.

In October, the UN Committee on the Elimination of Discrimination Against Women concluded its review of Oman, finding that it had made "very little progress in removing discrimination from marriage and family related law and practice."

## Migrant Workers

Migrant workers remained vulnerable to exploitation and abuse, due in part to the *kafala* (visa sponsorship) system that ties migrant workers to their employers and precludes them from changing employers without their current employer's consent.

Human Rights Watch found female domestic workers in particular at high risk of abuse, since Oman's labor law currently excludes domestic workers from its protections, and those who flee abuse have little avenue for redress.

Human Rights Watch documented abuse and exploitation of domestic workers, including employers frequently confiscating workers' passports despite a legal prohibition; not paying workers their salaries, in full or at all; forcing them to work excessively long hours without breaks or days off; and denying them adequate food and living conditions. In some cases, workers reported physical and sexual abuse.

Migrant domestic workers who fled abusive employers reported facing "absconding" charges that can lead to fines, imprisonment and deportation, trumped-up criminal charges by employers to force them to drop their cases, and lengthy delays when pursuing cases against employers. Workers reported that police at times returned them to their employers despite complaints of abuse, and Ministry of Manpower officials sided with employers during dispute-resolution processes despite workers' complaints of severe abuse.

## Key International Actors

In March 2016, Oman accepted 144 out of the 233 recommendations it received during its second Universal Periodic Review cycle in November 2015, including that it ratify the International Covenant on Economic, Social and Cultural Rights. However, authorities only noted 93 recommendations, including those on freedom of expression, assembly, allowing women to pass their nationality on to their children, and ratifying the International Covenant on Civil and Political Rights.

Both the US and UK provide significant economic and military aid to Oman. Oman's Western allies offered muted, if any criticism, of its human rights abuses in 2016, except in annual reports. In 2017, the US Trafficking in Persons Report maintained Oman's Tier 2 Watch List category, stating that "the Government of Oman does not fully meet the minimum standards of the elimination of trafficking, but is making significant efforts to do so."

# Pakistan

Political turmoil and instability engulfed Pakistan after Nawaz Sharif stepped down as prime minister in July after a five-member Supreme Court bench disqualified him based on investigations into corruption allegations.

Although Pakistan witnessed fewer attacks by Islamist militants than in previous years, scores of people were killed in attacks primarily targeting law enforcement officials and religious minorities.

Security forces remained unaccountable for human rights violations and exercised disproportionate political influence over civilian authorities, especially in matters of national security and counterterrorism. In March, parliament passed a constitutional amendment reinstating secret military courts to try terrorism suspects for another two years. Security forces were implicated in enforced disappearances and extrajudicial killings throughout the country.

The government muzzled dissenting voices in nongovernmental organizations (NGOs) and media on the pretext of national security. Militants and interest groups also threatened freedom of expression.

Women, religious minorities, and transgender people faced violent attacks, discrimination, and government persecution, with authorities failing to provide adequate protection or hold perpetrators accountable. The inclusion of the transgender population in the 2017 census and the first-ever proposed transgender law were positive developments.

The human rights crisis in Balochistan continued with reports of enforced disappearances and extrajudicial killings of suspected Baloch militants. Baloch nationalists and other militant groups continued attacking non-Baloch civilians.

Afghan refugees in Pakistan continued to face pressure from government authorities to return, although the number of repatriations decreased significantly from 2016.

## *Freedom of Expression and Attacks on Civil Society*

Journalists increasingly practiced self-censorship after numerous attacks by security forces and militant groups in retaliation for critical articles. Media outlets remained under pressure to avoid reporting on or criticizing human rights viola-tions during counterterrorism operations. The Taliban and other armed groups threatened media outlets and attacked journalists and activists because of their work.

In January, security forces abducted five men—Salman Haider, Waqas Goraya, Aasim Saeed, Ahmed Raza Naseer, and Samar Abbas—who were vocal critics of militant religious groups and Pakistan's security establishment. Four were re-leased after three weeks of public protests. Samar Abbas remained forcibly dis-appeared at time of writing.

In May, the Federal Investigation Agency's (FIA) counterterrorism wing sum-moned Taha Siddiqui, a journalist and the bureau chief for World Is One News (WION), for questioning about opinions expressed in his journalism. The same month, the FIA arrested six people for making "blasphemous" comments on the internet, and the interior minister announced new rules that can severely restrict online anonymity. According to media reports, the FIA interrogated at least 40 people for making comments criticizing the military on the internet, and seized their computers and phones for forensic evaluation.

In August, plainclothes men accompanied by police officials picked up Punhal Sario, a human rights activist and campaigner for victims of enforced disappear-ances; Partab Shivani, a teacher and activist; Naseer Kumbhar, a writer; and Muhammad Umar, a political party worker, from different cities in Sindh province. The same month, security forces raided the home of Amar Sindhu, a well-known poet in Sindh province. Sario returned home in October.

Human Rights Watch received several credible reports of intimidation, harass-ment, and surveillance of various NGOs by government authorities. The govern-ment used the "Regulation of INGOs in Pakistan" policy to impede the registration and functioning of international humanitarian and human rights groups.

In July, after its review of Pakistan, the United Nations Committee on Economic, Social and Cultural Rights said it is "deeply concerned at repeated reports of ab-duction, killings and intimidation of human rights defenders, particularly those fighting for economic, social and cultural rights, allegedly committed in some cases by State agents, including members of military intelligence services."

## *Freedom of Religion and Belief*

At least 19 people remained on death row in 2017 after being convicted under Pakistan's draconian blasphemy law, and hundreds awaited trial. Most of those facing blasphemy are members of religious minorities—including Aasia Bibi, the first woman to face a potential death sentence for blasphemy—and are often victimized by these charges due to personal disputes.

In 2017, Pakistan witnessed an increase in blasphemy-related violence while the government continued to encourage discriminatory prosecutions and other forms of discrimination against vulnerable groups by failing to repeal discriminatory laws and using religious rhetoric inciting hatred against minority groups. In March, the interior minister described blasphemers as "enemies of humanity," and stated he would take the issue to its "logical conclusion" in taking action against them.

In April, a mob dragged Mashal Khan, a 23-year-old student at a university in Mardan, Khyber Pakhtunkhwa province, from his dormitory and shot him dead over accusations that he made blasphemous remarks against Islamic injunctions. In May, a 10-year-old boy was killed when a mob tried to storm a police station in Balochistan to attack a man held on blasphemy charges.

The Pakistan Telecommunication Authority (PTA) sent out a mass text message in May to millions of users informing them that uploading and sharing blasphemous content is a punishable offense, and asking them to report such content.

In June, an counterterrorism court in Punjab province sentenced Taimoor Raza to death for committing blasphemy on Facebook. He was arrested in 2016 after a debate over Islam on Facebook with a man who later turned out to be a counterterrorism agent.

Provisions of Pakistan's penal code that perpetuate discrimination against members of the Ahmadi religious community remained unchanged: the code explicitly prohibits Ahmadis from "indirectly or directly posing as a Muslim," declaring or propagating their faith publicly, building mosques or referring to them as such, or making public calls to prayer.

Militant groups targeted Shia and followers of Sufi Islam. In February, a suicide attack on the shrine of Lal Shahbaz Qalandar in Sehwan, Sindh, claimed by the extremist group Islamic State (also known as ISIS), killed at least 88 people and injured hundreds.

In a positive development, parliament in March passed the Hindu Marriage Act, the country's first ever federal law recognizing and regulating marriages of the members of the minority Hindu community by allowing Hindu marriages to be registered.

## Women's and Children's Rights

Violence against women and girls—including rape, "honor" killings, acid attacks, domestic violence, and forced marriage—remained a serious problem. Pakistani activists estimate that there are about a 1,000 "honor" killings every year.

In June, a tribal council (jirga) in Khyber agency ordered the "honor" killing of Naghma, a 13-year-old girl, for "running away with men." Parliament had passed in February a controversial bill giving legal cover to tribal and village councils.

The Khyber Pakhtunkhwa draft domestic violence bill received wide public criticism for exempting parents and spouses when they use "corrective measures" against female family members, raising the concern that it will legitimize some forms of domestic violence. At least 180 cases of domestic violence were reported in Khyber Pakhtunkhwa province in 2017, including 94 women murdered by close family members.

Women from religious minority communities were particularly vulnerable. A report by the Movement for Solidarity and Peace in Pakistan found that at least 1,000 girls belonging to Christian and Hindu communities are forced to marry Muslim men every year. The government failed to act to stop such forced marriages.

Child marriage remained a serious concern, with 21 percent of girls in Pakistan marrying before the age of 18, according to the United Nations Children's Fund (UNICEF).

Attacks on schools and the use of children in suicide bombings by the Taliban and affiliated armed extremist groups continued during the year.

Over 5 million primary-school-age children are out of school, most of them girls. Human Rights Watch research found girls miss school for reasons including lack of schools, costs associated with studying, child bearing, and gender discrimination.

In June, the UN Committee on Economic, Social and Cultural Rights invited Pakistan to endorse the Safe Schools Declaration, which proposes steps to protect schools from attacks and military use during wartime. Pakistan has not yet endorsed the declaration.

## Sexual Orientation and Gender Identity

Violent attacks on transgender and intersex women in Pakistan continued in 2017, with unidentified assailants frequently targeting those involved in activism. In August, unknown gunmen shot dead a transgender woman in Karachi.

In a series of steps toward legally recognizing gender identity, the first bill safeguarding the rights of transgender persons was introduced in parliament in August. The 2017 national census included for the first time a category for Khawaja Siras, or transgender women. However, many transgender rights activists disputed the government figures claiming it underrepresented the transgender population. In June, the Pakistan government issued the first passport with a transgender category.

Pakistan's penal code continued to criminalize same-sex conduct, placing men who have sex with men and transgender women at risk of police abuse and other violence and discrimination.

## Terrorism and Counterterrorism

In its efforts to tackle security threats from armed extremists, security forces committed serious violations during counterterrorism operations, including torture, enforced disappearances, and extrajudicial killings. Suspects were frequently detained without charge or tried without proper judicial process. Counterterrorism laws also continued to be misused as an instrument of political coercion and to silence dissenting voices.

In March, parliament reinstated secret military courts empowered to try civilians after the term for military courts ended in January 2017. Pakistan human rights

groups said that many defendants facing military courts were secretly detained and tortured to coerce confessions. Several remain forcibly disappeared. Authorities do not allow independent monitoring of military court trials. The Pakistan government failed to sufficiently investigate and prosecute allegations of human rights violations by security forces.

In 2017, the practice of enforced disappearances targeting suspected militants—previously restricted to the conflict areas of Balochistan, Federally Administered Tribal Areas (FATA), and Khyber Pakhtunkhwa—became a nationwide policy with the targeting of bloggers and activists all over Pakistan.

## Refugees

Some of the 80,000 Afghans returning from Pakistan in the first eight months of the year reported that Pakistani police continue to extort money from registered and undocumented Afghans in Pakistan. In July, the authorities began to register some of the estimated 1 million unregistered Afghans in Pakistan, although the purpose was not clear, leading to fears authorities might deport them.

The uncertain residency status of Afghan refugees in Pakistan encouraged police harassment, threats, and extortion, particularly in Khyber Pakhtunkhwa, which hosts the majority of the Afghan population in the country. According to the International Organization for Migration (IOM), 82,019 refugees and undocumented Afghans returned or were deported to Afghanistan between January and August 2017.

## Death Penalty

At least 44 people on death row were executed in 2017, of whom 37 were executed after convictions by military courts.

## Key International Actors

In June, the Committee against Torture (CAT), in its concluding observations on Pakistan's compliance with commitments made under the Convention against Torture, called on the Pakistani government to prohibit the use of torture by law enforcement agencies and impartially investigate allegations of widespread torture.

In July, the UN Human Rights Committee, in its concluding observations on Pakistan's compliance and implementation of commitments made under the International Covenant on Civil and Political Rights (ICCPR), called on the Pakistani government to "review its legal provisions relating to freedom of expression … with a view to putting in place effective oversight mechanisms and procedural safeguards and bringing them in line with Article 19 of the Covenant."

The committee recommended, among other things, criminalizing enforced disappearances, reinstating the moratorium on death penalty, reviewing and reforming legislation governing military courts, prohibiting torture, and reviewing the vague legislation and policies governing the functioning of NGOs in Pakistan.

Pakistan's volatile relationship with United States, its largest development and military donor, deteriorated amid signs of mistrust. In August, US President Donald Trump accused Pakistan of failing to counter terrorist threats, and even actively fostering militant groups involved in attacks on civilian and military targets in Afghanistan. Pakistan denied the accusations. Later in August, the US administration notified Congress of its decision to provide US$255 million in military assistance to Pakistan, contingent on the government cracking down on internal terror networks.

Pakistan and China deepened extensive economic and political ties, and work continued on the China-Pakistan Economic Corridor, a long-term project consisting of construction of roads, railways, and energy pipelines.

In July, the European Union Foreign Affairs Council welcomed several positive measures taken by Pakistan, but also raised several concerns, including the death penalty; trial of civilians by military courts; inadequate protection for juveniles in the criminal justice system; the discrimination faced by minorities; misuse of blasphemy laws; lack of freedom of religion or belief; and restrictions on freedom of speech, particularly for journalists and activists, and related to NGO registration.

Historically tense relations between Pakistan and India showed no signs of improvement in 2017, with both countries accusing each other of facilitating unrest and militancy.

# Papua New Guinea

Almost 40 percent of the population in Papua New Guinea (PNG) lives in poverty. The government has not taken sufficient steps to address gender inequality, violence, excessive use of force by police, or corruption and relies heavily on religious groups and nongovernment organizations (NGOs) to provide services on a charitable basis to meet the economic and social rights of the population. Rates of family and sexual violence are among the highest in the world, and perpetrators are rarely prosecuted.

In August, Peter O'Neill was reappointed as prime minister following an election marred by widespread electoral irregularities and violence. Soldiers and extra police were sent to the Highlands in response to fighting triggered by the election, where dozens of people, including police, had been killed in election-related violence.

## Women's and Girls' Rights

More than three years after the 2013 Family Protection Act was adopted, parliament in May finally passed regulations to implement the law, which criminalizes domestic violence and allows victims to obtain protection orders.

Police and prosecutors rarely pursue investigations or criminal charges against people who commit family violence—even in cases of attempted murder, serious injury, or repeated rape—and instead prefer to resolve such cases through mediation and/or payment of compensation.

Police often demand money ("for fuel") from victims before acting, or simply ignore cases that occur in rural areas. There is also a severe lack of services for people requiring assistance after having suffered family violence, such as safe houses, qualified counselors, case management, financial support, or legal aid.

Violent mobs attacked individuals accused of sorcery or witchcraft, particularly women and girls. In March, a trial involving 122 defendants began in Madang. The defendants were charged in connection with the killing of five men and two children suspected of sorcery in 2014. The prosecution alleged that the men raided a village in search of sorcerers to kill, armed with "bush knives, bows and arrows, hunting spears, [and] home-made and factory-made shotguns." No further details were available at time of writing regarding the trial's progress.

PNG has one of the highest rates of maternal death in the world. Just over 50 percent of women and girls give birth in a health facility or with the help of a skilled birth attendant. Although the PNG government supports universal access to contraception, two out of three women still cannot access contraception due to geographic, cultural, and economic barriers. Abortion remains illegal in PNG, except when the mother's life is at risk.

## Security Force Abuses

Police abuse remained rampant in PNG. In May, police detained and assaulted a doctor at a police roadblock on his way home in Port Moresby. The case triggered a public outcry, but no one had been charged for the offence at time of writing.

Few police are ever held to account for beating or torturing criminal suspects, but in December 2016, a mobile squad commander was charged with the murder of a street vendor, six months after the alleged offence occurred. A court granted him bail in January 2017. In September, police charged a former police officer with the 2013 murder of two people in Central Province.

Despite the ombudsman and police announcing investigations into the 2016 police shooting of eight university students during a protest in Port Moresby, at time of writing no police had been charged or disciplined and neither body had issued a report.

In May, prison officers shot and killed 17 men who escaped from Buimo prison in Lae. Corrective Services ordered an inquiry, but no investigation had commenced by November 2017 due to lack of funding.

## Corruption

Corruption in PNG is widespread. Individuals in positions of power and government agencies lack accountability and transparency. In August, the National Court authorized the arrest of Prime Minister O'Neill in relation to a 2014 warrant obtained by anti-corruption police for corruption charges. But in August, the Supreme Court granted a stay against police executing the warrant pending appeal.

## *Asylum Seekers and Refugees*

About 770 male asylum seekers and refugees from countries including Afghanistan, Bangladesh, Burma, and Iran, live on Manus Island. Another 35 or so have signed settlement papers to remain in PNG, although only four of these are working and financially independent. About 70 are temporarily living in Port Moresby. All were forcibly transferred to PNG by Australia since 2013. Australia pays for their upkeep but refuses to resettle them, insisting refugees must settle in PNG or third countries, such as the United States.

Refugees and asylum seekers do not feel safe on Manus due to a spate of violent attacks by locals in the town of Lorengau. Local youths attacked refugees and asylum seekers with bush knives, sticks, and rocks and robbed them of mobile phones and possessions. Police failed to hold perpetrators to account.

In April, soldiers fired shots at the main regional processing center, injuring nine people including refugees and center staff. In June, locals carrying knives attacked and robbed a Bangladeshi man, seriously injuring his arm with a machete. He was transferred to Port Moresby for medical treatment. In July, locals attacked and robbed three refugees on Manus Island in three separate incidents; two of the men were seriously injured in knife attacks and one had to be transferred to Port Moresby for medical treatment.

In August, an Iranian with a mental health condition was found dead near the transit center on Manus. Police ruled his death a suicide, though an inquest was pending at time of writing. In October, a Sri Lankan refugee with a mental health condition was found dead at the hospital in Lorengau from a reported suicide, the sixth asylum seeker or refugee to die on Manus Island since 2013. In 2016, the UN Refugee Agency, UNHCR, surveyed 181 refugees and asylum seekers on Manus and found that 88 percent had anxiety, depression, and post-traumatic stress disorder.

In October, the Australian government ordered the main center closed, following a 2016 PNG Supreme Court ruling that detaining people there is unconstitutional. Hundreds of refugees refused to leave and remained in the squalid unguarded center without power, food, or water.

PNG and Australian officials pressed refugees and asylum seekers to move to other facilities on the island that are less secure, and offered financial incentives for both refugees and asylum seekers to return home "voluntarily." Approximately 200 men whose claims for asylum were rejected were told they must leave PNG, and will be moved to a separate accommodation facility on Manus pending deportation. In November, the PNG Supreme Court rejected an application by the refugees and asylum seekers to restore services to the main center.

## Children's Rights

Police often beat children in lock-ups and house them with adults, despite a juvenile justice law that states children should be kept separate from adults during all stages of the criminal justice process. A juvenile reception center in Port Moresby closed in 2016 due to a land dispute, so police refer children to Bomana adult prison which has separate accommodation for children.

While there have been efforts at reform and a new child reception facility established in Boroko, police abuse of children continues, and police target young people for "snake bails," where children are not charged but must pay a bribe for their release.

## Disability Rights

Despite the existence of a national disability policy, people with disabilities are often unable to participate in community life, go to school, or work because of lack of accessibility, stigma, and other barriers. Access to mental health support and services is limited, and traditional healers are the only option for many people with psychosocial disabilities.

## Sexual Orientation and Gender Identity

The PNG criminal code outlaws sex "against the order of nature," which has been interpreted to apply to consensual same-sex acts, and is punishable by up to 14 years' imprisonment. Gay asylum seekers on Manus Island have reported being harassed and sexually assaulted by other asylum seekers.

## Key International Actors

Australia remains PNG's most important international partner, providing over 70 percent of the country's total overseas development aid. The Australian government's aid to PNG for 2017-18 amounts to A$546.3 million (approximately US$438.7 million). In November 2018, PNG will host the annual Asia-Pacific Economic Cooperation forum.

HUMAN
RIGHTS
WATCH

# IMPLICATING HUMALA
Evidence of Atrocities and Cover-Up of Abuses Committed
during Peru's Armed Conflict

# Peru

In recent years, security forces have repeatedly wounded and killed civilians when responding to occasional violent protests over mining and other large-scale development projects. These killings have steeply decreased since 2016.

Efforts to prosecute grave human rights abuses committed during the 20-year armed conflict that ended in 2000 have had mixed results. Since May, new evidence became public implicating former President Ollanta Humala Tasso (2011-2016) in egregious human rights violations that security forces committed in the early 1990s.

## *Confronting Past Abuses*

Peru's Truth and Reconciliation Commission estimated that almost 70,000 people died or were subject to enforced disappearance during the country's armed conflict between 1980 and 2000. Many were victims of atrocities by the Shining Path and other insurgent groups; others were victims of human rights violations by state agents.

Authorities have achieved limited progress in prosecuting wartime abuses by government forces, in part due to lack of collaboration from the Defense Ministry. According to Peruvian human rights groups, prosecutors had only achieved rulings in 78 cases related to abuses committed during the armed conflict, as of May 2017, and only 17 convictions.

Since May, new evidence has become public corroborating longstanding allegations that former President Humala ordered egregious human rights violations committed by security forces in the early 1990s in the Madre Mía military base in the Alto Huallaga region. The evidence—including testimony from victims, witness, and soldiers involved in the abuses—strongly implicates Humala in crimes including torture, enforced disappearances, killings, and an attempt to conceal incriminating evidence when he ran for president in 2006. At time of writing, Humala remained under investigation for the abuses, and in pretrial detention on corruption charges.

Efforts to secure the early release of former President Alberto Fujimori gained strength during 2017. Fujimori was sentenced in a landmark trial in 2009 to 25 years in prison for killings, enforced disappearances, and kidnappings committed in 1991 and 1992. In May, Keiko Fujimori, his daughter and the runner-up in the 2016 tight presidential elections won by Pedro Pablo Kuczynski, filed a motion seeking to overturn her father's conviction for kidnappings. A Lima court rejected the motion, but her appeal remained pending at time of writing.

In June, President Kuczynski told *The Economist* that the time to secure Fujimori's release from prison was "about now." Although the president denies it, his announcement seemed to be a reaction to growing pressure from Fujimori supporters who control the country's Congress under the lead of Keiko Fujimori.

In 2016, prosecutors decided to close the investigation of Alberto Fujimori in connection with forced sterilizations of mostly poor and indigenous women committed during his administration. An appeal brought by victims' lawyers remained pending at time of writing. A national registry of victims of forced sterilizations committed between 1995 and 2001, was created in 2015 and more than 4,700 victims had been registered at time of writing.

Fujimori's intelligence advisor, Vladimiro Montesinos, three former army generals, and members of the Colina group—a state-sponsored death squad—are also serving sentences ranging from 15 to 25 years for the 1991 assassination of 15 people in the Lima district of Barrios Altos, and for six "disappearances."

Courts have made much less progress in addressing violations, including extrajudicial killings, disappearances, and torture, committed during the earlier administrations of Fernando Belaúnde (1980-1985) and Alan García (1985-1990).

## Police Abuse

In recent years, security forces have repeatedly wounded and killed civilians when responding to occasional violent protests over mining and other large-scale development projects. These killings have declined since 2016. Between July 2016, when President Kuczynski took office, and July 2017, security forces shot dead three protesters, according to human rights groups. Since 2006, security forces have reportedly killed more than 130 people during protests throughout Peru.

In August 2015, then-President Humala issued a decree that limited the use of force by police. Under the decree, police are permitted to employ lethal force only when it is "strictly necessary" in the face of a "serious and imminent risk" of grave harm. However, Law 30151, passed in January 2014, still grants legal immunity to "armed forces and police personnel who in fulfillment of their duty and using their weapons or other means of defense, cause injury or death." This amendment to the criminal code eliminated language that made immunity conditional on police using lethal force in compliance with regulations. The law may make it impossible to hold accountable police officers who use lethal force unlawfully.

In 2016, the Interior Ministry announced an investigation into a group of 28 policemen, including a general, who had allegedly carried out at least 20 extrajudicial killings between 2009 and 2015, and falsely reported the victims as criminals killed in combat, in order to receive promotions and awards. At least 11 policemen were awaiting trial for these crimes at time of writing.

## Freedom of Expression

Journalists investigating the corruption of regional government officials, mayors, and business people are frequent targets of physical attack, threats, and criminal defamation suits.

In November 2016, according to media reports, gunmen broke into the Camaná radio station in the southern state of Arequipa where Hernán David Choquepata Ordoñez was hosting his regular show, and shot him dead while he was on the air.

In February 2017, unknown men attacked journalist Marco Bonifacio Sánchez in the northern state of Cajamarca. The Institute of Press and Society (IPYS) in Peru, a respected nongovernmental organization (NGO) that monitors press freedoms, reported that the men beat him, forced him to get into a vehicle, and tried to cut out his tongue.

In March, a court in Lima convicted human rights lawyer and former prosecutor Ronald Gamarra of defamation and sentenced him to a suspended year in prison and ordered him to pay more than US$3,000 in compensation to Luz Guzmán. Gamarra had written a magazine piece in 2015 in which he alleged that Guzmán, a member of the National Council of Magistrates, had voted in favor of naming

Mirtha Chenguayén as a prosecutor, and that Chenguayén then dropped a pending investigation against Guzmán for forging documents.

## Women's and Girls' Rights

Gender-based violence is a significant problem in Peru. More than 382 women were victims of "femicides" (the killing of a woman in certain contexts, including domestic violence and gender-based discrimination) or attempted "femicide" in 2016, according to official statistics. Courts in Peru convicted 54 people for "femicide" between January 2015 and March 2016.

In August 2017, thousands demonstrated in Lima and other cities as part of the massive movement to call on authorities to do more to curb gender-based violence.

Women and girls in Peru have the right to access abortions only in cases of risk to their health or lives. In August, the human rights ombudsman's office asked the government to ensure an "integral attention and accompaniment" to a 10-year old girl in the city of Jaén who was pregnant and facing a risk to her life as a result of rape. A bill introduced in October 2016 to decriminalize abortion in cases of rape and if the fetus suffers severe conditions not compatible with life outside the womb remained pending in Congress at time of writing. But also pending in Congress remained a bill that would recognize the "right" of the fetus conceived as a result of rape to receive "protection from the state" until it is "adopted."

## Sexual Orientation and Gender Identity

Same-sex couples in Peru are not allowed to marry or engage in civil unions. In February, a group of lawmakers introduced a bill to legalize same-sex marriage. It remained pending in Congress at time of writing.

People in Peru are required to appear before a judge in order to revise the gender marker noted on their identification documents. In an August 2016 report, the human rights ombudsman noted that courts had rejected most of these requests, often applying inconsistent criteria. A bill allowing people to revise the gender noted on their identification documents without prior judicial approval remained pending in Congress at time of writing.

In May, opposition lawmakers in Congress abrogated a penal code reform supported by President Kuczynski that specifically sanctioned discrimination and crimes committed on the basis of sexual orientation or gender identity.

## Key International Actors

In July 2017, the UN Working Group on Business and Human Rights visited Peru. The experts noted that the high number of social conflicts in the country "suggests a failure of existing strategies to prevent and mitigate adverse human rights impacts related to foreign direct investment."

In November, the UN Human Rights Council released its draft report on the third cycle of Peru's Universal Periodic Review (UPR). Its recommendations included guaranteeing proportionate use of force by security forces, decriminalizing abortion, and ensuring justice for serious abuses committed during the armed conflict.

In October, United Nations High Commissioner for Human Rights Zeid Ra'ad Al Hussein visited Peru and recommended calling international experts to examine alleged health problems suffered by Fujimori. President Kuczynski said the recommendation was an "unnecessary interference in Peru's affairs."

President Kuczynski has played a leading role in regional efforts to help address the human rights crisis in Venezuela. In August, his government convoked a meeting at which foreign affairs ministers of 12 nations signed the Lima Declaration—a comprehensive statement that condemns the rupture of democratic order and the systematic violation of human rights in Venezuela.

Between January and March, more than 10,000 Venezuelans requested permission to stay in Peru. In January, President Kuczynski adopted a decree that lays out a special permission for Venezuelans to stay in the country. Under the decree, Venezuelans who arrived in the country before February 2—the date it entered into force—who do not have a criminal record, and whose legal permission to stay in the country had expired, may request a year-long temporary residency permit. Those who obtain the permit are allowed to work, enroll their children in school, and access health care.

# Philippines

President Rodrigo Duterte has plunged the Philippines into its worst human rights crisis since the dictatorship of Ferdinand Marcos in the 1970s and 1980s. His "war on drugs," launched after he took office in June 2016, has claimed an estimated 12,000 lives of primarily poor urban dwellers, including children.

Duterte has vowed to continue the abusive anti-drug campaign until his term ends in 2022. Throughout 2017 and the latter part of 2016, he engaged in harassment and intimidation of individuals and agencies tasked with accountability—including United Nations officials.

Duterte's most prominent critic, Senator Leila de Lima, remained in detention on politically motivated drug charges. Pro-Duterte lawmakers in 2017 sought to eliminate budgetary funding for the official Commission on Human Rights as apparent retaliation for its efforts to probe the anti-drug campaign. In the face of mounting international criticism, the Duterte government has adopted a tactic of denying as "alternative facts" well-substantiated reports by human rights and media organizations of high death tolls linked to the "drug war."

Violation of children's rights, attacks on journalists and media, and government policy failures contributing to the country's worsening HIV epidemic persisted in 2017.

## Extrajudicial Killings

The Duterte administration's "war on drugs" has resulted in the deaths of thousands of mostly poor Filipinos. Philippine Drug Enforcement Agency (PDEA) data indicates that police operations resulted in the deaths of 3,906 suspected drug users and dealers from July 1, 2016, to September 26, 2017. But unidentified gunmen have killed thousands more, bringing the total death toll to more than 12,000, according to credible media reports.

The government has frustrated efforts by media and other independent observers to maintain a verifiable and transparent tally of such deaths by issuing contradictory data. In August, the official Commission on Human Rights stated that the "[a]ctual number [of drug war killings] is certainly higher than what is suggested" by police.

A Human Rights Watch investigation found that the Philippine National Police and its agents have repeatedly carried out extrajudicial killings of drug suspects, and then falsely claimed self-defense. Police have planted guns, spent ammunition, and drug packets on victims' bodies to implicate them in drug activities. Masked gunmen taking part in killings appeared to be working closely with police, casting doubt on government claims that most killings have been committed by vigilantes or rival drug gangs.

No one has been meaningfully investigated, let alone prosecuted, for any of the "drug war" killings. Instead, Duterte has pledged to pardon policemen implicated in killings. In October, responding to a public outcry against killings notably committed against children, Duterte removed police from anti-drug operations, assigning the PDEA as the main agency to carry out the drug war.

However, journalists who closely cover the anti-drug campaign say that although the killings by uniformed police personnel have declined since that time, summary killings by "vigilantes" have continued uninterrupted. On November 22, Duterte warned of an imminent lifting of the suspension of police anti-drug operations, raising the likelihood of more extrajudicial executions by police and their agents.

## Human Rights Defenders

The Duterte administration has widened its "war on drugs" to include critics and political foes. Since February 2017, Senator Leila de Lima has been behind bars on politically motivated drug charges filed against her in apparent retaliation for leading a Senate inquiry into the drug war killings.

In August, Duterte encouraged police attacks against human rights groups and advocates, instructing police, "If they are obstructing justice, you shoot them."

Duterte has publicly condemned the Commission on Human Rights and threatened to abolish it. He also repeatedly subjected United Nations Special Rapporteur on Extrajudicial Killings Agnes Callamard to profanity-laced ridicule for her repeated efforts to secure an official visit to the Philippines. In August, he responded to Callamard's criticism of police extrajudicial killings of children by calling her a "son of a bitch" and a "fool."

## Children's Rights

In July, a Philippine children's rights group published data indicating that police have killed 56 children since the start of the "drug war." Most were killed while in the company of adults who were the apparent target of the shooting. Both Duterte and Justice Secretary Vitaliano Aguirre II have dismissed those child killings as "collateral damage."

In February, public opposition prompted Congress to reject a bill that would have lowered the age of criminal responsibility to nine from the current 15 years.

In August, the government approved mandatory drug testing for high school and college students and applicants. This will effectively allow the police to extend their abusive anti-drug operations to high schools and university campuses.

Child labor in small-scale gold mines remains a serious problem.

## Attacks on Journalists

In March, unidentified gunmen killed newspaper columnist Joaquin Briones in the Masbate province town of Milagros. In August, an unidentified gunman killed radio journalists Rudy Alicaway and Leo Diaz in separate incidents on the southern island of Mindanao. The National Union of Journalists estimates that 177 Filipino reporters and media workers have been killed since 1986.

Duterte has publicly vilified media outlets whose reporters have exposed police culpability in extrajudicial killings. In April, he threatened to block the renewal of the broadcasting franchise of ABS-CBN network. In July, Duterte publicly threatened the *Philippine Daily Inquirer* with tax evasion charges and falsely accused the media platform *Rappler* of being US-owned in an apparent effort to undermine its credibility.

Journalists who report critically on the Duterte administration are also subjected to harassment and threats online. In December 2016, the Foreign Correspondents Association of the Philippines issued a statement denouncing such attacks.

## *HIV Epidemic*

The Philippines is facing the fastest-growing epidemic of HIV in the Asia-Pacific region. According to the Joint United Nations Programme on HIV/AIDS (UNAIDS), the number of new HIV cases jumped from 4,300 to 10,000 between 2010 and 2016. Most new infections—up to 83 percent—are among men and transgender women who have sex with men. In August, the government declared the situation a "national emergency."

Despite recognition of the problem, the government is responsible for a legal and policy environment hostile to evidence-based policies and interventions have proven to help prevent HIV transmission, including the use of condoms and comprehensive sexuality education targeting the young.

Human Rights Watch research shows that many sexually active young Filipinos have little or no knowledge about the role of condoms in preventing sexually transmitted diseases because the government fails to provide adequate school programs on safe-sex practices. A bill amending the country's main law on HIV/AIDS to boost the government's response to the crisis remained pending in Congress at the time of writing.

## *Sexual Orientation and Gender Identity*

Students across the Philippines experience bullying and discrimination in school because of their sexual orientation and gender identity. In late 2016, Human Rights Watch documented a range of abuses against lesbian, gay, bisexual, and transgender (LGBT) students in secondary school. They include bullying, harassment, discriminatory policies and practices, and an absence of supportive resources that undermine the right to education under international law and put LGBT youth at risk. These students often face ridicule and even violence, including by teachers and administrators.

In September, the House of Representatives passed House Bill 4982, a proposed law against discrimination based on sexual orientation and gender identity and expression (SOGIE).

HUMAN
RIGHTS
WATCH

# "Just Let Us Be"

Discrimination Against LGBT Students in the Philippines

## Terrorism and Counterterrorism

On May 23, after Islamist rebels took over the predominantly Muslim city of Marawi, Mindanao, the Philippine government launched a counterattack. The fighting destroyed the city and left at least 1,112 people dead, mostly alleged rebels but also civilians and government soldiers, the government said. The government's figures could not be independently verified.

The fighting has displaced more than 400,000 residents of the city and nearby towns, many of whom were living in overcrowded evacuation camps. Duterte declared martial law across the entire Mindanao region in response to the fighting. The rebels, known as the Maute group, are residents of Marawi and nearby provinces who linked with elements of the Abu Sayyaf armed group, which had earlier pledged support for the extremist group Islamic State (ISIS).

## Key International Actors

The escalation in unlawful killings associated with the "war on drugs," and President Duterte's open defiance of international human rights standards and confrontational stance towards critics, have roiled the Philippines' relationships with its closest Western allies.

Duterte has repeatedly threatened to seek stronger ties with countries such as China and Russia, which have not been critical of his drug-campaign abuses. Historically, the Philippines has had close relationships with the United States and European Union countries.

In March, European Trade Commissioner Cecilia Malmström warned that unless the Philippine government addressed EU concerns about human rights abuses, the Philippines risks losing tariff-free export of up to 6,000 products under the EU's human rights benchmarks linked to the Generalized Scheme of Preferences Plus (GSP+) trade scheme.

In April, US President Donald Trump signaled a break with the Obama administration's criticism of Duterte's drug war killing campaign by praising it as a "great job" and inviting Duterte to the White House. In May, US senators introduced a bill, the Philippines Human Rights Accountability and Counternarcotics Act of 2017, which aims to restrict arms exports to the Philippines, support human rights groups, and assist the Philippines in dealing with the drug problem. The bill had been referred to the US Senate Foreign Relations Committee at time of writing.

The US remains a key source of military financial assistance, with the Trump administration allotting US$180 million for 2017. Australia, whose officials have criticized the "drug war" killings, has nevertheless promised to extend military aid to the Philippines, mainly for counterterrorism.

In January 2017, Japan pledged to the Philippines a five-year, $800 million Japanese government Overseas Development Assistance package to "promote economic and infrastructure development." Tokyo also promised financial support for drug rehabilitation projects in the Philippines. China has pledged assistance to the Philippines of as much as US$24 billion-worth of projects under Beijing's "One Belt, One Road" program.

In August, the education secretary expressed her commitment to see the Philippines join the Safe Schools Declaration, an intergovernmental political commitment to protect students, teachers, and schools from attack during armed conflict, but did not give a timeframe for doing so.

In May, the Philippines underwent its Universal Periodic Review, which focuses attention on the human rights record of each UN member state every four years. In its September response, the Philippines rejected nearly every recommendation to bring an end to extrajudicial killings and to ensure an independent investigation into the deaths. The High Commissioner for Human Rights expressed grave concern at Duterte's open support for a "shoot-to-kill" policy and the "apparent absence of credible investigations."

Iceland led a joint statement on behalf of 32 states at the June session of the Human Rights Council, and another on behalf of 39 states at the council's September session, condemning the extrajudicial killings and calling for credible independent investigations into these deaths.

# Qatar

Qatar faced a diplomatic crisis in 2017, as some of its neighbors cut diplomatic ties with it over its alleged support of terrorism and its closeness with Iran—claims that Qatar rejects.

The move in early June by Saudi Arabia, Bahrain, and the United Arab Emirates—and their subsequent issuance with Egypt of a list of 13 demands for ending the crisis, which Qatar rejected—isolated the Gulf state and precipitated serious human rights violations of individuals living in Qatar, infringing on their right to free expression, separating families, and interrupting medical care and education. At time of writing, travel to and from Qatar was restricted, and its border with Saudi Arabia remained closed.

## Gulf Crisis

On June 5, Saudi Arabia, Bahrain, and the UAE cut diplomatic relations with Qatar over its alleged support of terrorism and its closeness with Iran and ordered the expulsion of Qatari citizens and the return of their citizens from Qatar within 14 days.

On June 23, the three countries and Egypt issued a list of 13 demands for ending the crisis that included shutting down Al Jazeera and other media they claim are Qatar- funded; downgrading diplomatic ties with Iran; severing ties with "terrorist organizations," including the Muslim Brotherhood, and expelling people associated with such organizations from Qatar; and paying reparations to other Gulf countries for "loss of life" and "other financial losses" resulting from Qatar's policies.

Qatar rejected the demands.

## Residency Reforms

On August 3, 2017, the Qatari cabinet approved a draft law that will allow permanent residence for children of Qatari women married to non-Qataris, as well as expatriates who "provide outstanding services to Qatar."

Qatar does not allow dual nationality and discriminates against women by not allowing them to pass nationality to their children on the same basis as men.

Qatar allows men to pass citizenship to their children, whereas children of Qatari women and non-citizen men can only apply for citizenship under narrow conditions.

Under the 2005 law on acquisition of Qatari nationality, people who have lived in Qatar for more than 25 years may apply for nationality, with priority for those with Qatari mothers, under specific conditions. However, the government has not consistently approved such applications. If enacted, the draft law would help people whose mothers are Qatari nationals to secure resident status in Qatar even if they do not have valid passports from another country. However, it still falls short of granting women the same rights as Qatari men to pass citizenship to their children.

The Qatari draft law's provision of permanent residence to migrants who "provide outstanding services to Qatar" also could help Emirati, Egyptian, Bahraini, and Saudi nationals affected by the diplomatic crisis. Many have chosen to remain in Qatar for family or work reasons or because they fear persecution in their home countries.

Under the law, the Interior Ministry is to establish a committee to review requests for permanent residency IDs. But it was not clear at time of writing whether the committee would grant residency to those who fear persecution or harm in their countries of origin. Qatar does not have a law on asylum and has not ratified the 1951 Refugee Convention.

## *Migrant Domestic Workers*

On August 22, 2017, the emir of Qatar, Sheikh Tamim bin Hamad Al Thani, ratified Law No.15 on service workers in the home. The cabinet adopted the law in February, which will grant labor protections for the first time to Qatar's 173,742 domestic workers. The new law guarantees domestic workers a maximum 10-hour workday, a weekly rest day, three weeks of annual leave, an end-of-service payment of at least three weeks per year, and healthcare benefits.

However, the new law is still weaker than the Labor Law and does not fully conform to the International Labour Organization (ILO) Domestic Workers Convention, the global treaty on domestic workers' rights. The new law establishes fines for violations, but lacks provisions for enforcement, such as workplace inspections, including in homes where domestic workers are employed. The law does not state how workers can claim their rights if they have been breached except in cases of compensation for work injuries. Workers in Qatar are not allowed to form a union or entitled to a minimum wage established by law.

## Construction Workers

Qatar has a migrant labor force of nearly 2 million people, who comprise approximately 95 percent of its total labor force. Approximately 40 percent, or 800,000, of these workers are employed in construction. Current heat protection regulations for most workers in Qatar only prohibit outdoor work from 11:30 a.m. to 3 p.m. from June 15 to August 31. But climate data shows that weather conditions in Qatar outside those hours and dates frequently reach levels that can result in potentially fatal heat-related illnesses without rest.

In 2013, health authorities reported 520 deaths of workers of whom 385, or 74 percent, died from unexplained causes. Qatari public health officials have not responded to requests for information about the overall number and causes of deaths of migrant workers since 2012.

A 2014 report that the Qatari government commissioned from the international law firm DLA Piper noted that the number of worker deaths in Qatar attributed to cardiac arrest, a general term that does not specify cause of death, was "seemingly high." Authorities have failed to implement two of the report's key recommendations: reforming its laws to allow autopsies or post-mortem examinations in cases of "unexpected or sudden deaths" and commissioning an independent study into the seemingly high number of deaths vaguely attributed to cardiac arrest.

On October 26, the International Trade Union Confederation announced Qatar's agreement to extensive reforms of the current *kafala* (sponsorship) system, to institute a nondiscriminatory minimum wage, to improve payment of wages, to end document confiscation, to enhance labor inspections and occupational safety and health systems including by developing a heat mitigation strategy, to refine the contractual system to improve labor recruitment procedures, and to step up efforts to prevent forced labor.

These measures would be pathbreaking for Gulf countries where migrants make up most of the labor force, but the announcement gives little detail on how laws will be amended, how the changes will be carried out, or the timeframe for their implementation.

## Women's Rights, Sexual Orientation, and Gender Identity

Qatar's Law No. 22 of 2006 on Family and Personal Status continues to discriminate against women. Under article 36, a marriage contract is valid when a woman's male guardian concludes the contract and two male witnesses are present. Article 58 states that it is a wife's responsibility to look after the household and to obey her husband.

Other than article 57 of the family law forbidding husbands from hurting their wives physically or morally, and general provisions on assault, the penal code does not criminalize domestic violence or marital rape.

Qatar's penal code punishes "sodomy" with one to three years in prison. Muslims convicted of *zina* (sex outside of marriage) can be sentenced to flogging (if unmarried) or the death penalty (if married). Non-Muslims can be sentenced to imprisonment.

## Key International Actors

Qatar was a member of the Saudi-led coalition that began a military campaign in Yemen in March 2015 but Qatar withdrew its forces from the operation in June 2017. The coalition has conducted thousands of airstrikes in Yemen, including scores that appear to violate the laws of war, some of which may be war crimes. However, coalition members, including Qatar, have provided insufficient or no information about the role that particular countries' forces are playing in alleged unlawful attacks.

Qatar purchased at least US$18 billion in weapons during 2017, of which at least $12 billion was from the United States. In June, reacting to the isolation of Qatar by neighboring states, Turkey's parliament fast-tracked the approval of an April 2016 agreement with Qatar on the implementation of Turkish troops' deployment to a military base in Qatar, and the two countries began carrying out joint military exercises.

# Russia

As the March 2018 presidential election approached, the government increased its crackdown against political opposition and peaceful protesters and took new steps to stifle independent voices online. In Chechnya, local authorities carried out a large-scale anti-gay purge, rounding up and torturing dozens of men because of their presumed homosexuality. Parliament decriminalized acts of domestic violence not involving serious bodily harm. The government continued to support "separatists" in eastern Ukraine, who committed abuses in areas under their control, and it aimed to silence Crimean Tatars and other critics in occupied Crimea, including through criminal prosecution.

## *Freedom of Assembly*

In the first six months of 2017 alone, the number of people administratively punished by Russian authorities for supposedly violating the country's regulations on public gatherings was two-and-a-half times higher than throughout 2016.

In spring and summer, government critics in numerous cities across Russia held peaceful anti-corruption protests that authorities refused to authorize. Officials harassed and intimidated protesters, including schoolchildren and university students, and also parents whose children participated. University administrators directly or indirectly threatened students with expulsion for involvement. In July, a university in Kaliningrad expelled a law student, apparently for his active role in the protests.

Police arbitrarily detained hundreds of peaceful protesters on June 12 in Moscow and St. Petersburg. If protesters questioned their detentions, riot police handled them roughly, and in some cases beat them with truncheons and kicked and punched them. One protester in Moscow spent a week in a hospital with a concussion after a police officer hit her.

Police apprehended people who were not causing a disturbance, and in many cases were not even chanting slogans or carrying posters, and charged them groundlessly with various administrative violations. Most were fined or handed 10 to 15 days' jail time, following flawed, pro-forma court hearings. Protesters detained in St. Petersburg spent up to two nights sleeping on the floor or in chairs at overcrowded precincts, and had to rely on activists to bring food and drinking water. Police at some precincts denied detainees access to lawyers.

In February, the Constitutional Court ruled that criminal penalties for repeated breaches of public assembly regulations should not be applied in cases where protesters did not constitute a threat. Later in February, the Supreme Court quashed the two-and-a-half-year criminal sentence of Ildar Dadin, the first person convicted under that provision, and ordered his immediate release. Dadin's prior allegations of torture by penitentiary officials have seen no effective investigation.

## Suppression of Political Opposition Campaigning Activity

From spring 2017 onward, authorities systematically interfered with the presidential campaign of a leading opposition politician, Alexei Navalny. Formally disqualified from the race due to an outstanding criminal conviction resulting from a politicized, unfair trial, Navalny opened campaign offices in most of Russia's regions.

Police across Russia searched Navalny's offices and seized campaign materials. Authorities frequently refused to authorize campaign sidewalk displays, and detained campaigners on groundless charges. Police also raided the homes of local campaigners and their relatives.

Navalny campaigners and offices also faced increasing attacks by ultra-nationalist groups and pro-Kremlin activists. Attackers vandalized campaign offices or campaigners' homes, stormed into meetings, stole campaign materials, and damaged office equipment and campaigners' vehicles. They also physically assaulted campaigners, beating and throwing eggs and other objects at them. In some cases, police merely stood by or arrived too late to catch the attackers. Authorities registered complaints filed by campaigners, but typically failed to carry out effective investigations.

## Freedom of Association

Authorities used a 2015 law on "undesirable organizations" to ban four more foreign organizations, bringing the total to 11, and to intimidate protesters and independent groups.

HUMAN
RIGHTS
WATCH

## ONLINE AND ON ALL FRONTS
Russia's Assault on Freedom of Expression

Russians maintaining ties with "undesirables" face penalties ranging from fines to up to six years in prison. In June, a Krasnodar court fined an activist 15,000 rubles (US$260) for supposed involvement with the UK-based pro-democracy group Open Russia, banned in 2017, and in August, a Tula court fined another activist 1,000 rubles ($17) for the same.

Also, between June and November, the government filed charges against at least eight Russian groups for their supposed "participation in the activities of undesirable organizations." In September, the Moscow city prosecutor's office charged SOVA Center, an independent think tank, and its director, Alexander Verkhovsky, with involvement with "undesirable organizations." The charges stemmed from hyperlinks on SOVA's website to two US foundations, which had funded some of SOVA's projects until they were banned as "undesirable" in 2015. In November, a court in Moscow found the Andrei Rylkov Foundation, a prominent Russian group dedicated to responsible drug policy, in violation of the law on "undesirable organizations" and fined it 50,000 rubles (US$862). The charges stemmed from a hyperlink to the website of a banned US organization in an article published on the foundation's website.

Authorities also continued demonizing as "foreign agents" advocacy groups that accept foreign funding. The number of organizations on the government's "foreign agent" register dropped from almost 150 to 88 as some of the designated groups either abandoned foreign funding or closed. Over 30 groups, including several rights organizations and environmental groups, have closed since the foreign agents' law was adopted in 2012. In June, authorities in Rostov region brought criminal proceedings against Valentina Cherevatenko, a prominent rights activist, for "malicious evasion" of the foreign agents law, but dropped the case several weeks later.

## *Freedom of Expression Online and Freedom of Information*

Legislation adopted in July banned anonymous use of online messenger applications and software designed to circumvent internet censorship.

By February 2017, the number of people imprisoned for extremist speech spiked to 94, from 54 in 2015.

In December 2016, a court in Tyumen sentenced Alexey Kungurov, a journalist and blogger, to two-and-a-half years in prison for "publicly justifying terrorism." The charges had stemmed from his blog post criticizing Russia's actions in Syria.

In May, a court convicted video blogger Ruslan Sokolovsky for inciting hatred and insulting the feelings of religious believers, and handed down a three-and-a-half-year suspended sentence. The charges stemmed from a prank video mocking the Russian Orthodox Church, which Sokolovsky shared on social media. The sentence was reduced to two years and three months on appeal.

In June, a Moscow court convicted the director of the Moscow Library of Ukrainian Literature, Natalia Sharina, for "inciting hatred" for books in the library that authorities said were "extremist," and handed down a four-year suspended sentence. Sharina had spent one year and seven months under house arrest.

In November, the parliament amended Russia's media legislation to enable the government to designate any media organization or information distributor of foreign origin as "foreign media performing the functions of a foreign agent." Those designated must comply with the requirements for nongovernmental organizations (NGOs) set out in the 2012 "foreign agents" law.

## Freedom of Religion

In April, the Supreme Court banned as extremist the Jehovah's Witnesses organization, which has more than 100,000 worshippers across Russia.

Since July 2016, when the "Yarovaya Law" entered into force, authorities fined over 100 religious activists, mainly evangelist Christians, for either preaching without special authorization or distributing religious literature without the religious distributor's name on the cover.

In June, authorities stated that the Interior Ministry for Dagestan, in the south of Russia, was no longer placing "adherents of non-traditional Islam" on police watchlists. However, persecution of Salafi Muslims, including arbitrary detentions and harassment, continued.

## Chechnya

Early in 2017, Chechen security officials illegally detained and tortured presumed jihadists. *Novaya Gazeta* reported that in December 2016 and January 2017, Chechen police extrajudicially killed 27 detainees; Human Rights Center Memorial stated that, based on their investigation, 23 of the people on *Novaya Gazeta*'s list disappeared and two died following abduction-style detentions by local security officials.

From late February and through early April, security officials unlawfully rounded up dozens of men they believed were gay, searched their cell phones for contacts of other presumably gay men, and tried to coerce them, including through torture, into naming their gay acquaintances. They kept the men in several unofficial facilities, where Chechen authorities have for years held and tortured individuals suspected of dissent or sabotage. They exposed some of the captives to their families as gay and encouraged honor killings. At least two high-level local officials watched police humiliate and torture the detainees.

Chechen authorities responded to the allegations by denying the existence of gay people in Chechnya, suggesting obliquely that families kill their gay relatives, and accusing journalists and human rights defenders of seeking to destabilize the republic. Chechen officials and public figures made serious threats against *Novaya Gazeta*, the newspaper that broke the story.

The Russian LGBT Network opened a special hotline for those in immediate danger and provided evacuation-related assistance to 79 people. Most of them eventually found safe sanctuary abroad. Chechen police allegedly harassed relatives of those who fled, attempting to pressure them into disclosing the men's whereabouts, and forcing them to sign documents with false statements that the men were traveling outside Chechnya at the time the purge was ongoing.

The Kremlin initially dismissed reports about the violence but, faced with consolidated international pressure, federal authorities eventually investigated. By summer, the investigation apparently stalled. In September, Russian investigative authorities received an official complaint by one of the victims of the purge, Maxim Lapunov, detailing his abduction-style detention and torture by Chechen security officials in March. At time of writing, authorities had not carried out an effective investigation into Lapunov's complaint.

HUMAN
RIGHTS
WATCH

"They Have Long Arms
and They Can Find Me"
Anti-Gay Purge by Local Authorities in Russia's Chechen Republic

Chechen authorities also stepped up their "women's virtue campaign" aimed at ensuring that women wear headscarves in public and adhere to traditional family roles. With apparent approval by local authorities, Carthage, a Chechen online group published photos of numerous women and called for their punishment. In September, federal authorities blocked the website for "extremist" content.

In June, Chechnya's leader, Ramzan Kadyrov, launched a "family reunification" program, creating local councils of public officials and religious authorities, who draw up lists of divorced couples and approach the spouses separately, suggesting reconciliation. In September, Chechen media reported that the program led to the reuniting of over 1,000 divorced couples. Some of those reluctant to cooperate, including women who had fled abusive marriages, alleged pressure from the councils.

## *Sexual Orientation and Gender Identity*

Authorities continued to enforce discriminatory policies and laws against lesbian, gay, bisexual, and transgender (LGBT) people.

In May, St. Petersburg authorities refused to approve a flashmob on International Day against Homophobia, Biphobia and Transphobia, citing the "gay propaganda" ban.

In June, the European Court of Human Rights (ECtHR) ruled that the "gay propaganda" law violated freedom of expression, was discriminatory, and encouraged homophobia.

In October, a court in Samara fined a local activist 50,000 rubles (US$865) for violating the "gay propaganda" ban.

In a positive development in August, a court in Omsk ruled in favor of a man who sued a shop for denying him a job because of his apparent sexual orientation. The court found the refusal to hire him "unlawful" and awarded him 30,000 rubles ($505) in damages.

## *Abuses Linked to the 2017 FIFA Confederations Cup and 2018 World Cup*

Workers on stadiums being built for the 2017 FIFA Confederations Cup and 2018 World Cup reported exploitation, including non-provision of contracts, non-payment of wages, and retaliation for reporting abuses. The Building and Woodworkers International trade union reported at least 17 deaths on stadiums since construction began.

In April, authorities arbitrarily detained a Human Rights Watch researcher seeking to interview workers near the Volgograd stadium; he was released without charge after three hours. In June and July, police detained at least 33 people, citing a May presidential order unduly restricting peaceful assemblies in confederations and World Cup host cities.

## *Women's Rights*

Despite persistently high rates of domestic violence, in February the Russian government enacted a law decriminalizing acts of domestic violence that do not cause serious harm leading to hospital treatment, or which aren't reported more than once a year. The law leaves domestic violence victims more vulnerable to escalation of abuse. Moscow's mayor denied activists authorization to protest the law. A comprehensive domestic violence law has been stalled in parliament since 2014.

## *Disability Rights*

Reports persisted of discrimination against people with disabilities and abuse of children and adults with disabilities in state institutions. In July, a psychiatrist published videos showing several residents in an adult institution in Trubchevsk chained to beds, radiators, and other objects. Former staff publicly confirmed this practice. A criminal investigation is ongoing.

In March, the Prosecutor General's Office noted that violations of the rights of people with disabilities persist at high rates, including lack of physical accessibility, employment discrimination, and denial of medical treatment.

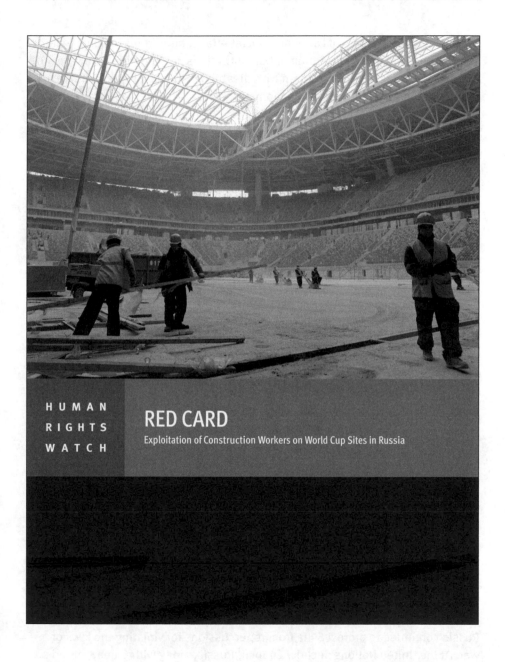

**HUMAN RIGHTS WATCH**

# RED CARD

Exploitation of Construction Workers on World Cup Sites in Russia

According to the Ministry of Labor and Social Affairs, authorities in some regions have taken steps to move children out of institutions and promote family-based care; education reforms for children with disabilities to study in mainstream schools with proper supports are ongoing.

## Russia and Ukraine (see also Ukraine chapter)

The government continued to provide political and material support to armed "separatists" in eastern Ukraine but took no measures to rein in their abuses, such as arbitrary detentions and torture. Russian authorities also continued repression against critics, primarily Crimean Tatars, in occupied Crimea. (See Ukraine chapter).

In September 2016, Russian authorities arrested Roman Sushchenko, a Ukrainian journalist with the state news service, Ukrinform, on dubious espionage charges. At time of writing, he remained in custody pending investigation.

Oleg Sentsov, a Ukrainian filmmaker, continued to serve a 20-year prison sentence resulting from his 2015 conviction on trumped-up charges of running "terrorist organizations" in Crimea.

## Russia and Syria (see also Syria chapter)

Between April and August, Russia conducted at least 13,000 air strikes. While the number of civilian casualties appeared to decrease, partially as a result of local ceasefires, monitoring groups reported hundreds of civilian deaths each month, including from unlawful aerial attacks. Syrian and Russian forces carried out unlawful attacks, including airstrikes on schools and hospitals, and air-dropped cluster munitions and incendiary weapons in populated areas.

Russian ground forces became more active in Syria. Russia also played a role in negotiating local ceasefires and evacuations and participated in the evacuation of fighters and civilians from opposition-controlled areas. Some evacuations could amount to forced displacement, where civilians may have been transferred to other areas without their informed consent and beyond the exceptions of imperative military or protection reasons.

Russia continued to protect Syria from repercussions for violating the laws of war. At the United Nations Security Council, Russia, along with China, vetoed a

February 2017 resolution proposing sanctions on those responsible for chemical attacks. Russia was also the only member to veto an April 2017 resolution condemning a chemical attack in northern Syria and calling for an international investigation.

Russia continued its efforts to shield the Syrian government from accountability by lobbying against the International, Impartial and Independent Mechanism (IIIM), established by the General Assembly in December 2016 to investigate serious crimes committed in Syria and prepare and preserve evidence.

Moscow has openly criticized the IIIM as illegitimate and suggested that the assembly had no authority to establish a quasi-special prosecutor's office. At the Security Council in November, Russia twice vetoed a proposed renewal of the Joint Investigative Mechanism (JIM) of the UN and Organization for the Prohibition of Chemical Weapons after JIM issued a report blaming the Syrian government for a sarin gas attack in April 2017. The vetoes brought to 11 the number of times Russia has cast its veto at the council since 2011.

## Key International Actors

Russia's role in the Syria conflict, sanctions against Russia for occupying Crimea, and engagement with Russian authorities to end hostilities in eastern Ukraine continued to dominate the agenda of key international actors. But many spoke out strongly against abuses.

In January, the European Union and the secretary general of the Council of Europe, Thorbjørn Jagland, spoke out against Russia's decriminalization of domestic violence.

In February, the EU called the repeated conviction of Alexei Navalny on embezzlement charges "an attempt to silence another independent political voice." The UK, French, and German governments raised similar concerns.

Also in February, Jagland welcomed the overturning of Ildar Dadin's verdict and his release from prison. He also called on Russia to amend its law on public gatherings.

Numerous international actors, both institutional and individual such as the EU, Jagland, UN human rights experts, and governments of the US, UK, France, and

Germany spoke out against the mass detentions of peaceful protesters at the March 26 and June 12 rallies.

In April, key international actors including the EU, the Organization for Security and Co-operation in Europe (OSCE) and UN human rights experts responded vocally and publicly to news of the anti-gay purge in Chechnya. The governments of Canada, the US, France, Germany, and the UK deplored the purge, and the foreign ministers of France, Germany, the Netherlands, the UK, and Sweden sent a joint letter to Russia's foreign minister urging the Russian government to investigate.

In a joint press conference with President Vladimir Putin, German Chancellor Angela Merkel raised the issue and asked him "to utilize his influence to protect these minority rights." French President Emmanuel Macron also raised the issue at his May summit with Putin. Canada and several EU member states provided refuge to some of the men who fled.

In April, UN human rights experts, officials of the OSCE, the UK human rights minister, the US State Department, and the EU expressed concern over Russia's Jehovah's Witnesses ban.

In June, the EU criticized Russia for labeling NGOs "foreign agents" and the Council of Europe Commissioner for Human Rights called the "foreign agents" law incompatible with international human rights standards.

In August, Russia was reviewed before the UN Committee on the Elimination of All Forms of Racial Discrimination, which raised concerns, including lack of protection from discrimination, vague and overly broad counter-extremism legislation, flawed laws on "foreign agents" and "undesirable organizations", hate crimes and hate speech. It also called on Russia to allow the Office of the UN High Commissioner for Human Rights (OHCHR) full access to Crimea, and address alleged violations against Crimean Tartars, Roma, indigenous peoples, migrant workers, and other vulnerable groups.

In September, Russia was reviewed before the UN Committee on Economic, Social and Cultural Rights, which raised concerns about a broad range of issues, including "foreign agent" restrictions on NGOs, harassment of human rights defenders, corruption, and discrimination.

In 2017, Russia-US relations hit a new low over the allegations of Russia's interference in the 2016 US presidential election.

# Rwanda

In a context of very limited free speech or open political space, President Paul Kagame overwhelmingly won a third term in August with a reported 98.8 percent of the vote, after a 2015 referendum allowed him to run for a seven-year term and two additional five-year terms thereafter. Before and after the August election, the Rwandan government continued to limit the ability of civil society groups, the media, international human rights organizations, and political opponents to function freely and independently or to criticize the government's policies and practices.

State security forces in the Western Province summarily killed at least 37 suspected petty offenders between April 2016 and March 2017, in what appeared to be part of a broader strategy to spread fear, enforce order, and deter any resistance to government orders or policies. Rwandan authorities continued to arrest and detain people in unofficial military detention centers, where scores of detainees have been tortured in recent years.

## *Freedom of Expression*

Civil society in Rwanda is very weak, due to many years of state intimidation and interference, leaving Rwandan human rights organizations largely unable to publicly document violations by state agents. While some private radio stations occasionally broadcast programs on politically sensitive issues, such as proposed changes to the penal code that would criminalize defamation, official government views dominated the domestic media and almost all election coverage. Government actors also intimidated international journalists. The BBC Kinyarwanda service remains suspended since 2014.

Sana Radio journalist John Ndabarasa, who had gone missing on August 8, 2016, resurfaced in the capital, Kigali, on March 6. Ndabarasa is a family member of Joel Mutabazi, a former presidential bodyguard sentenced to life imprisonment in 2014 for security-related offenses. In a story that raised suspicions for many, Ndabarasa told journalists that he had fled the country and later decided voluntarily to come back.

**HUMAN RIGHTS WATCH**

## "All Thieves Must Be Killed"

Extrajudicial Executions in Western Rwanda

## Political Pluralism

Three candidates contested the August presidential election: Kagame (Rwandan Patriotic Front, RPF); Frank Habineza (Democratic Green Party of Rwanda, DGPR); and an independent candidate, Philippe Mpayimana. Both Habineza and Mpayimana said they experienced harassment, threats, and intimidation ahead of the election. Neither posed a serious challenge to President Kagame.

Two other would-be independent candidates, Diana Rwigara and Gilbert Mwenedata, said that they had fulfilled all eligibility requirements, but the National Electoral Commission did not register them, claiming that many of the signatures supporting their candidacy were invalid. Another potential candidate, Thomas Nahimana, was denied access to Rwanda in January, when he tried to enter the country from France.

In the days after the vote, Human Rights Watch interviewed local activists and private citizens who spoke of intimidation and irregularities during the campaign and voting period.

Despite Kagame's overwhelming win, government authorities took no chances and arrested, forcibly disappeared, or threatened political opponents in the weeks following the August vote. On August 29, police showed up at Rwigara's office in Kigali and took her to her home, where they interrogated her and her family members and barred them from leaving their house. After several weeks of intimidation, questioning, and restrictions on their movements, Rwigara and her sister Anne and mother were arrested on September 23. At time of writing they were being held in police custody in Kigali.

In the days before her arrest, Rwigara spoke with international media outlets and criticized police actions and the accusations against her. Hours before her arrest, Rwigara told one outlet that her family was being "persecuted for critizing the government."

The FDU-Inkingi, an unregistered opposition party, also continued to face serious challenges, preventing the party from functioning effectively. Victoire Ingabire, president of the FDU-Inkingi, remained in prison since 2010. On September 6, seven FDU-Inkingi members were arrested, including four of the party's leaders: Boniface Twagirimana, first vice-president; Fabien Twagirayezu, head of party mobilization; Léonille Gasengayire, assistant treasurer; and Gratien Nsabiyaremye, assistant commissioner.

Théophile Ntirutwa, Kigali representative of the party, was arrested on September 6. He was held incommunicado for 17 days, before a family member was allowed to visit him at the Remera police station on September 23. Ntirutwa had previously been detained on September 18, 2016, allegedly by the military, in Nyarutarama, a Kigali suburb, where he said he was beaten, and questioned about his membership in the FDU-Inkingi, then released two days later.

Eight FDU-Inkingi members, including Ntirutwa, were charged in September with crimes linked to state security, including forming an irregular armed group and offenses against the president.

The police previously arrested Gasengayire after she visited Ingabire in prison in March 2016. She was detained for three days, beaten, questioned, and denied access to a lawyer. The police released her without charge, but rearrested her in August 2016, and charged her with inciting insurrection or disorder among the population. They also accused her of stirring-up local opposition to the expropriation of land belonging to residents in her home district and of promoting the FDU-Inkingi. Residents who tried to testify on her behalf at her trial were intimidated. A court acquitted and released her on March 23, 2017.

Violette Uwamahoro, a Rwandan-British woman married to a member of the Rwanda National Congress (RNC), an opposition group in exile, was reported missing on February 14. She was in Rwanda to attend her father's funeral. On March 3, the police announced that she was in government detention. She had been held incommunicado for more than two weeks. On March 13, Uwamahoro and a co-defendant were charged with revealing state secrets and offenses against the established government or the president. She was released on bail in late March because of insufficient evidence to warrant her detention, and on April 12 she returned to the United Kingdom.

## Extrajudicial Executions of Petty Offenders

State security forces in Rwanda summarily killed at least 37 suspected petty offenders and forcibly disappeared four others in Rwanda's Western Province between April 2016 and March 2017. Most victims were accused of stealing items such as bananas, a cow, or a motorcycle. Others were suspected of smuggling marijuana, illegally crossing the border from the Democratic Republic of Congo, or using illegal fishing nets.

Authorities used the extrajudicial executions to serve as a warning. In most of the cases, local military and civilian authorities told residents, often during public meetings, that the suspected petty offender had been killed and that all other thieves and criminals in the region would be arrested and executed. Government officials said the reports of the killings were "fake news."

## Arbitrary Detention, Ill-Treatment, and Torture

People accused of crimes against state security continued to be arrested and held unlawfully in military camps. Many people held in these camps were tortured in an attempt to force them to confess or accuse others. Authorities continued to round up street vendors, sex workers, street children, and other poor people and detained them in so-called transit centers across the country. Conditions in these centers are harsh and inhumane, and beatings are common.

## Justice for the Genocide

On September 15, the French constitutional court rejected a researcher access to the archives of Francois Mitterrand, president of France during the Rwanda genocide. The court cited a law protecting presidential archives for 25 years after the death of a head of state.

Jean Twagiramungu, the first genocide suspect extradited from Germany, arrived in Kigali on August 18. The former teacher who was arrested in 2015 in Frankfurt is alleged to have organized the killing of ethnic Tutsi during the genocide. His trial was ongoing at time of writing.

A UK High Court denied the extradition of five genocide suspects in July, citing concerns about a lack of judicial independence in Rwanda. Genocide suspect Wenceslas Twagirayezu was arrested in May in Denmark. He had not been extradited at time of writing. In June 2014, Rwandan authorities sent an international arrest warrant for Twagirayezu to Denmark.

HUMAN
RIGHTS
WATCH

# "We Will Force You to Confess"
Torture and Unlawful Military Detention in Rwanda

## *Key International Actors*

The United States voiced concern about irregularities and the lack of transparency in determining the eligibility of prospective candidates around the election. The European Union also expressed concern about a lack of transparency around the registration of candidates and the tabulation of results.

The UK said it was concerned about "irregularities with the counting of ballots and vote tabulation" and "by the arrests" and "targeting of opposition figures" after the vote. The US and UK embassies and the EU delegation commended the fact that the vote was peaceful.

A report by the United Nations secretary-general, released in September, identified Rwanda as one of 29 countries where human rights defenders face reprisals for cooperating with the UN on human rights.

In October, the Subcommittee on the Prevention of Torture, which oversees enforcement of the Optional Protocol to the Convention against Torture (OPCAT), ratified by Rwanda in 2015, conducted a state visit to Rwanda. It had to suspend their visit and leave sooner than planned, however, citing obstruction by Rwanda's government. Rwanda has yet to set up a national preventive mechanism for the prevention of torture at the domestic level, required by the OPCAT, despite a deadline to do so one year after ratification.

In November, Rwanda appeared before the Committee against Torture (CAT), a UN body that monitors implementation of the Convention against Torture by state parties. On December 6, CAT in its concluding observations, called for involuntary detention in transit centers to be abolished; an end to intimidation of political opponents, journalists, and human rights defenders; and prompt, impartial, and effective investigations into allegations of torture.

# Saudi Arabia

On June 21, King Salman removed Mohammed bin Nayef as interior minister and crown prince, and appointed his son, Mohammed bin Salman, as the new crown prince. Mohammed bin Salman also serves as minister of defense. The succession move followed the removal of the country's notorious prosecution service from the Interior Ministry and its transformation into an agency reporting directly to the royal court.

In addition, in July, King Salman removed the domestic intelligence agency and counterterrorism powers from the Interior Ministry and merged them into the newly created Presidency of State Security, which reports directly to the royal court. In September, the king decreed that women will be allowed to drive from June 2018, ending a long-standing ban.

Through 2017, the Saudi-led coalition continued a military campaign against the Houthi rebel group and their former allies, forces loyal to now-deceased former President Ali Abdullah Saleh in Yemen, which included scores of unlawful airstrikes that killed and wounded thousands of civilians. On June 5, Saudi Arabia, Bahrain, and the UAE cut off diplomatic relations with Qatar and ordered the expulsion of Qatari citizens and the return of their citizens from Qatar.

Saudi authorities continued their arbitrary arrests, trials, and convictions of peaceful dissidents. Dozens of human rights defenders and activists continued to serve long prison sentences for criticizing authorities or advocating political and rights reforms. Authorities continued to discriminate against women and religious minorities.

## Yemen Airstrikes and Blockade

As the leader of the nine-nation coalition that began military operations against Houthi-Saleh forces in Yemen on March 26, 2015, Saudi Arabia has committed numerous violations of international humanitarian law. As of November, at least 5,295 civilians had been killed and 8,873 wounded, according to the UN human rights office, although the actual civilian casualty count is likely much higher. In 2017, the Office of the UN High Commissioner for Human Rights (OHCHR) reported that airstrikes remained the single largest cause of civilian casualties.

Since March 2015, Human Rights Watch has documented 87 apparently unlawful attacks by the coalition, some of which may amount to war crimes, killing nearly 1,000 civilians and hitting homes, markets, hospitals, schools, and mosques. The coalition carried out six apparently unlawful airstrikes in Yemen between June and September 2017, that killed 33 children among 55 civilian deaths. Human Rights Watch also documented how the Saudi-led coalition repeatedly attacked civilian factories, warehouses, and other protected sites, in violation of the laws of war.

Human Rights Watch documented at least 18 coalition attacks using cluster munitions, which killed or wounded dozens of civilians. Saudi Arabia is not a party to the Convention on Cluster Munitions, which bans the weapon. In December 2016, the coalition announced it would stop using a British-made cluster munition, but in 2017 Human Rights watch documented the coalition's use of Brazilian-made cluster munitions.

The conflict exacerbated an existing humanitarian crisis. By 2017, an estimated 17 million Yemenis were unable to meet their food needs, according to the United Nations. The conflict also precipitated an unprecedented cholera outbreak, which by September had killed 2,000 people and was suspected to have infected up to 700,000. The war has largely destroyed Yemen's heath system.

By December, the Saudi-led coalition had announced findings of preliminary investigations into some 40 widely publicized coalition airstrikes causing civilian casualties. The coalition-appointed panel of investigators found that in almost every case the coalition was pursuing a legitimate military target and recommended compensation for victims in only a few attacks. Human Rights Watch is unaware of any steps to pay compensation to victims of these attacks or prosecute individuals who committed war crimes.

In September, the UN Human Rights Council (UNHRC) established an international, independent body to carry out comprehensive investigations into abuses in Yemen.

## Freedoms of Expression, Association, and Belief

Beginning on September 10, Saudi authorities carried out a wave of arrests of clerics and others in what appeared to be a coordinated crackdown on dissent.

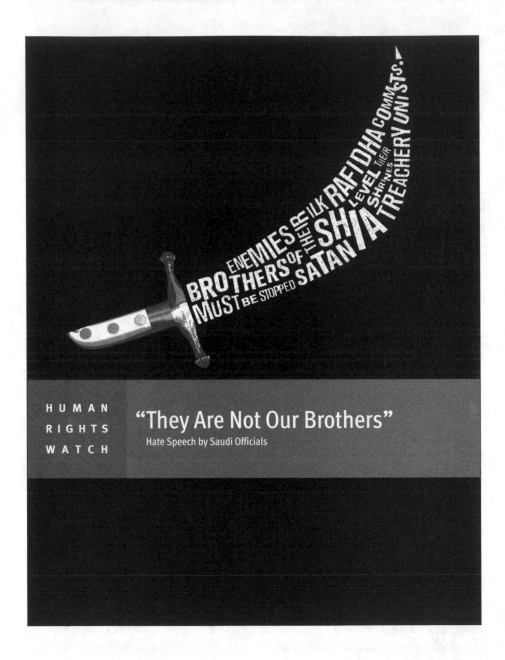

Saudi Arabia continued to repress pro-reform activists and peaceful dissidents. In early 2017, authorities arrested human rights activists Essam Koshak, Issa al-Nukheifi, Ali Shaban, and Ahmed al-Musheikhis. Authorities eventually referred Koshak and al-Nukheifi for trial in the country's notorious Specialized Criminal Court, the country's counterterrorism tribunal, on charges solely related to their human rights work. Saudi Arabia continues to use 2014 counterterrorism regulations to suppress political expression and dissent.

Over a dozen prominent activists convicted on charges arising from their peaceful activities were serving long prison sentences. Prominent activist Waleed Abu al-Khair continued to serve a 15-year sentence imposed by Saudi Arabia's Specialized Criminal Court that convicted him in 2014 on charges stemming solely from his peaceful criticism in media interviews and on social media of human rights abuses. Prominent blogger Raif Badawi served the fourth year of his 10-year sentence, but authorities did not flog him in 2016 and 2017, as they previously did in January 2015.

On January 18, Saudi Arabia's Specialized Criminal Court sentenced Nadhir al-Majid to seven years in prison and a seven-year ban on travel abroad. The conviction was based on his participation in protests in Saudi Arabia's Eastern Province in 2011 against discrimination against the country's minority Shia community, communication with international media and human rights organizations, and articles calling for an end to discrimination against the Shia.

By 2017 Saudi Arabia had jailed nearly all the founders of the banned Saudi Civil and Political Rights Association (ACPRA). In August, an appeals court upheld an eight-year sentence against ACPRA activist Abd al-Aziz al-Shubaily based solely on his peaceful pro-reform advocacy.

Saudi Arabia does not tolerate public worship by adherents of religions other than Islam and systematically discriminates against Muslim religious minorities, notably Twelver Shia and Ismailis, including in public education, the justice system, religious freedom, and employment. Government-affiliated religious authorities continued to disparage Shia and Sufi interpretations, versions, and understandings of Islam in public statements and documents.

Saudi Arabia has no written laws concerning sexual orientation or gender identity, but judges use principles of uncodified Islamic law to sanction people suspected of committing sexual relations outside marriage, including adultery, and extramarital and homosexual sex. If individuals are engaging in such relationships online, judges and prosecutors utilize vague provisions of the country's anti-cybercrime law that criminalize online activity impinging on "public order, religious values, public morals, and privacy."

In February 2017, Saudi police arrested 35 Pakistani citizens, some of whom were transgender women. One of them died in detention. Her family said her body bore signs of torture, while the Saudi authorities said she had died of a heart attack.

## *Criminal Justice*

Saudi Arabia applies Sharia (Islamic law) as its national law. There is no formal penal code, but the government has passed some laws and regulations that subject certain broadly-defined offenses to criminal penalties. In the absence of a written penal code or narrowly-worded regulations, however, judges and prosecutors can convict people on a wide range of offenses under broad, catch-all charges such as "breaking allegiance with the ruler" or "trying to distort the reputation of the kingdom."

Detainees, including children, commonly face systematic violations of due process and fair trial rights, including arbitrary arrest. Authorities do not always inform suspects of the crime with which they are charged, or allow them access to supporting evidence, sometimes even after trial sessions have begun. Authorities generally do not allow lawyers to assist suspects during interrogation and sometimes impede them from examining witnesses and presenting evidence at trial.

Judges routinely sentence defendants to floggings of hundreds of lashes. Children can be tried for capital crimes and sentenced as adults if there are physical signs of puberty.

During 2017, authorities continued to detain arrested suspects for months, even years, without judicial review or prosecution. In mid-September, Saudi authorities arrested dozens of people, including prominent clerics and intellectuals, in what appeared to be a coordinated crackdown on dissent. On November 4, Saudi authorities initiated a mass arrest of princes, current and former government officials, and prominent businessmen over corruption allegations, some of whom are reportedly held in a five-star hotel in Riyadh.

As of November, Ali al-Nimr, Dawoud al-Marhoun, Abdullah al-Zaher and Ab-dulkareem al-Hawaj remained on death row for allegedly committing protest-re-lated crimes while they were children in 2011 and 2012. Saudi judges based the capital convictions primarily on confessions that the defendants retracted in court and said had been coerced, and the courts did not investigate the allega-tions that the confessions were obtained by torture.

In mid-July, Saudi Arabia's Supreme Court upheld death sentences against four-teen members of the Saudi Shia community following an unfair trial for protest-related crimes. Courts convicted the 14 based on confessions they had repudiated in court, saying that they were coerced. In July, an appeals court up-held death sentences against another 15 men accused of spying for Iran. The ver-dict now requires approval by the Supreme Court and the king's signature.

In late July, Saudi security forces surrounded and sealed off the predominantly Shia town of Awamiya as they confronted an armed group hiding in a historic neighborhood slated for demolition. The violence in Awamiya, which began in May, resulted in deaths and injuries among the residents and caused significant damage to the town. Residents and activists said that security forces had fired at civilians in areas far from the clashes, and residents that remained in Awamiya lacked essential services such as medical care. Most residents fled the clashes.

According to Interior Ministry statements, Saudi Arabia executed 138 people be-tween January and early December, mostly for murder and drug crimes. Fifty-seven of those executed were convicted for non-violent drug crimes. Most executions are carried out by beheading, sometimes in public.

## Women's and Girls' Rights

Women in Saudi Arabia face formal and informal barriers when attempting to make decisions or take action without the presence or consent of a male rela-tive.

In April, King Salman issued an order stipulating that government agencies can-not deny women access to government services simply because they do not have a male guardian's consent unless existing regulations require it. If adequately enforced, the order could end arbitrary guardian consent requirements that government bureaucracies impose on women. Under the order, all government agencies were required to provide a list by mid-July of procedures that require male guardian approval, suggesting that authorities might review these rules and regulations and even eliminate some.

Nevertheless, Saudi Arabia's discriminatory male guardianship system remains intact despite government pledges to abolish it. Under this system, adult women must obtain permission from a male guardian—usually a husband, father, brother, or son—to travel abroad, obtain a passport, marry, or be discharged from prison. They may be required to provide guardian consent to work or access healthcare. Women regularly face difficulty conducting a range of transactions without a male relative, from renting an apartment to filing legal claims.

In July, authorities briefly detained a woman named "Khulood" after a Snapchat video appeared showing her wearing a short skirt and top, which revealed her partial midriff as she walked through the Heritage Village of Ushayqir, 100 miles north of Riyadh. Saudi Arabia maintains a strict public dress code—women must wear a loose black garment called an *abaya* and headscarf.

In September, the King decreed that women will be allowed to drive from June 2018. However, a ministerial committee is to make "the necessary arrangements to implement it" in 30 days. Reuters reported that the Saudi ambassador to the United States, Prince Khalid bin Salman, stated that women would not require their guardian's permission to obtain a license and would be permitted to drive without their guardian present. However, it is unclear if other restrictive rules will apply. Previous proposals to end the driving ban have included restrictions such as limiting driving licenses to women age 30 and over or allowing driving only during daylight hours.

Saudi Arabia continues to discriminate against women and girls by denying them the same opportunities to exercise and play sports as men and boys. In a positive step forward, however, Saudi Arabia's Education Ministry announced in July that Saudi girls' schools will offer a physical education program beginning in the fall 2017 school term "in accordance with Islamic law standards" and would scale up "according to the possibilities available in each school," including sports halls and competent women instructors. No public girls' schools currently have sports facilities, and the statement did not say whether physical education will be mandatory for girls, or if schools will require girls to get parental permission to enroll in physical education classes. In October, authorities announced that they would permit women to attend public sporting events for the first time.

## *Migrant Workers*

Over 9 million migrant workers fill manual, clerical, and service jobs, constituting more than half the workforce. Some suffer abuses and exploitation, sometimes amounting to conditions of forced labor.

The *kafala* (visa sponsorship) system ties migrant workers' residency permits to "sponsoring" employers, whose written consent is required for workers to change employers or leave the country under normal circumstances. Some employers confiscate passports, withhold wages, and force migrants to work against their will. Saudi Arabia also imposes an exit visa requirement, forcing migrant workers to obtain permission from their employer to leave the country. Workers who leave their employer without their consent can be charged with "absconding" and face imprisonment and deportation. Such a system traps many workers in abusive conditions and punishes victims who flee abuse.

In March, Saudi Arabia announced plans to deport foreign workers found in violation of existing labor laws, including those without valid residency or work permits, or those found working for an employer other than their legal sponsor. Authorities ordered that undocumented migrants must register their intention to leave with the Saudi authorities by August 24 or face detention, fines, and eventual deportation. Of the estimated 10 million migrant workers in Saudi Arabia, up to 500,000 are Ethiopian, a significant number of whom arrived after fleeing serious Ethiopian government abuses.

Saudi Arabia is not a party to the 1951 Refugee Convention and has not established an asylum system whereby people who fear being returned to places where their lives or freedom would be threatened may apply for asylum or to prevent their forced return.

Domestic workers, predominantly women, faced a range of abuses including overwork, forced confinement, non-payment of wages, food deprivation, and psychological, physical, and sexual abuse without the authorities holding their employers to account. Workers who attempted to report employer abuses sometimes faced prosecution based on counterclaims of theft, "black magic," or "sorcery."

## Key International Actors

The United States offered only muted criticism of Saudi human rights violations. Meanwhile, as a party to the armed conflict in Yemen, the US provided logistical and intelligence support to Saudi-led coalition forces, including refueling coalition planes on missions in Yemen. During a visit to Riyadh in May, President Trump announced US$110 billion worth of arms deals to Saudi Arabia, despite significant opposition from members of Congress concerned about Saudi conduct in Yemen. In June, a US Senate vote over the sale of about $500 million in precision-guided munitions to Saudi Arabia passed by a narrow margin, 53-47.

In April, United Nations member states elected Saudi Arabia to serve on the UN Commission on the Status of Women, a body "dedicated to the promotion of gender equality and the empowerment of women," despite its record of long-term, systematic discrimination against women. In May, UNESCO, the UN's educational, scientific, and cultural agency, held its 7th International Forum of NGOs in Riyadh, even though Saudi Arabia does not allow independent nongovernmental organizations (NGOs) or activists to function and puts advocates of human rights in jail. In June, Saudi Arabia was elected as a deputy member of the governing body of the International Labour Organization (ILO), even though unions are not permitted in Saudi Arabia and abuses against migrant workers remain widespread. Despite its bad human rights record at home and abroad, Saudi Arabia is currently serving its second term as a member of the UNHRC.

In September, the UNHRC set up by consensus a Group of Eminent Experts to conduct international investigations into violations and abuses in Yemen. In October, the UN secretary-general placed the Saudi-led coalition on his "list of shame" for violations against children in Yemen.

# Serbia

There was limited progress in closing the gap between Serbia's human rights obligations and its practice. Reception conditions for asylum seekers remained poor and the asylum system flawed, even though numbers of persons seeking protection fell. Journalists continued to work in a hostile environment. Progress on war crimes prosecutions remained slow.

## *Migrants, including Asylum Seekers, and Displaced Persons*

The number of new arrivals of asylum seekers to Serbia decreased again in 2017, reflecting ongoing restrictions along the Western Balkan migration route. Between January and October, Serbia registered 5,153 asylum seekers, compared to 10,201 during the same period in 2016. Afghans comprised the largest national group in 2017, followed by Iraqis and Syrians. By the end of August, the United Nations High Commissioner for Refugees (UNHCR) estimated that there were approximately 4,700 asylum seekers and migrants present in Serbia.

As of November, Serbia had granted refugee status to only one asylum seeker, a Syrian, and subsidiary protection to none. Since 2008, Serbia has granted refugee status to a total of 42 people and subsidiary protection to 49. The asylum procedure not only results in low recognition rates, but also in long delays before decisions are rendered.

By the end of October, the Ministry of Interior registered 132 unaccompanied children in Serbia, the majority from Afghanistan, compared to 127 during the same period in 2016. By November, there were a total of 250 unaccompanied children in Serbia. Serbia lacks formal age assessment procedures for unaccompanied children, putting older children at risk of being treated as adults instead of receiving special protection. Only three institutions exist in Serbia for unaccompanied children, with a total of 43 places. Other unaccompanied children stay in open asylum centers, such as reception and transit centers, often with unrelated adults, making them vulnerable to abuse and exploitation.

Progress was slow in finding durable solutions for refugees and internally displaced persons (IDPs) from the Balkan wars living in Serbia. According to the Serbian commissioner for refugees and migration, as of November, there were

27,802 such displaced persons in Serbia, compared to 35,300 during the same period in 2016, mostly from Croatia. There were 201,047 registered IDPs, majority from Kosovo, as of November, compared to 203,140 the previous year.

## Freedom of Media

Attacks and threats against journalists continued. The authorities' response was inadequate. Between January and mid-November, the Independent Journalists' Association of Serbia (NUNS) registered 75 incidents of violence, threats or intimidation against journalists, including six physical attacks. Pro-government media outlets continued to engage in smear campaigns against independent outlets and journalists.

In May, daily *Danas* journalist Lidija Valtner was covering the inauguration of Serbian President Aleksandar Vucic when two people dragged her away by the neck and tried to take her mobile phone. According to Valtner, two plain clothes police officers watched the assault without helping. Police were investigating the incident at time of writing. At the same event, journalists working for *Vice*, Radio Belgrade, and the daily *Insajder* claimed unidentified persons used physical force and threats to prevent them from reporting during the event.

In January, the High Court of Belgrade fined political weekly *NIN* for allegedly damaging the reputation of the Minister of Interior of Serbia in a June 2016 article concerning property demolitions in Belgrade's Savamala district.

A commission established to investigate the murders of three prominent journalists, Dada Vujasinovic in 1994, Slavko Curuvija in 1999, and Milan Pantic in 2001, made slow progress in its work. Two of the four state security officials charged with involvement in Curuvija's killing were released from custody to house arrest in July. A third defendant is serving a 40-year sentence for unrelated crimes, while the fourth is on the run. The other two killings remain unsolved.

## Accountability for War Crimes

War crimes prosecutions were hampered due to lack of political support, insufficient staff, and other resources at the Office of the War Crimes Prosecutor, and weak witness support mechanisms. The Serbian parliament finally appointed a new war crimes prosecutor in May, after an 18-month-long vacancy.

Few high ranking officials implicated in serious wartime abuses have been held to account in Serbian courts. Between January and August, 17 war crimes trials were pending before Serbian courts. The war crimes prosecutor issued two new indictments during the same period. Between January and August, first instance courts delivered no judgments. The appeals court overturned convictions of three people. Between January and August, 11 cases were still at investigation stage. Since the establishment of the War Crimes Prosecution Office in 2003, 124 judgments have been issued, 82 people convicted and 42 acquitted.

The first trials in Serbia for war crimes in Srebrenica started in February. Eight Bosnian Serb former police officers are charged with the killing in a warehouse of more than 1,300 Bosniak civilians from Srebrenica in July 1995. In July, the Belgrade Appeals Court dismissed the charges, stating that the prosecutor who filed the charges was not authorized to do so. The new war crimes prosecutor has yet to file new charges needed to schedule a trial.

In May, the Appeals Court in Belgrade confirmed charges against five Bosnian Serb former fighters indicted in 2015 for abducting and killing 20 civilians on a train in Strpci in Bosnia and Herzegovina in 1993.

Also in May, the Appeals Court acquitted two Bosnian Serb ex-fighters of all charges related to the killing of a Bosniak civilian in 1992.

In April, the war crimes prosecutor brought charges against a Bosnian-Serb ex-police reservist for war crimes against civilians in Sanski Most in Bosnia and Herzegovina in 1992.

Chief Prosecutor Serge Brammertz at the International Criminal Tribunal for the Former Yugoslavia (ICTY) urged Serbia in June to officially acknowledge the crimes committed in Srebrenica in 1995 as genocide.

Following the January arrest in France of former Kosovo Prime Minister and Kosovo Liberation Army fighter Ramush Haradinaj based on a Serbian arrest warrant, a French court in April rejected Serbia's extradition request. Haradinaj is wanted in Serbia on war crimes charges. He has been twice acquitted by the ICTY of war crimes during the 1998-1999 Kosovo conflict.

## Human Rights Defenders

Human rights defenders operate in a hostile environment. Online threats against human rights activists are commonplace and rarely investigated by authorities. Pro-government media smear human rights defenders as "traitors" and "foreign mercenaries."

In January, in the town of Beska, party members from the ruling Serbian Progressive Party attacked and ejected nine activists from the nongovernmental organization (NGO) Youth Initiative for Human Rights, who organized a protest during a pre-election campaign debate. Two of the human rights activists required hospitalization, and one activist's car was vandalized. Authorities were investigating at time of writing.

## Sexual Orientation and Gender Identity

Attacks on and harassment of lesbian, gay, bisexual, and transgender (LGBT) people and activists occurred regularly. Serbian LGBT rights organization DA SE ZNA!, between August 2016 and August 2017, recorded 79 incidents against LGBT people, including nine physical attacks, 12 threats and 56 cases of hate speech, mainly on social media. Investigations are often slow and prosecutions rare. The Pride parade in September took place without major incidents and was attended by the first female and openly lesbian prime minister of Serbia.

## Treatment of Minorities

Roma face discrimination, particularly in relation to housing. Police in Belgrade detained and abused a Romani couple in May after they reported their car was stolen, according to the European Roma Rights Centre.

## Key International Actors

Throughout the year, several visits by Federica Mogherini, high representative for foreign affairs and security policy; European Council President Donald Tusk; and Commissioner on European Neighbourhood Policy and Enlargement Johannes Hahn, focused on Serbia's European Union accession and the Belgrade-Pristina process, but failed to publicly address the need for improvements in human rights. In June, the European Parliament stressed the need for further reforms in the areas of human rights and the rule of law.

The 2016 US Department of State Human Rights report, published in June, identified discrimination and violence against Roma, harassment of journalists, overcrowding in prisons, and threats against members of the LGBT community as particularly serious human rights concerns.

The United Nations Committee on the Rights of the Child in its March concluding observations expressed concerns that children with disabilities continue to be over-represented in residential care institutions, and recommended authorities reduce the placement of children under three years in residential care.

In July, Serbia endorsed the Safe Schools Declaration, committing to do more to protect education during times of armed conflict.

In its April concluding observations, the UN Human Rights Committee expressed concern over the treatment of journalists, particularly through prosecutions, and recommended stronger protection for media workers. It also expressed concern about hate crimes, particularly against Roma, and recommended proper investigation and prosecution. The committee also called on Serbia to tackle delays in the asylum procedure, poor conditions in receptions centers, and inadequate age assessment procedures.

In February, Council of Europe Human Rights Commissioner Nils Muižnieks expressed concerns with regards to forced evictions of Roma, the lack of legal safeguards in the process of such evictions, and failure by authorities to provide alternative accommodation.

# Kosovo

Slow progress on human rights was marred by a political deadlock following snap elections in June, with a government only formed in September. The special court to try serious war crimes committed during the 1998-1999 Kosovo war was made operational and is expected to file its first indictments. Journalists faced threats and intimidation, and prosecutions of crimes against journalists were slow. Tensions between Serbs and Kosovo Albanians continued, particularly in the north. Roma, Ashkali, and Egyptian communities continue to face discrimination. The process of normalizing relations with Belgrade made limited progress.

## *Accountability for War Crimes*

In July, after months of delay, Kosovo's Constitutional Court approved the revised rules of procedure and evidence for the Specialist Chambers and Specialist Prosecutor's Office, the Hague-based court tasked with trying serious war crimes committed during the 1998-1999 Kosovo war. This allows the court to issue first indictments. The court is set to adjudicate cases investigated by the Special Investigative Task Force, prompted by a 2011 Council of Europe report accusing some Kosovo Liberation Army (KLA) members of abductions, beatings, summary executions, and the forced removal of human organs in Kosovo and Albania during and after the Kosovo war. Senior KLA fighters are expected to be indicted and stand trial. The court will operate under Kosovo laws, with 19 international judges, appointed by the European Union in February. The EU in June approved a one-year budget for the court.

In January 2017, Kosovo's special prosecutor charged an ex-paramilitary Serbian man with war crimes in Kosovo Polje in 1999. The suspect is charged with torturing civilian ethnic Albanians.

In February, the prosecutor issued 57 warrants of arrest of Serbian citizens suspected of war crimes, without providing further details of those wanted.

By early September, mixed panels consisting of the European Rule of Law Mission (EULEX) and local judges handed down five decisions related to war crimes. Formal investigations were underway in 34 cases, and 374 cases were pending at a preliminary investigation stage. EULEX has been involved in a total of 43 verdicts since established in 2008.

The Human Rights Review Panel, an independent body set up in 2009 to review allegations of human rights violations by EULEX staff, ruled in eight cases between January and October, four of which were follow-up decisions in earlier cases where violations had been found by the panel. Thirty cases were pending before the panel at time of writing.

## Accountability of International Institutions

The United Nations failed to follow recommendations made in 2016 by the Human Rights Advisory Panel (HRAP), an independent body set up in 2006 to examine complaints of abuses by the UN Interim Administration Mission in Kosovo (UNMIK), that the UN apologize and pay individual compensation to lead poison victims forced to live in UNMIK-run camps in northern Kosovo after the 1998-1999 war. Victims are displaced members of the Roma, Ashkali, and Balkan Egyptian communites.

In May, UN Secretary-General António Guterres proposed a watered-down plan to create a voluntary trust fund for community assistance projects not specifically targeting those affected by lead poisoning. At time of writing, no states have contributed to the trust fund.

## Treatment of Minorities

Roma, Ashkali, and Egyptians continue to face problems acquiring personal documents, affecting their ability to access health care, social assistance, and education.

There was slow implementation of a new strategy for the integration of Roma, Ashkali, and Egyptian communities. The strategy was adopted in 2016 and focused on improving civil registration, access to housing, education, health care, and employment. Public funds to finance the strategy's programs were lacking.

Inter-ethnic tensions continued during 2017 particularly in Kosovo's divided north. Kosovo police registered 15 cases of inter-ethnic violence between January and August 2017, involving disruption of public order, defamatory graffiti, incitement of religious, ethnic and racial hatred, and light bodily injury, without specifying the total number per category, making effective scrutiny of police response to inter-ethnic violence difficult. Kosovo police in August stated that cases were under investigation.

## Women's Rights

Domestic violence remained widespread in Kosovo. Inadequate police response, few prosecutions and failure by judges to issue restraining orders against abusive spouses contributed to the problem. The government in April adopted a new National Strategy and Action Plan against Domestic Violence, replacing a 2011-2014 strategy, and in May launched the Crime Victim Compensation Program. As a result victims are now able to seek compensation from the state for their injuries.

## Asylum Seekers and Displaced Persons

During the first nine months of the year, the United Nations High Commissioner for Refugees (UNHCR) registered 333 voluntary returns of members of ethnic minorities to Kosovo, up from 276 during that period in 2016.

The Kosovo Ministry of Internal Affairs registered 2,480 forced returns to Kosovo between January and October, including 159 Roma, 138 Ashkali, and 17 Egyptians. Ethnic data was missing for the month of June. Among those forcibly deported to Kosovo, 646 were children. Most of these forced returns were from Germany and returnees received limited assistance upon return.

## Sexual Orientation and Gender Identity

Gay rights activists reported an increase of hate speech online against lesbian, gay, bisexual, and transgender (LGBT) people in October, in connection with Gay Pride in Pristina. The October Pride event was the first of its kind ever held in Kosovo. In July, gay rights activists issued a call to challenge marriage laws in Kosovo, which define marriage as strictly between two people of different sexes, as being contrary to the constitution.

## Freedom of Media

Threats and attacks against journalists continued in 2017, while investigations and prosecutions were slow. Between January and August, the Association of Journalists of Kosovo registered nine cases of threats and violence against journalists, including one physical attack, two cases of intimidation, one of property damage, and five threats. Police were investigating at time of writing.

In August, Parim Olluri, an investigative journalist and director of online publication *Insajderi*, was physically attacked by unknown assailants outside his home in Pristina. Olluri received medical treatment for minor bodily injuries. He stated that he believes the assault was connected to his work as a journalist. Police were investigating at time of writing. The Organization for Security and Co-operation in Europe (OSCE) representative on freedom of the media, Harlem Desir, in August condemned the attack.

In April, Arbana Xharra, editor-in-chief of daily paper *Zeri*, was subjected to intimidation when an unknown assailant, or assailants, painted a cross in blood-red paint next to the apartment where she lives with her husband and child. The case remained unresolved at time of writing.

In October, the editor-in-chief of the online newspaper *Insajderi*, Vehbi Kajtazi, was physically attacked in a cafe in Pristina. Police were investigating the attack at time of writing. Kajtazi has been physically attacked and threatened in the past, and cases remained unresolved.

## Key International Actors

In his quarterly report on the situation in Kosovo, UN Secretary-General Guterres in May expressed concern about ethno-nationalist sentiments, and called on parties to act responsibly to diminish inter-ethnic tensions. Guterres also addressed the concerns of families whose relatives are still missing since the conflict, and urged authorities to do more to investigate what happened to them.

The US State Department Human Rights Report on Kosovo, published in March, raised concerns about violent obstructions of the parliament by opposition parties resulting in the blocking of free debate and passage of legislation, and the lack of accountability for government corruption. The report also noted societal violence and discrimination against members of religious and LGBT communities, intimidation of media, violence against displaced persons seeking to return to their homes, domestic violence and discrimination against women, and discrimination against ethnic minorities, particularly Ashkalis, Egyptians and Roma.

At the invitation of Kosovo, the EU deployed an Election Observation Mission, whose report highlighted some shortcomings including a disturbing pattern of intimidation within Serb-majority areas. In June, the European Parliament called on Kosovo to strengthen the role of the ombudsman and to increase efforts to protect minorities.

Over the year, EU leaders repeatedly met with their Kosovar counterparts but failed to raise human rights concerns, often focusing on the normalization of Kosovo's relations with Serbia.

# Singapore

Singapore's draconian restrictions on public assemblies tightened during 2017, with new limitations on the ability of foreigners in the country to organize, participate in, or even financially support, public gatherings. Event organizers and sometimes participants are subjected to investigations, home searches, and seizure of electronic devices. Critics of the judiciary continue to be targeted for "scandalizing the judiciary." The government lashed out at online media during the year, and threatened to pass new laws to deal with "misinformation" and "fake news."

## *Freedom of Peaceful Assembly and Expression*

The government maintains strict restrictions on the right to freedom of peaceful assembly through the Public Order Act, which requires a police permit for any "cause-related" assembly if it is held in a public place, or if members of the general public are invited. Permits are routinely denied for events addressing political topics. The law was amended in 2017 to tighten the restrictions, and now provides the police commissioner with specific authorization to reject any permit application for an assembly or procession "directed towards a political end" if any foreigner is involved.

The definition of what is treated as an assembly is extremely broad, and includes one person acting alone. In August, a man who held repeated solo protests in Singapore's central financial district calling for the resignation of the prime minister was sentenced to three weeks in prison and a fine of S$20,000 (US$14,850).

In early September, the police summoned for questioning the participants in a July 2017 vigil outside Changi prison to support the family of a man scheduled to hang, and banned them from leaving the country. In November, the police filed criminal charges against one of the participants in this event, Jolovan Wham, and indicated that the others involved remained under investigation. Wham was also charged with two other counts of violating the Public Order Act—one relating to an indoor forum at which Joshua Wong spoke from Hong Kong via Skype, and the other a silent protest to commemorate the 1987 arrests of activists under the Internal Security Act (ISA).

An area of Hong Lim Park known as "Speakers' Corner" is the only place in Singapore where an assembly can be held without a police permit, but only citizens are allowed to speak there, and only citizens or permanent residents may participate in assemblies there.

Under tightened restrictions put in place in October 2016, the government now considers the mere presence of a foreigner during an assembly to be unlawful participation that can result in criminal penalties for both the foreigner and the event organizer. To comply with the new rules, organizers of the annual Pink Dot festival in support of lesbian, gay, bisexual, and transgender (LGBT) rights had to put barricades around the park and check identity cards, quadrupling the cost of holding the event.

Although the government passed new legislation codifying the law of contempt in August 2016, the legislation had not gone into effect at time of writing, and the government continued to use common law contempt proceedings against those who criticize the judiciary.

Persons facing contempt proceedings in 2017 included a lawyer who posted a critical poem on his Facebook page after the execution of a client, an activist who asserted that her conviction for unlawful assembly and public nuisance was "political," and a relative of Prime Minister Lee Hsien Loong who referred in a private Facebook post to the judiciary as "pliant."

The Board of Film Censors must pre-approve all films and videos shown in Singapore. Theater productions must submit their scripts for government approval to obtain a mandatory license under the Public Entertainments and Meetings Act.

In September 2017, 18-year-old activist and blogger Amos Yee was granted political asylum in the United States on the grounds that Singapore had persecuted him for exercising his right to peaceful expression.

## Criminal Justice System

In January 2017, the Ministry of Home Affairs (MHA) announced that, starting in April 2017, all suspects below the age of 16 must be accompanied by an independent volunteer during police interviews. The government made the change in response to the case of Benjamin Lim, a 14-year-old who committed suicide in January 2016 after being released from the Ang Mo Kio police division headquarters after three hours of police questioning alone under suspicion of committing a crime.

Singapore uses the ISA and Criminal Law (Temporary Provisions) Act (CLTPA) to arrest and administratively detain persons for virtually unlimited periods without charge or judicial review. There is little publicly available information about the number of persons detained, their identities, or the basis for their detentions.

Singapore retains the death penalty, which is mandated for many drug offenses and certain other crimes. However, under provisions introduced in 2012, judges have some discretion to bypass the mandatory penalty and sentence low-level offenders to life in prison and caning. There is little transparency on the timing of executions, which often take place with short notice. Singapore executed Malaysian national S. Prabagaran in July for drug offenses despite a pending application to refer the case to the International Court of Justice.

Use of corporal punishment is common in Singapore. For medically fit males ages 16 to 50, caning is mandatory as an additional punishment for a range of crimes, including drug trafficking, violent crimes (such as armed robbery), and even some immigration offenses. Sentencing officials may also order caning for some 30 additional violent and non-violent crimes.

## *Sexual Orientation and Gender Identity*

The rights of Singapore's LGBT community are severely restricted. Sexual relations between two male persons remains a criminal offense, and there are no legal protections against discrimination on the basis of sexual orientation or gender identity.

The Media Development Authority effectively prohibits all positive depictions of LGBT lives on television or radio. In June 2017, the Advertising Standards Agency asked a shopping center to remove the phrase "Supporting the Freedom to Love" from a promotional ad for this year's annual Pink Dot festival on the grounds it "may affect public sensitivities."

The 8th annual Pink Dot festival took place at Hong Lim Park in June 2017. Under new rules passed in October 2016, any entity not incorporated in Singapore that does not have a majority of Singapore citizens on its board must apply for a permit to sponsor an event in Hong Lim Park. The 10 multinational corporations that applied for a permit to sponsor this year's Pink Dot festival were denied. However, over 100 Singaporean companies stepped forward to fill the funding gap, and Pink Dot exceeded its annual fundraising target.

T Project, which supports the transgender community in Singapore, has been denied the ability to register as a not-for-profit entity on grounds that doing so would be "against national security or interest." The group's appeal against the Registrar of Companies' rejection of their application was rejected in November 2017.

## Migrant Workers and Labor Exploitation

Foreign migrant workers are subject to labor abuse and exploitation through debts owed to recruitment agents, non-payment of wages, restrictions on movement, confiscation of passports, and sometimes physical and sexual abuse. Foreign women employed as domestic workers are particularly vulnerable to abuse.

The work permits of migrant workers in Singapore are tied to a particular employer, leaving workers vulnerable to exploitation. Foreign domestic workers are still excluded from the Employment Act and many key labor protections, such as limits on daily work hours. Labor laws also discriminate against foreign workers by barring them from organizing and registering a union or serving as union leaders without explicit government permission.

## Key International Actors

Singapore is a regional hub for international business, and maintains good political and economic relations with both the United States, which considers it a key security ally, and China. Prime Minister Lee Hsien Loong visited the White House in October. Neither the US nor any other government publicly criticized Singapore's poor human rights record.

# Somalia

Somalia's armed conflict, abuses by all warring parties, and a new humanitarian crisis continue to take a devastating toll on civilians.

Hundreds of civilians were killed in indiscriminate attacks by the Islamist armed group Al-Shabab, particularly in Mogadishu. Military operations against Al-Shabab, at times in violation of the laws of war, by Somali government forces and militia, African Union Mission in Somalia (AMISOM) troops, and other foreign forces resulted in deaths, injuries and displacement of civilians—as did inter-clan violence—across the country. On October 14, a bomb-laden truck in central Mogadishu killed at least 358 people, the deadliest single attack in the country's history; no group claimed responsibility. The United Nations Assistance Mission in Somalia (UNSOM) reported 1,228 civilian casualties between January and September 2017, about half by Al-Shabab.

In February, Mohamed Abdullahi Mohamed "Farmajo" was selected as the country's president following a protracted and controversial electoral process. Political infighting, including within federal member states, delayed greatly needed justice and security sector reforms and on occasion led to violence affecting civilians.

With parts of the country on the brink of famine, hundreds of thousands of Somalis were displaced bringing the total to over 2 million; while the new administration made addressing the humanitarian crisis a priority, many civilians faced serious abuses and very limited access to basic services.

The year saw little progress in holding security forces to account for attacks on journalists and arbitrary detentions, or improving protection for the internally displaced populations. Positively, the government took steps to establish a national human rights commission.

## *Abuses by Government and Allied Forces*

Security forces unlawfully killed and wounded civilians during infighting over land, control of roadblocks, disarmament operations, and aid distribution. On June 9, at least 13 civilians were killed and 20 injured when fighting broke out between government forces at an aid distribution site in Baidoa.

Civilians were targeted or faced indiscriminate attack during fighting over re-sources and political positions and control between clan militia and regional forces, particularly in Lower Shabelle, Hiraan, and Galguduud.

The National Intelligence and Security Agency (NISA) and the Puntland Intelligence Service (PIS), which operate without legal authority, arbitrarily arrested and detained individuals without charge or access to legal counsel and family visits. On several occasions, intelligence agents tortured and ill-treated alleged terrorism suspects to extract confessions or provide information.

Military courts continue to try a broad range of cases, including for terrorism-related offenses, in proceedings falling far short of international fair trial standards. By the third quarter of 2017 at least 23 individuals were executed following military court convictions, the majority on terrorism-related charges. Seven defendants, including a child, were sentenced to death for murder on February 13 in Puntland based largely on confessions obtained under coercion by PIS; five were executed in April.

According to UNSOM, AMISOM and other foreign forces were responsible for a significant number of civilian casualties during ground operations against Al-Shabab and in airstrikes. On September 26, an alleged Kenyan air force jet struck the village of Taraka in Somalia's Gedo region recently recaptured by Al-Shabab, wounding 4 civilians and killing 20 camels.

Accountability for abuses by security forces was almost nonexistent.

Measures at the disposal of troop-contributing countries to improve accountability have not been sufficiently used. AMISOM investigated the unlawful killings of 14 civilians by Ethiopian forces in July 2016 in a village in the Bay region, but never released the findings nor offered compensation to the affected families.

Somalia's penal code, currently being revised, classifies sexual violence as an "offense against modesty and sexual honor" rather than as a violation of bodily integrity, punishes same-sex intercourse, and imposes criminal penalties for speech considered insulting to authorities.

## Abuses by Al-Shabab

The Islamist armed group Al-Shabab committed serious abuses such as arbitrary executions, including those accused of spying, collaborating with the government, and at times adultery; forcibly recruiting adults and children; and extorting "taxes" through threats. On October 27, in Sakoow, a woman was stoned to death for allegedly committing adultery.

Attacks against civilians and civilian objects using vehicle-borne improvised explosive devices in Mogadishu resulted in a sharp rise in civilian casualties. The group also claimed responsibility for several targeted assassinations, particularly of government officials and electoral delegates.

In late May, Al-Shabab fighters abducted civilians, stole livestock, and committed arson in attacks that caused more than 15,000 people to flee their homes in the highly contested region of Lower Shabelle.

## Displaced Persons and Access to Humanitarian Assistance

By the year's end, the risk of famine persisted, with over half of the country's 12.4 million population still in need of emergency humanitarian assistance.

According to the UN, 1 million people were newly displaced in 2017, bringing the total internally displaced persons (IDP) population to 2.1 million. Many faced dire living conditions, with limited assistance, and faced a range of abuses, including indiscriminate killings, forced evictions, and sexual violence. Between November and May, at least 60,000 people were forcibly evicted, including by government forces. Hundreds of refugees returning from Kenya due to restrictions on asylum space became IDPs.

Humanitarian agencies faced serious challenges in accessing vulnerable populations due to insecurity, restrictions imposed by parties to the conflict, and targeted attacks on aid workers. Foreign counterterrorism legislation, notably US law that could interpret forms of aid as material support for terrorism, also hindered foreign assistance.

Al-Shabab banned most nongovernmental organizations and all UN agencies from areas under its control. It also imposed blockades on government-controlled towns and on occasion attacked civilians who broke them.

Government forces and clan militia also extorted civilians and aid convoys at checkpoints.

## Abuses against Children

Armed groups continued to kill and maim children and target schools. On April 18, unidentified rebel forces fired mortar rounds into a populated area of Mogadishu, hit a school and a home, killing at least two civilians, including an 8-year-old girl, and injuring eight others.

They have also recruited and used children in military operations. Al-Shabab increasingly focused on *duksis* (Quranic schools) to indoctrinate children, particularly in communities where it sought to assert control such as in Mudug, Galgadud, and Bay regions.

The federal government committed to rehabilitate children linked to Al-Shabab. However, military courts have prosecuted and sentenced children to heavy penalties for terrorism-related offenses in trials that do not meet international juvenile justice standards. In Puntland, at least 11 children were sentenced to death for terrorism-related offenses and murder by first instance military courts although all later had their sentences commuted.

## Sexual Violence

Internally displaced women and girls remain at particular risk of sexual and gender-based violence by armed men, including government soldiers and militia members, and civilians. According to the UN, incidents of reported sexual violence around displacement settlements increased in 2017.

While authorities adopted some measures to improve the capacity of government institutions to tackle impunity for sexual violence, including establishing a sexual violence unit within the Attorney General's Office, and passing a sexual offenses law in Puntland, implementation was limited. In early 2017, authorities in Puntland condoned a Sharia court-hearing of a group of young men accused of gang-raping two girls in Goldogob town instead of prosecutors pushing for the case to be transferred to criminal justice proceedings under its newly passed sexual offenses act.

## *Freedom of Expression and Association*

Targeted attacks on media, including harassment, and intimidation by federal and regional authorities and Al-Shabab, continued.

On March 12, Abdihamid Mohamed Osman, a technician and editor at Universal TV network, survived a bomb that exploded while he was in his vehicle.

In Puntland, authorities arbitrarily detained journalists and other civilians for criticizing the region's leadership and judicial decisions. On July 2, journalist Ahmed Ali Kilwe was detained by counterterrorism police and held for two weeks without charge, reportedly for criticizing the president.

Positively, the federal minister for information committed to reviewing the country's 2016 media law; proposed revisions failed to bring the law in line with international standards.

## *Somaliland*

Authorities in Somaliland continued to restrict free speech and expression, particularly on issues deemed sensitive, notably the construction of a port and military base by the United Arab Emirates in Berbera town and the relationship with Somalia. Authorities shut down social media for four days during Somaliland's electoral process, at the request of the national electoral commission. Authorities regularly temporarily detain journalists; on three occasions journalists were criminally charged.

## *Key International Actors*

International support focused on building Somalia's security sector, including regional forces, with limited attention to ensuring fair accountability for abuses. At a London conference on Somalia in May, partners endorsed a plan clarifying the structure of the security forces at national and regional levels.

International donors financially supported the federal government's controversial amnesty program for former Al-Shabab combatants. In August, one of Al-Shabab's former leaders, Sheikh Mukhtar Robow, was transferred to Mogadishu; foreign governments did not call for investigations into the serious abuses committed under his leadership.

In March, US President Donald Trump granted the US Defense Department greater authority to conduct operations in Somalia, declaring parts of the country an "area of active hostilities." The Pentagon acknowledged 30 strikes, 13 in November, and its involvement in at least four joint operations. The Pentagon said it was reviewing reports of civilian casualties in two operations conducted in August in Bariire and Jilib; despite media reports of civilian casualties its assessment found that those killed and wounded in Bariire were all "armed enemy combatants".

Gulf states, primarily the UAE, increased bilateral military and political support to Somalia's regional states. They used pressure and financial inducements to challenge the federal government's "neutral" stance on the diplomatic crisis between Qatar and other Gulf states, exacerbating regional tensions within Somalia.

# South Africa

South Africa has, over the years, built a robust and independent judiciary essential for respect for the rule of law; but in 2017, the government's record on human rights and respect for the rule of law was poor. Corruption, poverty, including high unemployment, and crime significantly restricted South Africans' enjoyment of their rights.

On October 13, the Supreme Court of Appeal (SCA) upheld a High Court decision to prosecute President Jacob Zuma on 18 charges and 783 counts of fraud, racketeering, and money laundering. Zuma and the National Prosecuting Authority (NPA) had asked the SCA to overturn the High Court decision, which found that the NPA's 2009 decision to drop corruption charges against Zuma was "irrational." Zuma called the SCA decision disappointing, and the NPA, due to procedural delay, has yet to reinstate the fraud and corruption charges against him at time of writing.

The government failed to realize the right to education for many children and young adults with disabilities. The absence of a national strategy to combat the high rate of violence against women, and the continued under-reporting of rape, remained a concern. In 2017, the government continued to send mixed signals on its support for the International Criminal Court (ICC), following a decision by domestic courts that the government's notice of withdrawal from the court was unconstitutional and invalid.

At the end of the year, the government indicated it would pursue the withdrawal through a future bill to be presented to parliament.

In August, South Africa took over as chairperson of the Southern African Development Community (SADC) for a year, but during 2017 did not use the leadership role to promote and support human rights improvements in the region.

## *Disability Rights*

In October, the South African Human Rights Commission (SAHRC) highlighted estimates that half-a-million children with disabilities still do not have access to education, with 11,461 children with disabilities on waiting lists for school placements (up from over 5,500 in 2015). The SAHRC expressed concern that children with disabilities constantly experience barriers to the enjoyment of basic human rights, including the right to education, healthcare, and family care.

Despite the government's international and domestic obligations, many children with disabilities do not have equal access to primary or secondary education, and face multiple forms of discrimination and barriers when they do access schools. They are turned away from mainstream schools, denied access to inclusive education, and referred instead to special schools by school officials or medical staff simply because they have a disability. The referrals system needlessly forces children to wait up to four years at care centers or at home for placement in a special school.

While education in public schools is free, children with disabilities who attend government special schools are required to pay school fees, and many who attend mainstream schools are asked to pay for their own class assistants as a condition for admission. In mainstream schools, many children with disabilities do not have access to the same curriculum as children without disabilities. In addition, many children with disabilities are exposed to high levels of violence and abuse by teachers and students.

In 2017, the government did not complete its efforts to publish accurate data on how many children and young people with disabilities are out of school across the country. It also failed to implement key aspects of the 2001 national policy, which calls for the provision of inclusive education for all children with disabilities, and is yet to adopt legislation that guarantees the right of children with disabilities to inclusive education.

However, the government continued to implement the Screening, Identification, Assessment, and Support (SIAS) policy designed to ensure that children with disabilities are provided full support when accessing education. The majority of the government's limited budget for students with disabilities continued to be allocated to special schools rather than to inclusive education.

In October 2017, an arbitration process, presided over by retired deputy chief justice Dikgang Moseneke, began between the state and families of former hospital patients who died following the Gauteng provincial government shut down of the

Life Esidimeni psychiatric hospice complex in Johannesburg, where more than 2,000 people with psychosocial disabilities lived.

Between March 2016 and October 2017, 141 former patients of the hospice died after about 1,700 patients were transferred to smaller institutions while others were discharged, sometimes without their families being notified. The Gauteng government, which terminated its contract with Life Esidimeni in October 2015 citing financial reasons, had a responsibility to ensure the hospice had adequate resources to support the patients.

## *Accountability for Xenophobic Attacks on Foreign Nationals*

Despite recurring waves of xenophobic attacks on businesses and the homes of refugees, asylum-seekers, and migrants, authorities appeared reluctant to even publicly acknowledge xenophobia and take decisive action to combat it, including ensuring proper police investigations. Virtually no one has been convicted over past outbreaks of xenophobic violence, including for the Durban violence of April 2015 that displaced thousands of foreign nationals, or the 2008 attacks, which resulted in the deaths of more than 60 people across the country.

In February, a group calling itself "The Mamelodi Concerned Residents" marched in Pretoria to protest against African immigrants in South Africa, blaming them for crime and stealing jobs meant for South Africans. The march triggered a wave of violent clashes and looting of shops owned by foreign nationals. In December 2016, Johannesburg Mayor Herman Mashaba made reckless public statements blaming illegal immigrants for crime and calling on them to leave the city.

In July 2017, the SAHRC condemned Deputy Minister of Police Bongani Mkongi's July 14, 2017 statement saying of Johannesburg: "How can a city in South Africa be 80 percent foreign national? That is dangerous. South Africans have surrendered their own city to the foreigners." The commission said the statement was inaccurate and could fuel xenophobia. The government took no action against Mkongi.

At time of writing, the government had yet to finalize the draft national action plan to combat racism, racial discrimination, xenophobia and related intolerance, or provide a mechanism for justice and accountability for xenophobic crimes.

## *Women's Rights*

Violence against women, including rape and domestic violence, remain widespread and underreported. According to research findings published in August 2017 by the Centre for the Study of Violence and Reconciliation and Oxfam South Africa, one in five women older than 18 has experienced physical violence, and three women die at the hands of their partner every day. The government has yet to introduce a national strategy to combat violence against women.

## *Sexual Orientation and Gender Identity*

In September, the Western Cape High Court ruled that individuals have the right to amend their gender description even if they were married as heterosexuals. Three women and their spouses had taken the Department of Home Affairs to court after it refused to change their gender description. Local rights group, the Legal Resources Centre (LRC), filed the case on behalf a client who had their marriage deleted from the National Population Register, and two others whom the department advised to get a divorce in order to give effect to their gender rights.

South Africa has a progressive constitution that prohibits discrimination on the basis of sexual orientation and protects the human rights of lesbian, gay, bisexual, and transgender (LGBT) people. The Department of Justice and Constitutional Development has taken significant steps to improve coordination between government and civil society in combatting violence (including rape and murder) against lesbians and transgender men.

In a historic victory for transgender students, in May 2017 the Seshego Magistrate's Court in Limpopo ordered the Limpopo Department of Education to pay R60 000 (approximately US$4,500) in personal compensation for discrimination to Nare Mphela, a transgender woman from Ga-Matlala village. The case was lodged by the SAHRC in November 2016 under the Promotion of Equality and Prevention of Unfair Discrimination Act (The Equality Act).

## Foreign Policy

In 2017, South Africa missed key opportunities to consistently place human rights at the center of its foreign policy. In August, the country took over the SADC for a year, but has refrained from criticizing Zimbabwe's poor human rights situation.

Although South Africa's governing party, the African National Congress, called for Swaziland to be referred to SADC for abuse of human rights and suppression of dissent in July, the government did not use the SADC chair to press for human rights respect in Swaziland. In October, President Zuma, during a visit to the Democratic Republic of Congo, did not publicly raise human rights concerns with President Joseph Kabila.

In his address to the United Nations General Assembly in September, President Zuma called on the UN to support the African Union (AU) to resolve conflicts on the continent through promoting "African solutions to African problems and challenges." He said South Africa stands ready to work with the UN to promote peace, human rights and sustainable development.

In February, South Africa's North Gauteng High Court ruled that the government's attempt to withdraw from the ICC was unconstitutional and invalid, as the government issued its withdrawal notice without consulting parliament. The court ordered President Zuma and the Ministries of Justice and Foreign Affairs to revoke the notice of withdrawal. The ICC debacle further dented South Africa's international image as a champion of human rights and international justice. The government proposed legislation to parliament on withdrawal, but removed it from consideration in March. In December, the government indicated at the ICC's Assembly of States Parties in New York that it would indeed pursue its intent to withdraw.

In July, the Pre-Trial Chamber of the ICC ruled that South Africa violated its legal obligations to the court in failing to arrest Sudanese President Omar al-Bashir in June 2015, when he attended the AU Summit in the country. Al-Bashir is the subject of two ICC arrest warrants on charges of genocide, crimes against humanity, and war crimes allegedly committed in Darfur. South African courts had previously confirmed the government had a duty to arrest al-Bashir. The chairperson of the ANC International Relations subcommittee, Edna Molema, in an op-ed published a week later, said the domestic court rulings on al-Bashir's arrest vindicated the ANC's initial decision to withdraw from the ICC.

In May 2017, UN member states recommended the implementation of measures to ensure inclusive education for all children with disabilities during South Africa's Universal Periodic Review before the UN Human Rights Council.

Some of South Africa's votes at the UN were inconsistent with the country's stated human rights principles, including the vote against a resolution at the Human Rights Council to renew the mandate of the Commission of Inquiry on Burundi.

# South Korea

The Republic of Korea (South Korea) is a democracy that generally respects basic civil and political liberties. However, it maintains unreasonable restrictions on freedom of expression, association, and assembly. Discrimination against lesbian, gay, bisexual, and transgender (LGBT) persons, women, racial and ethnic minorities, foreigners—especially refugees and migrants—and people with HIV remains a major problem.

South Korea faced one of its most tumultuous political years in recent memory when on December 9, 2016, the National Assembly voted to impeach President Park Geun-Hye. Charges against her included abuse of power, bribery, and extortion, and leaking classified government information. The action followed massive public protests.

On March 10, 2017, the Constitutional Court upheld the impeachment. Park was arrested on March 30 and was awaiting trial at time of writing. Moon Jae-In, a former human rights lawyer and the leader of the left-leaning Democratic Party of Korea, won the presidency on May 9, 2017, with 41 percent of the vote.

In May, South Korea was reviewed by the United Nations Committee against Torture, which expressed concern about detention conditions and excessive use of force.

## Freedom of Expression

Although South Korea has a free press and a lively civil society, successive South Korean governments and large corporations have at various times used draconian criminal defamation laws, the national security law, and restrictive interpretations of other laws to create a chilling effect that limits critical scrutiny of the government and corporations.

Criminal defamation law allows for up to seven years' imprisonment and a fine. The law focuses solely on whether what was said or written was in the public interest and does not allow for truth as a complete defense. Repeal of the criminal defamation law will be one of key tests of the new Moon administration's commitment to freedom of expression.

The National Security Law criminalizes any positive comments about North Korea or the dissemination of anything that the government classifies as North Korean "propaganda." The two Koreas are technically still at war, as the Korean War ended with only a ceasefire in 1953.

The law imposes significant restrictions on the freedom of South Koreans to create and join political associations by imposing severe criminal penalties on anyone who joins or induces others to join an "anti-government organization," a term not clearly defined in law. The law also imposes criminal penalties on anyone who "constitutes or joins an organization aimed at propagating, inciting, praising, or acting in concert with" an anti-government organization.

Lee Jin-Young, owner of the online library "Labour Books," was detained on January 5, 2017, for violating the National Security Law after distributing materials that authorities claimed, "benefit the enemy [referring to North Korea]." Seoul District Court declared him not guilty on July 20 and ordered him released from detention.

## Sexual Orientation and Gender Identity

Education ministry officials in Seoul stated in February 2017 that South Korea's new national sex education curriculum would not mention homosexuality. This follows the development in 2015 of a plan to train district education officials around the country on new sex education guidelines that do not mention sexual minorities.

A campaign by the military to identify and oust gay and bisexual male soldiers and officers started in April 2017. After a video of two servicemen having sex was posted on the internet by one of the men, the army investigated, interrogated, and compelled suspected gay and bisexual soldiers to admit their activities. Military investigators seized the mobile phones of more than 50 soldiers to identify other gay and bisexual servicemen.

The 1962 Military Criminal Act (Article 92-6) punishes sexual acts between soldiers with up to two years in prison under a "disgraceful conduct" clause, regardless of consent and whether they have sex in or outside military facilities. On May 24, a military court sentenced an army captain to six months in prison for having consensual sex with another man. In October, the UN Committee on

Economic, Social and Cultural Rights (CESCR) expressed concern at the criminalization of same-sex acts in the Military Criminal Act and recommended that the government abrogate the relevant provision in the law.

During a presidential debate in April, current president, Moon Jae-In, stated that he "opposed" homosexuality and marriage equality. However, he also later said he opposed "discrimination based on homosexuality."

## Freedom of Association for Workers

The government has not ratified the International Labour Organization's fundamental conventions on freedom of association (C.87), and on the right to organize and collectively bargain (C.98). Government officials are prohibited by law from exercising their right to form a union.

The South Korean government refuses to legally recognize the Korean Teachers and Education Workers' Union (KTU) and the Korean Government Employees Union (KGEU). The KTU was stripped of its legal status in October 2013 because it allows fired teachers to remain as members, while the KGEU has been repeatedly denied the ability to legally register as a union.

The Trade Union and Labour Relations Adjustment Act interferes with freedom of association by requiring a union to expel workers from membership if they are dismissed, even in cases where workers are fired for undertaking legal trade union activity.

The law also interferes with freedom of association by barring those who are not members from standing for trade union office. In October, the CESCR committee raised concerns about lack of protections for workers, including sub-contracted and dispatched labor, and those considered independent contractors, like truck drivers or construction equipment operators.

## Women's and Girls' Rights

Discrimination against women is widespread in South Korea. Gender-based stereotypes concerning the role of women in the family and society are common—including widespread social stigma and discrimination against unmarried mothers—and are often unchallenged or even encouraged by the government.

A relatively small proportion of women occupy decision-making positions in the business, political and public sectors, and there is a 37 percent wage gap between men and women. *The Economist* magazine's "Glass Ceiling Index," which evaluates women's higher education, women in managerial positions, and number of female members in parliament, gives ROK the lowest score among countries that belong to the Organisation for Economic Co-operation and Development (OECD), with 25 points out of 100.

South Korea's laws on abortion are punitive and harmful to women and girls. Abortion is considered a crime punishably by up to one year in prison or fines up to 2 million won (US$1,820). Healthcare workers who provide abortions can face up to two years in prison. Exceptions are permitted only in cases of rape or incest, if the parents are blood or matrimonial relatives that cannot marry legally, if continuing the pregnancy is likely to jeopardize the pregnant woman's health, or when the pregnant woman or her spouse has one of several hereditary disorders or communicable diseases that are designated by government decree.

Married women must have their spouse's permission to get an abortion. All abortions are prohibited after 24 weeks of pregnancy. In October, over 200,000 South Koreans signed a petition calling for legalization of abortion, which the government had pledged to respond to within a month. In November, the government's response ducked the issue by saying more research was needed.

## *Refugees*

South Korea is one of the few countries in Asia to be a party to the 1951 UN Refugee Convention and its 1967 Protocol. However, it continues to reject the vast majority of non-North Korean asylum seekers entering the country.

Since 1994, the government granted refugee status to approximately 2.5 percent of non-North Korean asylum applicants it screened. Between January and October 2017, 7,291 applied for refugee status; the government accepted just 96 cases, or approximately 1.31 percent of applications. North Koreans do not apply for asylum through this process, they are granted South Koran citizenship through the Promotion and Resettlement Support Act for North Korean Refugees.

While humanitarian visas are provided to some failed non-North Korean asylum seekers, most applicants are rejected outright. In 2017, the government gave 290 humanitarian visas. Asylum seekers complained about widespread discrimination and lack of basic social assistance.

## HIV Testing and Foreigners

In an important victory, on July 3, 2017, President Moon's new government abolished mandatory HIV testing for foreign teachers and overseas students seeking to study in South Korea—a policy that had contradicted guidance from the World Health Organization and other United Nations agencies.

## Policy on North Korean Human Rights

South Korea's "North Korean Human Rights Act" came into effect on September 4, 2016. The law requires that the government establish a foundation to support research on the rights situation in North Korea, develop a strategy to promote rights in the North, fund groups working on issues of North Korean human rights, and create the Center for North Korean Human Rights Records under the Ministry of Unification (MOU) to do research and act as an archive of North Korean human rights violations for possible use in future prosecutions.

The MOU created the database center and developed a required three-year plan of action that "consistently seeks to offer humanitarian assistance regardless of political situations and will simultaneously make efforts to improve North Korea's human rights record." However, at time of writing, the foundation had not yet been established.

HUMAN
RIGHTS
WATCH

"Soldiers Assume We Are Rebels"
Escalating Violence and Abuses in South Sudan's Equatorias

# South Sudan

In 2017, South Sudan's civil war entered its fourth year, spreading across the country with new fighting in Greater Upper Nile, Western Bahr al Ghazal, and the Equatorias, featuring highly abusive government counterinsurgency operations. The government continued to restrict media, suppress critics, and unlawfully detain people for perceived opposition.

Since the start of the conflict, almost 2 million people have been internally displaced, and another 2 million have sought refuge in neighboring countries, with 1 million in Uganda alone. More than 230,000 people are sheltering in six United Nations bases in towns across the country. Famine was declared in conflict-affected areas in the former Unity state in the first half of the year.

The war began as a political conflict between President Salva Kiir and his then Vice President Riek Machar in December 2013. A power sharing agreement, signed between the two parties in August 2015, did not end the fighting; following clashes in Juba in July 2016, Machar went into exile, where he remains.

Both sides have committed abuses that qualify as war crimes, including looting, indiscriminate attacks on civilians and the destruction of civilian property, arbitrary arrests and detention, beatings and torture, enforced disappearances, rape including gang rape, and extrajudicial executions. Some abuses may also constitute crimes against humanity.

Lack of accountability continued to fuel the violence, while progress on establishing the hybrid court envisioned in the 2015 peace agreement was slow. The United States imposed sanctions on three government officials in September.

## *Attacks on Civilians*

A range of human rights abuses took place during fighting in the former states of Upper Nile, Jonglei, Western Bahr el Ghazal, and in the Equatorias.

Starting in January, government forces conducted a series of offensives in Upper Nile, with soldiers attacking ethnic Shilluk villages and towns, killing civilians, burning and looting homes, and forcing tens of thousands to flee the areas to opposition areas or to Sudan. Many were stranded at Aburoc, a town north of

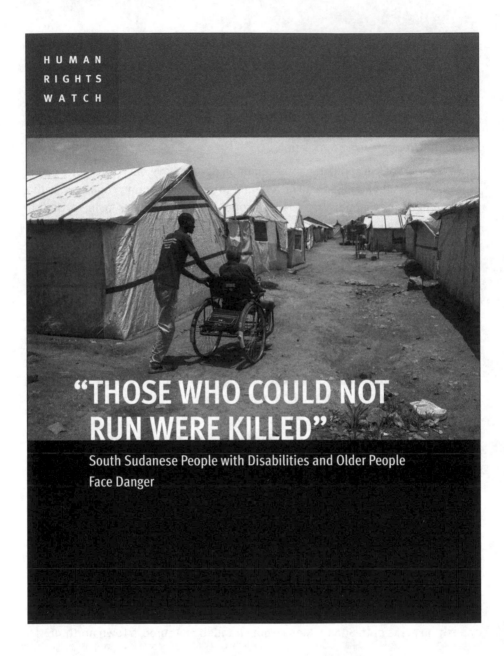

Kodok. Fighting in and around Pagak, in Jonglei, forced thousands to flee to Ethiopia.

In April, following clashes near Wau town and ambushes by opposition fighters, government forces attacked ethnic Fertit and Luo civilians in Wau town, killing at least 16 and forcing thousands to seek shelter at a displaced persons camp adjacent to the UN peacekeeping mission's base.

The same month, government soldiers killed at least 14 civilians during an attack against the town of Pajok, in Eastern Equatoria. Throughout the year, government forces also conducted highly abusive counter-insurgency operations across the Equatorias, causing hundreds of thousands of people to flee to Uganda.

The UN described South Sudan as one of the world's most dangerous places for aid workers—at least 83 killed since the conflict started in December 2013, with 16 in 2017 alone. In March, six aid workers were killed during an ambush on a convoy destined for Pibor. In September, a driver for the International Committee for the Red Cross was killed in the former state of Western Equatoria, prompting the organization to suspend operations there. Both sides obstructed delivery of aid—notably in famine affected areas of Unity and in Upper Nile—and attacked and looted humanitarian supplies and valuables in dozens of locations.

## *Sexual Violence*

Both government troops and opposition fighters were implicated in sexual violence against civilians in several locations, especially in and around Yei and Kajo Keji in the former state of Central Equatoria.

In April, the UN secretary general's report on conflict-related sexual violence noted a marked rise in cases of sexual violence by men in uniforms in South Sudan over the last two years, suggesting an increase in frequency as the conflict persists.

Little was done to hold soldiers accountable for sexual violence. Charges of rape of foreign aid workers are included in the ongoing trial of government soldiers for crimes committed during a July 2016 attack on an international humanitarian compound.

## *Arbitrary Detentions and Enforced Disappearances*

In August, South Sudanese authorities announced they had released 30 political prisoners since May; but during operations in the Equatorias, security forces arrested and detained individuals because of their perceived opposition to the government. Human Rights Watch documented clear patterns of arbitrary detention, abuse and torture by government forces since the conflict began.

In January 2017, a prominent lawyer, rights activist and civil society leader, Dong Samuel, and opposition humanitarian affairs officer, Aggrey Idri, were abducted and detained in Nairobi, Kenya, and forcibly deported to South Sudan. Kenyan authorities and South Sudanese authorities have denied knowledge of their fate, but credible sources told Human Rights Watch the men were detained in South Sudan. Their case amounts to an enforced disappearance, prohibited in all circumstances under international law.

The government brought charges against James Gadet Dak, a former spokesman for Machar's rebel group who had refugee status, for his public criticism of the government. He was forcibly deported from Kenya in late 2016 in violation of international refugee protections and detained in Juba.

## *Freedom of Expression*

Authorities harassed, detained, and interrogated journalists and editors. In July, the head of the state television was arrested for not broadcasting a presidential speech. The same month, authorities blocked at least four websites for publishing "subversive" information. In September, former newspaper editor Nial Bol told media that he narrowly escaped an attack by two government soldiers who raided his home in Juba.

South Sudanese authorities restricted international journalists from covering the conflict, including by refusing to grant them visas or accreditation, and accusing them of publishing articles critical of the government. The government blocked numerous independent online news sites, including Sudan Tribune.

In August, an American journalist was killed in fighting while embedded with opposition rebels in the town of Kaya, bordering Uganda. The government initially accused him of fighting with the rebels.

## Political and Legislative Developments

Implementation of the 2015 peace agreement effectively stalled, and the government used repressive tactics to silence opponents. In January, a year after a controversial decree created 28 states, President Kiir created four more states, bringing the number to 32. The creation of new states has contributed to intercommunal tensions in several locations.

In March, Kiir replaced legislators aligned with former Vice President Riek Machar with those aligned with Taban Deng Gai, whom Kiir appointed as first vice-president in the transitional unity government in July 2016. Riek Machar remained in exile at time of writing.

In May, Kiir sacked Paul Malong, the army chief of staff, and placed him under house arrest in Juba. Malong was allowed to leave the country in November, following a standoff between the army and his guards. A former deputy chief of staff, Lt. Gen. Thomas Cirillo, resigned in February, accusing the government of "ethnic cleansing," and started a new armed rebel movement, the National Salvation Front, which fought against Sudan People's Liberation Movement-in-Opposition forces in Central Equatoria.

Kiir launched a national dialogue process in May over objections from key opposition figures who declined to join. Kiir also announced plans to hold elections in 2018, originally slated for 2017 despite UN and Africa Union (AU) warnings that the country's conflict and conditions are not conducive to holding a free and fair election.

## Accountability and Justice

The government did little to end widespread abuses against civilians, or investigate and hold accountable individuals and commanders. Government investigations into violent episodes since the beginning of the conflict rarely led to credible prosecutions for human rights abuses.

The army established a court martial to try 13 soldiers for gang rape and other crimes committed during an attack on an international humanitarian compound in Juba in July 2016. The trial is a test of the government's commitment to accountability for human rights violations.

In July, a meeting of South Sudanese and AU officials in Juba to plan for the hybrid court was a step toward ensuring justice for the most serious crimes committed during the country's conflict, but much remains to be done. The government adopted a memorandum of understanding with the AU, but it had not endorsed the court's statute at time of writing.

## Key International Actors

In June, the regional Inter-Governmental Authority on Development, IGAD, embarked on efforts to "revitalize" the 2015 Agreement on Resolution of Conflict in South Sudan, ARCSS, which it had brokered with support from the US, United Kingdom, Norway, and the European Union.

Simultaneously, Ugandan president Yoweri Museveni pursued efforts to unify the ruling Sudan People's Liberation Movement, although several opposition figures did not participate.

In March, the UN Human Rights Council renewed and strengthened the mandate of the Commission on Human Rights in South Sudan, tasking it with gathering evidence and determining responsibility for violations with a view to providing accountability. The UN Mission in South Sudan, UNMISS, sheltered over 230,000 civilians in six sites, the highest number since the crisis started.

A UN "Regional Protection Force," mandated in the summer of 2016 by the UN Security Council, to protect Juba, began to deploy in August.

In September, the US imposed sanctions on three government officials: the former chief of staff, the army's deputy chief of staff, and the minister of information. The US also sanctioned three companies owned or controlled by former vice president Machar, and warned of UN sanctions and a UN arms embargo. However, Russia and China opposed the idea, along with other members of the Security Council, including from Africa. In November, Canada imposed sanctions on the same three government officials.

On May 18, the European Parliament adopted a resolution on South Sudan condemning abuses, including sexual violence and use of child soldiers, calling for accountability and supporting the establishment of a hybrid court. The European Parliament called on the EU to pursue an international arms embargo. The Troika and EU condemned government abuses.

# Sri Lanka

The general openness for media and civil society groups that emerged after the electoral defeat of the Mahinda Rajapaksa government in 2015 continued in 2017 under the administration of President Maithripala Sirisena. However, action stalled in 2017 on Sri Lanka's October 2015 pledges to the United Nations Human Rights Council (UNHRC) to address accountability and political reconciliation emerging from the country's 26-year civil war with the secessionist Liberation Tigers of Tamil Eelam (LTTE).

Despite a presidential pledge to release names of people in government custody, particularly those forcibly disappeared since the war's final months in 2009, the list was not produced. The government enacted a law to give effect to the International Convention for the Protection of All Persons from Enforced Disappearance, but made clear that the law would not be retroactive.

Religious minorities remained at risk. In June 2017, then Justice Minister Wijeyadasa Rajapakshe publicly threatened a lawyer who criticized the government's failure to protect minorities. In September, authorities took 31 Rohingya Muslim refugees into protective custody following threats by Buddhist extremists. There were further flares of violence in Galle and Vavuniya in November between Muslim and other communities, with allegations of mobs attacking Muslim homes and businesses.

## *Truth, Reconciliation, and Accountability for Past Abuses*

In October 2015, the UNHRC adopted a consensus resolution in which Sri Lanka pledged to undertake several human rights reforms, including transitional justice demands arising from the civil war, and to establish four transitional justice mechanisms, including a judicial mechanism with "participation of international judges, prosecutors, lawyers and investigators" with an independent investigative and prosecutorial body.

Civil society leaders, appointed by the government, conducted nationwide consultations in 2016, and handed a comprehensive report to the government in January 2017. It contained strong recommendations, including for a hybrid justice mechanism, acknowledging the need for independent international

participation to ensure justice for victims of war crimes and other grave human rights abuses by all sides. The report included the need for justice for all victims of the long conflict, regardless of ethnicity, religion, or political persuasion.

Neither the president nor the prime minister received the report publicly and it has since languished, with scant government attention. The government's response to the report since January 2017 has also been disappointing. Senior cabinet ministers explictly rejected the recommendation that foreign nationals particpate in the special court. Both the president and the prime minister publicly reiterated the point, and further emphasized that the government would not allow "war heroes" to be prosecuted.

## Enforced Disappearances

One of the four pillars of the 2015 resolution was to create an Office of Missing Persons (OMP). Although the government enacted a law in August 2016, efforts operationalize it remained stalled until September 2017. The OMP had yet to be formally set up at time of writing, and as of November, commissioners to the OMP had not been appointed.

Families of the disappeared said that the OMP was decided without proper consultation with affected groups, particularly as it was passed before the national consultation was finished. The act therefore does not address some of its central recommendations, including the need for psychosocial support, victim and witness protection measures, a minority rights commision, and symbolic gestures to allow public grieving, such as commemorating their dead.

The government failed to properly implement promised security sector reforms to ensure human rights protections. It failed to repeal or revise the draconian Prevention of Terrorism Act (PTA) and reform the Witness and Victim Protection Law. At least two separate drafts of the PTA were floated throughout the year, both of which could facilitate serious human rights abuses. Troubling provisions included overly broad definitions of terrorist offenses to possibly include peaceful political protesters. The government received feedback on the drafts from various UN offices specializing in counterterrorism, but at time of writing the drafts continued to fail international standards.

## Lack of Accountability

With a few exceptions, particularly in cases that generated considerable publicity, Sri Lankan police were not held accountable for routine torture and ill-treatment in custody.

In April-May 2016, the UN special rapporteur on torture visited Sri Lanka. The report, presented to the March 2017 Human Rights Council session expressed "extreme alarm" at the failure to investigate credible allegations of torture, and corroborated accounts of ongoing torture, including sexual abuse.

The UN special rapporteur on counterterrorism and human rights, following a visit in July 2017, similarly reported that use of torture by Sri Lankan security forces is routine, and continues despite government claims of security sector reforms.

The National Human Rights Commission, although limited in resources, actively visited and monitored prisons and places of detention throughout 2017; despite occasional difficulties, the commission experienced no obstacles securing access to detainees.

## Constitutional Reform

The government issued an interim report in September 2017, but it did not properly reflect recommendations from a 2016 national consultation. Nonetheless, its publication was welcomed by many political parties keen to see progress on constitutional reforms. However, the efforts stalled and parliament had yet to debate the report at time of writing, nor had the government issued timelines for when a final report on constitutional reform could be expected.

## Migrant Workers

The government took some steps to protect the rights of more than 1 million migrant workers in the Middle East and other parts of Asia, but many continued to face long working hours with little rest, delayed or unpaid wages, confinement in the workplace, and verbal, physical, and sexual abuse.

In June, the government announced the appointment of a committee to study strategies to reduce the number of domestic workers abroad and to end the *kafala* sponsorship system that operates in many Middle Eastern countries, restricting employment and transfer opportunities for migrant workers.

## Sexual Orientation and Gender Identity

The government failed to make progress during the year toward implementing a 2016 plan forwarded by the Ministry of Health to establish a clear procedure for transgender people to change their identity documents. State and non-state discrimination against the lesbian, gay, bisexual, transgender and intersex (LGBTI) population persisted. Sections 365 and 365A of the penal code prohibit "carnal knowledge against the order of nature" and "gross indecency," commonly understood in Sri Lanka to criminalize same-sex relations between consenting adults. At a UN review in November, Sri Lanka rejected recommendations to repeal sections 365 and 365A.

## Women's Rights

The UN Committee on the Elimination of Discrimination against Women (CEDAW) reviewed Sri Lanka in February 2017, noting in its concluding observations that the government had yet to fully implement the Convention on the Elimination of All Forms of Discrimination against Women, although it did note some progress on policies and plans designed to protect women against trafficking, and sexual and other violence.

## Key International Actors

Sri Lanka continued its engagement with the international community. UN special mandate holders made several visits to the country during the year. Sri Lanka appeared before the UN Universal Periodic Review Working Group in November.

The government engaged with the Human Rights Council and the Office of the High Commissioner for Human Rights regularly throughout the year. The UN High Commissioner for Human Rights called on Sri Lanka for speedier and more meaningful implementation of its promises during the September 2017 council sessions.

The Sri Lankan government, in responding to the CEDAW in February, seemed unable or unwilling to answer questions of concern that committee members put to the government delegation.

The United Nations expressed an interest in vetting Sri Lankan forces before sending them abroad for peacekeeping duties in light of the numerous wartime abuses attributed to the armed forces.

# Sudan

Sudan's human rights record continued to be defined by government repression and violations of basic civil and political rights, restriction of religious freedoms, and disregard for obligations on civilian protection under international humanitarian law.

In Darfur, Southern Kordofan and Blue Nile, Sudan's Rapid Support Forces (RSF) and other government-aligned forces attacked civilians. Sudan failed to provide accountability for serious crimes committed during the conflicts, or other serious human rights violations.

The national security agency detained student activists, human rights defenders, members of opposition parties and journalists. Authorities prosecuted activists and journalists for their reports and confiscated newspapers.

In January, then-United States President Barack Obama issued an executive order promising to lift broad economic sanctions if Sudan met certain conditions; these did not require measurable improvements in human rights.

## *Conflict and Abuses in Darfur, Southern Kordofan, and Blue Nile*

Despite the government's unilateral ceasefire and reduced fighting in all three war zones, government forces and allied militia attacked civilians including in displaced persons camps throughout the year.

In May and June, the RSF attacked villages in North and Central Darfur, forcing tens of thousands to flee. RSF fighters were responsible for large-scale attacks on villages during counterinsurgency campaigns from 2014 to 2016.

In Southern Kordofan and Blue Nile, the six-year conflict continued, with sporadic government attacks on civilians. In Blue Nile and in refugee camps in neighboring South Sudan, displaced communities fought along ethnic lines following a split within the leadership of the armed opposition, Sudan People's Liberation Army-North.

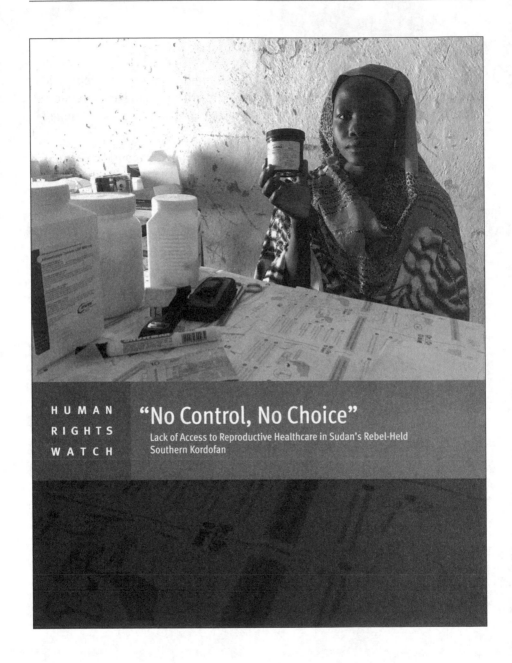

In the rebel held areas of both states, hundreds of thousands lacked sufficient food and basic supplies because the government and rebels failed to agree on modalities for the delivery of essential items.

## Human Rights Defenders

In December 2016 and January 2017, national security agents detained Dr. Mudawi Ibrahim Adam, a prominent rights defender, along with several other activists and held them for up to eight months. Mudawi and two others were charged with undermining the constitutional system and crimes against the state, which carry the death penalty. At least two detainees were badly beaten and one was forced to confess under torture. They were released by presidential pardon in August.

In March, authorities released three human rights defenders associated with the civil society organization Tracks for Training and Human Development, after nine months in detention. The men were convicted of trumped-up charges of espionage and dissemination of false information.

National security agents arrested the men along with other Tracks staff in May 2016. In August 2016, the United Nations Working Group of Arbitrary Detention found the detentions violated fair trial standards.

## Arbitrary Detentions, Ill-Treatment, and Torture

Security officials detained opposition members, journalists, and labor leaders throughout the year, often for long periods without charge or access to lawyers. They routinely beat detainees during interrogations.

Following the "civil disobedience" campaign to protest economic austerity measures in November and December 2016, agents detained dozens of opposition members. One Sudan Congress Party (SCP) member was held for 50 days without charge, and beaten so badly that he required surgery upon his release.

In December 2016, a British journalist and his Sudanese-American colleague were detained first in Darfur then transferred to Khartoum for almost two months without charge and said they were subjected to beatings, electric shocks, and mock execution. The two entered Darfur to investigate Amnesty International's allegations of chemical weapons use by the government.

In April, security officials detained for several days three doctors involved in a doctor's strike that began in late 2016 over work conditions. Several SCP members were detained in June from a sit-in about a cholera outbreak. In September, security officials detained a diaspora SCP member for seven weeks. In August, security officials detained Nasreddin Mukhtar, former head of a Darfur Student Union, and held him without charge in solitary confinement.

## Freedom of Association, Assembly, and Expression

Government security forces used excessive force to break up protests across the country. In September, government forces opened fire on protesters in the Kalma displaced persons camp in South Darfur, killing more than five and wounding two dozen. The residents were protesting President al-Bashir's visit to the camp.

Authorities also used excessive force on several occasions to disperse protests on university campuses. In May, following clashes over disputed elections at Bakht al-Rida university in White Nile state, police and security forces raided a dormitory, beat and shot students, wounding several, and arrested dozens. In response to the arrests, more than 1,000 Darfuri students withdrew from the university, alleging discrimination against Darfuri students. Nine students remained in detention by year's end.

In August and September, security officials detained dozens of members of the United Popular Front, a student branch of a Darfur rebel group, while protesting on the streets of Khartoum and Omdurman. Officials arrested many other student activists throughout the year.

By the end of 2017, there had been no justice for the killings of more than 170 people during violent government crackdowns on popular anti-austerity protests in September and October 2013.

## Freedom of Media

Security officials continued to restrict media by harassing and detaining journalists, charging them with crimes, and confiscating editions of newspapers that published articles deemed too sensitive.

In October, a court ordered the editor of *al-Tayyar* to pay a fine or spend six months in prison for publishing an article about alleged abuse of power in the president's family. Other journalists, including Hanadi el-Siddig, editor-in-chief of *Akhbar El Watan,* were interrogated or detained for content deemed too critical, such as allegations of abuse by security forces and an interview with an opposition leader. Marwa Tijani was detained for three days after publishing a piece of creative writing critiquing religion.

Three online activists were deported from Saudi Arabia to Sudan and detained there in July, allegedly for their writings in support of the 2016 "civil disobedience" campaign to protest austerity measures. Authorities confiscated both independent and pro-government newspapers, including *El Tayar, El Jareeda, Akhar Lahza, El Wifag, and El Sayha,* often without giving reason.

## Freedom of Religion

In early 2017, officials in Khartoum announced they would demolish at least 27 churches within Khartoum; the decision was being challenged by a church organization. In May, police and other security demolished a church in Soba area of Khartoum following a dispute over land ownership.

Officials have prohibited construction of new churches. In 2013, the minister of guidance and endowments claimed there was no need for new churches as South Sudanese Christians would have returned to South Sudan following its independence in 2011.

In October, police arrested five members of the Sudan Church of Christ, charging them with public nuisance for praying at a church that authorities closed, in a case that illustrates disputes over the administration of churches.

In February and May, al-Bashir pardoned two clerics—a Czech missionary and Sudanese pastor—and a Darfuri activist who had been detained since December 2015. The men were among five arrested in December 2015 and accused of links to armed opposition, and charged with espionage and other crimes.

## Refugees and Migrants

Sudan continued to receive large numbers of South Sudanese refugees. Approximately 183,500 arrived in 2017, bringing the total to more than 461,000 since war in South Sudan began in December 2013. Sudan agreed to open humanitarian aid corridors to South Sudan.

In August, Sudanese authorities deported 104 Eritrean refugees, including 30 minors. In September, the government reportedly deported another 36. None of the deportees appear to have had an opportunity to apply for asylum. The UN Refugee Agency, UNHCR, called on Sudan to refrain from further removals of potential refugees.

The head of the notoriously abusive Rapid Support Forces, Mohamed Hamdan "Hemeti," publicly claimed that his forces were assisting the European Union, raising concerns that the EU is funding the abusive forces as part of its migration assistance package.

## Law Reform

Following the conclusion of the national dialogue, a government initiative to address political grievances, President al-Bashir appointed a prime minister to implement recommendations and form a new government. Many opposition parties rejected the dialogue process.

In January, Sudan's parliament passed the Rapid Support Forces Act to regulate the force, but forces continued to operate under the same commander independently of the army.

Sudan has not reformed laws governing its security agency. The National Security Act of 2010 gave broad powers of arrest, detention, search, and seizure and violates accepted international standards, to which Sudan is bound. Sudan also retains the death penalty, despite international consensus to ban it.

Sudanese law discriminates against women and girls in various ways, including through application of Sharia (Islamic) law penalties for "morality crimes," such as adultery or dress code violations. Sudan also criminalizes same-sex sexual activity with harsh penalties such as life in prison or death.

## Key International Actors

In January, former US President Obama issued an executive order promising to lift broad economic sanctions on Sudan if Sudan made progress in five areas, which did not explicitly include human rights reforms. This step was welcomed by the EU. In October, the US permanently lifted the sanctions.

The EU has pledged hundreds of millions of euros to Sudan in support of the regional Khartoum Process, to manage migration. The aid programs have been widely criticized on grounds that they encourage or assist the RSF to carry out abusive operations.

In March, President al-Bashir attended a League of Arab States' summit In Amman, Jordan. Jordan did not comply with its obligation, as a party to the Rome Statute, to arrest and surrender him to the International Criminal Court (ICC).

EU High Representative for Foreign Affairs Federica Mogherini also attended the summit but did not publicly call on Jordanian authorities to comply with their obligation.

In July, the UN Security Council renewed the peacekeeping mission in Darfur through June 2018, agreeing to dramatic reductions as part of an exit plan lobbied for by Sudan, and extended the UN Interim Security Force for Abyei.

In September, the UN Human Rights Council renewed the mandate of the Independent Expert to monitor and advise on human rights for another year, but used language foreshadowing the end of the mandate if there is "continued and sustained improvement" to the situation in the country, risking prematurely ending the mandate in coming years.

The Security Council did not press Sudan to cooperate with the ICC in its investigation into crimes committed in Darfur, despite having referred the situation to the ICC in 2005. The ICC first announced charges in 2007. It currently has outstanding arrest warrants against five individuals, including President al-Bashir, for war crimes, crimes against humanity, and genocide allegedly committed in Darfur between 2003 and 2008.

# Swaziland

Ruled by absolute monarch King Mswati III since 1986, Swaziland continued to repress political dissent and disregard human rights and rule of law in 2017. Political parties remained banned, as they have been since 1973; the independence of the judiciary is severely compromised and repressive laws continued to be used to target critics of the government and the king, despite basic rights guarantees in Swaziland's 2005 constitution.

In 2017, Swaziland struggled to fulfil the rights of its estimated 1.4 million population amid numerous political and socio-economic challenges, including the highest HIV infection rate in the world at 26 percent according to the United Nations Children's Fund (UNICEF).

In September, King Mswati told the United Nations General Assembly in New York that Swaziland is committed to peace and a decent life for all. He said his government grants every citizen an opportunity to voice their views in order to constructively contribute to the social, economic, cultural, and political development of the country. He failed to mention, however, the recently passed amendments to the Public Order Act, which allow critics of the king or the Swazi government to be prosecuted, and upon conviction be fined E10,0000 (US$770), imprisoned for two years, or both for inciting "hatred or contempt" against cultural and traditional heritage.

The amendments to the Public Order Act grant sweeping powers to the national commissioner of police to arbitrarily halt pro-democracy meetings and protests, and crush any criticism of the government.

In the same month, the Swazi government approved a Ministry of Education and Training decision to introduce fees in schools, effectively ending free primary education, which had been available in the country since 2005. The Swaziland National Association of Teachers has criticized the decision as a violation of the right to primary education guaranteed in the country's constitution.

## *Freedom of Association and Assembly*

Restrictions on freedom of association and assembly continued. The government took no action to revoke the King's Proclamation of 1973, which prohibits formation and operations of political parties in the country. The police used the Urban Act, which requires protesters to give two weeks' notice before a public protest, to stop protests and harass protesters.

## *Human Rights Defenders*

Security legislation that severely curtails basic rights remained in force in 2017 despite calls for its amendment or repeal. The Suppression of Terrorism Act of 2008 placed severe restrictions on civil society organizations, religious groups, and media. Under the legislation, a "terrorist act" includes a wide range of legitimate conduct such as criticism of the government. The legislation was used by state officials to target perceived opponents through abusive surveillance, and unlawful searches of homes and offices.

Two leaders of a banned political party, the People's United Democratic Movement (PUDEMO), Mario Masuku and Maxwell Dlamini, remained on bail in 2017 pending the finalization of their trial on charges under the Suppression of Terrorism Act for allegedly criticizing the government by singing a pro-democracy song and shouting "viva PUDEMO" during a May Day rally in 2014. After more than a year in custody, they were granted bail in July 2015 by the Swaziland High Court. The trial continued at time of writing. If convicted, they could serve up to 15 years in prison. Both men attended the May Day rally of TUCOSWA in 2016, but their bail conditions prohibited them from addressing the workers.

## *Rule of Law*

Although the constitution provides for three separate organs of government—the executive, legislature, and judiciary—under Swaziland's law and custom, the powers of all three organs are vested in the king. The prime minister should exercise executive authority, but in reality, King Mswati holds supreme executive power and also controls the judiciary. The king appoints 20 members of the 30-member senate, 10 members of the house of assembly, and approves all legislation passed by parliament.

The constitution provides for equality before the law, but also places the king above the law. A 2011 directive, which protects the king from any civil law suits, issued by then-Swaziland Chief Justice Michael Ramodibedi after Swazi villagers claimed police had seized their cattle to add to the king's herd, remained in force in 2017.

The Sedition and Subversive Activities Act also remained in force in 2017. The act restricts freedom of expression by criminalizing alleged seditious publications and use of alleged seditious words, such as those which "may excite disaffection" against the king. Published criticism of the ruling party is also banned. Many journalists told Human Rights Watch that they practice self-censorship, especially with regards to reports involving the king, to avoid harassment by authorities.

## Women's and Girls' Rights

Article 20 of the Swazi Constitution provides for equality before the law and non-discrimination, but does not prevent discrimination on the grounds of sex, language, sexual orientation, and gender identity. Swaziland's dual legal system, where both Roman Dutch common law and Swazi customary law operate side by side, has resulted in conflicts leading to numerous violations of women's rights.

For example, under both Swazi customary law and the Marriage Act (1964), married women are assigned a disadvantaged status, granting men more privileges and rights. The act provides that married women require the consent of their husbands to enter into certain contracts, including accessing credit from financial institutions. The Marriage Act imposes on African spouses the customary consequences of marriage while granting to non-African spouses the common law consequences of marriage. This violates the right of married women to be free from racial discrimination under the constitution and international human rights treaties.

In August 2017, human rights groups Southern African Litigation Centre and Women and Law in Southern Africa (WLSA) Swaziland challenged these discriminatory laws in court on behalf of a married Swazi woman who, upon being deserted by her husband, was unable to sell any of the livestock she purchased with her own money because she did not have her husband's consent. At time of writing the matter had not been finalized in court.

The government has yet to pass into law the amended Marriage Act, which criminalizes marital rape, or the Sexual Offences and Domestic Violence Bill. The government developed the latter in 2009 to protect women's and girls' rights, and to outlaw child marriage.

On May 24, local trade unions, civil society groups, and the Swaziland Council of Churches held a protest march to raise awareness on the endemic gender-based violence. Survivors of gender-based violence have few avenues for help as both formal and customary justice processes discriminate against them.

## *Key International Actors*

In August, at the end of its one-year term, Swaziland handed over the leadership of the Southern African Development Community (SADC), the 15-nation regional economic institution, to South Africa. With a poor and deteriorating human rights record of its own, Swaziland failed to use its leadership of SADC to strengthen the regional body's ability to call for improved human rights standards across southern Africa. Both SADC and the African Union (AU) have done little to press Swaziland to improve respect for human rights.

At its national policy conference in July, South Africa's governing party, the African National Congress, called for Swaziland to be referred to SADC for abuse of human rights, suppression of dissent, and political activity. The ANC also pressed Swaziland to lift the ban on opposition political parties.

Swaziland ignored calls by the European Union to take steps to respect and promote freedom of expression, guarantee democracy and plurality, and establish a legislative framework allowing the registration, operation, and full participation of political parties.

Swaziland ratified the International Covenant on Civil and Political Rights (ICCPR) in 2004, but has since failed to submit reports in fulfilment of its obligations under the covenant. The Human Rights Committee, the treaty body overseeing the ICCPR's implementation, reviewed Swaziland's implementation of the treaty in the absence of a report in July 2017. The committee highlighted the issues of discrimination against HIV positive persons, and lesbian, gay, bisexual, transgender and intersex (LGBTI) people; inequality of women in marital status; and women's participation in political life.

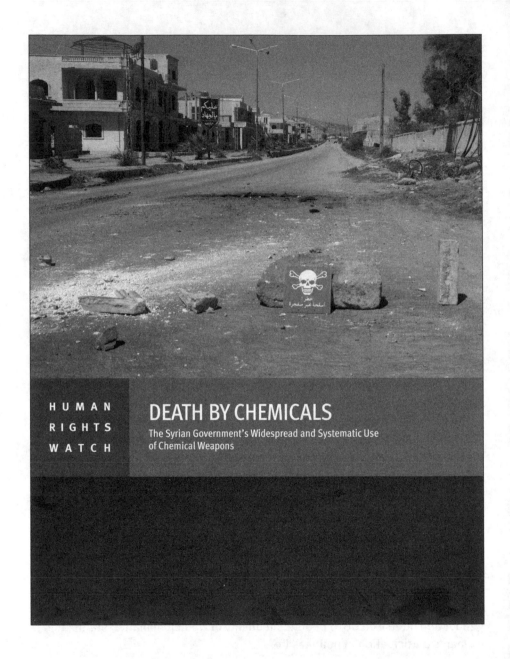

**HUMAN
RIGHTS
WATCH**

## DEATH BY CHEMICALS
The Syrian Government's Widespread and Systematic Use
of Chemical Weapons

# Syria

The fight against the extremist group Islamic State (also known as ISIS) emerged as the top priority for Syria's multiple warring parties in 2017. The government, with the assistance of Russia, Iran, and Hezbollah, retook large parts of central and eastern Syria from ISIS, while US-backed Syria Democratic Forces controlled Raqqa. The race to secure territory and consolidate gains was accompanied by grave violations of human rights and humanitarian law that have come to characterize the Syria conflict.

More than 400,000 have died because of the Syrian conflict since 2011, according to the World Bank, with 5 million people seeking refuge abroad and over 6 million displaced internally, according to United Nations agencies. By June 2017, the UN also estimated that 540,000 people were still living in besieged areas.

The Syrian government has launched numerous chemical weapons attacks on civilians in opposition-held areas. With Russia and Iran's support, the Syrian government has conducted deliberate and indiscriminate attacks against civilians and civilian infrastructure, withheld humanitarian aid, employed starvation as war tactic, and forcibly displaced Syrians in contravention of international law. The Syrian government's practices of torture and ill-treatment in detention and enforced disappearances continue.

Non-state armed groups have also committed a host of violations. The groups have launched deliberate and indiscriminate attacks against civilians, abducted, and arbitrarily detained activists, used excessive force to stifle protests and interfered with humanitarian aid delivery. ISIS has reportedly used civilians as human shields, and employed landmines and other IEDs causing significant harm to civilians and civilian infrastructure.

Civilian casualties from airstrikes by the US-led coalition fighting ISIS increased. According to the Syrian Network for Human Rights, a local group, 2,286 civilians had died since the beginning of the campaign until September 2017. A number of these strikes raise concerns that the coalition failed to take necessary precautions to avoid and minimize civilian casualties.

While accountability efforts remained blocked at the Security Council, the UN General Assembly established in December 2016 a mechanism to assist in the

HUMAN
RIGHTS
WATCH

## ATTACK ON THE
## OMAR IBN AL-KHATAB MOSQUE
Authorities' Failure to Take Adequate Precautions

investigation of serious crimes, preserve evidence, and prepare cases for future criminal proceedings.

## Targeting Civilians, Indiscriminate Attacks, Continued Use of Cluster Munitions and Incendiary Weapons

Unlawful attacks against civilians and civilian structures in Syria persisted, with attacks on medical facilities, schools, and mosques.

The Syrian government regained control over opposition-held parts of Aleppo at the end of 2016. In its operation, the Russian-Syrian military coalition conducted indiscriminate air attacks, including strikes on several medical facilities, and used incendiary weapons and cluster munitions. The Violations Documentation Center (VDC), a local monitoring group, documented the killing of 446 civilians, including 91 children, in aerial attacks in eastern Aleppo between September 19 and October 18.

While the number of civilian deaths in Southern Syria decreased after local ceasefire agreements, unlawful attacks persisted. In June, for example, Russian-Syrian airstrikes and artillery attacks targeted the town of Tafas, south of Daraa, killing 10 civilians in and near a school.

In September, the Russian-Syrian Joint Military Operation launched an offensive on Idlib province. Airstrikes targeted several towns and surrounding areas in the province, destroying at least six hospitals and five civil defense centers, resulting in the death of over 150 civilians, according to the Syrian Civil Defense.

Cluster munition attacks by Syrian government forces on opposition-held areas continued unabated. At least 238 separate attacks using cluster munitions in Syria between August 2016 and July 2017 were reported by local activists, first responders, and medical personnel.

Human Rights Watch recorded at least 22 air attacks with incendiary weapons in 2017. In April 2017, Human Rights Watch documented the use of ZAB incendiary submunitions, containing thermite, and delivered by RBK-500 bombs used to attack the city of Saraqeb, northwest of Saraqeb.

## Unlawful Restrictions on Humanitarian Aid, Sieges, and Forced Displacements

The siege of civilian areas and restrictions on humanitarian aid by government and pro-government forces and by armed opposition groups continued in 2017. The UN Office for the Coordination of Humanitarian Affairs (OCHA) estimate that around 540,000 people were trapped in besieged areas as of June 2017 with the majority besieged by government forces in Eastern Ghouta.

Humanitarian conditions in besieged opposition enclaves rapidly deteriorated in 2017, forcing communities in several besieged areas to surrender to the terms of brokered ceasefire and evacuation deals with the government.

Several local "reconciliation" agreements were finalized in 2017, including the "Four Towns Agreement" signed in March, resulted in the evacuation of the government-besieged towns of Madaya and Zabadani in exchange for evacuating the towns of Fouah and Kefraya, encircled by armed opposition groups. The UN Commission of Inquiry and Amnesty International have found that some of these evacuations are unlawful and constitute forced displacement.

## Unlawful Use of Chemical Weapons and Nerve Agents

The Syrian government's forces continued to use chemical weapons repeatedly, with nerve agents being deployed on at least four occasions since late 2016—in eastern Hama on December 11 and 12, 2016, northern Hama, on March 30, and Khan Sheikhoun on April 4.

Clinical symptoms affecting victims of the chemical weapons attack in Khan Sheikhoun suggested that an organophosphorus compound, which targets the nervous system, was used. The attack killed at least 92, including 30 children, and injured hundreds more.

In September, the UN-appointed commission of inquiry's report concluded that "the Syrian air force used sarin in Khan Sheikhoun, Idlib, killing dozens, the majority of whom were women and children." The commission says it has evidence the attack was conducted by a Sukhoi SU-22 aircraft, a type that only Syrian government forces use. In October, the Joint Investigative Mechanism (JIM) of the UN and Organization for the Prohibition of Chemical Weapons (OPCW) found that the Syrian government was responsible for the chemical weapons attack in Khan

HUMAN
RIGHTS
WATCH

# ALL FEASIBLE PRECAUTIONS?
Civilian Casualties in Anti-ISIS Coalition Airstrikes in Syria

Sheikhoun. Russia vetoed the renewal of the JIM whose mandate ended in November.

Human Rights Watch also documented government helicopters dropping chlorine on at least eight occasions in the offensive to recapture Aleppo, indicating widespread and systematic use of chemical weapons.

## US-Led Coalition Airstrikes

In March, a US warplane struck a mosque in al-Jinah village in Aleppo killing at least 38 people. The US said it struck a meeting of Al-Qaeda members but local residents said that the victims were all civilians attending evening prayers. Statements by US military after the attack indicate they failed to understand the targeted building was a mosque, that prayer was about to begin, and that a religious lecture was taking place at the time of the attack.

The United States conducted an investigation into the airstrike, and found it legal, though it failed to clarify the factors that led to that determination or consult external actors. The UN Commission of Inquiry found the strike was unlawful as US forces failed to take all feasible precautions to minimize loss of civilian life.

According to the Syrian Observatory for Human Rights, a Britain-based monitoring group, around 1,100 civilians died in airstrikes launched by coalition planes since the campaign to retake the city of Raqqa began.

Human Rights Watch investigated several airstrikes in towns near Raqqa, including one on a school housing displaced persons in Mansourah on March 20 and a market and a bakery in Tabqa on March 22 that killed at least 84 civilians, including 30 children. According to local residents, the Mansourah school had long hosted displaced civilians fleeing other parts of Syria, and civilians had used the Tabqa market throughout the war. The strikes raise concerns that US-led coalition forces did not take adequate precautions to minimize civilian casualties.

## *Enforced Disappearances, Death in Custody, Arbitrary Arrests, and Torture*

Arbitrary detention, ill-treatment, torture and enforced disappearances continued to run rampant in Syria. In 2017, the Syrian Network for Human Rights (SNHR) documented more than 4,252 individual arbitrary arrests, most of them conducted by government forces. As of August 2017, over 80,000 individuals remain disappeared, according to SNHR.

In August, the wife of Bassel Khartabil, a computer engineer and freedom of expression advocate who was arrested in 2012, revealed that she had received confirmation that government forces had executed her husband in detention in 2015 but had kept his fate secret. The Syrian government also conducted arbitrary arrests under a law that criminalizes "unnatural sexual intercourse."

## *Non-State Armed Groups' Abuses*

### Hay'et Tahrir al-Sham

In January, a coalition of Jabhat Fateh al-Sham, which changed its name from Jabhat al-Nusra after stating that it was breaking off ties with Al-Qaeda, and other opposition factions formed Hay'et Tahrir Al-Sham (HTS), which became the dominant group in Idlib province. During 2017, HTS committed a host of violations including arbitrary detention of civilians and local activists in Idlib. In response to protests by civilians in Idlib province contesting HTS's control, the group reportedly shot at protesters, killing and injuring civilians. HTS also interfered with humanitarian aid delivery, in contravention of international humanitarian law.

HTS also targeted religious minorities through car bombings. In March, HTS claimed responsibility for two explosions in the Bab al-Saghir cemetery, a well-known Shia pilgrimage site south of Damascus which, according to the UN Commission of Inquiry, killed 44 civilians, including 8 children, and injured another 120.

## ISIS

Abuses by ISIS against civilians continue unabated despite the group losing control of wide areas. ISIS used civilians as human shields in its defense of Raqqa and other towns, and employed internationally banned landmines to hold off the advance of attacking forces.

In May, ISIS militants attacked the town of Aqarib al-Safiyah, predominantly populated by Ismailis, a minority Shia Muslim community. While attempting to flee, residents were killed in the streets by snipers positioned at the village's water reservoir and on the roofs of houses. In total, 52 civilians were killed, including 12 children according to the UN Commission of Inquiry. Another 100 were injured, including two girls who suffered serious head wounds.

The UN-OPCW's joint investigation into the use of chemical weapons in Syria has previously confirmed that ISIS has used chemical weapons, specifically sulfur mustard gas, against civilians.

## Other Armed Groups

Fighting among different non-state armed groups increased risk to civilians. The UN Commission of Inquiry has documented the death of an 11-year-old child in Daraa City, as well as destruction of civilian infrastructure, as a result of indiscriminate shelling by armed groups. The commission estimated that practices of torture and arbitrary detention continued in areas under the control of armed groups, including Eastern Ghouta.

## *Areas Under Kurdish Democratic Union Party (PYD) Control*

The security forces in PYD-controlled areas conducted a series of raids to close opposing political parties' offices, and detained and harassed members of the political opposition and activists. Most were detained without any charges brought against them. Most prisoners were released after a few months.

Human Rights Watch has received reports of torture and ill-treatment in detention facilities controlled by the Syrian Democratic Forces (SDF)—a coalition of forces fighting ISIS primarily made up of the YPG. SDF held individuals without charge in violation of fair trial guarantees, according to local residents. Local activists report the SDF restricted the freedom of movement of displaced persons from Raqqa and Deir-Ezzor province who end up in displacement camps in SDF-controlled areas, and deteriorating humanitarian conditions for the displaced.

## Displacement Crisis and Forcible Evacuations

Neighboring countries, including Lebanon, Jordan, and Turkey, sought to curb the massive inflow of refugees with unlawful administrative, legal, and even physical barriers. Incidents of Turkish border guards shooting at Syrians and smugglers attempting to cross the border continue to be reported, including the fatal shooting of a three-year-old child in September.

Lebanon maintained visa-like restrictions for Syrians seeking entry and stringent residency renewal regulations, negatively impacting refugees' freedom of movement, access to education, and access to healthcare. Deteriorating conditions for Syrians in the Lebanese border town of Arsal led to almost 10,000 Syrians returning to Idlib largely under agreements negotiated between Hezbollah and different Syrian groups, as well as ISIS.

In the first five months of 2017, Jordanian authorities deported about 400 registered Syrian refugees per month to unsafe conditions in Syria. Another estimated 500 refugees each month returned to Syria from Jordan under circumstances that are unclear. Authorities produced little evidence of wrongdoing by these refugees and did not give any real opportunity for the refugees to contest their removal or to seek legal help prior to deportation.

## Key International Actors

Peace talks held by the United Nations in Geneva have failed to achieve momentum. In January 2017, Russia, Iran, and Turkey met in Astana, Kazakhstan, along with representatives of the parties to the conflict to pursue a de-escalation of the conflict. While consecutive Astana meetings have resulted in a decrease in violence following a May agreement on four de-escalation zones, they have failed to realize a complete end to the violence completely. The Syrian government, Russia, and other actors repeatedly violated these ceasefires. In October, Turkey deployed troops inside Idlib province.

The Syrian government continued to violate Security Council resolutions demanding safe and unhindered humanitarian access; cessation of "indiscriminate employment of weapons in populated areas, including shelling and aerial bombardment, such as the use of barrel bombs;" and an end to the practices of arbitrary detention, disappearance, and abductions, and the release of everyone who has been arbitrarily detained.

In addition to persistently discouraging or pre-emptively rejecting suggestions for meaningful Security Council action to curb violations by the Syrian government, Russia, along with the Iranian government, continued to provide the Syrian government with military assistance in 2017.

The United States also continued to lead a coalition of other states targeting ISIS in Iraq and Syria, as well as to support the Syrian Democratic Forces in the same offensive. In April, the US also launched an attack on a Syrian airfield in response to the Syrian government's use of chemical weapons. In July, the US, Jordan, and Russia agreed to a ceasefire zone in southern Syria.

In December 2016, the UN General Assembly passed a resolution creating the "International, Impartial and Independent Mechanism" to gather, preserve, and analyze potential evidence of serious crimes in Syria for use in courts that may have a mandate over the abuses now or in the future.

In April, foreign ministers of EU member states adopted the EU strategy for Syria, which includes political and humanitarian actions and provides for efforts to promote accountability for war crimes and serious human rights violations. In May, the European Parliament welcomed the adoption of the strategy and stressed the need for accountability, at international and domestic levels.

In April, the EU hosted the "Brussels Conference on Supporting the Future of Syria and the Region," in which donors pledged €5.6 billion for 2017 and €3.5 billion for the 2018-2020 period. In June, the European Commission announced €1.5 million to support the IIIM. In September, the EU announced the intention to host a second donors conference in Brussels in spring 2018.

Police and prosecutors in several countries, including Sweden, Germany, and France, were also investigating some individuals alleged to have committed serious crimes, such as torture, war crimes, and crimes against humanity in Syria under the principle of universal jurisdiction.

# Tajikistan

Tajikistan's human rights record worsened further in 2017, as authorities deepened a severe, widespread crackdown on free expression and association, peaceful political opposition activity, the independent legal profession, and the independent exercise of religious faith.

Well over 150 political activists, including a number of lawyers and journalists, remain unjustly jailed, and the relatives of dissidents who peacefully criticize the government from outside the country are subjected to violent retaliation orchestrated by authorities, including arbitrary detention, threats of rape, confiscation of passports and property, and vigilante justice at the hands of sometimes-violent mobs.

Torture remains a serious concern. Since 2016, the Coalition against Torture, a collection of Tajik rights groups, has reported at least 90 instances of torture or ill-treatment in detention. Although a law on domestic violence has been in place since 2013, legal protections for victims remain insufficient and impunity for perpetrators of domestic violence continues as the norm.

## *Harassment of Dissidents and Dissidents' Families*

Since mid-September 2015, following the forced closure of Tajikistan's leading opposition party, the Islamic Renaissance Party of Tajikistan (IRPT), authorities have subjected party members and their relatives to arbitrary detention and imprisonment, in addition to persons associated with the opposition movement Group 24 and other critical groups. Authorities regularly harass relatives of critics living abroad.

In December 2016, prison officials tortured imprisoned IRPT activist Rahmatulloi Rajab in retaliation for the critical journalistic work of his son Shukhrati Rahmatullo. Rajab was sentenced to 28 years in prison in June 2016, alongside at least 12 other high-ranking IRPT officials.

The same month, Tajik security officials harassed the relatives of several peaceful protestors, including Vaisiddin Odinaev, who were demonstrating in Prague during President Rahmon's official visit with Czech president Milos Zeman. A few days after the demonstrations in Prague, security service officers in Tajikistan forcibly took Odinaev's 75-year-old grandfather to the Shahrinav district police station and interrogated him for five hours.

Also in December 2016, authorities confiscated the passports of the mother, daughter, and several relatives of Shabnam Khudoydodova, an independent activist living in Warsaw. Since late 2016, every few months following Khudoy-dodova's participation in the 2016 Organization for Security and Co-operation in Europe Human Dimension Implementation Meeting (OSCE/HDIM), a human rights conference, authorities have regularly threatened and harassed Khudoy-dodova's relatives in Kulob.

Their intimidation includes visiting their home to remind them they are under surveillance and threatening that if Khudoydodova's mother attempts to leave the country with Khudoydodova's 10-year-old daughter authorities will "shave her bald" and place her in a state orphanage. Following the intervention of local human rights defenders, authorities returned the passports only in November 2017, holding them for almost a year.

In January 2017, Said Ziyoyev, a resident of the Qubodiyon district in Khatlon province, was sentenced to seven years in jail for participating in a Group 24 meeting in the Russian city of Yekaterinburg in November 2014.

In July, security service officers in seven cities across Tajikistan arbitrarily detained and interrogated the relatives of at least ten peaceful activists who, earlier that month, had attended a conference in Dortmund, Germany commemorating the signing of the peace accords that formally ended Tajik-istan's civil war. Authorities retaliated against the activists' relatives, publicly shaming them for their family members' activism.

One of the opposition activists was Jamshed Yorov, Germany-based lawyer and brother of jailed human rights lawyer Buzurgmehr Yorov. Tajik authorities visited his family home in Tajikistan and informed Jamshed's wife, Dilbar Zuhurova, that she and her children would be imprisoned if they tried to leave the country. Officers also pressured Zuhurova to divorce Yorov, and threatened to rape Zuhurova's 15-year-old daughter.

## Imprisonment and Harassment of Lawyers

Since 2014, authorities have arrested or imprisoned at least seven human rights lawyers: Shukhrat Kudratov, Fakhriddin Zokirov, Buzurgmehr Yorov, Jamshed Yorov, Nuriddin Makhkamov, Dilbar Dodojonova, Fayzinisso Vohidova, and two sons of deceased lawyer Ishoq Tabarov, Firuz Tabarov and Daler Tabarov.

In May 2017, authorities barred Fayzinisso Vohidova from leaving the country and threatened her with a criminal case. Before the ban, Vohidova had publicly criticized the imprisonment of Yorov and Makhkamov.

In October 2016, the government jailed Buzurgmehr Yorov and Nurridin Makhkamov on politically motivated charges, to 21 and 23 years' imprisonment, respectively. In 2017, in two additional trials, authorities extended Yorov's prison sentence by two years for insulting a government official, and again for citing a stanza of the 11th century Persian poet Omar Khayyam, during his own trial.

At time of writing, prosecutors were seeking Yorov's imprisonment for up to five more years in relation to additional charges of fraud and "insulting the president," increasing Yorov's total possible jail term from 25 to 30 years.

Lawyer Shukhrat Kudratov remains behind bars despite promises by authorities to release him in late 2016. Kudratov was initially imprisoned in 2015 after acting as defense counsel for opposition figure Zayd Saidov.

## Freedom of Media

Over the past year, at least 20 journalists have fled the country, fearing persecution for their professional activities. Journalists perceived to be critical of the government are subjected to harassment and intimidation. As a cult of personality around President Rahmon has risen, journalists are subjected to ever stricter provisions regarding the way they must refer to him and his family. As of April 2017, a new law mandates that all media must refer to Rahmon as "The Founder of Peace and National Unity, Leader of the Nation, President of the Republic of Tajikistan, His Excellency Emomali Rahmon."

In November 2016, authorities reversed a decision made weeks earlier to deny the accreditation of six Radio Ozodi journalists, a US government-supported station, after the radio station reported that Rahmon's third daughter had been appointed a deputy head of the foreign ministry's international organizations department.

In July, parliament passed amendments allowing security services to monitor individuals' online activities, including by keeping records of mobile messages and social media comments. Citizens who visit "undesirable" websites are subject to surveillance, fines, and detention. The legislation does not define what qualifies as an "undesirable website." For several years, the government has blocked access to popular social media sites, including VKontakte, Facebook, and YouTube. Authorities denied initiating blocks, despite multiple reports by internet service providers confirming government orders to censor websites.

In March, Tajikistan's Culture Ministry announced that books may not be brought into or taken out of the country without written approval, regardless of the language of the texts. Travelers are required to fill out an application "citing the name of the books, stating their language, the place of publication (and) the name of the authors…" Tajikistan's State Religious Affairs Committee and Interior Ministry have compiled a blacklist of banned books, most religious in nature, but also including books of spells.

## Freedom of Religious Expression

In August, continuing a multi-year campaign of strict control of religious practices, authorities introduced a new law urging citizens to "stick to traditional and national dress." While carrying no penalties, the law appears to specifically discourage women from wearing the Islamic hijab, and was accompanied by a campaign in the streets of the capital, Dushanbe, and other cities during which members of the State Women's Committee stopped women from wearing the hijab on the street, and urged them to replace it with the traditional Tajik scarf, in which the neck is left uncovered.

Also in 2017, authorities installed surveillance cameras in numerous mosques and subjected men wearing long beards to harassment and intimidation, in some cases forcibly shaving their beards.

In July, Protestant Pastor Bakhrom Kholmatov was sentenced to three years in prison for "singing extremist songs in church and so inciting 'religious hatred.'" Authorities raided Kholmatov's church and neighboring affiliate churches in

Sughd, harassing and beating church members. Kholmatov was previously arrested in April and kept in secret police custody. No action has been taken to investigate or prosecute the officials involved.

## Key International Actors

In September, the Tajik government did not attend the OSCE/HDIM, a longstanding human rights conference attended by governments and civil society activists, citing the participation of political activists the government believes are "terrorists." The decision to boycott the conference followed a year of Tajik authorities harassing the relatives of the activists who attended the 2016 HDIM.

As of July 1, the OSCE downgraded its presence in Tajikistan from a full-fledged mission to a Program Office. The restricted mandate, believed to be a result of the Tajik government's protests about the 2016 HDIM, led to the disbanding of five OSCE field offices, leaving the Dushanbe office as the sole OSCE monitoring mechanism in the country. The US Mission to the OSCE expressed dismay, emphasizing that field operations provide invaluable support to their host countries and facilitate open dialogue between the government and civil society.

Following a country visit to Tajikistan in June, the UN Special Rapporteur on the Right to Freedom of Expression David Kaye expressed concern regarding the government's repression of independent media, religious expression, and opposition voices, particularly those of detained IRPT members. Kaye urged the government to fully decriminalize defamation, make regulations regarding the operation of NGOs transparent and fair, and release all unlawfully imprisoned political activists, lawyers, and journalists.

In its annual report, the US Commission on International Religious Freedom (US-CIRF) once again designated Tajikistan as a "country of particular concern" with respect to religious freedom, and called on Tajikistan to achieve "major legal reform, an end to police raids, prisoner releases, and greater access to foreign coreligionists."

During his Central Asia tour in June, UN Secretary-General António Guterres traveled to Dushanbe, but failed to publicly articulate clear expectations for reform on human rights issues. Guterres mainly engaged with Tajik officials regarding climate change and anti-drug initiatives. He announced that the UN would help Tajikistan implement recommendations by the UN Human Rights Council.

HUMAN
RIGHTS
WATCH

"I Had a Dream to Finish School"
Barriers to Secondary Education in Tanzania

# Tanzania and Zanzibar

Upon taking office in October 2015, President John Pombe Magufuli committed to stamp out corruption in government and to be accountable to ordinary citizens, but instead has restricted basic freedoms through repressive laws and decrees. Critical journalists, politicians, human rights defenders, civil society activists and senior United Nations officials have faced various threats, intimidation and arbitrary detention by government authorities.

While the government made some progress in expanding access to free secondary education, it reinforced a discriminatory ban against pregnant students. It further stalled on a legal reform process to increase the age of marriage to 18 for boys and girls.

## *Freedom of Expression*

Authorities arbitrarily arrested or otherwise threatened and harassed rights activists and numerous prominent members of opposition parties who were critical of the government or the president.

On December 13, 2016, police arrested Maxence Melo, a prominent human rights defender and the owner of Jamii Forums, an independent whistleblower and reporting website, and Mike William, a shareholder of Jamii media, which hosts the site. The site hosted articles and debates exposing public sector corruption and criticizing government actions.

Police searched the offices of Jamii Forums and Melo's home without warrants. They reportedly made copies of several documents. On December 16, 2016, the Resident Magistrate Court of Dar es Salaam brought charges against Melo, under Tanzania's controversial Cyber Crimes Law, including obstruction of investigations for refusing to reveal the names of anonymous contributors to Jamii Forums, and "managing a domain not registered in Tanzania." Their trial began in August 2017 and continued at time of writing.

In March, police in Morogoro, about 200 kilometers west of Dar es Salaam, arrested Emmanuel Elibariki, a popular Tanzanian rapper known as Ney wa Mitego, following the release of his song that allegedly insulted the president. He was released without charges.

In July, Dar es Salaam's district commissioner ordered the arrest of Halima Mdee, a member of parliament and head of Bawacha, the women's wing of the opposition political party Chadema. Mdee had been critical of the president's decision to ban pregnant girls from public schools. Police charged her with insulting the president.

In August, police arrested Ester Bulaya, a Chadema member of parliament for Bunda, for conducting political activities outside her constituency. In separate events, police also arrested Godbless Lema, a Chadema member of parliament for Arusha Urban, and Salum Mwalimu, the party's deputy secretary general in Zanzibar, accusing both politicians of sedition.

In September, unidentified attackers shot and wounded Tundu Lissu, an outspoken member of parliament critical of the president, in Dodoma. Lissu, Chadema's chief whip, and president of the Tanganyika Law Society, was arrested multiple times in 2017, including for "hate speech" and for "insulting words that are likely to incite ethnic hatred."

In October, police arrested Zitto Kabwe, leader of ACT Wazalendo, an opposition party, and charged him with sedition, on grounds of breaching the Cyber Crime Act and the Statistics Act of 2015, which criminalizes the publication of statistics that are not endorsed by the National Bureau of Statistics.

On October 17, police raided a workshop organized by the Initiative for Strategic Litigation in Africa (ISLA), a Pan African organization advancing women's and sexual rights. Dar es Salaam's head of police ordered arbitrary arrests of 12 lawyers and activists, including two South Africans, one Ugandan and nine Tanzanian nationals, on spurious charges of "promoting homosexuality." Police released them on October 26, and deported all foreign lawyers a day later. The case against nine nationals remained open at time of writing.

On November 14, Tanzanian government officials in Dar es Salaam prevented Human Rights Watch from holding a news conference to launch a report on the abuse of Tanzanian migrant domestic workers in Oman and the United Arab Emirates.

On June 25, Home Affairs Minister Mwigulu Nchemba threatened to deregister organizations that challenged the president's controversial June 22 statement banning pregnant girls and teen mothers from attending school, and threats to prosecute or deport anyone working to protect rights of lesbian, gay, bisexual, and transgender (LGBT) people.

In September, Tanzania's National Assembly passed the Electronic and Postal Communications (Online Content) Regulations, which aim to control content used on social media, and impose onerous fines on individual users and online providers.

## Freedom of Media

The government shut down or threatened privately owned radio stations and newspapers, ended live transmissions of parliamentary debates, and ordered the prosecution of at least 10 individuals over posts on social media. In March, President Magufuli publicly warned media outlets to "be careful, watch it."

In March, Dar es Salaam's regional commissioner, Paul Makonda, who leads all executive functions in the region, raided, with armed security, the offices of Clouds FM Media Group, an independent broadcaster, and demanded the airing of a defamatory video implicating a local pastor. The station refused to broadcast the video.

In June, authorities banned the independent newspaper Mawio for two years over articles linking former presidents to alleged mismanagement of mining deals. In September, the government banned Mwanahalisi, a weekly newspaper, for two years, on claims of "unethical reporting" and "endangering national security" for an article calling for prayers for Tundu Lissu, an opposition party member. In October, authorities banned Raia Mwema, a weekly newspaper, for 90 days for publishing an article deemed critical of Magufuli's presidency.

## Women's and Girls' Rights

In July 2016, Tanzania's Constitutional Court declared child marriage unconstitutional and ordered the government to set 18 as the minimum age of marriage within one year of its ruling. The ruling settled a January 2016 case filed by the Msichana Initiative, a girls' rights organization, challenging Tanzania's discriminatory marriage law. In September, Tanzania's attorney general, George Masaju, appealed the ruling.

In December 2016, the government abolished tuition fees and indirect costs for primary and lower secondary schools. The measure boosted secondary school enrollment, but the poorest students still face obstacles, including long distances to school and costs.

Many girls regularly experience sexual harassment and exploitation by teachers in schools. Schools lack adequate protection and confidential reporting mechanisms.

Corporal punishment of students is a widespread, lawful practice in Tanzania's secondary schools, which violates international standards.

Girls also face discrimination in schooling. School officials can automatically expel pregnant girls and married girls from school. In May, the Ministry of Education, Science and Technology presented re-entry guidelines to amend the regulations and ensure that girls can return to school after pregnancy. Tanzania's National Assembly did not endorse the guidelines.

Thousands of Tanzanian women working as domestic workers in the Middle East face labor rights violations and other abuses. Tanzania has no law to protect migrant workers overseas, and weak safeguards facilitate abuse of workers.

## Sexual Orientation and Gender Identity

In mid-2016, the government initiated an unprecedented crackdown on the rights of LGBT people and their advocates. Senior government officials threatened to arrest gays and their social media followers and to deregister organizations "promoting" homosexuality. They banned the distribution of water-based lubricant, raiding and closing drop-in centers and private clinics that provide services targeting key populations, including men who have sex with men (MSM), sex workers, and people who use drugs.

In December 2016, Dar es Salaam police raided a workshop on HIV prevention among key populations, and briefly detained eight participants. In Zanzibar, police detained nine men for several days on suspicion of homosexual conduct, and subjected them to forced anal examinations, a form of torture.

In March, police arrested a man, 19, suspected of homosexuality based on his Instagram posts and subjected him to an anal exam. Several activists were arrested for holding meetings. In July, President Magufuli stated that "even cows disapprove of" homosexuality. In September, Zanzibar police arrested 20 people at a workshop for parents of key populations and accused them of homosexuality.

Several organizations reported that the crackdown has resulted in HIV-positive men failing to access their anti-retroviral treatment, while other MSM have stopped accessing testing and preventive services.

## Asylum Seekers and Refugees

In 2017, Tanzania hosted over 240,000 refugees who entered the country from Burundi since April 2015, following the political unrest in Burundi. In July, President Magufuli ordered the suspension of registration and naturalization of thousands of Burundian refugees, and publicly urged them to voluntarily return to Burundi.

## Key International Actors

Tanzania summarily expelled three heads of UN agencies, including Awa Dabo, the United Nations Development Programme (UNDP) country director. UNDP was reportedly critical of the conduct of elections in Zanzibar.

In June, Tanzania withdrew from the Open Government Partnership Initiative, a multilateral initiative aimed at promoting government openness, and improving service delivery, government responsiveness, combatting corruption and building greater trust.

In August, three African regional rights experts issued a joint letter of appeal to Tanzania's president regarding his June 22 statement on pregnant girls.

In July, the UN independent expert on the enjoyment of human rights by persons with albinism, Ikponwosa Ero, visited Tanzania, welcoming government measures to decrease attacks against persons with albinism, but finding that people with albinism live in a "very fragile situation." She further expressed concern on the use of schools as protection centers for children with albinism.

In September, the UN Committee on the Rights of Persons with Disabilities heard the case of a man with albinism who was attacked by two men, and had not received government compensation for the abuses suffered. The committee concluded that the government had failed to take all necessary measures to prevent acts of violence and to efficiently investigate and punish those acts. The committee further urged the government to promptly prosecute attacks against persons with albinism and to criminalize using body parts for witchcraft.

# Thailand

Thailand's National Council for Peace and Order (NCPO) junta failed in 2017 to keep its repeated promises made at the United Nations and elsewhere to respect human rights and restore democratic rule. The government announced the national human rights agenda in November, but did not end repression of civil and political liberties, imprisonment of dissidents, and impunity for torture and other abuses.

## *Sweeping, Unchecked, and Unaccountable Military Powers*

Section 44 of the 2014 interim constitution allows Prime Minister Gen. Prayuth Chan-ocha, in his concurrent position as NCPO chairman, to wield absolute power without oversight or accountability. The 2017 constitution, promulgated in March, endorses the continuance of this power, thereby guaranteeing that both the NCPO and officials operating under its orders cannot be held accountable for their rights violations. An unelected Senate and other elements of the new constitution lay the foundations for prolonged military control even if the junta fulfills its promise to hold elections in November 2018.

## *Freedom of Expression*

Media outlets face intimidation, punishment, and closure if they publicize commentaries critical of the junta and the monarchy, or raise issues the NCPO considers to be sensitive to national security—including the repression of basic rights.

Media outlets that refused to fully comply, including Voice TV, Spring News Radio, Peace TV, and TV24, were temporarily forced off the air in March, April, August, and November respectively. These stations were later allowed to resume broadcasting when they agreed to practice self-censorship, either by excluding outspoken commentators or avoiding political issues altogether.

In August, government officials charged prominent academic Dr. Chayan Vaddhanaphuti and four other participants at the International Conference on Thai Studies, held in August in Chiang Mai province, with violating the NCPO ban on public assembly by more than five people. The real reason for the charges appears to have been academic discussions that the junta deemed critical of military rule, and the fact that some participants took photos of themselves holding messages criticizing the military's heavy-handed monitoring of proceedings.

On November 27, Thai security forces violently dispersed a peaceful protest in Songkhla province and stopped protesters from submitting a petition to General Prayuth against the construction of a coal-fired power plant. At least 16 protest leaders were arrested.

The junta continued to use sedition (article 116 of the criminal code) and the Computer-Related Crime Act (CCA) to criminalize criticism and peaceful opposition to military rule. Since the 2014 coup, at least 66 people have been charged with sedition. In August, authorities charged veteran journalist Pravit Rojanaphruk and two prominent politicians—Pichai Naripthaphan and Watana Muangsook—with sedition and violating the CCA for their Facebook commentaries about Thailand's political and economic problems.

Thailand's revised CCA, which became effective in May, provides the government with broad powers to restrict free speech and enforce censorship. The law uses vague and overbroad grounds for the government to prosecute any information online that it deems to be "false" or "distorted," including allegations against government officials regarding human rights abuses. Even internet content that is not found to be illegal under the act can be banned if a government computer data screening committee finds the information is "against public order" or violates the "good morals of the people."

People charged with *lese majeste* (article 112 of the penal code, insulting the monarchy) are systematically denied bail and held in prison for months or years while awaiting trial. In August, after eight months of pre-trial detention, prominent student activist Jatupat (Pai) Boonphatthararaksa was sentenced to two years and six months in jail for posting on his Facebook page a critical BBC Thai profile of Thailand's new king, Maha Vajiralongkorn Bodindradebayavarangkun.

Since the coup, authorities have arrested at least 105 people on lese majeste charges, mostly for posting or sharing critical commentary online. Some have been convicted and sentenced to decades of imprisonment, including a man sent to prison in June for 35 years (a 50 percent reduction of the original sentence because he confessed to the alleged crime) based on 10 critical Facebook posts.

### Secret Military Detention, Torture, and Military Courts

Under NCPO Orders 3/2015 and 13/2016, military authorities can secretly detain people for a wide range of offenses, and hold them for up to seven days without charge, access to lawyers, or any safeguards against mistreatment. The government also regularly uses military detention, in which abuses during interrogation occur with impunity, in its counterinsurgency operations against suspected separatist insurgents in the southern border provinces of Pattani, Yala, and Naradhiwat.

The NCPO in 2017 rejected calls by human rights groups to disclose information about persons held in secret military detention, and summarily dismissed all allegations that soldiers tortured detainees. The junta did not move 369 cases (involving the prosecution of approximately 1,800 civilians) out of military courts and into civilian courts as required by international law.

The NCPO continued to summon members of the opposition Pheu Thai Party and the United Front for Democracy Against Dictatorship (UDD), as well as anyone accused of opposing military rule, for "attitude adjustment." Failure to report to the junta's summons is considered a criminal offense.

### Enforced Disappearances

Since 1980, the UN Working Group on Enforced or Involuntary Disappearances has recorded 82 cases of enforced disappearance in Thailand. Many of these cases implicated government officials, including the enforced disappearances of prominent Muslim lawyer Somchai Neelapaijit in March 2004 and ethnic Karen activist Por Cha Lee "Billy" Rakchongcharoen in April 2014. None had been resolved at time of writing.

In July, Thai security officials were reportedly involved in the abduction of exiled anti-monarchy activist Wuthipong "Ko Tee" Kachathamakul in Laos. Police did not make any progress in investigating what happened to land rights activist Den Khamlae, another suspected victim of enforced disappearance who went missing near his home in Chaiyaphum province in April 2016.

Thailand signed the International Convention for the Protection of All Persons from Enforced Disappearance in January 2012, but has yet to ratify the treaty. The penal code still does not recognize enforced disappearance as a criminal offense. In February, the junta-appointed National Legislative Assembly suddenly suspended its consideration of the Prevention and Suppression of Torture and Enforced Disappearance Bill, and the government still has not clarified whether the bill will be reintroduced.

The government-appointed Committee to Receive Complaints and Investigate Allegations of Torture and Enforced Disappearance is an administrative body with little authority or political will to seriously act in cases. It falls far short of what can be considered to be an adequate substitute for domestic legislation criminalizing torture, ill-treatment, and enforced disappearance.

## Lack of Accountability for Politically Motivated Violence

In spite of evidence showing that soldiers were responsible for most casualties during the 2010 political confrontations with the UDD, or "Red Shirts," that left at least 90 dead and more than 2,000 injured, no military personnel or officials from the government of former Prime Minister Abhisit Vejjajiva have been charged for killing and wounding civilians at the time. On the other hand, numerous UDD leaders and supporters faced serious criminal charges for their street protests in 2010.

In August, the Supreme Court's Criminal Division for Political Office Holders acquitted former Prime Minister Somchai Wongsawat and other senior government officials for their roles in the violent crackdown on the People's Alliance for Democracy (PAD) protesters in October 2008, which left two people dead and more than 400 injured.

There was no significant progress during the year in investigating and prosecuting alleged abuses and criminal offenses committed by the People's Democratic Reform Committee (PDRC) during political confrontations in Bangkok in 2013 and 2014.

## Human Rights Defenders

The killings of more than 30 human rights defenders and other civil society activists since 2001 remained unresolved.

Government pledges to develop measures to protect human rights defenders remained unfulfilled. Meanwhile, Thai authorities and private companies continued to frequently use defamation lawsuits and other criminal charges to retaliate against individuals reporting human rights violations.

Authorities charged Sirikan Charoensiri of the Thai Lawyers for Human Rights (TLHR) with sedition and other criminal offenses that could result in at least 10 years' imprisonment. The junta initiated these lawsuits in retaliation for her professional activities representing 14 student activists arrested in June 2015 after staging peaceful protests in Bangkok.

In March 2017, in response to domestic and international pressure, the Internal Security Operations Command announced it would end its legal action against Somchai Homlaor, Pornpen Khongkachonkie, and Anchana Heemmina, who accused the military of torturing suspected separatist insurgents in the southern border provinces. On October 24, prosecutors informed the police that the case had formally been dropped.

In August, the National Legislative Assembly approved the revised law on the National Human Rights Commission of Thailand that will seriously weaken the agency and strip away its independence, thus transforming it into a de facto government mouthpiece.

## Violence and Abuses in Southern Border Provinces

Since January 2004, Barisan Revolusi Nasional (BRN) insurgents have committed numerous violations of the laws of war. More than 90 percent of the 6,800 people killed in the ongoing armed conflict in Thailand's southern border provinces have been civilians.

In April, BRN issued a statement opposing a Malaysia-brokered peace dialogue between the Thai government and separatist groups in the loose network of Majlis Syura Patani. BRN insurgents pointed to abusive, heavy-handed tactics by government security forces to recruit new members to the insurgency and justify their acts of violence. In May, suspected insurgents detonated two bombs at Big C Supermarket in Pattani province, injuring at least 61 people, including children.

The government has not prosecuted members of its security forces responsible for illegal killings and torture against ethnic Malay Muslims. In many cases, Thai authorities provided financial compensation to the victims or their families in exchange for their agreement not to pursue criminal prosecution of officials.

## Refugees, Asylum Seekers, and Migrant Workers

Thailand has not acceded to the 1951 Refugee Convention and its 1967 protocol. Thai authorities continued to treat asylum seekers, including those whom the United Nations recognizes as refugees, as illegal migrants subject to arrest and deportation.

In May, the government transferred M. Furkan Sökmen—a Turkish educator allegedly connected to the Gulen movement, which Turkey blames for orchestrating the 2016 coup attempt—to the custody of Turkish authorities despite UN warnings that he would face persecution and serious rights violations if returned to Turkey.

In September, the Internal Security Operations Command (ISOC) announced a policy to push back Rohingya refugees seeking to enter Thailand by boat. The government also refused to allow the UN Refugee Agency, UNHCR, to conduct refugee status determinations for Rohingya asylum seekers, and planned to put those who landed in indefinite detention in squalid immigration lockups. Over 60 ethnic Uighurs from China have been held in indefinite detention since March 2014.

Migrant workers from Burma, Cambodia, Laos, and Vietnam are vulnerable to physical abuses, indefinite detention, and extortion by Thai authorities; severe labor rights abuses and exploitation by employers; and violence and human trafficking by criminals who sometimes collaborate with corrupt officials.

Migrant workers remained fearful of reporting abuses to Thai authorities due to lack of effective protection. In June, 14 Burmese migrant workers were brought to court on criminal defamation charges after they filed a complaint with the National Human Rights Commission of Thailand alleging that their employer—Thammakaset Company Limited, a chicken farm in Lopburi province—violated their rights.

When the government in June enacted the Decree Concerning the Management of Foreign Workers' Employment, tens of thousands of registered and unregistered migrant workers from Cambodia, Burma, Laos, and Vietnam fled Thailand, fearing arrest and harsh punishment.

The government declared that combating human trafficking was a national priority, including by enforcing the Human Trafficking Criminal Procedure Act. In July, the Bangkok Criminal Court sentenced 62 people—including former army advisor Lt. Gen. Manas Kongpan—to prison terms of up to 94 years for trafficking and mistreatment of Rohingya migrants. However, improvements in suppressing human trafficking in the fishing sector were still limited.

The US State Department maintained Thailand on its Tier 2 (Watch List) in its annual Trafficking in Persons (TIP) Report. The European Commission raised concerns about human trafficking and forced labor on Thai fishing boats and put Thailand on formal notice for possible trade sanctions connected to illegal, unreported, and unregulated fishing.

## Anti-Narcotics Policy

The government failed to pursue criminal investigations of extrajudicial killings related to anti-drug operations, especially the more than 2,800 killings that accompanied then-Prime Minister Thaksin Shinawatra's "war on drugs" in 2003.

There has been no progress in the government's plan to remove methamphetamine from category 1, the most serious classification in the controlled substance list, in order to ease prison overcrowding and facilitate drug users' access to rehabilitation. The Interior Ministry and military continued to operate boot camp-style forced rehabilitation of drug users.

## Key International Actors

The UN and Thailand's major allies urged the junta to respect human rights and return the country to democratic civilian rule through free and fair elections. During the Human Rights Committee's review of Thailand's obligations under the ICCPR in March, the Office of the UN High Commissioner for Human Rights (OHCHR), as well as many foreign governments and human rights groups, expressed concerns regarding violations of fundamental rights and freedoms since the coup.

US President Donald Trump received Prime Minister Prayuth at the White House on October 2 but did not publicly raise rights concerns. The US military sought to restore its previous close engagement with Thailand's military.

Australia's foreign minister and defense minister separately visited Thailand in August; neither publicly mentioned human rights concerns.

# Tunisia

Seven years after ousting its authoritarian president, Zine el-Abidine Ben Ali, Tunisia is still facing numerous challenges in consolidating human rights protection.

Tunisian lawmakers have made important steps for the consolidation of women's and detainees' rights but have failed to establish key institutions mandated by the constitution for human rights protection, such as the Constitutional Court. They have also adopted laws that threaten the democratic transition, such as the administrative reconciliation law, which grants amnesty for state officials accused of corruption.

Authorities arbitrarily imposed travel restrictions on hundreds under a state of emergency declared in November 2015. Civilians continued to face prosecution in military courts for certain offenses. Laws criminalizing sodomy continued to send men accused of consensual homosexual conduct to prison, often after compulsory anal testing to prove their sexual conduct, although Tunisia committed to taking steps to end the use of forced anal exams. There was no progress on accountability for torture, as most complaints, filed years ago, including for ill-treatment and torture during the dictatorship, remained stalled at the prosecution phase.

## Constitution

The 2014 constitution upheld many key civil, political, social, economic, and cultural rights. However, the constitution does not abolish the death penalty, even though authorities have observed a de facto moratorium on its application since the early 1990s.

Authorities made some progress in harmonizing legislation with the constitution.

For example, the 2014 constitution guarantees judicial independence and called for establishing a Supreme Judicial Council (SJC) to make judicial appointments and oversee the discipline and career progression of judges. On November 16, 2015, parliament approved a law creating the SJC. On October 23, 2016, 33 out of 45 members of the council were elected by their peers (judges, lawyers, bailiffs, notaries, and law professors), a radical change from the previous system under Ben Ali where government officials appointed them, undermining judicial independence.

The constitution envisages the creation of a Constitutional Court empowered to rule on the constitutionality of laws, and to invalidate laws that do not conform with human rights standards affirmed in the constitution. On December 3, 2015, parliament adopted a law creating the Constitutional Court, but at time of writing, authorities had yet to set up the court and appoint its members.

## *Freedom of Expression*

In 2011, the transitional authorities liberalized the press code and law pertaining to the broadcast media, eliminating most of the criminal penalties these laws impose on speech offenses. However, authorities continued to resort to the penal code and the Code of Military Justice, to prosecute people for speech offenses.

A Tunis court used article 128 of the penal code, which criminalizes "accusing, without proof, a public agent of violating the law," to sentence Walid Zarrouk, a former prisons officer and member of the Union for a Republican Police, on November 23, 2016, to one year in prison for a television interview in which he accused Tunisian authorities of fabricating charges against those who criticize them. The same day, another chamber of the same court sentenced Zarrouk to eight months for his criticism of the interior minister in a daily newspaper. And on February 7, 2017, a Tunis court sentenced him to one year in prison for Facebook posts that criticized an investigative judge and a judiciary spokesperson. Zarrouk was still serving his time in prison at time of writing. The charges were defamation in both cases.

Nabil Rabhi, a Tunisian blogger arrested on July 23, was sentenced on August 5 to six months in prison and fined 1,200 dinars (US$487) under article 125 for Facebook posts "insulting" public figures. In his social media posts, published on July 21, Rabhi used vulgar language in describing Hafedh Caïd Essebsi, the executive director of the Nidaa Tounes Party and son of the Tunisian president, as well as other Nidaa Tounes members.

Penal code article 125 that criminalizes "insulting a public official" has served in practice as a means by which the police can arrest individuals—some of whom ended up being prosecuted and imprisoned—merely for arguing with police, being slow to heed orders, or were suspected when they filed a complaint of being likely to file a complaint against police.

Salam and Salwa Malik, two journalists, were sentenced in May 2017 to six months in prison, later reduced to a fine. They were accused of insulting the police during a raid on their house seeking to arrest their brother, during which a policeman threatened to "blast" their 7-year-old nephew, according to Salwa Malik.

Separate trials of two prominent bloggers, Mariem Mnaouer and Lina Ben Mhenni, continued in 2017. The first was prosecuted in 2012 for insulting a state official, and the second in 2014 under the same charge, shortly after each had filed complaints against police officers for using violence against them.

In October, a couple was sentenced to several months in prison for public indecency and insulting a state official under article 125 of the penal code after police found them kissing in their car.

## *Transitional Justice and Accountability*

On December 24, 2013, the National Constituent Assembly (NCA) adopted the Law on Establishing and Organizing Transitional Justice.

The law established a Truth and Dignity Commission tasked with uncovering the truth about abuses committed between July 1955, shortly before Tunisia's independence from France, and the law's adoption in 2013. The commission declared, in June 2016, that it had received 62,065 complaints from people alleging human rights abuses and had begun processing them.

On November 17 and 18, 2016, the Truth and Dignity Commission held the first public hearings of victims of human rights violations, which were aired live on national TV and radio stations. Since then, the commission has held 11 more hearings covering various human rights violations during the Ben Ali and Bourguiba presidencies, such as torture, abuses against union rights, sexual assault against women imprisoned for political reasons, and violations of economic rights.

The transitional justice process suffered a major setback with the adoption, on September 13, 2017, of a law on "reconciliation in the administrative field" by a vote of 117 votes to nine, with one abstention. The law offers blanket impunity for those civil servants implicated in corruption and embezzlement of public funds but who did not benefit personally. For this category of persons, the law terminates any ongoing prosecutions and trials and preempts future trials. The law would thus impair the work of the commission, which had a mandate to investigate economic crimes and situate them within the larger picture of systematic corruption under President Ben Ali.

The transitional justice process suffered also from lack of criminal accountability for serious human rights violations. Authorities have failed in the seven years since Ben Ali's overthrow to investigate or hold anyone accountable for the vast majority of torture cases, including notorious cases of death in custody as a result of torture. The transitional justice law mandates the establishment of specialized chambers within the civil court system to try human rights violations that occurred between July 1955 and December 2013. To date, the specialized chambers have not been set up.

## *Security and State of Emergency*

The state of emergency President Beji Caïd Essebsi declared after a suicide attack on a bus that killed 12 presidential guards in November 2015 remained in effect at time of writing. It is based on a 1978 decree that empowers authorities to ban strikes or demonstrations deemed to threaten public order, and to prohibit gatherings "likely to provoke or sustain disorder." It gives the government broad powers to restrict media and to place persons under house arrest.

Authorities arrested Chafik Jarraya, a well-connected businessman, and several other men in May 2017 and placed them under "house arrest" in an unknown location, a procedure allowed under the state of emergency. Authorities said the men were involved in corruption and represented a threat to state security and later transferred them to prisons.

During their house arrest, they were not allowed to see their lawyers or to contact their families for more than 10 days, a clear breach of due-process rights. Jarraya and the previous head of the anti-terror unit, Saber Lajili, are being prosecuted before a military court on charges of treason and sharing intelligence with a foreign army, punishable by the death penalty. The other men are being prosecuted before a financial court for financial crimes.

Since the emergency law came into force in November 2015, at least 139 Tunisians have been confined without charge under indefinite house arrest orders that the police deliver orally, thus hindering the ability of the affected person to mount a court challenge. The measures have created economic hardship, stigmatized those targeted, and prevented them from pursuing their study or business.

Authorities eased the measures in 2016; however, many of those affected remain subject to a travel ban procedure called "S17," applied to anyone the state suspects of intending to join a fighting group abroad. The procedure allows restrictions on movement both abroad and inside Tunisia. A person placed under S17 procedure risks lengthy questioning whenever they are stopped at a routine police check. The procedure is based on vague language in the law regulating the work of the Ministry of Interior. Authorities have also imprisoned around 200 fighters who returned from Syria, Iraq, or Libya.

## Women's Rights

Tunisia continued to make progress towards the consolidation of women's rights.

On July 26, parliament adopted a comprehensive law on fighting violence against women, which includes key elements that are essential to prevent violence against women, protect domestic violence survivors, and prosecute abusers. The law eliminated from the penal code a provision that allowed a rapist to escape punishment if he married his victim.

On September 14, the Ministry of Justice announced that it had rescinded a 1973 directive prohibiting the marriage of a Tunisian woman to a non-Muslim man unless the man provides a certificate of conversion to Islam. If a Tunisian woman married a non-Muslim abroad, who lacked this certificate, Tunisian authorities would refuse to register their marriage.

In August, Caïd Essebsi called for reforming this discriminatory legislation. But Tunisia's personal status code continues to retain some discriminatory gender provisions, including designating the man as the head of the household and allowing males in certain instances to receive double the share of inheritance than their female relatives.

## Drug Law

On April 25, parliament adopted an amendment to ease the harsh drug law, the enforcement of which lands hundreds of young people each year in prison on charges of possessing small quantities of marijuana for personal use.

The Ben Ali-era Law 92-52 imposes a mandatory one-year jail sentence for narcotics use or possession. The amendment gives judges discretion to weigh mitigating circumstances in order to reduce the punishment.

## Sexual Orientation and Gender Identity

Article 230 of the penal code punishes consensual same-sex conduct with up to three years in prison. Anal testing is used as the main form of evidence in order to convict men of sodomy. Shams, a Tunisian LGBTI association, said that at least 10 men were prosecuted under article 230 in various parts of Tunisia in 2017, and two were sentenced to two years in prison.

In April, The National Council of the Medical Order urged doctors to cease conducting forced anal and genital examinations, calling it "a practice which is contrary to human dignity and physical and moral integrity of the human being." On September 21, during the adoption of the report from its Universal Periodic Review (UPR) at the United Nations Human Rights Council (UNHRC), Tunisia accepted a recommendation from Ireland to immediately cease the practice of forced anal examinations, but it did not accept 11 other recommendations to repeal article 230 of the penal code.

## Key International Actors

On September 21, the outcome report from the third UPR of Tunisia was adopted during session 27 of the UNHRC. Tunisia accepted 198 recommendations out of the 264 made by states parties, including pledging to boost accountability for abuses by security forces, eliminate torture and other ill-treatment, and ensure that counterterrorism and national security measures do not jeopardize human rights.

On April 13, Tunisia signed a declaration to the African Court on Human and Peoples' Rights that grants individuals and nongovernmental organizations the right to access the court directly with human rights complaints against it.

# Turkey

An April 2017 referendum, which voters approved by a slim margin, introduced constitutional amendments switching Turkey to a presidential system of governance, the most significant change to its political institutions in decades. The referendum took place under a state of emergency imposed after the July 15, 2016 attempted military coup, and in an environment of heavy media censorship, with many journalists and parliamentarians from the pro-Kurdish opposition in jail.

The new presidential system, which consolidates the incumbent's hold on power, is a setback for human rights and the rule of law. It lacks sufficient checks and balances against abuse of executive power, greatly diminishing the powers of parliament, and consolidating presidential control over most judicial appointments. The presidential system will come fully into force following elections in 2019.

## *State of Emergency Measures*

Under the state of emergency in place since July 2016, the president presides over the cabinet, which can pass decrees without parliamentary scrutiny or the possibility of appeal to the constitutional court. Many decrees adopted contained measures that undermine human rights safeguards and conflict with Turkey's international human rights obligations.

Public officials continued to be dismissed or suspended by decree without due process, with more than 110,000 dismissed since July 2016. Hundreds of media outlets, associations, foundations, private hospitals, and educational establishments that the government shut down by decree remained closed in 2017, their assets confiscated without compensation.

In January, the government ruled on the establishment of an ad hoc commission to review decisions made under the state of emergency. The commission lacks independence since its seven members are appointed by the same authorities responsible for approving dismissals and closures. There is a right of further appeal, but mechanisms for redress and compensation are likely to take many years. In the meantime, those affected have no right to work in public service, their bank accounts are frozen, and passports confiscated. At time of writing, over 102,000 people had applied to the commission, which had not yet begun to issue decisions such as overturning dismissals and closures.

People continued to be arrested and remanded to pretrial custody on terrorism charges, with at least 50,000 remanded to pretrial detention and many more prosecuted since the failed coup. Those prosecuted include journalists, civil servants, teachers and politicians as well as police officers and military personnel. Most were accused of being followers of the US-based cleric Fethullah Gülen. Turkey's government and courts say the Gülen movement masterminded the coup attempt, and deem it a terrorist organization, labelled the Fethullahist Terrorist Organization (FETÖ). Prosecutions of individuals charged with FETÖ membership often lacked compelling evidence of criminal activity.

Among many ongoing trials against soldiers alleged to have participated in the coup attempt, in October a court in Muğla sentenced 40 military personnel to life imprisonment in connection with the attempted assassination of President Erdoğan on July 15, 2016.

## *Freedom of Expression, Association, and Assembly*

The prosecution and jailing of journalists for doing their work continued after the closing of media outlets since the coup attempt. Turkey is the world leader in jailing journalists and media workers as they face criminal investigations and trials, with around 150 behind bars at time of writing. Most newspapers and television channels lack independence and promote the government's political line.

Several major, politically motivated trials of journalists on terrorism-related charges began in 2017. The evidence consisted of writing and reporting, which did not advocate violence, alongside unsupported allegations of connections with terrorist organizations or involvement in the coup attempt. That trials continued despite the lack of credible evidence to substantiate the charges demonstrated lack of judicial independence.

At the first trial hearing in March of a group of journalists accused of FETÖ membership, the court decided to release on bail 21 defendants who had been held in prolonged pretrial detention. However, following criticism of the decision by a pro-government journalist, there was an appeal against the release of eight of the 21, and a new investigation against the other 13. As a result, none were released from detention. The High Council of Judges and Prosecutors subsequently suspended the three judges who had ruled to release the journalists, plus the prosecutor at the hearing.

The trial of 19 journalists, board members and other personnel from the *Cumhuriyet* newspaper on charges of FETÖ links began on July 24. Well-known reporter Ahmet Şık is among five defendants still in prolonged pretrial detention.

In a separate case concerning *Cumhuriyet* reporting on Turkish intelligence services supplying arms to Syrian opposition groups, an Istanbul court in June sentenced Enis Berberoğlu, member of parliament for the opposition Republican People's Party (CHP), to 25 years' imprisonment for providing video of the weapons to the newspaper. He remained in prison at time of writing, although a court of appeal overturned his conviction and ordered a retrial. Proceedings against *Cumhuriyet* Ankara bureau chief Erdem Gül and former editor Can Dündar on related allegations continued.

The trial of 31 *Zaman* newspaper journalists and media workers on coup attempt charges began in September, a full 14 months after many of the defendants were remanded to pretrial detention. They face life imprisonment if convicted for writings that did not advocate violence.

During 2017, Kurdish journalists were prosecuted and detained on charges of links with the armed Kurdistan Workers' Party (PKK) over their reporting. Dozens of journalists and public figures who participated in a solidarity campaign with the now closed pro-Kurdish *Özgür Gündem* newspaper were prosecuted for terrorist propaganda. While most received suspended sentences and fines, in May an Istanbul court sentenced Murat Çelikkan, a journalist and human rights defender, to 18 months' imprisonment. He was released after two months.

The blocking of websites and removal of online content continued, with an April court order upholding the request by the state Information and Communication Technologies Authority to block the entire Wikipedia website. Turkey made 45 percent of global requests to Twitter to remove online content in the first six months of 2017.

Authorities frequently imposed arbitrary bans on public assemblies and violently dispersed peaceful demonstrations.

Nuriye Gülmen and Semih Özakça, an academic and teacher respectively, dismissed under the state of emergency, were repeatedly detained and released by police as they carried out a sit-in, and later hunger strike in Ankara to demand reinstatement. In May, a court remanded them to prison pending trial charged with terrorist membership. Özakça was released in October and Gülmen in December. In advance of their first trial hearing in September, 16 lawyers representing them were detained and 14 subsequently remanded to prison. In November, their lead defense lawyer Selçuk Kozağaçlı, head of the shuttered Contemporary Lawyers Association, was also arrested.

Under the state of emergency in Turkey over 500 lawyers have been jailed pending trial, and over 1,000 prosecuted. Most lawyers facing prosecution are accused of alleged FETÖ links.

For a third year, the Istanbul governor's office banned the annual Istanbul Gay and Trans Pride marches in June 2017, citing concerns about security threats and public order.

## Human Rights Defenders

In 2017, the crackdown on critical voices in Turkey was extended to human rights defenders. In June, Taner Kılıç, chair of Amnesty International Turkey, was detained and placed in pretrial detention for alleged FETÖ links. The politically motivated and unsubstantiated charges against him are grounded on the claim he had an encryption app known as ByLock on his phone, which the government claims links him to FETÖ. Kılıç denies the accusation, and his legal team produced two expert reports demonstrating that ByLock was never downloaded on his phone.

In July, 10 human rights defenders were detained during a routine meeting in Istanbul, accused of aiding unnamed terrorist organizations. Eight were remanded to pretrial detention, including Amnesty Turkey director İdil Eser, Citizens' Assembly member and Amnesty Turkey founder Özlem Dalkıran, and two defenders of German and Swedish nationality.

The charges are based on random material, including Amnesty International campaign material, and a grant application, gathered from the defenders' phones and laptops. On October 25, a court ordered their release on bail. The

**HUMAN
RIGHTS
WATCH**

## IN CUSTODY
Police Torture and Abductions in Turkey

two foreign nationals left the country. The case against Taner Kılıç was combined with that against the 10 defenders, and the trial against the 11 continued.

In November, Osman Kavala, a businessman and well-known figure in civil society in Turkey, was jailed pending investigation on trumped up charges, including involvement in the July 2016 coup.

## Torture and Ill-Treatment in Custody

Cases of torture and ill-treatment in police custody were widely reported through 2017, especially by individuals detained under the anti-terror law, marking a reverse in long-standing progress, despite the government's stated zero tolerance for torture policy. There were widespread reports of police beating detainees, subjecting them to prolonged stress positions and threats of rape, threats to lawyers, and interference with medical examinations.

There were credible reports of unidentified perpetrators believed to be state agents abducting men in at least six cases, and holding them in undisclosed places of detention in circumstances that amounted to possible enforced disappearances. At least one surfaced in official custody and three others were released after periods of two to three months. The men had all been dismissed from civil service jobs for Gülenist connections.

## Resumption of Conflict and Crackdown on Kurdish Opposition

In parallel with the resumption of armed clashes between the military and the armed Kurdistan Workers' Party (PKK) in the southeast, the government pursued a crackdown on elected parliamentarians and municipalities from pro-Kurdish parties.

During 2017, up to 13 Peoples' Democratic Party (HDP) deputies were held in prolonged pretrial detention on terrorism charges. Two of them, party co-leader Selahattin Demirtaş and former co-leader Figen Yüksekdağ, have been in detention since November 2016. Yüksekdağ was stripped of her parliamentary seat in February after an earlier terrorism propaganda conviction was upheld. Demirtaş' trial began in Ankara on December 7 but, allegedly due to security concerns, he was not permitted to appear in court, a failure to respect his due process rights.

In the southeast, the government took control in 89 municipalities won by the HDP's sister party in the region, the Democratic Regions Party (DBP), and suspended their democratically elected co-mayors under suspicion of terrorism offenses, with at least 70 jailed pending trial at time of writing. This violates the rights to political association and participation and freedom of expression of the elected officials, and denies the right to political representation for those who elected them.

## Refugees and Migrants

Turkey continues to host the largest number of refugees in the world. Of the 3.4 million in Turkey, most come from Syria, but Turkey also hosts asylum seekers from Afghanistan, Iraq and other countries. A migration deal with the European Union, which offers aid in exchange for preventing onward migration to the EU, continued. Restrictions on the Syrian border impeded access to Turkey for refugees.

There remained high rates of child labor and large numbers of child refugees and asylum seekers not attending school, with a particularly precarious situation for non-Syrians. As of the latest available update, nearly half a million Syrian refugee children are currently enrolled in school, but at least 380,000 remain out of school. Lack of access to full protection is compounded by exploitative labor conditions and poverty.

## Key International Actors

The EU-Turkey relationship deteriorated further in 2017, with a resolution in the European Parliament and some member states calling for a suspension of the EU accession process over the country's worsening rights record.

Relations between Turkey and several EU member states and the US were marked with tensions over arbitrary detention of their nationals on trumped up terrorism charges.

Germany's Chancellor Angela Merkel ruled out greater EU-Turkey economic cooperation through a renewed Customs Union in the current political context. In June, the German cabinet decided to relocate troops from a Turkish airbase to one in Jordan.

While the US State Department raised concerns on matters relating to human rights in Turkey, relations between the US and Turkish governments were dominated by Turkey's objection to US backing for PKK-affiliated Kurdish forces in Syria in operations against the extremist Islamic State (IS) forces. Turkey sees the extradition of US-based cleric Fethullah Gülen as another priority.

In April, the Council of Europe Parliamentary Assembly voted to reinstate a full monitoring procedure against Turkey after 13 years, citing "serious concerns" about respect for human rights, democracy and the rule of law. The Venice Commission, the Council of Europe's constitutional advisory body, criticized Turkey's state of emergency measures and move to a presidential system, citing "excessive concentration of executive power in the hands of the president" and lack of "necessary checks and balances."

In July, United Nations experts on the right to assembly and association, human rights defenders, arbitrary detention, and judges and lawyers, jointly called the arrests of human rights defenders in Turkey a "witch-hunt" and called on the UN Human Rights Council to address the deterioration of human rights in the country.

The Council of Europe Commissioner for Human Rights and UN special rapporteur on freedom of expression both published reports on Turkey's deeply problematic record on free speech and media freedom.

# Turkmenistan

Turkmenistan remains one of the world's most closed and oppressively governed countries. President Gurbanguly Berdymukhamedov and his associates control all aspects of public life. Elections extended Berdymukhamedov's presidential term for another seven years.

The government effectively bans all forms of religious and political expression not approved by authorities, tightly controls media, and allows no independent monitoring groups. Dozens of people remain victims of enforced disappearance.

In 2017, Turkmenistan hosted the 5th Asian Indoor and Martial Arts Games (AIMAG), marking a rare departure from the country's self-imposed isolation, but prompting the government to clamp down further on expression and other rights.

## Presidential Elections

In February, Berdymukhamedov was re-elected to a third term with 97.7 percent of the vote in an election that lacked meaningful political competition. The election assessment mission of the Organization for Security and Co-operation in Europe's Office for Democratic Institutions and Human Rights (OSCE/ODIHR) noted that it "took place in a strictly controlled political environment" that lacked pluralism and media independence.

In October, Berdymukhamedov announced the revival of the People's Council, in theory the state's highest representative body, headed by the president. Composed of a wide variety of elected and unelected officials, it can change and pass constitutional laws and issue decrees, further eviscerating separation of powers in Turkmenistan.

## Freedom of Media and Information

The government keeps a tight grip on all print and electronic media in Turkmenistan. Activists and correspondents who provide information to foreign outlets face government retaliation. Authorities withdrew press accreditation and visas for several foreign reporters who planned to cover the AIMAG, claiming lack of capacity to accommodate them.

Saparmamed Nepeskuliev—a freelance contributor for Alternative News of Turkmenistan (ANT), a Europe-based news website and Radio Free Europe/Radio Liberty (RFE/RL)—convicted on bogus charges in 2015, continued to serve a three-year sentence.

In four separate incidents during July, and again in November, unidentified men severely harassed Soltan Achilova, an RFE/RL reporter, including with death threats.

In December 2016, authorities in Dashoguz province beat and arrested Khudayberdy Allashov, an RFE/RL Turkmen-language service correspondent, and his mother on charges of possessing chewing tobacco. Allashov had reported on such topics as wage delays and food shortages. Both were released in February after a court convicted them and issued a three-year suspended prison sentence.

In November 2016, authorities threatened to enforce a suspended sentence against another RFE/RL contributor, Rovshen Yazmuhamedov, if he did not stop working with the outlet.

Internet access in Turkmenistan remains limited and heavily state-controlled.

## Civil Society

Independent groups that carry out human rights work can operate openly only in exile. Legal regulations impose serious challenges for organizations to register. Unregistered work by nongovernmental organizations (NGOs) is illegal.

In March, Yazdursun Gurbannazarov was elected Turkmenistan's first ombudsperson, following the 2016 ombudsmen law's entry into force. It is unclear whether authorities will allow this new institution independence and impartiality.

Anyone who exposes or questions government policies faces constant threat of reprisal. The Turkmen government ignored calls by several international actors to free Gaspar Matalaev, an ANT activist, imprisoned in October 2016 on false fraud charges in retaliation for his work monitoring state-sponsored forced labor in the cotton harvest.

In October 2016, Galina Vertryakova was convicted on bogus extortion charges after she criticized, on Russian social media, government policies, and was freed through amnesty in December 2016. In October, police accused Vertyakova of spreading secret state information.

In September, on the eve of the AIMAG, police threatened Galina Kucherenko, an animal rights activist, with 25 years' imprisonment for her posts on Russian-language social media. For several weeks in September, October and November, her internet was inexplicably cut off and she has been under constant surveillance. In November, unidentified officials came to her home and threatened to have her imprisoned.

In August, unknown people verbally assaulted Natalia Shabunts, one of the few openly active human rights defenders inside Turkmenistan. They publicly shouted racial slurs at Shabunts, and demanded that she go to Russia.

## Freedom of Movement

The government arbitrarily bans from foreign travel people it considers disloyal, including the families of dissidents and prisoners. The Ruzimatov family, relatives of an exiled former official, remained banned from traveling abroad.

## Housing and Property Rights

Authorities in Ashgabat failed to provide adequate compensation or redress to residents whose homes were expropriated and demolished for large-scale renewal and beautification projects in the five years before the AIMAG. Authorities denied justice to, harassed, and intimidated some residents who sought fair compensation.

In May and August, officials in Ashgabat ordered residents of several neighborhoods to remove air conditioners in multi-story apartment buildings to improve the city's appearance before the AIMAG. In many cases, authorities forcibly removed them, damaging property and leaving residents without air conditioning despite heat often exceeding 40 degrees Centigrade (104 degrees Farenheit).

## Freedom of Religion

The government forbids unregistered religious groups and congregations and severely punishes religious activity not approved by authorities. The state strictly censors religious literature. Turkmenistan does not allow conscientious objection to military service.

According to Forum 18, an independent religious freedom group, only two religious communities are known to have successfully re-registered under a March 2016 religious law.

In June, TIHR reported that a court sentenced to lengthy prison terms 12 military officers accused of spreading non-traditional Islam.

In January, ANT reported the deaths in 2016 of Lukman Yaylanov and Narkuly Baltayev. In July, ANT reported the death in June of Aziz Gafurov. Yavlanov and Baltayev were sentenced in 2013, and Gafurov in 2015, for involvement in an informal Sunni study group. All three were inmates at Ovadan-Tepe, known for torture and long-term incommunicado detention. Authorities forced the deceased's families to sign a nondisclosure agreement about the bodies of the deceased.

ANT also reported that in December 2016, 52-year-old Yoldash Khojamuradov committed suicide at home after police accused him of being a Wahhabi (the term used by the government to designate people as extremists) and interrogated him for several weeks, pressuring him to name other Wahhabis.

## Political Prisoners, Enforced Disappearances, and Torture

Torture and ill-treatment are widespread and continue with impunity. It is impossible to determine the exact number of people jailed on politically motivated grounds due to the complete lack of transparency in the justice system, closed trials, and severe repression that precludes independent monitoring of these cases.

Political dissident Gulgeldy Annaniyazov, arrested in 2008 and sentenced to 11 years on charges that were not made public, remained imprisoned. Turkmen authorities have said he is being held in a penal colony in Tejen, however this has not been independently confirmed.

In October 2016, Turkmen authorities accused an estimated 100 men of having links to the Gülen movement and its leader, Fethullah Gulen, accused by the

Turkish government of organizing the 2016 coup attempt in Turkey. In February, 18 were sentenced in closed trials to up to 25 years in prison on various charges, including incitement to hatred and involvement in a criminal organization. In July, authorities sentenced another 40 men from Lebap province to lengthy prison terms, reportedly on similar charges. The authorities' isolation of these men and intimidation of their families made it impossible to independently confirm some aspects of these reports, including that the men were tortured in custody.

Dozens of people arrested in the late 1990s and early 2000s remain forcibly disappeared in Turkmen prisons. Following their arrest, the government denied their families access to them and information on their whereabouts. In 2017, the fate and whereabouts of these men remained unknown, except in the cases of three who died and whose bodies authorities returned to families, confirmed by Prove They Are Alive, an international campaign against enforced disappearances in Turkmenistan. Among them is Tirkish Tyrmyev, former head of the State Border Service, sentenced to 10 years on abuse of office charges.

In 2012, just before his scheduled release, authorities arbitrarily extended his sentence by nearly eight years for supposedly violating prison rules. Prove they Are Alive reported new enforced disappearances, especially among people convicted on religious extremism charges.

Authorities continued to ignore the United Nations Human Rights Committee's decision to release Boris Shikhmuradov, the former foreign minister and a victim of an enforced disappearance as determined by the committee.

## Sexual Orientation and Gender Identity

Homosexual conduct is a criminal offense under Turkmen law, punishable by a maximum two-year prison sentence.

## Key International Actors

Turkmenistan's international partners spoke out more than in previous years about human rights abuses. An exception was UN Secretary-General António Guterres, who met President Berdymukhamedov in June but who only mentioned "commitments to respect human rights" in the context of countering terrorism.

Another exception was the Olympic Council of Asia (OCA), owner and operator of the AIMAG. Despite its commitment within its own constituent charter to uphold the principles of human dignity and press freedoms in host countries, the OCA was silent on Turkmenistan's abuses. When asked at a press conference in Ashgabat about Turkmenistan's violation of media freedoms, a top OCA official said, "We have instructed the organising committee not to cooperate with media that is unwilling to ... report positively about sport. Our attention is directed at the development of sport and positive, real media".

In February, the European Union highlighted several shortcomings in Turkmenistan's presidential elections and called on the Turkmen authorities to address them.

During its annual human rights dialogue with Turkmenistan, the EU raised concerns about torture and conditions in detention and suppression of fundamental freedoms.

Several international actors spoke against press freedom violations. In a December 2016 media interview, Nisha Desai Biswal, then-US assistant secretary of state for south and central Asian affairs deplored the government's treatment of RFE/RL journalists. A March EU statement called "on Turkmenistan to immediately release Saparmamed Nepeskuliev."

In its annual human rights report on Turkmenistan, the US Department of State flagged general human rights concerns, and for the first time reported the status of Shikhmuradov and others on the Prove They Are Alive list under the section on disappearances.

During a January meeting of the OSCE Permanent Council, Switzerland—acting also on behalf of Iceland and Canada—called on Turkmenistan to investigate Tirkish Tyrmyev's death and raised concern about enforced disappearances.

In their respective concluding observations, the UN Human Rights Committee and the UN Committee Against Torture urged the government to investigate enforced disappearances. The former also urged the government to, among other things, end informal travel bans, allow "a truly independent media," "decriminalize sexual relations between consenting adults of the same sex," and provide effective remedies to people affected by forced evictions.

13 UN experts have requested, but not received, access to the country.

573

# Uganda

The government of President Yoweri Museveni, in power since 1986, continues to violate free association, expression, and assembly rights.

Protests over constitutional amendments that would entrench the power of the ruling elites—one to remove the presidential age limit, allowing Museveni to run for office in 2021, and another to dramatically ease government's ability to acquire land without meaningful advance consultation and adequate compensation—met with heavy-handed partisan response from police.

Security officials' continue to use excessive use of force with impunity, for example there was no investigation into the November 2016 military and police assault in Kasese that left over 100 people, including children, dead.

## Freedom of Assembly

The police unjustifiably block, restrict, and disperse peaceful assemblies and demonstrations by opposition groups, relying on the vague and overbroad 2013 Public Order Management Act (POMA) which grants police wide discretionary powers over public and private gatherings.

In July, police arrested and detained 56 members of the opposition Forum for Democratic Change (FDC) for three days on charges of holding an "unlawful assembly" at a private home on the outskirts of Kampala. Police also arrested and detained members of the opposition Democratic Party in July and August as they prepared to address the public to oppose the draft constitutional amendment lifting the age limit of presidential candidates. In contrast, in August and September police in Arua, West Nile and Kabale escorted demonstrators advocating in favor of the constitutional amendment.

In September and October, police arrested several prominent opposition leaders and protestors in several towns during protests againt the lifting of presidential age limits. Police killed at least two people in Rukungiri and one in Amolatar while using excessive force to disperse what they deemed "illegal rallies." And yet, in October, police charged opposition leader Kizza Besigye and two colleagues with murder, assault, inciting violence, and unlawful assembly for the deaths of protestors in Rukungiri.

## Freedom of Expression and Media

The government consistently uses a variety of laws to curtail media freedom and free expression. Government regulatory bodies, particularly the Uganda Communications Commission, applies laws and broadcasting guidelines selectively to arbitrarily shut down radio stations and curtail speech critical of the president or the government.

After parliamentarians clashed during age limit debates in September, the commission issued a directive banning any live broadcasts of the controversial issue. Police arrested four journalists in Lira for providing coverage of public protests and two Kampala-based editors were charged with offensive communication in October for their newspapers' ongoing reporting.

Dr. Stella Nyanzi, a research fellow at Makerere University, faced charges of "cyber harassment" and "offensive communication" in April for Facebook posts challenging the president and his wife, the education minister, for failure to fulfil a campaign pledge to provide sanitary pads to school girls. Nyanzi spent more than a month in prison before being released on bail; charges remain pending.

Television journalist Getrude Tumusiime Owitware received threats online and was later abducted and beaten by unknown assailants, after posting on social media in support of Nyanzi's campaign. Owitware was later found at a police station in Kampala. No one had been arrested at time of writing for her abduction and beating.

Journalists, at times, were interrogated and faced charges of criminal defamation, which remains law, despite a 2014 ruling from the African Court on Human and People's Rights that such laws are an unnecessary restriction on free expression.

## Extrajudicial Killings and Absence of Accountability

The government refused to investigate the conduct of its forces during military and police operations at the palace compound of the region's cultural institution and other locations in Kasese, western Uganda from November 26 to 27, 2016. Over 100 civilians were killed including at least 15 children, in operations the government argued were required to curtail activities of the institution's royal guards.

In March, the police increased previous figures they claimed were inaccurate, stating the death toll was 103. Without credible independent investigations, the true death toll remains unknown. Witnesses report government-orchestrated efforts to silence them from speaking about the events on November 27.

At least 180 people, including six children, face murder, treason, and terrorism charges, among other crimes, for the November violence, including deaths of 14 police. Charges remain pending.

Government spokespeople argued Uganda "does not lack independent investigative capability", but deflected calls for such investigations into the role of government forces in the killings of civilians in Kasese, arguing that there could not be interference as the matter was before a court and therefore *sub-judice, or* pending litigation. However, none of the ongoing prosecutions involve soldiers or police.

## *Illegal Detention and Torture*

Police and prosecutors consistently failed to investigate cases of illegal detention and torture of suspects and did not charge a single security personnel under Uganda's Prevention and Prohibition of Torture Act.

Human Rights Watch and other organizations have documented numerous instances of mistreatment and torture, particularly in Nalufenya police post in Jinja, eastern Uganda over several years. Suspects are often held at the post for periods well beyond the 48 hours, permitted by law. Defendents arrested after the Kasese violence and detained in Nalufenya showed clear signs of mistreatment and torture during court hearings. The magistrate ordered an investigation, which remained pending at time of writing.

In May, defendants charged in the March murders of police commander Andrew Kaweesi, his driver and bodyguard also had visible injuries and complained in open court of severe beatings by police in Nalufenya. In July, the high court ordered medical examinations of 19 suspects. Photos later emerged of the mayor of Kamwenge, in western Uganda, bearing horrific injuries which he said resulted from beatings by police investigating the same murders.

## Freedom of Association

In September, police raided three nongovernmental organizations (NGOs) offices, alleging "illicit financial transactions" and "subversive activities" and froze bank accounts. The organizations publicly opposed amending constitutional limits on presidential age. The raids were widely seen as part of a crackdown on civic activism opposed to the change.

The 2016 Non-Governmental Organisations Act includes troubling and vague "special obligations" of NGOs, such as a requirement that groups should "not engage in any act which is prejudicial to the interests of Uganda or the dignity of the people of Uganda." Another provision criminalizes activities by organizations that have not been issued with a permit by the government regulator, fundamentally undermining free association rights. A separate provision allows imprisonment for up to three years for violating the act.

Police failed to make progress on accountability for over two dozen break-ins at NGO offices, all known for work on sensitive subjects—including human rights and corruption. In two instances, guards were killed, but no one was arrested.

## Sexual Orientation and Gender Identity

Same-sex conduct remained criminalized under Uganda's colonial-era law, which prohibits "carnal knowledge" among people of the same sex. Concerns remain that the 2016 NGO law effectively criminalizes legitimate advocacy on rights of lesbian, gay, bisexual, and transgender (LGBT) people.

In August, activists canceled Pride celebrations in Kampala and Jinja after the minister of ethnics and integrity threatened organizers with arrest and violence.

Police failed to end the practice of forced anal examinations of men and transgender women accused of consensual same-sex conduct. These examinations lack evidentiary value and are a form of cruel, inhuman, and degrading treatment that may constitute torture.

## Lord's Resistance Army

The Lord's Resistance Army (LRA) remains active in central Africa, but allegations of killings and abductions have reduced. In May, the Ugandan military withdrew its forces mandated to fight the LRA in Central African Republic. (See Chapter on Central African Republic.)

The trial of former LRA commander, Dominic Ongwen—charged with 70 counts of war crimes and crimes against humanity as part of attacks on internally displaced persons (IDP) camps, including murder, enslavement, sexual and gender-based crimes, and conscription of child soldiers—continued before the International Criminal Court (ICC). Warrants for four other LRA commanders have been outstanding since 2005; three are believed dead. Joseph Kony is the only LRA ICC suspect at large.

In February, prosecutors in the case against former LRA fighter Thomas Kwoyelo, charged before Uganda's International Crimes Division (ICD), brought 93 counts including wilful killing, taking hostages, and extensive destruction of property under article 3 of the Geneva conventions and Uganda's penal code. Kwoyelo has been imprisoned since March 2009 and the start of his trial has been postponed numerous times.

## Key International Actors

The United States and European Union publicly raised serious concerns over the disproportionate use of force by security forces in Kasese and repeatedly called for independent investigations. European Union member states also offered to support witness protection and evidence protection for investigations into the Kasese violence but the government declined. The US also criticized the government's curtailing of dissent on the constitutional amendment as "heavy-handed."

The US ended providing military advisors and support to Uganda's army for the counter-LRA operations but continues to provide significant funding for logistics and training to the African Union Mission in Somalia, where Uganda contributes troops.

The US provides over US$440 million annually to support Uganda's health sector. US President Trump reinstated the Mexico City policy, which stops organizations from supporting safe abortion care, negatively affecting Ugandan organizations working to clarify the legal status of abortion services.

In August 2016, the World Bank suspended new lending to Uganda due in part to weaknesses in social *safeguards* monitoring after allegations emerged that workers on a bank-funded road project sexually abused children. In May, the bank resumed funding, arguing improved compliance.

# Ukraine

Throughout 2017, all sides in the armed conflict in eastern Ukraine frequently ignored the 2015 Minsk Agreements and endangered civilians and civilian infrastructure as they continued hostilities. Total impunity for conflict-related torture and arbitrary, unacknowledged detention persisted on both sides. The government failed to hold perpetrators of attacks on journalists to account. New government measures further contracted media pluralism, new regulations curbed freedom of expression and association, and new draft laws propose further restrictions. In Crimea, Russian authorities persecuted pro-Ukraine activists and the Crimean Tatar community for their peaceful opposition to Russia's occupation of the peninsula.

## *Hostilities in Eastern Ukraine*

The armed conflict in eastern Ukraine between the Ukrainian government and separatist armed groups supported by Russia entered its fourth year. In late January and early February, all sides to the conflict engaged in massive shelling of populated areas, severely damaging essential civilian infrastructure and killing civilians. According to the Organization for Security and Co-operation in Europe (OSCE) Special Monitoring Mission (SMM), as of mid-November, at least 425 civilians were injured or killed in 2017, more than the previous year.

In April, a paramedic with the OSCE's SMM was killed when the car he was riding in blew up on a landmine in eastern Ukraine.

Ukrainian authorities took several positive steps to facilitate civilians' crossing of the contact line. But lack of adequate sanitary and other infrastructure at crossing points, especially from the nongovernment-controlled side, exposure to landmines and shelling, and long waits in extreme temperatures continued to cause civilians undue hardship.

## *Cruel and Degrading Treatment and Arbitrary Detention*

In the self-proclaimed Donetsk People's Republic (DPR) and Luhansk People's Republic (LPR) Russia-backed de facto authorities continued to carry out arbitrary detentions and enforced disappearances, holding civilians for weeks without any contact with lawyers, families, or the outside world. Local security services operated without checks and balances. The overall absence of the rule of law in separatist-controlled areas leaves detainees extremely vulnerable to abuse.

In February, security officials in Donetsk forcibly disappeared and held incommunicado two Russian activists, releasing them two weeks later without explanation.

In May, a military tribunal in Donetsk convicted Igor Kozlovsky, a local academic with pro-Ukrainian views, on trumped-up charges of illegal weapons possession and sentenced him to 32 months in prison. The circumstances of Kozlovsky's arrest, his prolonged incommunicado detention, and the use of clearly fabricated evidence indicate political motivation.

In June, security officials in Donetsk arbitrarily detained and forcibly disappeared a pro-Ukrainian blogger and a regular contributor to Radio Free Europe/Radio Liberty, Stanyslav Aseev, who was still in custody at time of writing.

By the end of 2016, the Security Service of Ukraine (SBU) released all detainees it had been unlawfully holding, in secret, in its Kharkiv branch. However, the SBU's leadership continued to deny its responsibility for secret detentions and enforced disappearances. The military prosecutor's probe into these practices yielded no meaningful results.

In August, SBU officials in the Dnipropetrovsk region unlawfully detained and tortured Daria Mastikasheva, later charging her with treason for allegedly working as a Russian agent. At time of writing, no one was found responsible for Mastikasheva's ill-treatment.

## Rule of Law, Accountability for Past Abuses

Justice for conflict-related abuses and crimes committed during the 2014 Maidan protests, which led to the ouster of the Ukrainian government and mass disturbances in Odesa, remained elusive.

In September, an Odesa court acquitted all 19 defendants who were on trial for offenses related to the May 2, 2014 mass disturbances, which pitted pro-Maidan and anti-Maidan groups against each other, and in which 48 people died and more than 200 were injured. All 19 were anti-Maidan activists, five of them were in pretrial custody since 2014. The court stated that the prosecution "did not even try to prove their guilt." The SBU immediately accused two of them of separatism, and a court remanded them to custody. A crowd of Ukrainian nationalists attempted to storm the courtroom as judges announced the verdict, using tear gas and stones, and injuring about 20 police officers. Police investigated, but at time of writing no one was held accountable. One pro-Maidan suspect remains at liberty, pending trial.

In two ongoing trials against former members of the Berkut riot police battalion, charged with killing and injuring protestors in the February 2014 Maidan protests, several of the defendants were on the run, and others repeatedly failed to appear in court. Five more former Berkut members are currently on trial in Kyiv on similar charges. In July, another former Berkut member, Sergei Loboda, was detained and is under house arrest pending investigation.

On April 7, a Kyiv court sentenced seven former members of the Tornado police battalion to 8 to 10 years in prison, and its leader to 11 years in prison, for torture and rape of civilians. Four others received suspended sentences.

## Freedom of Expression and Media

The government took several steps to restrict freedom of expression and media freedom, justifying them by the need to counter Russia's military aggression in eastern Ukraine and anti-Ukraine propaganda.

In April, President Petro Poroshenko signed a law requiring activists and journalists investigating corruption to publicly declare their personal assets, much like government officials. On July 10, the president introduced amendments that would annul the requirement but instead introduced burdensome and unjustified reporting requirements for all nonprofit organizations and individuals working for them.

On May 16, Poroshenko signed a decree banning major Russian companies and their websites from operating in Ukraine, citing national security. The ban targeted Russian social media used by millions of Ukrainians daily; language and accounting software; the websites of many Russian television stations and other media; and Yandex, an internet browser, and its many affiliates.

In June, a court annulled the 2016 acquittal of Ruslan Kotsaba, a journalist who had been prosecuted on treason charges for calling for boycotting conscription. His re-trial was ongoing at time of writing.

Ukrainian authorities made no meaningful effort to investigate a pro-government site, Myrotvorets, which in 2016 and 2017 leaked the personal data of hundreds of journalists working in separatist-controlled regions. Some government officials publicly supported Myrotvorets' actions.

In July and August, the SBU expelled or denied entry to several foreign journalists—three from Russia and two from Spain—for allegedly engaging in anti-Ukrainian "propaganda."

The 2016 murder of renowned journalist Pavel Sheremet remained unsolved. The 2016 attacks on the offices of Inter, a television station widely perceived to be pro-Russian, also remained uninvestigated.

## Sexual Orientation and Gender Identity

Ukraine has taken several significant steps to improve the protection and inclusion of the country's lesbian, gay, bisexual, and transgender (LGBT) people. In February, the Ministry of Health proposed a medical form for patients choosing a family doctor, which acknowledges transgender people and allows people to choose whether to indicate their gender.

Law enforcement ensured the safety of participants in Marches for Equality in June and July 2017 in Kyiv and Odesa, but everyday homophobia and transphobia remains widespread.

In May 2017, around 30 young men assaulted several LGBT activists at a small rally in Kharkiv, burned their rainbow flag, and injured one activist and two police officers. Four of the attackers were detained.

## Palliative Care

Tens of thousands of patients with advanced cancer suffer from severe pain every year. The regulatory reforms adopted in recent years that made oral morphine available to patients have not been fully implemented. Healthcare workers lack proper education and training in pain treatment, or simply refuse to change their practices.

## Crimea

The human rights crisis in Crimea that began with Russia's occupation of the peninsula in 2014 persisted. Russian authorities thoroughly suppressed public criticism of Russia's actions there and criminally prosecuted people for criticizing the occupation. Most independent media and rights activists have had to leave. The few who remain are under increasing pressure from authorities.

Russian authorities in Crimea have targeted Crimean Tatars for their pro-Ukraine position, using criminal prosecutions for separatism and baseless terrorism-related charges. Authorities in Crimea also detained and imposed fines on Crimean Tatars who peacefully staged single-person pickets to protest the arrest and prosecution of others.

On September 11, a Russian court in Crimea found a prominent Crimean Tatar leader, Akhtem Chiygoz, guilty on charges of organizing "mass riots," following an unfair trial, and sentenced him to eight years in prison. In August, a court in Simferopol sentenced Server Karametov, a 76-year old Crimean Tatar, to 10 days' detention for "disobeying police orders" while holding a peaceful, single-person picket to protest Chiygoz's trial.

Chiygoz is deputy chairman of the Mejlis, the Crimean Tatars' elected representative body. In September, another Mejlis deputy chairman, Ilmi Umerov, was sentenced on separatism charges for stating in a media interview that Crimea should be returned to Ukraine. Russia's Supreme Court in 2016 declared the Mejlis an "extremist" organization and banned it. On October 25, after negotiations between Turkey and Russia, Russian authorities allowed Chiygoz and Umerov to leave Crimea for Turkey. On October 27, they arrived in Kyiv.

In January 2017, Russian authorities in separate incidents detained Nikolai Polozov and Emil Kurberdinov, lawyers representing Chiygoz and Umerov. A court sentenced Kurbedinov to 10 days' detention on bogus extremism charges, and the security service released Polozov after several hours.

On September 23, a Simferopol court convicted journalist Mykola Semena and handed him a 30-month suspended sentence for articles criticizing Russia's occupation.

The number of students in Crimea in classes with Ukrainian as the language of instruction plummeted from 13,589 in 2013 to 371 in 2016, according to a report by the Crimean Human Rights Group, a nongovernmental organization. Local law enforcement intimidated pro-Ukraine activists into canceling peaceful cultural and political events. One of the few remaining activists, Leonid Kuzmin, fled Crimea in August.

## Key International Actors

In September, the OSCE SMM's chief monitor, Ambassador Ertugrul Apakan, urged the sides to the conflict to "prioritise the protection of the civilian population" and to stop "positioning personnel and hardware in and around residential areas, and [...] imprecise weapons [...] in civilian-populated areas."

In a September report, the United Nations High Commissioner for Human Rights condemned repeated ceasefire violations in eastern Ukraine and their impact on civilian lives. In a separate September report, he noted that the human rights situation in Crimea "significantly deteriorated under Russian occupation."

In July, the European Union ratified a key trade agreement with Ukraine, and introduced visa-free travel for Ukrainian citizens. Its condemnation of abuse by Russia in Crimea and of abuses by Russia-backed armed groups in Donetsk and Luhansk regions is consistently strong. It raised concerns about media freedoms, torture prevention, and other issues at the EU-Ukraine human rights dialogue.

During the July EU-Ukraine summit, the EU underscored the need for Ukraine to pursue stronger in-country reforms against corruption. But the EU's willingness to press the government on rights issues did not always match its level of commitment to expanding and deepening its overall relationship. Except for its strong reaction to the measures targeting anti-corruption activists, the EU has failed to engage with the government on limitations to freedom of expression and association.

During a July visit to Kyiv, US Secretary of State Rex Tillerson highlighted the importance of anti-corruption and judiciary reforms as "critical to the success of Ukraine."

# United Arab Emirates

The United Arab Emirates' intolerance of criticism continued in 2017 with the detention of prominent Emirati rights defender Ahmed Mansoor for exercising his right to free expression. The government arbitrarily detains and forcibly disappears individuals who criticize authorities.

The UAE continued to play a leading role in the Saudi-led coalition, which has conducted scores of unlawful attacks in Yemen. The UAE was implicated in detainee abuse at home and abroad.

Labor abuses persist. Migrant construction workers face serious exploitation. The UAE introduced a domestic workers law providing them labor rights for the first time, but some provisions are weaker than those accorded to other workers under the labor law.

The UAE continued to ban representatives of international human rights organizations from visiting.

## *Freedom of Expression*

UAE authorities have launched a sustained assault on freedom of expression and association since 2011. UAE residents who have spoken about human rights issues are at serious risk of arbitrary detention, imprisonment, and torture. Many are serving long prison terms or have left the country under pressure.

The UAE's 2014 counterterrorism law provides for the death penalty for people whose activities "undermine national unity or social peace," neither of which the law defines.

In March, the UAE detained Ahmed Mansoor, an award-winning human rights defender, who is facing speech-related charges that include using social media websites to "publish false information that harms national unity." Before his arrest, Mansoor had called for the release of Osama al-Najjar, who remains in prison despite having completed a three-year prison sentence on charges related to his peaceful activities on Twitter.

In March, the UAE imposed a 10-year prison sentence on prominent academic Nasser bin-Ghaith, whom authorities forcibly disappeared in August 2015, for charges that included peaceful criticism of the UAE and Egyptian authorities.

Authorities imposed a three-year prison sentence on UAE-based Jordanian journalist Tayseer al-Najjar related to his online criticism of Israeli and Egyptian military actions in and near the Gaza Strip.

## Yemen Airstrikes and Detainee Abuse

The UAE is a leading member of the Saudi-led coalition operating in Yemen. Human Rights Watch has documented 87 apparently unlawful coalition attacks, some likely war crimes, that have killed nearly 1,000 civilians since March 2015.

Coalition members have provided insufficient information about the role their forces are playing in the campaign to determine which are responsible for unlawful attacks. In March 2015, the Emirati State news agency reported that the UAE had deployed 30 aircraft to take part in coalition operations. In March 2017, after a helicopter attacked a boat carrying Somali migrants and refugees off Yemen's coast, killing and wounding dozens, a member of the UAE armed forces said UAE forces were operating in the area but denied carrying out the attack.

The UAE leads counterterror efforts, including by supporting Yemeni forces carrying out security campaigns, in southern Yemen. Human Rights Watch has documented abuses by these forces, including excessive force during arrests, detaining family members of wanted suspects to pressure them to "voluntarily" turn themselves in, arbitrarily detaining men and boys, detaining children with adults, and forcibly disappearing dozens.

The UAE runs at least two informal detention facilities in Yemen and its officials appear to have ordered the continued detention of people despite release orders, forcibly disappeared people, and reportedly moved high-profile detainees outside the country. Former detainees and family members reported abuse or torture inside facilities run by the UAE and UAE-backed forces. Yemeni activists who have criticized these abuses have been threatened, harassed, detained, and disappeared.

### Arbitrary Detention, Torture, and Mistreatment of Detainees

The UAE arbitrarily detains and forcibly disappears individuals who criticize authorities within the UAE's borders. In February, a group of United Nations human rights experts criticized the UAE's treatment of five Libyan nationals who had been arbitrarily detained since 2014. The special rapporteur on torture said he received credible information that authorities subjected the men to torture. In May 2016, the Federal Supreme Court acquitted the men of having links to armed groups in Libya.

### Migrant Workers

Foreign nationals account for more than 88.5 percent of the UAE's population, according to 2011 government statistics. Many low-paid migrant workers remain acutely vulnerable to forced labor, despite some reforms.

The *kafala* (visa-sponsorship) system continues to tie migrant workers to their employers. Those who leave their employers can face punishment for "absconding," including fines, prison, and deportation.

The UAE's labor law excludes domestic workers, who face a range of abuses, from unpaid wages, confinement to the house, workdays up to 21 hours with no breaks, to physical or sexual assault by employers, from its protections. Domestic workers face legal and practical obstacles to redress.

The UAE has made some reforms to increase domestic worker protection. In September, the president signed a bill on domestic workers that guarantees domestic workers labor rights for the first time including a weekly rest day, 30 days of paid annual leave, sick leave, and 12 hours of rest a day. In some cases, the law allows for inspections of recruitment agency offices, workplaces, and residences, and sets out penalties for violations. But, the 2017 law does not prohibit employers from charging reimbursement for recruitment expenses and requires that workers who terminate employment without a breach of contract compensate their employers with one month's salary and pay for their own tickets home.

### Women's Rights

Discrimination on the basis of sex and gender is not included in the definition of discrimination in the UAE's 2015 anti-discrimination law.

HUMAN
RIGHTS
WATCH

# "Working Like a Robot"
Abuse of Tanzanian Domestic Workers in Oman
and the United Arab Emirates

Federal Law No. 28 of 2005 regulates personal status matters. Some of its provisions discriminate against women. For a woman to marry, her male guardian must conclude her marriage contract; men have the right to unilaterally divorce their wives, whereas a woman must apply for a court order to obtain a divorce; a woman can lose her right to maintenance if, for example, she refuses to have sexual relations with her husband without a lawful excuse; and women are required to "obey" their husbands. A woman may be considered disobedient, with few exceptions, if she decides to work without her husband's consent.

UAE law permits domestic violence. Article 53 of the penal code allows the imposition of "chastisement by a husband to his wife and the chastisement of minor children" so long as the assault does not exceed the limits of Islamic law. Marital rape is not a crime. In 2010, the Federal Supreme Court issued a ruling, citing the penal code, that sanctions husbands' beating and infliction of other forms of punishment or coercion on their wives, provided they do not leave physical marks.

## Sexual Orientation and Gender Identity

Article 356 of the penal code criminalizes (but does not define) "indecency" and provides for a minimum sentence of one year in prison. UAE courts use this article to convict and sentence people for zina offenses, which include same-sex relations as well as consensual heterosexual relations outside marriage.

Different emirates within the UAE's federal system have laws that criminalize same-sex sexual relations, including Abu Dhabi, where "unnatural sex with another person" can be punished with up to 14 years in prison.

In August, the UAE sentenced two Singaporean nationals who had been arrested in an Abu Dhabi shopping mall to one year in prison "for attempting to resemble women." An appeals court converted their sentence to a fine and deportation.

# United States

The strong civil society and democratic institutions of the United States were tested in the first year of the administration of President Donald Trump. Across a range of issues in 2017, the US moved backward on human rights at home and abroad.

Trump has targeted refugees and immigrants, calling them criminals and security threats; emboldened racist politics by equivocating on white nationalism; and consistently championed anti-Muslim ideas and policies. His administration has embraced policies that will roll back access to reproductive health care for women; championed health insurance changes that would leave many more Americans without access to affordable health care; and undermined police accountability for abuse. Trump has also expressed disdain for independent media and for federal courts that have blocked some of his actions. And he has repeatedly coddled autocratic leaders and showed little interest or leadership in pressing for the respect of human rights abroad.

The individuals most likely to suffer abuse in the United States—including members of racial and ethnic minorities, immigrants, children, the poor, and prisoners—are often least able to defend their rights in court or via the political process. Many vulnerable groups endured renewed attacks on their rights during the year. Other longstanding US laws and practices—particularly related to criminal and juvenile justice, immigration, and national security—continued to violate internationally recognized human rights.

## *Harsh Criminal Sentencing*

On any given day in the US, there are 2.3 million people in state and federal prisons and jails, the world's largest reported incarcerated population. Concerns about over-incarceration in prisons—partly due to mandatory minimum sentencing and excessively long sentences—have led some states and the US Congress to propose reforms. At time of writing, a bipartisan proposal for sentencing and corrections reform was gaining momentum in Congress, but the Trump administration had given no indication of support.

Thirty-one US states impose the death penalty. At time of writing, 23 people in eight states had been executed in 2017, all by lethal injection. Debate over lethal injection protocols continued, with several US states continuing to use experimental drug combinations and refusing to disclose their composition.

## Racial Disparities, Drug Policy, and Policing

Racial disparities permeate every part of the US criminal justice system, including in the enforcement of drug laws. Black people make up 13 percent of the population and 13 percent of all adults who use drugs, but 27 percent of all drug arrests. Black men are incarcerated at nearly six times the rate of white men.

Police continue to kill black people in numbers disproportionate to their overall share of the population. Black people are 2.5 times as likely as white to be killed by police. An unarmed black person is five times as likely to be killed by police as an unarmed white person.

The Trump administration has expressed almost unconditional support for the prerogatives of law enforcement officers, scaling back or altogether removing police oversight mechanisms. The US Department of Justice began to discontinue investigations into, and monitoring of, local police departments reported to have patterns and practices of excessive force and constitutional violations.

The administration reversed an order from the Obama administration limiting acquisition of offensive military weaponry by local police departments. In a speech in July, President Trump encouraged officers to use unnecessary force on suspects. Congress introduced the "Back the Blue Act," which would severely restrict civilians' rights to sue police officers who unlawfully injure them.

Despite voicing concern over the opioid crisis, the Trump administration signaled an intent to re-escalate the "war on drugs" and de-emphasize bipartisan public health approaches to drug policy. Attorney General Jeff Sessions rescinded his predecessor's Smart on Crime initiative, which had prioritized federal prosecutions of individuals accused of high-level drug offenses, reduced racial disparities in federal drug sentencing, and improved re-entry opportunities.

# SYSTEMIC INDIFFERENCE
Dangerous & Substandard Medical Care in US Immigration Detention

HUMAN
RIGHTS
WATCH

CIV|C
end isolation

## *Youth in the Criminal Justice System*

Nearly 50,000 youth age 17 and younger are held in juvenile prisons or other confinement facilities on any given day in the US, and approximately 5,000 more are incarcerated in adult jails or prisons. Every year, 200,000 people under 18 have contact with the adult criminal system, with many children tried automatically as adults.

The US continues to sentence children to life in prison without parole, although states increasingly reject its use: as of 2017, 25 states and Washington, DC had banned or did not use the sentence for children.

## *Poverty and Criminal Justice*

Poor defendants throughout the United States are locked up in pretrial detention because they cannot afford to post bail. A 2017 Human Rights Watch report demonstrated that pretrial detention—often resulting from failure to pay bail—coerces people, some innocent, into pleading guilty just to get out of jail. A movement to reduce the use of money bail is growing in the US, with several states implementing, and others considering, reform.

Many states and counties fund their court systems, including judges, prosecutors, and public defenders, partly or entirely via fees and fines imposed on criminal and traffic defendants. The privatization of misdemeanor probation services by several US states has led to abuses, including fees structured by private probation companies to penalize poor offenders.

## *Rights of Non-Citizens*

One week after his January 20, 2017 inauguration, President Trump issued an executive order to suspend the US refugee program, cut the number of refugees who could be resettled into the US in 2017, and temporarily ban entry of nationals from seven Muslim-majority countries. This and later versions of the order banning entry from various countries have been the subject of ongoing federal litigation.

In October, Trump signed an executive order resuming the refugee program but with new screening measures. The annual cap for refugee admissions for 2018 was set at 45,000, the lowest annual limit since Congress passed the Refugee Act in 1980.

On the back of rhetoric falsely conflating illegal immigration with increased crime, Trump also moved to make all deportable immigrants "priority" targets for deportation, penalize so-called sanctuary cities and states that have limited local police involvement in federal immigration enforcement; expand abusive fast-track deportation procedures and criminal prosecutions for immigration offenses; and increase the prolonged detention of immigrants, despite evidence, documented by Human Rights Watch and others, of abusive conditions in immigration detention.

In August, President Trump repealed a program protecting from deportation immigrants who arrived in the United States as children, putting hundreds of thousands of people who grew up in the US at risk of deportation. President Trump signalled he would support legislation that provided legal status for undocumented immigrants brought to the United States as children. However, in October the White House released a hard-line set of immigration principles and policies—including weakening protections for child migrants and refugees—it considers necessary components of any such legislative deal.

Some cities and states sought to increase protections for immigrants by creating funds for legal services, limiting local law enforcement involvement in federal immigration enforcement, and resisting efforts to defund "sanctuary" cities. Others sought to pass laws punishing such localities.

In December, Human Rights Watch reported on the impact of the Trump administration on immigration policies, profiling dozens of long-term residents with strong family and other ties within the US who were summarily deported. US law rarely allows for individualized hearings that weigh such ties, and most immigrants do not have attorneys to help them fight deportation.

At time of writing, seizures for deportation of undocumented people from the interior without criminal convictions had nearly tripled to 31,888 between the inauguration and the end of September 2017, compared with 11,500 during approximately the same period in 2016.

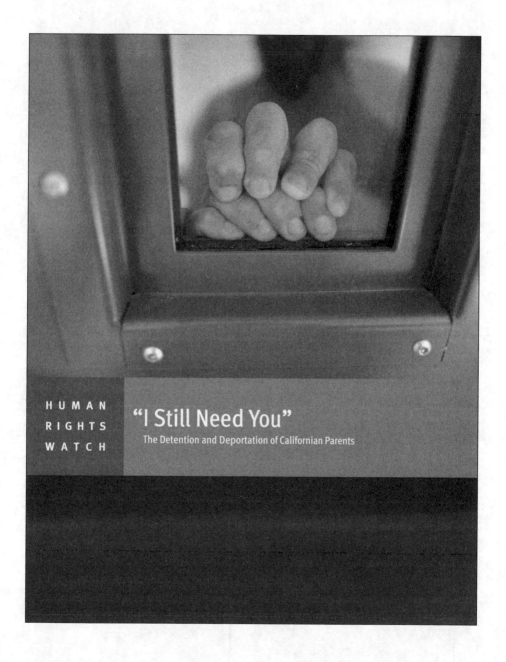

HUMAN
RIGHTS
WATCH

## "I Still Need You"
The Detention and Deportation of Californian Parents

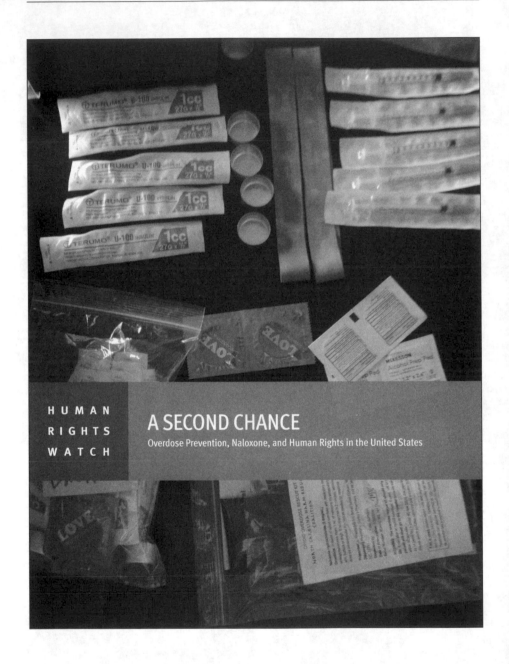

HUMAN
RIGHTS
WATCH

# A SECOND CHANCE
Overdose Prevention, Naloxone, and Human Rights in the United States

## Right to Health

To date, attempts in Congress to repeal the Affordable Care Act (ACA)—legislation that has greatly expanded access to health care for millions of Americans—have failed. However, the Medicaid program, private insurance subsidies, non-discrimination protections for lesbian, gay, bisexual, and transgender (LGBT) people, and other key elements of the ACA remained vulnerable to regulatory action by the Trump administration.

The Trump administration's opioid commission released an interim report endorsing numerous public health approaches, but did not recommend protecting Medicaid, which currently covers drug dependence treatment. The commission endorsed increased access to naloxone, the overdose reversal medication, but did not recommend that it be available over the counter, a potential game-changer in addressing the more than 90 deaths per day from opioid overdose in the US.

Around 1.5 million Americans live in nursing homes, where inappropriate and nonconsensual use of antipsychotic medications—for staff convenience or to discipline residents without a medical purpose—is widespread. To date, government agencies have not taken sufficient steps to end this practice.

## Disability Rights

The Trump administration's proposed cuts to the ACA, which provides crucial services to people with disabilities, and a proposed rollback of accessibility obligations under the Americans with Disabilities Act, could undermine the rights of people with disabilities. In July 2017, a man with a psychosocial disability, William Charles Morva, was executed in Virginia, 2017, despite pleas from lawmakers and UN experts to commute his sentence.

A 2017 Ruderman Foundation study found that one-third to one-half of all use of force by police in the US involve people with psychosocial or intellectual disabilities.

"I Want to Be Like Nature Made Me"

Medically Unnecessary Surgeries on Intersex Children in the US

## Women's and Girls' Rights

President Trump, his cabinet appointees, and the Republican-controlled Congress rolled back some important women's rights protections, domestically and in foreign policy, and pledged to dismantle others. Some state governments also eroded women's rights by introducing new laws with absurd restrictions on women's reproductive rights. Several high-profile media revelations related to sexual harassment and misconduct reinvigorated discussions around abuses suffered by women at work and in public places.

Congress passed legislation dismantling a rule protecting family planning funds in Title X, a national program that funds services to more than 4 million Americans, ensuring access to reproductive health care. The new legislation makes it easier for states to restrict Title X grants by creating eligibility requirements that could exclude certain family planning providers, like Planned Parenthood. This will leave many women without affordable access to cancer screenings, birth control, and testing and treatment for sexually transmitted infections.

Congressional proposals to repeal the ACA would have dealt a major blow to essential women's health services, including by preventing the nongovernmental organization Planned Parenthood from receiving federal funding, and allowing states to limit insurance coverage for an array of essential women's health benefits. Trump's proposed federal budget also called for massive Medicaid cuts.

Trump also issued an executive order on "promoting free speech and religious liberty," which will cut women off from access to reproductive health services. It invites agencies to issue regulations that would allow more employers and insurers to assert "conscience-based objections" to the preventive-care mandate of the ACA, which includes contraception. Religious employers are already exempt, and religious non-profits and certain closely held corporations also have accommodations. Following Trump's order, the Department of Health and Human Services effectively reversed the contraceptive coverage mandate by expanding exemptions to cover nearly any objecting employer.

The White House announced in August that it would scrap an equal pay initiative that was to go into effect in 2018. As a result, large employers and federal contractors will not be required to provide disaggregated information about employees' compensation to civil rights enforcement agencies. It also revoked executive orders that required federal contractors to comply with fair pay measures and a ban on forced arbitration of sexual harassment and discrimination claims. The Department of Education announced its intention to review and change guidelines on campus sexual assault, notably the Obama-era guidance on Title IX of Education Amendments Act of 1972.

Several states adopted highly restrictive laws on abortion and reproductive health. These include new bans on abortion in some circumstances or other restrictive measures in Texas, Arkansas, Kentucky, Iowa, Tennessee. Some states increased efforts to deny public family planning funds to providers who also offer abortion services.

Despite these significant assaults on women's human rights, the picture was not entirely grim. Congress passed the 2017 National Defense Authorization Act, which includes new protections for whistleblowers in military sexual assault cases and requires training on preventing sexual assault. Trump signed into law the Women, Peace, and Security Act of 2017, which aims to increase women's participation in conflict prevention and security.

New York State's 2017 law reform on child marriage dramatically reduces the circumstances under which children can marry.

Millions gathered for Women's Marches in Washington, DC, and in cities around the world to demand equality and justice.

## *Sexual Orientation and Gender Identity*

In the first five months of 2017, legislators in several states introduced more than 100 bills that would attack or undermine LGBT rights. In March 2017, North Carolina partially repealed a 2016 law requiring transgender people to use government facilities according to their sex assigned at birth and barring local governments from prohibiting discrimination against LGBT people. The 2017 provisions bar local governments from passing transgender-inclusive policies and prohibit local non-discrimination ordinances from protecting LGBT people until 2020.

In April, Mississippi enacted a law protecting individuals who discriminate based on their religious convictions regarding same-sex marriage, extramarital sex, and transgender people.

# A CHANGING PARADIGM

US Medical Provider Discomfort with Intersex Care Practices

Tennessee enacted a law permitting therapists and counselors to decline to serve LGBT people based on their religious beliefs.

At time of writing, 20 states have laws banning workplace and housing discrimination based on sexual orientation and gender identity, while two states prohibit discrimination based on sexual orientation but not gender identity.

## *National Security*

President Trump made statements during the presidential campaign and once in office supporting the use of torture of detainees and other counterterrorism policies that would amount to violations of US and international law. Trump later backtracked on these proposals saying he would defer to Defense Secretary James Mattis, who was outspoken against torture, on interrogation matters.

In November, the Office of the Prosecutor for the International Criminal Court (ICC) requested judicial authorization to open an investigation into alleged war crimes and crimes against humanity committed in the armed conflict in Afghanistan, including by US personnel in secret detention sites in Afghanistan and elsewhere.

At time of writing, media reported that US forces interrogated detainees in secret prisons run by foreign forces in Yemen. Defense Department officials denied that abuses had occurred when US forces were present, although their statements did not preclude possible US complicity in torture. Following the reports, the Senate Armed Services Committee sent a letter to Mattis demanding an investigation into the matter. Mattis' response remained classified at time of writing.

Trump promised to keep the US prison at Guantanamo Bay open and send new detainees there. The US continues to hold 31 men at the facility indefinitely without charge, nearly all of whom have been there for more than a decade. The Obama administration failed to release five that it had cleared for release. It claimed the remaining 26 could neither be prosecuted nor released but did not adequately explain the basis for these determinations or allow detainees to meaningfully challenge them.

The US continues to prosecute seven men for terrorist offenses, including the 9/11 attacks on the US, in Guantanamo's fundamentally flawed military commissions system, which does not meet international fair trial standards. It also is holding three men who have already been convicted by the commissions.

## *Surveillance*

Throughout 2017, the US continued to carry out large-scale warrantless intelligence surveillance programs without transparency or oversight. Authorities used Section 702 of the Foreign Intelligence Surveillance Act to target non-citizens (except lawful permanent residents) outside the country for warrantless communications monitoring and to "incidentally" gather large numbers of communications to or from people in the US.

Section 702 was scheduled to end at the end of 2017 unless Congress renewed it; at time of writing federal appeals courts had differing conclusions about the constitutionality of certain aspects of the law.

US surveillance of global communications under Executive Order 12333 remained shrouded in secrecy, with neither Congress nor the courts providing meaningful oversight. In January, the government disclosed procedures for the National Security Agency (NSA) to share data with domestic law enforcement agencies obtained by surveillance under the order. Documents disclosed to Human Rights Watch during the year revealed a Defense Department policy under the order sanctioning otherwise prohibited forms of monitoring of people inside the United States designated as "homegrown violent extremists." The Defense Department has not revealed how it designates "extremists" or what types of monitoring may result.

In May 2017, the Trump administration approved a proposal that asks US visa applicants for social media handles and accounts from the past five years as part of its enhanced vetting process. The US also continues to assert broad authority to search electronic devices and copy data at the border without any suspicion of wrongdoing.

## *Freedom of Expression and Assembly*

In one of his last acts in office, President Obama commuted the sentence of Chelsea Manning, a soldier who had received a 35-year prison term for disclosing US diplomatic cables to WikiLeaks and endured abuse while in custody. However, the US government continued to seek the extradition from Russia of Edward Snowden, the whistleblower who revealed the scope of US mass surveillance in 2013.

In June 2017, the Justice Department indicted NSA contractor Reality Winner for allegedly disclosing classified information about possible Russian government interference in the 2016 US election. Under current US law and contrary to international human rights law, Winner will not have a chance to claim that she made her disclosures in the public interest.

President Trump repeatedly criticized journalists and posted comments and videos denigrating them during the year, prompting concerns over the chilling of freedom of speech. In August 2017, the UN High Commissioner for Human Rights expressed concern that "freedom of the press" in the United States was "under attack from the President."

Two UN experts expressed alarm about state legislative proposals seeking to "criminalize peaceful protests," and a third described "a militarized, at times violent, escalation of force..." against protesters opposing the Dakota Access Pipeline. In August, a woman protesting at a rally held by white supremacists in Charlottesville, Virginia, was killed when a man allegedly drove a car into the crowd; the driver was charged with murder.

In July 2017, the US Justice Department served a warrant on a company that hosted a website used to coordinate protests at the inauguration, demanding information that included more than 1.3 million Internet Protocol addresses that could identify site visitors.

## Foreign Policy

During his inaugural address, Trump articulated a vision of foreign policy that placed "America First," vowing to defeat terrorism, strengthen the US military, and embrace diplomacy based on US interests. Some foreign dignitaries invited to the White House early in his presidency included those with poor reputations on human rights, including Egyptian President Abdel Fattah al-Sisi, Malaysian Prime Minister Najib Razak, and Turkish President Recep Erdoğan.

On his first full day in office, President Trump reinstated and dramatically expanded the Mexico City Policy, or "Global Gag Rule." This strips US health funding from foreign nongovernmental organizations if they use funds from any source to supply information about abortions, provide abortions, or advocate to liberalize abortion laws. The expanded Global Gag Rule will have disastrous effects beyond previous gag rules—restricting some $8.8 billion in foreign assistance for health services such as family planning, maternal healthcare, and services to treat HIV, malaria, and tuberculosis in 60 countries.

Affected organizations cannot easily replace these funds, which help prevent millions of unintended pregnancies, unsafe abortions, and tens of thousands of maternal deaths. The US government also severed support for the UN Population Fund, limiting the agency's ability to provide life-saving care for women and girls, often in crisis zones.

Secretary of State Rex Tillerson has sought to overhaul the US State Department's structure by sharply reducing the State Department's staffing and global role, including by requesting a 29 percent decrease in funding for the State Department and international aid.

In April, the US carried out a targeted military strike on the al Shayrat Syrian airfield in response to a chemical weapons attack that killed more than 80 civilians. The April strike was not accompanied by a clear strategy for continued engagement in Syria.

During his first foreign trip in May, which began in Saudi Arabia, Trump announced a US$110 billion weapons deal with Saudi Arabia, and pledged to address human rights concerns through "gradual reforms." Secretary Tillerson voiced concern during the same trip about lack of free speech in Iran, while ignoring equally onerous restrictions in Saudi Arabia.

In June, the US Senate voted 53-47 against a proposal that would have banned $510 million in arms sales to Saudi Arabia because of its role in the conflict in Yemen; a similar measure garnered only 27 votes in 2016. Also that month, the Trump administration announced it might withdraw from the UN Human Rights Council (UNHRC) over purported bias against Israel, among other concerns.

In July 2016, the US Congress extended through 2019 its authority to freeze assets and ban visas of Venezuelan officials accused of abuses against anti-government demonstrators. In 2017, the Trump administration imposed additional sanctions on Venezuelan officials, including President Maduro, and economic sanctions that prohibit dealings in new securities that the Venezuelan government and its state oil company issue. President Trump's August threat to use military force against Venezuela met with widespread criticism in the region.

In August, the State Department announced that it had re-allocated some of Egypt's US assistance and had frozen additional monies and military assistance, subject to democracy and human rights conditions.

However, joint military exercises that had been on hiatus resumed the next day. After months of review, President Trump announced his administration's new policy on Afghanistan, calling for more US troops, expanded airstrikes, and looser rules of engagement governing anti-Taliban combat operations. The policy also calls on Pakistan to do more to prevent terrorists from harboring there, and on India to play a more influential regional role.

Speaking at the UN General Assembly in September, Trump reaffirmed his commitment to an "America First" agenda and threatened to "totally destroy North Korea," and referred to Iran as a "rogue nation" and to the Iran nuclear deal as an "embarrassment."

The US did not publicly support calls at the UNHRC for a commission of inquiry into abuses in Yemen, but was active during negotiations and ultimately joined consensus on a resolution to create an international investigation.

In November, Trump traveled to Asia, visiting China, Japan, South Korea, and Vietnam while in the region for the ASEAN summit in the Philippines. During the trip, Trump boasted of his good relations with authoritarian leaders and did not publicly comment on core human rights concerns, including the Rohingya crisis.

As the fighting against the extremist group Islamic State (ISIS) in Iraq and Syria continued, the number of US airstrikes and the number of civilian casualties increased significantly with little acknowledgement by the Pentagon. Strikes also resumed in Libya and increased in pace in Somalia. Trump reportedly changed US policy for drone strikes outside conventional war zones to allow attacks on lower-level terrorism suspects in more countries, with less oversight, and greater secrecy. The CIA was reportedly granted authority to carry out covert drone strikes in Afghanistan.

The Trump administration was considering withdrawing from the UNHRC, primarily because of concerns about the body's membership and its dedicated agenda item on the Occupied Palestinian Territories. Although the council's membership includes some serial rights violators, this has not prevented it from successfully addressing a wide range of human rights issues.

# Uzbekistan

In the year-and-a-half since Uzbekistan's President Shavkat Mirziyoyev assumed power following the death of his predecessor, Islam Karimov, he has taken some steps to improve the country's abysmal human rights record, such as releasing some political prisoners, relaxing certain restrictions on free expression, removing citizens from the security services' notorious "black list," and increasing accountability of government institutions to the citizenry.

These moves, coupled with Tashkent's efforts to improve ties with its Central Asian neighbors, have contributed to a sense of hope in Uzbekistan about the possibility for change not witnessed in many years. At the same time, Uzbek security services brought fresh charges against journalists, raising fears of a "revolving door" for political arrests. It is far from clear if Uzbekistan's still-authoritarian government will follow up the modest steps it has taken thus far with institutional change and sustainable human rights improvements. Grave rights violations such as torture, politically motivated imprisonment, and forced labor in the cotton fields remain widespread.

## *Politically Motivated Imprisonment*

Authorities released at least 17 people imprisoned on politically motivated charges since September 2016, including Solijon Abdurakhmanov, Muhammad Bekjanov, Botirbek Eshkuziev, Azam Farmonov, Bahrom Ibragimov, Davron Kabilov Muhammadali Karabaev, Samandar Kukanov, Ganihon Mamatkhanov, Erkin Musaev, Bobomurod Razzakov, Davron Tojiev, Kobuljon Tulashev, Akzam Turgunov, Rustam Usmanov, and Ravshanbek Vafoev. In March, authorities also released Jamshid Karimov, an independent journalist and nephew of former ruler Karimov, from forced psychiatric treatment.

The number of prisoner releases compared to the one or two prisoners released on average per year during Karimov's rule signaled some hope that President Mirziyoyev could move toward freeing all of Uzbekistan's numerous political prisoners. However, prison authorities continued in 2017 to use Article 221 of Uzbekistan's criminal code regarding "violations of prison rules" to arbitrarily extend the sentences of political prisoners.

Thousands of individuals imprisoned on politically motivated charges remain behind bars and many have experienced torture or ill-treatment. Human rights activists in prison include Mehriniso Hamdamova, Zulhumor Hamdamova, Isroiljon Kholdorov, Gaybullo Jalilov, Chuyan Mamatkulov, Zafarjon Rahimov, Yuldash Rasulov, and Fahriddin Tillaev. Journalists in prison include Bobomurod Abdullaev, Gayrat Mikhliboev, Hayot Nasreddinov, Yusuf Ruzimuradov, and Dilmurod Saidov. Imprisoned religious figures and other perceived government critics include Aramais Avakyan, Ruhiddin Fahriddinov, Sobir Hamidkariyev, Nodirbek Yusupov, and Dilorom Abdukodirova. Kudratbek Rasulov, an opposition activist, also remains behind bars.

## *Civil Society Activists and Freedom of Expression*

Authorities have slightly relaxed restrictions on the holding of modest peaceful demonstrations. But the activities of critical voices, including independent rights activists, journalists, and lawyers, are still largely suppressed.

In March, authorities refused to release long-time rights activist Elena Urlaeva from a psychiatric hospital for nearly a month. Many observers believed the detention to be retaliation for Urlaeva's human rights work, which in recent years has included the monitoring of forced labor in Uzbekistan's cotton fields.

In June, relatives of imprisoned rights defender Nuraddin Jumaniyazov reported that Jumaniyazov had died in prison on December 31, 2016, of tuberculosis and diabetes-related complications. Authorities jailed Jumaniyazov in 2014 on politically motivated charges, tortured him, and denied him contact with his attorney. In May, Jumaniyazov's attorney, Polina Braunerg, known for taking on numerous politically sensitive cases, died of a stroke. For three years Braunerg had sought an exit visa to obtain medical treatment abroad but had been repeatedly denied permission.

This year, President Mirziyoyev announced that the country's exit visas—a Soviet relic that authorities have used as a tool to prevent a wide array of perceived critics, including artists and activists, from foreign travel—would be abolished by January 2019.

While the media sphere remains highly controlled, some public criticism of Karimov appeared in July, when a new 24-hour news channel, Uzbekistan 24, featured criticism of Karimov's economic and social policies. Local media outlets such as kun.uz have acquired a reputation for more critical reporting, and the government indicated it would invite the BBC's Uzbek service to base a correspondent in Tashkent.

On September 27, Uzbek security services detained Bobomurod Abdullaev, an independent journalist, in Tashkent, for "attempts to overthrow the constitutional regime." He has been denied meaningful access to a lawyer, nor has his family been granted access, and he faces up to 20 years in prison.

On the same day, police also detained Nurullo Muhummad Raufkhon, an Uzbek author, at Tashkent airport, after he arrived from Turkey following two years of exile. He was charged with extremism for his book *Bu Kunlar* (*These Days*), which criticizes Karimov. He was released on October 1, but still faces charges. On October 20, security services arrested another journalist, Hayot Nasreddinov, on extremism charges.

In September, a Human Rights Watch delegation visited Uzbekistan, seven years after the government banned the organization's researcher from working in the country.

## *Forced Labor*

Forced labor in Uzbekistan's cotton sector in 2017 remained systematic, both during the spring weeding season and the fall cotton harvest. The government issued a public decree prohibiting the forced mobilization of public sector workers, including teachers, medical personnel, and students into the cotton fields in August, and re-iterated the ban in September, which resulted in many forced laborers returning to their homes and places of work and study. However, various authorities continued to mobilize public sector workers and students to pick cotton on threat of punishment or loss of employment, despite the public decree. In various regions, such as Bukhara, public sector workers were forced to sign forms that they would "voluntarily" pick cotton. Human Rights Watch learned of instances, such as in the Parkent district of the Tashkent region, where authorities forced teachers and medical personnel to conceal their actual professions when signing up to participate in the harvest.

## "We Can't Refuse to Pick Cotton"

Forced and Child Labor Linked to World Bank Group Investments
in Uzbekistan

HUMAN
RIGHTS
WATCH

UGF

Responding to significant pressure to end forced child and adult labor in the cotton sector, the Uzbek government in 2017 again allowed the International Labour Organization (ILO) to conduct monitoring in the country's cotton fields, but serious concerns remained as to the ILO's methodology in conducting monitoring, as their teams included officials from Uzbekistan's Federation of Trade Unions, which despite its title is governed mainly by representatives from government and employers, not workers.

During 2017, the World Bank, increased its lending commitments to Tashkent for irrigation and agriculture projects to US$300 million, compared to $63 million during the previous fiscal year. While the World Bank's continued loan agreements are contingent on confirmation by the ILO that cotton laborers are working voluntarily in the bank's project areas, rights groups have repeatedly found evidence to the contrary.

Global corporations have engaged closely on the issue of forced labor in Uzbekistan's cotton sector, with over 300 companies, as of June, pledging not to knowingly source Uzbek cotton in their supply chains until the government ends forced labor.

## Sexual Orientation and Gender Identity

Consensual sexual relations between men are criminalized, with a maximum prison sentence of three years. Lesbian, gay, bisexual, and transgender (LGBT) people face deep-rooted homophobia and discrimination.

## Freedom of Religion

Uzbekistan maintains some of the world's most restrictive policies on the exercise of worship or belief. Authorities highly regulate religious worship, clothing, the sermons delivered by the country's imams, and ban all forms of proselytism.

The government maintains a "black list" made up of thousands of individuals suspected of belonging to unregistered or extremist groups. Those on the list are barred from obtaining various jobs, from travel, and must report regularly for interrogations with the police.

Authorities in August announced a reduction of the total number of people on the "black list" from 17,582 to 1,352. In public remarks accompanying the move,

President Mirziyoyev emphasized the need to rehabilitate citizens who had been "misled" by radical groups. In a speech to the United Nations General Assembly in September, he touted Uzbekistan's identity as a center for Islamic education and enlightenment.

Despite this positive move, thousands of religious believers, religious Muslims who practice their religion outside strict state controls, remain imprisoned on vague charges of extremism. In May, authorities sentenced 11 Muslims on extremism charges that appeared fabricated. Rights activist Surat Ikramov said the men's confessions were procured through torture.

Meanwhile, authorities also continued to harass Christian communities. In April, in the north-western Karakalpakstan autonomous region, four Protestant men were sentenced to short prison terms on charges of meeting for worship in a home.

## *Key International Actors*

The Uzbek government moved to re-establish ties with a number of international organizations in 2017, meeting in Tashkent with delegations including the European Bank for Reconstruction and Development (EBRD) and the Organization for Security and Co-operation in Europe's Office for Democratic Institutions and Human Rights (OSCE/ODIHR).

Signaling a willingness to engage more closely with UN human rights mechanisms, President Mirziyoyev received High Commissioner for Human Rights Zeid Ra'ad Al Hussein in Tashkent in May—the first ever visit by a high commissioner to Uzbekistan. Zeid commended Mirziyoyev for his stated commitment to reforms and urged him to follow through on releasing wrongfully imprisoned activists, to cooperate with UN human rights monitors, end forced labor, and lift restrictions on media.

During the visit, the Uzbek government agreed to resume cooperation with the high commissioner's regional office in Bishkek. UN Special Rapporteur on Freedom of Religion Ahmed Shaheed visited Uzbekistan in October. At a press conference, he stated that "resilience against religious extremism can be built on strengthening diversity as well as freedom of religion or belief," adding that religious freedom rights "cannot be sacrificed in preventing or countering violent extremism."

As part of his Central Asia tour in June, UN Secretary-General António Guterres travelled to Samarkand to meet with President Mirziyoyev. Guterres raised issues of climate change, regional security, and sustainable development, but failed to publicly raise specific rights abuses.

In July, the EU and Uzbekistan held their 13th Cooperation Council meeting, a few weeks after a Textile Protocol had entered into force. The protocol lowers tariffs on Uzbek cotton, allowing it to reach European markets more easily. In adopting the protocol, the European Parliament underlined the need to maintain efforts to ensure that both child and forced labor are fully eradicated, in cooperation with the ILO and other relevant stakeholders.

In November, European Union High Representative for Foreign Affairs Federica Mogherini visited Samarkand for the 13th EU-Central Asia Ministerial meeting with foreign ministers of all five Central Asian countries. The EU and Central Asian government delegations issued a "joint communique," which stated the importance of "strengthening of democracy, the protection of human rights, fundamental freedoms and the rule of law in order to enable them to effectively and flexibly tackle threats from violent extremism, terrorism and drug trafficking, and to respond to financial and political challenges."

In 2017, the US State Department's human trafficking report again placed Uzbekistan in the lowest category, "Tier III", based on Tashkent's systematic use of forced labor. For the 11th consecutive year, the US State Department also designated Uzbekistan as a "country of particular concern" due to its serial violations of religious freedom, but the White House waived the sanctions envisaged under both statutes, citing national security grounds.

**CRACKDOWN ON DISSENT**

Brutality, Torture, and Political Persecution in Venezuela

# Venezuela

In Venezuela today, no independent government institutions remain to act as a check on executive power. The Venezuelan government—under Maduro and previously under Chávez—has stacked the courts with judges who make no pretense of independence.

The government has been repressing dissent through often-violent crackdowns on street protests, jailing opponents, and prosecuting civilians in military courts. It has also stripped power from the opposition-led legislature.

Due to severe shortages of medicines, medical supplies, and food, many Venezuelans cannot adequately feed their families or access the most basic healthcare. In response to the human rights and humanitarian crisis, hundreds of thousands of Venezuelans are fleeing the country.

Other persistent concerns include poor prison conditions, impunity for human rights violations, and harassment by government officials of human rights defenders and independent media outlets.

## *Persecution of Political Opponents*

The Venezuelan government has jailed political opponents and disqualified them from running for office. At time of writing, more than 340 political prisoners were languishing in Venezuelan prisons or intelligence services headquarters, according to the Penal Forum, a Venezuelan network of pro-bono criminal defense lawyers.

In mid-2017, the Supreme Court sentenced five opposition mayors, after summary proceedings that violated international norms of due process, to 15 months in prison and disqualified them from running for office. At time of writing, one was being held at the intelligence services' headquarters in Caracas; the rest had fled the country. At least nine more mayors were subject to a Supreme Court injunction that could lead to similarly long prison sentences if they are accused of violating it.

Opposition leader Leopoldo López is serving a 13-year sentence for allegedly inciting violence during a demonstration in Caracas in February 2014, despite the lack of any credible evidence against him.

After three-and-a-half years in prison, López was moved to house arrest in July 2017, but was again detained in the middle of the night weeks later after he publicly criticized the government. That same night, intelligence agents detained Antonio Ledezma, a former opposition mayor who has been under house arrest since 2015 and had published a critical video while under house arrest.

The Supreme Court later issued a statement saying López was forbidden from carrying out "political proselytism" and that Ledezma could not "issue statements to any media," adding that "intelligence sources" said they had a plan to flee. Both men were returned to house arrest days later. In November, Ledezma fled Venezuela.

Several others arrested in connection with the 2014 anti-government protests or subsequent political activism remain under house arrest or in detention awaiting trial.

## Crackdown on Protest Activity

Venezuelan security forces, together with armed pro-government groups called "*colectivos*," have violently attacked anti-government protests—some of them attended by tens of thousands of Venezuelans—between April and July 2017. Security force personnel have shot demonstrators at point-blank range with riot-control munitions, run over demonstrators with an armored vehicle, brutally beaten people who offered no resistance, and staged violent raids on apartment buildings.

The Attorney General's Office reported that, as of July 31, 124 people had been killed during incidents related to the protests. The UN High Commissioner for Human Rights reported in August that more than half of the deaths had been caused by security agents or *colectivos*. The Venezuelan government claims that 10 security force officers died in the context of the demonstrations, and reported several instances of violence against government supporters.

In late July, before the Constituent Assembly fired Attorney General Luisa Ortega Díaz, her office was investigating nearly 2,000 cases of people injured during the crackdown. While the number appears to have included cases in which protesters and security forces were the alleged perpetrators, in more than half of the cases the office had evidence suggesting fundamental rights violations.

About 5,400 people were arrested in connection with demonstrations between April and November, including demonstrators, bystanders, and people taken away from their homes without warrants, according to the Penal Forum. Around 3,900 had been conditionally released at time of writing but remained subject to criminal prosecution.

Security forces have committed serious abuses against detainees that in some cases amount to torture—including severe beatings, the use of electric shocks, asphyxiation, and sexual abuse. Military courts have prosecuted more than 750 civilians in violation of international law.

In early 2014, the government had also responded to massive anti-government protests with excessive force. Security forces often held protestors incommunicado on military bases for 48 hours or more, and in some cases, committed egregious human rights violations, including severe beatings, electric shocks or burns, and forcing detainees to squat or kneel without moving for hours.

No senior officers have been prosecuted for these abuses.

## Constituent Assembly

In May, Maduro convened a Constituent Assembly through a presidential decree, despite a constitutional requirement that a public referendum be held beforehand in order to rewrite the constitution. The assembly is made up exclusively of government supporters chosen through an election in July that Smartmatic, a British company hired by the government to verify the results, later alleged was fraudulent.

The Constituent Assembly has sweeping powers that go well beyond drafting a constitution. In August, as soon as the assembly started operating, its members assumed all legislative powers and fired Attorney General Ortega Díaz, a former government loyalist who had become an outspoken critic in late March, and appointed a government supporter to the position. In November, together with the Supreme Court, it stripped Freddy Guevara, the National Assembly's vice president, of his parliamentary immunity.

## *Operation Peoples' Liberation*

Beginning in July 2015, President Maduro deployed more than 80,000 members of security forces nationwide in an initiative called "Operation Peoples' Liberation" (OLP) to address rising security concerns. Police and military raids in low-income and immigrant communities led to widespread allegations of abuse, including extrajudicial killings, mass arbitrary detentions, maltreatment of detainees, forced evictions, destruction of homes, and arbitrary deportations.

In November 2017, the attorney general said more than 500 people had been killed during OLP raids between 2015 and 2017. Government officials typically said that those killed died during "confrontations" with armed criminals, claims denied in many cases by families of victims or witnesses. In several cases, victims were last seen alive in police custody.

## *Humanitarian Crisis*

Venezuelans are facing severe shortages of medicine, medical supplies, and food, seriously undermining their rights to health and food. In 2017, the Venezuelan health minister released official data for 2016 indicating that, in one year, maternal mortality increased 65 percent, infant mortality increased 30 percent, and cases of malaria increased 76 percent.

Days later, the minister was fired. Cases of severe malnutrition of children under 5 years old increased from 10.2 percent in February 2017 to 14.5 percent in September 2017, crossing the World Health Organization crisis threshold, according to Cáritas Venezuela.

## *Judicial Independence*

Since former President Chávez and his supporters in the National Assembly conducted a political takeover of the Supreme Court in 2004, the judiciary has ceased to function as an independent branch of government. Members of the Supreme Court have openly rejected the principle of separation of powers, and publicly pledged their commitment to advancing the current administration's political agenda.

Since the opposition assumed the majority in the National Assembly in January 2016, the Supreme Court has struck down almost every law it has passed. In March 2017, it took over all legislative powers, and partially backtracked only after strong criticism in Venezuela and abroad.

## *Freedom of Expression*

For more than a decade, the government has expanded and abused its power to regulate media and has worked aggressively to reduce the number of dissenting media outlets. Existing laws grant the government power to suspend or revoke concessions to private media if "convenient for the interests of the nation," allow for arbitrary suspension of websites for the vaguely defined offense of "incitement," and criminalize expression of "disrespect" for high government officials. While some newspapers, websites, and radio stations criticize the government, fear of reprisals has made self-censorship a serious problem.

Security forces detained, interrogated, and confiscated the equipment of several journalists in 2017. Some international journalists were barred from entering the country, or were detained after covering anti-government protests or the health crisis. Several cable news channels and radios were taken off the air.

In November, the Constituent Assembly adopted a "Law Against Hatred" that includes vague language that undermines free speech. It forbids political parties that "promote fascism, hatred, and intolerance," and imposes prison sentences of up to 20 years on those who publish "messages of intolerance and hatred" in media outlets or social media.

## *Human Rights Defenders*

Government measures to restrict international funding of nongovernmental organizations—combined with unsubstantiated accusations by government officials and supporters that human rights defenders are seeking to undermine Venezuelan democracy—create a hostile environment that limits the ability of civil society groups to promote human rights.

In 2010, the Supreme Court ruled that individuals or organizations receiving foreign funding can be prosecuted for treason. That year, the National Assembly enacted legislation blocking organizations that "defend political rights" or "monitor the performance of public bodies" from receiving international assistance.

## Political Discrimination

According to Venezuelan media reports, hundreds of government workers were fired in 2016 for having supported the recall of President Maduro, and many others were threatened with the same in 2017 for supporting an unofficial plebiscite organized by the opposition against the Constituent Assembly proposal. Other reports say a government program that distributes food and basic goods at government-capped prices discriminates against government critics.

## Prison Conditions

Corruption, weak security, deteriorating infrastructure, overcrowding, insufficient staffing, and poorly trained guards allow armed gangs to exercise effective control over inmate populations within prisons. In August, 37 inmates—nearly half the detainee population—at the Judicial Detention Center of Amazonas in Puerto Ayacucho died and 14 security guards were injured when security forces reportedly tried to take control of the prison.

## Key International Actors

In March and July, OAS Secretary General Luis Almagro presented two comprehensive reports on the humanitarian and human rights crisis in Venezuela, as part of ongoing discussions of Venezuela's compliance with the Inter-American Democratic Charter—an agreement protecting human rights and democratic guarantees in OAS member states. Between September and November, the OAS held a series of public hearings in which victims provided information to three experts evaluating whether abuses committed by Venezuelan security forces could constitute crimes against humanity.

In August, the regional trade bloc Mercosur indefinitely suspended Venezuela, applying the Ushuaia Protocol, an agreement that allows the bloc to suspend a member when there's a "rupture of [its] constitutional order."

Also in August, 17 foreign affairs ministers from the Americas met in Perú to address Venezuela's crisis. Twelve of them—11 Latin American governments and

Canada—signed the Lima Declaration, a comprehensive statement that condemns the assault on democratic order and the systematic violation of human rights in Venezuela. The 12 stated they would recognize neither the Constituent Assembly nor its resolutions, pledged to stop the transfer of weapons to Venezuela, and expressed concern about the humanitarian crisis and the government's refusal to accept international humanitarian aid. They also indicated their willingness to support efforts toward credible and good faith negotiations aimed at restoring democracy in the country peacefully.

The Venezuelan government withdrew from the American Convention on Human Rights in 2013, leaving citizens and residents no longer able to request intervention by the Inter-American Court of Human Rights when local remedies for abuses are ineffective or unavailable. The Inter-American Commission on Human Rights (IACHR) continues to monitor Venezuela, however, applying the American Declaration of Rights and Duties of Man, which is not an instrument subject to states' ratification.

The UN High Commissioner for Human Rights released a report in August 2017, concluding that Venezuelan authorities had committed extensive human rights violations and abuses in responding to anti-government protests. The "generalized and systematic use of excessive force during demonstrations and the arbitrary detention of protestors and perceived political opponents indicate that these were not the illegal or rogue acts of isolated officials," the report said.

In September the high commissioner presented his findings to the UN Human Rights Council, saying "crimes against humanity may have been committed" in Venezuela and calling for an international investigation. Numerous states expressed serious concern about human rights violations in the country.

In 2015, US President Barack Obama issued an executive order imposing targeted sanctions against seven Venezuelan government officials. In July 2016, the US Congress extended through 2019 its authority to freeze assets and deny visas to officials accused of committing abuses against anti-government demonstrators during the 2014 protests.

In 2017, the US government issued additional sanctions targeting key Venezuelan officials, including President Maduro, as well as financial sanctions that include a ban on dealings in new stocks and bonds issued by the Venezuelan government and its state oil company. President Trump's August threat to use military force against Venezuela, however, was met with widespread criticism in the region.

The European Union has repeatedly expressed concern over the deteriorating situation in Venezuela, condemning the violent repression of peaceful protests and the persecution of political opponents. In November, it imposed an arms embargo on Venezuela and targeted sanctions against Venezuelan officials.

International efforts to mediate between the government and the opposition to restore democratic order in Venezuela have not delivered meaningful results.

As a member of the UN Human Rights Council, Venezuela has regularly voted to prevent scrutiny of human rights violations in other countries, opposing resolutions that spotlight abuses in countries including Syria, Belarus, Burundi, and Iran.

# Vietnam

Vietnam's human rights situation seriously deteriorated in 2017. Police arrested at least 21 people for sweeping "national security" offenses that are used to punish critical speech and peaceful activism.

## *Freedom of Expression*

Vietnam frequently used vaguely worded penal code provisions during the year to crack down on dissent, including "carrying out activities that aim to overthrow the people's administration," "undermining national great unity," "conducting propaganda against the state," and "abusing the rights to democracy and freedom to infringe upon the interests of the state." Other laws, such as disrupting public order and resisting officials carrying out their public duty, are also used to repress exercise of basic civil and political liberties.

In June 2017, the National Assembly, which operates under the effective control of the ruling Communist Party, revised sections of the penal code to criminalize actions related to preparing to perform forbidden acts involving national security. Those found guilty face up to five years in prison. The revised penal code also holds lawyers criminally responsible if they fail to report their own clients to authorities for a number of crimes, including national security violations.

During 2017, authorities arrested at least 21 rights bloggers and activists, including former political prisoners Nguyen Bac Truyen, Truong Minh Duc, Nguyen Van Tuc, Nguyen Trung Ton, and Pham Van Troi, for exercising their civil and political rights in a way that the government views as threatening national security. At time of writing, at least 10 other people had already been put on trial, convicted, and sentenced to between 5 to 10 years in prison.

Authorities continued to detain many people without trial, including blogger Ho Van Hai (also known as Dr. Ho Hai), held since November 2016, and rights campaigners Nguyen Van Dai and Le Thu Ha, detained since December 2015.

In May, an appeals court upheld the long prison sentences given to Tran Anh Kim and Le Thanh Tung. In December 2016, the People's Court of Thai Binh sentenced Tran Anh Kim and Le Thanh Tung to 13 and 12 years in prison, respectively, for al-

HUMAN
RIGHTS
WATCH

# NO COUNTRY FOR
# HUMAN RIGHTS ACTIVISTS
Assaults on Bloggers and Democracy Campaigners in Vietnam

legedly founding a pro-democracy group called the National Force to Raise the Flag of Democracy.

In June, a court in Khanh Hoa sentenced prominent blogger Nguyen Ngoc Nhu Quynh (also known as Mother Mushroom) to 10 years in prison for critical online posts and documents she published on the Internet collected from public sources, including state-sanctioned media. In July, a court in Ha Nam province sentenced prominent activist Tran Thi Nga to nine years in prison for her internet posts.

Physical assaults against human rights activists occur frequently. In June 2017, Human Rights Watch published a report highlighting 36 incidents in which men in civilian clothes beat activists between January 2015 and April 2017, often resulting in serious injuries. Attacks by thugs on rights campaigners took place in many regions, sometimes in the presence of uniformed police who did nothing to stop the attacks.

A typical case occurred in February 2017, when a group of men in civilian clothes abducted former political prisoner Nguyen Trung Ton and his friend Nguyen Viet Tu off the street, dragged them into a van, and drove away. While in the van, the men stripped off Ton's and Tu's clothes, covered their heads with their jackets, threatened them, and repeatedly hit them with iron pipes before dumping them in a forest, far from where they had been seized. Nguyen Trung Ton required surgery at a local hospital for the severe injuries he incurred. Police failed to seriously investigate the case or apprehend any suspects. In July, Nguyen Trung Ton was arrested and charged with "carrying out activities that aim to overthrow the people's administration."

## *Freedom of Assembly, Association, and Movement*

Vietnam prohibits the establishment or operation of independent political parties, labor unions, and human rights organizations. Authorities require approval for public gatherings and refuse permission for meetings, marches, or public assemblies they deem to be politically unacceptable. In September, police used excessive force while dispersing protesters in front of the entrance of a Hong Kong-owned textile factory in Hai Duong province. Many people were injured.

Hundreds of people in central provinces including Quang Binh, Ha Tinh, and Nghe An held regular protests against Formosa, a Taiwanese steel corporation that dumped toxic waste in the ocean, causing a massive marine environment disaster in April 2016.

Land confiscation that displaces local people without providing adequate compensation is one of biggest problems in the country. In April, the people of Dong Tam commune in Hanoi took a nationally unprecedented move by holding 38 policemen and local government officials hostage for a week over a long-unresolved land dispute. The villagers released the hostages after Chairman of Hanoi People's Committee Nguyen Duc Chung promised to conduct a comprehensive inspection.

Local police use force and intimidation to prevent activists from participating in protests and human rights discussions, or attending trials of fellow activists. In May, authorities prevented prominent activists Pham Doan Trang, Nguyen Quang A, and Nguyen Dan Que from leaving their houses during the bilateral human rights dialogue between Vietnam and the United States government.

Police also stop rights activists from traveling abroad, sometimes citing vague national security reasons. In January 2017, police prohibited former political prisoner Pham Thanh Nghien from leaving the country for a personal trip to Thailand. In April, they prevented political detainee Nguyen Van Dai's wife, Vu Minh Khanh, from going to Germany to receive a human rights award from the German Association of Judges on her husband's behalf.

In May, police stopped Polish-Vietnamese activist Phan Chau Thanh from entering Vietnam, and in June, stopped former political prisoner Do Thi Minh Hanh from leaving for Austria to visit her ill mother. The same month, authorities stripped former political prisoner Pham Minh Hoang of his Vietnamese citizenship and deported him to France.

## Freedom of Religion

The government monitors, harasses, and sometimes violently cracks down on religious groups operating outside government-controlled institutions. Unrecognized branches of the Cao Dai church, Hoa Hao Buddhist church, independent Protestant and Catholic house churches, Khmer Krom Buddhist temples, and the

Unified Buddhist Church of Vietnam face constant surveillance. In June, An Giang province authorities set up a barrier to block people from Quang Minh Pagoda celebrations on the founding day of Hoa Hao Buddhism.

Ethnic Montagnards face surveillance, intimidation, arbitrary arrest, and mistreatment by securlty forces. Authorities compelled members of independent Christian Montagnard religious groups to publicly denounce their faith.

Government repression caused hundreds of Montagnards to flee to Cambodia and Thailand. Vietnam responded to the flight of Montagnards into Cambodia by pressuring Cambodian authorities to prevent border crossings and deny the asylum claims of those who arrive in Cambodia. According to the United Nations Refugee Agency, UNHCR, Vietnam pressured the UN and refugee resettlement countries to not accept Montangnards.

In April, the People's Court of Gia Lai province sentenced at least five Montagnards to 8 to 10 years in prison for the so-called crime of participating in independent religious groups not approved by the government.

## *Criminal Justice System*

Vietnamese courts remained firmly under government control. Trials of human rights activists consistently failed to meet international fair standards. Police regularly intimidated family members and friends who tried to attend trials of activists.

Police brutality, sometimes leading to deaths in police custody, was common during the year. In May 2017, Vinh Long police arrested Nguyen Huu Tan on charges of conducting propaganda against the state. Police later claimed he committed suicide with a knife left in the interrogation room by a policeman. His family protested, pointing out many discrepancies between what they saw on his body and a blurry police video recording shown to them briefly.

In August, Tran Anh Doanh told a reporter that police in Son Tay, Hanoi, beat him severely to force him to confess to a theft charge. In September, Vo Tan Minh died in police custody in Phan Rang-Thap Cham, Ninh Thuan province, and his family found bruises on his back, legs, and arms. The police initially claimed Vo Tan Minh was involved in a fight, but later suspended five police officers and opened a case of "using corporal punishment."

People dependent on drugs, including children, are frequently held in government detention centers where they are forced to perform menial work in the name of "labor therapy." Violations of center rules and failure to meet work quotas are punished by beatings and confinement to disciplinary rooms where detainees claim they are deprived of food and water. State media reported that during the first six months of 2017, authorities sent 3,168 people to centers in Ho Chi Minh City, increasing the number of drug detainees held in the city to 11,317. In August, the government issued Decree 97 that expands the categories of people who can be sent to compulsory drug rehabilitation centers.

## Key International Actors

China remained the biggest trade partner of Vietnam, but maritime territorial disputes continued to complicate the relationship between the two countries.

Despite the US pullout from the Trans-Pacific Partnership in January 2017, the two countries pursued improved military and economic relations. During his May visit to the White House, Prime Minister Nguyen Xuan Phuc promised that Vietnam would cooperate with the US on trade, regional security, and immigration issues.

In November, US President Donald Trump traveled to Vietnam for a regional summit and meetings with officials in Hanoi, but did not publicly raise human rights or democracy concerns during the visit.

In August, Germany protested the abduction in Berlin of asylum seeker Trinh Xuan Thanh, a former PetroVietnam executive, and expelled two Vietnamese diplomats who allegedly were involved in the incident.

During the year, the European Union delegation to Vietnam voiced concerns over the arrest and conviction of several activists, but Brussels remained silent on human rights violations in the country. In February, the European Parliament (EP) Subcommittee on Human Rights visited Vietnam.

The EP delegation recognized that Vietnam has made economic and social progress and begun a process of advancing economic and social rights, but voiced concerns over Vietnam's record on civil and political rights, including freedom of expression, association, religion, or belief. In September, the chair of the EP Committee on International Trade said that human rights are at the center of Vietnam-EU trade talks.

# Yemen

The Saudi Arabia-led coalition continued its aerial and ground campaign in Yemen with little let-up. In September 2014, Houthi forces and forces loyal to former President Ali Abdullah Saleh took control of Yemen's capital, Sanaa, and much of the country. In March 2015, the coalition, with military assistance from the United States, attacked Houthi-Saleh forces in support of President Abdu Rabbu Mansour Hadi.

After clashes broke out between the former allies in Sanaa, Houthi forces killed former President Ali Abdullah Saleh on December 4 as he tried to leave the city.

The armed conflict has taken a terrible toll on the civilian population. The coalition has conducted scores of indiscriminate and disproportionate airstrikes hitting civilian objects that have killed thousands of civilians in violation of the laws of war, with munitions that the US, United Kingdom, and others still supply. Houthi-Saleh forces have fired artillery indiscriminately into cities such as Taizz and Aden, killing civilians, and launched rockets into southern Saudi Arabia.

As of November, at least 5,295 civilians had been killed and 8,873 wounded, according to the UN human rights office, although the actual civilian casualty count is likely much higher.

The war is also exacerbating the world's largest humanitarian catastrophe. Both sides are unlawfully impeding the delivery of desperately needed humanitarian aid.

The coalition has used cluster munitions, while Houthi-Saleh forces have used antipersonnel landmines—both weapons are banned by international treaties.

Both sides have harassed, threatened, and attacked Yemeni activists and journalists. Houthi-Saleh forces, government-affiliated forces, and the United Arab Emirates and UAE-backed Yemeni forces have arbitrarily detained or forcibly disappeared scores.

None of the states party to the conflict carried out meaningful investigations into their forces' alleged violations.

## *Unlawful Airstrikes*

Human Rights Watch has documented 85 apparently unlawful coalition airstrikes, which have killed nearly 1,000 civilians and hit homes, markets, hospitals, schools, and mosques. Some of these attacks may amount to war crimes. In March, a helicopter attacked a boat carrying Somali migrants and refugees off Yemen's coast, killing and wounding dozens.

In 2017, Saudi Arabia pledged to reduce civilian harm in coalition attacks. Since then, Human Rights Watch documented six coalition attacks that killed 55 civilians, including 33 children; one killed 14 members of the same family. The UN Office of the UN High Commissioner for Human Rights (OHCHR) office reported in September that coalition airstrikes remain "the leading cause of civilian casualties."

## *Indiscriminate Artillery Attacks*

Houthi-Saleh forces have repeatedly fired artillery indiscriminately into Yemeni cities and into southern Saudi Arabia.

Human Rights Watch documented attacks by both Houthi-Saleh and government-aligned forces inside Yemen that have struck populated neighborhoods, killing and wounding civilians. Over three days in May, artillery attacks in Taizz, most of them carried out by Houthi-Saleh forces, killed at least 12 civilians, including four children, and wounded 29, including 10 children. The OHCHR called the shelling of Taizz "unrelenting."

## *Landmines*

Landmines appear to have killed and maimed hundreds of civilians, disrupted civilian life in affected areas, and will pose a threat to civilians long after the conflict ends.

Houthi-Saleh forces have used landmines in at least six governorates. Human Rights Watch investigated 10 incidents where landmines laid by Houthi-Saleh forces in Sanaa, Marib, Aden, and Taizz killed two people and wounded eight.

Yemen suffers from a shortage of equipped and trained personnel who can systematically clear mines and explosive remnants of war.

Yemen is a party to the 1997 Mine Ban Treaty.

## Cluster Munitions

Human Rights Watch has documented the Saudi-led coalition using six types of widely banned cluster munitions, including those produced in the US and Brazil, in attacks that targeted populated areas, killing and wounding dozens.

The US suspended transfers of cluster munitions to Saudi Arabia in 2016. On December 19, 2016, the coalition announced it would stop using a UK-made cluster munition. A few days earlier, a cluster munition attack hit near two local schools in northern Yemen, killing two civilians and wounding six, including a child. Another attack in February 2017 hit a farm, wounding two boys. In both attacks, the coalition used Brazilian-made cluster munitions.

Yemen, Saudi Arabia, and other coalition states are not party to the 2008 Convention on Cluster Munitions.

## Arbitrary Detentions, Torture, and Enforced Disappearances

Houthi-Saleh forces, the Yemeni government, and the UAE and UAE-backed Yemeni forces arbitrarily detained people, including children, abused detainees and held them in poor conditions, and forcibly disappeared people perceived to be political opponents or security threats. The number of the "disappeared" is growing.

Houthi-Saleh forces have cracked down on dissent, closing several dozen NGOs, carrying out enforced disappearances, torturing detainees, and arbitrarily detaining numerous activists, journalists, tribal leaders, political opponents, and members of the Baha'i community. Since August 2014, Human Rights Watch has documented the Sanaa-based authorities' arbitrary or abusive detention of dozens of people, including two deaths in custody and 11 cases of alleged torture or other ill-treatment.

In areas of southern Yemen nominally under government control, Human Rights Watch has documented more than 50 people, including four children, arbitrarily detained or disappeared. UAE-backed security forces abusively detained or disappeared most of these individuals. The UAE runs at least two informal detention facilities, where they have continued to detain people despite release orders and reportedly moved high-profile detainees outside the country.

The committee set up by the Hadi government to investigate arbitrary detention has not made any results public. The UAE has denied any role in detainee abuse. Houthi-Saleh forces do not appear to have conducted investigations into detainee abuse.

Yemeni human rights groups and lawyers have documented hundreds more cases of arbitrary detentions and forcible disappearances in northern and southern Yemen.

## Terrorism and Counterterrorism

Both Al-Qaeda in the Arabian Peninsula (AQAP) and the Islamic State in Yemen (IS-Y) claimed responsibility for numerous suicide and other bombings.

After President Donald Trump took office, the number of US drone attacks in Yemen increased significantly. According to the Bureau of Investigative Journalism, the US carried out 37 drone attacks in Yemen in 2016, the last year of the Obama administration, but by October, the US had carried out 105 drone attacks in 2017. The US said it targeted AQAP in the majority of attacks but announced in late 2017 it carried out attacks on IS-Y that killed "dozens."

The US has conducted at least two ground raids in Yemen since January, reportedly alongside the UAE, one of which killed at least 14 civilians, including nine children. The US may be complicit in detainee abuse by UAE forces. According to the Associated Press, the US has sent interrogators to Yemen and sent questions to and seen transcripts from UAE interrogations. The US has not made public any investigations conducted into its raids in Yemen or participation in UAE or Yemeni abuse of detainees.

In 2017, the US transferred four Yemeni detainees from Guantanamo Bay to Saudi Arabia, news agencies reported.

## Blocking and Impeding Humanitarian Access

Yemen is the world's largest humanitarian crisis, with at least 8 million people on the brink of famine and nearly 1 million suspected to be infected with cholera. This crisis is linked directly to the ongoing armed conflict.

The Saudi-led coalition's restrictions on imports have worsened the dire humanitarian situation. The coalition has delayed and diverted fuel tankers, closed critical ports and stopped goods from entering seaports controlled by the Houthis. Fuel needed to power generators to hospitals and pump water to civilian residences has also been blocked.

In November, the coalition temporarily blocked all entry points to Yemen in response to a Houthi-Saleh missile attack on Riyadh, gravely worsening the humanitarian situation. Key restrictions remain. In August 2016, the coalition suspended all commercial flights to Sanaa, "having serious implications for patients seeking urgent medical treatment abroad," according to the UN. Since May, the coalition has blocked international human rights organizations, including Human Rights Watch, from traveling to areas of Yemen under Houthi control.

Houthi-Saleh forces have blocked and confiscated food and medical supplies and denied access to populations in need. They have imposed onerous restrictions on aid workers and interfered with aid delivery. Aid groups have ceased working in some areas due to these restrictions. The cumulative impact of Houthi-Saleh obstruction and interference with humanitarian assistance has significantly harmed the civilian population.

Aid workers have been kidnapped, arbitrarily detained, and killed while engaged in humanitarian operations in Yemen.

## Children and Armed Conflict

The UN secretary-general included the Houthis, government forces, pro-government militias, AQAP, and the Saudi-led coalition on his annual "list of shame" for grave violations against children during armed conflict. In 2016, then-Secretary-General Ban Ki-moon removed the coalition from the list after Saudi Arabia and its allies threatened to withdraw millions of dollars of funding from critical UN relief programs.

Houthi forces, government and pro-government forces, and other armed groups have used child soldiers, an estimated one-third of the fighters in Yemen. By August 2017, the UN had documented 1,702 cases of child recruitment since March 2015, 67 percent of which were attributable to Houthi-Saleh forces. About 100 were younger than 15. Under Yemeni law, 18 is the minimum age for military service. In 2014, Yemen signed a UN action plan to end the use of child soldiers. Due to the conflict and without an effective government in place, the action plan has not been implemented.

In October, Yemen endorsed the Safe Schools Declaration, thereby committing to do more to protect students, teachers, and schools during conflict, including by implementing the Guidelines for Protecting Schools and Universities from Military Use During Armed Conflict.

## Women's and Girls' Rights

Violence against women has increased 63 percent since the conflict escalated, according to UNFPA. Forced marriage rates, including child marriage, have increased. Yemen has no minimum age of marriage. Women in Yemen face severe discrimination in law and practice. They cannot marry without the permission of their male guardian and do not have equal rights to divorce, inheritance or child custody. Lack of legal protection leaves them exposed to domestic and sexual violence.

## Accountability

None of the warring parties carried out credible investigations into their forces' alleged laws-of-war violations. In September, the OHCHR concluded that efforts towards accountability were "wholly insufficient."

The coalition-appointed Joint Incidents Assessment Team (JIAT) did not conduct credible investigations, failing to release full investigation reports or detailed information on their methodology, including how they determine which strikes to investigate, or whether or not they have the power to ensure prosecutions of individuals responsible for war crimes. JIAT has not clarified which state's forces participated in the attacks it investigated. While in a few strikes JIAT recommended the coalition pay compensation, the coalition does not appear to have made any concrete progress toward creating a compensation system.

The US is not known to have conducted investigations into any alleged unlawful attacks in which its forces have taken part.

In September, for the third time, the UN High Commissioner for Human Rights recommended establishing an independent, international mechanism to investigate alleged abuses by all sides in Yemen. That month, the UN Human Rights Council (UNHRC) adopted by consensus a resolution creating a Group of Eminent Experts to conduct an international investigation into violations and abuses in Yemen.

## Key International Actors

Members of the coalition have sought to avoid international legal liability by refusing to provide information on their role in unlawful attacks. The Saudi-led coalition consists of Saudi Arabia, Bahrain, Kuwait, the UAE, Egypt, Jordan, Morocco, and Sudan; Qatar withdrew in June.

The US is a party to the conflict and risks being complicit in unlawful coalition attacks in which it takes part. The US continues to provide in-air refueling and other support to the coalition, but has not provided detailed information on the extent and scope of its engagement.

The UK has provided diplomatic support, training, and weaponry to members of the coalition. UK arms sales to Saudi Arabia are the subject of ongoing litigation in the UK.

The US, UK, and France continued to provide arms to Saudi Arabia and other coalition states, despite the coalition's use of US and UK-supplied weapons in apparently unlawful attacks. US and UK lawmakers have repeatedly challenged the continuation of these sales.

In April, European Union foreign ministers called for the removal of all obstacles preventing the delivery of life-saving humanitarian assistance to Yemen. In September, the European Parliament reiterated its call on member states to suspend weapons sales to Saudi Arabia due to its conduct in Yemen.

The Netherlands, joined by Canada, Belgium, Ireland, and Luxembourg, successfully led efforts at the UNHRC to create an international investigation.

# Zimbabwe

In November 2017, President Robert Mugabe was ousted in a military coup and was replaced by his former deputy, Emmerson Mnangagwa, who has his own long record of rights violations. During the military takeover between November 14 and 24, the army arrested and detained a number of Mugabe's associates without providing information about the arrest, or places and conditions of detention.

In his inaugural speech on November 24, Mnangagwa confirmed that elections will take place as scheduled, by August 2018, but did not address the issue of meaningful security sector, media, and electoral reforms to ensure credible, free, and fair elections. There was no indication that the Mnangagwa administration intended to ensure the independence and enhance the professionalism of the Zimbabwe Electoral Commission (ZEC), or update the voters' roll under ZEC's exclusive control.

Prior to his ouster, Mugabe had presided over intensified repression of peaceful protests against human rights violations and an economy on the brink of collapse. His administration disregarded the rights provisions in the country's 2013 constitution, and implemented no meaningful human rights reforms. In July, the parliament passed a constitutional amendment granting the president powers to directly appoint senior members of the judiciary, further eroding the independence of the judiciary. Police abuse continued, using excessive force to crush dissent. Human rights defenders, civil society activists, journalists, and government opponents were harassed, threatened or faced arbitrary arrest by the police. Widespread impunity for abuses by the police and state security agents remained.

## *Freedom of Expression and Media*

In 2017, several journalists and activists were subject to arbitrary arrest, harassment, and intimidation while participating in protests or reporting on demonstrations.

On September 24, police arrested and charged rights activist Pastor Evan Mawarire with "subverting a constitutional government," which carries a maximum 20-year prison sentence. Mawarire is a prominent critic of the government and leader of the #ThisFlag campaign, which organizes protests against the government for failing to address Zimbabwe's rights problems and failing economy. Mawarire was released after three days. The police previously arrested Mawarire in February on the same charge of subverting a constitutional government. A court had cleared him of similar charges in July 2016.

On July 28, the Media Institute of Southern Africa (MISA, Zimbabwe) led a journalists' march to the Harare Central Police Station protesting police assault on three journalists of the privately owned *NewsDay* daily newspaper. Police had assaulted journalists Obey Manayiti, Shepherd Tozvireva, Abigail Mutsikidze, and their driver, Raphael Phiri, the previous day for allegedly taking photographs of the police beating protesters in Harare.

On June 22, police in Rusape, 170 kilometers east of Harare, arrested and briefly detained freelance journalists Garikai Chaunza and Frank Chikowore, who were investigating forced evictions at Lesbury farm in Rusape. The journalists said police ordered them to delete all pictures they took at the farm before being released. In the same month, Harare police summoned and interrogated *NewsDay editor* Wisdom Mdzungairi and reporter Everson Mushava over a story they published about alleged ZANU-PF party infighting.

State media remains partisan in favor of the ruling ZANU-PF party while limiting coverage of opposition political parties. The government has not repealed or amended the Access to Information and Protection of Privacy Act (AIPPA), the Public Order and Security Act (POSA), and other laws that severely restrict basic rights and infringe on freedom of expression.

## Women's and Girls' Rights, Sexual Orientation, and Gender Identity

Two years after Zimbabwe's Constitutional Court declared child marriage unconstitutional and set 18 as the minimum marriage age, the government has yet to amend or repeal all existing marriage laws that still allow child marriage. It also has not put structures in place to implement the court decision and ensure that girls under 18 are not forced into marriage.

A January 2017 Human Rights Watch report found that widows are routinely evicted from their marital homes and their property confiscated by in-laws with little recourse to the formal justice system. Many of the victims struggled to claim rights for reasons unique to their status as widows. Few women formally own the property held during their marriage. As a result, they were unable to keep jointly held property upon the death of their husband. They are required to prove they were in fact married, which can pose great challenges, due to lack of access to the courts and the high cost of obtaining the necessary documents to ward off in-laws' intent on property grabbing. The government has yet to raise awareness, review inheritance and marriage laws, and improve access to justice for women.

Section 73 of the Criminal Law Act punishes consensual same-sex conduct between men with up to one year in prison or a fine or both.

## Rule of Law

Authorities continued to ignore human rights provisions in the country's 2013 constitution. The government did not enact new laws or amend existing legislation to bring them in line with the constitution and Zimbabwe's international and regional human rights obligations.

In July, the parliament amended the constitution to give the president absolute powers to appoint the chief justice (the head of the judiciary), the deputy chief justice, and the judge president of the high court. Zimbabwe's ruling ZANU-PF party used its parliamentary majority to approve the amendment despite the opposition's objections.

Then-president Mugabe signed the retrogressive constitutional amendment into law, further eroding the rule of law through executive control over the judiciary. The amendment also undermines Zimbabwe's international human rights legal obligations to respect judicial independence under the African Charter on Human and Peoples' Rights (ACHPR) and the International Covenant on Civil and Political Rights (ICCPR).

On March 17, about 100 anti-riot police demolished homes at Arnolds Farm—a farm linked to former president Mugabe's family—forcing residents onto trucks and dumping them by the roadside 40 kilometers away. On March 24, the farm residents obtained a High Court order to stop the evictions and bar police from harassing them, demolishing their homes or attempting to evict them without a valid court order. The anti-riot police, claiming to be acting on behalf of former First Lady Grace Mugabe, ignored the court order, and on several occasions ordered some 200 families to leave the farm. The anti-riot police then demolished homes, destroyed property, and beat up those who resisted.

Authorities have not fully investigated the March 9, 2015 abduction and enforced disappearance of pro-democracy activist and human rights defender Itai Dzamara. Dzamara remained missing at time of writing.

## Key International Actors

Following the November 2017 military coup, the leadership of the Southern African Development Community (SADC) called on all stakeholders in Zimbabwe to peacefully resolve the nation's political challenges. When Mugabe resigned under military pressure, SADC leaders welcomed his decision, pledging to support the August 2018 elections. The African Union (AU) initially condemned the military takeover, but later welcomed Mugabe's resignation. The AU said it recognized that the Zimbabwean people have expressed their will to have a peaceful transfer of power, and Mugabe's decision to resign paves the way for a transition process, owned and led by the people of Zimbabwe.

The AU and SADC have also not yet spoken publicly on the need for Zimbabwe's new government to establish a roadmap to democratic elections and to ensure the political neutrality and non-interference of the security forces in civilian and electoral affairs. Zimbabwe is party to the SADC Principles and Guidelines Governing Democratic Elections, established to promote regular free and fair, transparent, credible and peaceful democratic elections.

Boris Johnson, foreign secretary of the United Kingdom, Zimbabwe's former colonial ruler, expressed hope that a "stable and successful Zimbabwe" would emerge from the ouster of Mugabe.

The United Nations, United States, and UK have provided support for social services such as health, water, sanitation, and education projects. The US and the UK have had little influence with the government of Zimbabwe during Mugabe's 37 years as leader. While the UN may be more influential, UN officials have rarely made public comments critical of human rights abuses by the Zimbabwean government.

Following the November military takeover, two UN independent human rights experts, Idriss Jazairy, special rapporteur on the negative impact of the unilateral coercive measures on the enjoyment of human rights, and Alfred de Zayas, independent expert on the promotion of a democratic and equitable international order, welcomed "the avoidance of bloodshed" during the change of power, and called on the international community to respond by lifting sanctions.